COMPUTATIONAL METHODS IN DRUG DISCOVERY AND REPURPOSING FOR CANCER THERAPY

COMPUTATIONAL METHODS IN DRUG DISCOVERY AND REPURPOSING FOR CANCER THERAPY

Edited by

GANJI PURNACHANDRA NAGARAJU
Department of Hematology and Oncology, School of Medicine, University of Alabama, Birmingham, AL, United States

VENKATESAN AMOUDA
Department of Bioinformatics, Pondicherry University, Puducherry, India

AMPASALA DINAKARA RAO
Department of Bioinformatics, Pondicherry University, Puducherry, India

Academic Press is an imprint of Elsevier
125 London Wall, London EC2Y 5AS, United Kingdom
525 B Street, Suite 1650, San Diego, CA 92101, United States
50 Hampshire Street, 5th Floor, Cambridge, MA 02139, United States
The Boulevard, Langford Lane, Kidlington, Oxford OX5 1GB, United Kingdom

ISBN 978-0-443-15280-1

For information on all Academic Press publications
visit our website at https://www.elsevier.com/books-and-journals

Publisher: Stacy Masucci
Acquisitions Editor: Linda Versteeg-Buschman
Editorial Project Manager: Michaela Realiza
Production Project Manager: Sajana Devasi P K
Cover Designer: Greg Harris

Typeset by STRAIVE, India

This book is dedicated to our families, teachers, contributors, and friends.

Contents

Contributors

Shloka Adluru
Altrincham Grammar School for Girls, Altrincham, United Kingdom

Sarfraz Ahmad
AdventHealth Cancer Institute, FSU and UCF Colleges of Medicine, Orlando, FL, United States

Dinakara Rao Ampasala
Department of Bioinformatics, Pondicherry University, Puducherry, India

Anand Anbarasu
Medical and Biological Computing Laboratory; Department of Biotechnology, School of Biosciences and Technology, Vellore Institute of Technology, Vellore, Tamil Nadu, India

Jayamuruga Pandian Arunachalam
Central Inter-Disciplinary Research Facility, Sri Balaji Vidyapeeth (Deemed to be University), Pondicherry, India

Gayathri Ashok
Medical and Biological Computing Laboratory; Department of Bio-Sciences, School of Biosciences and Technology, Vellore Institute of Technology, Vellore, Tamil Nadu, India

Angshuman Bagchi
Department of Biochemistry and Biophysics, University of Kalyani, Kalyani, West Bengal, India

Grace Persis Burri
Department of Hematology and Oncology, School of Medicine, University of Alabama, Birmingham, AL, United States

Subbulakshmi Chidambaram
Department of Biochemistry and Molecular Biology, Pondicherry University, Puducherry, India

Manabendra Dutta Choudhury
Department of Life Science and Bioinformatics, Assam University, Silchar, Assam, India

Rajesh Das
Department of Bioinformatics, Pondicherry University, Puducherry, India

Subrata Das
Department of Botany and Biotechnology, Karimganj College, Karimganj, Assam, India

Asmita Dasgupta
Department of Biochemistry and Molecular Biology, Pondicherry University, Pondicherry, India

Bassel F. El-Rayes
Department of Hematology and Oncology, School of Medicine, University of Alabama, Birmingham, AL, United States

Shabnam Farisha
Department of Biochemistry and Molecular Biology, Pondicherry University, Pondicherry, India

Sanjukta Ghosh
Department of Biochemistry and Molecular Biology, Pondicherry University, Pondicherry, India

Yuvasri Golivi
Department of Hematology and Oncology, School of Medicine, University of Alabama, Birmingham, AL, United States

Manoj Kumar Gupta
Department of Biotechnology and Bioinformatics, Yogi Vemana University, Kadapa, India

Akriti Gupta Jain
Department of Hematology-Oncology, H. Lee Moffitt Cancer Center and Research Institute, Tampa, FL, United States

Anum Jalil
Department of Hospital Medicine, PeaceHealth Southwest Medical Center, Vancouver, WA, United States

Kastro Kalidass
Department of Biochemistry and Molecular Biology, Pondicherry University, Pondicherry, India

Arunasree M. Kalle
Department of Animal Biology, School of Life Sciences, University of Hyderabad, Hyderabad, TS, India

Muthuramalingam Karpagavalli
Department of Biochemistry and Molecular Biology, Pondicherry University, Puducherry, India

Umamahesh Katike
Department of Bioinformatics, Pondicherry University, Puducherry, India

Vedavathi Katneni
Department of Computer Science, GSS, GITAM (Deemed to be University), Visakhapatnam, Andhra Pradesh, India

Angelina Job Kolady
Department of Genomic Science, Central University of Kerala, Kasaragod, India

Hithesh Kumar
Medical and Biological Computing Laboratory; Department of Bio-Sciences, School of Biosciences and Technology, Vellore Institute of Technology, Vellore, Tamil Nadu, India

Ranjith Kumavath
Department of Genomic Science, Central University of Kerala, Kasaragod; Department of Biotechnology, School of Life Sciences, Pondicherry University, Puducherry, India

Tha Luong
Department of Hematology and Oncology, School of Medicine, University of Alabama, Birmingham, AL, United States

Rama Rao Malla
Cancer Biology Lab, Department of Biochemistry and Bioinformatics, GSS, GITAM (Deemed to be University), Visakhapatnam, Andhra Pradesh, India

Rajalakshmi Manikkam
DBT-BIF Centre; Department of Zoology; Department of Biotechnology, Holy Cross College (Autonomous), Tiruchirappalli, Tamil Nadu, India

Neha Merchant
Department of Bioscience and Biotechnology, Banasthali Vidyapith, Banasthali, Rajasthan, India

Sravan Kumar Miryala
Medical and Biological Computing Laboratory; Department of Bio-Sciences, School of Biosciences and Technology, Vellore Institute of Technology, Vellore, Tamil Nadu, India

Saswati Sarita Mohanty
Department of Bioinformatics, Pondicherry University, Puducherry, India

Ganji Purnachandra Nagaraju
Department of Hematology and Oncology, School of Medicine, University of Alabama, Birmingham, AL; Franklin College of Arts and Sciences, University of Georgia, Athens, GA, United States

Deepa Nath
Department of Botany, Gurucharan College, Silchar, Assam, India

Ishwar Patidar
Department of Bioinformatics, Pondicherry University, Puducherry, India

Dahrii Paul
Department of Bioinformatics, Pondicherry University, Puducherry, India

Honey Pavithran
Department of Genomic Science, Central University of Kerala, Kasaragod, India

Vijayalakshmi Periyasamy
DBT-BIF Centre; Department of Biotechnology, Holy Cross College (Autonomous), Tiruchirappalli, Tamil Nadu, India

P. Priyamvada
Medical and Biological Computing Laboratory; Department of Bio-Sciences, School of Biosciences and Technology, Vellore Institute of Technology, Vellore, Tamil Nadu, India

Sudha Ramaiah
Medical and Biological Computing Laboratory; Department of Bio-Sciences, School of Biosciences and Technology, Vellore Institute of Technology, Vellore, Tamil Nadu, India

Athira Ramesh
Department of Biochemistry and Molecular Biology, Pondicherry University, Puducherry, India

Rishabh Rege
Franklin College of Arts and Sciences, University of Georgia, Athens, GA, United States

Rupa Roy
Department of Biochemistry and Molecular Biology, Pondicherry University, Puducherry, India

Indu Sabapathy
DBT-BIF Centre; Department of Biotechnology, Holy Cross College (Autonomous), Tiruchirappalli, Tamil Nadu, India

Sudha Rani Sadras
Department of Biochemistry and Molecular Biology, Pondicherry University, Puducherry, India

Vemula Sarojamma
Department of Microbiology, Government Medical College, Anantapur, India

Jeelan Basha Shaik
Department of Chemistry, Yogi Vemana University, Kadapa, India

Bhavini Singh
Franklin College of Arts and Sciences, University of Georgia, Athens, GA, United States

Vigneshwar Suriya Prakash Sinnarasan
Department of Bioinformatics, Pondicherry University, Puducherry, India

Anupam Das Talukdar
Department of Life Science and Bioinformatics, Assam University, Silchar, Assam, India

Tulsi
Department of Bioinformatics, Pondicherry University, Puducherry, India

Ramakrishna Vadde
Department of Biotechnology and Bioinformatics, Yogi Vemana University, Kadapa, India

Anbumani Velmurugan Ilavarasi
Department of Bioinformatics, Pondicherry University, Puducherry, India

Aparna Vema
Department of Animal Biology, School of Life Sciences, University of Hyderabad, Hyderabad, TS, India

Amouda Venkatesan
Department of Bioinformatics, Pondicherry University, Puducherry, India

James Wert
Department of Hematology-Oncology, University of Mississippi Medical Center, Jackson, MS, United States

About the editors

Ganji Purnachandra Nagaraju

Assistant Professor, School of Medicine, Division of Hematology and Oncology, University of Alabama, Birmingham, AL, United States.

Dr. Nagaraju obtained his MSc. and his PhD, both in Biotechnology, from Sri Venkateswara University in Tirupati, Andhra Pradesh, India. He received his DSc. from Berhampur University in Berhampur, Odisha, India. Dr. Nagaraju's research focuses on translational projects related to gastrointestinal malignancies. He has published more than 120 research and review papers in highly reputed international journals and has presented more than 50 abstracts at various national and international conferences. Dr. Nagaraju is the author and editor of several books published by Elsevier and Springer Nature. He serves as editorial board member of several internationally recognized academic journals. Dr. Nagaraju has received several international awards, including FAACC. He also holds memberships of the Association of Scientists of Indian Origin in America (ASIOA), the Society for Integrative and Comparative Biology (SICB), the Science Advisory Board, the RNA Society, the American Association for Clinical Chemistry (AACC), and the American Association of Cancer Research (AACR).

Venkatesan Amouda

Assistant Professor, Department of Bioinformatics, School of Life Sciences, Pondicherry University, Puducherry, India.

Dr. Amouda received her Doctorate in Computer Science and Engineering from Pondicherry University, Puducherry, India. Her research focuses on computational approaches for different biological applications using artificial intelligence and big data analytics. She has published 36 research papers in highly reputed international journals and book chapters. She has completed three major extramural projects. Dr. Amouda has organized 22 national and international conferences and attended 20 workshops and conferences related to various platforms in the bioinformatics and computer science fields. She is associated with a number of government scientific bodies and NGOs, and is a member of learned societies of national professional agencies. Dr. Amouda has experience of coordinating many academic, administration, and extension activities.

Ampasala Dinakara Rao
Professor and Chairperson, Department of Bioinformatics, School of Life Sciences, Pondicherry University, Puducherry, India.

Dr. Dinakara Rao earned his PhD degree in biochemistry from Sri Venkateswara University. He spent 12 years in research and teaching at Pondicherry University, Puducherry, India, and 10 years in postdoctoral studies in cancer research in the United States and Canada. Dr. Dinakara Rao's current research focuses are on functional genomics, the molecular mechanisms of cancer, signal transduction, and computational neurobiology, and he has published nearly 70 peer-reviewed scholarly research articles and book chapters, which are extensively cited globally. He is a reviewer and editorial member for several biomedical/bioinformatics journals and has received several competitive research grants for his research accomplishments/contributions. Dr. Dinakara Rao has been honored with the Fellow Award from the Society of Plant Research (2019), and he has gained other prestigious awards, such as DST-Young Scientist (2008), DBT-Young Investigator (2015), Science Communicator-ISCA (2013, 2014), and the Best Teacher Award (2011, Pondicherry University). He received the VA Merit Award from Wayne State University, Detroit, MI, United States (2005–2007) for his postdoctoral studies; a research associate fellowship funded by Genomic Canada, Canada (2001–2005); and a postdoctoral fellowship funded by DBT, Indian Institute of Science (1999–2001).

Preface

Designing anticancer drugs that selectively target tumor cells and exhibit high specificity is a major challenge of the modern era. Machine learning processes not only support the optimization of novel anticancer agents but also expedite the rate of research at which new treatment strategies are discovered. Computation approaches support the treatment of tumors by targeting abnormal metabolism in cancerous cells. With the advancement of technology, virtual screening has permitted the testing of a large number of chemicals in a short time at a much lower cost. Consequently, scientists are making in silico breakthrough progress with computer-assisted drug discovery and design.

The first set of articles deliberate about the role of artificial intelligence in cancer therapy. The rapid development of advanced and high-throughput techniques acts as a catalyst in the discovery of novel drugs. The advancement of genetic information associated with the molecular biology of tumors has led to the identification of potential molecular targets for anticancer drug discovery and development. Molecular modeling approaches help in obtaining target protein information, such as atomic coordinates, secondary structure assignments, and atomic connectivity. The application of artificial intelligence in the field of cancer therapy assists in diagnosing the root cause of tumor advancement and assessing drug doses for maximum effectiveness. The fourth review specifically discusses the significance of artificial intelligence in colorectal cancer and in precision medicine. With the advancement of artificial intelligence, a personalized therapeutic regimen called precision medicine can be established. The fifth article demonstrates the application of artificial intelligence in breast cancer treatment and diagnosis. The combination of artificial intelligence, especially machine learning approaches and digital imaging techniques, can assist in decreasing the false diagnosis of breast cancer. The review elucidates the fundamentals of machine learning algorithms and machine learning models for breast cancer prediction, model assessment, as well as the present knowledge on machine learning-based methods for breast cancer diagnosis. The use of molecular modeling, such as quantitative structure-activity relationships (QSARs), has been extremely important in evaluating the potential of various molecules and their applicability. In the seventh article, a structure-based virtual screening strategy to identify novel great wall kinase (GWL) inhibitors is described.

The second set of review articles discusses important drug repurposing strategies that provide time and cost savings. Incorporating statistical techniques, bioinformatic resources, chemoinformatic tools, as well as experimental methods can result in effective and efficient drug repurposing methods. The principles of computational drug designing and drug repurposing have also been outlined. A synopsis of diverse computational techniques used for drug development has been explored along with some basic information on the principles of thermodynamics. The next article discusses strategies to search effective treatment approaches against astrocytic tumors, and tumors of the central nervous system. Drug repositioning for astrocytic tumors aims at using anticancer therapies that are originally approved or designed for tumors of organs other than the brain. Next, the repurposing of phytochemical-derived novel bioactive compounds that possess anticancer properties are assessed via molecular docking, MD simulation, and ADMET studies. Drug repurposing specifically designed for colon cancer treatment has also been elucidated. Principles and tools used in drug repurposing, various drugs classes against colorectal cancer, previously repurposed drugs used in colon cancer, and computational methods used in the development of drugs through drug repurposing have been outlined in detail. The anticancer properties of cardiac glycosides (CGs), a class of FDA-approved drugs to increase rhythmic heart conditions, have been discussed.

The final set of review articles focus on discovering potential drug targets and biological markers that are effective for cancer therapeutics. The systems biology method using gene interaction networks is a developing field that can assist cancer biomarker discovery as well as new drug target identification. The significance of human body fluid biomarkers in liver cancer has been discussed along with its systematic analysis and clinical significance. Endometrial cancer (EC) is a female-associated cancer and possible diagnostic biomarkers are warranted to enhance EC diagnosis. An integrated bioinformatics and machine learning analysis is carried out on publicly available data to explore the identification of novel biomarkers to diagnose EC. In the eighteenth chapter, the involvement of PIWI/piRNA in multiple tumors is discussed with a focus on its therapeutic use for retinoblastoma. Abnormal PIWI/piRNA expression in various tumors makes it a potential biomarker and therapeutic target for cancer diagnosis and treatment. The nineteenth chapter discusses the role of biosimilars and their essential roles in hepatocellular carcinoma. Finally, the twentieth chapter explores computational approaches to identify precision medicine for cancer therapy. This chapter also discusses the present scenario and future prospects.

Twenty chapters are presented in this book that discusses the emerging role of computational analysis for cancer therapy. We present this book with immense gratitude to the scientific community and hope that it will provide better understanding of artificial intelligence, drug repurposing, and targeting biomarkers in cancer treatment. We also hope that this will spark novel ideas and breakthrough research for the benefit of clinicians and patients who suffer with these fatal malignancies.

CHAPTER 1

Computational approaches for anticancer drug design

Tha Luong, Grace Persis Burri, Yuvasri Golivi, Ganji Purnachandra Nagaraju, and Bassel F. El-Rayes
Department of Hematology and Oncology, School of Medicine, University of Alabama, Birmingham, AL, United States

Abstract

Computational strategies have been playing an essential role in the development of anticancer medicines. The rapid growth of newly advanced, high-throughput in silico techniques significantly fosters the discovery of novel drugs. These techniques are applied in many steps of drug development, from target identification, and ligand- or structured-based screening of hits to lead optimization. Additionally, the increasing generations of new hardware, software, computational networks, and algorithms highly contribute to the decline in labor, time, and cost required to create administrable cancer drugs. Crizotinib, axitinib, and luminespib are successful examples of this state-of-the-art method. Despite difficulties, the benefits still outweigh the challenges, and computational applications are still a promising strategy for anticancer drug creations.

Abbreviations

ECFP extended-connectivity fingerprints
FDA Food and Drug Administration
GH Güner-Henry
GNN Graph Neural Network
HGFR hepatocyte growth factor receptor
HSP90 heat shock protein 90
IUPAC International Union of Pure and Applied Chemistry
MCSS multiple copy simultaneous search
MLR multilinear regression
PR polynomial regression
QSAR quantitative structure-activity relationship
RCC renal cell carcinoma
RF random forest
ROCS rapid overlay of chemical structures
SVM support vector machine
VEGF vascular endothelial growth factor
VEGFR vascular endothelial growth factor receptor

Computational Methods in Drug Discovery and Repurposing for Cancer Therapy
https://doi.org/10.1016/B978-0-443-15280-1.00009-1

1. Introduction

Cancer is among the leading causes of death in many countries, particularly in low- and middle-income nations [1]. It is a global challenge in public health and accounts for roughly 10 million deaths in 2020 [2]. A promising direction for discovering new anti-cancer medicines is the utility of computational methods. These approaches not only bring about valued and appealing resources but also speed up the process of drug discovery through decreasing the time, labor, and cost of drug development [3]. Computational approaches can be applied in many steps of drug discovery and development, including target prediction, hit identification, and lead optimization [1]. The overall strategy is to use the chemical, molecular, and quantum properties of potential compounds to screen, optimize, and assess their biological activity against a drug target. Consequently, the relationship between the structure and the activity of a molecule can be evaluated, and drug candidates can be designed and optimized. Computer-aided drug designing generally consists of two main groups: structure-based and ligand-based strategies, which relies on whether the structure of the protein target is known or not. In this chapter, we aim to present a general knowledge of computational methods and provide typical examples of these approaches as well as how they are applied in designing anticancer drugs. We also highlight current challenges and future directions in this research area (Fig. 1).

2. Current computational approaches for cancer drug designs

It is estimated that around 7000 positions in the human genome are potential targets for drug development, but only a small amount of them are proved as effective sites [4]. Cancer is among diseases with many potential targets for pharmacological development [1]. In 2020, 18 out of 53 new products approved by the US Food and Drug Administration (FDA) were for cancer treatment [5]. One of the main contributors to this notable

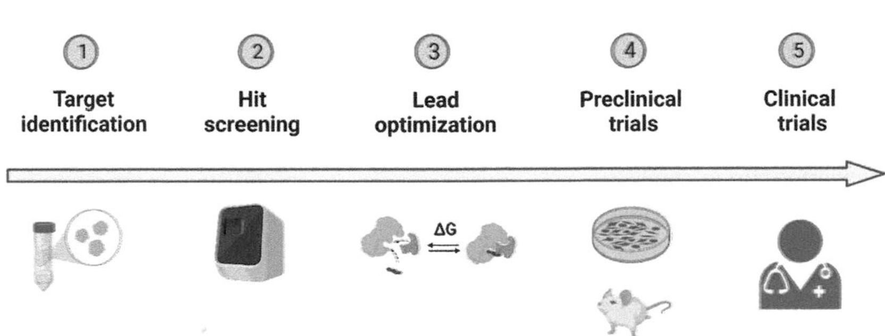

Fig. 1 A pipeline of new drug development. Five main steps in this process include target identification, hit screening, lead optimization, preclinical trials, and clinical trials.

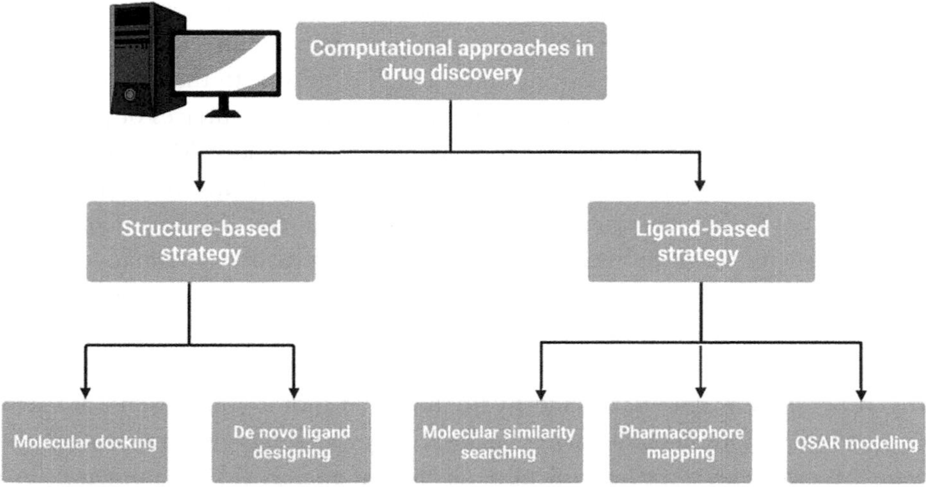

Fig. 2 A category of computational approaches. Two major strategies in computational methods are structure-based and ligand-based. While the former method typically contains molecular docking and de novo ligand designing, the latter approach generally comprises molecular similarity searching, pharmacophore mapping, and quantitative structure-activity relationship.

accomplishment is computational research. Overall, studies applying computational methods to discover novel drugs mostly focus on designing drug candidates based on the structure of protein targets or their ligands. The next steps of drug discovery consist of the selection of high-scoring compounds, optimization of leads, in vitro and/or in vivo experimental assessment, identification of drug candidates, and finally pharmacological testing in a preclinical and clinical study [3] (Fig. 2).

2.1 Structure-based methods

In this strategy, the three-dimensional structure of the target is known and can be detected via many means such as X-ray crystallography, homology modeling, and nuclear magnetic resonance spectroscopy [3]. The structure is needed to determine binding and active sites on the target molecules. From the information of these sites, a quantity of chemical compounds is assessed based on their binding affinity and interactions against the target. Subsequently, potential binding candidates are selected and evaluated based on their steric configurations and molecular interactions with the active site of the protein. High-scoring compounds or leads are analyzed further by biochemical assays. Next, positive leads are surveyed for their stableness in the complex with the target. To improve the efficacy and lessen the side effects to work as a drug, the selected molecules may go through chemical modifications. With the general principles mentioned above, there are various ways to construct a new drug compound, such as molecular docking and de novo ligand designing.

Molecular docking has been applied for decades to predict interactions between proteins and their ligands such as DNA and other protein molecules. It is used to forecast the conformation of a molecule that possesses a high affinity with the target compound [6]. To form a stable complex, a suitable orientation of protein surfaces or poses of two molecules needs to interact with each other like a lock and its key. Most of the existing docking procedures contain two steps: sampling and scoring. Generally, from the target structure, active sites are identified and utilized to create spheres that have representative configurations with them. Subsequently, the representing globes are employed to build possible binding sites. Depending on the binding features in terms of thermodynamics and kinetics, the interaction between a ligand and its target is evaluated and screened to obtain possible pharmacophores. Five molecular forces, namely, covalent bonds, hydrogen bonds, van der Waals, and hydrophobic and ionic interactions, are able to impact the interactions via influencing binding affinity and energy. Numerous docking software has been developed to calculate all the parameters [7]. For instance, in the sampling step, while MedusaDock, MCDOCK, ProDock, and GOLD begin with an initial pose and gradually screen for more accurate poses, FlexX that adopts a fragment-based method starts seeking low-binding-affinity fragments. In all the above methods, the initial searching is relied on random seed and requires lots of times to invoke the software, which may take up to several days to gain the final docking pose of a complex. In the scoring process, the binding affinity of the protein-ligand complex is evaluated via the free energy and constructed by two major functions: physics-based and knowledge-based. Recently, many machine learning-based functions have been developed to improve the scoring, including AGL-Score, AtomNet, Kdeep, TopologyNet, and Graph Neural Network (GNN)-based approaches. Although this advanced software can enhance the scoring process, they are all dependent on conventional sampling software.

De novo ligand designing is a methodology in which computational systems are applied to construct ligands that possess functional groups and suitable configurations enabling them to interact with protein targets [6]. The ultimate goal of this strategy is to combine unattached functional groups in a simulated molecule fulfilling chemical fundamentals. Then, the compound can be used as a model to search existing molecules against databases or to build synthetic products. From ligand models, the structure of protein-ligand complexes is noted, and the structure of ligands can be altered so that the interaction affinity of the aggregate is fostered. Fragment-growing and fragment-linking are two main approaches of de novo ligand designing. The former approach initiates with seeding molecules into the target and follows by linking fragments matching the target for each seed and from that build a complete ligand compound. In contrast, the latter method starts incorporating molecular fragments into the target so that the best interaction energy is achieved. The fragments are also combined to form a whole ligand structure. A lot of software is built to design novel ligands and is mostly based on the calculation of molecular interactions between protein target and the modeling ligands.

For example, while LUDI focuses on hydrophobic interactions and hydrogen bonds created by the fragments and target sites, GRID evaluates van der Waals interaction, hydrogen bonds, and electrostatic bonds to calculate the interaction energy [8,9]. Conversely, multiple copy simultaneous search (MCSS) considers force fields to assess the interactions between molecular fragments and active sites on protein targets [10].

2.2 Ligand-based strategies

In this approach, although the three-dimensional structure of the protein target is unknown, the structural information of its ligand is declared [1]. Generally, in the first process, the structure of the known ligand is used as a template to search for and to identify new chemical compounds with high similarity [3]. Second, the bioactivities of the novel molecules are predicted based on the development of the quantitative structure-activity relationship (QSAR). There are three major methodologies in this category, namely, molecular similarity searching, QSAR modeling, and pharmacophore mapping.

In molecular similarity searching, the structure of ligands is used as a query molecule to screen novel chemical compounds with similar characteristics [11]. The underlying principle of this method is that molecules sharing similar structures are likely to possess similar biological activities. Because it requires only structural knowledge of small active molecules, ligand-based strategies are commonly utilized to identify new ligands and optimize their biological activities in terms of pharmacokinetics. Moreover, physicochemical characteristics such as molecular weight, charges, logP as well as two- and three-dimensional shape-similarity are considered in the search. Several 2D fingerprints and 3D shape-similarity, including Molprin 2D and Unity 2D, extended-connectivity fingerprints (ECFP), and rapid overlay of chemical structures (ROCS), respectively, are widely used in virtual screening.

In addition to similarity searching, QSAR modeling is also one of the common chemo-informatics approaches of the ligand-based method [12]. QSAR models are developed based on biological activity analyses of a group of known ligands that respond to a certain target protein [3]. To illustrate, a training set accounting for 80% of ligands with known activity from experimental data is utilized to derive initial QSAR models. This group contains compounds that react against a certain target protein. Next, the initial models are evaluated using a test set contributing to 20% of the data set of known-activity ligands. This step is considered as an internal valuation, and its outcome is the input for an external assessment, which is performed using datasets of other experimental references. There are many machine learning and deep learning methods used to construct QSAR models, including random forest (RF), support vector machine (SVM), polynomial regression (PR), artificial neural network, and multilinear regression (MLR). The developed models can not only be used to predict the biological activities of novel ligands but also illustrate the relation between physicochemical features and biological activity of a set of molecules. Interestingly, they can provide both positive and negative influences on bioactivities according to molecular characteristics such as spatial orientation, electronic information, molecular interactions, and conformational features. Furthermore, QSAR analyses, including Gusar, ChemDes, BioPPSy, and PHASE, can recommend necessary alternations in the chemical properties and structure of the lead molecule to enhance its pharmacological features.

Pharmacophore mapping is another example of ligand-based methods. It is a precise technique enabling the discovery of novel drugs by analyzing numerous pharmaceutical characteristics from an ample chemical space [3]. According to the International Union of Pure and Applied Chemistry (IUPAC), a pharmacophore is a group of spatial and electronic properties needed to assure optimal supramolecular interactions with particular biological objects and to foster (or restrict) their biological activities [13]. Therefore, a pharmacophore is generated by a combination of chemical characteristics instead of chemical categories. In detail, the main goal of pharmacophore-based approaches is to search for a set of common pharmacophores within ligands possessing particular chemical bonds, electronic information, and hydrophobic interactions to treat as active sites of ligand-target complex [6]. They produce assessable hypotheses about spatially interacting sites on functional groups. To illustrate, the hypotheses are developed using training sets comprising a statistically significant number of compounds with different, obvious, non-redundant structures. The set also needs to include compounds possessing the highest activity to provide critical information for pharmacophore production. The underlying principles of pharmacophore processes are that: (i) compounds in a training set share the same binding motif with the same protein targets, and (ii) the more binding interactions of the compounds, the higher activity they have. There are many tools that are used to develop pharmacophore models, including MOE, Ligand-Scout, Phase, and Catalyst/Discovery Studio [3]. These models mostly based on pharmacophore properties can be utilized for compound library searching, ligand de novo design, and lead optimization. Pharmacophore techniques, thereby, become a primary approach for drug discovery.

3. Applications of computational approaches in cancer drug designing

Depending on whether the structure of ligand and protein target is known or not, different strategies of computational approaches can be selected [6]. For instance, if both ligand and target structure are known, structure-based approaches such as molecular docking can be applied. If only the structure of protein target is known, de novo ligand designing can be used to enhance the compound design. Fragment responses to active sites are chosen and combined to form a new compound with a structure satisfying chemical principles. In contrast, if only the structure of ligands is known, QSAR modeling and pharmacophore mapping can be employed. While the former techniques focus on compounds sharing similar structures with different activities, the latter approach analyzes compounds with various structures with alike bioactivity. After that, generated lead compounds are evaluated using Lipinski's rule [14]. Finally, the quality of drug candidates is validated by the analyses of a cost function, Fisher's Cross, and Güner-Henry (GH) test. While the cost function assesses the complexity, bias, and differences between forecasted and the real outcomes of developed models, Fisher's cross examines proposed compounds if their predicted activities are correlated with their actual activities. On the other hand, GH test centers on screening datasets and validates them if they are statistically significant.

Regardless of which strategies are being used, computational applications play a critical role in discovering anticancer drugs [1]. Recently, computational approaches have turned into a powerful technique with multiple successful examples of the development of new anticancer medicines. The first instance is crizotinib, which is approved by the FDA in 2011 as a potent inhibitor of cMet/ALK [15]. c-Met is a protein in tyrosine-protein kinase family known as hepatocyte growth factor receptor (HGFR) and contributes to many cellular signaling activities. It is commonly overexpressed in many human cancers and thereby a promising pharmaceutical target. Beginning with a set of a novel synthesized class of tyrosine kinase inhibitors, 3-substituted indolin-2-ones, structured-based approaches were applied to identify a strong activity derivative against c-Met phosphorylation, PHA-665752. Despite possessing biological activities both in vitro and in vivo, this compound showed poor pharmacological properties. However, by analyzing the interacting complex of PHA-665752 and c-Met, a crucial binding site for inhibitor is unraveled. From that, a new class of 5-substituted 3-benzyloxy-2-aminopyridine was designed and utilized to screen compounds owning inhibition activity against c-Met. To further foster the inhibitory ability, an optimal process occurred, and among the derivatives, a molecule possessing a suitable functional group and chiral center with an effective inhibition and good drug-like features, crizotinib, was attained. Strikingly, this drug has shown a significant clinical effect on the replication of c-Met gene in lymphoma, esophageal cancers, and lung cancers [16]. The second example of computational applications is axitinib (AG-013736), which was approved by FDA in 2012 to treat advanced renal cell carcinoma (RCC). This drug is a potent, selective inhibitor of vascular endothelial growth factor receptor (VEGFR), another tyrosine kinase protein. Vascular endothelial growth factor (VEGF) is an essential regulator in several signaling pathways, including angiogenesis, which considerably contributes to malignant growth [1]. Hence, preventing the binding of VEGF and VEGFR is an efficient means to restrict tumor development. The discovery of novel VEGFR inhibitors was initiated by analyzing the relationship between the structure and activity of phosphorylated p-VEGFR2Δ50 and the binding complex of inhibitor-unphosphorylated VEGFR2Δ50. From that, a group of hits was assessed, in which pyrazole and benzamide were selected. The pyrazole indicated promising features and was modified into indazole compounds that present novel kinase inhibition activities. Among the derivatives, a compound having a styryl group at 3′ of the indazole ring was identified to possess a high inhibitory effect and used for further optimization. Lastly, a truncation strategy was applied to finalize the novel inhibitor, axitinib, which has a high cellular potency and appealing physiochemical characteristics. The drug now is used as the first-line anticancer medicine to treat RCC in combination with pembrolizumab. Another illustration for computational utilization is the generation of luminespib, an inhibitor of heat shock protein 90 (HSP90). HSP90 is a key protein with identified biological functions in maintaining the proper performance of other proteins. Changes in its structure are related to cancer development, and thereby, it has become a promising target for designing anticancer drugs. The structure of HSP90 is well known with three functional domains, namely, an N-terminal domain that can bind to ATP, a middle domain, and a C-terminal domain determining protein dimerization [17]. Starting from the structure information of HSP90, a large-scale screening was performed and found an active inhibitor CCT018159. A crystal structure of the complex HSP90-CCT018159 revealed important information that was useful for further modification of this inhibitor. It was disclosed that alternations of particular functional groups lead to pharmacokinetic improvement. The modified molecule, luminespib, carrying a new amide group and isoxazole ring, showed a high inhibition and strong anticancer effect. Recently, this medicine is enrolled in different clinical trials with or without other combination drugs.

4. Challenges and future directions

Although computational approaches bring about many advantages in anticancer drug discovery, most of them bear limitations [3]. Overall, computational outcomes need to be examined in real systems because all designing processes are based on theoretical biochemical parameters, mathematical algorithms, and computational functions. Unfortunately, many developed pharmacophores are not associated with real solutions and do not fulfill the required characteristics for physiological reactions. One of the reasons for this fact is the lack of experimental data and the reliability of computational tools that hardly consider all necessary parameters. Thus, a solution for this problem is to generate more precise, desirable experimental data as well as to create verified algorithms, and accurate functions.

In spite of the above concerns, computational applications in drug discovery are still a growing trend [1]. A recent direction of this approach is drug repurposing. In this strategy, licensed or studied drugs are assessed for new applications on other diseases rather than current treatment. In this way, time and budget spending on preclinical examinations, safety evaluations, and formulations significantly decrease because they have already been done. The second path is a combinatorial treatment where a mixture of multiple single-target drugs is given to patients. It is particularly desirable to treat complicated diseases. Nevertheless, many parameters are needed to consider, such as the interactions and different pharmacokinetic features among drugs. Another orientation is the development of multitarget pharmacophores. With the ability to target several objects at the same time, these drugs provide benefits in the treatment of multifactorial diseases, including cancers. Interestingly, new advances in computational drug discovery reveal that nucleic acids may be a promising target, particularly RNA and certain tertiary-structure-forming motifs such as G-quadruplexes [18]. However, one of the main challenges of this approach is the high flexibility of the target structures.

5. Conclusion

Cancer is still a definite thread worldwide. Anticancer drugs are in urgent need, but due to complicated processes that consume a vast time and money, the treatments are still lacking. In this context, the applications of computational approaches to design anticancer medicines are promising and able to facilitate the discovery of novel drugs. Notwithstanding challenges, these in silico techniques are bright and worth further investigation.

References

[1] W. Cui, A. Aouidate, S. Wang, Q. Yu, Y. Li, S. Yuan, Discovering anti-cancer drugs via computational methods, Front. Pharmacol. 11 (2020) 733.

[2] J. Ferlay, M. Colombet, I. Soerjomataram, D.M. Parkin, M. Piñeros, A. Znaor, F. Bray, Cancer statistics for the year 2020: an overview, Int. J. Cancer 149 (4) (2021) 778–789.

[3] A. Tiwari, S. Singh, Computational approaches in drug designing, in: Bioinformatics, Elsevier, 2022, pp. 207–217.

[4] X. Chen, M.-X. Liu, G.-Y. Yan, Drug–target interaction prediction by random walk on the heterogeneous network, Mol. Biosyst. 8 (7) (2012) 1970–1978.

[5] A. Mullard, 2020 FDA drug approvals, Nat. Rev. Drug Discov. 20 (2) (2021) 85–91.

[6] C.L. Hung, C.C. Chen, Computational approaches for drug discovery, Drug Dev. Res. 75 (6) (2014) 412–418.

[7] H. Jiang, J. Wang, W. Cong, Y. Huang, M. Ramezani, A. Sarma, N.V. Dokholyan, M. Mahdavi, M.T. Kandemir, Predicting protein–ligand docking structure with graph neural network, J. Chem. Inf. Model. 62 (12) (2022) 2923–2932.

[8] P. Prathipati, A.K. Saxena, Evaluation of binary QSAR models derived from LUDI and MOE scoring functions for structure based virtual screening, J. Chem. Inf. Model. 46 (1) (2006) 39–51.

[9] M.A. Kastenholz, M. Pastor, G. Cruciani, E.E. Haaksma, T. Fox, GRID/CPCA: a new computational tool to design selective ligands, J. Med. Chem. 43 (16) (2000) 3033–3044.

[10] A. Caflisch, A. Miranker, M. Karplus, Multiple copy simultaneous search and construction of ligands in binding sites: application to inhibitors of HIV-1 aspartic proteinase, J. Med. Chem. 36 (15) (1993) 2142–2167.

[11] A. Zhavoronkov, Y.A. Ivanenkov, A. Aliper, M.S. Veselov, V.A. Aladinskiy, A.V. Aladinskaya, V.A. Terentiev, D.A. Polykovskiy, M.D. Kuznetsov, A. Asadulaev, Deep learning enables rapid identification of potent DDR1 kinase inhibitors, Nat. Biotechnol. 37 (9) (2019) 1038–1040.

[12] A.R. Leach, V.J. Gillet, An Introduction to Chemoinformatics, Springer, 2007.

[13] D.R. Buckle, P.W. Erhardt, C.R. Ganellin, T. Kobayashi, T.J. Perun, J. Proudfoot, J. Senn-Bilfinger, Glossary of terms used in medicinal chemistry. Part II (IUPAC Recommendations 2013), Pure Appl. Chem. 85 (8) (2013) 1725–1758.

[14] C.A. Lipinski, F. Lombardo, B.W. Dominy, P.J. Feeney, Experimental and computational approaches to estimate solubility and permeability in drug discovery and development settings, Adv. Drug Deliv. Rev. 23 (1–3) (1997) 3–25.

[15] J.J. Cui, M. McTigue, R. Kania, M. Edwards, Case history: Xalkori^{TM}(crizotinib), a potent and selective dual inhibitor of mesenchymal epithelial transition (MET) and anaplastic lymphoma kinase (ALK) for cancer treatment, Annu. Rep. Med. Chem. 48 (2013) 421–434. Elsevier.
[16] J.J. Cui, M. Tran-Dubé, H. Shen, M. Nambu, P.-P. Kung, M. Pairish, L. Jia, J. Meng, L. Funk, I. Botrous, Structure based drug design of crizotinib (PF-02341066), a potent and selective dual inhibitor of mesenchymal–epithelial transition factor (c-MET) kinase and anaplastic lymphoma kinase (ALK), J. Med. Chem. 54 (18) (2011) 6342–6363.
[17] A. Hoter, M.E. El-Sabban, H.Y. Naim, The HSP90 family: structure, regulation, function, and implications in health and disease, Int. J. Mol. Sci. 19 (9) (2018) 2560.
[18] M. Castelli, S.A. Serapian, F. Marchetti, A. Triveri, V. Pirota, L. Torielli, S. Collina, F. Doria, M. Freccero, G. Colombo, New perspectives in cancer drug development: computational advances with an eye to design, RSC Med. Chem. 12 (9) (2021) 1491–1502.

CHAPTER 2

Molecular modeling approach for cancer drug therapy

Bhavini Singh[a], Rishabh Rege[a], and Ganji Purnachandra Nagaraju[b]
[a]Franklin College of Arts and Sciences, University of Georgia, Athens, GA, United States
[b]Department of Hematology and Oncology, School of Medicine, University of Alabama, Birmingham, AL, United States

Abstract

The adverse effects and therapeutic resistance development are among the most potent clinical issues for cancer treatment. The increase in genetic understanding and information relating to the molecular biology of cancer has resulted in the identification of numerous potential molecular targets for anticancer drug discovery and development. However, the complexities of cancer treatment and the extensive accessibility to experimental data have made computer-aided approaches necessary. The dynamic nature of protein structure makes it difficult to portray an accurate model for certain proteins. In the case where a 3D structure cannot be obtained by experimental methods, molecular modeling methods can be utilized to obtain the target protein's information, including atomic coordinates, secondary structure assignments, and atomic connectivity. Molecular modeling describes the generation, representation, and/or manipulation of the 3D structure of chemical and biological molecules, along with the determination of physicochemical and pharmacokinetic properties that can help to interpret the structure-activity relationship (SAR) of the biological molecules. This review paper aims to summarize approaches in molecular modeling and their applications in cancer research.

Abbreviations

FGFR fibroblast growth factor receptors
HTS high-throughput screening
MD molecular dynamics
MDR multidrug-resistant
MRP1 multidrug resistance-associated protein 1
MRP2 multidrug resistance-associated protein 2
RMSD root-mean-square deviation

1. Introduction

The overprescription and overuse of antibiotics have dramatically led to resistance against them in recent decades. Only three new classes of antibiotics have been implemented in the past 40 years, and most antibiotics use a similar mechanism and target similar pathways and biological markers in the bacteria [1]. These factors further compromise the effectiveness of antibiotics. Additional studies must be conducted to discover antibacterial

Computational Methods in Drug Discovery and Repurposing for Cancer Therapy
https://doi.org/10.1016/B978-0-443-15280-1.00002-9

agents that can be effective against a wider range of essential molecular targets and pathways. In recent years, the molecular mechanisms underlying drug resistance have been successfully studied and have revealed new and specific molecules that interplay with active receptors [2]. Computational studies can be used to analyze mechanisms of drug resistance, improve new drugs, and reveal the specificity of drug molecules [2]. With the collaboration of theoretical and experimental scientists dealing with cancer research from a molecular approach, these functionalities can be used to assist in preclinical studies.

2. Drug designing

A crucial aspect of cell function is molecular pathways and protein interaction. Any morphological or chemical change can disrupt the pathway and alter or disable the function of the cell, including uncontrolled cell division, or cancer [3]. Prevention of abnormal protein-protein interaction can induce cancer cell death [1]. A common challenge with anticancer drugs is that they are not designed specifically to target abnormal proteins and can interfere with healthy proteins [1]. Therefore, drug design must be adjusted to impact only the intended proteins involved in the molecular pathway.

The pharmacokinetic properties of molecules can also be determined computationally. These include ADMET properties such as absorption (A), distribution (D), metabolism (M), excretion (E), and toxicity (T). These properties are crucial to understanding the drug being developed inside our bodies. Early detection of unsuitable ADMET properties can save resources such as money, time, and physical labor. In silico tools can be of great help in this regard and in some circumstances, are an alternative to animal testing in predicting these properties [4].

Drug design is the approach of finding drugs using their biological targets [1]. Typically, the biological target is a molecule critically involved in a metabolic or signaling pathway that is specific to the disease, its infectivity, or its survival. Therefore, to develop a drug, various ligands and protein binding sites must be examined. Determining the protein structure can further assist in how the protein responds to different mutations. Methods such as X-ray crystallography and nuclear magnetic resonance spectroscopy reveal information regarding the 3D structure of the protein that can assist in structure-based drug design. However, these methods have their limitations in accurately predicting the shape of the dynamic protein landscape [4].

A crucial aspect of the computational approach in chemistry is to identify the drug-like molecules that can bind to and inhibit the function of proteins [4]. Standard experimental methods use a structure of the target protein bound to an inhibitor and identify molecules that are structurally similar to that inhibitor, which can then be fitted into the binding site, and the complexes are refined and studied by the use of computer simulation methods such as molecular dynamics [4]. However, often this approach does not yield any improvements or has already been exhausted; therefore, it is necessary to identify chemically novel molecules using the molecular modeling approaches [4].

3. Molecular modeling

Molecular modeling is the application of computer-generated models to simulate processes utilizing anywhere from a few atoms to a multitude of biomolecules [4]. The accuracy and level of detail of the output depend on the size and timescale of the system. The technology allows for the study of differences at the sub-Ångström level (unit of length equal to 10^{-10} m), which can have a large influence on the depiction of the binding of a drug molecule to its receptor [4,5]. This is significant as the size of protein complexes is three orders of magnitude larger and necessitates the use of computational resources.

Molecular modeling in cancer studies is performed at the atomic level using existing structural data. However, certain limitations are posed due to size and timescale. Soluble proteins can be studied for 10^{-7}–10^{-6} s, which is enough time to gather the domain motions of the protein. However, larger processes such as conformational changes or activation of channels are not collected [4]. Molecular modeling studies are especially useful in analyzing multidrug, or efflux transporter proteins. This is because efflux transporter proteins have limitations in analyzing 3D structures due to their hydrophobic transmembrane interfering with crystallization [2]. Therefore, molecular modeling methods such as quantum mechanics, molecular docking, and molecular dynamics simulation applications are frequently used to investigate noncovalent interactions [2]. For example, a study conducted on breast cancer multidrug-resistant (MDR) proteins utilized molecular modeling. This is because the 3D structures of the target protein, which were previously available on protein banks, were retrieved, leaving no source for 3D interpretation of the required proteins. Molecular modeling was applied to the MRP2 (multidrug resistance-associated protein 2) protein where MRP1 (multidrug resistance-associated protein 1) protein was used as a template [2,6,7].

4. Methods of molecular modeling

There are several methods for molecular modeling. These methods include atomistic simulation, modeling proteins and protein complexes, and modeling protein-drug interactions [4].

Molecular dynamics is based on Newton's well-known equation of motion, $F = ma$, where F is the force operating on a particle, m is its mass, and a is its acceleration [4]. For example, a molecule(s) coordinates can be obtained using an enzyme-inhibitor complex's crystallographic structure. The forces that act on the atoms are calculated, and the system is propagated in time according to Newton's equation of motion [4]. The force is calculated by differentiating the potential energy at the positions of every atom in the system where potential energy will depend on all other atoms present in their locations. In practice, the force field, a set of equations and parametric, is used to estimate the potential energy of the system. Simulations are calculated in steps that are 1–4 femtoseconds (fs, 10^{-15} s) [4]. A simulation that is 0.1 μs typically requires 50 million steps. An illustration

1. Potential energy of the system, V, as a function of atom positions.

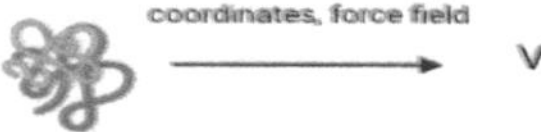

2. Different potential energy using the forces acting upon each atom with respect to the atomic coordinates

3. Update the configuration and velocities.

Fig. 1 The process of calculating 1 step of the Molecular Docking Simulation.

of the method is given in Fig. 1. The MD simulation produces the particle velocities with respect to its coordinates, which is referred to as particle trajectory [4].

- The ab initio MD uses a simulation based on Newtonian mechanics to bridge molecular dynamics with quantum mechanics. It is unique in that the forces acting on the atoms are calculated from quantum-mechanical principles, which is greater in accuracy. However, the complexity in the usage of ab initio MD renders the method in being a widely used method [4].
- Homology modeling is an approach that uses preexisting data as a baseline to determine the structural model of a complex involving a dynamic protein [4].
- Computational molecular docking is a research technique for predicting whether one molecule will bind to another, where docking is the ability to position a ligand in the active site of a protein and calculate specific binding affinities [1]. Molecular docking utilizes the orientation of the molecules inside the cavity and the scoring of each pose to evaluate the quality of the obtained binding mode [8]. The orientations of the ligand inside the binding pocket are calculated and assigned scoring values [8]. Most scoring functions are physics-based molecular mechanics force fields that estimate the energy of the pose; a low (negative) energy indicates a stable system and thus a likely binding interaction [1]. Therefore, the conformation with the lowest scoring value among all considered receptors with their respective ligands will resemble the overall orientation of the ideal compound [2].

5. Applications of molecular modeling

In a study using *Escherichia coli*, the ligand and receptor conformation scoring was evaluated using the root-mean-square deviation (RMSD), which is the average deviation between the corresponding atoms of two proteins [2,9]. The RMSD was measured for the common core of the inhibitors relative to the experimental orientation of the compound. Visual inspection of the predicted binding was used to determine whether the interactions observed in the X-ray structure were reproduced [2,9]. These results are summarized in Fig. 2, which plots the RMSD of the common core of each

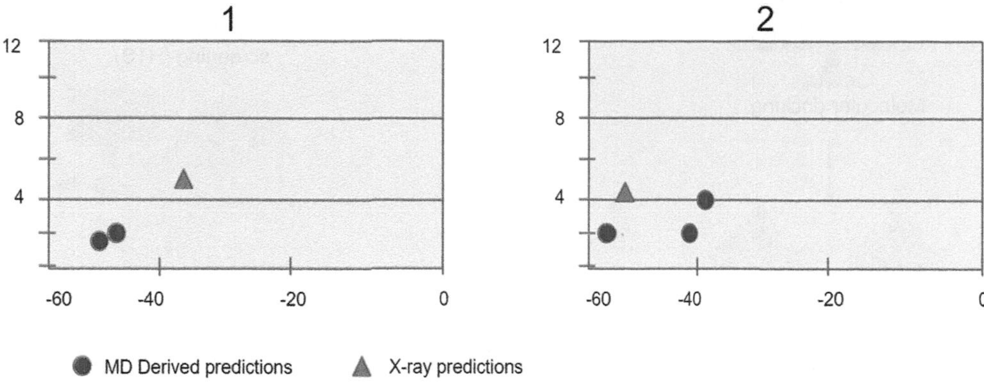

Fig. 2 RMSD and the X-ray structure of each compound versus its scoring value. The *circle markers* represent the binding poses of the MD extracted receptor conformations, and the *triangular markers* represent the X-ray structures.

compound relative to the X-ray structure of the compound with the scoring value. The figure only shows the lower scored (most efficient) pose of each compound on each receptor conformation.

6. Applications in multidrug-resistant proteins

A method to reverse MDR is by conjugation of anticancer drugs with targeting ligand molecules, hence rendering them specific to the target cancer cell [2,10]. To do this, the Basic Local Alignment Search Tool database is scanned to determine the protein structures that show high homology to the 3D structures of relevant proteins [2,11,12]. Therefore, molecular modeling can be used to generate a 3D structure using homology-modeling tools in the software. The best molecule to use as a template can be determined using the SWISS-Model and I-TASSER web servers that show the homology ratios [2]. By choosing one of these templates, the user can obtain the 3D structure of the desired protein. For homology, modeling studies carried out with the ABC transporter family, and studies using both computational software and web servers, are possible [2,13].

High-throughput screening (HTS) is a drug discovery process that allows automated testing of large numbers of chemical and/or biological compounds for a specific biological target, for example, through binding assays [14]. HTS allows a researcher to effectively conduct millions of biochemical, genetic, or pharmacological tests in a short period of time [1].

Fig. 3 shows an overview of molecular docking and HTS inputs and outputs.

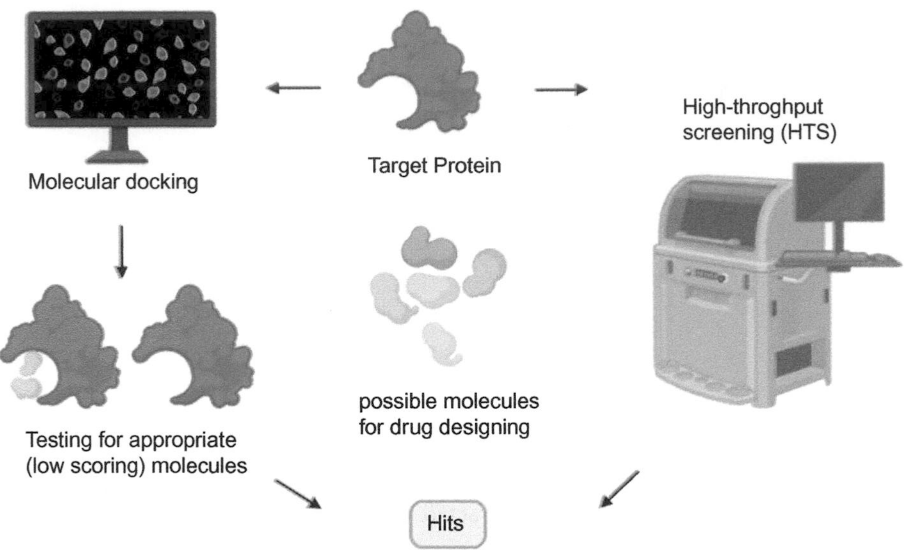

Fig. 3 The process of molecular docking is visualized (left) with a high-throughput drug screening assay (HTS) (right). In the drug screening process, molecular docking techniques and virtual HTS are used to identify molecules that are best situated for drug design.

A study conducted on MDR in breast cancer involved the P-glycoprotein (P-gp). P-glycoprotein is overexpressed in many MDR cancer cell lines, and the efficacy of anticancer drugs increases when P-gp is inhibited [2]. Due to the lack of X-ray crystallography structures of the human P-gp protein, molecular docking was used to examine the 3D structures of P-gp [2].

A similar study that utilized molecular docking in breast cancer focused on the eugenol molecules. Eugenol is extracted from cloves and exhibits anticancer and antibacterial properties, and has a significant affinity for breast cancer receptors [8,15]. The aim of the study has been on the eugenol compounds and chemokines receptors inhibition. Molecular docking was used to determine the structure of the protein-like interactions that play a vital role in drug development. The results were evaluated using RMSD to indicate protein-ligand complex stability [8]. The results confirm that eugenol and cinnamaldehyde have the best docking score for breast cancer, followed by aspirin eugenol ester and 4-allyl-2-methoxyphenyl cinnamate [8]. From the results obtained from in silico studies, the selected eugenols can be further investigated and evaluated for further lead optimization and drug development.

A study regarding fibroblast growth factor receptor (FGFR), which is an important factor in tumor progression, used molecular modeling to interpret a receptor-ligand complex that was optimized, and the hydrogen network was oriented [16]. FGFRs act as receptor tyrosine kinases, and FGFR-targeted anticancer therapy is obstructed by a gatekeeper mutation that leads to chemotherapeutic resistance [16,17]. The gatekeeper residue is present in the first part of the hinge region that connects the N-terminal and C-terminal lobes of the amino acid. For the ligands used in the receptor-ligand complexes, the physiological conditions were maintained in the simulation cell by applying pH 7.4, 310 K temperature, and 0.9% NaCl [16]. A protein complex's low radius of gyration (Rg) profile reflects compactness, whereas a high Rg profile reflects flexibility [16]. The Rg profile of the complex under investigation was nearly similar until the end of the simulation period, which indicates the complex maintained a stable and rigid status during the entire simulation. The number of hydrogen bonds in this complex was found near uniform in the trajectories, which also implies stable ligand binding [16]. A total estimated fitness score was calculated using the van der Waals energy, hydrogen bonding energy, and electrostatic energy [16]. The molecular docking studies revealed that other FGFR gatekeeper mutant proteins and the ligand can also efficiently bind with all these mutants. Details of the predicted ADMET properties revealed that there are minor differences in various properties between the ligands [16].

7. Conclusion

With the growing number of cancer cases worldwide, humans are likely to develop increased resistance to cancer treatments. The use of molecular modeling to design drugs that are specific to the protein and molecular level will allow researchers to efficiently target these cancer-causing cells. Theoretical questions, such as applying known drug molecules to proteins, and understanding the impact of mutations on drug resistance can now easily be explored with computational approaches. Different molecular modeling methods pose their respective strengths and weaknesses; however, their increasing accessibility and preproduction drug evaluation make them exceedingly valuable for improving public health.

References

[1] G.D. Geromichalos, Importance of molecular computer modeling in anticancer drug development, J. BUON 12 (2007) S101–S118.

[2] G. Yalcin-Ozkat, Molecular modeling strategies of cancer multidrug resistance, Drug Resist. Updat. 59 (2021) 100789.

[3] G. Cooper, The Cell: A Molecular Approach, second ed., Sinauer Associates, Sunderland (MA), 2000. Boston University [Google Scholar].

[4] R. Friedman, K. Boye, K. Flatmark, Molecular modelling and simulations in cancer research, Biochim. Biophys. Acta 1836 (2013) 1–14.

[5] W. Gao, C. Addiego, H. Wang, X. Yan, Y. Hou, D. Ji, C. Heikes, Y. Zhang, L. Li, H. Huyan, Real-space charge-density imaging with sub-ångström resolution by four-dimensional electron microscopy, Nature 575 (2019) 480–484.

[6] Y. Fang, W. Cao, F. Liang, M. Xia, S. Pan, X. Xu, Structure affinity relationship and docking studies of flavonoids as substrates of multidrug-resistant associated protein 2 (MRP2) in MDCK/MRP2 cells, Food Chem. 291 (2019) 101–109.
[7] Z.L. Johnson, J. Chen, Structural basis of substrate recognition by the multidrug resistance protein MRP1, Cell 168 (2017) 1075–1085. e1079.
[8] H.O. Rasul, B.K. Aziz, D.D. Ghafour, A. Kivrak, In silico molecular docking and dynamic simulation of eugenol compounds against breast cancer, J. Mol. Model. 28 (2022) 1–18.
[9] B.A. Reva, A.V. Finkelstein, J. Skolnick, What is the probability of a chance prediction of a protein structure with an rmsd of 6 Å? Fold. Des. 3 (1998) 141–147.
[10] S. Dallavalle, V. Dobričić, L. Lazzarato, E. Gazzano, M. Machuqueiro, I. Pajeva, I. Tsakovska, N. Zidar, R. Fruttero, Improvement of conventional anti-cancer drugs as new tools against multidrug resistant tumors, Drug Resist. Updat. 50 (2020), 100682.
[11] S.F. Altschul, W. Gish, W. Miller, E.W. Myers, D.J. Lipman, Basic local alignment search tool, J. Mol. Biol. 215 (1990) 403–410.
[12] H.M. Berman, J. Westbrook, Z. Feng, G. Gilliland, T.N. Bhat, H. Weissig, I.N. Shindyalov, P.E. Bourne, The protein data bank, Nucleic Acids Res. 28 (2000) 235–242.
[13] O. Silakari, P.K. Singh, Concepts and Experimental Protocols of Modelling and Informatics in Drug Design, Academic Press, 2020.
[14] R.P. Hertzberg, A.J. Pope, High-throughput screening: new technology for the 21st century, Curr. Opin. Chem. Biol. 4 (2000) 445–451.
[15] J.H. Hoofnagle, LiverTox: a website on drug-induced liver injury, in: Drug-Induced Liver Disease, Elsevier, 2013, pp. 725–732.
[16] A. Mahfuz, M.A. Khan, S. Biswas, S. Afrose, S. Mahmud, N.M. Bahadur, F. Ahmed, In search of novel inhibitors of anti-cancer drug target fibroblast growth factor receptors: insights from virtual screening, molecular docking, and molecular dynamics, Arab. J. Chem. 15 (2022), 103882.
[17] M. Azam, M.A. Seeliger, N.S. Gray, J. Kuriyan, G.Q. Daley, Activation of tyrosine kinases by mutation of the gatekeeper threonine, Nat. Struct. Mol. Biol. 15 (2008) 1109–1118.

CHAPTER 3

Discovery of anticancer therapeutics: Computational chemistry and Artificial Intelligence-assisted approach

Subrata Das[a], Anupam Das Talukdar[b], Deepa Nath[c], and Manabendra Dutta Choudhury[b]

[a]Department of Botany and Biotechnology, Karimganj College, Karimganj, Assam, India
[b]Department of Life Science and Bioinformatics, Assam University, Silchar, Assam, India
[c]Department of Botany, Gurucharan College, Silchar, Assam, India

Abstract

Nowadays, cancer is causing a serious health issue worldwide. Due to inadequate detection, heterogeneity in tumor formation, chemoresistance, drug resistance, and also manifestation of metastases, the death rate is increasing. Hence, managing of these challenges needs more potent and effective anticancer drugs. The new drug development requires longer time and more cost. Therefore, in the recent technological advancement, search for alternate methods to develop new drugs is a necessary step, which can remove the complex processes, lessen cost, shorten time, and improves success rates. Drug repurposing, computational chemistry, and Artificial Intelligence-assisted approaches are new and novel way of thinking toward the development of anticancer drugs. Drug repurposing with AI can develop a novel effective and specific anticancer drug for the treatment of cancer. The application of AI helps to diagnose the actual cause of cancerous development in the patient and also to determine the doses of effective drugs to be applied for particular cancer. AI together with computational chemistry provides an enhancement to the medical system for the effective diagnosis and treatment of cancer.

Abbreviations

ACE angiotensin-converting enzyme
ADMET absorption, distribution, metabolism, excretion, toxicity
AI Artificial Intelligence
CDSS clinical decision support system
CT scan computed tomography scan
DL deep learning
FDA Food and Drug Administration
IARC International Agency for Research on Cancer
MD molecular dynamics
ML machine learning
MRI magnetic resonance imaging
NGS next generation sequencing
NMR nuclear magnetic resonance

Computational Methods in Drug Discovery and Repurposing for Cancer Therapy
https://doi.org/10.1016/B978-0-443-15280-1.00007-8

QSAR quantitative structure-activity relationship
WHO World Health Organization

1. Introduction

Cancer is one of the global health issues of modern day, and it shares the second most cause of death worldwide. A report of WHO and IARC demonstrated that approximately 9.6 million deaths were noted globally due to cancer in 2018, 606,520 in 2020, and expected to 13 million new cancer-related deaths by 2030 [1,2]. The most common cancer-related deaths are due to lung, female breast, and colorectal carcinoma. These are ranked among the top five together with stomach and pancreatic cancer along with mortality rate, for which therapeutic choices are very minimal. The increased death rate in these cancer patients depends on several factors, such as inadequate detection, heterogeneity in tumor formation, chemoresistance, and also manifestation of metastases. About 60% patients are diagnosed at late stages with metastasis, where survival chances become very minimal as cells proliferate very quickly in this phase [3]. Cancer in metastatic phase is very aggressive, in which patients' mortality rate stands above 90%. High rate of proliferation and metastasis, and drug resistance with nonspecific target activity are important challenges in the management and treatment of cancer [4]. A number of lead molecules have been isolated and developed as drugs for the prevention and treatment of cancer. Because of low specificity and high toxicity of the drugs, the effectiveness becomes very limited. Hence, managing of these challenges needs more potent and effective anticancer drugs. The development of novel anticancer drugs progresses through a series of steps, which include identification, isolation, optimization, and pharmacological activity testing with preclinical and clinical evaluation. This developmental process for the generation of new drugs costs approximately 161–1800 million US dollars and takes 11.4–13.5 years per drug. Furthermore, below 5% of the identified molecules pass through clinical trial phase I, and some of them fall short of clinical trial phase II [5,6]. Therefore, in the recent technological advance time, exploration of alternate methods or ways to generate new drugs is a necessary step, which can remove the complex processes, lessen cost and time, and improves the success rate. Drug repurposing, computational chemistry, and Artificial Intelligence-assisted approaches are a new and novel way of thinking toward the development of anticancer drugs [7].

2. Drug repurposing

Repurposing of drug has gained a serious attention in the recent time as an alternate approach in the process of drug development [8,9]. Repurposing of drug or redirection or repositioning is the use of an approved drug for other specific indication (Fig. 1). The key advantage of using repurposed drug is accessibility of information that lessens the requirement of added studies of tolerability, pharmacokinetics, and toxicity of the drugs (Fig. 2). Due to these properties, the repurposed drugs go for speedy clinical trials [7]. The

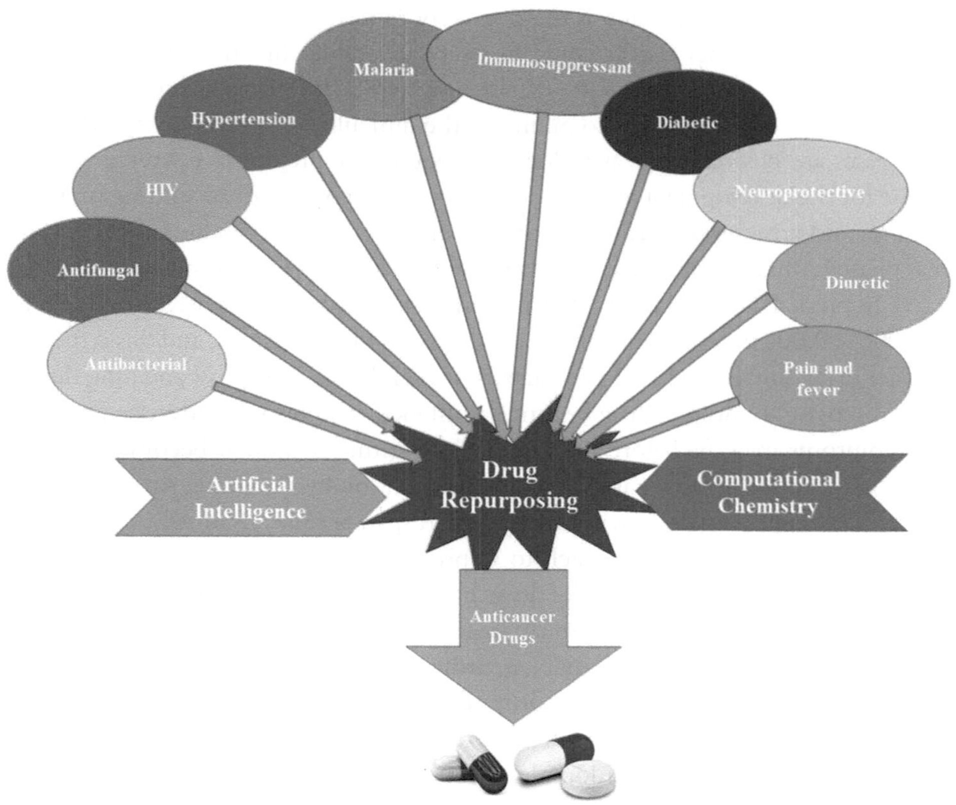

Fig. 1 Schematic representation of development of anticancer drug through repurposing of drugs with the help of artificial intelligence and computational chemistry.

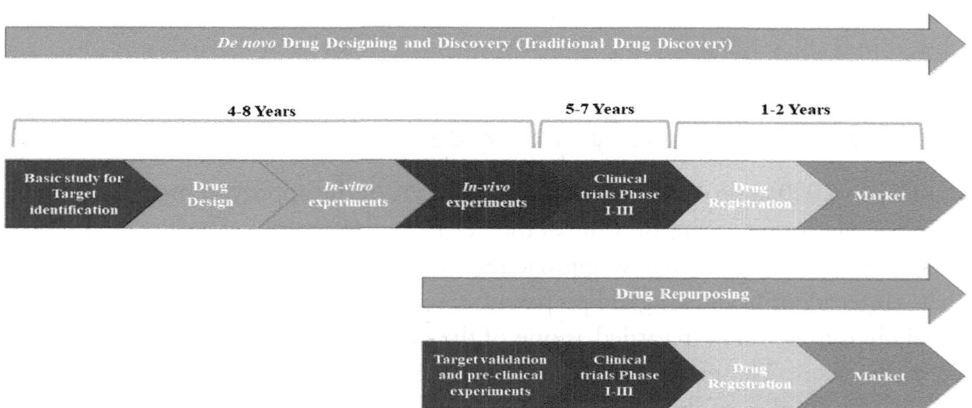

Fig. 2 Graphic illustration of estimated time and steps of traditional drug discovery and drug repurposing.

ultimate aim of drug repurposing is the discovery of new application for existing drugs [10]. While various other factors could be accredited with this strategy, the economic advantage remains the driving force. In this strategy, the pharmaceutical companies get the extension of their patents to minimize the difficulties in productivity. Moreover, the processes are cost-effective as it does not require the preliminary screening of new molecule for the development of drugs. The discovery of new anticancer drug is a tedious procedure, and it requires thorough testing for efficacy and safety in human clinical trials such as phase I, phase II, phase III, and phase IV clinical trials [11]. Commonly, if a drug is effective in phase III clinical trials, FDA provides the approval for its use. But only one in every 5000–10,000 potential anticancer leads receives FDA approval, and this is the 5% of anticancer drugs entering phase I clinical trials [6,12]. In the rising cost and long duration for new discovery of drug, if drug becomes resistance, patients with advanced condition of the symptoms may die before the potential substitute treatment becomes accessible. Here, drug repurposing will make a serious contribution by providing a treatment strategy with FDA-approved drugs within a very short span of time. Gradually, clinicians and researchers are applying this approach to improve the situation of drug deficiency for anticancer therapies [13]. A number of drugs have been effectively repurposed from non-cancer uses to cancer therapeutics: aspirin in colorectal cancer [14]; valproic acid for leukemia, an antiepileptic drug; celecoxib, an arthritis drug for colorectal, breast, and lung cancers [15]; metformin, antidiabetic drug, for breast, prostate, and colorectal cancers [16]; losartan, antihypertensive (angiotensin receptor blockers) used for breast and pancreatic cancer [17–20]; and thalidomide, a drug for morning sickness now effectively being used to treat multiple myeloma [21,22]. Several nononcologic drugs newly identified and repurposed for anticancer therapy can act by the inhibition of proliferation and induction of cell death in vitro, in vivo, and in clinical trials [23,24]. All these drugs earlier have been used for other complications, have validated drug safety information, and are economical (particularly when they are accessible as generics) [25]. A few of these drugs are listed in Tables 1 and 2.

3. Computational chemistry in drug designing

The FDA in 2020 approved 53 new leads, and 35% of the approved products are anti-cancer, which dominate the list. One of the key factors responsible for this revolutionary success is the development of new approaches and knowledge of computational methods, such as target identification, ligand preparation, screening, and drug designing. Computational chemistry is now regarded as one of the prominent approaches in the drug discovery processes. The growth of new software, hardware, and their amalgamation to interpret activity data of drugs coupled with new algorithms can potentially contribute to lessen the time and costs required to generate a novel administrable drug [81]. The working process of computational chemistry in drug designing relies on structure-based

Table 1 Nononcologic drugs repurposed as anticancer therapeutics.

Sl. no.	Repurposed drugs	Original application	Cancer clinical trials	Citation
1	Rapamycin	Antirestenosis agent immunosuppressant	Breast, rectum, prostate cancer, etc.	[26,27]
2	Prazosin	Hypertension	Adrenal incidentalomas	[28]
3	Indomethacin	Rheumatic disease	Esophageal, colorectal, ovarian cancer, etc.	[29,30]
4	Quinacrine	Giardiasis, malaria, rheumatoid arthritis	Nonsmall-cell lung, prostatic cancer, etc.	[31,32]
5	Ritonavir	HIV	Breast cancer, Kaposi's sarcoma, etc.	[33,34]
6	Artemisinin and related derivatives	Malaria	Lung, breast, colorectal cancer, etc.	[35,36]
7	Chloroquine	Rheumatoid arthritis, malaria	Breast cancer, pancreatic cancer, etc.	[37–39]
8	Curcumin	Dermatological diseases	Breast, prostate cancer, multiple myeloma, etc.	[40–42]
9	Genistein	Menopause, osteoporosis, obesity	Colorectal, bladder, breast cancer, etc.	[43,44]
10	Thalidomide	Sedative, antiemetic	Prostate, ovarian, colorectal cancer, etc.	[45,46]
11	Itraconazole	Antifungal agent	Lung, prostate cancer, etc.	[47–49]
12	Berberine	Bacterial diarrhea	Lung, gastric, colorectal cancer, etc.	[50,51]
13	Niclosamide	Antihelmintic drug	Prostate, colorectal cancer, etc.	[52–54]
14	Triamterene	Diuretic	Acute myelocytic leukemia, etc.	[55]
15	Mebendazole and related derivatives	Intestinal helminthiasis	Medulloblastoma, glioma, astrocytoma, etc.	[56,57]
16	Aspirin	Pain, fever	Esophageal, gastrointestinal cancer, etc.	[58,59]
17	Thiocolchicoside	Rheumatologic, orthopedic disorders	Leukemia, myeloma, and squamous cell carcinoma	[60]
18	Spironolactone	High blood pressure and edema	Breast and prostate cancer	[61]
19	Metformin	Obese type 2 diabetes	Breast, prostate, colorectal cancer, etc.	[62,63]
20	Disulfiram	Alcohol-aversion drug	Breast, prostate cancer, melanoma etc.	[64]
21	Ivermectin	Antiparasitic	Breast cancer cells	[65]

Continued

Table 1 Nononcologic drugs repurposed as anticancer therapeutics—cont'd

Sl. no.	Repurposed drugs	Original application	Cancer clinical trials	Citation
22	Brefeldin A	Antibiotic	Colorectal cancer	[66]
23	Lenalidomide	Immunomodulatory drugs	Multiple myeloma, follicular or marginal lymphoma	[67]
24	Pomalidomide	Immunomodulatory drugs	Relapsed and/or refractory multiple myeloma	[68]
25	Hydralazine	Antihypertensives	Breast, ovarian, cervical cancer, and rectal cancer, refractory solid tumors	[69]
26	Valproate	Bipolar disorder Epilepsy Migraine headaches	Inhibits cancer cell proliferation and angiogenesis, induce apoptosis	[70–72]
27	Levomepromazine	Schizophrenia Psychosis Antiemetic	Promotes differentiation of cancer stem cell; antiproliferative effect in leukemic cells	[73]
28	Olanzapine	Bipolar disorder in Schizophrenia	Interrupts cholesterol balance to kill cancer cells	[74]
29	Citalopram	Obsessive-compulsive disorder	Induce apoptosis and decreases proliferation in carcinoma cells	[75–77]
30	Fluoxetine	Eating disorders	Induce apoptosis by inhibition of proliferation in cancer cells	
31	Paroxetine	Stroke recovery	Synergistic antiproliferative interaction by downregulating pAKT	
32	Sertraline	Premature ejaculation	Synergistic antiproliferative interaction by downregulating pAKT	
33	Imipramine	Major sadness, insomnia, chronic pain, attention-deficit hyperactivity disorder	Induces apoptosis and prevents proliferation in neuroendocrine tumors	[78,79]
34	Trimipramine			
35	Amitriptyline			

Table 2 Drugs undergoing preclinical study for repurposing in cancer treatment.

Sl. no.	Repurpose drugs	Chemical structure	Citation
1	Telmisartan	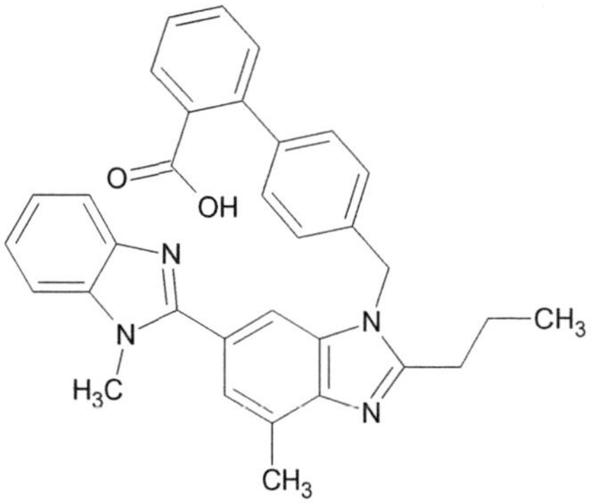	[80]
2	Candesartan	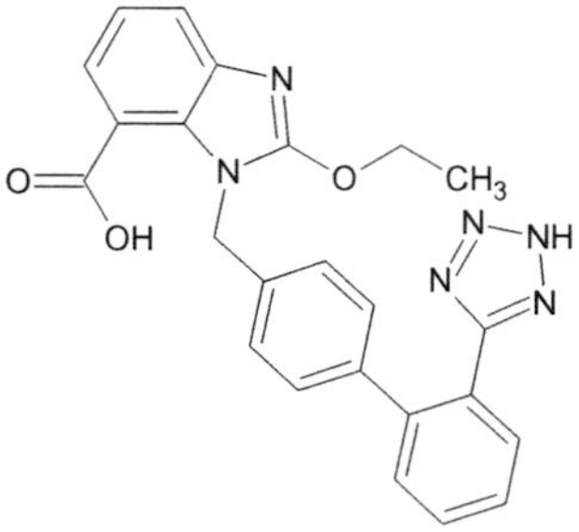	
3	Irbesartan	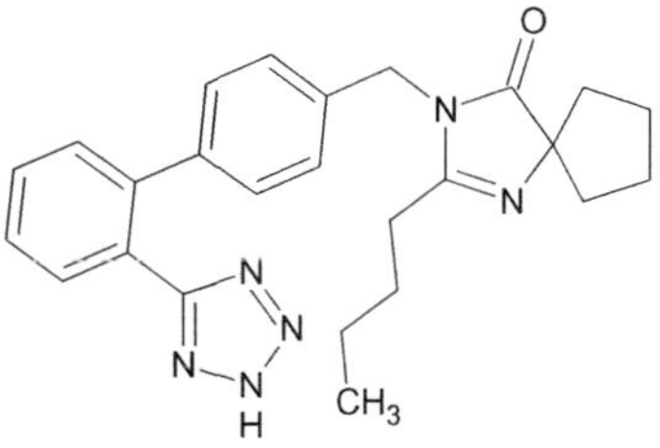	Dinić (2020)
4	Amiloride	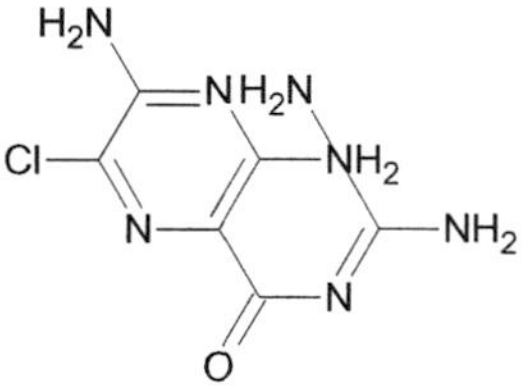	
5	Cariporide	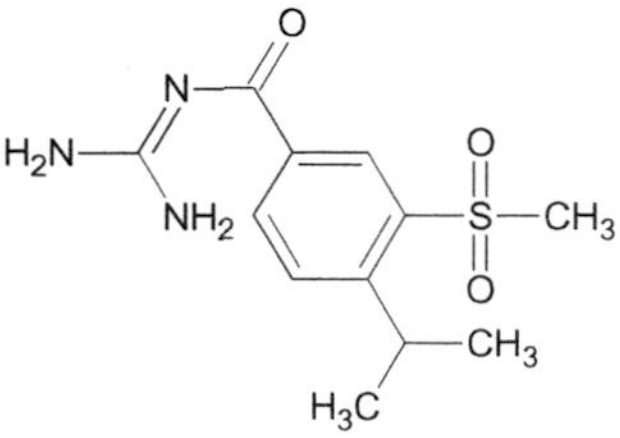	

Continued

Table 2 Drugs undergoing preclinical study for repurposing in cancer treatment—cont'd

Sl. no.	Repurpose drugs	Chemical structure	Citation
6	Furosemide	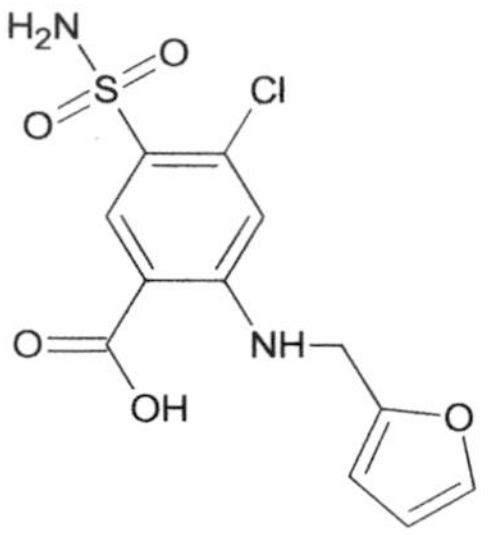	
7	Ethacrynic acid	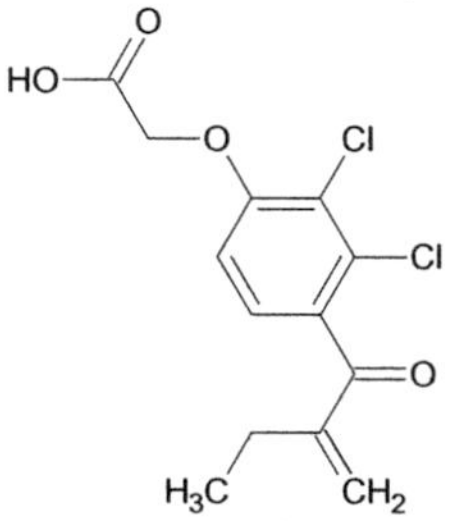	Dinić (2020)
8	Carvedilol	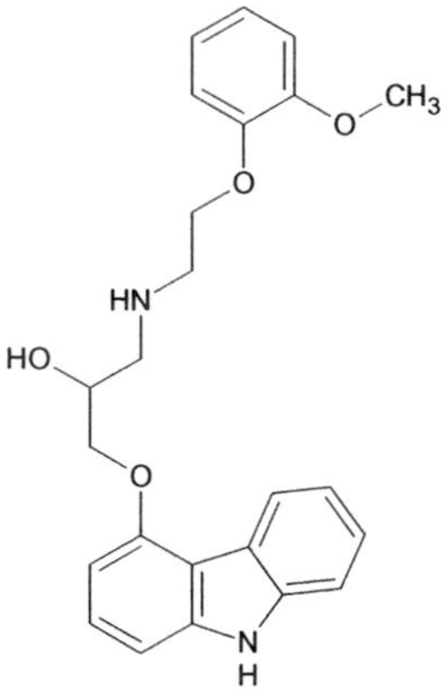	
9	Rosiglitazone	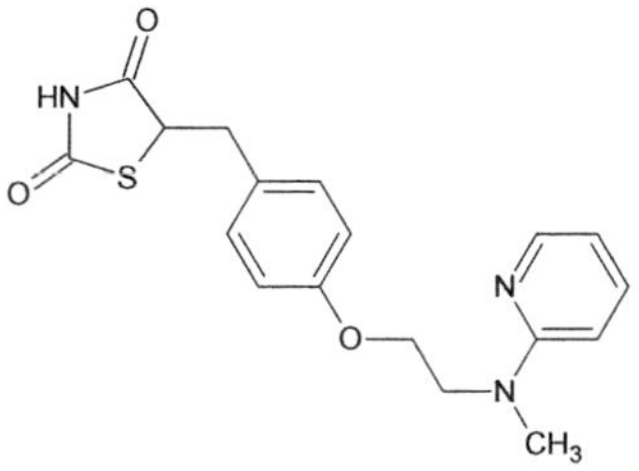	

Table 2 Drugs undergoing preclinical study for repurposing in cancer treatment—cont'd

Sl. no.	Repurpose drugs	Chemical structure	Citation
10	Anisomycin	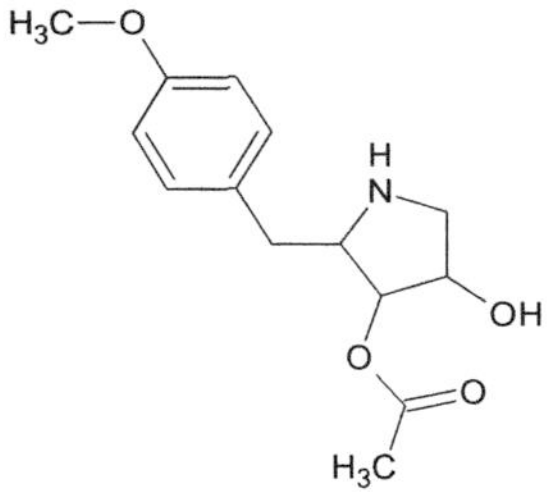	
11	Troglitazone	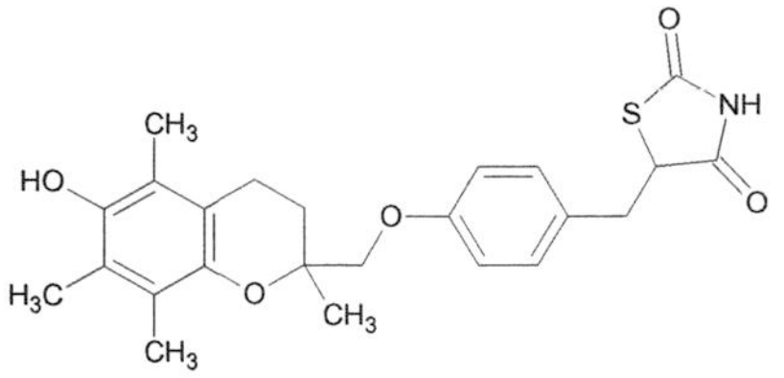	
12	Albendazole	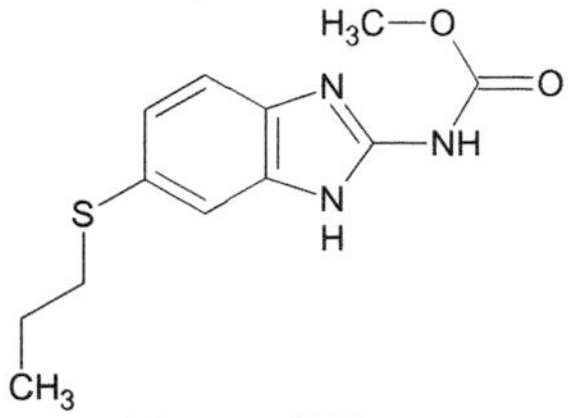	
13	Salinomycin	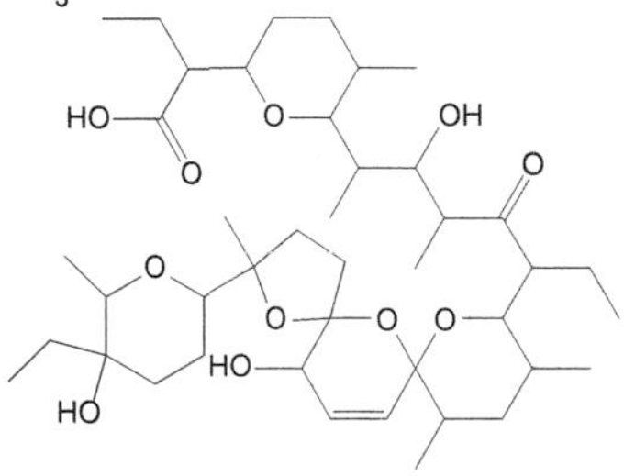	Dinić (2020)
14	Monensin	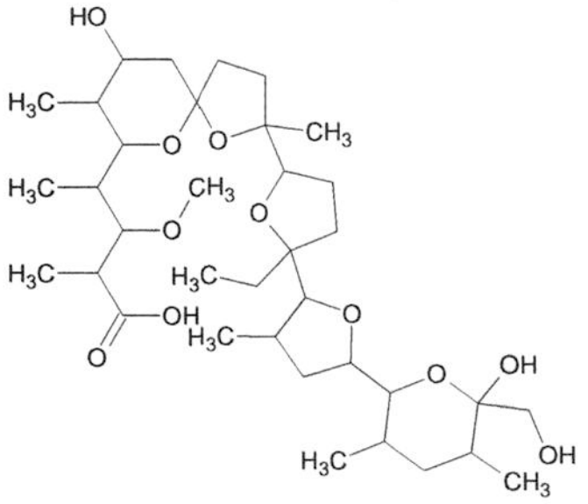	

Continued

Table 2 Drugs undergoing preclinical study for repurposing in cancer treatment—cont'd

Sl. no.	Repurpose drugs	Chemical structure	Citation
15	Primaquine	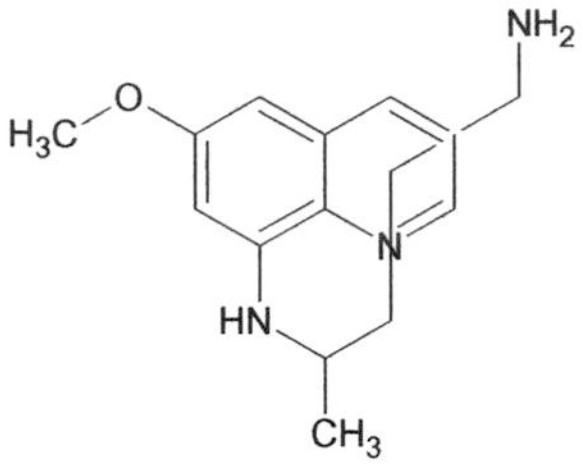	
16	Amodiaquine	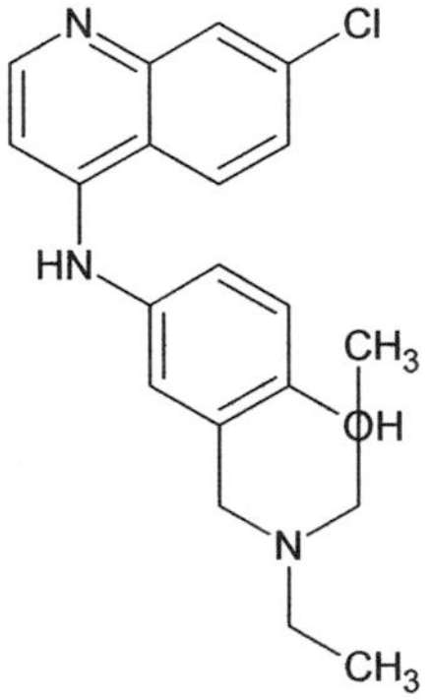	
17	Brivudine	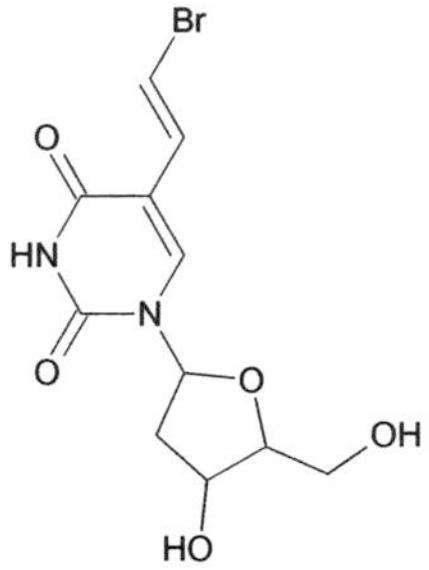	
18	Thioridazine	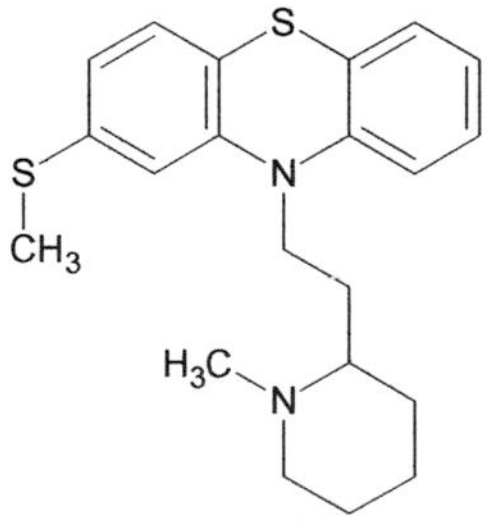	Dinić (2020)
19	Trifluoperazine	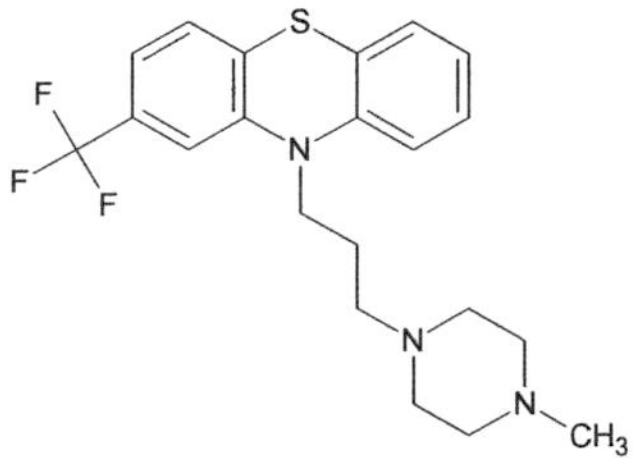	

Table 2 Drugs undergoing preclinical study for repurposing in cancer treatment—cont'd

Sl. no.	Repurpose drugs	Chemical structure	Citation
20	Chlorpromazine	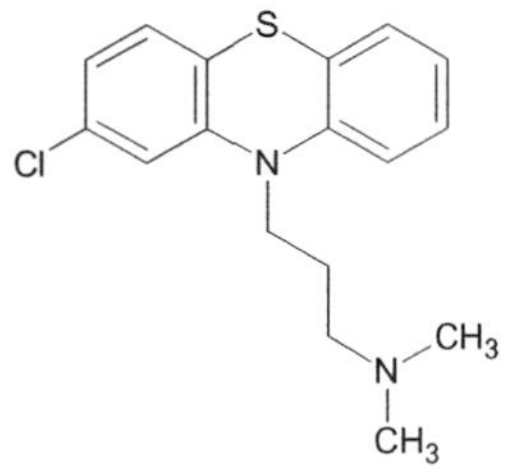	Dinić (2020)
21	Mefloquine	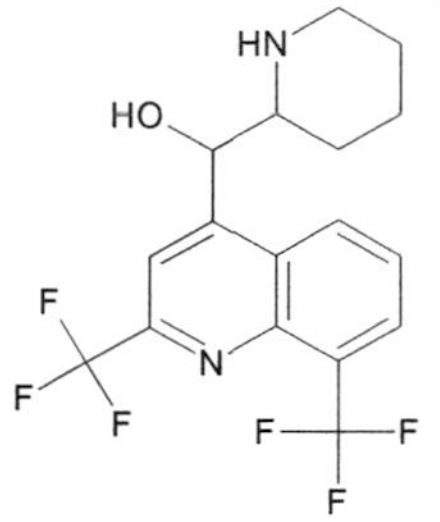	
22	Minocycline	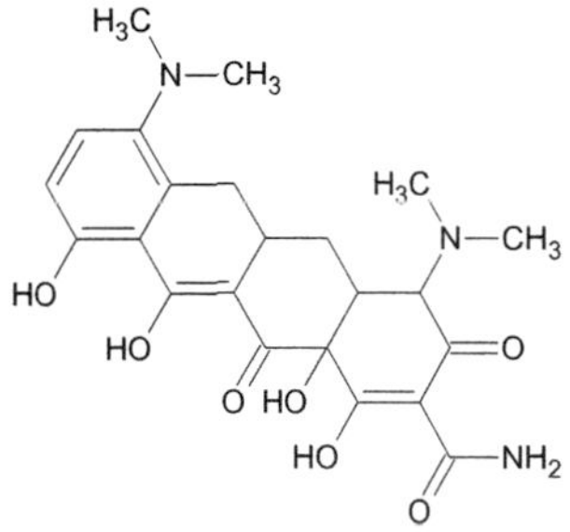	

drug designing, which includes two strategies, i.e., target-based and ligand-based drug designing. For anticancer drug development, the drug target prediction is one of the tedious jobs. Human body consists of nearly 30K genes, in which approximately 6K to 8K positions are assessed as potent drug targets. Though, only 400 encoded proteins have been verified to be efficient for drug design [82,83]. Cancer comprises several vital molecular drug targets for the development of therapeutics [84]. New and accurate in silico target prediction procedures are essential for the precise drug targets prediction. Several drug target interactive web servers are now available, which consist of several databases of drug-target (Table 3) and prediction tools (Table 4). A few FDA-approved anticancer drugs are listed in Table 5.

Table 3 Drug target databases [83].

Databases	Websites
MATADOR	http://matador.embl.de/
TTD	http://bidd.nus.edu.sg/group/ttd/ttd.asp
TDR targets	http://tdrtargets.org/
SuperTarget	http://insilico.charite.de/supertarget/
DrugBank	https://www.drugbank.ca/
PDTD	http://www.dddc.ac.cn/pdtd/
BindingDB	http://www.bindingdb.org/
STITCH	http://stitch.embl.de/
DCDB	http://www.cls.zju.edu.cn/dcdb/
CancerDR	http://crdd.osdd.net/raghava/cancerdr/
ChEMBL	https://www.ebi.ac.uk/chembldb

Table 4 Computational tools for target prediction [83].

Computational tools	Websites
Pharmmapper	http://www.lilab-ecust.cn/pharmmapper/
SwissTarget Prediction	http://www.swisstargetprediction.ch/
Chemmapper	https://omictools.com/chemmapper-tool
SuperPred	http://prediction.charite.de/
DINIES	http://www.genome.jp/tools/dinies/
SEA	https://omictools.com/sea-2-tool
Tide	http://sysbio.molgen.mpg.de/tide

The discovery of web server and target prediction tools makes the computational chemistry approach of drug designing more interesting and reliable in terms of time and cost-saving.

4. Structure-based drug designing

Structure-based drug designing relies on the interaction between receptor protein and the bioactive ligand molecule when three-dimensional structural information is available [102]. Through the advancement of spectroscopic techniques like NMR and X-ray crystallography, a revolutionary advancement has been attained in the process of drug designing, leading to the better understanding of structural elucidation of drug targets and ligands. Based on 3D structure of proteins, novel lead molecule can be designed to induce medicinal activity. Hence, this strategy of structure-based drug designing could deliver a serious insight into novel drug design through discovery and optimization of lead molecule [83,103]. Angiotensin-converting enzyme (ACE) inhibitor, Capoten (captopril), was known to be the foremost efficacious specimens of exploring structural data to

Table 5 Few FDA-approved anticancer drugs developed with the aid of computational chemistry.

Sl. no.	Drug name	Therapeutic area	Citation
1	Darolutamide	Prostate cancer	[85]
2	Cladribine	Hairy cell leukemia	[86]
3	Selinexor	Multiple myeloma	[87]
4	Entrectinib	Solid tumors and nonsmall-cell lung cancer	[88]
5	Alpelisib	Breast cancer	[89]
6	Fedratinib Hydrochloride	Myelofibrosis	[90]
7	Erdafitinib	Urothelial carcinoma	[91]
8	Zanubrutinib	Mantle cell lymphoma	[92]
9	Dacomitinib	Nonsmall-cell lung cancer	[93,94]
10	Apalutamide	Prostate cancer	[88]
11	Binimetinib	Melanoma	[95]
12	Glasdegib Maleate	Acute myeloid leukemia	[96]
13	Larotrectinib Sulfate	Solid tumors	[97]
14	Encorafenib	Melanoma and colorectal cancer	[95]
15	Ivosidenib	Acute myeloid leukemia	[98]
16	Gilteritinib Fumarate	Acute myeloid leukemia	[99]
17	Duvelisib	Follicular lymphoma (FL), chronic lymphocytic leukemia (CLL)	[93]
18	Abemaciclib	Breast cancer	[100]
19	Lorlatinib	Nonsmall-cell lung cancer	[101]

optimize drug designing in the 1980s [104]. Since then, structure-based drug designing process has been in use as one of the novel and effective algorithms for cheaper, faster, and more efficacious drug development against cancer. During the past decade, the structure-based drug designing strategy has been played an important role in the development of therapeutic research [105–108]. There are two strategies of structure-based drug designing: one is target-based drug design, where target is a receptor protein and its structure is known. The search for suitable ligand molecule is undertaken to obtain an effective protein-ligand interaction for the development of novel drug. And the other is ligand-based drug design, where ligand's structure is known and search for suitable target for the specific diseases is undertaken to obtain an effective ligand-target interaction for drugs.

5. ADME/Tox screening and drug-likeness prediction

Absorption, distribution, metabolism, excretion, and toxicity (ADMET) screening and drug likeness prediction of ligands are much needed criterion in the designing of drug. A molecule to be drug must be easily absorbable, distributed to the specific place of action, is easy to metabolize, and after performing its action, it should be excreted properly so that no toxicity or harm could be developed in the body. Drug likeness prediction is also a necessary step in the development of drug. Drug likeness of molecule relies on Rule of 5 provided by C. Lipinski, molecule that obeys the Lipinski filter that may be treated as drug like. ADME/Tox screening can be executed by login to the web server, viz., FAF-Drugs3 of Mobyle@rpbs, ADMET Predictor, OSIRIS Property Explorer, ADMET Modeler, etc., and drug likeness can be checked with Molsoft L.L.C. online portal [102].

6. Molecular docking

It is a structure-based method used in the drug design process. In this strategy, the ligand and target are allowed to interact among each other based on their affinity. Docking relies on an algorithm that describes the intermolecular interaction between the specific target receptor and the ligand. Ligand molecule goes on interaction with the receptor protein at a definite binding pocket of protein with favorable conformations [102,109]. Molecular docking can be performed in two situations: the rigid docking and flexible docking [83]. The binding and interaction in rigid docking process relies on the static condition of chemical, geometrical, and physical complementarity between the target proteins and the ligand molecules, while it overlooks the induced-fit theory and flexibility [110]. The docking in rigid condition is more preferred than flexible docking, because it is swift and highly effective and applicable to the high-throughput virtual screening with large number of ligands and is time-efficient. However, the flexible docking process is considered to be more accurate and detailed. With the technology advancement in computing system, flexible docking method is developing continuously with more accessibility. There are several types of molecular docking software available in the computational domain, such as AutoDock, Glide, DOCK, FlexX, Discovery Studio, Molegro virtual docker, Sybyl, etc. [83].

7. Quantitative structure-activity relationship modeling

Quantitative structure activity relationship (QSAR) is a ligand-based method that analyzes the bioactivities of lead molecule with several molecular descriptors. Based on the descriptor of the ligands, a mathematical model is generated by the algorithm of the software. These generated models illustrate the responses of targets based on the activities of the ligand's structural appearances. QSAR is determined by evaluating the correlations and regression between the chemical characteristics and the biological activities of the ligands. Evaluation of quantifiable bioactivities is attained as concentration of a chemical element essential to deliver a biological response. The structure-activity relationship of ligand can be determined with the available software, such as QSARPro, cQSAR, Easy-QSAR and McQSAR, etc. [102,111].

8. Molecular dynamics simulation

Molecular dynamics simulation is a structure-based methods of computational drug design. In MD simulation, the interaction between the protein and the ligand molecule is calculated in a dynamic state of environment as inside the human body. A dynamic virtual living environment is created to check the interaction among the ligands and the target protein. The interaction is recorded in each fraction of time in all possible pockets or residue of bonding protein. The water molecule in the MD simulation environment plays a crucial role in determining the interaction between the protein and drug, which also takes part toward the affinity of the protein-drug interaction. The energy minimization and free energy calculation also help to know the conformational changes during the interactions of the molecules. MD simulation is a step forward toward the understanding of behavior of molecules that take part in the interaction under the several mechanical stresses that arise in a cellular environment [81,112,113].

9. Artificial Intelligence in drug discovery

In 1956 at the Dartmouth Summer Workshop, the term "Artificial intelligence" (AI) was first coined, which stated as "thinking machines." Simply, AI may be described as the capability of a machines to recognize and learn relationships and patterns from a pool of samples and use this dataset efficiently for creating decisions on new data. And in other words, AI describes the capability of a machine to act in superficially intellectual ways, creating decisions in reply to new inputs without a specific programmed to do so. However, typical computer programs create outputs only after receiving a set of instructions. The term "AI" is broadly comprising of deep learning (DL) and machine learning (ML). The subfield of AI is ML, and the subset of ML is deep learning that emphases on deep artificial neural networks to mimic the capability of human brains for processing data to identify objects, images, improve drug discovery, process languages, improve diagnosis, advancement in precision medicines and support humans to take decisions. Nowadays, deep learning has grown massive importance due to its extraordinary achievement in computer-aided face recognition and image sorting, among others. Due to these characteristics of deep learning, extensive applicability is noted in several research fields of cancer and medicine. Such as use of robotics in precisely detection of malignancy from tumor images of radiology [114–118]. AI is now become a reliable technique to predict or analyze anticancer activity of drug molecule during the development of drugs. A particular drug molecule may have an effective inhibitory activity to different cancer and experimental information from big data often explores the connection between genomic instability of cancerous cells and drugs activity [119]. A model of AI was developed by incorporating ML and screening data, which can interpret the action of anticarcinogenic drugs in accordance with changing state of genome of cancer cell [120]. A group of researchers developed a model of drug sensitivity test with machine learning (elastic net regression) technique. The model was evidenced to fruitfully predict the sensitivity of drugs in patient with gastric cancer, ovarian cancer, and endometrial cancer [121–123]. AI plays a vital role in determining drug resistance in cancer cells. It can swiftly recognize how cancerous cells develop resistance to anticancer drugs by analyzing and learning information on cancer cells having drug-resistant activity, which can benefit the development of improved quality of drugs and also regulate drug use [124,125]. An AI algorithm developed by Hu et al. [126] can interpret the digital images of cervix of women and precisely recognize the precarcinogenic symptoms that required the treatment to avoid patient's overtreatment. Another machine learning device can identify which breast inflammation is probable to become cancerous, benefiting doctors and patients to take the right decisions for treatment and diminish redundant surgery [127]. Deep learning technology provides a boost in treatment choices of cancer in very intelligent way. The development of NGS and advanced imaging technologies like CT scan, MRI, and other radiological technologies on AI platforms generate a large number of clinical information of cancerous patients. Based on the clinical information of cancerous patients, AI can discover the appropriate treatment strategy for doctors [128–130]. Printz invented a clinical decision support system (CDSS) taking the platform of deep learning technology of AI. This can collect and assess a big volume of clinical information from health histories and produce cancer treatment opportunities. The newer study reveals the status of AI technology in serving oncologists to improve cancer handling tactics in patients [131]. The AI platform is also providing a skill to doctors toward determining the personalized medicine and precision medicine strategy for the treatment of cancerous patient [132].

10. Conclusion

Cancer is causing a serious damage to humankind worldwide, and if its damaging activity is not hindered today, it will be late to handle. Due to increase in drug resistance and mutating behavior of cancerous lesions, the available drug molecule to treat cancer remains in the side-line and could not make a hindrance to the cancer cells. In the recent times, the advancement in technology and novel research activity toward the development of cancer therapeutics and treatment procedure is proving to be fruitful to mitigate cancer. The development of computational chemistry and artificial intelligence have been proved to be an effective strategy to find the actual diagnosis and treatment of cancer patient. Drug repurposing is also a new strategy toward searching of effective control of cancer. Several noncancerous drugs are being approved by the FDA or remain in the clinical phase for the development of anticancer therapeutics through drug repurposing. AI together with drug repurposing is a novel strategy toward the development of effective anticancer therapeutics.

References

[1] J. Huang, D. Zhao, Z. Liu, F. Liu, Repurposing psychiatric drugs as anti-cancer agents, Cancer Lett. 419 (2018) 257–265.

[2] R.L. Siegel, K.D. Miller, A. Jemal, Cancer statistics, 2020, CA Cancer J. Clin. 70 (1) (2020) 7–30.

[3] S. Das, D. Nath, M.D. Choudhury, Molecular docking analysis of flupenthixol and desmethylastemizole with the apoptotic regulator proteins CFLAR and TRAF2 linked to lung carcinoma, Bioinformation 17 (4) (2021) 470–478.

[4] C. Mottini, F. Napolitano, Z. Li, X. Gao, L. Cardone, Computer-aided drug repurposing for cancer therapy: approaches and opportunities to challenge anticancer targets, Semin. Cancer Biol. 68 (2021) 59–74.

[5] C.P. Adams, V.V. Brantner, Estimating the cost of new drug development: is it really $802 million? Health Aff. 25 (2) (2006) 420–428.

[6] S.M. Paul, D.S. Mytelka, C.T. Dunwiddie, C.C. Persinger, B.H. Munos, S.R. Lindborg, A.L. Schacht, How to improve R&D productivity: the pharmaceutical industry's grand challenge, Nat. Rev. Drug Discov. 9 (3) (2010) 203–214.

[7] S.K. Srivastava, Drug repurposing for cancer therapy, Semin. Cancer Biol. 68 (2021) 1–2.

[8] S.C. Gupta, B. Sung, S. Prasad, L.J. Webb, B.B. Aggarwal, Cancer drug discovery by repurposing: teaching new tricks to old dogs, Trends Pharmacol. Sci. 34 (9) (2013) 508–517.

[9] P. Pantziarka, G. Bouche, L. Meheus, V. Sukhatme, V.P. Sukhatme, P. Vikas, The repurposing drugs in oncology (ReDO) project, Ecancermedicalscience 8 (2014) 442.

[10] S. Pushpakom, F. Iorio, P.A. Eyers, K.J. Escott, S. Hopper, A. Wells, A. Doig, T. Guilliams, J. Latimer, C. McNamee, Drug repurposing: progress, challenges and recommendations, Nat. Rev. Drug Discov. 18 (1) (2019) 41–58.

[11] R. Kurzrock, H.M. Kantarjian, A.S. Kesselheim, E.V. Sigal, New drug approvals in oncology, Nat. Rev. Clin. Oncol. 17 (3) (2020) 140–146.

[12] G.A. Petsko, When failure should be the option, BMC Biol. 8 (1) (2010) 1–3.

[13] Z. Zhang, L. Zhou, N. Xie, E.C. Nice, T. Zhang, Y. Cui, C. Huang, Overcoming cancer therapeutic bottleneck by drug repurposing, Signal Transduct. Target. Therapy 5 (1) (2020) 1–25.

[14] P.M. Rothwell, F.G.R. Fowkes, J.F. Belch, H. Ogawa, C.P. Warlow, T.W. Meade, Effect of daily aspirin on long-term risk of death due to cancer: analysis of individual patient data from randomised trials, Lancet 377 (9759) (2011) 31–41.

[15] R.D. Brandão, J. Veeck, K.K. Van de Vijver, P. Lindsey, B. De Vries, C.H. Van Elssen, M.J. Blok, K. Keymeulen, T. Ayoubi, H.J. Smeets, A randomised controlled phase II trial of pre-operative celecoxib treatment reveals anti-tumour transcriptional response in primary breast cancer, Breast Cancer Res. 15 (2) (2013) 1–12.

[16] R.J. Dowling, S. Niraula, M.C. Chang, S.J. Done, M. Ennis, D.R. McCready, W.L. Leong, J.M. Escallon, M. Reedijk, P.J. Goodwin, Changes in insulin receptor signaling underlie neoadjuvant metformin administration in breast cancer: a prospective window of opportunity neoadjuvant study, Breast Cancer Res. 17 (1) (2015) 1–12.

[17] V.P. Chauhan, I.X. Chen, R. Tong, M.R. Ng, J.D. Martin, K. Naxerova, M.W. Wu, P. Huang, Y. Boucher, D.S. Kohane, Reprogramming the microenvironment with tumor-selective angiotensin blockers enhances cancer immunotherapy, Proc. Natl. Acad. Sci. 116 (22) (2019) 10674–10680.

[18] R. Coulson, S.H. Liew, A.A. Connelly, N.S. Yee, S. Deb, B. Kumar, A.C. Vargas, S.A. O'Toole, A.C. Parslow, A. Poh, The angiotensin receptor blocker, Losartan, inhibits mammary tumor development and progression to invasive carcinoma, Oncotarget 8 (12) (2017) 18640.

[19] A.J. George, A. Allen, A.L. Chand, Repurposing ARBs as treatments for breast cancer, Aging (Albany NY) 9 (5) (2017) 1357.

[20] J.E. Murphy, J.Y. Wo, D.P. Ryan, J.W. Clark, W. Jiang, B.Y. Yeap, L.C. Drapek, L. Ly, C.V. Baglini, L.S. Blaszkowsky, Total neoadjuvant therapy with FOLFIRINOX in combination with losartan followed by chemoradiotherapy for locally advanced pancreatic cancer: a phase 2 clinical trial, JAMA Oncol. 5 (7) (2019) 1020–1027.

[21] A. Palumbo, T. Facon, P. Sonneveld, J. Blade, M. Offidani, F. Gay, P. Moreau, A. Waage, A. Spencer, H. Ludwig, Thalidomide for treatment of multiple myeloma: 10 years later, Blood 111 (8) (2008) 3968–3977.

[22] P.S. Thilakasiri, R.S. Dmello, T.L. Nero, M.W. Parker, M. Ernst, A.L. Chand, Repurposing of drugs as STAT3 inhibitors for cancer therapy, Semin. Cancer Biol. 68 (2021) 31–46.

[23] J.J. Hernandez, M. Pryszlak, L. Smith, C. Yanchus, N. Kurji, V.M. Shahani, S.V. Molinski, Giving drugs a second chance: overcoming regulatory and financial hurdles in repurposing approved drugs as cancer therapeutics, Front. Oncol. 7 (2017) 273.

[24] Q. Zhang, S. Wang, D. Yang, K. Pan, L. Li, S. Yuan, Preclinical pharmacodynamic evaluation of antibiotic nitroxoline for anticancer drug repurposing, Oncol. Lett. 11 (5) (2016) 3265–3272.

[25] T. Efferth, From ancient herb to modern drug: Artemisia annua and artemisinin for cancer therapy, Semin. Cancer Biol. 46 (2017) 65–83.

[26] D.J. McHugh, J. Chudow, M. DeNunzio, S.F. Slovin, D.C. Danila, M.J. Morris, H.I. Scher, D.E. Rathkopf, A Phase I trial of IGF-1R inhibitor cixutumumab and mTOR inhibitor temsirolimus in metastatic castration-resistant prostate cancer, Clin. Genitourin. Cancer 18 (3) (2020) 171–178. e172.

[27] H.S. Rugo, O. Trédan, J. Ro, S.M. Morales, M. Campone, A. Musolino, N. Afonso, M. Ferreira, K.-H. Park, J. Cortes, A randomized phase II trial of ridaforolimus, dalotuzumab, and exemestane compared with ridaforolimus and exemestane in patients with advanced breast cancer, Breast Cancer Res. Treat. 165 (3) (2017) 601–609.

[28] S. Assad Kahn, S.L. Costa, S. Gholamin, R.T. Nitta, L.G. Dubois, M. Fève, M. Zeniou, P.L.C. Coelho, E. El-Habr, J. Cadusseau, The anti-hypertensive drug prazosin inhibits glioblastoma growth via the PKC δ-dependent inhibition of the AKT pathway, EMBO Mol. Med. 8 (5) (2016) 511–526.

[29] C.-C. Lin, K.M. Suen, A. Stainthorp, L. Wieteska, G.S. Biggs, A. Leitão, C.A. Montanari, J.E. Ladbury, Targeting the Shc-EGFR interaction with indomethacin inhibits MAP kinase pathway signalling, Cancer Lett. 457 (2019) 86–97.

[30] S. Mazumder, R. De, S. Debsharma, S. Bindu, P. Maity, S. Sarkar, S.J. Saha, A.A. Siddiqui, C. Banerjee, S. Nag, Indomethacin impairs mitochondrial dynamics by activating the PKCζ–p38–DRP1 pathway and inducing apoptosis in gastric cancer and normal mucosal cells, J. Biol. Chem. 294 (20) (2019) 8238–8258.

[31] E. Nesher, A. Safina, I. Aljahdali, S. Portwood, E.S. Wang, I. Koman, J. Wang, K.V. Gurova, Role of chromatin damage and chromatin trapping of FACT in mediating the anticancer cytotoxicity of DNA-binding small-molecule drugs, Cancer Res. 78 (6) (2018) 1431–1443.

[32] S. Park, A.-Y. Oh, J.-H. Cho, M.-H. Yoon, T.-G. Woo, S.-M. Kang, H.-Y. Lee, Y.-J. Jung, B.-J. Park, Therapeutic effect of quinacrine, an antiprotozoan drug, by selective suppression of p-CHK1/2 in p53-negative malignant cancers, Mol. Cancer Res. 16 (6) (2018) 935–946.

[33] M.S. Ahluwalia, C. Patton, G. Stevens, T. Tekautz, L. Angelov, M.A. Vogelbaum, R.J. Weil, S. Chao, P. Elson, J.H. Suh, Phase II trial of ritonavir/lopinavir in patients with progressive or recurrent high-grade gliomas, J. Neuro-Oncol. 102 (2) (2011) 317–321.

[34] R.B. Batchu, O.V. Gruzdyn, C.S. Bryant, A.M. Qazi, S. Kumar, S. Chamala, S.T. Kung, R.S. Sanka, U.S. Puttagunta, D.W. Weaver, Ritonavir-mediated induction of apoptosis in pancreatic cancer occurs via the RB/E2F-1 and AKT pathways, Pharmaceuticals 7 (1) (2014) 46–57.

[35] G.-Q. Chen, F.A. Benthani, J. Wu, D. Liang, Z.-X. Bian, X. Jiang, Artemisinin compounds sensitize cancer cells to ferroptosis by regulating iron homeostasis, Cell Death Differ. 27 (1) (2020) 242–254.

[36] J. Du, T. Wang, Y. Li, Y. Zhou, X. Wang, X. Yu, X. Ren, Y. An, Y. Wu, W. Sun, DHA inhibits proliferation and induces ferroptosis of leukemia cells through autophagy dependent degradation of ferritin, Free Radic. Biol. Med. 131 (2019) 356–369.

[37] J.M.M. Levy, C.G. Towers, A. Thorburn, Targeting autophagy in cancer, Nat. Rev. Cancer 17 (9) (2017) 528–542.

[38] M. Mauthe, I. Orhon, C. Rocchi, X. Zhou, M. Luhr, K.-J. Hijlkema, R.P. Coppes, N. Engedal, M. Mari, F. Reggiori, Chloroquine inhibits autophagic flux by decreasing autophagosome-lysosome fusion, Autophagy 14 (8) (2018) 1435–1455.

[39] V.W. Rebecca, M.C. Nicastri, C. Fennelly, C.I. Chude, J.S. Barber-Rotenberg, A. Ronghe, Q. McAfee, N.P. McLaughlin, G. Zhang, A.R. Goldman, PPT1 promotes tumor growth and is the molecular target of chloroquine derivatives in cancer, Cancer Discov. 9 (2) (2019) 220–229.

[40] M. Hosseini, S.M. Hassanian, E. Mohammadzadeh, S. ShahidSales, M. Maftouh, H. Fayazbakhsh, M. Khazaei, A. Avan, Therapeutic potential of curcumin in treatment of pancreatic cancer: current status and future perspectives, J. Cell. Biochem. 118 (7) (2017) 1634–1638.
[41] M. Kanai, Therapeutic applications of curcumin for patients with pancreatic cancer, World J. Gastroenterol. 20 (28) (2014) 9384.
[42] Y. Shen, Z. Han, S. Liu, Y. Jiao, Y. Li, H. Yuan, Curcumin inhibits the tumorigenesis of breast cancer by blocking tafazzin/yes-associated protein axis, Cancer Manag. Res. 12 (2020) 1493.
[43] C. Naujokat, D.L. McKee, The "Big Five" phytochemicals targeting cancer stem cells: curcumin, EGCG, sulforaphane, resveratrol and genistein, Curr. Med. Chem. 28 (22) (2021) 4321–4342.
[44] C. Spagnuolo, G.L. Russo, I.E. Orhan, S. Habtemariam, M. Daglia, A. Sureda, S.F. Nabavi, K.P. Devi, M.R. Loizzo, R. Tundis, Genistein and cancer: current status, challenges, and future directions, Adv. Nutr. 6 (4) (2015) 408–419.
[45] S. Lindner, J. Krönke, The molecular mechanism of thalidomide analogs in hematologic malignancies, J. Mol. Med. 94 (12) (2016) 1327–1334.
[46] T. Liu, F. Guo, X. Zhu, X. He, L. Xie, Thalidomide and its analogues: a review of the potential for immunomodulation of fibrosis diseases and opthalmopathy, Exp. Therap. Med. 14 (6) (2017) 5251–5257.
[47] S. Chen, K. Zhuang, K. Sun, Q. Yang, X. Ran, X. Xu, C. Mu, B. Zheng, Y. Lu, J. Zeng, Itraconazole induces regression of infantile hemangioma via downregulation of the platelet-derived growth factor–D/PI3K/Akt/mTOR pathway, J. Investig. Dermatol. 139 (7) (2019) 1574–1582.
[48] M.S. Copley, M. Waldron, V. Athans, S.C. Welch, K.D. Brizendine, E. Cober, C. Siebenaller, Itraconazole vs. posaconazole for antifungal prophylaxis in patients with acute myeloid leukemia undergoing intensive chemotherapy: a retrospective study, Int. J. Antimicrob. Agents 55 (3) (2020), 105886.
[49] H. Tsubamoto, T. Ueda, K. Inoue, K. Sakata, H. Shibahara, T. Sonoda, Repurposing itraconazole as an anticancer agent, Oncol. Lett. 14 (2) (2017) 1240–1246.
[50] W. Ma, M. Zhu, D. Zhang, L. Yang, T. Yang, X. Li, Y. Zhang, Berberine inhibits the proliferation and migration of breast cancer ZR-75-30 cells by targeting Ephrin-B2, Phytomedicine 25 (2017) 45–51.
[51] Y. Wang, S. Zhang, Berberine suppresses growth and metastasis of endometrial cancer cells via miR-101/COX-2, Biomed. Pharmacother. 103 (2018) 1287–1293.
[52] L. Lu, J. Dong, L. Wang, Q. Xia, D. Zhang, H. Kim, T. Yin, S. Fan, Q. Shen, Activation of STAT3 and Bcl-2 and reduction of reactive oxygen species (ROS) promote radioresistance in breast cancer and overcome of radioresistance with niclosamide, Oncogene 37 (39) (2018) 5292–5304.
[53] R. Ma, Z.G. Ma, J.L. Gao, Y. Tai, L.J. Li, H.B. Zhu, L. Li, D.L. Dong, Z.J. Sun, Injectable pegylated niclosamide (polyethylene glycol-modified niclosamide) for cancer therapy, J. Biomed. Mater. Res. A 108 (1) (2020) 30–38.
[54] R.L. Stewart, B.L. Carpenter, D.S. West, T. Knifley, L. Liu, C. Wang, H.L. Weiss, T.S. Gal, E.B. Durbin, S.M. Arnold, S100A4 drives non-small cell lung cancer invasion, associates with poor prognosis, and is effectively targeted by the FDA-approved anti-helminthic agent niclosamide, Oncotarget 7 (23) (2016) 34630.
[55] D. Guillotin, P. Austin, R. Begum, M.O. Freitas, A. Merve, T. Brend, S. Short, S. Marino, S.A. Martin, Drug-repositioning screens identify Triamterene as a selective drug for the treatment of DNA Mismatch Repair deficient cells, Clin. Cancer Res. 23 (11) (2017) 2880–2890.
[56] T. Williamson, T.B. Mendes, N. Joe, J.M. Cerutti, G.J. Riggins, Mebendazole inhibits tumor growth and prevents lung metastasis in models of advanced thyroid cancer, Endocr. Relat. Cancer 27 (3) (2020) 123–136.
[57] L. Zhang, M.B. Dratver, T. Yazal, K. Dong, A. Nguyen, G. Yu, A. Dao, M.B. Dratver, S. Duhachek-Muggy, K. Bhat, Mebendazole potentiates radiation therapy in triple-negative breast cancer, Int. J. Radiat. Oncol. Biol. Phys. 103 (1) (2019) 195–207.
[58] M.M. Gilligan, A. Gartung, M.L. Sulciner, P.C. Norris, V.P. Sukhatme, D.R. Bielenberg, S. Huang, M.W. Kieran, C.N. Serhan, D. Panigrahy, Aspirin-triggered proresolving mediators stimulate resolution in cancer, Proc. Natl. Acad. Sci. 116 (13) (2019) 6292–6297.
[59] C.-C. Hsieh, C.-H. Wang, Aspirin disrupts the crosstalk of angiogenic and inflammatory cytokines between 4T1 breast cancer cells and macrophages, Mediators Inflamm. 2018 (2018) 1–12.

[60] S. Reuter, S. Prasad, K. Phromnoi, J. Ravindran, B. Sung, V.R. Yadav, R. Kannappan, M.M. Chaturvedi, B.B. Aggarwal, Thiocolchicoside exhibits anticancer effects through downregulation of NF-κB pathway and its regulated gene products linked to inflammation and cancer, Cancer Prev. Res. 3 (11) (2010) 1462–1472.
[61] K. Beckmann, H. Garmo, B. Lindahl, L. Holmberg, P. Stattin, J. Adolfsson, J.K. Cruickshank, M. Van Hemelrijck, Spironolactone use is associated with lower prostate cancer risk: a population-wide case-control study, Prostate Cancer Prostatic Dis. 23 (3) (2020) 527–533.
[62] K. Petchsila, N. Prueksaritanond, P. Insin, M. Yanaranop, N. Chotikawichean, Effect of metformin for decreasing proliferative marker in women with endometrial cancer: a randomized double-blind placebo-controlled trial, Asian Pac. J. Cancer Prev. 21 (3) (2020) 733.
[63] Z.-J. Zhang, J. Yuan, Y. Bi, C. Wang, Y. Liu, The effect of metformin on biomarkers and survivals for breast cancer-a systematic review and meta-analysis of randomized clinical trials, Pharmacol. Res. 141 (2019) 551–555.
[64] E. Ekinci, S. Rohondia, R. Khan, Q.P. Dou, Repurposing disulfiram as an anti-cancer agent: updated review on literature and patents, Recent Pat. Anticancer Drug Discov. 14 (2) (2019) 113–132.
[65] Q. Dou, H.-N. Chen, K. Wang, K. Yuan, Y. Lei, K. Li, J. Lan, Y. Chen, Z. Huang, N. Xie, Ivermectin induces cytostatic autophagy by blocking the PAK1/Akt axis in breast cancer, Cancer Res. 76 (15) (2016) 4457–4469.
[66] L. Zhou, W. Gao, K. Wang, Z. Huang, L. Zhang, Z. Zhang, J. Zhou, E.C. Nice, C. Huang, Brefeldin A inhibits colorectal cancer growth by triggering Bip/Akt-regulated autophagy, FASEB J. 33 (4) (2019) 5520–5534.
[67] A.K. Stewart, How thalidomide works against cancer, Science 343 (6168) (2014) 256–257.
[68] L. Sundaresan, P. Kumar, J. Manivannan, U.M. Balaguru, D. Kasiviswanathan, V. Veeriah, S. Anishetty, S. Chatterjee, Thalidomide and its analogs differentially target fibroblast growth factor receptors: thalidomide suppresses FGFR gene expression while pomalidomide dampens FGFR2 activity, Chem. Res. Toxicol. 32 (4) (2019) 589–602.
[69] S. Garcés-Eisele, B. Cedillo-Carvallo, V. Reyes-Núñez, L. Estrada-Marín, R. Vázquez-Pérez, M. Juárez-Calderón, M. Guzmán-García, A. Dueñas-González, A. Ruiz-Argüelles, Genetic selection of volunteers and concomitant dose adjustment leads to comparable hydralazine/valproate exposure, J. Clin. Pharm. Ther. 39 (4) (2014) 368–375.
[70] S. Berendsen, M. Broekman, T. Seute, T. Snijders, C. van Es, F. de Vos, L. Regli, P. Robe, Valproic acid for the treatment of malignant gliomas: review of the preclinical rationale and published clinical results, Expert Opin. Investig. Drugs 21 (9) (2012) 1391–1415.
[71] M. Michaelis, H.W. Doerr, J. Cinatl Jr., Valproic acid as anti-cancer drug, Curr. Pharm. Des. 13 (33) (2007) 3378–3393.
[72] C.H. Ryu, W.S. Yoon, K.Y. Park, S.M. Kim, J.Y. Lim, J.S. Woo, C.H. Jeong, Y. Hou, S.-S. Jeun, Valproic acid downregulates the expression of MGMT and sensitizes temozolomide-resistant glioma cells, J. Biomed. Biotechnol. 2012 (2012) 1–9.
[73] G. Fond, A. Macgregor, J. Attal, A. Larue, M. Brittner, D. Ducasse, D. Capdevielle, Antipsychotic drugs: pro-cancer or anti-cancer? A systematic review, Med. Hypotheses 79 (1) (2012) 38–42.
[74] E.D. Wiklund, V.S. Catts, S.V. Catts, T.F. Ng, N.J. Whitaker, A.J. Brown, L.H. Lutze-Mann, Cytotoxic effects of antipsychotic drugs implicate cholesterol homeostasis as a novel chemotherapeutic target, Int. J. Cancer 126 (1) (2010) 28–40.
[75] A. Serafeim, M.J. Holder, G. Grafton, A. Chamba, M.T. Drayson, Q.T. Luong, C.M. Bunce, C.D. Gregory, N.M. Barnes, J. Gordon, Selective serotonin reuptake inhibitors directly signal for apoptosis in biopsy-like Burkitt lymphoma cells, Blood 101 (8) (2003) 3212–3219.
[76] I. Gil-Ad, A. Zolokov, L. Lomnitski, M. Taler, M. Bar, D. Luria, E. Ram, A. Weizman, Evaluation of the potential anti-cancer activity of the antidepressant sertraline in human colon cancer cell lines and in colorectal cancer-xenografted mice, Int. J. Oncol. 33 (2) (2008) 277–286.
[77] F. Liu, J. Huang, B. Ning, Z. Liu, S. Chen, W. Zhao, Drug discovery via human-derived stem cell organoids, Front. Pharmacol. 7 (2016) 334.
[78] J. Huang, C. Zeng, J. Xiao, D. Zhao, H. Tang, H. Wu, J. Chen, Association between depression and brain tumor: a systematic review and meta-analysis, Oncotarget 8 (55) (2017) 94932.

[79] N.S. Jahchan, J.T. Dudley, P.K. Mazur, N. Flores, D. Yang, A. Palmerton, A.F. Zmoos, D. Vaka, K.Q. Tran, M. Zhou, K. Krasinska, A drug repositioning approach identifies tricyclic antidepressants as inhibitors of small cell lung cancer and other neuroendocrine tumors, Cancer Discov 3 (12) (2013) 1364–1377.

[80] J. Dinić, T. Efferth, A.T. García-Sosa, J. Grahovac, J.M. Padrón, I. Pajeva, F. Rizzolio, S. Saponara, G. Spengler, I. Tsakovska, Repurposing old drugs to fight multidrug resistant cancers, Drug Resist. Updat. 52 (2020) 100713.

[81] M. Castelli, S.A. Serapian, F. Marchetti, A. Triveri, V. Pirota, L. Torielli, S. Collina, F. Doria, M. Freccero, G. Colombo, New perspectives in cancer drug development: computational advances with an eye to design, RSC Med. Chem. 12 (9) (2021) 1491–1502.

[82] X. Chen, C.C. Yan, X. Zhang, X. Zhang, F. Dai, J. Yin, Y. Zhang, Drug–target interaction prediction: databases, web servers and computational models, Brief. Bioinform. 17 (4) (2016) 696–712.

[83] W. Cui, A. Aouidate, S. Wang, Q. Yu, Y. Li, S. Yuan, Discovering anti-cancer drugs via computational methods, Front. Pharmacol. 11 (2020) 733.

[84] J.S. Lazo, E.R. Sharlow, Drugging undruggable molecular cancer targets, Annu. Rev. Pharmacol. Toxicol. 56 (2016) 23–40.

[85] A. Markham, S. Duggan, Darolutamide: first approval, Drugs 79 (16) (2019) 1813–1818.

[86] H.M. Bryson, E.M. Sorkin, Cladribine, Drugs 46 (5) (1993) 872–894.

[87] Y.Y. Syed, Selinexor: first global approval, Drugs 79 (13) (2019) 1485–1494.

[88] Z.T. Al-Salama, Apalutamide: a review in non-metastatic castration-resistant prostate cancer, Drugs 79 (14) (2019) 1591–1598.

[89] A. Markham, Alpelisib: first global approval, Drugs 79 (11) (2019) 1249–1253.

[90] Q. Zhang, Y. Zhang, S. Diamond, J. Boer, J.J. Harris, Y. Li, M. Rupar, E. Behshad, C. Gardiner, P. Collier, The Janus kinase 2 inhibitor fedratinib inhibits thiamine uptake: a putative mechanism for the onset of Wernicke's encephalopathy, Drug Metab. Dispos. 42 (10) (2014) 1656–1662.

[91] A. Markham, Erdafitinib: first global approval, Drugs 79 (9) (2019) 1017–1021.

[92] Y.Y. Syed, Zanubrutinib: first approval, Drugs 80 (1) (2020) 91–97.

[93] H.A. Blair, Duvelisib: first global approval, Drugs 78 (17) (2018) 1847–1853.

[94] P. Sidaway, Cemiplimab effective in cutaneous SCC, Nat. Rev. Clin. Oncol. 15 (8) (2018) 472.

[95] M. Shirley, Encorafenib and binimetinib: first global approvals, Drugs 78 (12) (2018) 1277–1284.

[96] N. Shaik, B. Hee, H. Wei, R.R. LaBadie, Evaluation of the effects of formulation, food, or a proton-pump inhibitor on the pharmacokinetics of glasdegib (PF-04449913) in healthy volunteers: a randomized phase I study, Cancer Chemother. Pharmacol. 83 (3) (2019) 463–472.

[97] Z. Gajdosik, Larotrectinib sulfate, Drugs Future 42 (2017) 275–280.

[98] S. Dhillon, Ivosidenib: first global approval, Drugs 78 (14) (2018) 1509–1516.

[99] S. Dhillon, Gilteritinib: first global approval, Drugs 79 (3) (2019) 331–339.

[100] E.S. Kim, Abemaciclib: first global approval, Drugs 77 (18) (2017) 2063–2070.

[101] Y. Su, X. Long, Y. Song, P. Chen, S. Li, H. Yang, P. Wu, Y. Wang, Z. Bing, Z. Cao, Distribution of ALK fusion variants and correlation with clinical outcomes in Chinese patients with non-small cell lung cancer treated with crizotinib, Target. Oncol. 14 (2) (2019) 159–168.

[102] S. Das, M.A. Laskar, S.D. Sarker, M.D. Choudhury, P.R. Choudhury, A. Mitra, S. Jamil, S.M.A. Lathiff, S.A. Abdullah, N. Basar, Prediction of anti-Alzheimer's activity of flavonoids targeting acetylcholinesterase in silico, Phytochem. Anal. 28 (4) (2017) 324–331.

[103] P. Lu, D.R. Bevan, A. Leber, R. Hontecillas, N. Tubau-Juni, J. Bassaganya-Riera, Computer-aided drug discovery, in: Accelerated Path to Cures, Springer, 2018, pp. 7–24.

[104] C.S. Anthony, G. Masuyer, E.D. Sturrock, K.R. Acharya, Structure based drug design of angiotensin-I converting enzyme inhibitors, Curr. Med. Chem. 19 (6) (2012) 845–855.

[105] S. Debnath, M. Kanakaraju, M. Islam, R. Yeeravalli, D. Sen, A. Das, In silico design, synthesis and activity of potential drug-like chrysin scaffold-derived selective EGFR inhibitors as anticancer agents, Comput. Biol. Chem. 83 (2019), 107156.

[106] J.Y. Hong, I.R. Price, J.J. Bai, H. Lin, A glycoconjugated SIRT2 inhibitor with aqueous solubility allows structure-based design of SIRT2 inhibitors, ACS Chem. Biol. 14 (8) (2019) 1802–1810.

[107] Y. Itoh, Drug discovery researches on modulators of lysine-modifying enzymes based on strategic chemistry approaches, Chem. Pharm. Bull. 68 (1) (2020) 34–45.

[108] A.R. Tondo, L. Caputo, G.F. Mangiatordi, L. Monaci, G. Lentini, A.F. Logrieco, M. Montaruli, O. Nicolotti, L. Quintieri, Structure-based identification and design of angiotensin converting enzyme-inhibitory peptides from whey proteins, J. Agric. Food Chem. 68 (2) (2019) 541–548.
[109] S. Das, A.D. Talukdar, R. Nath, D. Nath, A. Rahaman, S. Bhattacharjee, M.D. Choudhury, Molecular docking analysis of flupenthixol and desmethylastemizole with the apoptotic regulator proteins CFLAR and TRAF2 linked to lung carcinoma, Bioinformation 17 (4) (2021) 470–478.
[110] V. Salmaso, S. Moro, Bridging molecular docking to molecular dynamics in exploring ligand-protein recognition process: an overview, Front. Pharmacol. 9 (2018) 923.
[111] J. Mendenhall, J. Meiler, Improving quantitative structure–activity relationship models using Artificial Neural Networks trained with dropout, J. Comput. Aided Mol. Des. 30 (2) (2016) 177–189.
[112] P.-C. Do, E.H. Lee, L. Le, Steered molecular dynamics simulation in rational drug design, J. Chem. Inf. Model. 58 (8) (2018) 1473–1482.
[113] M. Garofalo, G. Grazioso, A. Cavalli, J. Sgrignani, How computational chemistry and drug delivery techniques can support the development of new anticancer drugs, Molecules 25 (7) (2020) 1756.
[114] Z.J. Baum, X. Yu, P.Y. Ayala, Y. Zhao, S.P. Watkins, Q. Zhou, Artificial intelligence in chemistry: current trends and future directions, J. Chem. Inf. Model. 61 (7) (2021) 3197–3212.
[115] B. Bhinder, C. Gilvary, N.S. Madhukar, O. Elemento, Artificial intelligence in cancer research and precision medicine, Cancer Discov. 11 (4) (2021) 900–915.
[116] T. Davenport, R. Kalakota, The potential for artificial intelligence in healthcare, Future Healthc. J. 6 (2) (2019) 94.
[117] M.J. Iqbal, Z. Javed, H. Sadia, I.A. Qureshi, A. Irshad, R. Ahmed, K. Malik, S. Raza, A. Abbas, R. Pezzani, Clinical applications of artificial intelligence and machine learning in cancer diagnosis: looking into the future, Cancer Cell Int. 21 (1) (2021) 1–11.
[118] Y. LeCun, Y. Bengio, G. Hinton, Deep learning, Nature 521 (7553) (2015) 436–444.
[119] G. Liang, W. Fan, H. Luo, X. Zhu, The emerging roles of artificial intelligence in cancer drug development and precision therapy, Biomed. Pharmacother. 128 (2020), 110255.
[120] A.P. Lind, P.C. Anderson, Predicting drug activity against cancer cells by random forest models based on minimal genomic information and chemical properties, PLoS One 14 (7) (2019), e0219774.
[121] M.A. Hossain, S.M.S. Islam, J.M. Quinn, F. Huq, M.A. Moni, Machine learning and bioinformatics models to identify gene expression patterns of ovarian cancer associated with disease progression and mortality, J. Biomed. Inform. 100 (2019), 103313.
[122] A. Stanzione, R. Cuocolo, R. Del Grosso, A. Nardiello, V. Romeo, A. Travaglino, A. Raffone, G. Bifulco, F. Zullo, L. Insabato, Deep myometrial infiltration of endometrial cancer on MRI: a radiomics-powered machine learning pilot study, Acad. Radiol. 28 (5) (2021) 737–744.
[123] Y. Wang, Z. Wang, J. Xu, J. Li, S. Li, M. Zhang, D. Yang, Systematic identification of non-coding pharmacogenomic landscape in cancer, Nat. Commun. 9 (1) (2018) 1–15.
[124] J.T. Beck, M. Rammage, G.P. Jackson, A.M. Preininger, I. Dankwa-Mullan, M.C. Roebuck, A. Torres, H. Holtzen, S.E. Coverdill, M.P. Williamson, Artificial intelligence tool for optimizing eligibility screening for clinical trials in a large community cancer center, JCO Clin. Cancer Inform. 4 (2020) 50–59.
[125] K. Leventakos, J. Helgeson, A. Mansfield, E. Deering, A. Schwecke, A. Adjei, J. Molina, C. Hocum, T. Halfdanarson, R. Marks, Implementation of artificial intelligence (AI) for lung cancer clinical trial matching in a tertiary cancer center, Ann. Oncol. 30 (2019) ii74.
[126] L. Hu, D. Bell, S. Antani, Z. Xue, K. Yu, M.P. Horning, N. Gachuhi, B. Wilson, M.S. Jaiswal, B. Befano, An observational study of deep learning and automated evaluation of cervical images for cancer screening, J. Natl. Cancer Inst. 111 (9) (2019) 923–932.
[127] M. Bahl, R. Barzilay, A.B. Yedidia, N.J. Locascio, L. Yu, C.D. Lehman, High-risk breast lesions: a machine learning model to predict pathologic upgrade and reduce unnecessary surgical excision, Radiology 286 (3) (2018) 810–818.
[128] M.D. Blackledge, J.M. Winfield, A. Miah, D. Strauss, K. Thway, V.A. Morgan, D.J. Collins, D.-M. Koh, M.O. Leach, C. Messiou, Supervised machine-learning enables segmentation and evaluation of heterogeneous post-treatment changes in multi-parametric MRI of soft-tissue sarcoma, Front. Oncol. 9 (2019) 941.

[129] C. Liu, X. Liu, F. Wu, M. Xie, Y. Feng, C. Hu, Using artificial intelligence (Watson for Oncology) for treatment recommendations amongst Chinese patients with lung cancer: feasibility study, J. Med. Internet Res. 20 (9) (2018), e11087.
[130] P. Meyer, V. Noblet, C. Mazzara, A. Lallement, Survey on deep learning for radiotherapy, Comput. Biol. Med. 98 (2018) 126–146.
[131] C. Printz, Artificial intelligence platform for oncology could assist in treatment decisions, Cancer 123 (6) (2017) 905.
[132] D. Ho, Artificial intelligence in cancer therapy, Science 367 (6481) (2020) 982–983.

CHAPTER 4

Artificial intelligence in oncological therapies

Shloka Adluru
Altrincham Grammar School for Girls, Altrincham, United Kingdom

Abstract

Artificial intelligence (AI) is slowly becoming infused into many aspects of everyday life. Healthcare is a field that could be greatly improved by AI as one of the main goals of modern healthcare is to move toward personalized medicine. This chapter will focus on the integration of AI techniques into the field of oncology with the main objective being to assess the advantages and disadvantages of involving AI models in cancer drug design and treatment. The whole process of cancer treatment, from diagnosis to the development of new drugs, to the design of personalized treatment plans, will be detailed in this chapter with comments on the future prospects of AI in oncology.

Abbreviations

ACP	anticancer peptides
AI	artificial intelligence
ALK	anaplastic lymphoma kinase
CNN	convolutional neural network
DL	deep learning
DNA	deoxyribose nucleic acid
DTI	drug-target interactions
EGFR	epidermal growth factor receptor
FDA	Food and Drug Administration
HPV	human papillomavirus
KRAS	Kirsten rat sarcoma virus
LRP	layer-wise relevance propagation
ML	machine learning
NSCLC	nonsmall cell lung cancer
PPM	phenotypic personalized medicine
RAS	rat sarcoma virus
RNA	ribose nucleic acid
TKI	tyrosine kinase inhibitors

1. Introduction

Cancer is a very broad umbrella term that encompasses a large range of different oncological diseases. Depending on where carcinogenesis occurs, you will get different categories of cancer, such as lung cancer or breast cancer, which will each need to be

Computational Methods in Drug Discovery and Repurposing for Cancer Therapy
https://doi.org/10.1016/B978-0-443-15280-1.00014-5

tackled differently depending on how they arise, how they proliferate, and how they can be killed. For example, cancers such as breast and prostate cancer use hormones for proliferation so may be dealt with using hormone treatment [1] or for bone cancers, radiotherapeutics can be used [2]. Even when considering patients with the same category of cancer, it must be remembered that there are subcategories within a cancer type; e.g., some lung cancers involve a mutated EGFR gene and some other lung cancers involve a mutated ALK gene, and depending on the genetic makeup of the lung cancer, you would be given different drugs in your treatment [3]. Furthermore, even when focusing on a single individual's cancer, there is tumor heterogeneity, meaning that the cells between primary and secondary tumors differ in phenotype and gene expression (intertumor heterogeneity) or even that the cells within a single tumor differ (intratumor heterogeneity) [4].

This further complicates the matter of designing treatment plans for patients as it would be difficult to identify the characteristics of all the different cells across all the tumors in the body and it would be difficult to come up with a combination of therapies and drugs that could target and eradicate all of the cancer cells to avoid recurrence of cancer [4]. Therefore, a single approach cannot be used to efficiently treat all patients, and thus, research into personalizing cancer therapies is necessary. This is where AI demonstrates significant potential for advances in oncological therapies, due to its capacity to work with large quantities of information points to reveal the most optimal approach with the highest chance of success.

2. Importance of early diagnosis

It is well known that survival rates for cancer patients are significantly improved if the cancer is diagnosed and treated at an early stage. For example, in the case of lung cancer (the second most common cancer worldwide) [5], survival rates have been seen to drastically increase the earlier the stage at which the cancer is diagnosed according to UK national statistics [6]. In addition, early detection of cancer has been seen to have economic benefits as the cost of treatment is reduced for less advanced forms of cancer and patients are more able to continue financially supporting their families [7]. According to the World Health Organization, studies have shown that in high-income countries, diagnosing cancer at the early stages can make treatment two to four times less expensive [8].

This is because the longer cancer goes untreated, the higher the likelihood that it has spread to other organs in the body via the blood and lymph system to form secondary tumors. In such cases, surgery to remove the tumor is no longer a viable option [9], and instead, systemic treatments such as chemotherapy and radiotherapy may have to instead be utilized and such therapies often cause severe side effects due to their influence on healthy body cells (especially cells that divide rapidly such as cells in the hair, bone marrow, skin, and intestines) [10]. In a study on the side effects of chemotherapy on patients with breast, lung, or colorectal cancer, 67% were recorded to have endured at least six side effects [11].

Furthermore, the later the stage at which the cancer is treated, the higher the rate of recurrence, which would raise medical costs as patients are more likely to require repeated treatment until the cancer goes into remission. This was demonstrated by a study investigating the differences in recurrence patterns in early- and advanced-stage NSCLC (nonsmall-cell lung cancer) [12]. The data were taken from patients who were treated with resection with a portion of patients having been treated when their cancer was at an early stage (stage I–II) and a portion of patients having been treated when their cancer had already advanced to a later stage (stage IIIA) [12]. 20% of patients who were treated for early-stage (stage I–II) NSCLC experienced recurrences, whereas 52% of patients who were treated for advanced-stage (stage IIIA) cancer experienced recurrences [12].

3. How AI can improve accuracy and speed of cancer diagnoses

With this in mind, seeking to improve the accuracy of cancer diagnoses can ensure that more cases are detected at an early stage, thus improving the survival chances of cancer patients and reducing the need for more invasive (and thus more expensive) cancer treatments while decreasing the likelihood of recurrence. Furthermore, the reduction in the cost of healthcare can alleviate some of the financial burden cancer that can have on health services (where healthcare is generalized) or upon cancer patients (where healthcare is privatized), which may allow for investment in higher-quality care.

Artificial intelligence (AI) can demonstrably reduce false positives and false negatives that arise from misjudgment of cancer screenings by clinical specialists. Organizations such as Google's DeepMind have developed AI systems capable of accurately interpreting mammographs to correctly diagnose cancer [13]. In the case of breast cancer (the most common cancer in the world) [14], two large datasets from the United States and the United Kingdom were used and it was recorded that false positives were decreased by 5.7% (US data)/1.2% (UK data) and false negatives were decreased by 9.4% (US data)/2.7% (UK data) [13] with the AI's diagnoses. The reduction in false negatives is promising as it demonstrates that AI can reduce the number of people who are incorrectly judged not to have cancer, thus allowing for earlier treatment to increase their likelihood of survival.

The datasets used to train the Google DeepMind AI were large—25,856 women in the UK dataset and 3097 women in the United States—so initially it appears that the use of AI in detecting cancer is restricted to countries developed enough to have large sets of data on cancer since the AI would struggle to learn how to predict cancer accurately if the data it is fed is not abundant. For example, people with cancer in countries like Niger and

Sudan lack access to facilities where they can get their cancer diagnosed [15], and thus, there may be a lack of recorded data on cancer in such countries.

However, the study conducted by Google's DeepMind suggests that the AI system is highly capable of generalizing what it has learned to apply to a fresh new dataset that it has not encountered before [13]. In the study, the AI's training dataset was the UK dataset only [13]. This AI system that has only encountered UK data was then tested for its accuracy in predicting cancer in the US dataset [13]. The AI still managed to outperform the experts when diagnosing cancer [13]. The paper published about this experiment suggested that these results support the idea that the AI system is reliable enough to be used in regions that lack data on screening mammography (and thus cannot use their own data to train an AI model) [13].

Although this would appear to be a reasonable suggestion, it could be argued that because the quality of life in the United Kingdom and the United States is relatively similar considering they are both developed countries, the variables that could increase or decrease the risk of cancer may also remain somewhat constant between them. For example, China has a more prominent secondary sector [16] that contributes to the economy; i.e., there are many citizens employed in factories. Since 1960, almost 14 million tons of chrysotile has been consumed, which is predicted to have increased the risk of lung cancer and mesothelioma (a type of cancer that affects the surface of some organs) [17]. Therefore, it could be said that in certain countries, especially less developed countries with fewer policies on limiting people's exposure to carcinogens, the average risk of certain cancers may be elevated. If an AI system was to be trained using the US or UK dataset for lung cancer and then tested on scans presenting potential lung cancer from patients in China, the AI may underpredict the average risk of lung cancer since its bias toward a positive diagnosis is less than it would have been if the AI was trained on data from China. This could mean a higher proportion of scans presenting cancer would be falsely diagnosed as negative for cancer.

It is also said that 15%–20% of cancer worldwide is a result of viral, bacterial, or parasitic infection with a prominent example being the HPV [18]. There are different types of HPV with some being more high risk than others; for example, research illustrates that types 16 and 18 are a causing factor in 70% of all cervical cancer cases and precancerous cells in the cervix [18]. HPV can be transmitted sexually [18] so it can be expected that individuals from countries with less established sexual or family planning education are more frequently infected by HPV and thus have an increased risk of cancer. This would appear to coincide with studies showing that around 90% of cervical cancer cases arise in low- or middle-income countries [19].

The study conducted by Google's DeepMind was based on breast cancer, and not cervical or lung cancer, but the point that should be emphasized is that although AI systems may be able to generalize their ability to diagnose various cancers between countries of similar socioeconomic status or with similar environmental conditions/regulations, they may not produce the same accurate results when employed in countries with different socioeconomic statuses/countries with different policies with regard to exposure to carcinogens. If a country's general population is on average more at risk of developing a particular type of cancer than the country from which the AI was trained, then the AI system's level of bias toward a positive diagnosis would be inaccurate.

Therefore, although Google's DeepMind study does demonstrate a potential for AI to be utilized in countries, which lack sufficient data on a particular type of cancer, the process of making this work in real life may be far more complex.

4. How AI can assess patient background information to determine risk of cancer

Individuals who have been identified to have cancerous cells and tissues are not the only ones that medical staff should draw their attention to. Some may have precancerous cells, which display abnormal activity but do not have the malignant spreading capabilities of cancer cells [20]. Although precancerous cells are not guaranteed to develop into cancer cells and are in fact likely to either turn back to normal or remain harmless for the rest of the individual's life, people with precancerous cells are still at a higher risk of developing cancer [21]. There are different degrees of abnormality within the cells, which are more often described as different degrees of dysplasia [22]. There is mild, moderate, and severe dysplasia, with mild dysplasia having the lowest risk of developing into cancerous cells and severe dysplasia, which is much more likely to turn into carcinoma in situ (cancer in place, i.e., cancer that has not spread) [22].

Precancerous cells can surgically be removed but medical staff must assess the risk of these cells turning into cancer since as mentioned before, most precancerous cells, especially those found in mild dysplasia, are most likely to remain harmless [21]. Ideally, medical centers should be made more efficient at allocating resources and time to different at-risk individuals. There has been an AI algorithm, which was developed to analyze signs of precancerous cells in mammograms and then predict the risk of those precancerous cells developing into breast cancer within the next 5 years [23]. Based on this risk assessment, medical staff can make a more informed decision as to how frequently the patient should be screened [23]. This personalized approach can help hospitals keep track of at-risk individuals so that any potential cancer that develops can be identified early and the patient can be given the treatment they need, perhaps before the cancer progresses to malignancy, meaning less invasive procedures can be used.

5. Diagnosis of cancer subtype and stage

As mentioned before, most cancer display great heterogeneity within just one patient, and thus, a detailed diagnosis, regarding the subtype of cancer (which depends on which mutated gene was involved in making the cell cancerous) and the stage to which the cancer has progressed, is also important to know before starting a treatment plan.

Deep learning (DL) systems have been able to pick out genetic as well as epigenetic variations between tumor cells [24]. For example, a CNN model named "Inception v3" was able to differentiate between and predict six mutations within lung cancer cells [25]. The Inception v3 was trained using data from the Genomics Data Commons database [25]; however, other AI systems have been developed that could yield even more personalized and tailored results. For example, CURATE.AI is a platform that can predict what the outcomes of a certain type or intensity of treatment would be, i.e., it can recommend the right combination of drugs as well as the ideal dosage needed for the patient to experience the best outcome [26]. The data that it is trained on comes not from records of previous cancer patients, but rather data from just the patient being treated with each patient getting their own unique CURATE.AI profile, which will take in any observations about the progression of the patient's cancer as well as any changes to their treatment plan and then use the information to recalibrate and adjust the treatment plan accordingly [26]. CURATE.AI is able to function despite the small amount of data collected from just a single individual because it uses a PPM (phenotypic personalized medicine) approach, which is a system that learns through the phenotypic feedback it receives, i.e., information about how the cancer responded to a certain combination of drugs, unlike other AI systems that train on the big data collected from thousands of different patients [26]. This approach to AI training could have its own advantages because often, when it comes to a patient's response to a treatment, there may be too big of a standard deviation for each individual patient, meaning that the AI model will still have too much of a generalized approach when designing treatment plans, whereas, with the PPM strategy, the AI is directly monitoring the response of the patient, allowing for the most optimal and most tailored therapies to be applied.

An example of the CURATE.AI platform at work was in a patient suffering from prostate cancer, which had become metastatic and was castration-resistant (meaning it no longer responded to hormone therapy) [26,27]. Before having a personal CURATE.AI profile for himself, he was given the maximum doses of drugs that were tolerable (which is what is often done in standard treatment) but the CURATE.AI system was able to recommend reduced doses, which would minimize the unpleasant side effects of the drug and very accurately predicted how this dosage would change as the treatment progressed [26]. After a 24-week period, the lesion shrunk from 6 to 4 mm and no newly formed lesions were detected in the radiograph [26].

This demonstrates how AI can very much be infused throughout the entire treatment process, with the AI system not only observing the patient's condition at the point of diagnosis but also regularly tracking how the patient's cancer is progressing and making adjustments to its recommendations in accordance with this. Such an AI platform could also assist in avoiding the emergence of resistant tumor cells as the right dosage of medicine as well as the right combination of drugs can prevent the survival of cancerous cells.

Finally, AI can help individuals even after their treatment has come to an end by predicting the likelihood of recurrence more accurately than human experts [28]. Recurrence of cancer happens when small clusters of tumor cells still remain after the treatment, and sometimes these clusters of cells are hard to detect using the standard screening tools but AI can aid in making a more accurate prognosis [29]. Furthermore, AI can factor in the genetic makeup of the tumor as well as information on the patient (e.g., sex, age, history of disease in the family, etc.) to assess the likelihood of recurrence [30]. This can, in turn, provide clinicians with guidance on how to follow-up treatment; e.g., if the risk of recurrence is high, chemotherapy can be used to try and kill off any more undetectable cancer cells [30].

6. AI in cancer drug discovery and development

In the past, the process of discovering a medical drug consisted of mostly trial and error or often some drugs were revealed through chance such as is the case with penicillin [31]. However, in the modern era, the emergence of a rational drug design strategy means that now scientists have a better idea of which properties they would look for in a drug candidate when treating a certain disease and would have vast amounts of data to explore when looking for a suitable candidate [32]. This is aided by advances in our ability to fully analyze and identify the structures and properties of chemicals as well as increasing computational power, allowing for the storage of large amounts of data to form comprehensive libraries of information on millions of compounds; for example, PubChem is the largest publicly available database storing information on millions of different chemicals regarding their structure, biological activities, toxicity, etc. [33].

Navigating such large amounts of data would become too time-consuming if the information were to be analyzed by humans, no matter the level of their expertise. It must also be considered that attrition rates are very high in the drug development process; analyzing statistics from pharma companies in the United States and in Europe indicates that only one in nine compounds will reach the final approval stage and become approved [34]. Furthermore, in a paper published in the *Nature* journal article, detailing the biopharmaceutical benchmarks from 2014 to 2018, it was observed that only 52% of approved products could be distinguished as new with 48% considered to be biosimilars, which resembled drugs that were already available in the market [35]. These factors indicate that the lack of a quick, efficient, and thorough method for retrieving information could lead to large amounts of time and resources that were spent in research being wasted on developing compounds that fail to be approved. The biopharmaceutical industry cannot afford such inefficiencies when the demand for better medicine is ever growing.

AI can assist in accelerating the drug development and design process due to its ability to thrive when presented with large amounts of data. For example, in a collaboration project between the RAS initiative and a research team, a simulation of how a KRAS protein would behave on a cell surface membrane was created (since the mutated gene for the KRAS protein is something that often leads to cancer) [36]. Through this model, researchers could better understand what kind of drug could inhibit the KRAS protein to prevent cancer, which could help scientists come up with ideal drug candidates to target KRAS [37].

However, it could be argued that the current chemical descriptors that are used by AI systems to predict the progression of organic chemical reactions (or the events that happen in signaling cascades) are too inadequate to allow the AI to come up with accurate predictions as all the factors are not being accounted for [38]. Some researchers contend that for AI to reach its full potential, new descriptors must be created to account for nuances since even small differences between molecules can mean that the reactions that occur differ drastically [38].

7. De novo drug design

De novo design is a drug design strategy that involves creating a completely new ligand from scratch, with the ligand having a complementary shape to the target receptor [39]. With the aid of 3D modeling techniques, researchers can determine if the drug they design will interact favorably with the target [39]. The concept of chemical space appears often when discussing the creation of novel drugs, with the term used to describe the practically infinite number of chemical compounds that could be made [40]. The number of potential drug compounds that have already been discovered and manufactured reaches staggering numbers from between 10^8 to 10^{10} and even still this pales in comparison with the estimated number of potential therapeutic compounds that have yet to be designed and developed [41].

Although techniques such as high-throughput screening, which involve testing lots of similar compounds to identify a lead compound, are commonly used in the drug development industry [42], they are limited to only exploring compounds that have already been synthesized, i.e., compounds that can be found in chemical data libraries [41]. Arguably, the advantage of utilizing AI for de novo drug design is that completely new drugs that may not have been synthesized or even imagined can emerge [41]. When presented with the target, an AI system can navigate the undiscovered chemical space to present some possible drug candidates that could interact with the target.

For example, in a study exploring anticancer peptides (ACPs), an AI model capable of designing effective ACPs is introduced [43]. Specifically, the AI model was trained to identify compounds that would combat breast cancer, lung cancer, or both [43]. The model produced 1000 de novo designs, out of which 14 were tested in vitro on breast and lung cancer cells and 6 of these 14 demonstrated an ability to kill cancer cells [43]. These peptides that the AI system came up with had not been discovered before, illustrating the ability of AI to go beyond human imagination to explore undiscovered areas of chemical space [43].

However, one disadvantage to exploring chemical space in this way is that these molecule-generating AI systems may sometimes disregard the practical aspects of making a chemical in real life, meaning the system generates chemicals that may not be feasible to produce in practice even if they are theoretically possible to make [41]. This can be fixed by adding penalties to discourage the DL model, e.g., from breaking valency rules [41], so many of the issues that arise when using AI in de novo drug design may be resolved in the near future.

8. AI in recommending drug combinations and repurposing drugs

Due to the high attrition rates in the Biopharma Industry, billions of dollars' worth of money on decade-long research projects can be wasted on compounds that fail to become approved medical drugs. This is especially the case when developing oncological drugs as more drugs fail to get approval in the field of oncology than in any other category of disease [34]. However, by focusing energy on repurposing already-approved medical drugs to solve the issues of a different disease, the time and money taken can be dramatically cut down. For example, it has been observed the drugs that have been repurposed can get approval in a shorter period of time (3–12 years) with the overall cost being decreased to 50%–60% of what it would originally cost [44] because many experiments testing the efficacy and toxicity of the drug will have already been conducted so the data on the drug's safety does not have to be collected again with repeated experiments.

Because of the capacity of AI systems to analyze large chemical profiles as well as their ability to draw connections between information points that a human may overlook, AI has recently become a promising tool for repurposing drugs. For example, a human expert may be more likely to associate a drug compound with its intended on-target effects and ignore its off-target effects. Off-target effects may be overlooked in the context of the original disease that the drug is treating as they are seen as undesirable but an AI system can use its broad knowledge of the compound's target activity to connect these off-target effects to biochemical pathways associated with completely separate diseases [45]. For example, a drug called "metformin" was originally only used to treat type 2 diabetes as it reduces the cell's resistance to insulin, allowing for the uptake of glucose and decreasing the level of insulin in the blood, which can indirectly help slow the growth and spread of cancer as insulin encourages tumor growth [46]. In addition, metformin has also been observed to inhibit tumor growth by having an effect on important pathways within the cell, giving it great potential for being used in cancer treatment [46].

9. AI in identifying drug-target interactions

Often when a drug is developed to combat a disease, one important factor to consider is if the drug will interact with the cells being targeted. For example, a compound's ligands may bind to an enzyme or a receptor in such a way that a certain process within a cell is inhibited or stimulated. However, there may be many compounds that could interact with the target so researchers may find it cost-efficient to focus on the drug compounds that interact the best by ranking the binding affinities of a drug to its target [47]. However, predicting the binding affinities of drug-target interactions or DTIs would prove challenging without the aid of computational methods since researchers would have to conduct several experiments to test just one of the drugs' interactions with a target to predict a quantifiable value for the strength of binding, not to mention several other drugs this process would have to be repeated on [47]. However, using an AI deep learning system to predict the binding affinities could cut out the need for repeated experiments, thus drastically cutting down the cost [47].

This knowledge of the interactions between a drug and its target allows AI to assist in recommending targeted therapies with the optimal efficacy by preventing the development of drug resistance [48]. For example, tyrosine kinase inhibitors (TKIs) are a category of compounds that inhibit the action of enzymes called tyrosine kinases, which normally in the context of healthy cells regulate the signaling cascades that control processes related to growth as well as metabolism [49]. However, in cancer cells, it has been observed that tyrosine kinases can promote uncontrolled growth leading to cancer [49]. By inhibiting tyrosine kinases, cancer growth can be suppressed [49]. In spite of the positive implications of such a treatment, there is a risk that the cancer will become resistant to the TKIs if one or more cells within the tumor express the ability to elude the TKI treatment in its phenotype; even if most of the other tumor cells are left unable to function and divide, the resistant tumor cells will simply divide into more resistant clones via rapid mitosis, rendering the initial TKI as ineffective [48]. Since drug resistance can arise due to a multitude of factors, the process of understanding how resistance develops and consequently producing a strategic plan for targeted therapy is complex and unique to each patient, which is precisely why AI may be better equipped to analyze the multiple processes that could contribute to TKI resistance and aid in creating a treatment plan that is likely to yield the best outcomes with the lowest chances of recurrence after treatment [48].

10. Deep learning, black boxes, and hidden layers

DL is a type of machine learning (ML) under the AI umbrella that has a neural network resembling that of a human brain [50]. Like the human brain, it has neurons that connect to one another in layers, one neuron receiving the inputs from neurons in the previous layer and sending output signals to the neurons in the next layer [51] and like how biological neurons need to have enough excitation to fire, the weighted inputs that a neuron receives from a previous layer will determine the "strength" of the output the neurons in the next layer receive [52]. A DL model can learn to distinguish between objects within images, which is useful for diagnosing cancer from medical screenings [24] or recognizing patterns and connections between data points, which is useful for designing anticancer drug combinations [53].

The very first layer is the input layer where the features in the image are initially perceived, and the final layer is the output layer which is where we will get our prediction [54]; e.g., in the case of cancer screening, the output layer may contain the DL model's prediction of whether the patient does or does not have cancer as well as the model's assessment on what type of tumor is shown. There are also many hidden layers in between which are assigned their own weights during the time when the DL model is being trained by an expert; e.g., the expert informs the DL model how much its output, in this case its diagnosis, strays from what the medical screening shows in actuality, and thus via the process of backpropagation, the DL algorithm adjusts the weights and biases of the neurons in the hidden layers [55].

The issue with these hidden layers is that it is challenging for oncologists and other medical professionals to understand the reasoning behind the DL model's judgment, with their elusive nature often earning these models the description of being a "black box" [56]. In order for a DL algorithm to accurately predict an outcome in a dataset, it needs to consider all the conditions and factors that contribute to that outcome; i.e., it needs to be able to process many different input parameters [53]. The overwhelmingly multifactorial aspects that have to be accounted for by the algorithm further complicate the issue that medical professionals would have to face if they were to make sense of the DL system's judgment [53]. Training the DL system could prove difficult, requiring clinicians to receive training on how to guide the DL model's learning, which would demand lots of time and money [57].

Let us consider the context of using DL methods to identify DTIs or effective drug combinations: it can be deduced that the researchers' lack of knowledge of the justifications behind the algorithm's choice of drug candidates could pose a major issue since the drug's efficacy and toxicity need to be sufficiently explained in order for it to be approved. For example, for a drug to be approved in the United States, a review team consisting of experts from across different scientific disciplines would have to be convinced of the functionality and safety of the drug, which would be hard to achieve due to the DL system's lack of transparency [58].

These difficulties could somewhat diminish the hope that AI systems could be integrated into the field of cancer therapy as the original goal is for AI to work together to assist medical professionals in their treatment planning or to aid researchers in identifying suitable drug candidates. Fortunately, this issue could be on the path to being resolved. For example, a research team has developed a DL model called DeepSignalingSynergy, which they describe to be a model simpler than previous DL models [59]. This is because rather than inputting an inordinate amount of parameters associated with the many different chemical identifiers of a drug and information on gene expression, they have instead prioritized pathways responsible for cancer signaling, simulating a multiomics approach to investigating the synergy in drug combinations [59]. Such a model could introduce a less complicated method of developing drug combinations that can combat cancer and drug resistance [59]. Furthermore, this layout, which employs the LRP (layer-wise relevance propagation) technique, also makes it more straightforward for experts to understand and delineate the way in which the DL model navigates through its inputs to reach its output [53].

Similarly, in order to help oncologists comprehend and visualize what parts of a cancer screening an AI system is focusing on to use as evidence for its diagnosis, the Grad-CAM technique can be used to produce Activation Heatmaps [24]. Activation Heatmaps work by pointing out (using colors from red being the most active to blue being the least active) which parts of an image are "stimulating" the most neurons to fire [60].

Images on the left show a Grad-CAM of a histopathology image (taken from the cells of a patient with ovarian cancer), which highlights groups of tumor cells in red [61].

11. Future of AI in oncology

At present, AI is already making leaps of progress in the field of oncology. So far, the FDA has approved 71 devices related to AI [62], demonstrating that AI is no longer just promising in theory but is already making a difference to cancer treatment in practice. Currently, there are a few challenges that stand as obstacles to the progress of AI in cancer therapy.

For example, many AI systems do not always succeed at generalizing, i.e., accurately working with samples outside of the dataset they were trained on. In a study conducted by Zech et al. on AI in pneumonia screenings [63], multiple CNNs were trained either using data from one hospital or from a collection of hospitals, and the results highlighted how the CNNs could not always generalize what they had learned when tested on patients in hospitals outside their training dataset [63]. This may indicate that currently, AI cannot be relied upon for accurate predictions unless the AI is to be trained using data from the same location, as it will assist in. However, as mentioned before, new methods of building AI systems may involve far fewer parameters which allow for the models to be more simplified and easier to interpret by medical staff compared to previous data models, which in turn could make it easier for the AI model to generalize. Therefore, the problem of generalization may soon be resolved.

Another area that could be improved is the application of AI for rarer types of cancer. Most of the AI-related devices created focus on cancers such as breast, lung, and prostate cancers, which makes sense as these cancers tend to be the most common and thus have the most data for AI models to be trained in [62]. However, rarer cancers lack large datasets on them and are often less researched or less understood due to the scarcity of individuals having them [62]. Often when experts are diagnosing cancer from medical screenings, they rely on their past experience to inform their decisions, meaning that for rarer cancers, there may be fewer clinicians with enough expertise to diagnose or treat the cancer or there may be fewer standardized treatment plans for clinicians to rely on [62]. This means that AI is lacking in the areas of oncology in which it is most needed and necessary [62]. If, however, more effort is put into recording or collecting more data related to rare tumor types, then in the future, there may be a larger database [62] for future AI models to work with, making it more feasible to use AI as a tool for treating these rare cancer types.

In my opinion, the future of AI in cancer treatment is optimistic and AI is likely to revolutionize not only the field of oncology but many other diseases due to the vast array of different tasks it can tackle. AI could provide a pathway for medical professionals to take a more holistic approach to treatment, allowing them to extract meaningful information from overwhelmingly large datasets. Instead of viewing the different types of analyses (e.g., screening, biopsy, DNA, and RNA tests [62]) as completely separate, AI can integrate details from these diagnostic methods to create a clearer bigger picture. Many AI models have proven themselves to be accurate in initial tests but many currently fail to prove that they are fully functional in realistic hospital settings [64]. Despite some of these obstacles that are currently hindering certain aspects of progress in AI, these obstacles appear to have feasible solutions, raising hopes for the future.

12. Conclusion

In conclusion, the use of AI algorithms has repeatedly proven to have significant advantages over traditional cancer treatment and drug discovery methods, often yielding results of higher accuracy at a much faster speed and at a much lower price than if the cancer data were to only be analyzed by human experts. There seem to be a few final gaps that AI would need to cross if it was to be more successful at being integrated into modern healthcare. These gaps are the lack of interpretability of some neural networks due to the "black box" that are their hidden layers, the inability of some AI models to generalize, and finally, the fact that many medical experts may be unfamiliar with how to work in synergy with an AI algorithm. However, many of these issues have attainable potential solutions that could materialize in the foreseeable future. In conclusion, it is reasonable to expect AI to have a net positive impact on cancer treatment with its list of uses and benefits ever growing.

References

[1] L.M. Wu, A. Amidi, Cognitive impairment following hormone therapy: current opinion of research in breast and prostate cancer patients, Curr. Opin. Support. Palliat. Care 11 (2017) 38.

[2] G. Bauman, M. Charette, R. Reid, J. Sathya, T.R.G.G. of Cancer, Radiopharmaceuticals for the palliation of painful bone metastases—a systematic review, Radiother. Oncol. 75 (2005) 258. E251-258. E213.

[3] W. Pao, N. Girard, New driver mutations in non-small-cell lung cancer, Lancet Oncol. 12 (2011) 175–180.

[4] A. Marusyk, K. Polyak, Tumor heterogeneity: causes and consequences, Biochim. Biophys. Acta 1805 (2010) 105–117.

[5] R.L. Siegel, K.D. Miller, H.E. Fuchs, A. Jemal, Cancer statistics, CA Cancer J. Clin. 72 (2022) (2022) 7–33.

[6] N. Bannister, J. Broggio, Cancer Survival by Stage at Diagnosis for England (Experimental Statistics): Adults Diagnosed 2012, 2013 and 2014 and Followed Up to 2015, Produced in Collaboration with Public Health England, 2016.

[7] A. Hackshaw, S.S. Cohen, H. Reichert, A.R. Kansal, K.C. Chung, J.J. Ofman, Estimating the population health impact of a multi-cancer early detection genomic blood test to complement existing screening in the US and UK, Br. J. Cancer 125 (2021) 1432–1442.

[8] J. Sheringham, A. King, R. Plackett, A. Khan, M. Cornes, A.P. Kassianos, Physician associate/assistant contributions to cancer diagnosis in primary care: a rapid systematic review, BMC Health Serv. Res. 21 (2021) 1–12.

[9] R. Sullivan, O.I. Alatise, B.O. Anderson, R. Audisio, P. Autier, A. Aggarwal, et al., Global cancer surgery: delivering safe, affordable, and timely cancer surgery, Lancet Oncol. 16 (11) (2015) 1193–1224.

[10] S. Yao, Z. Wang, L. Li, Application of organic frame materials in cancer therapy through regulation of tumor microenvironment, Smart Mater. Med. 3 (2022) 230–242.

[11] A. Pearce, M. Haas, R. Viney, S.-A. Pearson, P. Haywood, C. Brown, R. Ward, Incidence and severity of self-reported chemotherapy side effects in routine care: a prospective cohort study, PLoS One 12 (2017), e0184360.

[12] F. Lou, C.S. Sima, V.W. Rusch, D.R. Jones, J. Huang, Differences in patterns of recurrence in early-stage versus locally advanced non-small cell lung cancer, Ann. Thorac. Surg. 98 (2014) 1755–1761.

[13] S.M. McKinney, M. Sieniek, V. Godbole, J. Godwin, N. Antropova, H. Ashrafian, T. Back, M. Chesus, G.S. Corrado, A. Darzi, International evaluation of an AI system for breast cancer screening, Nature 577 (2020) 89–94.

[14] K. Freeman, J. Geppert, C. Stinton, D. Todkill, S. Johnson, A. Clarke, S. Taylor-Phillips, Use of artificial intelligence for image analysis in breast cancer screening programmes: systematic review of test accuracy, BMJ 374 (2021) n1872.

[15] C. Caglevic, C. Rolfo, I. Gil-Bazo, A. Cardona, J. Sapunar, F.R. Hirsch, D.R. Gandara, G. Morgan, S. Novello, M.-C. Garassino, The armed conflict and the impact on patients with cancer in Ukraine: urgent considerations, JCO Global Oncol. 8 (2022), e2200123.

[16] J.-L. Fan, J.-D. Wang, L.-S. Kong, X. Zhang, The carbon footprints of secondary industry in China: an input–output subsystem analysis, Nat. Hazards 91 (2018) 635–657.

[17] N. van Zandwijk, J.E. Rasko, A.M. George, A.L. Frank, G. Reid, The silent malignant mesothelioma epidemic: a call to action, Lancet Oncol. 23 (10) (2022) 1245–1248.

[18] F. Martín-Hernán, J.G. Sánchez-Hernández, J. Cano, J. Campo, J. del Romero, Oral cancer, HPV infection and evidence of sexual transmission, Med. Oral Patol. Oral Cir. Bucal 18 (2013), e439.

[19] E.R. Allanson, K.M. Schmeler, Preventing cervical cancer globally: are we making progress? Cancer Prev. Res. 14 (2021) 1055–1060.

[20] J.P. Richardson, C. Smith, S. Curtis, S. Watson, X. Zhu, B. Barry, R.R. Sharp, Patient apprehensions about the use of artificial intelligence in healthcare, NPJ Digit. Med. 4 (2021) 1–6.

[21] M. Crawford, E.H. Johnson, K.Y. Liu, C. Poh, R.Y. Tsai, On the cutting edge of oral cancer prevention: finding risk-predictive markers in precancerous lesions by longitudinal studies, Cells 11 (2022) 1033.

[22] J. Roelands, M. van der Ploeg, H. Dang, L. Hawinkels, H. Morreau, N. de Miranda, 673 (Re-) Solving the biology of colorectal cancer onset and progression to improve treatment and prevention, J. Immunother. Cancer 9 (Suppl. 2) (2021) A1–A1054.

[23] A. Sahu, S. Qazi, K. Raza, A. Singh, S. Verma, Machine learning-based approach for early diagnosis of breast cancer using biomarkers and gene expression profiles, in: Computational Intelligence in Oncology, Springer, 2022, pp. 285–306.
[24] Z.H. Chen, L. Lin, C.F. Wu, C.F. Li, R.H. Xu, Y. Sun, Artificial intelligence for assisting cancer diagnosis and treatment in the era of precision medicine, Cancer Commun. 41 (2021) 1100–1115.
[25] N. Coudray, P.S. Ocampo, T. Sakellaropoulos, N. Narula, M. Snuderl, D. Fenyö, A.L. Moreira, N. Razavian, A. Tsirigos, Classification and mutation prediction from non–small cell lung cancer histopathology images using deep learning, Nat. Med. 24 (2018) 1559–1567.
[26] A. Blasiak, J. Khong, T. Kee, CURATE. AI: optimizing personalized medicine with artificial intelligence, SLAS Technol. 25 (2020) 95–105.
[27] A.T. Truong, L.W. Tan, K.A. Chew, S. Villaraza, P. Siongco, A. Blasiak, C. Chen, D. Ho, Harnessing CURATE. AI for N-of-1 optimization analysis of combination therapy in hypertension patients: a retrospective case series, Adv. Therap. 4 (2021) 2100091.
[28] B. Bhinder, C. Gilvary, N.S. Madhukar, O. Elemento, Artificial intelligence in cancer research and precision medicine, Cancer Discov. 11 (2021) 900–915.
[29] K. Bera, N. Braman, A. Gupta, V. Velcheti, A. Madabhushi, Predicting cancer outcomes with radiomics and artificial intelligence in radiology, Nat. Rev. Clin. Oncol. 19 (2022) 132–146.
[30] R. Rattan, T. Kataria, S. Banerjee, S. Goyal, D. Gupta, A. Pandita, S. Bisht, K. Narang, S.R. Mishra, Artificial intelligence in oncology, its scope and future prospects with specific reference to radiation oncology, BJR Open 1 (2019) 20180031.
[31] R. Gaynes, The discovery of penicillin—new insights after more than 75 years of clinical use, Emerg. Infect. Dis. 23 (2017) 849.
[32] S. Mandal, S.K. Mandal, Rational drug design, Eur. J. Pharmacol. 625 (2009) 90–100.
[33] S. Kim, P.A. Thiessen, E.E. Bolton, J. Chen, G. Fu, A. Gindulyte, L. Han, J. He, S. He, B.A. Shoemaker, PubChem substance and compound databases, Nucleic Acids Res. 44 (2016) D1202–D1213.
[34] I. Kola, J. Landis, Can the pharmaceutical industry reduce attrition rates? Nat. Rev. Drug Discov. 3 (2004) 711–716.
[35] G. Walsh, Biopharmaceutical benchmarks 2018, Nat. Biotechnol. 36 (2018) 1136–1145.
[36] T.H. Tran, A.H. Chan, L.C. Young, L. Bindu, C. Neale, S. Messing, S. Dharmaiah, T. Taylor, J.-P. Denson, D. Esposito, KRAS interaction with RAF1 RAS-binding domain and cysteine-rich domain provides insights into RAS-mediated RAF activation, Nat. Commun. 12 (2021) 1–16.
[37] A. Wadood, A. Ajmal, A.U. Rehman, Strategies of targeting KRAS, challenging drug target, Curr. Pharm. Des. 28 (23) (2022) 1897–1901.
[38] G. Skoraczyński, P. Dittwald, B. Miasojedow, S. Szymkuć, E. Gajewska, B.A. Grzybowski, A. Gambin, Predicting the outcomes of organic reactions via machine learning: are current descriptors sufficient? Sci. Rep. 7 (2017) 1–9.
[39] Q. Bai, S. Tan, T. Xu, H. Liu, J. Huang, X. Yao, MolAICal: a soft tool for 3D drug design of protein targets by artificial intelligence and classical algorithm, Brief. Bioinform. 22 (2021) bbaa161.
[40] C. Lipinski, A. Hopkins, Navigating chemical space for biology and medicine, Nature 432 (2004) 855–861.
[41] X. Xia, J. Hu, Y. Wang, L. Zhang, Z. Liu, Graph-based generative models for de Novo drug design, Drug Discov. Today Technol. 32 (2019) 45–53.
[42] R. Choi, M. Zhou, R. Shek, J.W. Wilson, L. Tillery, J.K. Craig, I.A. Salukhe, S.E. Hickson, N. Kumar, R.M. James, High-throughput screening of the ReFRAME, Pandemic Box, and COVID Box drug repurposing libraries against SARS-CoV-2 nsp15 endoribonuclease to identify small-molecule inhibitors of viral activity, PLoS One 16 (2021), e0250019.
[43] F. Grisoni, C.S. Neuhaus, M. Hishinuma, G. Gabernet, J.A. Hiss, M. Kotera, G. Schneider, De novo design of anticancer peptides by ensemble artificial neural networks, J. Mol. Model. 25 (2019) 1–10.
[44] J.J. Hernandez, M. Pryszlak, L. Smith, C. Yanchus, N. Kurji, V.M. Shahani, S.V. Molinski, Giving drugs a second chance: overcoming regulatory and financial hurdles in repurposing approved drugs as cancer therapeutics, Front. Oncol. 7 (2017) 273.

[45] Z. Tanoli, M. Vähä-Koskela, T. Aittokallio, Artificial intelligence, machine learning, and drug repurposing in cancer, Expert Opin. Drug Discovery 16 (2021) 977–989.
[46] I. Ben Sahra, Y. Le Marchand-Brustel, J.-F. Tanti, F. Bost, Metformin in cancer therapy: a new perspective for an old antidiabetic drug? Mol. Cancer Ther. 9 (2010) 1092–1099.
[47] H. Öztürk, A. Özgür, E. Ozkirimli, DeepDTA: deep drug–target binding affinity prediction, Bioinformatics 34 (2018) i821–i829.
[48] R. Alves, A.C. Gonçalves, S. Rutella, A.M. Almeida, J. De Las Rivas, I.P. Trougakos, A.B. Sarmento Ribeiro, Resistance to tyrosine kinase inhibitors in chronic myeloid leukemia—from molecular mechanisms to clinical relevance, Cancers 13 (2021) 4820.
[49] M.K. Paul, A.K. Mukhopadhyay, Tyrosine kinase–role and significance in cancer, Int. J. Med. Sci. 1 (2004) 101.
[50] R.Y. Choi, A.S. Coyner, J. Kalpathy-Cramer, M.F. Chiang, J.P. Campbell, Introduction to machine learning, neural networks, and deep learning, Transl. Vis. Sci. Technol. 9 (2020) 14.
[51] Y. LeCun, Y. Bengio, G. Hinton, Deep learning, Nature 521 (2015) 436–444.
[52] M. Parsajoo, D.J. Armaghani, A.S. Mohammed, M. Khari, S. Jahandari, Tensile strength prediction of rock material using non-destructive tests: a comparative intelligent study, Transp. Geotech. 31 (2021), 100652.
[53] K. Fan, L. Cheng, L. Li, Artificial intelligence and machine learning methods in predicting anti-cancer drug combination effects, Brief. Bioinform. 22 (2021) bbab271.
[54] Y.H. Qu, H.T. Zhu, K. Cao, X.T. Li, M. Ye, Y.S. Sun, Prediction of pathological complete response to neoadjuvant chemotherapy in breast cancer using a deep learning (DL) method, Thorac. Cancer 11 (2020) 651–658.
[55] A. Pavone, A. Plebe, How neurons in deep models relate with neurons in the brain, Algorithms 14 (2021) 272.
[56] D.S. Watson, J. Krutzinna, I.N. Bruce, C.E. Griffiths, I.B. McInnes, M.R. Barnes, L. Floridi, Clinical applications of machine learning algorithms: beyond the black box, BMJ 364 (2019) l886.
[57] O. Elemento, C. Leslie, J. Lundin, G. Tourassi, Artificial intelligence in cancer research, diagnosis and therapy, Nat. Rev. Cancer 21 (2021) 747–752.
[58] D. Baptista, P.G. Ferreira, M. Rocha, Deep learning for drug response prediction in cancer, Brief. Bioinform. 22 (2021) 360–379.
[59] H. Zhang, J. Feng, A. Zeng, P. Payne, F. Li, Predicting tumor cell response to synergistic drug combinations using a novel simplified deep learning model, in: AMIA Annual Symposium Proceedings, American Medical Informatics Association, 2020, p. 1364.
[60] T. Chakraborty, U. Trehan, K. Mallat, J.-L. Dugelay, Generalizing adversarial explanations with Grad-CAM, in: Proceedings of the IEEE/CVF Conference on Computer Vision and Pattern Recognition, 2022, pp. 187–193.
[61] K.-H. Yu, V. Hu, F. Wang, U.A. Matulonis, G.L. Mutter, J.A. Golden, I.S. Kohane, Deciphering serous ovarian carcinoma histopathology and platinum response by convolutional neural networks, BMC Med. 18 (2020) 1–14.
[62] C. Luchini, A. Pea, A. Scarpa, Artificial intelligence in oncology: current applications and future perspectives, Br. J. Cancer 126 (2022) 4–9.
[63] J.R. Zech, M.A. Badgeley, M. Liu, A.B. Costa, J.J. Titano, E.K. Oermann, Variable generalization performance of a deep learning model to detect pneumonia in chest radiographs: a cross-sectional study, PLoS Med. 15 (2018), e1002683.
[64] V. Kaul, S. Enslin, S.A. Gross, History of artificial intelligence in medicine, Gastrointest. Endosc. 92 (2020) 807–812.

CHAPTER 5

Approach of artificial intelligence in colorectal cancer and in precision medicine

Grace Persis Burri[a], Yuvasri Golivi[a], Tha Luong[a], Neha Merchant[b], and Ganji Purnachandra Nagaraju[a]

[a]Department of Hematology and Oncology, School of Medicine, University of Alabama, Birmingham, AL, United States
[b]Department of Bioscience and Biotechnology, Banasthali Vidyapith, Banasthali, Rajasthan, India

Abstract

Artificial Intelligence (AI) is a computer-based technology where the computer is programmed to identify, learn, reason, and act like humans. AI has a groundbreaking resolution to different medical problems especially in cancer. Colorectal cancer (CRC) is the third most fatal cancer and upsurging in men and young adults due to unhealthy diet, heavy consumption of alcohol, smoking, and genetic and environmental conditions. The applications of AI to CRC include detection, diagnosis, grading, characterization, drug discovery, treatment, and prevention. With the increase in AI technology and research, a personalized medicine therapy called precision medicine is developed. This helps with accurate, unique drug design and medical treatment for the patients. CRC is a heterogeneous disease and is considered as model disease for the complete implementation of precision medicine concept. The applications, benefits, drawbacks, current challenges, and further prospects of AI in CRC and precision medicine are discussed in the article.

Abbreviations

AI artificial intelligence
ANN artificial neural networks
CAD computer-aided detection
CADx computer-aided diagnosis
CNN convolutional neural networks
CRC colorectal cancer
CTC computed tomographic colonoscopy
DL deep learning
ML machine learning
NPV negative predictive value

1. Introduction

1.1 History

In the year 1950, Alan Turing a famous mathematician and computer scientist conducted a test to check computers ability to display intelligent behavior like the human

Computational Methods in Drug Discovery and Repurposing for Cancer Therapy
https://doi.org/10.1016/B978-0-443-15280-1.00016-9

intelligence. It is known as Turing test. Many of the works of Artificial Intelligence (AI) was done before and after this test, but they came with different names. John McCarthy first coined the name AI at Dartmouth conference in the year 1956.

1.2 Artificial intelligence

AI is defined as intelligence displayed by the machines to act, learn, reasons, and identify patterns parallel to human cognitive operations [1]. Machine learning (MI) is a subfield of AI that deals with making decisions or predictions by performing different tasks and comparing them. The more MI is exposed to the data, the better can it function overtime. Deep learning (DL) is subset of the ML that focus on artificial neural networks (ANN) programmed after how human brain functions. It can process huge quantity of data and recognize patterns not only in the written data but also in the complex images. DL became a huge success due to its recent works such as visual recognition, virtual assistants, image classification, and language translation [2]. The positive results lead to the application of AI in oncology to improve speed, accuracy of diagnosis, and to aid specific drug discovery.

1.3 AI in colorectal cancer (CRC)

Use of AI algorithm and codes with genetic tests showed many promising outcomes for CRC. Hu et al. [3] performed an experiment of AI in CRC. The results showed that reoccurrence of cancer after surgery is high in normal treatment methods compared to AI implemented Surgeries. It was because, AI can identify the accurate mutations occurred in the genes. In the year 2015, a group developed ANN to analyze the relation between genetical and environmental conditions of DNA mutations in CRC [4]. Wan et al. proposed another AI method using the tumor-derived cell-free DNA (cf DNA), which resulted in the high specificity and sensitivity. This technique paved promising future for the detection of CRC at early stage [5].

1.4 Precision medicine

Precision medicine also known as personalized medicine or customized therapy is one of the most effective and promising approach for many clinical treatment methods including cancer [6]. It refers to the customized medical treatment for individual patients. It literally does not mean design of drugs and treatment plants that are specific to each patient but differentiates the patients based on their profile including age, gender, gene variability, environmental conditions, lifestyle, and pre-existing conditions [7], and it presents best therapy suitable for the patients.

In 2015, U.S. President Barack Obama started precision medicine initiative to research cancer genomics for better treatment and preventive strategies [8].

2. Applications of AI in CRC

- CRC screening and diagnosis.
- Genomic characterization of polyps.
- Drug discovery and repurposing.
- Treatment and prevention.

2.1 CRC screening and diagnosis

CRC is a fatal disease and does not have cure. Early detection and treatment may enhance patient mortality rate [9]. Effective screening and diagnostic methods are developed for the identification of abnormal tissues, tumors, and detection of premalignant lesions and colon polyps by different techniques such as colonoscopy, virtual colonoscopy (VC), capsule endoscopy, and blood tests [10,11].

2.1.1 Colonoscopy

Colonoscopy has been considered as the golden standard for the screening and detection of CRC [12]. It is a process used to examine the insides of colon and rectum by a long, flexible tube attached with a camera to give us an idea where the polyps are present. With this test, we can evaluate any gastrointestinal symptoms, bleeding, bowel habit alterations, and the presence of adenoma or polyps. The ADR adenoma detection rate is a standard to measure the percentage of adenoma present in the large intestine during colonoscopy. The ADR differs from 7% to 52%, the higher the percentage, the higher the chance of CRC [13]. Above 25% is considered as positive and dangerous.

But there are some cases where colonoscopy failed to show the accurate results. Sometimes with the false alarms of CRC and sometimes with negative results ended up being positive. Not only that but also the polyps which were detected and excised during colonoscopy are diminutive polyps (<5mm) and benign [14]. Polypectomy increased the risk of bleeding and perforations. To overcome these, computer-aided detection (CAD) and diagnosis (CADx) has been introduce to characterize histology of adenoma or polyps in vivo [15]. To improve ADRs, convolutional neural networks (CNN) are used for accurate detection and localization of premalignant polyps [16].

The first use of CAD for the detection of colorectal polyps was in 2003 [17] [18]. Karkanis et al. with the help of wavelet transformation method detected polyps with sensitivity 93.6% and specificity 99.3% [19]. After many years to CAD, DL technology was applied. This helped in real-time research studies. The first real-time research to detect polyps was done by Urban et al. [20]. They studied nine standard colonoscopy test videos. During normal colonoscopy, 28 polyps were detected and excised. But with the addition of CAD 17 extra polyps were exposed and the accuracy of this test increased to 96.4%.

Klare et al. applied CAD to the study of 55 colonoscopies in vivo and in real time. The results of this test were slightly lower (29.1%) compared to expert endoscopies (30.9%). This is because it could not detect the diminutive polyps [21].

Recently, randomized control trails (RCTs) were operated in real-time detection of colorectal polyps. In Wang et al. [22], unblinded study of 1058 CRC patients, 536 patients were grouped to conventional colonoscopy, and 522 patients were grouped to colonoscopy with (CAD). The ADR of conventional colonoscopy was 20.3%, whereas the ADR of CAD was 29.1%. Here CAD did not miss detecting any diminutive polyps but gave 39 incorrect positive alarms of polyps [23]. Wang et al. again performed double-blinded RCT with 478 conventional colonoscopy cases and 484 CAD colonoscopy cases with sham system. The ADR of conventional colonoscopy to CAD was 28% and 34%, respectively [22].

Su et al. performed partially blinded RCT with automatic quality control system (AQCS) in 315 patients to conventional colonoscopy and 308 to AQCS colonoscopy. The ADR of AQCS was 28.9%, and the ADR of conventional colonoscopy was only 16.5%. But the withdrawal time of AQCS was longer (7.03 ± 1.01 min) compared to conventional colonoscopy (5.68 ± 1.26 min). With all the above studies, CAD was proved to perform better than novice colonoscopy [24].

2.1.2 Virtual colonoscopy

VC, also known as computed tomographic colonoscopy (CTC), is a modified subset of computed tomography (CT) and was first discussed by Vining et al. in 1994 [25]. It is considered as an alternative screening method for conventional colonoscopy and has better polyp detection and classification. In VC, AI presented virtual pathological prototype to explore image quality and differentiation.

Song et al. developed a virtual pathological prototype to survey the images with the help of AI. More advanced differentiations such as gradient and curvature were taken into consideration for the detection of colorectal lesions [26]. This study results showed that the zone under ROC (receiver operating characteristic) improved in distinguishing neoplastic and non-neoplastic colon lesions from 0.74 to 0.85. In study of Grosu et al., they developed an AI method to differentiate benign and premalignant colorectal polyps. The result of this study showed specificity of 85%, sensitivity of 82%, and AUC (area under the curve) of 0.91. In previous studies, Taylor et al. developed a CAD prototype to evaluate its diagnostic potential of early-stage colon cancer (T1) by CTC technique. The CAD model detected inverse relation between polyp sensitivity and the sphericity (83.3% at sphericity 0, 70.8% at 0.75, and 54.1% at 1). It also detected direct relation between sphericity and accuracy [27]. The addition of AI to normal detection methods increases accuracy, specificity, and sensitivity, and they become cost effective and less risky.

2.2 Genomic characterization of polyps

Generally, the characterization of tumors or polyps is done by genomics sequence. It is a complex process and takes both time and effort. To reduce that AI methods are used for the detection of specific or accurate gene mutations occur in tumor pathology. With AI, the origin of polyps can be detected along with the characterization of colon polyps during colonoscopy [28,29]. Use of AI in real-time diagnosis may help to determine the most suitable treatment method and to avoid unnecessary polypectomies and complications. To increase the development of endoscopy technology, the preservation and incorporation of value endoscopic innovations (PIVI) proposed that the novel technologies should be able to achieve >90% of negative predictive value (NPV) for optical diagnosis and characterization of diminutive polyps [30].

For the polyp characterization, many methods were developed. The most used and discussed methods are narrow-band imaging (NBI), endoscopy, and white light endoscopy (WLE).

2.2.1 Magnification endoscopy with NBI

NBI is an ultra-advanced imaging technique that helps in detailed visualization and analysis of colonic mucosa thus increasing the potential for detection of colon polyps [31]. This is essential for the differentiation of benign and premalignant lesions [32]. It also helps in evaluating depth of the submucosal infiltration. When NBI is combined with magnifying colonoscopy, it improves accuracy of the real-time diagnosis.

The first evaluation of this classification system was done by Tischendorf et al. [33] on 128 CRC patients who had 209 colon polyps. But the accuracy of NBI was relatively less compared to expert endoscopists. Gross et al. [34] in 2011, designed a computer-assisted mode for colon polyp classification. This yielded with a sensitivity of 95%, specificity of 90.3%, and accuracy of 93.1% from 214 patients of CRC with 434-colon polyps. In this classification, results were superior to that of conventional endoscopy, which has sensitivity of 86%, specificity of 87.8% and accuracy of 86.8%. For the better polyp characterization, the research team at Hiroshima University of Japan developed CADx system to differentiate neoplastic and non-neoplastic colon polyps. This showed higher accuracy even in real-time diagnosis [35].

2.2.2 Endoscopy

Endocytoscopy is an advanced magnification endoscopic imaging technique, which helps in real-time diagnosis and in vivo analysis of lesions or polyps found in large intestine [36]. This test is simple and requires only 10–20 min. This was first discovered in the year 2003 and was developed regularly. The critical factor of this test is CM double staining, which results in best and accurate endoscopic images. This technique uses a light microscope fixed to colonoscopy, which produces images with higher magnifications by 520 times.

Mori et al. [37] performed a pilot study on 152 patients with 176 colon polyps. They used CAD for characterization of polyps. The results showed sensitivity of 92%, specificity of 79.5%, and accuracy of 89.2%. Takeda et al. [38] in retrospective study of 5543 EC images using CAD for classification showed higher accuracy of 94%, sensitivity of 89.4%, specificity of 98.9%, NPV of 90.1%. Moris et al. [37] in an open-label and prospective study of 325 patients with 466 diminutive polyps used CAD in real-time diagnosis of colonoscopy. The results of this showed sensitivity of 93.8%, specificity of 90.3%, accuracy of 98.1%, and NPV of 89.8%. Kudo et al. [39] in retrospective study of 89 patients with 100 polyps used CAD with EndoBRAIN for classification of colon polyps. The results showed sensitivity of 96.9%, specificity of 100%, accuracy of 98%, and NPV of 94.6%.

2.2.3 White light endoscopy (WLE)

WLE is an endoscopic technique, which can be used with combination of AI models to differentiate neoplastic and non-neoplastic lesions. Komeda et al. [40] in his recent study applied CNN system for the classification of polyps using WLE. This study resulted with accuracy of only 75.1%. This showed that this method is inferior compared to NBI or endoscopy with the presence or absence of magnification.

2.2.4 Studies of polyp characterization

In 2016, Kominami et al. [41], in the prospective study of colon polyps, studied 41 patients using support vector machines (SVM) an AI algorithm, which is used for classification and regressive analysis. In real-time diagnosis, the results showed sensitivity of 93%, specificity of 93.3%, accuracy of 93.2%, and NPV of 93.3%. It also detected the diminutive polyps. In 2017, Takeda et al. [38] studied 76 CRC patients retrospectively by endoscopy method. In this study, they also used SVM for classification of polyps. The results of the study were sensitivity: 89.4%, specificity: 98.9%, accuracy: 94.1%, NPV: 90.1%. Here, CADx system is also used for the differentiation of adenomatous polyps and invasive CRC.

In 2018, Renner et al. [42], in retrospective study of colon polyps, found about 100 polyps using NBI and WLE. For accurate characterization, they used deep neural network (DNN). The results were sensitivity of 92.3%, specificity of 62.5%, accuracy of 78%, and NPV of 88.2%. The diminutive polyps were also detected. Lui et al. 2019 [43] in the study of colon polyps using WLE and NBI found 76 polyps. They introduced CNN and CADx system for polyp classification. The results were sensitivity of 88.2%, specificity of 77.9%, and accuracy of 85.5%. Kudo et al. (2020) in retrospective study of colon polyps found 2000 polyps using endocytoscopy along with NBI and staining modes of MB (44). For accurate classification, they used EndoBRAIN, an ai algorithm. The results showed NBI sensitivity of 96.9%, specificity of 94.3%, accuracy of 96%, and NPV of 94.3%. The diminutive polyps were also detected. In 2020, Rodriquez-diaz et al. [44] in the prospective real-time diagnosis of 119 patients found 280 polyps using magnifying

NBI. In this study, DeepLab V3+, a semantic segmentation of DL, is used for better classification of colon polyps. The results of this study showed sensitivity of 96%, specificity of 84%, and NPV of 91%. This not only detected diminutive polyps but also classified them. The results showed sensitivity of 95%, specificity of 88%, and NPV of 93%. Till now, many polyp characterization and classification modes have been introduced and developed. The application of AI showed promising and accurate results for colon polyp characterization.

2.3 Drug discovery and repurposing

The application of AI to drug discovery accelerates the process and provide new options for CRC patients. It detects the target molecules (nucleic acids, proteins) or cells where the mutations takes place and predicts new drugs for the target molecules it also helps to evaluate the effect of drugs. This make AI more proficient in drug discovery, and it also has developing models, which helps in providing drugs for different types of cancers. The DepMap consortium [45] contains large data sets available for researchers to implement diverse AI techniques. The ECLIPSE, an AI approach predicts accurate drugs to specific cancer based on cell line and gene specific data present on DepMap [46]. You et al. developed a graphed CNN approach to generate drugs for molecules having certain properties. The drugs also showed high accuracy rate [47].

MolGAN, [48] a system for generating the molecules with certain properties used reinforcement learning method and GAN (Generative Adversarial networks) resulted with high performance of drug similarities of 62%, solubility of 89%, and synthesizability of 95%. Neural network-based methods dominated molecule generation, while non-neural network-based methods were successful in predicting specific drug properties. Shen et al. [49] produced a SVM model for the prediction of various properties of drugs such as absorption, diffusion, metabolism, and exudation (ADME) and verified their applications accurately. Reinforcement learning, the subset of AI deals with problems of complex objectives and gives interactive feedback of activity of new drugs.

AI has a new feature called drug repurposing, here with the help of AI new therapeutic uses of the existing drugs are found and developed. It is a safe, speedy, and cost-benefit method. New programs such as Library of Integrated Network-Based Cellular Signatures (LINCS) database consists different experimental data and drug history and protocols that accelerate the drug repurposing effects by AI [50]. Recently, a research class used AI methods and specific phenotype studies including chemical genetics, biochemical assays for the prediction of disease–drug match to repurpose, and develop existing drugs. They are used for different diseases including CRC treatment.

2.4 Treatment and prevention

The traditional treatment methods of CRC include chemotherapy, nCRT (neo adjuvant chemo radiotherapy), surgery, and some other approaches [51]. Just like any other cancers, CRC has also 4 stages that determine the condition of the cancer. Different treatment methods are recommended based on the stage of CRC.

STAGE-0: Common treatment is polypectomy where the polyps and tumors are removed during colonoscopy. There will be no need for surgery.

STAGE-1: Removal of polyps and the lymph nodes during surgery is required.

STAGE-2: Surgery is mandatory and the additional chemotherapy may also be recommended.

STAGE-3: For stage 3 CRC, surgery followed by the adjuvant chemotherapy is required. The duration of chemotherapy depends on rate of recurrence. In case of rectal cancer, the radiation therapy is given along with chemotherapy.

STAGE-4: This stage is also called metastatic stage, and it spreads from colon and rectum to the distant organs like liver, ovaries, and lungs. At this stage, there is no cure for CRC, but the treatment may increase the life span of the patient. A combination of surgery, immunotherapy, chemotherapy, and radiation therapy is usually required. However, the common treatment methods takes more time, labor, recovery time, they are risky, and may have side effects and perforations. Application of AI to CRC helps clinicians to choose suitable treatment options and enhances treatment efficiency.

3. Robotic-assisted surgery

CRC treatment takes a new leap with the application of robotic-assisted colorectal surgery. This is an advanced method of minimally invasive surgical treatment. Da Vinci system is the most known and used to perform minimally invasive surgical treatment.

Based on recent studies, when compared to open surgeries, robotic surgeries resulted in less inflammatory response, less complications, and lower conversion rates [52]. The postoperative recovery of robotic surgery was also high compared to laparoscopy for CRC. Park et al. [53] stated that conversion rate of laparoscopy is higher (7.1%) to robotic surgery (0%). Laparoscopic surgery for the rectal cancer is technically challenging for obese patients and patients with complex pelvic anatomy. Use of robotic platform helps in providing access for hard-to-reach and difficult areas like narrow pelvis. Jayne et al. in ROLARR randomized medical trials reported that robotic surgery has lower conversion rate than laparoscopy in males, in patients with low anterior resection (LAR) and in obese patients [54].

This method allows surgeons in the surgery to perform easily and delicately during complex procedures. It is not only beneficial to patients but also to the surgeons. The advantages of this method include fast recovery, minimal scarring, less inflammation rate, low risk of surgical infections, and less blood loss. Hirano et al. suggested that use of this system as safe, effective, precise, and accurate surgical treatment for CRC patients.

As the precision medicine helps to identify the detection of molecular alterations or mutations in patients, the accurate therapy is provided. Therefore, the reoccurrence of CRC is less. Precision medicine is more effective as preventive method. The preventive strategies of AI in precision medicine include study of molecular profile, biomarker-based analysis, and studies of genomic sequence.

4. Precision medicine in CRC

Precision medicine is an important medical paradigm for achieving personalized and accurate therapy for patients with specific conditions. It also provides new therapeutic strategies. In 2019, an AI algorithm was developed by research team and it differentiated patients into cancer subgroups based on their genetic biomarkers and type of cancer [55]. It also identifies and enhances the drug combinations and design for the patients. Lee et al. with the application of ML developed an AI algorithm for the prediction of protein–protein reactions of S100A9 [56]. It interacts with the drugs and evaluates drug specificity. In another study, their developed a model that can identify the drugs that detects cancer-specified metabolisms.

"Watson for Oncology" (IBM Corporation, WFO, US) developed an AI model that can assist in precision oncology. When this is trailed clinically and applied it resulted with 90% treatment recommendations equal to the human experts in cancer treatment [57]. A research study in Japan applied IBM Watson to cancer patients for whole genome sequence (WGS) and analysis. It delivered results within 4 days only [58]. With all the advanced approaches of AI and treatment techniques, precision medicine is believed as the key for effective treatment strategies in future.

5. Benefits

- Accelerates the rate of diagnosis, accuracy, and medical decision making, leading to better outcomes.
- Prescribes more suitable drugs, which decrease negative side effects.
- Reduces time, expense, failure rate, and labor.
- Customized treatment and preventive strategies.

6. Limitations

- Requires a high quantity and quality of data, but there is a limited research and work done on approach of AI in CRC treatment.
- It is not widely accepted as much as traditional methods.
- It requires proper care and attention to study and learn the techniques.

7. Current challenges and prospects

Application of AI in the CRC treatment still is in research and in infancy state compared to the other oncology studies such as breast and lung cancers [59]. Even though the results tend to be promising and effective, there is no solid evidence for the application of AI in CRC. The clinical practice is required to validate the use of AI. There is no proper funding for the study of predictive models of AI and precision medicine. It requires high amount of medical or clinical data of patients with CRC and needs privacy protection, which raise ethical issues.

AI technology could be operated to design a model that can check healthy people for early warning and occurrence of the cancer. More accurate and staging systems had to be developed. Reoccurrence prediction and survival prediction can also be studied by focusing AI methods on specific stages [60].

8. Conclusion

Overall, with the application of AI models to CRC in screening, diagnosis, drug discovery, and treatment may enhance better clinical performance and prognosis. The ML models can assist physicians in detecting precancerous polyps at early stage. Several AI algorithms showed promising results and gave accurate treatment strategies with the help of precision medicine. This increased the research and study of AI in CRC.

Conflict of interest

None.

Funding

None.

References

[1] S.J. Russell, P. Norvig, Artificial Intelligence: A Modern Approach, Harlow, Pearson Education, 2003.
[2] Y. LeCun, Y. Bengio, G. Hinton, Deep learning, Nature 521 (2015) 436–444.
[3] H. Hu, Z. Niu, Y. Bai, X. Tan, Cancer classification based on gene expression using neural networks, Genet. Mol. Res. 14 (2015) 17605–17611.
[4] F. Coppedè, E. Grossi, A. Lopomo, R. Spisni, M. Buscema, L. Migliore, Application of artificial neural networks to link genetic and environmental factors to DNA methylation in colorectal cancer, Epigenomics 7 (2015) 175–186.
[5] Q. Wang, J. Wei, Z. Chen, T. Zhang, J. Zhong, B. Zhong, P. Yang, W. Li, J. Cao, Establishment of multiple diagnosis models for colorectal cancer with artificial neural networks, Oncol. Lett. 17 (2019) 3314–3322.
[6] M.A. Aziz, Z. Yousef, A.M. Saleh, S. Mohammad, B. Al Knawy, Towards personalized medicine of colorectal cancer, Crit. Rev. Oncol. Hematol. 118 (2017) 70–78.
[7] L. Timmerman, What's in a name? A lot, when it comes to 'precision medicine', Xconomy (2013). 4 February.
[8] J.M. Brant, D.K. Mayer, Precision medicine: accelerating the science to revolutionize cancer care, Clin. J. Oncol. Nurs. 21 (2017).

[9] E. Sinagra, M. Badalamenti, M. Maida, M. Spadaccini, R. Maselli, F. Rossi, G. Conoscenti, D. Raimondo, S. Pallio, A. Repici, Use of artificial intelligence in improving adenoma detection rate during colonoscopy: might both endoscopists and pathologists be further helped, World J. Gastroenterol. 26 (2020) 5911.

[10] R.A. Smith, K.S. Andrews, D. Brooks, S.A. Fedewa, D. Manassaram-Baptiste, D. Saslow, R.C. Wender, Cancer Screening in the United States, A review of current American Cancer Society guidelines and current issues in cancer screening, CA Cancer J. Clin. 69 (2019) (2019) 184–210.

[11] I.A. Issa, M. Noureddine, Colorectal cancer screening: an updated review of the available options, World J. Gastroenterol. 23 (2017) 5086.

[12] B. Bressler, L.F. Paszat, Z. Chen, D.M. Rothwell, C. Vinden, L. Rabeneck, Rates of new or missed colorectal cancers after colonoscopy and their risk factors: a population-based analysis, Gastroenterology 132 (2007) 96–102.

[13] D.A. Corley, C.D. Jensen, A.R. Marks, W.K. Zhao, J.K. Lee, C.A. Doubeni, A.G. Zauber, J. de Boer, B.H. Fireman, J.E. Schottinger, Adenoma detection rate and risk of colorectal cancer and death, N. Engl. J. Med. 370 (2014) 1298–1306.

[14] B. Zheng, E. Rieder, M.A. Cassera, D.V. Martinec, G. Lee, O.N.M. Panton, A. Park, L.L. Swanström, Quantifying mental workloads of surgeons performing natural orifice transluminal endoscopic surgery (NOTES) procedures, Surg. Endosc. 26 (2012) 1352–1358.

[15] Y. Mori, S.-E. Kudo, T.M. Berzin, M. Misawa, K. Takeda, Computer-aided diagnosis for colonoscopy, Endoscopy 49 (2017) 813–819.

[16] A. Nogueira-Rodríguez, R. Domínguez-Carbajales, H. López-Fernández, Á. Iglesias, J. Cubiella, F. Fdez-Riverola, M. Reboiro-Jato, D. Glez-Peña, Deep neural networks approaches for detecting and classifying colorectal polyps, Neurocomputing 423 (2021) 721–734.

[17] K.O. Kim, E.Y. Kim, Application of artificial intelligence in the detection and characterization of colorectal neoplasm, Gut Liver 15 (2021) 346.

[18] S.E. Kudo, Y. Mori, M. Misawa, K. Takeda, T. Kudo, H. Itoh, M. Oda, K. Mori, Artificial intelligence and colonoscopy: current status and future perspectives, Dig. Endosc. 31 (2019) 363–371.

[19] S.A. Karkanis, D.K. Iakovidis, D.E. Maroulis, D.A. Karras, M. Tzivras, Computer-aided tumor detection in endoscopic video using color wavelet features, IEEE Trans. Inf. Technol. Biomed. 7 (2003) 141–152.

[20] G. Urban, P. Tripathi, T. Alkayali, M. Mittal, F. Jalali, W. Karnes, P. Baldi, Deep learning localizes and identifies polyps in real time with 96% accuracy in screening colonoscopy, Gastroenterology 155 (2018) 1069–1078 (e1068).

[21] P. Klare, C. Sander, M. Prinzen, B. Haller, S. Nowack, M. Abdelhafez, A. Poszler, H. Brown, D. Wilhelm, R.M. Schmid, Automated polyp detection in the colorectum: a prospective study (with videos), Gastrointest. Endosc. 89 (2019) 576–582 (e571).

[22] P. Wang, X. Liu, T.M. Berzin, J.R.G. Brown, P. Liu, C. Zhou, L. Lei, L. Li, Z. Guo, S. Lei, Effect of a deep-learning computer-aided detection system on adenoma detection during colonoscopy (CADe-DB trial): a double-blind randomised study, Lancet Gastroenterol. Hepatol. 5 (2020) 343–351.

[23] P. Wang, T.M. Berzin, J.R.G. Brown, S. Bharadwaj, A. Becq, X. Xiao, P. Liu, L. Li, Y. Song, D. Zhang, Real-time automatic detection system increases colonoscopic polyp and adenoma detection rates: a prospective randomised controlled study, Gut 68 (2019) 1813–1819.

[24] J.-R. Su, Z. Li, X.-J. Shao, C.-R. Ji, R. Ji, R.-C. Zhou, G.-C. Li, G.-Q. Liu, Y.-S. He, X.-L. Zuo, Impact of a real-time automatic quality control system on colorectal polyp and adenoma detection: a prospective randomized controlled study (with videos), Gastrointest. Endosc. 91 (2020) 415–424 (e414).

[25] D. Vining, Technical feasibility of colon imaging with helical CT and virtual reality, AJR 162 (1994) 104.

[26] K. Manjunath, P. Siddalingaswamy, G. Prabhu, Measurement of smaller colon polyp in CT colonography images using morphological image processing, Int. J. Comput. Assist. Radiol. Surg. 12 (2017) 1845–1855.

[27] S. Grosu, P. Wesp, A. Graser, S. Maurus, C. Schulz, T. Knösel, C.C. Cyran, J. Ricke, M. Ingrisch, P.M. Kazmierczak, Machine learning–based differentiation of benign and premalignant colorectal polyps

detected with CT colonography in an asymptomatic screening population: a proof-of-concept study, Radiology 299 (2021) 326–335.
[28] T.K. Lui, C.-G. Guo, W.K. Leung, Accuracy of artificial intelligence on histology prediction and detection of colorectal polyps: a systematic review and meta-analysis, Gastrointest. Endosc. 92 (2020) 11–22 (e16).
[29] R. Bisschops, J.E. East, C. Hassan, Y. Hazewinkel, M.F. Kamiński, H. Neumann, M. Pellisé, G. Antonelli, M.B. Balen, E. Coron, Advanced imaging for detection and differentiation of colorectal neoplasia: European Society of Gastrointestinal Endoscopy (ESGE) Guideline–Update 2019, Endoscopy 51 (2019) 1155–1179.
[30] D.K. Rex, C. Kahi, M. O'Brien, T. Levin, H. Pohl, A. Rastogi, L. Burgart, T. Imperiale, U. Ladabaum, J. Cohen, The American Society for Gastrointestinal Endoscopy PIVI (preservation and incorporation of valuable endoscopic innovations) on real-time endoscopic assessment of the histology of diminutive colorectal polyps, Gastrointest. Endosc. 73 (2011) 419–422.
[31] S.B.D.L.R. Castrob, M. Dinis-Ribeirob, P. Pimentel-Nunesb, Narrow-Band Imaging: Clinical Application in Gastrointestinal Endoscopy, 2018.
[32] Y. Takemura, S. Yoshida, S. Tanaka, R. Kawase, K. Onji, S. Oka, T. Tamaki, B. Raytchev, K. Kaneda, M. Yoshihara, Computer-aided system for predicting the histology of colorectal tumors by using narrow-band imaging magnifying colonoscopy (with video), Gastrointest. Endosc. 75 (2012) 179–185.
[33] J. Tischendorf, S. Gross, R. Winograd, H. Hecker, R. Auer, A. Behrens, C. Trautwein, T. Aach, T. Stehle, Computer-aided classification of colorectal polyps based on vascular patterns: a pilot study, Endoscopy 42 (2010) 203–207.
[34] S. Gross, C. Trautwein, A. Behrens, R. Winograd, S. Palm, H.H. Lutz, R. Schirin-Sokhan, H. Hecker, T. Aach, J.J. Tischendorf, Computer-based classification of small colorectal polyps by using narrow-band imaging with optical magnification, Gastrointest. Endosc. 74 (2011) 1354–1359.
[35] T. Hirakawa, T. Tamaki, B. Raytchev, K. Kaneda, T. Koide, Y. Kominami, S. Yoshida, S. Tanaka, SVM-MRF segmentation of colorectal NBI endoscopic images, in: 2014 36th Annual International Conference of the IEEE Engineering in Medicine and Biology Society, IEEE, 2014, pp. 4739–4742.
[36] H. Neumann, F.S. Fuchs, M. Vieth, R. Atreya, J. Siebler, R. Kiesslich, M. Neurath, In vivo imaging by endocytoscopy, Aliment. Pharmacol. Ther. 33 (2011) 1183–1193.
[37] Y. Mori, S.-E. Kudo, K. Wakamura, M. Misawa, Y. Ogawa, M. Kutsukawa, T. Kudo, T. Hayashi, H. Miyachi, F. Ishida, Novel computer-aided diagnostic system for colorectal lesions by using endocytoscopy (with videos), Gastrointest. Endosc. 81 (2015) 621–629.
[38] K. Takeda, S.-E. Kudo, Y. Mori, M. Misawa, T. Kudo, K. Wakamura, A. Katagiri, T. Baba, E. Hidaka, F. Ishida, Accuracy of diagnosing invasive colorectal cancer using computer-aided endocytoscopy, Endoscopy 49 (2017) 798–802.
[39] S.-E. Kudo, M. Misawa, Y. Mori, K. Hotta, K. Ohtsuka, H. Ikematsu, Y. Saito, K. Takeda, H. Nakamura, K. Ichimasa, Artificial intelligence-assisted system improves endoscopic identification of colorectal neoplasms, Clin. Gastroenterol. Hepatol. 18 (2020) 1874–1881. e1872.
[40] Y. Komeda, H. Handa, T. Watanabe, T. Nomura, M. Kitahashi, T. Sakurai, A. Okamoto, T. Minami, M. Kono, T. Arizumi, Computer-aided diagnosis based on convolutional neural network system for colorectal polyp classification: preliminary experience, Oncology 93 (2017) 30–34.
[41] Y. Kominami, S. Yoshida, S. Tanaka, Y. Sanomura, T. Hirakawa, B. Raytchev, T. Tamaki, T. Koide, K. Kaneda, K. Chayama, Computer-aided diagnosis of colorectal polyp histology by using a real-time image recognition system and narrow-band imaging magnifying colonoscopy, Gastrointest. Endosc. 83 (2016) 643–649.
[42] J. Renner, H. Phlipsen, B. Haller, F. Navarro-Avila, Y. Saint-Hill-Febles, D. Mateus, T. Ponchon, A. Poszler, M. Abdelhafez, R.M. Schmid, Optical classification of neoplastic colorectal polyps – a computer-assisted approach (the COACH study), Scand. J. Gastroenterol. 53 (2018) 1100–1106.
[43] T.K. Lui, K.K. Wong, L.L. Mak, M.K. Ko, S.K. Tsao, W.K. Leung, Endoscopic prediction of deeply submucosal invasive carcinoma with use of artificial intelligence, Endosc. Int. Open 7 (2019) E514–E520.

[44] E. Rodriguez-Diaz, G. Baffy, W.-K. Lo, H. Mashimo, G. Vidyarthi, S.S. Mohapatra, S.K. Singh, Real-time artificial intelligence–based histologic classification of colorectal polyps with augmented visualization, Gastrointest. Endosc. 93 (2021) 662–670.
[45] A. Tsherniak, F. Vazquez, P.G. Montgomery, B.A. Weir, G. Kryukov, G.S. Cowley, S. Gill, W.F. Harrington, S. Pantel, J.M. Krill-Burger, Defining a cancer dependency map, Cell 170 (2017) 564–576 (e516).
[46] C. Gilvary, N.S. Madhukar, K. Gayvert, M. Foronda, A. Perez, C.S. Leslie, L. Dow, G. Pandey, O. Elemento, A machine learning approach predicts essential genes and pharmacological targets in cancer, BioRxiv (2019) 692277.
[47] J. You, B. Liu, Z. Ying, V. Pande, J. Leskovec, Graph convolutional policy network for goal-directed molecular graph generation, Adv. Neural Inf. Proces. Syst. 31 (2018).
[48] N. De Cao, T. Kipf, MolGAN: An implicit generative model for small molecular graphs, arXiv preprint arXiv:1805.11973, 2018.
[49] J. Shen, F. Cheng, Y. Xu, W. Li, Y. Tang, Estimation of ADME properties with substructure pattern recognition, J. Chem. Inf. Model. 50 (2010) 1034–1041.
[50] A. Subramanian, R. Narayan, S.M. Corsello, D.D. Peck, T.E. Natoli, X. Lu, J. Gould, J.F. Davis, A.A. Tubelli, J.K. Asiedu, A next generation connectivity map: L1000 platform and the first 1,000,000 profiles, Cell 171 (2017) 1437–1452 (e1417).
[51] P. Bondeven, S. Laurberg, R. Hagemann-Madsen, B. Ginnerup Pedersen, Suboptimal surgery and omission of neoadjuvant therapy for upper rectal cancer is associated with a high risk of local recurrence, Color. Dis. 17 (2015) 216–224.
[52] A. Hussain, A. Malik, M.U. Halim, A.M. Ali, The use of robotics in surgery: a review, Int. J. Clin. Pract. 68 (2014) 1376–1382.
[53] E.J. Park, M.S. Cho, S.J. Baek, H. Hur, B.S. Min, S.H. Baik, K.Y. Lee, N.K. Kim, Long-term oncologic outcomes of robotic low anterior resection for rectal cancer: a comparative study with laparoscopic surgery, Ann. Surg. 261 (2015) 129–137.
[54] D. Jayne, A. Pigazzi, H. Marshall, J. Croft, N. Corrigan, J. Copeland, P. Quirke, N. West, T. Rautio, N. Thomassen, Effect of robotic-assisted vs conventional laparoscopic surgery on risk of conversion to open laparotomy among patients undergoing resection for rectal cancer: the ROLARR randomized clinical trial, JAMA 318 (2017) 1569–1580.
[55] N. Keshava, T.S. Toh, H. Yuan, B. Yang, M.P. Menden, D. Wang, Defining subpopulations of differential drug response to reveal novel target populations, NPJ Syst. Biol. Appl. 5 (2019) 1–11.
[56] J. Lee, S. Kumar, S.-Y. Lee, S.J. Park, M.-H. Kim, Development of predictive models for identifying potential S100A9 inhibitors based on machine learning methods, Front. Chem. 7 (2019) 779.
[57] C. Schmidt, MD Anderson breaks with IBM Watson, raising questions about artificial intelligence in oncology, JNCI: J. Natl. Cancer Inst. 109 (2017).
[58] S. Miyano, Artificial intelligence for cancer genomic medicine: understanding cancer is beyond human ability, Brain and Nerve = Shinkei Kenkyu no Shinpo 71 (2019) 25–32.
[59] R. Hamamoto, K. Suvarna, M. Yamada, K. Kobayashi, N. Shinkai, M. Miyake, M. Takahashi, S. Jinnai, R. Shimoyama, A. Sakai, Application of artificial intelligence technology in oncology: towards the establishment of precision medicine, Cancers 12 (2020) 3532.
[60] J. Li, Y. Tian, Y. Zhu, T. Zhou, J. Li, K. Ding, J. Li, A multicenter random forest model for effective prognosis prediction in collaborative clinical research network, Artif. Intell. Med. 103 (2020), 101814.

CHAPTER 6

Artificial intelligence in breast cancer: An opportunity for early diagnosis

Rama Rao Malla[a] and Vedavathi Katneni[b]

[a]Cancer Biology Lab, Department of Biochemistry and Bioinformatics, GSS, GITAM (Deemed to be University), Visakhapatnam, Andhra Pradesh, India

[b]Department of Computer Science, GSS, GITAM (Deemed to be University), Visakhapatnam, Andhra Pradesh, India

Abstract

One of the serious women's cancer types across the globe is breast cancer (BC). It occurs due to complex heterogeneity as well as multiple etiological factors. Early diagnosis will increase the survival of the patients and reduce mortality to a great extent. Generally, different types of biopsy procedures, mammography, ultrasonography, PET scan, and magnetic resonance imaging (MRI) scan are used to detect breast tumors. However, for the accurate diagnosis of BC, there is a complex necessity for a reliable system. Nowadays, a combination of artificial intelligence (AI), especially a machine learning (ML) approach with digital imaging techniques, has assisted in reducing the false diagnoses of BC. This review presents the fundamentals of ML algorithms and ML models for BC prediction, model assessment, and current knowledge on ML-based approaches for BC diagnosis. Finally, it presents the challenges and scope of AI in precision medicine for BC. Therefore, AI could be useful for achieving groundbreaking progress in precision medicine for BC.

Abbreviations

ANN	artificial neural network
AUC	area under the curve
BC	breast cancer
BCRAT	breast cancer risk assessment tool
BN	Bayesian network
BOADICEA	breast and ovarian analysis of disease incidence and carrier estimation algorithm
CT	computed tomography
DFS	disease-free survival
DRS	digital risk score
ELM	extreme learning machine
FNR	false-negative rate
FNR	false-positive rate
GA	genetic algorithm
GBM	generalized boosted models
GWAS	genome-wide association studies
IHC	immune histochemistry
KNNs	k-nearest neighbors

https://doi.org/10.1016/B978-0-443-15280-1.00004-2

LDA	linear discriminant analysis
LLM	logic learning machine
lncRNAs	long non-coding RNAs
MALDI	matrix-assisted laser desorption/ionization
MDP	Markov decision process
ML	machine learning
MRI	magnetic resonance imaging
NGS	next generation sequence
PAM	prediction analysis for microarrays
PET	positron emission tomography
RF	random forest
RPART	recursive partitioning and regression trees
SDAE	stacked denoising autoencoder
SL	supervised learning
SNP	single nucleotide polymorphism
SVM	support vector machine
TCGA	the cancer genome atlas
TNR	true negative rate
TOC	total operating characteristic
TPR	true positive rate
TRS	thermalytix risk score
US	ultrasound

1. Machine learning

Machine learning (ML) is a scientific study of algorithms concerning statistical models that uses computer systems to execute a specific task by relying on patterns and inference but without precise instructions. ML can analyze a very high quantity of data with faster delivery and accuracy in identifying risks. ML uses statistical computation that directs attention over the accomplishment of predictions. The use of optimization studies comes across with application domains of ML [1]. The algorithms used in ML are concerned with statistical modeling that uses computers for processing large volumes of data to identify hidden patterns and draw inferences based on the instructions given. ML can analyze a very high quantity of data with faster delivery and accuracy in identifying risks. ML uses statistical computation that directs attention to the accomplishment of predictions. The use of optimization studies comes across application domains of ML [2].

1.1 Machine learning algorithms

Supervised and unsupervised learning are ML algorithms. They can be used to develop mathematical models. These models are obtained from "sample data" or "training data" to make forecasts without a need for specific programming [3]. For supervised learning (SL) algorithms, a sample data set is used to build a mathematical model that includes both inputs and expected outputs. An incomplete training data is utilized to develop a mathematical model for semi-SL algorithms. In the beginning, the SL algorithms perform data analysis from known training sets that produce inferred functions to make predictions about the output that will provide targets for new input. The model is trained by modifying the inferred functions by comparing its output with the correct and desired output [4]. SL algorithms deal with two popular algorithms: algorithms for classification and regression. The classification algorithms will find a model using outputs that are a limited set of discrete values, while regression algorithms find a model that predicts continuous values based on the input value within a range [5].

Unsupervised learning, also known as clustering, is a data mining technique that focuses on analyzing exploratory data through identifying patterns in the input data and clustering the data into groups called classes [6]. In the case of the unsupervised learning algorithm, a mathematical model development takes place only from the input data set without a labeled output class. The clustering algorithm is employed to determine the hidden pattern of unlabeled data, extract useful information, and group similar data. To obtain class labels for training data, the learning algorithms access the desired outputs for a subset of inputs. The reinforcement learning algorithm is a dynamic algorithm that receives feedback that may be either positive or negative [7]. Dynamic programming is the most used technique in many reinforcement learning algorithms [8]. Markov decision process (MDP) in ML represents this dynamic environment [9]. It does not know an exact mathematical model in contrast to reinforcement learning. Also, reinforcement learning is used when the exact models are not feasible [10].

1.2 Implementation of ML models

Implementing the ML model involves creating and then training the model with training data. If the model gives satisfactory results, it can also be applied to forecast new data. Research has been carried out to develop different types of models by using ML. One such development is an artificial neural network (ANNs) [11]. It is an interconnected collection of nodes. It is like that of the network of neurons in the brain of humans or animals. It is also a connectionist system. In ANN, a node simulates the function of a neuron, and the directed arrow represents how the nodes are connected in the network. The connection in the network is established by connecting the output of one node to the input of another node [12].

Learning in these systems is done by considering examples but not through a program that follows specific rules. Each artificial node in the network transmits the information from one artificial neuron to another in the network through a "signal." A signal received by the artificial neuron is processed at that node and then sends the output signal to other neurons linked to it in the network. The input signal to the node is a real number [13]. A nonlinear function is used in the algorithm [14]. To calculate the output at a node in the network, a sum of all inputs received at that node is obtained. This network can be represented as a graph, where the connection between neurons is named "edges." Each edge has a weight, and this weight for the edge is adjusted during the learning process. This weight may either increase or decrease the strength of the signal in the connection. The signal in the artificial neurons is broad-casted only when the aggregate signal at that node crosses the threshold. Typically, ANN is composed of multiple layers, where each layer has a collection of nodes. Based on the inputs, each layer performs different transformations. The first layer of the network, also known as the input layer, receives the input signals. The output emerges from the network through the last layer, called the output layer. ANN is developed to decipher problems like our brains. Nevertheless, it has gained momentum to perform specific tasks and deviated from biology. Among these, medical diagnosis is one of the important areas [15]. Deep learning is a special case of ANN composed of several hidden layers. An application of deep learning can be mentioned as computer vision and speech recognition.

The decision tree approach is another commonly used predictive modeling technique. It has been used widely in ML [16]. The decision tree resembles a tree-like structure. The leaf of the tree is used to denote the class label, with the branch indicating the attribute that directs to the class label. If the target variable of the tree considers a discrete set of values, then the tree is a classification tree. Alternatively, if the target variable considers continuous values i.e., real numbers, then the tree is a regression tree. Learning in a decision tree starts from the node represented as a branch and travels towards the next level of the tree until the threshold is satisfied. By traversing the root node to the leaf node, one can attain a decision in the form of if-then rules. In data mining, the decision tree is used to describe attributes as nodes in the tree, and the subtrees result in a classification tree, which is the input for decision making. The decision tree model also represents probability and decision making in ML [17]. A conditional statement narrows down the input values and predicts the probability of the outcome. It splits the data into a node until every input gives an outcome. The internal node splits further, while external nodes stop splitting and show a stop sign.

Support vector machine (SVM) is a support vector network of ML [18]. It consists of a collection of interrelated SL methods. It is used for classification as well as regression processes. Here two categories are defined for the given set of training examples, i.e., each sample will belong to one and only one category. A model is built with an SVM training algorithm, and once a new example is given, the model will forecast which category the new example falls in [19]. It is labeled as a binary linear classifier. In a probabilistic classification setting, the Platt scaling exists to use SVM. In addition, SVMs use the Kernel trick to perform a nonlinear classification with inputs into high-dimensional feature space through implicit mapping.

Bayesian network (BN) is a stochastic graphical model, representing a group of random variables and their conditional independence [20]. For instance, a BN may denote the probable association between diseases and its symptoms. BN predicts the probability of the presence or absence of a disease based on the symptoms of the disease. The algorithms can be used to draw inferences and may be used in learning. Dynamic BNs are the BNs that will model sequences of signals and sequence of proteins [21]. The influence diagrams are the generalizations of BNs, represent as well as solve decision problems.

Another heuristic search algorithm is the genetic algorithm (GA). During the 1990s, ML used GAs [22]. Also, ML has been used to expand the efficiency of GAs as well as evolutionary algorithms. Extensive data is required for ML models to obtain accurate results. During the training phase of the model, a large representative sample of data needs to be considered from a training set. This data extracted from the training set is diverse like corpus. While training an Ml model, care must be taken in overfitting. Another new ML model training approach is federated learning [23]. These federal models will decentralize the training process. Also, the users' privacy is maintained by not sending their data to a central server. This implements decentralization of the training process to several devices, which increases efficiency. For example, Gboard federated ML is applied to train search query prediction. It is used to design an aggregation logic for a given network and to train a robust and generalizable network. For example, it uses a validation dataset for total tumor mass, tumor core, and tumor progression [24].

1.3 Assessment of ML models

The validation of the developed ML model by classification or SL can be performed with accuracy estimation techniques. One such method is the Holdout method [25]. It partitions the whole data into a training set and a test set. Normally, 2/3 of the data collected is considered a training set and 1/3 as a test set. The model is fitted with the training set. The accuracy of the developed model is obtained by applying the model to the test datasets. The K-fold-cross-validation method will arbitrarily separate the data into subsets. Each subset is evaluated on the model trained using (K-1) subsets. The other methods used are cross-validation methods and bootstrapping. These will sample "n" instances with displacement from the dataset and can also be used to evaluate model precision. The other metrics include sensitivity and specificity metrics. They are obtained by determining the true-positive rate (TPR) and true-negative rate (TNR) [26]. TPR determines the fraction of actual positives that are exactly identified as such, for example, the percentage of sick people correctly identified as having the symptom. A TNR measures the proportion of actual negatives that are correctly identified as such, for instance, the percent of healthy individuals accurately identified as normal without having the symptoms. Also, the false-positive rate (FPR) and the false-negative rate (FNR) are also obtained to validate the model's performance. Another method used to measure the model efficiency is the total operating characteristic (TOC) [27]. This method is more accurate compared to conventional methods like receiver-operating characteristic as well as area under the curve (AUC) [28].

1.4 ML in cancer prediction and diagnosis

ML has a massive impact on cancer diagnostics, specifically developing novel computational tools for stratification, grading, and prognosis to improve patient outcome [29]. ML has tremendous potential in medicine, especially in the interpretation of images [30]. Even ML finds applications in the development of drugs as well as in the prediction of epidemiology to translate the medical landscape [31]. ML is essential in multimodal imaging of tumors, image-guided treatment, computer-aided diagnosis of cancers, as well as annotation and retrieval of tumor image database [32]. ML approaches are important in health care, especially in recognizing cancer images [33] and lung cancer [34]. ML algorithms have integrated to imaging devices to detect breast cancer (BC) [35]. These advances fuel the rapid growth of commercial ML-based health care in clinical oncology.

2. Breast cancer

BC is one of the most common cancer types worldwide and is a severe threat to health. This type of cancer is complex; it is a hereditary disease and does not result from a single cause. The diagnosis of cancer starts with a biopsy. Various methods are used to detect and recognize cancer cells, from microscopic images and mammography to ultrasonography and magnetic resonance imaging (MRI). With the early diagnosis of BC, survival will increase from 56% to more than 86%. Therefore, an accurate and reliable system is necessary for the early diagnosis of this cancer.

ML would be preferred over heterogeneous predictors with large number of noisy and intricate problems. In the current era, transforming biomedical big data into precious information is a major challenge in biomedical informatics. However, applying various ML techniques, simultaneously biomedical field, shows state-of-the-art performance, especially for computational genomics [36]. ML constitutes an important area that deals with computers to learn through knowledge representation, processing, and storing and offers solutions to health care [37]. For example, Srđan Jović et al., developed the best predictive model for the early detection of prostate cancer using various ML techniques [38].

2.1 ML in breast cancer

The combination of ML and DL approaches was linked to digital mammography images for early detection of BC. This model can substantially reduce false diagnoses of BC [39]. The clinical data of 140 confirmed BC cases along with ultrasound (US) images were examined retrospectively to differentiate BC subtypes. US images from the grayscale as well as color Doppler images were utilized with logistic regression for classification by ML. The analysis of breast US images by ML attains an accurate differentiation of BC subtypes [40].

2.2 ML in BC risk prediction

ML method was used to validate the classification of tissue microarray data from the primary tumor ($N=1299$) during a nationwide BC screening along with long-term follow-up. It categorized BC patients into two groups based on low or high digital risk score (DRS). It also predicted survival of BC patients with a hazard ratio of 2.10 and confidence interval of 95% [41]. Stark et al., have designed ML models using only the Gail model inputs and models using both Gail model inputs and additional personal health data relevant to BC risk [42]. Advancements are constantly being made in oncology, improving the prevention and treatment of cancers. They must be detected early to help reduce the impact and deadliness of cancers. Additionally, there is a risk of cancers recurring after potentially curative treatments are performed. Predictive models that build using cancer patient data predict the cancer relapse or risk of recurrence in a wide range of diverse patients [43]. BC risk prediction models used in clinical practice have low discriminatory accuracy (0.53–0.64). ML-based BC Risk Assessment Tool (BCRAT) and Breast and Ovarian Analysis of Disease Incidence and Carrier Estimation Algorithm (BOADICEA) models offer an alternative approach to standard prediction modeling for the classification of women with and without BC at high accuracy, which is important in personalized medicine since they facilitate the stratification of prevention strategies and individualized clinical management [44]. Behravan et al., adopted a gradient tree boosting method and adaptive iterative SNP search to capture complex nonlinear SNP-SNP interactions. This model obtained interacting SNPs with high BC risk-predictive potential and classified BC cases and controls using an SVM [45]. Ricvan Dana Nindrea conducted a meta-analysis on the diagnostic test accuracy of ML algorithms for BC risk calculation. The meta-analysis confirmed that the SVM algorithm is able to calculate BC risk with a better accuracy value than other ML algorithms [46]. Recently, Kakileti et al. proposed a Thermalytix Risk Score (TRS) based on the AI for computational prediction of BC risk with an AUC of 0.89 compared to age-normal and healthy individuals of 0.68. This method empowers the physician to develop personalized care for BC patients based on the TRS score. It is useful for mass screening of risk group individuals to diagnose at an early stage [47] (Table 1).

2.3 ML in breast cancer diagnosis

A rule-based classification method was proposed for predicting survival of BC patients using ML techniques. According to this study, Trees Random Forest (TRF) model predicts survival of BC with high accuracy [48]. Another study developed a multistep DL-based model for the quantification of in situ expression of proteins involved associated with immune regulation in TNBC patients [49].

The supervised and unsupervised ML approaches with “handcrafted” and “data-driven” molecular descriptors are usually used in health care [50]. Supervised

Table 1 Applications of machine leaning approaches in prediction of risk factors of BC.

Approaches used	Application in BC	Reference
Machine Leaning and Deep Leaning with digital mammography	Early diagnosis with reduced false positivity.	[39]
Ultrasound imaging and Machine Learning	Attain an accurate differentiation of BC subtypes.	[40]
Machine Leaning	Categorization of BC patients based on low or high digital risk score and predicts survival of BC patients.	[41]
Machine Leaning model and Gail model	Predict risk of cancers recurring after potentially curative treatments	[42]
Statistical and machine learning methods	Predict the cancer relapse or risk of recurrence in a wide range of diverse patients	[43]
ML-based BC Risk Assessment Tool (BCRAT) and Breast and Ovarian Analysis of Disease Incidence and Carrier Estimation Algorithm (BOADICEA) models.	Offer an alternative approach for the classification of women with and without BC at high accuracy.	[44]
Support vector machine	Predicts BC risk potential and classified BC cases and controls.	[45]
ML algorithms	Calculate BC risk with a better accuracy value.	[46]
Thermalytix Risk Score (TRS) based on the AI	Predicts BC risk with an AUC of 0.89. It is useful for mass screening of risk group individuals to diagnose at an early stage.	[47]

methods of ML, such as SVMs and k-nearest neighbors (kNNs), are applied for pattern-recognition problems in biology and medicine [50]. ML platforms can gather and integrate information from diverse sources that can aid decision-making processes for highly skilled workers [51].

ML explores learning approaches and uses examples from medicine to introduce basic concepts. ML also identifies the obstacles that are changing the practice of medicine through statistical learning approaches [52]. The application of ML to laboratory data helps physician-scientists to support pathology and laboratory medicine [53]. ML is an expanding field of medicine with considerable resources to solve medical problems by fusing computer science with statistics [54]. ML has applications in analyzing light microscopy images with typical tasks of segmentation using the SL method and active learning for tracking individual cells using and modeling reconstructed lineage trees [55]. ML can recommend the treatment trial to cure cancer based on genome, history, imaging, and pathology, which are coupled with information on available cancer treatments [56]. Data-driven ML identifies similarities and differences in patient phenotypes and genomes, improves existing therapies, identifies new drug targets, optimizes prediction rules, avoids clinical errors due to human cognitive bias and fatigue, and delivers precision medicine [57].

ML is rapidly progressing in radiology in clinical predictive modeling [58], and passing the input image layer forward through links (weights), to several hidden layers that process the image to produce an output [59]. Over the decades, IHC, MRI, CT, and PET images have been used for cancer diagnosis, staging, and prognosis. ML programs help radiologists prioritize work lists by identifying suspicious or positive cases for early review. They can be applied to extract "radiomic" information from images that are not apparent by visual inspection, potentially increasing the diagnostic and prognostic value derived from image datasets [60].

IHC remains a common diagnostic method for rare type tumors due to a lack of molecular markers. Still, it has several challenges due to heterogeneity in tumor cells or similarity between different types. The expansion of ML computational tools can analyze histological data and classify tumors [61,62]. Application of deep learning for ultrasound image analysis to diagnose BC showed high accuracy comparable to human readers because a DL algorithm learns faster and better than a human reader without prior experience with the same training data [63]. Zou et al., applied a novel primer on DL applications for genome analysis, including regulatory genomics, variant calling, and pathogenicity scores, and provided general guidance for efficiently using deep learning methods [64].

Mass spectrometry imaging (MSI) permits simultaneous detection and visualization of lipids, proteins, peptides, glycans, metabolites, and therapeutics in various biological samples. ML algorithms are implemented to detect patterns and structures within the data. Specifically, supervised and unsupervised ML algorithms are widely used for data classification and clustering [65]. In the study by Braman et al., DL predicts the response of HER2-positive BC patients to HER2-targeted neoadjuvant chemotherapy using pretreatment MRI images [66]. Further, they applied a neural network to predict responses with a maximal accuracy of 0.93 based on the MRI datasets compared to the multivariate clinical model (0.67).

Supervised ML algorithms describe tumor margins and microenvironment in the clinic. An analysis using ML methods to identify the margins of clear cell renal cell carcinoma suggested that adapting such approaches can better define tumor margins, resulting in more thorough tumor extirpation and reducing local recurrence [67]. SVM-based classification and RF algorithms were utilized to accurately and reliably discriminate different cancer types, including thyroid cancer, BC, colon cancer, and liver cancer, by analyzing MALDI imaging data acquired from biopsy samples, thus assisting in determining the origin of the tumorigenesis irrespective of the metastatic sites [68,69].

Infrared digital imaging with DL detects BC based on a thermal comparison between a BC and healthy breast, which predicts precancerous tissues as well as surrounding area of breast tumor by enhancing thermal activity [70]. GWAS and NGS data that contribute to big genomic data could be translated to recognize clinically important changes that could be useful for designing precision medicine to BC patients. Applying deep learning algorithms to whole-slide pathology images can improve diagnostic accuracy and efficiency [71]. Bejnordi et al., assessed the performance of automated deep learning algorithms at detecting metastases in hematoxylin and eosin-stained tissue sections of lymph nodes of women with BC and compared it with pathologists' diagnoses in a diagnostic setting [72,73]. Zexian Zeng et al., developed a model using natural language processing and ML to identify local recurrences in BC patients. The authors claimed that the development provides an automated way to identify BC local recurrences with significant accuracy (AUC: 0.93 in cross-validation, 0.87 in held-out testing) compared to full MetaMap concepts, filtered MetaMap concepts, and bag of words [74].

Toprak developed an Extreme Learning Machine (ELM) method for detecting and characterizing malignant as well as benign tumors by employing image processing-based segmentation for early diagnosis of BC. This method used 9 features for classification based on image segmentation in the BC Wisconsin (Diagnostic) dataset with 98.99% accuracy [75]. Alakwaa et al., tested the accuracy of the feedforward networks, DL framework. They compared it with six widely used ML models, namely, random forest (RF), SVM, recursive partitioning and regression trees (RPART), linear discriminant analysis (LDA), prediction analysis for microarrays (PAM), and generalized boosted models (GBM). The authors found that the DL framework predicted metabolomics-based ER status in BC patients with prediction accuracy (AUC=0.93) [76].

The characterization of tumor heterogeneity as well as conversion of radiomics data into mineable data helps for effective diagnosis and treatment monitoring [77]. Lavdas et al., developed the ML method to improve the diagnostic performance and reduce the radiology reading time of whole-body MRI scans in patients with different stages of cancer [78]. BC outcomes are usually prognosticated by using surface markers of tumor cells and serum-based tests. Yi-Ju Tseng reported that a combination of serum HER2 and clinicopathological features predicts BC metastasis using ML algorithms, namely, RF, SVM, logistic regression, and Bayesian classification algorithms. The model developed using a RF algorithm can predict BC metastasis based on (sHER2) at least 3 months in advancc [79].

The identification of genes, which are vital for diagnosing BC, using the DL approach can be used as biomarkers. This model was developed by extracting functional features from high-dimensional gene expression profiles using Stacked Denoising Autoencoder (SDAE); performance of the extracted representation was evaluated through supervised classification models to verify the usefulness of the new features in cancer detection, and a set of highly interactive genes were identified by analyzing the SDAE connectivity matrices [80]. Masih explored the miRNA expression dataset of BC patients from the TCGA database to develop a prediction model. In this study, a tree-based ML classification model was used to extract rules and identify a minimal set of biomarkers. Empirical negative control miRNAs were used to normalize the dataset, and the model was trained using hsa-miR-139 with hsa-miR-183 to classify breast tumors from normal samples and hsa-miR4728 with hsa-miR190b to further classify these tumors into three major subtypes of BC [81].

Takada et al., developed two mathematical tools using an ML method to predict the likelihood of disease-free survival (DFS) (DFS model) and brain metastasis within 5 years after surgery based on the data of 776 patients from a multicenter retrospective cohort study. These models predicted DFS and BM of HER2-positive patients treated with NAC plus trastuzumab with high accuracy [82]. Extracting information manually from electronic medical records is time-consuming and expensive. However, the ML model trained on 91,505 breast pathology reports and extracted pertinent tumor characteristics. The model accuracy was tested on 500 reports that did not overlap with the training set. The model achieved an accuracy of 90% for correctly parsing all carcinoma and atypia categories for a given patient [83]. Recently, Petrillo et al., reported that AI could enhance the histological outcome of BC patients in advanced mammography with an accuracy of 83.65% in the grading classification while slightly lower accuracy (81.65%) in the classification of BC based on hormone receptors [84].

Long non-coding RNAs (lncRNAs) are widely involved in the initiation and development of BC. Logic learning machine (LLM) is an innovative method of supervised analysis capable of constructing models based on simple and intelligible rules. The performance of LLM in classifying patients with cancer was tested using a set of eight publicly available gene expression databases for cancer diagnosis and compared in cross-validation with standard supervised methods such as decision tree, ANN, SVM, and kNN classifier. The method showed significant accuracy (AUC = 0.99, 95% CI: 0.98–1.0) [85] (Table 2).

Table 2 Applications of machine leaning approaches in diagnosis of BC.

AI approaches used	Application in BC	Reference
Machine Leaning and Trees Random Forest model (TRF)	Predicts survival of BC with high accuracy.	[48]
Multistep DL-based model	Quantification of in situ expression of proteins involved associated with immune regulation in TNBC patients	[49]
Machine Learning Neural Networks	Predict toxicology	[50]
Machine Leaning model and Gail model	Integrate information from diverse sources that can aid decision-making processes for highly skilled workers.	[51]

Continued

Table 2 Applications of machine leaning approaches in diagnosis of BC—cont'd

AI approaches used	Application in BC	Reference
Machine Learning	Explores learning approaches and uses examples from medicine to introduce basic concepts. It also identifies the obstacles that are changing the practice of medicine through statistical learning approaches.	[52]
Machine Learning	Helps physician-scientists to support pathology and laboratory medicine.	[53]
Machine Learning	Expands field of medicine with considerable resources to solve medical problems by fusing computer science with statistics.	[54]
Machine Learning	Analyzes light microscopy images with typical tasks of segmentation using the supervised learning method and active learning for tracking individual cells using and modeling reconstructed lineage trees.	[55]
Machine Learning	Recommends the treatment trial to cure cancer based on genome, history, imaging, and pathology, which are coupled with information on available cancer treatments.	[56]
Machine Learning	Identifies similarities and differences in patient phenotypes and genomes, improves existing therapies, identifies new drug targets, optimizes prediction rules, avoids clinical errors due to human cognitive bias and fatigue, and delivers precision medicine.	[57]
Machine Learning-based predictive model	Useful in image analysis, clinical predictive modeling, and trainee education.	[58]
Machine Learning models	Classify images, image interpretation, and provides consistent analysis for a given input or series of input parameters.	[59]
Machine Learning models	Help radiologists prioritize work lists by identifying suspicious or positive cases for early review	[60]
Machine Learning models	Analyze histological data and classify tumors	[61,62]
Deep learning for ultrasound image	Diagnoses BC high accuracy comparable to human readers	[63]

Table 2 Applications of machine leaning approaches in diagnosis of BC—cont'd

AI approaches used	Application in BC	Reference
Deep learning	Helps in genome analysis, including regulatory genomics, variant calling, and pathogenicity scores	[64]
Supervised and unsupervised ML algorithms	Useful for data classification and clustering.	[65]
Deep learning and MRI images	Predict the response of HER2-positive BC patients to HER2-targeted neoadjuvant chemotherapy using pretreatment MRI images	[66]
ML methods	Define tumor margins of clear cell renal cell carcinoma	[67]
SVM-based classification and RF algorithms	Discriminate different cancer types by analyzing MALDI imaging.	[68,69]
Infrared digital imaging with DL	Predicts precancerous breast tissues as well as surrounding area of breast tumor by enhancing thermal activity.	[70]
Deep machine learning and artificial intelligence	Examine the integrative clinical and -omics datasets to inform, educate, and help cancer treatment and research.	[71]
Automated deep learning algorithms	Detect metastases in hematoxylin and eosin-stained tissue sections of lymph nodes of women with BC and compared it with pathologists' diagnoses in a diagnostic setting.	[72,73]
Natural language processing and ML models	Identify BC local recurrences with significant accuracy.	[74]
Extreme Learning Machine (ELM) method	Detects and characterizes malignant as well as benign tumors by employing image processing-based segmentation for early diagnosis of BC.	[75]
DL framework	Predicts metabolomics-based ER status in BC patients with prediction accuracy.	[76]
Deep learning	Quantifies and characterizes tumor heterogeneity as well as conversion of radiomics data into mineable data for effective diagnosis and treatment monitoring.	[77]
ML learning approaches	Improve the diagnostic performance and reduce the radiology reading time of whole-body MRI scans in patients with different stages of cancer.	[78]
Random forest, support vector machine, logistic regression, and Bayesian classification algorithms	Predict BC metastasis in combination with serum HER2 and clinicopathological features.	[79]

Continued

Table 2 Applications of machine leaning approaches in diagnosis of BC—cont'd

AI approaches used	Application in BC	Reference
DL approach with supervised classification models	Verifies the usefulness of the new features in cancer detection and identifies a set of highly interactive genes by analyzing the SDAE connectivity matrices.	[80]
Tree-based machine learning classification model	Classifies breast tumors from normal samples and hsa-miR4728 with hsa-miR190b to be further used to classify these tumors into three major subtypes of BC.	[81]
Mathematical tools along with ML method	Predict the likelihood of disease-free survival (DFS) and brain metastasis within 5 years after surgery.	[82]
ML model	Correctly parsing all carcinoma and atypia categories for a given patient.	[83]
AI methods	Enhance the histological outcome of BC patients in advanced mammography with an accuracy in the grading classification.	[84]
Decision tree, artificial neural network, SVM, and k-nearest neighbor classifier	Classifying patients with cancer was tested using a set of eight publicly available gene expression databases for cancer diagnosis.	[85]

3. Conclusion

The ML algorithms rapidly explore variables and experimental data to predict BC risk factors and diagnostic markers with optimistic performance and accuracy.

References

[1] R.Y. Choi, et al., Introduction to machine learning, neural networks, and deep learning, Transl. Vis. Sci. Technol. 9 (2) (2020) 14.

[2] K. El Bouchefry, R.S. de Souza, Chapter 12—learning in big data: introduction to machine learning, in: P. Škoda, F. Adam (Eds.), Knowledge Discovery in Big Data from Astronomy and Earth Observation, Elsevier, 2020, pp. 225–249.

[3] I.H. Sarker, Machine learning: algorithms, real-world applications and research directions, SN Comput. Sci. 2 (2021) 160.

[4] S. Uddin, et al., Comparing different supervised machine learning algorithms for disease prediction, BMC Med. Inform. Decis. Mak. 19 (1) (2019) 281.

[5] S. Ray, A quick review of machine learning algorithms, in: 2019 International Conference on Machine Learning, Big Data, Cloud and Parallel Computing (COMITCon), IEEE, 2019.

[6] N. Verbeeck, R.M. Caprioli, R. Van de Plas, Unsupervised machine learning for exploratory data analysis in imaging mass spectrometry, Mass Spectrom. Rev. 39 (3) (2020) 245–291.

[7] S. Chander, P. Vijaya, Unsupervised learning methods for data clustering, in: Artificial Intelligence in Data Mining, Elsevier, 2021, pp. 41–64.
[8] M. Botvinick, et al., Reinforcement learning, fast and slow, Trends Cogn. Sci. 23 (5) (2019) 408–422.
[9] R. Li, Defect Detection for Additive Manufacturing with Machine Learning and Markov Decision Process, 2022.
[10] Y. Li, et al., Deep reinforcement learning (DRL): another perspective for unsupervised wireless localization, IEEE Internet Things J. 7 (7) (2019) 6279–6287.
[11] T. Guillod, P. Papamanolis, J.W. Kolar, Artificial neural network (ANN) based fast and accurate inductor modeling and design, IEEE Open J. Power Electron. 1 (2020) 284–299.
[12] S.H. Han, et al., Artificial neural network: understanding the basic concepts without mathematics, Dement. Neurocogn. Disord. 17 (3) (2018) 83–89.
[13] G.D. Saxena, N.P. Tembhare, Analytical and Systematic Study of Artificial Neural Network, 2022.
[14] M. Stoffel, F. Bamer, B. Markert, Artificial neural networks and intelligent finite elements in non-linear structural mechanics, Thin-Walled Struct. 131 (2018) 102–106.
[15] M.M. Bukhari, et al., An improved artificial neural network model for effective diabetes prediction, Complexity 2021 (2021).
[16] B. Charbuty, A. Abdulazeez, Classification based on decision tree algorithm for machine learning, J. Appl. Sci. Technol. Trends 2 (01) (2021) 20–28.
[17] A. Arabameri, et al., Decision tree based ensemble machine learning approaches for landslide susceptibility mapping, Geocarto Int. (2021) 1–35.
[18] J.S. Raj, J.V. Ananthi, Recurrent neural networks and nonlinear prediction in support vector machines, J. Soft Comput. Paradigm 1 (01) (2019) 33–40.
[19] M. Zeng, et al., Accelerated design of catalytic water-cleaning nanomotors via machine learning, ACS Appl. Mater. Interfaces 11 (43) (2019) 40099–40106.
[20] K. Zhong, et al., Bayesian network structure learning approach based on searching local structure of strongly connected components, IEEE Access 10 (2022) 67630–67638.
[21] R. Gupta, Expression and order of assembly of protein complexes–applying dynamic Bayesian networks to RNA-Seq data, in: Beyond Gene Expression, 2021, p. 121.
[22] J. Shapiro, Genetic algorithms in machine learning, in: Machine Learning and Its Applications: Advanced Lectures, Springer, 2001, pp. 146–168.
[23] A. Vaid, et al., Federated learning of electronic health records to improve mortality prediction in hospitalized patients with COVID-19: machine learning approach, JMIR Med. Inform. 9 (1) (2021), e24207.
[24] S. Nalawade, et al., Federated learning for brain tumor segmentation using MRI and transformers, in: International MICCAI Brainlesion Workshop, Springer, 2022.
[25] K. Pal, B.V. Patel, Data classification with k-fold cross validation and holdout accuracy estimation methods with 5 different machine learning techniques, in: 2020 Fourth International Conference on Computing Methodologies and Communication (ICCMC), IEEE, 2020.
[26] A.S. Jadhav, A novel weighted TPR-TNR measure to assess performance of the classifiers, Expert Syst. Appl. 152 (2020), 113391.
[27] M. Merry, P.J. Riddle, J. Warren, Human versus machine: how do we know who is winning? ROC analysis for comparing human and machine performance under varying cost-prevalence assumptions, Methods Inf. Med. 61 (S 01) (2022) e45–e49.
[28] A.G. Singal, et al., Machine learning algorithms outperform conventional regression models in predicting development of hepatocellular carcinoma, Am. J. Gastroenterol. 108 (11) (2013) 1723.
[29] Machine learning in cancer diagnostics, EBioMedicine 45 (2019) 1–2.
[30] A.S. Adamson, H.G. Welch, Machine learning and the cancer-diagnosis problem—no gold standard, N. Engl. J. Med. 381 (24) (2019) 2285–2287.
[31] W.L. Bi, et al., Artificial intelligence in cancer imaging: clinical challenges and applications, CA Cancer J. Clin. 69 (2) (2019) 127–157.
[32] P. Punde, Computer aided diagnosis model of glaucoma with eye tracking data, Turk. J. Comput. Math. Edu. 12 (12) (2021) 3529–3533.
[33] A. Esteva, et al., A guide to deep learning in healthcare, Nat. Med. 25 (1) (2019) 24–29.

[34] L. Ubaldi, et al., Strategies to develop radiomics and machine learning models for lung cancer stage and histology prediction using small data samples, Phys. Med. 90 (2021) 13–22.
[35] J. Kim, et al., Artificial intelligence in breast ultrasonography, Ultrasonography 40 (2) (2021) 183–190.
[36] C.H. Lee, H.J. Yoon, Medical big data: promise and challenges, Kidney Res. Clin. Pract. 36 (1) (2017) 3–11.
[37] G.A. Papakostas, K.I. Diamantaras, F.A.N. Palmieri, Emerging trends in machine learning for signal processing, Comput. Intell. Neurosci. 2017 (2017) 6521367.
[38] S. Jović, et al., Prostate cancer probability prediction by machine learning technique, Cancer Invest. 35 (10) (2017) 647–651.
[39] A. Akselrod-Ballin, et al., Predicting breast cancer by applying deep learning to linked health records and mammograms, Radiology 292 (2) (2019) 331–342.
[40] G.G. Wu, et al., Artificial intelligence in breast ultrasound, World J. Radiol. 11 (2) (2019) 19–26.
[41] R. Turkki, et al., Breast cancer outcome prediction with tumour tissue images and machine learning, Breast Cancer Res. Treat. 177 (1) (2019) 41–52.
[42] G.F. Stark, et al., Predicting breast cancer risk using personal health data and machine learning models, PLoS One 14 (12) (2019), e0226765.
[43] A.N. Richter, T.M. Khoshgoftaar, A review of statistical and machine learning methods for modeling cancer risk using structured clinical data, Artif. Intell. Med. 90 (2018) 1–14.
[44] C. Ming, et al., Machine learning techniques for personalized breast cancer risk prediction: comparison with the BCRAT and BOADICEA models, Breast Cancer Res. 21 (1) (2019) 75.
[45] H. Behravan, et al., Machine learning identifies interacting genetic variants contributing to breast cancer risk: a case study in Finnish cases and controls, Sci. Rep. 8 (1) (2018) 13149.
[46] R.D. Nindrea, et al., Diagnostic accuracy of different machine learning algorithms for breast cancer risk calculation: a meta-analysis, Asian Pac. J. Cancer Prev. 19 (7) (2018) 1747.
[47] S.T. Kakileti, et al., Personalized risk prediction for breast cancer pre-screening using artificial intelligence and thermal radiomics, Artif. Intell. Med. 105 (2020), 101854.
[48] M. Montazeri, et al., Machine learning models in breast cancer survival prediction, Technol. Health Care 24 (1) (2016) 31–42.
[49] L. Keren, et al., A structured tumor-immune microenvironment in triple negative breast cancer revealed by multiplexed ion beam imaging, Cell 174 (6) (2018) 1373–1387.e19.
[50] I.I. Baskin, Machine learning methods in computational toxicology, Methods Mol. Biol. 1800 (2018) 119–139.
[51] Ascent of machine learning in medicine, Nat. Mater. 18 (5) (2019) 407.
[52] R.C. Deo, Machine learning in medicine, Circulation 132 (20) (2015) 1920–1930.
[53] F. Cabitza, G. Banfi, Machine learning in laboratory medicine: waiting for the flood? Clin. Chem. Lab. Med. 56 (4) (2018) 516–524.
[54] G.S. Handelman, et al., eDoctor: machine learning and the future of medicine, J. Intern. Med. 284 (6) (2018) 603–619.
[55] A. Kan, Machine learning applications in cell image analysis, Immunol. Cell Biol. 95 (6) (2017) 525–530.
[56] S.A. Bini, Artificial intelligence, machine learning, deep learning, and cognitive computing: what do these terms mean and how will they impact health care? J. Arthroplasty 33 (8) (2018) 2358–2361.
[57] I.A. Scott, Machine learning and evidence-based medicine, Ann. Intern. Med. 169 (1) (2018) 44–46.
[58] R.D. Meek, M.P. Lungren, J.W. Gichoya, Machine learning for the interventional radiologist, AJR Am. J. Roentgenol. 213 (4) (2019) 782–784.
[59] P. Brotchie, Machine learning in radiology, J. Med. Imaging Radiat. Oncol. 63 (1) (2019) 25–26.
[60] J.H. Thrall, et al., Artificial intelligence and machine learning in radiology: opportunities, challenges, pitfalls, and criteria for success, J. Am. Coll. Radiol. 15 (3 Pt B) (2018) 504–508.
[61] D. Komura, S. Ishikawa, Machine learning methods for histopathological image analysis, Comput. Struct. Biotechnol. J. 16 (2018) 34–42.
[62] A.S. Becker, et al., Classification of breast cancer in ultrasound imaging using a generic deep learning analysis software: a pilot study, Br. J. Radiol. 91 (1083) (2018) 20170576.

[63] L.M. Pehrson, C. Lauridsen, M.B. Nielsen, Machine learning and deep learning applied in ultrasound, Ultraschall. Med. 39 (4) (2018) 379–381.
[64] J. Zou, et al., A primer on deep learning in genomics, Nat. Genet. 51 (1) (2019) 12–18.
[65] L. Zhang, et al., Deep learning-based multi-omics data integration reveals two prognostic subtypes in high-risk neuroblastoma, Front. Genet. 9 (2018) 477.
[66] N. Braman, et al., Deep learning-based prediction of response to HER2-targeted neoadjuvant chemotherapy from pre-treatment dynamic breast MRI: a multi-institutional validation study, arXiv (2020). preprint arXiv:2001.08570.
[67] S.R. Oppenheimer, et al., Molecular analysis of tumor margins by MALDI mass spectrometry in renal carcinoma, J. Proteome Res. 9 (5) (2010) 2182–2190.
[68] M. Galli, et al., Machine learning approaches in MALDI-MSI: clinical applications, Expert Rev. Proteomics 13 (7) (2016) 685–696.
[69] S. Meding, et al., Tumor classification of six common cancer types based on proteomic profiling by MALDI imaging, J. Proteome Res. 11 (3) (2012) 1996–2003.
[70] S.J. Mambou, et al., Breast cancer detection using infrared thermal imaging and a deep learning model, Sensors (Basel) 18 (9) (2018).
[71] S.K. Low, H. Zembutsu, Y. Nakamura, Breast cancer: the translation of big genomic data to cancer precision medicine, Cancer Sci. 109 (3) (2018) 497–506.
[72] B. Ehteshami Bejnordi, et al., Diagnostic assessment of deep learning algorithms for detection of lymph node metastases in women with breast cancer, JAMA 318 (22) (2017) 2199–2210.
[73] B. Ehteshami Bejnordi, et al., Using deep convolutional neural networks to identify and classify tumor-associated stroma in diagnostic breast biopsies, Mod. Pathol. 31 (10) (2018) 1502–1512.
[74] Z. Zeng, et al., Using natural language processing and machine learning to identify breast cancer local recurrence, BMC Bioinf. 19 (Suppl 17) (2018) 498.
[75] A. Toprak, Extreme learning machine (elm)-based classification of benign and malignant cells in breast cancer, Med. Sci. Monit. 24 (2018) 6537.
[76] F.M. Alakwaa, K. Chaudhary, L.X. Garmire, Deep learning accurately predicts estrogen receptor status in breast cancer metabolomics data, J. Proteome Res. 17 (1) (2018) 337–347.
[77] S. Napel, et al., Quantitative imaging of cancer in the postgenomic era: radio(geno)mics, deep learning, and habitats, Cancer 124 (24) (2018) 4633–4649.
[78] I. Lavdas, et al., Histogram analysis of apparent diffusion coefficient from whole-body diffusion-weighted MRI to predict early response to chemotherapy in patients with metastatic colorectal cancer: preliminary results, Clin. Radiol. 73 (9) (2018) 832.e9–832.e16.
[79] Y.-J. Tseng, et al., Predicting breast cancer metastasis by using serum biomarkers and clinicopathological data with machine learning technologies, Int. J. Med. Inform. 128 (2019) 79–86.
[80] P. Danaee, R. Ghaeini, D.A. Hendrix, A deep learning approach for cancer detection and relevant gene identification, Pac. Symp. Biocomput. 22 (2017) 219–229.
[81] M. Sherafatian, Tree-based machine learning algorithms identified minimal set of miRNA biomarkers for breast cancer diagnosis and molecular subtyping, Gene 677 (2018) 111–118.
[82] M. Takada, et al., Prediction of postoperative disease-free survival and brain metastasis for HER2-positive breast cancer patients treated with neoadjuvant chemotherapy plus trastuzumab using a machine learning algorithm, Breast Cancer Res. Treat. 172 (3) (2018) 611–618.
[83] A. Yala, et al., Using machine learning to parse breast pathology reports, Breast Cancer Res. Treat. 161 (2) (2017) 203–211.
[84] A. Petrillo, et al., Prediction of breast cancer histological outcome by radiomics and artificial intelligence analysis in contrast-enhanced mammography, Cancers (Basel) 14 (9) (2022).
[85] D. Verda, et al., Analyzing gene expression data for pediatric and adult cancer diagnosis using logic learning machine and standard supervised methods, BMC Bioinf. 20 (Suppl 9) (2019) 390.

CHAPTER 7

Quantitative structure-activity relationship and its application to cancer therapy

Bhavini Singh, Rishabh Rege, and Ganji Purnachandra Nagaraju
Franklin College of Arts and Sciences, University of Georgia, Athens, GA, United States

Abstract

In the analysis of molecules and drugs today, computational techniques have become increasingly relied upon as the core of efficient advancement. Of these techniques, molecular modeling and, more specifically, quantitative structure-activity relationships (QSARs) have been extremely influential in assessing the qualities of molecules and their application to the real world. The QSAR modeling technique evaluates the properties, structure, and biological activity to provide further insight into the function and utility of chemical studies. Furthermore, QSAR has a variety of applications in the pharmaceutical world, allowing researchers to understand the mechanisms of biological structures and their receptors. It allows for the study of the interaction between drugs and their targets using public databases to further identify chemicals with specific properties. QSAR provides researchers and pharmacists with low-cost and efficient methods to discover innovative molecules and treatments for diseases like cancer. Though subject to some concerns, the rapid development of QSAR alongside the improvement in technology elicits a promising future.

Abbreviations

AD applicability domains
kNN K nearest neighbors
QSAR quantitative structure-activity relationship
QSPR quantitative structure-property relationship

1. Introduction

Quantitative structure-activity relationship (QSAR) is a quantitative study of the activity between small organic molecules and biological macromolecules. The study considers relationships between the measured properties of molecules (such as metabolism of small organic molecules, absorption, and distribution) and their experimentally determined biological activity [1]. Biological activity is a broad measurement considering numerical values such as bioavailability, inhibitory concentration, and the presence or absence of a condition like infection [2]. Furthermore, QSAR is also classified on the dimensions of

Computational Methods in Drug Discovery and Repurposing for Cancer Therapy
https://doi.org/10.1016/B978-0-443-15280-1.00012-1

the molecular descriptors, or the information about the molecular structure obtained via different dimensional planes. For example, the 0D plane represents the count, the 1D plane represents the fingerprints, the 2D plane represents the topological plane, and the 3D plane represents a geometrical plane [2]. These planes deviate even further and serve to improve the prediction accuracies of the modeling. However, the popular strategy of 3D-QSAR is more computationally complex and demanding than its predecessors [3].

QSAR is practiced widely in industry, academics, and government institutions around the world. After more than 50 years of improvement, breakthroughs, and community-driven development, QSAR is one of the most employed approaches to modeling the biological and physical properties of chemicals today. Furthermore, as chemical data and databases continue to grow, published literature has indicated that QSAR publications will grow concurrently [4]. However, the broad impact of the application of QSAR is not limited to human health but can also assess the effect of chemicals, materials, and nanomaterials on ecological systems as well [4]. Government agencies are expanding QSAR to the use of predictive models for regulatory purposes as a growing number of specialized regulatory tools and databases are being developed and endorsed.

2. Function

The QSAR approach can be described as the application of data analysis methods and statistics to develop models that can accurately predict the biological activities and properties of compounds based on their structure [5]. These mathematical and statistical methods are applied to discover empirical relationships of the form $P_i = k'(D_1, D_2, \ldots, D_n)$, where P_i represents biological activities and other properties of molecules, $D_1, D_2, \ldots, D_n$ are calculated structural properties, and k' is empirically established mathematical transformation applied to descriptors to calculate property values for all the molecules. QSAR modeling aims to establish a trend in the descriptor values to imply a simple similarity principle: compounds with similar structures are expected to have similar biological activities [5]. This is the foundation of experimental medicinal chemistry.

Many laboratories deviate in their QSAR application process. We can consider generally that the process of QSAR molecular modeling begins with careful curation of chemical structures and, if possible, their biological activities to create a dataset for subsequent calculations [5]. The data utilized for the design of the QSAR model has a large influence on its quality. Thus, when creating the model, researchers must understand clearly the relevant problem, any influencing factors, related literature, proper datasets, division of data, molecular descriptors, and statistical methods for model development [2]. The data must be preprocessed to remove any noise and redundant data. A fraction of the compounds (10%–20%) is selected at random and designated as an external evaluation set. The remaining subset of compounds is randomly divided into multiple training and test sets for model development and validation, respectively [5]. The training set is used to formulate the QSAR and develop its function, while the testing set is used to evaluate its accuracy and predictability [2].

Then, the QSAR algorithms are employed to establish the model and test it with the aforementioned parameters. In some laboratories, multiple QSAR techniques are used simultaneously based on the combinatorial exploration of the multitude of possible pairs of descriptor sets and a variety of supervised data analysis techniques (combi-QSAR) [5]. This allows researchers to select the models characterized by high accuracy in predicting both training and test sets of data. The model acceptability thresholds are frequently characterized by the lowest acceptable value of the leave-one-out cross-validated R^2 (q^2) for the training set and by conventional R^2 for the test set [5]. Then, the validated models are tested using the external evaluation set. The crucial step within external validation is the use of applicability domains (AD), which estimate the prediction accuracy for each modeled compound individually [6]. Once external validation demonstrates the significant predictive power of the models, they are employed for virtual screening of available chemical databases to identify putative active compounds and to work with collaborators who could approve of such hits experimentally [5] (Fig. 1).

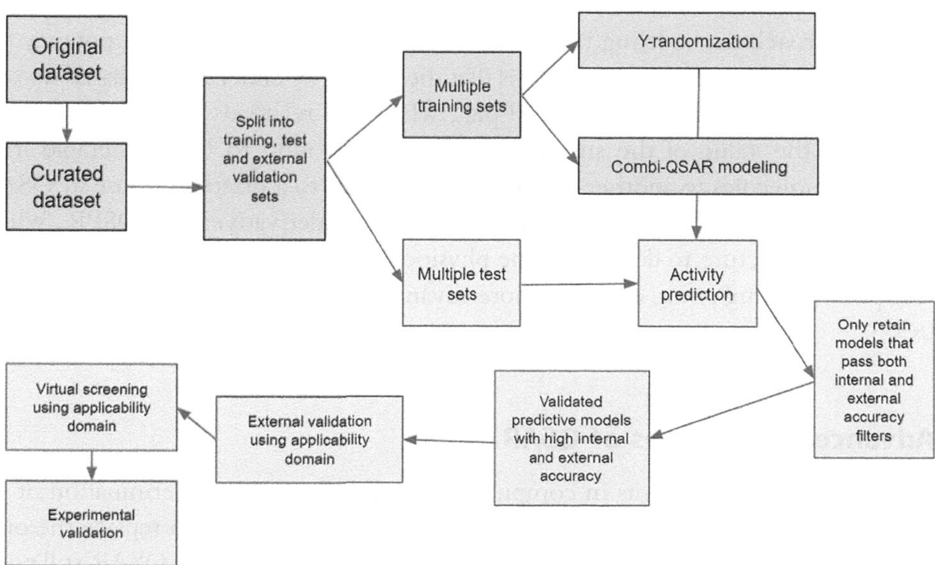

Fig. 1 Predictive QSAR workflow.

3. Origin of QSAR

Initially idealized to be a logical extension of physical organic chemistry, QSAR modeling has grown and expanded from its application to small series of congeneric compounds using simple regression methods to the analysis of extensive datasets comprising thousands of diverse molecular structures while using a large variety of statistical and machine learning techniques [4]. The conception of QSAR is thought to have begun in 1868 with researchers Brown and Fraser who created a formulation positing that the biological activity of molecules was based on their composition [5]. This concept accumulated in a 1962 publication by Hansch et al., of which many mark to be the founding of modern QSAR practice. In this paper, the researchers struggled to understand the basis of the structure-activity relationships (SARs) of plant growth regulators. Unable to find a clear relationship, Hansch investigated the effect of lipophilicity on biological potency and worked with Fujita to experimentally measure octanol-water partition coefficients (log P), a surrogate measure of lipophilicity [7]. They discovered that log P was an additive property and that the partial contribution of a substituent to the log P of one molecule was often the same as the contribution of that substituent to the log P of another molecule, terming this effect on hydrophobicity as "Π" [7].

As additional research built up on this concept, biochemists were prompted to endorse the central role of hydrophobicity in the determinance of protein structure, with earlier work emphasizing the role of partitioning to the biological target [4]. Hansch and Fujita further developed their equation between log P and biological potency to include Hammett's "σ," which accounts for the reactivity differences explanation of substituent effects [7]. The publications following this formulation successfully demonstrated a computational approach to modeling the quantitative effects of substituents on potency [8]. One factor in the attraction to this work is that the substituent effects were based on partition coefficients, model equilibria, and pK_a, which are relatively easy to understand. Furthermore, the value of the substituent effects was found to be transferable from one series of molecules to another [4]. This interest leads to a drastic increase in QSAR modeling growth, leading to the development of many derivatives like QSPR, which uses molecular structure to determine the physiochemical properties of a molecule like melting point, boiling point, etc., and more advanced techniques like 3D-QSAR in the 1980s [2].

4. Advanced techniques of QSAR

Since the 1990s, improvements in computing power and accurate determination of the 3D structure of biomacromolecules have led structure-based design to replace the once dominant position of QSAR in the field of drug design. While standard QSAR still posits many advantages like small amounts of calculation and good predictive ability,

3D-QSAR is able to further build on this trend. Based on the structural characteristics of ligands and targets, 3D-QSAR analyzes the 3D form of bioactive molecules, reflects the energy changes and patterns between bioactive molecule and receptor interactions, and reveals the drug-receiving mechanism of body interactions [1]. Then, the physiochemical parameters and 3D structural parameters of a drug series are fitted into the quantitative relationship, predicting and optimizing the structure of new compounds [1]. Thus, 3D-QSAR is a research method that combines QSAR with computational chemistry and molecular graphics. It allows for efficient studying of the interactions between drugs and target macromolecules, speculating the images of simulated targets, establishing the relationship of drug structure-activity, and finally designing drugs.

5. Application in drug design

Pharmaceutical science is increasingly reliant on the study of chemical compounds and drugs along with their activity and capabilities. Furthermore, it is interested in the structure of biological structures like ligands and receptors and the interaction between the aforementioned drugs with these structures [9]. Drug discovery often utilizes QSAR to identify chemical structures that display potential in their inhibitory effects on specific targets and have low toxicity (nonspecific activity) [1]. This study is called pharmacophore modeling and introduces an important application of QSAR within the realm of pharmaceutical science. In pharmaceutical research, it can often take 10–12 years for a molecule to be discovered and approved as a drug [2]. Furthermore, most fail the preclinical and clinical trials. The expenses needed to fund such endeavors can be extensive. Thus, pharmacophore has become an important player in research design and testing as its computational aspect allows researchers to save on time and funds [2]. Additionally, pharmacophore's use of a large database of compounds allows chemical laboratories and pharmaceutical companies to identify and purchase only the molecules with potential for further activity studies [2].

Pharmacophore modeling is initiated by using the activity values of ligands. These values are determined by the relationship between the IC50 values and the chemical components of the compound or by the alignment of the ligand-receptor interactions [10]. In QSAR drug development studies, thousands of molecular descriptors are scanned through web serves such as E-DRAGON, PaDEK, and Molecular Operating Environment (MOE) software to identify possible models, though sometimes machine learning methods are also utilized [9]. Models can then be obtained showing which functional groups are more suitable when deriving molecules. It is predominant in the literature for pharmacophore modeling studies to aim to determine the key structural features, especially with natural products, to surmount cancer MDR.

The advantages of QSAR in throughput, cost-saving, turn-around-time, and, possibly the most important, the ability to test compounds before their production make it frequently used in drug discovery optimization [10]. The combination of QSAR and pharmacophore modeling studies is also extremely effective in determining the derivatives of a lead compound whose activity has been determined before, along with the detection of brand-new drug precursor models [9].

6. Application in cancer therapy

A combined approach of QSAR modeling and virtual screening was applied to the discovery of novel tylophorine derivatives as anticancer agents [11]. QSAR models were first developed for 52 chemically diverse phenanthrene-based tylophorine derivatives (PBTs) with known EC50 using chemical topological descriptors and variable selection k nearest neighbor (kNN) method. Several validation protocols were applied to achieve robust QSAR models. To do this, the original dataset was divided into multiple training and test sets, and the models were only considered acceptable if the leave-one-out cross-validated R^2 (q^2) values were greater than 0.5 for the training sets and the correlation coefficient R^2 values were greater than 0.6 for the test sets. The q^2 values were found to be significantly greater than those obtained from the dataset with randomized target properties, indicating that the models were statistically significant. The 10 best models were then sent to mine a commercially available ChemDiv Database, resulting in 34 hits with moderate to high predicted activities [12]. Ten structurally diverse hits were then experimentally tested and eight were confirmed to be active with the highest experimental EC50 of 1.8 uM, implying an extremely high hit rate of 80%.

Another example of application in cancer treatment is the research of histone deacetylases (HDAC) which play a critical role in transcription regulation. Small HDAC molecular inhibitors have recently become an emerging target for the treatment of cancer and other cell proliferation diseases [11]. To design QSAR models, researchers employed variable selection kNN and support vector machines (SVM) approach to generate QSAR models for 59 chemically diverse compounds with inhibition activity on class 1 HDAC. 2D descriptors (MOE22 and MolConnZ65) were combined with kNN and SVM to improve the predictive power of the models, followed by vigorous model validation approaches like the randomization of target activity (Y-randomization test) and external dataset assessments. Highly predictive QSAR models were generated with 0.81 R^2 (q^2) values for the training set and 0.80 R^2 values for the test set. The validated QSAR models were used to mine four chemical databases, namely, the National Cancer Institute (NCI) database, Maybridge database, ChemDiv database, and ZINC database (a total of over 3 million compounds). The mining resulted in 48 consensus hits, including two reported HDAC inhibitors not included in the original dataset. Four database hits with novel structural features were purchased and tested with the same biological assay used to assess the inhibition activity of the training set compounds. Three of the four compounds were confirmed active with the best inhibitory activity (IC50) of 1 uM [11].

7. Concerns

While QSAR modeling techniques have large utility in the discovery and analysis of chemical compounds, it suffers from some drawbacks. The first is that any error in the structure translates into an inability to calculate descriptors for erroneous chemical records or into erroneous descriptors [11]. Models developed with incomplete or inaccurate descriptors are either restricted only to a fraction of formally available data or completely inaccurate. A recent study showed that on average, there are two structural errors per medicinal chemistry publication with an error rate for compounds indexed in the WOMBAT database as high as 8% [13,14]. In a similar study, the researchers investigated several public and commercial databases to calculate their rate of error and found that they ranged from 0.1% to 3.4% depending on the database [15].

This addresses an increasingly important problem, for as data, data models, and scholarly publications in cheminformatics continue to grow, the dependence on the quality of data increases [11]. Furthermore, recent benchmarking studies by a large group of collaborators from six laboratories have demonstrated that the type of chemical descriptors has a much greater influence on the prediction performances of QSAR models than the nature of the model optimization techniques [16]. These factors raise the importance of the need to develop and systematically employ standard chemical record curation protocols that are to be helpful in the preprocessing of chemical datasets. Some important steps to be made to clean the chemical records in a database include the removal of small amounts of data that cannot be handled by conventional cheminformatics techniques, inorganic and organometallic compounds, salts, and mixtures, ring aromatization, etc., along with the deletion of duplicates [11].

The number of compounds used in the dataset for QSAR studies is another concern, as they cannot be too small nor have too many. The upper limit is often defined by the computer and time resources available based on laboratory methodologies. The kNN QSAR approach is frequently practiced to perform discriminant analysis when reliable parametric estimates are unknown or difficult to determine [11,17]. Many approaches can be implemented for large datasets such as selecting a diverse subset of compounds, clustering a dataset and building separate QSAR models, and possibly excluding some compounds from model development [11].

Training sets used in model development are also subject to size constraints. If they are too small, chance correlation and overfitting become major problems that negatively impact the predictability of a model. Though an exact minimum number of compounds is not known, in the case of continuous response variable activity, the number of compounds in the training set should be at least 20 and about 10 should be in each test and external evaluation set [11]. In the case of classification or category response variable, the training set should contain at least 10 compounds of each class, while the test and external evaluation sets should contain no less than five compounds per class. Finally, the best situation is when the number of compounds in the dataset is between these two extremes (150–300 compounds in total) where an equal number of compounds should be in each class or category [11].

Finally, one of the main deficiencies of many chemical datasets is their lack of appreciation of the main hypothesis of all QSAR studies: similar compounds have similar biological activities or properties. Often, "cliffs" exist in the descriptor space where the properties change so rapidly that the adding or deleting of one small chemical group can lead to a dramatic change in the compound's property [18]. In this case, there could not be just one outlier but a subset of compounds whose properties are different from those on the other "side" of the cliff. We can consider cliffs as areas where the QSAR hypothesis does not hold [15]. Intervention methods need to be determined in order to discover these cliffs and remove them accordingly.

8. Conclusion

As the expansion of chemical discovery and biological understanding continue to induce extensive amounts of research, the dependence on processes that enhance the procedures amplify similarly. QSAR and its deviations provide such an apparatus, making the means of chemical analysis and application in the real world ever so simple. Furthermore, its investigation into the biological activity of molecules and drugs along with their interactions within ecology makes the application of QSAR revolutionary for the modern world. Ultimately, QSAR's current and future facilitation of cancer therapy and disease-drug development make it essential in the improvement of public health.

References

[1] X. Lin, X. Li, X. Lin, A review on applications of computational methods in drug screening and design, Molecules 25 (2020) 1375.

[2] S.C. Peter, J.K. Dhanjal, V. Malik, N. Radhakrishnan, M. Jayakanthan, D. Sundar, Quantitative structure-activity relationship (QSAR): modeling approaches to biological applications, in: S. Ranganathan, M. Gribskov, K. Nakai, C. Schönbach (Eds.), Encyclopedia of Bioinformatics and Computational Biology, Academic Press, 2019, pp. 661–676, ISBN: 9780128114322.

[3] K.Z. Myint, X.-Q. Xie, Recent advances in fragment-based QSAR and multi-dimensional QSAR methods, Int. J. Mol. Sci. 11 (2010) 3846–3866.

[4] A. Cherkasov, E.N. Muratov, D. Fourches, A. Varnek, I.I. Baskin, M. Cronin, J. Dearden, P. Gramatica, Y.C. Martin, R. Todeschini, QSAR modeling: where have you been? Where are you going to? J. Med. Chem. 57 (2014) 4977–5010.

[5] S. Gad, Reference Module in Biomedical Sciences From Encyclopedia of Toxicology, Academic Press, 2014.

[6] I. Sushko, S. Novotarskyi, R. Körner, A.K. Pandey, A. Cherkasov, J. Li, P. Gramatica, K. Hansen, T. Schroeter, K.-R. Müller, Applicability domains for classification problems: benchmarking of distance to models for Ames mutagenicity set, J. Chem. Inf. Model. 50 (2010) 2094–2111.
[7] C. Hansch, P.P. Maloney, T. Fujita, R.M. Muir, Correlation of biological activity of phenoxyacetic acids with Hammett substituent constants and partition coefficients, Nature 194 (1962) 178–180.
[8] S. Hochreiter, G. Klambauer, M. Rarey, Machine learning in drug discovery, J. Chem. Inf. Model. 58 (9) (2018) 1723–1724, https://doi.org/10.1021/acs.jcim.8b00478. Epub 2018 Aug 15. PMID: 30109927.
[9] G. Yalcin-Ozkat, Molecular modeling strategies of cancer multidrug resistance, Drug Resist. Updat. 59 (2021), 100789.
[10] D. Schaller, D. Šribar, T. Noonan, L. Deng, T.N. Nguyen, S. Pach, D. Machalz, M. Bermudez, G. Wolber, Next generation 3D pharmacophore modeling, Wiley Interdiscip. Rev.: Comput. Mol. Sci. 10 (2020), e1468.
[11] A. Tropsha, Best practices for QSAR model development, validation, and exploitation, Mol. Inf. 29 (2010) 476–488.
[12] S. Zhang, L. Wei, K. Bastow, W. Zheng, A. Brossi, K.-H. Lee, A. Tropsha, Antitumor agents 252. Application of validated QSAR models to database mining: discovery of novel tylophorine derivatives as potential anticancer agents, J. Comput. Aided Mol. Des. 21 (2007) 97–112.
[13] M. Olah, M. Mracec, L. Ostopovici, R. Rad, A. Bora, N. Hadaruga, I. Olah, M. Banda, Z. Simon, M. Mracec, WOMBAT: world of molecular bioactivity, in: Chemoinformatics in Drug Discovery, vol. 1, Wiley-VCH, 2005.
[14] M. Olah, R. Rad, L. Ostopovici, A. Bora, N. Hadaruga, D. Hadaruga, R. Moldovan, A. Fulias, M. Mractc, T.I. Oprea, WOMBAT and WOMBAT-PK: bioactivity databases for lead and drug discovery, in: Chemical Biology: From Small Molecules to Systems Biology and Drug Design, vol. 1, WILEY-VCH Verlag GmbH & Co KGaA, Weinheim, 2007, pp. 760–786.
[15] D. Young, T. Martin, R. Venkatapathy, P. Harten, Are the chemical structures in your QSAR correct? QSAR Comb. Sci. 27 (2008) 1337–1345.
[16] H. Zhu, A. Tropsha, D. Fourches, A. Varnek, E. Papa, P. Gramatica, T. Oberg, P. Dao, A. Cherkasov, I.V. Tetko, Combinatorial QSAR modeling of chemical toxicants tested against Tetrahymena pyriformis, J. Chem. Inf. Model. 48 (2008) 766–784.
[17] L.E. Peterson, K-nearest neighbor, Scholarpedia 4 (2009) 1883.
[18] G.M. Maggiora, On outliers and activity cliffs—why QSAR often disappoints ACS Publications, J. Chem. Inf. Model. 46 (4) (2006) 1535, https://doi.org/10.1021/ci060117s. PMID: 16859285.

CHAPTER 8

Structure-based virtual screening for the identification of novel Greatwall kinase inhibitors

Anbumani Velmurugan Ilavarasi, Tulsi, Saswati Sarita Mohanty, Umamahesh Katike, Ishwar Patidar, Amouda Venkatesan, and Dinakara Rao Ampasala
Department of Bioinformatics, Pondicherry University, Puducherry, India

Abstract

Over the last few decades, research has substantially enhanced our understanding of cancer biology. Regulating the functioning of mitotic machinery helps to halt cancer progression because uncontrolled cell division is a unifying hallmark of cancer. The complex cell division process is balanced by various kinases and phosphatases. Greatwall kinase (GWL), also known as microtubule-associated serine/threonine kinase-like (MASTL), an AGC family protein kinase required for mitotic control, has received far less attention than Polo-like kinase 1 (PLK1) and Aurora kinases. GWL has emerged as a novel oncogenic candidate in the therapy of several cancer types associated with chromosomal instability (CIN) and poor patient survival where GWL is overexpressed. Hence, identifying novel molecular scaffolds to inhibit the GWL is essential. Therefore, in the current work, structure-based virtual screening was carried out to shortlist the compounds with good efficacy toward the active site of GWL, which led to the identification of 10 compounds with a good binding affinity toward GWL. Compared to Greatwall kinase inhibitor-1 (GKI-1), these 10 top-scoring compounds have a better docking score and a higher Prime MM-GBSA score with favorable interactions. The results revealed that the compounds Z1526916456, Z1657074241, Z951212238, Z1274223489, and Z241520898 showed good binding affinity and good interactions compared to other selected compounds. Thus, these compounds warrant further confirmation by in vitro and in vivo studies.

Abbreviations

2D	two-dimensional
3D	three-dimensional
ARPP19	cAMP-regulated phosphoprotein 19
CDKs	cyclin-dependent kinases
CIN	chromosomal instability
ENSA	α-endosulfine
FDA	Food and Drug Administration
GKI-1	Greatwall kinase inhibitor-1
GLIDE	grid-based ligand docking with energetics
GLOBOCAN	Global Cancer Observatory

Computational Methods in Drug Discovery and Repurposing for Cancer Therapy
https://doi.org/10.1016/B978-0-443-15280-1.00005-4

GWL	Greatwall kinase
HeLa	Henrietta Lacks
HTVS	high-throughput virtual screening
MASTL	microtubule-associated serine/threonine kinase-like
MEP	MASTL-ENSA-PP2A-B55 axis
MM-GBSA	molecular mechanics-generalized born and surface area solvation
NSCLC	nonsmall cell lung cancer
OPLS	optimized potential for liquid simulations
PDB	Protein Data Bank
PLK1	Polo-like kinase-1
PP2A-B55	protein phosphatase 2A holoenzyme containing a B55-family regulatory subunit
RMSD	root mean square deviation
SP	standard-precision
VSGB	variable-dielectric generalized born
WHO	World Health Organization
XP	extra-precision

1. Introduction

Cancer is a prominent cause of death worldwide and a substantial obstacle to increasing life expectancy [1]. Cancer is the leading or secondary cause of death before the age of 70 in 112 out of 183 countries, and it ranks third or fourth in another 23 countries, according to data from the World Health Organization (WHO) [2]. The significant declines in mortality rates from coronary heart disease and stroke in many countries have contributed to the emergence of cancer as the major cause of mortality [1]. In 2020, there are expected to be roughly 10 million cancer deaths and 19.3 million new cancer diagnoses, according to the GLOBOCAN 2020 forecasts. The most prevalent cancer diagnosed in women is breast cancer, which has overtaken lung cancer in terms of new occurrences, with an estimated 2.3 million cases. Lung, colorectal, prostate, and stomach cancers are next in the frequency of diagnosis. The scenario could become worse due to risk factors brought on by globalization and a booming economy [2]. Thus, the development of sustainable cancer treatment methods is critical. The prevalence of cancers that are resistant to current therapies is increasing, and this means that more research is required to find novel cancer therapies [3]. Furthermore, an improved understanding of the molecular pathways underlying oncogenesis is essential for cancer prevention, identification, and superior prognosis. If the crucial molecular mechanisms that lead to cancer cells developing resistance are understood, the development of cancer-specific treatments will proceed more quickly. Notably, malignant cancer is distinguished by abnormal cell proliferation, which, in the case of metastasis, disrupts the regular function of adjacent or distant organs and is a significant contributor to cancer-related fatalities [4]. Cell division is a coordinated series of events that involves the distribution of identical DNA and other cellular components equally between two daughter cells [5]. Cell cycle checkpoints are control mechanisms that guarantee the appropriate completion of cell cycle stages [6,7]. The rate of genomic mutation is accelerated by CIN, which is connected to oncogenic transformation. This is mostly accomplished by circumventing cell cycle checkpoints [8,9]. As a direct consequence, cell cycle watchdogs such as PLK1 [10], Aurora kinases [11,12], and cyclin-dependent kinases (CDKs) have therefore emerged as critical regulators of mitosis for cell cycle progression and chromosomal integrity [13–15]. Due to the overexpression of these cell cycle regulatory kinases in a variety of cancers [10,16], several small-molecule inhibitors that target these kinases are also currently being tested in clinical trials for the treatment of cancer [12].

MASTL, also known as GWL, was first identified in *Drosophila melanogaster* as an indispensable kinase necessary for proper chromosomal condensation, as well as cell cycle progression through mitosis and meiosis [17–19]. The role of MASTL in the regulation of mitosis has gained prominence in recent years [20]. GWL is a crucial kinase for mitosis progression and maintenance because it inhibits PP2A-B55, a key protein phosphatase that counteracts the influence of cyclin B-Cdk1 [21,22]. GWL inhibits the activity of the PP2A-B55 by phosphorylating α-endosulfine (ENSA) and cAMP-regulated phosphoprotein 19 (ARPP19) [23–25]. While the inhibitory function of GWL is required to prevent mitotic collapse, in order to cause mitotic exit, GWL must be inhibited, and PP2A must be reactivated [26]. Thus, GWL knockdown in HeLa cells caused serious mitotic abnormalities, such as chromosomal misalignment, missegregation, and serious cytokinesis problems [27]. These findings collectively offer compelling evidence for the role of GWL in regulating PP2A-B55 activity to govern the progression of mitosis through the phosphorylation of a number of key substrates linked to anaphase entrance, cytokinesis, and nuclear pore reformation [28,29].

Numerous studies have shown that GWL is overexpressed in a variety of human cancers [30]. Increased GWL overexpression has been associated with adverse prognosis in head and neck [31], oral [32], breast [33], gastric [34], and colon cancers [35], implying that GWL is an important player in the development of oncogenesis. Multiple mitotic defects and CIN, a cancer hallmark [30], result from disruption of the MASTL-ENSA-PP2A-B55 (MEP) axis [20,27,28]. Recent research has found that GWL increases Wnt signaling [30] and the oncogenic AKT kinase activity in cancer cells [32], promoting oncogenesis and therapeutic resistance [35]. Furthermore, overexpression of GWL has been linked to recurrence after initial therapy, lowering patient survival in a variety of cancers [31,35,36]. Similar research on breast cancer patients has revealed that GWL expression is highly correlated with increased CIN, poor survival, and a significant risk of metastatic relapse [33]. In patients with gastric cancer, GWL overexpression was associated with tumor recurrence, poor survival, and metastasis, indicating that it could be a therapeutic target as well as a useful prognostic marker [34]. According to Cao et al., the development of liver cancer linked to chronic hepatitis is significantly influenced by GWL [37]. GWL has also been identified as a key target for thyroid carcinoma cells by Cetti et al. [38]. In patients with recurrent head and neck squamous cell carcinoma,

Wang et al. found that GWL overexpression is related to cancer progression and tumor recurrence following initial cancer therapy [31]. GWL has also been shown to be a therapeutic candidate for radiosensitization of nonsmall cell lung cancer (NSCLC) by Nagel et al. [39]. GWL knockdown in recurrent tumor cells increased their susceptibility to chemotherapy-induced cell death and restored their responsiveness to cancer therapy [33,35,36]. Additionally, it has been proven that suppressing GWL is advantageous for DNA damage-based therapies [40].

Targeting mitotic kinase as a therapeutic method for selective anticancer treatment has been found appealing, as mentioned earlier. Given its importance in cancer progression and drug resistance, there has been a surge in interest in using GWL as a therapeutic target for cancer treatment in recent years. Recent research has also shown that DNA-damaging agents can be used to target GWL in therapy [31,33,38]. These findings show that inhibiting GWL with small-molecule inhibitors has a huge amount of potential for cancer therapy. These findings suggest that GWL kinase is a promising target candidate in cancer because it regulates the activation of critical oncogenic signaling pathways linked to chemoresistance [35], metastasis [30,33], and poor patient outcomes [34,36]. Chemotherapy has long dominated cancer treatment, but kinase inhibitors have lately been shown to be effective as well. Over 25 kinase inhibitors have been approved by the FDA for cancer treatment, with many more in clinical trials [41]. GWL, on the other hand, has received less attention than other kinases such as PLK1 and Aurora. To date, only one inhibitor, Greatwall kinase inhibitor-1 (GKI-1), has been identified as a first-line GWL inhibitor [42]. To that goal, a few researchers have looked into the virtual screening of diverse drug databases, including natural and synthetic component sources [43]. Despite numerous attempts by researchers, none of the inhibitors proved to be effective with significant in vivo efficacy. Thus, new molecular scaffolds that can efficiently bind to GWL and block its oncogenic activity are needed. Small-molecule drugs that can specifically block this GWL will be extremely useful in cancer treatment. Hence, in this study, a structure-based drug design approach was opted to discover novel compounds for GWL on the basis of its three-dimensional biological structure. The obtained compounds with good binding energies were assigned to Prime MM-GBSA calculations to study the reliability of MASTL inhibition.

2. Computational methods

2.1 Software and hardware used in this investigation

Schrödinger's Maestro version 11.4 was used to perform all computational studies, including high-throughput virtual screening, molecular docking, and Prime MM-GBSA calculations on a Hewlett-Packard computer with a 2GB Nvidia Geforce GT 610 graphics card, 16GB RAM, and an Intel Core i5-4440 processor running Ubuntu 18.04.1 LTS.

2.2 Protein preparation and receptor grid generation

The human GWL kinase domain crystal structure with a resolution of 3.10 Å (PDB: 5LOH) was used for structure-based screening investigations (www.rcsb.org/pdb) [42]. Water molecules, counter-ions, and any other hetero groups not connected to inhibitor binding were eliminated from the PDB file. The protein preparation wizard in Schrödinger's Maestro (Schrodinger, LLC, NY, United States, 2019) was used to process the protein structure. Schrödinger's Prime (Schrödinger LLC, NY, United States, 2019) was used to predict the protein's missing residues and loops from the structure. Bond orders were corrected, steric conflicts were fixed, missing hydrogen atoms were added, disulfides were treated, protonation and ionization states were assigned, and missing residues and loops were filled. The protein structure's integrity was examined and corrected. Using the PROPKA software, the protonation states of GWL kinase residues were assigned to neutral pH 7. The hydrogen bonds were optimized using sample water orientation. The neutral and protonated rotameric states of His, Asp, and Glu residues were flipped and sampled to improve the hydrogen bonding network. The protein structure was finally minimized by bringing the heavy atoms to a root mean square deviation (RMSD) of 0.30 Å using the Optimized Potentials for Liquid Simulations (OPLS) 2005 force field [44]. The active site residues were identified through a literature search and SiteMap calculations based on the inhibitor-bound crystal structure complex of human GWL protein. The receptor grid was created by specifying amino acid residues with a van der Waals scaling factor of 1.00 and a partial charge cutoff of 0.25 using the Grid-Based Ligand Docking with Energetics (GLIDE) receptor grid generation panel. No constraints were added to the default settings.

2.3 Database retrieval and ligand preparation

The kinase library (Library code: KNS-65, Version: 16 March 2021) containing 65,200 diverse kinase inhibitors was obtained in SDF format from the Enamine database (https://enamine.net/). These ligands, as well as the reference inhibitor molecule, GKI-1, which was sketched from the 2D workspace sketcher, were prepared using the ligand preparation module of Schrödinger's Maestro suite (Schrödinger, LLC, NY, 2019). After checking and correcting the bond orders and angles, hydrogen atoms were added, and then the metal ions were desalted. All possible tautomers and ionization states at a pH of 7.0 ± 2.0 were generated using the Epik module (Schrödinger, LLC, NY, 2019) [45,46]. Chiralities were defined for each ligand to retain one low-energy ring conformation from their 3D structure. Furthermore, the OPLS2005 force field was used to minimize energy in these ligands.

2.4 High-throughput structure-based virtual screening

The obtained compounds were then docked in Schrödinger's Maestro suite utilizing the GLIDE standard Virtual Screening Workflow (Schrödinger, LLC, NY, 2019). Three phases were involved in docking operations: phase (i) high-throughput virtual screening (HTVS), phase (ii) standard-precision (SP), and phase (iii) extra-precision (XP). The receptor structure was kept rigid while ring conformations were created for the ligand groups to maintain flexibility during the docking process. Nonpolar amide bond conformations were penalized. A partial cutoff charge of 0.15 and a van der Waals scaling factor of 0.80 were used to construct the grid map. 20% of the molecules from HTVS, 20% of all SP excellent-scoring molecules, and 20% of only the highest-scoring molecules from XP docking were designed to be retained by the procedure [47–49]. This sequential filtration method allows for more rigorous sampling as well as the elimination of false positives. The ligand geometries were optimized using postdocking minimization with the OPLS2005 force field, with one pose per ligand retained. The GLIDE pose-viewer tool was used to examine the hydrogen bond and hydrophobic interactions of docked protein-ligand complexes over a 5 Å range. The top docked compound poses were classified based on their docking scores and binding orientations. Compounds with a higher docking score than the reference compound were chosen for further investigation.

2.5 Protein-ligand free energy binding calculations

The hit compounds were subjected to Prime Molecular Mechanics-Generalized Born Surface Area (MM-GBSA) analysis in the Schrödinger Maestro suite after the virtual screening. This method combined a Generalized Born and Surface Area Continuum implicit solvation solvent model with a fast-force field-based technique. A default parameter with an OPLS2005 force field, a Variable-Dielectric Generalized Born (VSGB) solvent model, and rotamer search algorithms is used to calculate the binding free energy of a GWL-ligand complex. The binding free energy (DGbind) was calculated using the differences in energies of the complex, ligand, and protein in the solution. All ligand atoms and GWL residues located within 5 Å of the ligand were configured to be flexible during the calculations. The protein-ligand complexes were then sorted based on their computed MM-GBSA DGbind values. The following equation is used in the Prime MM-GBSA calculation to determine the binding free energy between a receptor and a ligand.

$$\text{DGbind} = \text{minimisedEcomplex} - \text{minimisedEligand} - \text{minimisedEreceptor}$$

where Ecomplex, Eligand, and Ereceptor are the energies of the optimized complex, ligand, and receptor, respectively.

3. Results and discussion

3.1 High-throughput virtual screening and molecular docking studies of GWL kinase

Using the gene names “MASTL” AND “GWL,” a comprehensive search for the crystal structure of the human GWL kinase was conducted in PDB. The following search yielded a single entry displaying the X-ray diffracted kinase domain structure of human

GWL (PDB ID: 5LOH). The retrieved structure was processed in protein preparation wizard in Maestro's suite where the crystallographic irregularities were fixed and optimized and missing residues and loops were modeled and energy minimized for the virtual screening process. The active site residues of GWL kinase were obtained from the literature and sitemap calculations. ILE41, SER42, VAL49, ALA60, MET110, GLU111, TYR112, LEU113, GLY116, ASP117, ASP160, ASN161, LEU163, THR173, ASP174, and SER178 are active site amino residues used in receptor grid generation. Before the virtual screening, the precision and reliability of the docking methodology were tested by molecular docking of inhibitor GKI-1 into the GWL active site. In the virtual screening experiment, the GKI-1 was used as a control. GKI-1 was docked in GWL's active site. The GKI-1 glide docking score was found to be −7.243 kcal/mol. The glide docking score value was the same as the glide gscore. It had a glide emodel score of −40.730 kcal/mol, a glide energy of −29.930 kcal/mol, and a glide ligand efficiency of −0.381 kcal/mol. GKI-1 established two hydrogen bonds with GLU111 and LEU113. It made eight hydrophobic interactions with the amino acids ILE41, VAL49, ALA60, GLY111, TYR112, GLY116, ASP117, and LEU163. It also formed 10 van der Waal interactions with ILE41, SER42, LYS62, VAL94, MET110, TYR112, GLY116, ASP117, SER120, and THR173. GKI-1 also had Pi-alkyl interactions with VAL49, ALA60, LEU113, and LEU163. For the virtual screening of potential compounds, Enamine databases were investigated. Virtual screening was performed on a kinase library set containing around 65,200 diverse inhibitors to identify the possible inhibitors of GWL. These compounds were processed with the ligprep application in the Maestro suite, yielding approximately 186,928 compounds. Following the initial screening, 186,928 compounds were targeted for HTVS. Then, from the HTVS output, a total of 37,385 compounds were subjected to SP docking, where 7477 compounds were chosen from the SP output. Finally, the top 20% of compounds were chosen for XP docking based on the previous SP docking score, where 1495 compounds were chosen from the XP output.

These compounds were then ranked according to their glide docking scores followed by glide gscore, glide emodel, glide energy, and glide ligand efficiency values. These compounds' interactions were further examined manually using different visualization programmers. The screening resulted in the identification of around 10 compounds with docking scores better than GKI-1. These top 10 hits with high docking scores were retrieved and analyzed for their chemistry and interactions profiles. Z1567950091, Z147200608, Z340464784, Z1526916456, Z1657074241, Z951212238, Z1274223489, Z241520898, Z18357062, and Z639025220 were identified as 10 potential compounds with good energies and interactions based on the virtual screening results.

3.1.1 Z1567950091

Z1567950091 was the top-scoring compound in the virtual screening, with docking, glide gscore, emodel, energy, and ligand efficiency scores of −10.058, −10.469,

−80.379, −55.614, and −0.347 kcal/mol, respectively. GWL amino acid residues LYS62, GLU111, LEU113, ASN161, and ASP174 formed five hydrogen bonds, while ILE41, ALA60, MET110, TYR112, GLY116, LEU163, and THR173 formed hydrophobic interactions with Z1567950091. Furthermore, van der Waal interactions with amino residues such as VAL94, TYR112, ILE114, GLY116, ASP117, ASP156, ASP160, THR173, SER178, and ARG736 helped to stabilize Z1567950091's binding to GWL. Z1567950091's binding to the GWL active site residues was dominated by hydrophobic and van der Waal's interactions. Pi-alkyl interactions with residues ILE41, VAL49, LYS62, ALA60, LEU113, and LEU163 were also significant. In addition, Z1567950091 formed one Pi-sulfur interaction with the MET110 residue and Pi-cation interaction with LYS62.

3.1.2 Z147200608

Z147200608 was the second highest scoring compound, with docking, gscore emodel, energy, and ligand efficiency scores of −9.957, −9.973, −50.874, −30.554, and − 0.474 kcal/mol, respectively. This compound formed three hydrogen bonds with GLU111, LEU113, and ASP117 amino acid residues from GWL. Z1760158796 also formed hydrophobic interactions with ILE41, ALA60, VAL94, MET110, TYR112, ILE114, GLY116, and LEU163. And the residues that established van der Waal's interactions with Z147200608 were LYS62, ILE114, SER120, and THR173. The compound Z147200608, like Z1567950091, established one Pi-sulfur interaction with the MET110 residue. It was also observed to form Pi-alkyl interactions with ILE41, VAL49, ALA60, VAL94, LEU113, and LEU163 residues.

3.1.3 Z340464784

Z340464784 was the third highest-scoring compound on the list, with a docking score and glide gscore of −9.847 kcal/mol. It has glide emodel, energy, and ligand efficiency values of −69.531, −47.461, and −0.379 kcal/mol, respectively. This compound formed five hydrogen bonds with amino acid residues LYS62, LEU113, ASN161, and ASP174. Out of these four residues, LEU113 formed two hydrogen bonds. It made hydrophobic interactions with the amino acid residues ILE41, ALA60, GLU111, TYR112, GLY116, ASP117, ASP160, and LEU163. It formed van der Waal's interactions with the amino acid residues VAL49, VAL94, MET110, ILE114, ASP117, ASP160, and THR173. This compound formed one unique Pi-sigma bond interaction with GLY116 residue, which was not observed in any other selected compounds. It also made four Pi-alkyl interactions with GWL residues ILE41, ALA60, LEU113, and IEU163.

3.1.4 Z1526916456

Z1526916456 was the fourth highest scoring compound, with the same docking score and glide gscore of −9.348 kcal/mol. It has glide emodel, energy, and ligand efficiency values of −53.878, −36.904, and −0.390 kcal/mol, respectively. It has three hydrogen bonds, one with LYS39 and two in LEU113 residues and formed nine hydrophobic interactions with ILE41, LEU51, LEU58, ALA60, MET110, GLU111, ILE114, GLY116, and LEU163 amino acid residues. Z1526916456 also made van der Waal's interaction with VAL38, VAL49, LEU58, ILE114, GLY115, GLY116, and THR173 residues. It formed four Pi-alkyl interactions with the residues ILE41, LEU51, ALA60, and LEU163.

3.1.5 Z1657074241

The fifth compound Z1657074241 has the same docking score and glide gscore of −9.275 kcal/mol. It has glide emodel, energy, and ligand efficiency values of −65.855, −46.545, and −0.371 kcal/mol, respectively. It made one hydrogen bond with TYR112 and three hydrogen bonds with LEU113. It made hydrophobic interaction with ILE41, VAL49, ALA60, MET110, GLU111, GLY116, ASP160, ASN161, LEU163, THR173, and ASP174 amino acid residues. It also made van der Waal's interactions with LYS39, ARG43, VAL49, LEU51, LYS62, VAL94, MET110, ILE114, GLY116, ASP117, ASP160, ASN161, THR173, and ASP174 amino acid residues. Furthermore, it formed four Pi-alkyl interactions with ILE41, ALA60, and LEU163.

3.1.6 Z951212238

The compound Z951212238 is ranked sixth on the list, with a −9.264 kcal/mol docking score and a −9.345 kcal/mol glide gscore. It also had glide emodel, energy, and ligand efficiency values of −59.481, −43.885, and −0.386 kcal/mol, respectively. This compound formed two hydrogen bonds with LEU113 and one hydrogen bond with ILE114 amino acid residue. It also made five van der Waal's interaction with amino acid residues SER42, GLU111, GLY115, GLY116, and THR173. It formed seven hydrophobic interactions with amino acid residues ILE41, ALA60, MET110, TYR112, GLY116, LEU163, and THR173, as well as seven Pi-alkyl interactions with ILE41, VAL49, ALA60, and LEU163.

3.1.7 Z1274223489

With a docking score of −9.240 kcal/mol, the compound Z1274223489 is ranked seventh on the list. Glide gscore, glide emodel, glide energy, and glide ligand efficiency values for the compound are −9.651, −57.940, −41.207, and −0.385 kcal/mol, respectively. It formed five hydrogen bonds with the GWL amino acid residues GLU111, LEU113, ASP117, and SER120. van der Waal interactions were formed by Z1274223489 with LYS62, VAL94, TYR112, ILE114, and THR173 amino acid residues. It also made hydrophobic interactions with the amino acid residues ILE41, VAL49, ALA60, VAL94, MET110, TYR112, ILE114, GLY116, and LEU163. It also interacted with ILE41, ALA60, LEU113, and LEU163 via Pi-alkyl interactions.

3.1.8 Z241520898

Z241520898 is ranked eighth on the list, with a docking score of −9.222 kcal/mol. The compound has glide gscore, glide emodel, glide energy, and glide ligand efficiency values of −9.250, −48.418, −41.060, and −0.401 kcal/mol, respectively. It created two hydrogen bonds with LEU 113 and one with ILE114. van der Waal's interactions were formed by Z241520898 with LYS62, GLU111, GLY115, GLY116, and THR173 amino acid residues. It also had hydrophobic interactions with the amino acid residues ILE41, ALA60, MET110, TYR112, GLY115, GLY116, LEU163, and THR173. Pi-alkyl interactions were also observed with ILE41, VAL49, ALA60, and LEU163.

3.1.9 Z18357062

Z18357062 has a docking score of −8.485 kcal/mol, a glide gscore of −9.705, and an emodel score of −79.185 kcal/mol, a glide energy of −54.471 kcal/mol, and a glide ligand efficiency of −0.293 kcal/mol. Z18357062 formed one hydrogen bond with ILE41 and two with LEU113 and ASP117. Z18357062 formed van der Waal interactions by interacting with SER42, ARG43, LYS62, GLU111, ILE114, SER120, ASP160, and THR173. It also made hydrophobic interactions with the amino acid residues SER42, ALA60, MET110, GLU111, TYR112, ILE114, GLY116, SER120, and LEU163. Pi-alkyl interactions were aided by ILE41, VAL49, ALA60, and LEU163.

3.1.10 Z639025220

Compound Z639025220 had a docking score of −8.470 kcal/mol, with a glide gscore of −8.501 kcal/mol, a glide emodel −54.127 kcal/mol, a glide energy of −42.629 kcal/mol, and a glide ligand efficiency value of −0.339 kcal/mol. Similar to the eighth compound, it established two hydrogen bonds with LEU113 and one hydrogen bond with ILE114. The compound formed hydrophobic interactions with the amino acid residues ILE41, ALA60, MET110, GLU111, TYR112, GLY115, GLY116, and LEU163. It also formed van der Waal interactions with the amino acid residues LYS62, GLU111, GLY115, GLY116, SER120, THR173, and PHE850. Furthermore, Z639025220 formed Pi-alkyl interactions with ILE41, VAL49, ALA60, and LEU163.

The top 10 compounds had docking scores ranging from −8.470 to − 10.058 kcal/mol, which were greater than the GKI-1 docking value of −7.243 kcal/mol. These compounds also have glide emodel scores ranging from −48.418 to −80.379 kcal/mol. The greater the emodel score, the more reliable the predicted docking pose of the compound. All of the compounds were found to have good emodel values, indicating that the poses produced from virtual screening were reliable. The Glide docking score, Glide gscore, Glide emodel, Glide energy, and Glide ligand efficiency values for the shortlisted compounds and control GKI-1 are shown in Table 1. Fig. 1 depicts the best binding pose of the shortlisted compounds and the control GKI-1 in the active site of the human GWL kinase domain obtained from virtual screening using the PDB structure 5LOH. In the active site region of the GWL kinase domain, the compounds Z951212238,

Table 1 The Glide docking energetics and Prime MM-GBSA values for the shortlisted compounds and the control, GKI-1.

S. no.	Catalogue IDs	Glide docking score (kcal/mol)	Glide gscore (kcal/mol)	Glide emodel (kcal/mol)	Glide energy (kcal/mol)	Glide ligand efficiency (kcal/mol)	Prime MMGBSA dG Bind (kcal/mol)	Prime MMGBSA ligand efficiency (kcal/mol)
1	Z1567950091	−10.058	−10.469	−80.379	−55.614	−0.347	−47.19	−1.627
2	Z147200608	−9.957	−9.973	−50.874	−30.554	−0.474	−43.43	−2.068
3	Z340464784	−9.847	−9.847	−69.531	−47.461	−0.379	−48.41	−1.862
4	Z1526916456	−9.348	−9.348	−53.878	−36.904	−0.390	−54.82	−2.284
5	Z1657074241	−9.275	−9.275	−65.855	−46.545	−0.371	−50.43	−2.017
6	Z951212238	−9.264	−9.325	−59.481	−43.885	−0.386	−54.28	−2.262
7	Z1274223489	−9.240	−9.651	−57.940	−41.207	−0.385	−51.91	−2.163
8	Z241520898	−9.222	−9.250	−48.418	−41.060	−0.401	−55.26	−2.402
9	Z18357062	−8.485	−9.704	−79.185	−54.471	−0.293	−60.10	−2.072
10	Z639025220	−8.470	−8.501	−54.127	−42.629	−0.339	−62.70	−2.508
11	GKI-1	−7.243	−7.243	−40.730	−29.930	−0.381	−37.58	−1.978

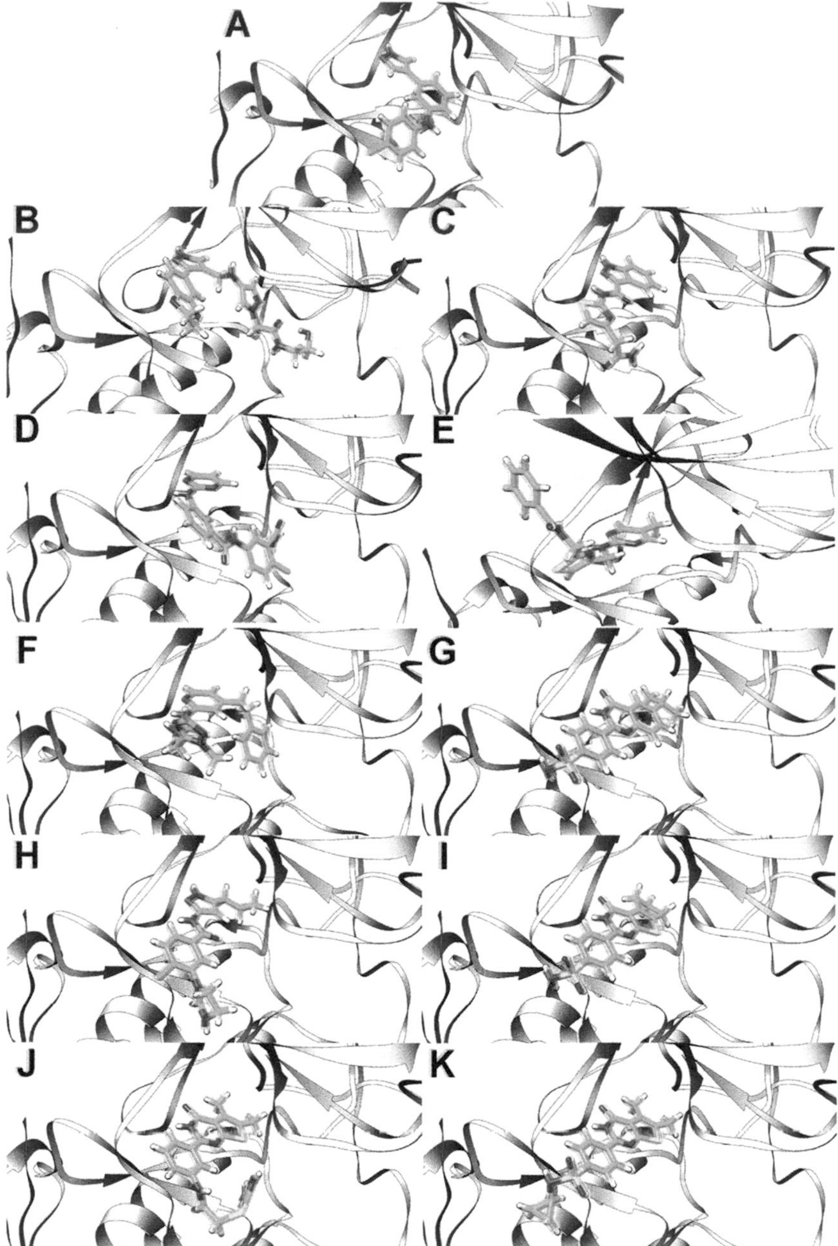

Fig. 1 The binding poses of the 10 top-scoring compounds and the control, GKI-1, in the active site region of GWL. (A) GKI-1, (B) Z1567950091, (C) Z147200608, (D) Z340464784, (E) Z1526916456, (F) Z1657074241, (G) Z951212238, (H) Z1274223489, (I) Z241520898, (J) Z18357062, and (K) Z639025220.

Z1274223489, Z241520898, Z18357062, and Z639025220 had similar binding orientations. When compared to other compounds, Z1526916456 had a unique binding orientation. The compounds Z1567950091, Z147200608, and Z1274223489 retained the GLU111 and LEU113 hydrogen bond interactions seen in the GKI-1 interaction with GWL. However, the remaining compounds only had one hydrogen bond interaction with the LEU113 residue.

3.2 Estimation of the binding free energy for the top-scoring compounds

The influence of solvent on the interaction between GWL and inhibitors was investigated by calculating the Prime MM-GBSA values of the 10 shortlisted compounds that demonstrated a good docking score and favorable interactions. In general, the lower the Prime MM-GBSA score for the compound, the higher the binding energy to the target protein. The Prime MM-GBSA scores of the Z1567950091, Z147200608, Z340464784, Z1526916456, Z1657074241, Z951212238, Z1274223489, Z241520898, Z18357062, and Z639025220 were −47.19, −43.43, −48.41, −54.82, −50.43, −54.28, −51.91, −55.26, −60.10, and −62.70 kcal/mol, respectively. The compounds Z639025220 and Z18357062 had the best lowest MM-GBSA scores of −62.70 and −60.10 kcal/mol, respectively. The compounds Z1526916456, Z1657074241, Z951212238, Z1274223489, and Z241520898 had well-balanced MM-GBSA scores ranging from −50.43 to −55.26 kcal/mol. It is important to note that the MM-GBSA score of the screened compounds was lower than that of GKI-1, which had an MM-GBSA value of −37.58 kcal/mol.

Similarly, the compound Z639025220 exhibited the best lowest MM-GBSA ligand efficiency value of −2.508 kcal/mol. The compounds Z147200608, Z1526916456, Z1657074241, Z951212238, Z1274223489, Z241520898, and Z18357062 had good MM-GBSA ligand efficiency values ranging from −2.017 to −2.402 kcal/mol. These compounds had greater ligand efficiency values than GKI-1, except Z1567950091 and Z340464784, which had ligand efficiency scores of −1.627 and − 1.862 kcal/mol, respectively, which were below the GKI-1 MM-GBSA ligand efficiency score of −1.978 kcal/mol. The MM-GBSA values for the top 10 scoring compounds and the control GKI-1 inhibitor are shown in Table 1.

4. Conclusion

This study employed a computational approach to virtually screen 65,200 diverse protein kinase inhibitors against GWL. The docking scores, Prime MM-GBSA scores, number of hydrogen bonds, and various nonbonded interactions of the resulting receptor-ligand complexes were used to evaluate the binding affinities of these shortlisted compounds for GWL inhibition. We identified 10 potential inhibitors with strong binding traits for the GWL protein. Among the 10 inhibitors, we found that Z1567950091 had the best docking score of −10.058 kcal/mol, while Z639025220 had the best Prime MM-GBSA score of −62.70 kcal/mol. It is worth noting that none of the screened compounds had a lower MM-GBSA score than GKI-1, which had an MM-GBSA value of −37.58 kcal/mol. When compared to GKI-1, all selected inhibitors had a superior interaction profile with GWL. In comparison with GKI-1, compounds Z1526916456, Z1657074241, Z951212238, Z1274223489, and Z241520898 had balanced values for docking score, glide score, emodel, and energy and glide ligand efficiency. These compounds also exhibited essential hydrogen bonding and nonbonded interactions similar to the GKI-1 inhibitor. The major hydrogen bond contributing residues involved in GWL inhibition were shown to be GLU111 and LEU113. Furthermore, these compounds exhibited a variety of nonbonded interactions, which will significantly contribute to the compound's ability to bind effectively with the GWL. Hence, these five compounds can be prioritized over other selected compounds for confirmation in future studies. Nonetheless, the contributions of Z1567950091, Z147200608, Z340464784, Z18357062, and Z639025220 are equally important and cannot be overlooked in the study. The findings of this study may warrant additional in vitro and in vivo research to develop novel and potentially effective GWL inhibitors for cancer treatment.

Acknowledgements

The authors would like to thank the ICMR (No. ISRM/12(134)/2020-IDNo.2020-5540), and the Government of India, for financial support. All the authors thank the Department of Bioinformatics, Pondicherry University, and the Bioinformatics Resources and Applications Facility (BRAF), Centre for Development of Advanced Computing (C-DAC), Pune—India, which provided necessary computational facilities for the research work.

Conflict of interest

No potential conflicts of interest were disclosed.

References

[1] F. Bray, M. Laversanne, E. Weiderpass, I. Soerjomataram, The ever-increasing importance of cancer as a leading cause of premature death worldwide, Cancer 127 (16) (2021) 3029–3030.

[2] H. Sung, J. Ferlay, R.L. Siegel, M. Laversanne, I. Soerjomataram, A. Jemal, et al., Global cancer statistics 2020: GLOBOCAN estimates of incidence and mortality worldwide for 36 cancers in 185 countries, CA Cancer J. Clin. 71 (3) (2021) 209–249.

[3] G. Housman, S. Byler, S. Heerboth, K. Lapinska, M. Longacre, N. Snyder, et al., Drug resistance in cancer: an overview, Cancer 6 (2014) 1769–1792. MDPI AG.

[4] I. Fatima, A.B. Singh, P. Dhawan, MASTL: a novel therapeutic target for cancer malignancy, Cancer Med. 9 (2020) 6322–6329. Blackwell Publishing Ltd.

[5] Y. Saka, C.V. Giuraniuc, H. Ohkura, Accurate chromosome segregation by probabilistic self-organisation, BMC Biol. 13 (1) (2015) 65.

[6] L.H. Hartwell, T.A. Weinert, Checkpoints: controls that ensure the order of cell cycle events, Science 246 (4930) (1989) 629–634.

[7] K.J. Barnum, M.J. O'Connell, Cell cycle regulation by checkpoints, Methods Mol. Biol. 1170 (2014) 29–40.

[8] A.B. D'Assoro, R. Busby, K. Suino, E. Delva, G.J. Almodovar-Mercado, H. Johnson, et al., Genotoxic stress leads to centrosome amplification in breast cancer cell lines that have an inactive G1/S cell cycle checkpoint, Oncogene 23 (23) (2004) 4068–4075.

[9] J.A. Knauf, B. Ouyang, E.S. Knudsen, K. Fukasawa, G. Babcock, J.A. Fagin, Oncogenic RAS induces accelerated transition through G2/M and promotes defects in the G2 DNA damage and mitotic spindle checkpoints, J. Biol. Chem. 281 (7) (2006) 3800–3809.

[10] S.-Y. Lee, C. Jang, K.-A. Lee, Polo-like kinases (Plks), a key regulator of cell cycle and new potential target for cancer therapy, Dev. Reprod. 18 (1) (2014) 65–71.

[11] H. Katayama, W.R. Brinkley, S. Sen, The Aurora kinases: role in cell transformation and tumorigenesis, Cancer Metastasis Rev. 22 (2003) 451–464.

[12] T. Otto, P. Sicinski, Cell cycle proteins as promising targets in cancer therapy, Nat. Rev. Cancer 17 (2017) 93–115. Nature Publishing Group.

[13] T. Chibazakura, S.G. McGrew, J.A. Cooper, H. Yoshikawa, J.M. Roberts, Regulation of cyclin-dependent kinase activity during mitotic exit and maintenance of genome stability by p21, p27, and p107, Proc. Natl. Acad. Sci. U. S. A. 101 (13) (2004) 4465–4470.

[14] M.C. Casimiro, M. Crosariol, E. Loro, Z. Li, R.G. Pestell, Cyclins and cell cycle control in cancer and disease, Genes Cancer 3 (11–12) (2012) 649–657.

[15] U. Asghar, A.K. Witkiewicz, N.C. Turner, E.S. Knudsen, The history and future of targeting cyclin-dependent kinases in cancer therapy, Nat. Rev. Drug Discov. 14 (2) (2015) 130–146.

[16] A.B. D'Assoro, T. Haddad, E. Galanis, Aurora—a kinase as a promising therapeutic target in cancer, Front. Oncol. 5 (January) (2016) 1–8.

[17] J. Yu, S.L. Fleming, B. Williams, E.V. Williams, Z.X. Li, P. Somma, et al., Greatwall kinase: a nuclear protein required for proper chromosome condensation and mitotic progression in Drosophila, J. Cell Biol. 164 (4) (2004) 487–492.

[18] V. Archambault, X. Zhao, H. White-Cooper, A.T.C. Carpenter, D.M. Glover, Mutations in Drosophila Greatwall/scant reveal its roles in mitosis and meiosis and interdependence with polo kinase, PLoS Genet. 3 (11) (2007) 2163–2179.

[19] D.M. Glover, The overlooked Greatwall: a new perspective on mitotic control, Open Biol. 2 (March) (2012), 120023.

[20] A. Castro, T. Lorca, Greatwall kinase at a glance, J. Cell Sci. 131 (20) (2018), jcs222364.

[21] J. Yu, Y. Zhao, Z.X. Li, S. Galas, M.L. Goldberg, Greatwall kinase participates in the Cdc2 autoregulatory loop in Xenopus egg extracts, Mol. Cell 22 (1) (2006) 83–91.

[22] E. Okumura, A. Morita, M. Wakai, S. Mochida, M. Hara, T. Kishimoto, Cyclin B-Cdk1 inhibits protein phosphatase PP2A-B55 via a Greatwall kinase-independent mechanism, J. Cell Biol. 204 (6) (2014) 881–889.

[23] S. Vigneron, E. Brioudes, A. Burgess, J.C. Labbé, T. Lorca, A. Castro, Greatwall maintains mitosis through regulation of PP2A, EMBO J. 28 (18) (2009) 2786–2793.

[24] B.C. Williams, J.J. Filter, K.A. Blake-Hodek, B.E. Wadzinski, N.J. Fuda, D. Shalloway, et al., Greatwall-phosphorylated Endosulfine is both an inhibitor and a substrate of PP2A-B55 heterotrimers, Elife (3) (2014) 1–34.

[25] M.J. Cundell, L.H. Hutter, R.N. Bastos, E. Poser, J. Holder, S. Mohammed, et al., A PP2A-B55 recognition signal controls substrate dephosphorylation kinetics during mitotic exit, J. Cell Biol. 214 (5) (2016) 539–554.

[26] M. Álvarez-Fernández, M. Sanz-Flores, B. Sanz-Castillo, M. Salazar-Roa, D. Partida, E. Zapatero-Solana, et al., Therapeutic relevance of the PP2A-B55 inhibitory kinase MASTL/Greatwall in breast cancer, Cell Death Differ. 25 (5) (2018) 828–840.

[27] A. Burgess, S. Vigneron, E. Brioudes, J.C. Labbé, T. Lorca, A. Castro, Loss of human Greatwall results in G2 arrest and multiple mitotic defects due to deregulation of the cyclin B-Cdc2/PP2A balance, Proc. Natl. Acad. Sci. U. S. A. 107 (28) (2010) 12564–12569.

[28] E. Voets, R.M.F. Wolthuis, MASTL is the human orthologue of Greatwall kinase that facilitates mitotic entry, anaphase and cytokinesis, Cell Cycle 9 (17) (2010) 3591–3601.

[29] M. Álvarez-Fernández, R. Sánchez-Martínez, B. Sanz-Castillo, P.P. Gan, M. Sanz-Flores, M. Trakala, et al., Greatwall is essential to prevent mitotic collapse after nuclear envelope breakdown in mammals, Proc. Natl. Acad. Sci. U. S. A. 110 (43) (2013) 17374–17379.

[30] K. Marzec, A. Burgess, The oncogenic functions of MASTL kinase, Front. Cell Dev. Biol. 6 (2018) 162. Frontiers Media S.A.

[31] L. Wang, V.Q. Luong, P.J. Giannini, A. Peng, Mastl kinase, a promising therapeutic target, promotes cancer recurrence, Oncotarget 5 (22) (2014) 11479–11489.

[32] J. Vera, L. Lartigue, S. Vigneron, G. Gadea, V. Gire, M. Del Rio, et al., Greatwall promotes cell transformation by hyperactivating AKT in human malignancies, Elife (4) (2015) 1–24.

[33] S. Rogers, R.A. McCloy, B.L. Parker, D. Gallego-Ortega, A.M.K. Law, V.T. Chin, et al., MASTL overexpression promotes chromosome instability and metastasis in breast cancer, Oncogene 37 (33) (2018) 4518–4533.

[34] X.J. Sun, Y.L. Li, L.G. Wang, L.Q. Liu, H. Ma, W.H. Hou, et al., Mastl overexpression is associated with epithelial to mesenchymal transition and predicts a poor clinical outcome in gastric cancer, Oncol. Lett. 14 (6) (2017) 7283–7287.

[35] S.B. Uppada, S. Gowrikumar, R. Ahmad, B. Kumar, B. Szeglin, X. Chen, et al., MASTL induces colon cancer progression and chemoresistance by promoting Wnt/β-catenin signaling, Mol. Cancer 17 (1) (2018) 1–5.

[36] Y.N. Yoon, M.H. Choe, K.Y. Jung, S.G. Hwang, J.S. Oh, J.S. Kim, MASTL inhibition promotes mitotic catastrophe through PP2A activation to inhibit cancer growth and radioresistance in breast cancer cells, BMC Cancer 18 (1) (2018) 1–13.

[37] L. Cao, W.J. Li, J.H. Yang, Y.U. Wang, Z.J. Hua, D. Liu, et al., Inflammatory cytokine-induced expression of MASTL is involved in hepatocarcinogenesis by regulating cell cycle progression, Oncol. Lett. 17 (3) (2019) 3163–3172.

[38] E. Cetti, T. Di Marco, G. Mauro, M. Mazzoni, D. Lecis, E. Minna, et al., Mitosis perturbation by MASTL depletion impairs the viability of thyroid tumor cells, Cancer Lett. 442 (2019) 362–372.

[39] R. Nagel, M. Stigter-Van Walsum, M. Buijze, J. Van Den Berg, I.H. Van Der Meulen, J. Hodzic, et al., Genome-wide siRNA screen identifies the radiosensitizing effect of downregulation of MASTL and FOXM1 in NSCLC, Mol. Cancer Ther. 14 (6) (2015) 1434–1444.

[40] P.Y. Wong, H.T. Ma, H.J. Lee, R.Y.C. Poon, MASTL(Greatwall) regulates DNA damage responses by coordinating mitotic entry after checkpoint recovery and APC/C activation, Sci. Rep. 6 (2016) 1–12.

[41] S. Gross, R. Rahal, N. Stransky, C. Lengauer, K.P. Hoeflich, Targeting cancer with kinase inhibitors, J. Clin. Investig. 125 (2015) 1780–1789. American Society for Clinical Investigation.

[42] C.A. Ocasio, M.B. Rajasekaran, S. Walker, D. Le Grand, J. Spencer, F.M.G. Pearl, et al., A first generation inhibitor of human Greatwall kinase, enabled by structural and functional characterisation of a minimal kinase domain construct, Oncotarget 7 (44) (2016) 71182–71197.

[43] U. Ammarah, A. Kumar, R. Pal, N.C. Bal, G. Misra, Identification of new inhibitors against human Great wall kinase using in silico approaches, Sci. Rep. 8 (1) (2018) 1–12.

[44] G. Madhavi Sastry, M. Adzhigirey, T. Day, R. Annabhimoju, W. Sherman, Protein and ligand preparation: parameters, protocols, and influence on virtual screening enrichments, J. Comput. Aided Mol. Des. 27 (3) (2013) 221–234.

[45] J.C. Shelley, A. Cholleti, L.L. Frye, J.R. Greenwood, M.R. Timlin, M. Uchimaya, Epik: a software program for pKa prediction and protonation state generation for drug-like molecules, J. Comput. Aided Mol. Des. 21 (12) (2007) 681–691.

[46] J.R. Greenwood, D. Calkins, A.P. Sullivan, J.C. Shelley, Towards the comprehensive, rapid, and accurate prediction of the favorable tautomeric states of drug-like molecules in aqueous solution, J. Comput. Aided Mol. Des. 24 (2010) 591–604.

[47] R.A. Friesner, J.L. Banks, R.B. Murphy, T.A. Halgren, J.J. Klicic, D.T. Mainz, et al., Glide: a new approach for rapid, accurate docking and scoring. 1. Method and assessment of docking accuracy, J. Med. Chem. 47 (7) (2004) 1739–1749.

[48] T.A. Halgren, R.B. Murphy, R.A. Friesner, H.S. Beard, L.L. Frye, W.T. Pollard, et al., Glide: a new approach for rapid, accurate docking and scoring. 2. Enrichment factors in database screening, J. Med. Chem. 47 (7) (2004) 1750–1759.

[49] R.A. Friesner, R.B. Murphy, M.P. Repasky, L.L. Frye, J.R. Greenwood, T.A. Halgren, et al., Extra precision glide: docking and scoring incorporating a model of hydrophobic enclosure for protein-ligand complexes, J. Med. Chem. 49 (21) (2006) 6177–6196.

CHAPTER 9

Strategies for drug repurposing

Aparna Vema and Arunasree M. Kalle
Department of Animal Biology, School of Life Sciences, University of Hyderabad, Hyderabad, TS, India

Abstract

Drug discovery process is both time-consuming and costly affair. Repurposing of "old drugs" for a new indication/disease can aid in combating the effects of high-attrition rates, substantial costs, and slow timelines of the drug discovery process. Integration of statistical methods, bioinformatic resources, chemoinformatic tools, and experimental methods resulted in various drug repurposing approaches. In this chapter, we summarize various computational and experimental approaches for drug repurposing with use-cases. We also discuss the limitations of these methods to help in addressing these limitations and realize the full potential of these approaches.

Abbreviations

AI	artificial intelligence
BiGG	Biochemical Genetic and Genomic
CMap	Connectivity Map
CML	chronic myelogenous leukemia
COMT	catechol-*O*-methyl transferase
COX-2	cyclooxygenase-2
DART	Drug Adverse Reaction Target Database
DGIdb	Drug Gene Interaction Database
EHRs	electronic health record
GDSC	Genomics of Drug Sensitivity in Cancer
GEO	Gene Expression Omnibus
GIST	gastrointestinal stromal tumor
GPCRs	G-protein coupled receptors
GWAS	genome-wide association studies
HIV-1	human immuno deficiency virus-1
HMDB	Human Metabolome Database
IBD	inflammatory bowel disease
KEGG	Kyoto Encyclopaedia of Genes and Genomes
KLIFS	Kinase-Ligand Interaction Fingerprints and Structure
LINCS	Library of Integrated Network-Based Cellular Signatures
NCBI	National Centre For Biotechnology Information
NLP	natural language processing
NSCLC	nonsmall cell lung cancer
OMIM	Online Mendelian Inheritance in Man
PDB	Protein Data Bank
PharmGKB	Pharmacogenomics Knowledge Database

Computational Methods in Drug Discovery and Repurposing for Cancer Therapy
https://doi.org/10.1016/B978-0-443-15280-1.00017-0

PINA	Protein Interaction Network Analysis
ProBis	Protein Structure Binding Sites
RA	rheumatoid arthritis
RIOK1	RIO protein kinase-1
RNA	ribo-nucleic acid
ROCK	Rho-associated protein kinase
SDE	signature of differential gene expression
SFINX database	Swedish, Finnish, INteraction X-referencing database
SMPDB	Small Molecule Pathway Database
SRP	Signature Reversion Principle
TMFS	Train Match Fit Streamline
TNFSF11	tumor necrosis factor super family member 11
TTD	Therapeutic Target Database
VEGFR2	vascular endothelial growth factor receptor 2

1. Introduction

Drug repurposing (or repositioning, reprofiling, retasking) is best defined as a strategy for identifying new uses for approved drugs, outside the scope of the original indication [1]. Approved drugs have already undergone all phases of clinical trials to reach the market and thus have a known and accepted safety profile. Identification of a new clinical indication for an already-approved drug allows the drug to re-enter the clinical trials process directly at Phase-II level, reducing the cost substantially and facilitating rapid clinical translation.

Drug repositioning has two alternative and complementary approaches, namely, computational approach and experimental approach.

2. Computational drug repurposing

Computational drug repurposing strategies integrate data from disparate sources and reveal connections that are otherwise hidden. They involve systematic analysis of genomic, transcriptomic, proteomic, metabolomic, and clinical data, including electronic health records (EHRs), and identify drugs that can be repurposed for other diseases not intended for use.

Any computational drug repurposing study follows a typical workflow (Fig. 1) of data mining and extraction from a wide variety of data sources. Table 1 includes the resources of data at molecular structure, proteome, transcriptome, and genome levels that can be used for the application of various drug repurposing strategies [20]. Once the data is obtained, computational methods like machine learning, text mining, natural language processing, deep learning, and network analysis are used to obtain models. These models are further validated using various evaluation metrics. A model with reasonable metrics can be used for predicting novel indications.

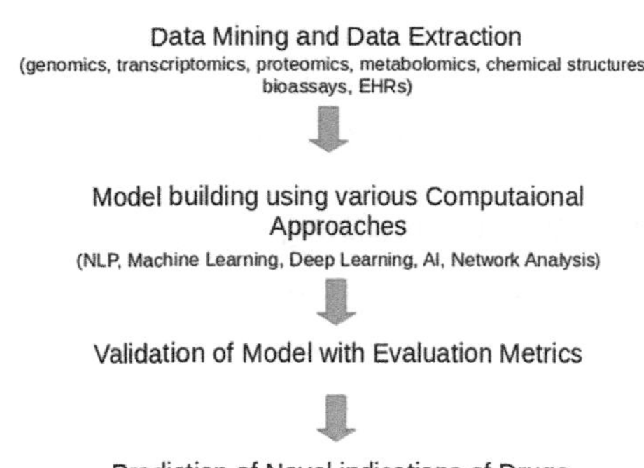

Fig. 1 Workflow of computational drug repurposing.

Table 1 Data resources used for computational drug repurposing.

Information level	Database
Small molecules	PubChem, ChEMBL, DrugBank
	Drug Adverse Reaction Target Database (DART) [2]
	Drug Drug interaction Database (SNIFX) [3]
	Small Molecule Pathway Database (SMPDB) [4]
Protein	Protein Data Bank (PDB)
	Therapeutic Target Database (TTD) [5]
	Protein Binding Sites (ProBis)
	Kinase-Ligand Interaction Fingerprints and Structure (KLIFS)
	Protein Interaction Network Analysis (PINA) [6]
Transcriptome	Connectivity Map (CMap)
	Library of Integrated Network-based Cellular Signatures (LINCS) [7]
Gene	Genome Wide Association Studies (GWAS) [8]
	Kyoto Encyclopaedia of Genes and Genomes (KEGG) [9]
	Drug Gene Interaction Database (DGIdb) [10]
	Online Mendelian Inheritance in Man (OMIM)
	Database of Gene Disease Association (DisGeNET)
	Human Disease Network Database (DnetDB) [11]
	Human Gene Networks (HumanNet) [12]
	Genomics of Drug Sensitivity in Cancer (GDSC) [13]
	Gene Expression Omnibus (GEO) [14]
	Pharmacogenomics Knowledge Database (PharmGKB) [15]
Metabolism	Human Metabolome Database (HMDB) [16]
	Biochemical Genetic and Genomic (BiGG) [17]
Clinical	RepoDB [18]
	Clinical Trials
	Side Effect Resource (SIDER) [19]

Computational approaches for drug repurposing are broadly classified as (i) profile-based or signature mapping, (ii) GWAS-based, (iii) network-based, and (iv) data-based approaches [21,22]. Drug repurposed using different strategies are listed in Table 2.

2.1 Profile-based or signature mapping

The basic principle of profile-based drug repurposing or signature mapping is the comparison of bioactive profiles, or unique characteristics ("signatures") of a drug in tandem with any other drug or disease profile. The signature of a drug can be derived from three types of data: (i) transcriptomic (RNA), proteomic, or metabolomic data; (ii) chemical structures, and (iii) adverse-effects profile.

2.1.1 Transcriptome mapping

Transcriptomic signatures of a drug can be used to make drug-disease similarity and drug-drug similarity. Initially, a transcriptomic signature of a particular disease is obtained by differential gene expression analysis between healthy and diseased conditions.

(a) Drug-disease similarity: If certain genes are upregulated in a disease condition, identifying a drug that has a profile where these genes are downregulated (upon treatment with drug) can be promising. This approach named as "Signature Reversion Principle" is successfully utilized to repurpose drugs [23]. For example, Connectivity Map (CMap) [24], which is a massive collection of transcriptomes of cell lines treated with more than 1300 drug-like substances, can be used in signature mapping to identify differences and similarities in diseases, thereby revealing the functional connections between drugs, genes, and diseases. Numerous studies have been carried out to integrate CMap with other functional genomic databases like National Centre for Biotechnology Information (NCBI) Gene Expression Omnibus (GEO) to discover the associations between genes, drugs, and diseases. Topiramate, an antiepileptic drug, is one such example where "SRP" is utilized to identify its efficacy against inflammatory bowel disease (IBD) [25].

(b) Drug-drug similarity: Comparing the expression profile of a cell, before and after exposure to a drug, can quantitatively assess the changes brought by that drug. The corresponding signature of differential gene expression (SDE) can be considered as the drug effect. If two drugs elicit similar SDEs, despite acting on different targets, they share a common mechanism of action. This principle is called a "Guilt-by-Association."

Based on this concept, Iorio et al. used CMap to identify large number of drug-drug associations based on the similarity between their SDEs [26]. A novel similarity score ("drug distance") was used to construct a network where each drug is treated as a node and each edge indicates the similarity between the SDEs of the connected nodes. The entire drug network was divided into "communities" of densely interconnected nodes, where each community contains drugs eliciting similar SDEs. They have identified that

Table 2 Examples of repurposed drugs obtained from different strategies.

Strategy	Drug	Existing indication	Identified target	New indication
Molecular Docking, Binding site comparison	Nelfinavir	Human immunodeficiency virus 1 (HIV-1)		Colorectal cancer, lung cancer
	Entacapone	Parkinson's disease	COMT	Multidrug resistance tuberculosis
	Celecoxib	Pain and inflammation	Carbonic anhydrase	Glaucoma, cancer
	Levosimendan	Acute heart failure	RIOK1	Colorectal and gastric cancer
Signature matching	Phenoxybenzamine	Antihypertensive		Analgesic, antinociceptive
	Fasudil			Amyotrophic lateral sclerosis
	Thioridazine	Antipsychotic		Ovarian cancer
	Albendazole	Anthelmintic		Gaucher disease
	Auranofin	Rheumatoid arthritis (RA)		Gastrointestinal stromal tumor (GIST)
	Crizotinib			Nonsmall-cell lung cancer (NSCLC)
	Imatinib	Chronic myeloid leukemia (CML)	KIT	Gastrointestinal stromal tumors (GIST)
Pathway mapping	Pranlukast	Asthma		Antiviral
	Amrinone	Congestive heart failure		Antiviral
Network mapping	Vismodegib	Hedgehog signaling pathway		Gorlin syndrome
	Iloperidone	Schizophrenia		Hypertension
	Donepezil	Alzheimer's disease		Parkinson's disease
	Methotrexate	Antirheumatic		Crohn's disease
	Gabapentin	Anticonvulsant		Anxiety disorder
	Risperidone	Antipsychotic		Obsessive compulsive disorder
	Cisplatin	Lymphoma		Breast cancer
Adverse effect mapping	Minoxidil	Hypertension		Hair loss
GWAS	Alosetron	Irritable bowel syndrome		Bladder cancer
	Denosumab	Osteoporosis	TNFSF11	Crohn's disease
Clinical data analysis	Sildenafil	Angina		Erectile dysfunction
	Aspirin	Analgesia		Colorectal cancer
	Raloxifene	Osteoporosis		Breast cancer
	Propranolol	Hypertension		Osteoporosis
	Terbutaline sulfate	Antiasthmatic		Amyotrophic lateral sclerosis

each community was strikingly populated by drugs with similar mode of action or share a common therapeutic application. Using this network, fasudil, a Rho-Kinase (ROCK) inhibitor, was identified to be in proximity to known autophagy enhancers such a 2-deoxy-D-glucose and tamoxifen. Thus, fasudil was repurposed for treating amyotrophic lateral sclerosis where autophagy plays a key role.

2.1.2 Chemical structure mapping

"Guilt-by-association" principle is also widely implemented with chemical structure similarities. Traditional drug discovery methods use molecular similarity to infer the drug-target binding. Ligand-based virtual screening methods have long been successfully implemented to identify molecules with similar pharmacophoric features, despite lacking prior knowledge of target receptor. On the other hand, if the structure of the target receptor is known, structure-based studies (like molecular docking) are carried out to identify drugs binding with similar interaction patterns. Dakshanamurthy et al., implemented computational proteochemometric method—train, match, fit, streamline (TMFS), to map drug target interaction space on 3671 FDA-approved drugs across 2335 protein crystal structures [27]. They identified that mebendazole, an antiparasitic drug, can be repurposed to inhibit vascular endothelial growth factor receptor 2 (VEGFR2) and confirmed it experimentally. Binding site comparisons of the receptor is another popular approach to predict similar pharmacological profiles of the drugs. For example, binding site similarity between cyclooxygenase-2 (Cox-2) and carbonic anhydrase makes celecoxib to repurpose it against glaucoma and cancer [28].

2.1.3 Mapping of adverse effects profile

Adverse effects of the drugs are mainly due to the binding of drugs to "off-targets" other than intended. Every drug has a unique adverse-effect profile. If any two drugs cause same adverse effects, then the probability of these drugs sharing same protein/pathway is high. Campillos et al. identified novel drug-target relationships for 746 drugs by applying adverse-effect similarity approach. Adverse drug effects can also be mapped to diseases [29]. Yang et al., extracted 3175 adverse effect-disease relationships by combining the adverse effect-drug relationships from drug labels and the drug-disease relationships from PharmGKB [30]. Using this data, a Naive-Bayes model has been developed using adverse effects as features to predict 145 disease indications.

2.2 Genome-wide association studies

Genome-wide association studies (GWAS) aim at the identification of genetic variants associated with common diseases, thereby providing valuable insights to the biology of diseases. GWAS-based studies follow phenotype-to-genotype concept, where millions of genetic variants across the genomes of many individuals are tested to identify genotype-phenotype associations. If a genome-wide significant variant is plausibly mapped to a gene modulated by a known drug, this signal can be leveraged to repurpose a drug that can target the gene. Sanseau et al. used GWAS to find genes that are associated with a disease trait [31]. These genes were evaluated against drug targets for novel indications and drug repurposing opportunities. For example, denosumab, an antibody targeting tumor necrosis factor ligand super family member 11 (TNFSF11), is used in the treatment of postmenopausal women having high risk of bone fracture with osteoporosis. TNFSF11 genetic variant (rs2062305) was identified to be associated with Crohn's disease using GWAS. Hence, the authors have indicated that denosumab can be repurposed to treat Crohn's disease. Grover et al., integrated drug information obtained from Drug Bank, Therapeutic Target database, and PharmGKB to match gene targets identified for coronary artery disease and identify potential drug repurposing opportunities.

2.3 Network or pathway mapping

Constructing drug or disease networks based on gene expression patterns, GWAS data, protein interactions is the key for network-based drug repurposing strategy. Many a times, targets found by GWAS, or other studies may not be druggable; in such cases, network or pathway-based analysis aids in exploiting either genes associated with connected networks or upstream/downstream genes respectively. Drugs targeting these genes can be repurposed [32].

Network-based methods build drug-disease networks based on various data like protein-protein interactions, gene expression, and GWAS. DrugNet is one such tool that utilizes network-based approach to integrate information of drugs, protein targets, and diseases to perform drug-drug and drug-disease prioritization [33].

Pathway analysis of gene expression datasets obtained from studies on respiratory viruses in human host infection models identified 67 recurrent biological pathways [34]. Mapping these pathways against Drug Bank database identifies several drugs that can be repurposed against viral targets. Pranlukast, a leukotriene receptor 1 agonist used in asthma, and amrinone, a phosphodiesterase inhibitor used in treating congestive heart failure, are identified as potential drugs for treating viral infections, are derived from pathway mapping studies.

2.4 Data based

Electronic health records (EHRs) cover huge data on clinical history of patients that includes disease history, symptom description, laboratory test results, image data, drug prescription etc. Application of text mining, natural language processing (NLP), and machine learning techniques on EHRs can be utilized in drug repurposing [35]. Example of one such repurposed drug is metformin. Application of machine learning methods on EHRs identified the association of metformin with decreased mortality rates after cancer diagnosis [36]. Postmarketing surveillance data and clinical data are other important sources that can be used for drug repurposing.

2.4.1 Challenges and limitations of computational drug discovery strategies

Computational drug repurposing approaches are largely data dependent. Much of the limitations arise with the data collection and the assumptions made during that process. For example, CMap is derived from exposing drug candidates to isolated cell lines, which may not accurately reflect the physiological scenario. Repurposing strategies based on chemical structure similarity become error prone when the physiological effects are a result of the drug metabolite rather than the original drug itself. Further, inadequate availability of high-resolution membrane-bound proteins limits the usage of structure-based methods like docking on GPCRs. Also, binding affinity predictions depend on scoring functions that are highly approximated and cannot be generalized for all the target proteins and all types of interactions. Adverse-effect profiles of drugs are comparatively less documented, providing a narrow scope of exploration in this direction.

At times strategies based on GWAS are biased, as this data does not provide detailed pathophysiology. In addition to this, since the current understanding of human genome is not final, there could be large unexplored areas and new genes that are yet to be identified. Drug repurposing strategies based on EHRs confront ethical and legal issues that limit the access to the data. Moreover, there is great difficulty in extracting unstructured information from EHRs.

3. Experimental drug repurposing

Experimental drug repurposing strategies include in vitro and in vivo screening [37,38]. The two major approaches of experimental drug repurposing are phenotypic screens and target-based screens for which cell-based assays, disease-based animal models, or clinical samples would be used as model systems.

3.1 Phenotypic screening

In this approach, the approved drug is screened to identify any phenotypic changes using in vitro cell-based assays or relevant disease-based animal models. Historically, phenotypic screening has been the traditional drug discovery approach by nature. For instance, the discovery of penicillin, although accidental, was mainly due to the phenotypic observation of the inability of the bacteria to grow in the presence of a fungus, and this has paved the way for the identification of all other antibiotics [39]. In this approach, the drug's activity and efficacy alone are determined using specific assays such as killing cancer cells without effecting normal cells, killing pathogens in culture, etc., although the mechanism and the target remain unknown.

A classic example of this is aspirin, which was initially marketed as an analgesic and was later repurposed as "blood thinner" for cardiovascular diseases based on the phenotypic observation by Dr. Lawrence Craven that aspirin when administered for analgesia for his tonsillectomy patients resulted in adverse effect of increased bleeding. This observation then led to the target identification and mechanism of action of aspirin for which J.R. Vane received Nobel Prize in Medicine in the year 1982, 100 years after aspirin discovery [40]. The same phenotypic screening has also resulted in aspirin's repurposing as an anticancer agent where long-term administration of daily aspirin prevents cancer development, specifically colorectal cancers.

3.2 Target-based screening

In target-based screens, the new activity of the existing drugs would be discovered using enzymatic assays. In 2006, Chong et al. identified astemizole, an antihistamine, as a potential antimalarial drug using target-based screening method wherein they screened a library of 2687 existing drugs for inhibitors of human *Plasmodium falciparum* parasite [41].

Target-based drug discovery also called "reverse pharmacology" started in early 20th century and was shown to be a better approach than phenotypic screening, the forward pharmacology. Recently, a study by Swinney and Anthony [42] indicated that among the total drugs approved by the FDA between 1999 and 2008, 28 of them were discovered using phenotypic screening approach in contrast to 17 drugs by target-based approach. Currently, researchers are trying to identify new uses of existing drugs using both computational and phenotypic screens.

4. Conclusions and perspectives

Traditional drug discovery process is complex and time-consuming, incurring huge cost to the pharmaceutical company. Drug repurposing has been shown to be a best alternative to identify existing drugs for another disease. In contrast to the computational approaches, the experimental approaches provide direct evidence for the drug repositioning. In recent years, the computational, artificial intelligence, and machine learning methods have improved the performance of the drug repurposing process. However, the computational methods need to be validated by the experimental approaches using suitable animal and clinical models. With the current technology advancements such as genomics, transcriptomics, proteomics, and metabolomics, the identification of new targets and new therapeutics for several diseases is increasingly on demand and drug repurposing offers an opportunity to be exploited by the pharma companies. However, every opportunity comes with a challenge. Two of the major challenges the drug repositioning faces are the identification of a right therapeutic area or disease for the existing drugs and the intellectual property protection of the repositioned drug for new indication. Therefore, for successful drug repositioning, researches need to gain more in-depth understanding of the complex process of the disease biology using network biology and systems biology approaches, execute the repositioning by integrating the computational and experimental strategies, and thus develop effective therapeutic indications for human diseases.

Author contributions

All of the authors have equally contributed to the conception, development, and preparation of this manuscript. All of the authors have read and approved the final draft.

Financial disclosures

None to disclose.

Conflict of interest

No potential conflicts of interest were disclosed.

References

[1] T.T. Ashburn, K.B. Thor, Drug repositioning: identifying and developing new uses for existing drugs, Nat. Rev. Drug Discov. 3 (8) (2004) 673–683, https://doi.org/10.1038/NRD1468.

[2] Z.L. Ji, L.Y. Han, C.W. Yap, L.Z. Sun, X. Chen, Y.Z. Chen, Drug Adverse Reaction Target Database (DART), Drug Saf. 26 (10) (2003) 685–690, https://doi.org/10.2165/00002018-200326100-00002.

[3] Y. Böttiger, K. Laine, M.L. Andersson, T. Korhonen, B. Molin, M.L. Ovesjö, T. Tirkkonen, A. Rane, L.L. Gustafsson, B. Eiermann, SFINX—a drug-drug interaction database designed for clinical decision support systems, Eur. J. Clin. Pharmacol. 65 (6) (2009) 627–633, https://doi.org/10.1007/S00228-008-0612-5.

[4] A. Frolkis, C. Knox, E. Lim, T. Jewison, V. Law, D.D. Hau, P. Liu, B. Gautam, S. Ly, A.C. Guo, J. Xia, Y. Liang, S. Shrivastava, D.S. Wishart, SMPDB: The small molecule pathway database, Nucleic Acids Res. 38 (Database issue) (2010), https://doi.org/10.1093/NAR/GKP1002.

[5] Y. Zhou, Y. Zhang, X. Lian, F. Li, C. Wang, F. Zhu, Y. Qiu, Y. Chen, Therapeutic target database update 2022: facilitating drug discovery with enriched comparative data of targeted agents, Nucleic Acids Res. 50 (D1) (2022) D1398–D1407, https://doi.org/10.1093/NAR/GKAB953.

[6] J. Wu, T. Vallenius, K. Ovaska, J. Westermarck, T.P. Mäkelä, S. Hautaniemi, Integrated network analysis platform for protein-protein interactions, Nat. Methods 6 (1) (2009) 75–77, https://doi.org/10.1038/nmeth.1282.

[7] V. Stathias, J. Turner, A. Koleti, D. Vidovic, D. Cooper, M. Fazel-Najafabadi, M. Pilarczyk, R. Terryn, C. Chung, A. Umeano, D.J.B. Clarke, A. Lachmann, J.E. Evangelista, A. Ma'Ayan, M. Medvedovic, S.C. Schürer, LINCS Data Portal 2.0: next generation access point for perturbation-response signatures, Nucleic Acids Res. 48 (D1) (2020) D431–D439, https://doi.org/10.1093/NAR/GKZ1023.

[8] E. Uffelmann, Q.Q. Huang, N.S. Munung, J. de Vries, Y. Okada, A.R. Martin, H.C. Martin, T. Lappalainen, D. Posthuma, Genome-wide association studies, Nat. Rev. Methods Prim. 1 (1) (2021) 1–21, https://doi.org/10.1038/s43586-021-00056-9.

[9] M. Kanehisa, M. Furumichi, M. Tanabe, Y. Sato, K. Morishima, KEGG: new perspectives on genomes, pathways, diseases and drugs, Nucleic Acids Res. 45 (D1) (2017) D353–D361, https://doi.org/10.1093/NAR/GKW1092.

[10] M. Griffith, O.L. Griffith, A.C. Coffman, J.V. Weible, J.F. Mcmichael, N.C. Spies, J. Koval, I. Das, M.-B. Callaway, J.M. Eldred, C.A. Miller, J. Subramanian, R. Govindan, R.D. Kumar, R. Bose, L.

Ding, J.R. Walker, D.E. Larson, D.J. Dooling, S.M. Smith, T.J. Ley, E.R. Mardis, R.K. Wilson, DGIdb: mining the druggable genome, Nat. Methods 10 (12) (2013) 1209–1210, https://doi.org/10.1038/NMETH.2689.

[11] J. Yang, S.J. Wu, S.Y. Yang, J.W. Peng, S.N. Wang, F.Y. Wang, Y.X. Song, T. Qi, Y.X. Li, Y.Y. Li, DNetDB: the human disease network database based on dysfunctional regulation mechanism, BMC Syst. Biol. 10 (1) (2016) 1–8, https://doi.org/10.1186/S12918-016-0280-5.

[12] S. Hwang, C.Y. Kim, S. Yang, E. Kim, T. Hart, E.M. Marcotte, I. Lee, HumanNet v2: human gene networks for disease research, Nucleic Acids Res. 47 (D1) (2019) D573–D580, https://doi.org/10.1093/NAR/GKY1126.

[13] W. Yang, J. Soares, P. Greninger, E.J. Edelman, H. Lightfoot, S. Forbes, N. Bindal, D. Beare, J.A. Smith, I.R. Thompson, S. Ramaswamy, P.A. Futreal, D.A. Haber, M.R. Stratton, C. Benes, U. McDermott, M.J. Garnett, Genomics of drug sensitivity in cancer (GDSC): a resource for therapeutic biomarker discovery in cancer cells, Nucleic Acids Res. 41 (Database issue) (2013), https://doi.org/10.1093/NAR/GKS1111.

[14] E. Clough, T. Barrett, The Gene Expression Omnibus database, Methods Mol. Biol. 1418 (2016) 93–110, https://doi.org/10.1007/978-1-4939-3578-9_5/FIGURES/3.

[15] L. Gong, M. Whirl-Carrillo, T.E. Klein, PharmGKB, an integrated resource of pharmacogenomic knowledge, Curr. Protoc. 1 (8) (2021), e226, https://doi.org/10.1002/CPZ1.226.

[16] D.S. Wishart, D. Tzur, C. Knox, R. Eisner, A.C. Guo, N. Young, D. Cheng, K. Jewell, D. Arndt, S. Sawhney, C. Fung, L. Nikolai, M. Lewis, M.A. Coutouly, I. Forsythe, P. Tang, S. Shrivastava, K. Jeroncic, P. Stothard, G. Amegbey, D. Block, D.D. Hau, J. Wagner, J. Miniaci, M. Clements, M. Gebremedhin, N. Guo, Y. Zhang, G.E. Duggan, G.D. MacInnis, A.M. Weljie, R. Dowlatabadi, F. Bamforth, D. Clive, R. Greiner, L. Li, T. Marrie, B.D. Sykes, H.J. Vogel, L. Querengesser, HMDB: the human metabolome database, Nucleic Acids Res. *35* (Database issue) (2007), https://doi.org/10.1093/NAR/GKL923.

[17] J. Schellenberger, J.O. Park, T.M. Conrad, B.T. Palsson, BiGG: a Biochemical Genetic and Genomic knowledgebase of large scale metabolic reconstructions, BMC Bioinf. 11 (1) (2010) 1–10, https://doi.org/10.1186/1471-2105-11-213/FIGURES/4.

[18] A.S. Brown, C.J. Patel, A standard database for drug repositioning, Sci. Data 4 (1) (2017) 1–7, https://doi.org/10.1038/sdata.2017.29.

[19] M. Kuhn, I. Letunic, L.J. Jensen, P. Bork, The SIDER database of drugs and side effects, Nucleic Acids Res. 44 (Database issue) (2016) D1075, https://doi.org/10.1093/NAR/GKV1075.

[20] Z. Tanoli, U. Seemab, A. Scherer, K. Wennerberg, J. Tang, M. Vähä-Koskela, Exploration of databases and methods supporting drug repurposing: a comprehensive survey, Brief. Bioinform. 22 (2) (2021) 1656–1678, https://doi.org/10.1093/BIB/BBAA003.

[21] S. Pushpakom, F. Iorio, P.A. Eyers, K.J. Escott, S. Hopper, A. Wells, A. Doig, T. Guilliams, J. Latimer, C. McNamee, A. Norris, P. Sanseau, D. Cavalla, M. Pirmohamed, Drug repurposing: progress, challenges and recommendations, Nat. Rev. Drug Discov. 18 (1) (2018) 41–58, https://doi.org/10.1038/nrd.2018.168.

[22] Y. Ko, Computational drug repositioning: current progress and challenges, Appl. Sci. 10 (15) (2020), https://doi.org/10.3390/app10155076.

[23] K.K.M. Koudijs, A.G.T. Terwisscha Van Scheltinga, S. Böhringer, K.J.M. Schimmel, H.J. Guchelaar, Transcriptome signature reversion as a method to reposition drugs against cancer for precision oncology, Cancer J. (United States) 25 (2) (2019) 116–120, https://doi.org/10.1097/PPO.0000000000000370.

[24] J. Lamb, E.D. Crawford, D. Peck, J.W. Modell, I.C. Blat, M.J. Wrobel, J. Lerner, J.P. Brunet, A. Subramanian, K.N. Ross, M. Reich, H. Hieronymus, G. Wei, S.A. Armstrong, S.J. Haggarty, P.A. Clemons, R. Wei, S.A. Carr, E.S. Lander, T.R. Golub, The connectivity map: using gene-expression signatures to connect small molecules, genes, and disease, Science (80-.) 313 (5795) (2006) 1929–1935, https://doi.org/10.1126/SCIENCE.1132939.

[25] J.T. Dudley, M. Sirota, M. Shenoy, R.K. Pai, S. Roedder, A.P. Chiang, A.A. Morgan, M.M. Sarwal, P.J. Pasricha, A.J. Butte, Computational repositioning of the anticonvulsant topiramate for inflammatory bowel disease, Sci. Transl. Med. 3 (96) (2011), https://doi.org/10.1126/SCITRANSLMED.3002648.

[26] F. Iorio, R. Bosotti, E. Scacheri, V. Belcastro, P. Mithbaokar, R. Ferriero, L. Murino, R. Tagliaferri, N. Brunetti-Pierri, A. Isacchi, D. Di Bernardo, Discovery of drug mode of action and drug repositioning from transcriptional responses, Proc. Natl. Acad. Sci. U. S. A. 107 (33) (2010) 14621–14626, https://doi.org/10.1073/pnas.1000138107.
[27] S. Dakshanamurthy, N.T. Issa, S. Assefnia, A. Seshasayee, O.J. Peters, S. Madhavan, A. Uren, M.L. Brown, S.W. Byers, Predicting new indications for approved drugs using a proteochemometric method, J. Med. Chem. 55 (15) (2012) 6832–6848, https://doi.org/10.1021/JM300576Q.
[28] A. Weber, A. Casini, A. Heine, D. Kuhn, C.T. Supuran, A. Scozzafava, G. Klebe, Unexpected nanomolar inhibition of carbonic anhydrase by COX-2-selective celecoxib: new pharmacological opportunities due to related binding site recognition, J. Med. Chem. 47 (3) (2004) 550–557, https://doi.org/10.1021/JM030912M.
[29] M. Campillos, M. Kuhn, A.C. Gavin, L.J. Jensen, P. Bork, Drug target identification using side-effect similarity, Science (80-.) 321 (5886) (2008) 263–266, https://doi.org/10.1126/SCIENCE.1158140.
[30] L. Yang, P. Agarwal, Systematic drug repositioning based on clinical side-effects, PLoS One 6 (12) (2011), e28025, https://doi.org/10.1371/JOURNAL.PONE.0028025.
[31] P. Sanseau, P. Agarwal, M.R. Barnes, T. Pastinen, J.B. Richards, L.R. Cardon, V. Mooser, Use of genome-wide association studies for drug repositioning, Nat. Biotechnol. 30 (4) (2012) 317–320, https://doi.org/10.1038/nbt.2151.
[32] C.S. Greene, B.F. Voight, Pathway and network-based strategies to translate genetic discoveries into effective therapies, Hum. Mol. Genet. 25 (R2) (2016) R94–R98, https://doi.org/10.1093/HMG/DDW160.
[33] V. Martínez, C. Navarro, C. Cano, W. Fajardo, A. Blanco, DrugNet: network-based drug–disease prioritization by integrating heterogeneous data, Artif. Intell. Med. 63 (1) (2015) 41–49, https://doi.org/10.1016/J.ARTMED.2014.11.003.
[34] S.B. Smith, W. Dampier, A. Tozeren, J.R. Brown, M. Magid-Slav, Identification of common biological pathways and drug targets across multiple respiratory viruses based on human host gene expression analysis, PLoS One 7 (3) (2012), e33174, https://doi.org/10.1371/JOURNAL.PONE.0033174.
[35] H. Xu, J. Li, X. Jiang, Q. Chen, Electronic health records for drug repurposing: current status, challenges, and future directions, Clin. Pharmacol. Ther. 107 (4) (2020) 712–714, https://doi.org/10.1002/cpt.1769.
[36] H. Xu, M.C. Aldrich, Q. Chen, H. Liu, N.B. Peterson, Q. Dai, M. Levy, A. Shah, X. Han, X. Ruan, M. Jiang, Y. Li, J.S. Julien, J. Warner, C. Friedman, D.M. Roden, J.C. Denny, Validating drug repurposing signals using electronic health records: a case study of metformin associated with reduced cancer mortality, J. Am. Med. Inform. Assoc. 22 (1) (2015) 179–191, https://doi.org/10.1136/AMIAJNL-2014-002649.
[37] T.I. Oprea, J.P. Overington, Computational and Practical Aspects of Drug Repositioning, Assay Drug Dev. Technol. 13 (6) (2015) 299–306, https://doi.org/10.1089/ADT.2015.29011.TIODRRR.
[38] K. Shameer, B. Readhead, J.T. Dudley, Computational and experimental advances in drug repositioning for accelerated therapeutic stratification, Curr. Top. Med. Chem. 15 (1) (2015) 5–20, https://doi.org/10.2174/1568026615666150112103510.
[39] A.S. Pina, A. Hussain, A.C.A. Roque, An historical overview of drug discovery, Methods Mol. Biol. 572 (2009) 3–12, https://doi.org/10.1007/978-1-60761-244-5_1/COVER/.
[40] J.R. Vane, Inhibition of prostaglandin synthesis as a mechanism of action for aspirin-like drugs, Nat. New Biol. 231 (25) (1971) 232–235, https://doi.org/10.1038/newbio231232a0.
[41] C.R. Chong, X. Chen, L. Shi, J.O. Liu, D.J. Sullivan, A clinical drug library screen identifies astemizole as an antimalarial agent, Nat. Chem. Biol. 2 (8) (2006) 415–416, https://doi.org/10.1038/nchembio806.
[42] D.C. Swinney, J. Anthony, How were new medicines discovered? Nat. Rev. Drug Discov. 10 (7) (2011) 507–519, https://doi.org/10.1038/nrd3480.

CHAPTER 10

Principles of computational drug designing and drug repurposing—An algorithmic approach

Angshuman Bagchi
Department of Biochemistry and Biophysics, University of Kalyani, Kalyani, West Bengal, India

Abstract

The rates of infections and onsets of diseases are increasing day by day. With the passage of time, new microbial pathogenic strains are evolving and they claim the lives of thousands and people worldwide. Development of new drugs is a very important endeavor. Medicinal chemists and biologists are working day and night to come up with new drug molecules to combat the onset and subsequent spreading of the diseases. However, the traditional process of drug development is extremely time-consuming, labor-intensive, and above all highly expensive. With the advent of high-end computing systems, the process of drug development has achieved new directions. Computer algorithms are being used constantly to screen millions of databases to choose the appropriate structures of drug-like candidates. The process is called virtual screening of ligand libraries. There are other methods called molecular docking, which is used to measure the affinity of a ligand with the target protein receptor. Nowadays, there is an approach called drug repurposing, which involves the use of an existing drug specific for a particular type of disease to be tested for subsequent use to treat other related ailments. In this chapter, an overview of the different computational techniques used for the purpose of drug development is explored. The basics of thermodynamic principles used in the process of computational drug development are also mentioned. This chapter aims to provide the key points in the process involved in computational drug designing.

Abbreviations

BM binding mode
G Gibb's free energy
H enthalpy
L ligand
LJ Lennard-Jones potential
PDB Protein Data Bank
R receptor
RL ranking of ligands
S entropy
SDP scoring of a docking pose
U internal energy
VS virtual screening

Computational Methods in Drug Discovery and Repurposing for Cancer Therapy
https://doi.org/10.1016/B978-0-443-15280-1.00011-X

1. Introduction

With the rise in the rates of various types of infections and onsets of different diseases, developments of new drugs have become an essential part of industry and academia. Development of new drug candidates is not a new subject [1–10]. The process of drug development is a truly multidisciplinary subject, and it requires the knowledge of Chemistry, Biochemistry, Physiology, Physics, Statistics, and other related disciplines. The traditional drug development process involves the following steps [11–20]:

- Identification of target(s) and validations: The first and foremost important step of a drug development process is the identification of the target. A typical target is a biological entity that has a significant role in the disease onset. Analyses of the characteristics of the drug target could provide valuable insights into the mechanism of the disease onset. The details of the target can be obtained from different sources like literature and wet-lab experimentations.
- Identification and validation of drug-like candidates: The method is also referred to as the hit identification. A hit is a putative candidate that has affinity toward the target. The identification of a hit can be done by different ways, like high-throughput screening, fragment-based screening, virtual screening, and phenotypic screening, to name a few.
- Choosing a lead compound from the collection of hits: The next step is the processing of the hits to determine the best candidate to bind to the target. The best candidate is referred to as the lead. The lead molecule(s) has/have the most favorable interactions with the target among all the hit molecules. The binding of the lead(s) with the target is guided by the principles of thermodynamics, which will be discussed in the next section.
- Optimization of lead: The lead molecule(s) chosen from the collection of hits is/are then subjected to structural optimizations. Sometimes, the chosen lead molecule might have lower than desired affinity toward the target. The affinities of the chosen lead molecule(s) are enhanced by chemical modifications. Another important aspect to consider is to minimize the undesirable off-target interactions by the lead molecule(s).
- Preclinical and clinical trials: The final stage of drug development process is the testing of the drug candidate. The efficacy of the drug candidate is measured first in vitro. On the basis of the results obtained from in vitro analysis, the drug candidates are tested in vivo.

The aforementioned steps are the basics of new drug development methodologies. In general, development of a new drug for a disease takes a long time to complete. However, with the advent of advanced computational methodologies, the screenings of molecular libraries to select hit molecules for a particular target have become much easier. An algorithm is a basic workflow of a process. In terms of computational methodologies, algorithms determine how to interpret and analyze the data. The drug designing endeavors would depend on molecular modeling, molecular docking, and virtual screening of molecular libraries. Computational algorithms are cost-effective and require much less time than the wet-lab-based screening methodologies [21–40]. There are different software tools available for the purpose of computational drug designing [41–50]. However, the basic principles of all the tools, i.e., the algorithms behind the computational techniques, are based on thermodynamic principles [51–60].

2. Overview of basic thermodynamic principles involved in computational algorithms

As mentioned before, with the advent of computational methodologies, the endeavor for new drug development has become much easier in terms of cost and time. The different algorithms depend on basic principles of thermodynamics. In this section, the basics of thermodynamics will be covered.

System: It is a part of the universe that is under observation.

Surroundings: Anything that is not included inside the system is called surroundings.

Universe: The universe refers to the study of the properties of the system and surroundings together.

Open system: If a system can transfer matter and energy both with the external environment, it is referred to as an open system.

Closed system: If a system can transfer energy only with outside, it is called closed system.

Isolated system: It is a system incapable of exchanging any of the aforementioned two parameters with outside.

Reversible process: A process that can go back and forth from one direction to the other direction within an infinitesimally small time period.

Irreversible process: A process that goes in one direction only.

Internal energy (U): It is the energy inherent within a system that is necessary for the existence of the system.

Enthalpy (H): It is net heat content of a system. It is the additive product of the internal energy of the system and the pressure-volume work associated with the system. In general, the absolute value of enthalpy is not important but the change in enthalpy is measured.

Entropy (S): It is the measure of randomness of a system. The more is the entropy, the more stable is the system. In this case, the change in entropy is measured by dividing the reversible heat change with the temperature at which the change occurs. For a spontaneous process, the entropy change should be positive.

Free energy (G): It is measured as the change. Free energy change determines the amount of available work at a constant temperature. For a process to be spontaneous, the change in free energy should be negative.

The van der Waals potential: This is a model to calculate the weak, short-range forces arising out of the movements of electrons in an atom. The model includes various types of dipolar interactions. The van der Waals potential is often determined by the Lennard-Jones potential.

The Lennard-Jones potential (LJ): This is a model to calculate the nonbonded interactions between a pair of atoms. The potential involves repulsive and attractive interactions between pairs of atoms. This potential model is applicable to neutral molecules.

3. Fundamentals of computational algorithms

There are essentially many different software tools available for the drug development process. The algorithms behind the software tools more or less follow the same principles [61–80]. The basic workflow of such tools can be expressed as the following flowchart:

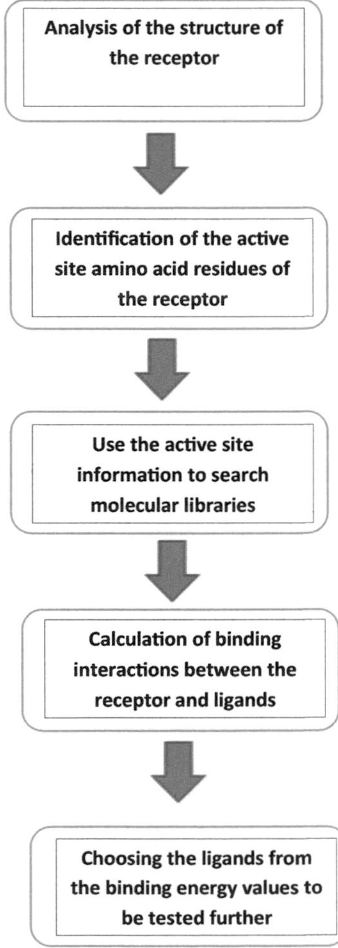

(a) Analysis of the structure of the receptor

The first and foremost important part of computational drug designing efforts is to analyze the structure of the receptor. In general, the receptor is a protein and the structure of the protein is extracted from the Protein Data Bank (PDB). (https://www.rcsb.org/). If the structure of the receptor protein is not available, then its structure is generated from the amino acid sequence by the process called molecular modeling.

(b) Identification of the active site amino acid residues in the receptor

There are different methods to identify the amino acid residues present at the active site of the receptor protein. The active site is defined as the region where the ligands bind. If the structure of the receptor is available, the active site information may be obtained from PDB and the corresponding literature. However, if no such information can be obtained, then there are different tools to predict the active site regions in proteins [81–85]. The tools provide an insight into the amino acid residues that might be involved in interactions with ligands.

(c) Use the active site information to search molecular libraries: virtual screening (VS)

The active site information is used to search molecular libraries to find suitable ligands to bind to the receptor using computer algorithms [86–90]. The method of virtual screening is broadly classified in two different categories:

- **Ligand-based virtual screening:** In this method, first the database of ligands is explored to derive some common features from the sets of ligands. The common feature may include physicochemical parameters, structural and molecular features, shapes of the ligands to name a few. These common features are used to extract their functional characteristics. Using the functional characteristics, the details of their putative binding partners are determined. This method is less computer-intensive [91–95].
- **Receptor-based virtual screening:** This method is opposite to the method mentioned before. The method involves the use of the structural information of the receptors to find the putative ligands. The process involves the principle of molecular docking. This method uses parallel processing approach [96–100].
- **Hybrid methods:** Hybrid methods involve analysis of similarity between structure of receptor and ligand. The methods utilize the concept of evolutionary computation to identify the nature of small-molecule ligands binding to protein target receptors [22,101]. The structures of the protein target receptors are analyzed, and a 2D fingerprint region from the structure is extracted. This fingerprint region is used to search the ligand libraries.

One of the fundamental aspects of computational drug designing endeavors is molecular docking. The problem of docking is to use the principle of lock and key technique. The receptor protein is considered as the lock, whereas the ligand is the key. The docking is basically a problem of optimization through which the best possible orientation of the ligand bound to a receptor is determined [77,78,96–118]. There are different tools available for the purpose of molecular docking. Before going into the algorithmic details of the docking procedure, the basics of molecular docking is worth a revisit.

- Docking: This is a procedure to find and analyze the binding interactions between a receptor and a ligand. The receptor and ligand may be proteins, nucleic acids, small molecules to name a few. The main aim of docking is to predict the structure of the biomolecular complexes. The docking tools generate a number of solutions, and each solution represents a plausible conformation of the biomolecular complex. The solutions are generated by searching the six-dimensional conformational spaces for the receptor and the ligand. The solutions are ranked as per the docking scores.
- Receptor (R) and ligand (L): Receptor and ligand are two components of a docking procedure. The receptor is generally a macromolecule to which a ligand binds. On the other hand, a ligand is either a macromolecule or a small molecule.
- Rigid body and flexible docking methods: While sampling the docking solutions in three-dimensional spaces of each of the receptor and the ligand, if the bond lengths, bond angles, and torsion angels of the molecules are kept fixed, the process is referred to as rigid body docking. On the other hand, when these bond parameters are allowed to move, the docking procedure is called flexible docking. Flexible docking generally provides a better representation of the structure of the docked complex as compared to rigid body docking. However, the flexible docking method is extremely expensive in terms of computational power.
- Binding mode (BM): This is the relative orientation of the ligand with respect to the receptor. It also represents the conformation of the receptor and ligand when they are bound together.
- Scoring of a docking pose (SDP): This is the quantitative estimate of the quality of the docked complex. This is calculated by analyzing the total number of favorable interactions in the docked complex.
- Ranking of ligands (RL): This is a method to identify the nature of a ligand that fits best to the target receptor. This is obtained from the free energy of binding of the ligands with the receptor.

Overview of docking algorithm: The main approaches of molecular docking use the principles of shape complementarity and molecular simulations. Both the approaches have certain levels of accuracy as well as disadvantages.

Principle of shape complementarity: The principle of shape complementarity involves features of the surfaces of the ligand and its corresponding binding partner. The surface of the binding partner is expressed by its solvent-accessible surface area. On the other hand, the surface of the ligand is expressed by the nature of its exposed surface, which is complimentary to the surface of the receptor protein. The complementarity between the surfaces of the receptor and the ligand is analyzed, and the docking poses are generated on the basis of the complementarity in the shapes of the receptor and the ligand. While measuring the shape complementarity, the hydrophobic surfaces of the receptor and the ligand are considered. These hydrophobic patches are considered to be stacked together [80,119–121]. The process of shape complementarity is very fast and robust. It can be used to scan the binding affinities of many ligands to the binding partner. However, the main drawback of the process is that the process ignores the flexibility in ligands. The process only provides information about a ligand's ability to be attached to the surface of a target protein receptor.

Principle of simulation: In this technique, the target protein receptor and the ligand are kept at a certain distance and the ligand is allowed to move under the influence of an external force. The process involves changing in the translational, rotational degrees of freedom of the ligand. The movement of the ligand is also associated with changes in the torsions of the ligand. All these changes would lead to some energetic cost of the ligand. The same technique is applied to the binding partner as well. Therefore, every move of the ligand and the corresponding binding partner involve the estimation of the total energetic cost of the system. The process is more accurate than the shape complementarity-based technique. However, this principle is highly computationally intensive.

4. Searching the conformational space

It is a process to analyze all the modes of the movements of the binding partner as well the ligand. However, given the computational resources, it is simply not possible to analyze all the degrees of freedom of both the ligands and the receptor proteins. Most of the docking algorithms use the entire three-dimensional region where the ligand is able to move and try to fit the ligand to the receptor protein molecule in a specific orientation. The searching of the conformational space of the ligand may be carried out by different approaches. One of such approaches is the exhaustive conformational search process [122,123]. In this approach, the different degrees of freedom of the ligand are analyzed by manipulating all the dihedral angles considering the geometrical and chemical constraints. Ligand flexibility makes the problem complicated as there will be more sampling spaces available for the ligand.

Another search method is called incremental construction. In this approach, the ligand is divided into smaller fragments. The skeletal fragment is then docked into the receptor protein. The docked ligand is then joined together with the remaining fragments while in bound condition [124–126].

Another widely used algorithm is stochastic method. In this method, all the modes of the movements of the ligand are varied and new sets of poses are generated at each step. The suitability of the ligand poses is determined on the basis of probabilistic approaches. Though the process would provide a great deal of solutions, it is always very difficult to choose the optimum ligand pose [122].

The third most widely used algorithm of molecular docking is referred to as the deterministic method. In this method, the final docking solution is obtained based on the structure of the input molecule. The process depends on energy minimization and molecular dynamics simulations. Energy minimization methods are used to identify the energetically favorable structure based on the direction of the energy gradient of the system potential energy. As a suitable alternative, molecular dynamics simulation methods determine the final structure of the docked complex in the presence of some external physical parameters like temperature and pressure with the passage of time [127].

5. Analysis of protein flexibility

Analyzing the three-dimensional space for the movement of the binding partner is a challenging task as the process is very costly in terms of computational speed. Nonetheless, the proteins inside cells are considered to be present as a combination of the different energetically favorable conformational states available to the protein [123,128]. One of such conformational states of the receptor protein would become available to the ligand for binding and the ligand would tend to stabilize that conformational state [128–131]. As mentioned, searching of the conformational space of the protein receptor is a real challenge. There are several algorithms available for finding the conformational space. The algorithms are classified as soft docking, flexibility of side-chain, relaxation of molecular structure, docking of an ensemble structure, and collective information on the modes of the movements.

The soft docking: This approach considers restrained movements of protein side chains. Such movements might bring about certain changes in the ligand binding process. The method is suitable to study local motions of the receptor protein [123,132]. The most important aspect of the docking procedure is the speed. However, the process is an approximated one.

Side-chain flexibility: An alternative to the soft docking approach is to analyze the side-chain flexibility of the amino acid residues. Rotamer libraries are used to predict the conformations of the side chains of the amino acid residues in the binding partner. The torsional degrees of freedom of the side-chain atoms of the amino acid residues of the binding partner are considered here to find the suitable pose of the binding partner, which will be used to dock with the ligand [133–136].

Molecular relaxation: This method is employed on the docked molecule of the binding partner-ligand complex. In this case, the backbone and side chain movements of the atoms of the amino acids of the receptor protein are considered in ligand-bound state. The method involves minimization of energy of the system, Monte-Carlo methods, and molecular dynamics simulations [137–140].

Docking of the ensemble structure: In this method, the flexibility in the structure of the binding partner is considered while docking the ligand. A multitude of conformations of the binding partner is considered while docking the ligand. The different sites on the structure of the binding partner are also taken into consideration [141–147].

Collective degrees of freedom: This method considers the full protein motion. The method considers only the dominant modes of movement of the receptor protein. However, such a process requires a huge computational time [148–150].

Analysis of the quality of the docking procedure [151–157]**:** Every docking program comes up with different solutions of the structures of the binding partner-ligand complex. The qualities of the docked complexes are estimated by scoring of the complexes. The docking tools utilize several scoring functions to rank the results obtained after the docking simulation run. The scoring functions provide the result with the most favorable orientations of the ligands bound to the receptor protein. The scoring functions are used to discriminate between native and nonnative forms of the docked complexes. The scoring functions tend to discriminate between the appropriate and inappropriate ligands for a specific receptor protein. The scoring functions are classified as:

- Scoring functions on the basis of force field
- Scoring functions based on empirical knowledge
- Scoring functions on existing knowledge

Scoring functions on the basis of force field: This is a popular method. It is dependent on the various energy potentials as obtained from the laws of thermodynamics. The energy terms are the ones that are associated with van der Waal's energy, hydrogen bond potential, and entropy.

Scoring functions based on empirical knowledge: This is another popular method. It is obtained from the calculation of the binding affinity data from the protein-ligand complexes as obtained from wet-lab-based techniques. The main difference between the scoring functions on the basis of force-field and empirical knowledge is the number of energy terms involved in calculations.

Scoring functions on existing knowledge: This method depends on the available structures of protein-ligand complexes. The interactions holding the receptor and the ligand are determined from the existing structures present in the databases. This information is utilized as a training dataset, and based on the training dataset, a model is created. The model is then employed to judge the quality of docked structures.

Some success stories of computational drug development: There are different examples of drugs, which have been developed by the protocols of computer-aided drug discovery. Some of the examples are listed below:

- **Carbonic anhydrase inhibitor dorzolamide:** This particular drug was approved in 1995 as a medicine to treat glaucoma. It reduces intraocular pressure [158].
- **Angiotensin-converting enzyme (ACE) inhibitor captopril:** This particular medicine was approved to be used as a potential drug for the treatment of high blood pressure and heart failure. In the year 1981, this molecule has been approved to be a medication for the treatment of hypertension [159].
- **Drugs for the treatment of HIV:** There are three of the most important drugs that are being used for the treatment of infection by HIV. The drugs are saquinavir, ritonavir, and indinavir [160].

6. Drug repurposing [161–167]

The drug repurposing is the process of using an old and established drug which is meant for the treatment of a specific disease to be used further for the treatment of another disease. Nowadays, the technique of drug repurposing is used frequently. Specially, during the ongoing COVID-19 pandemic, the drug repurposing has become a very popular approach. This is because, for the treatment of COVID-19, it is really a challenge to identify a new drug candidate within a small span of time. Therefore, the alternative avenue for the treatment is to use older drugs. Some of the examples of repurposed drugs are as follows:

Zidovudine: This drug is used for the treatment of cancer. However, it shows its efficacy against retroviral infections as well.

Miltefosine: This drug is used for the treatment of cancer. However, it can be used to treat leishmaniasis.

Sildenafil: This drug is used for the treatment of pulmonary arterial hypertension. However, it is active against erectile dysfunction as well.

Bupropion: This is an antidepressant. However, it also helps the smokers to quit the habit.

Rituximab: This drug is used for the treatment of cancer. However, it can be used to treat rheumatoid arthritis.

Raloxifene: This is used for the treatment of osteoporosis. It shows its further action in the treatment of breast cancer as well.

Minoxidil: This is used for the treatment of hypertension. However, it can be used for the treatment of alopecia as well.

7. Conclusion

Development of new candidate drugs is a very important aspect. The traditional wet-lab-based approach on drug development is labor-intensive and time-consuming as well as very costly. The discovery of modern in silico platforms for the initial screening of drug candidates has become much easier. There are different computational tools available for the purpose of drug development. These tools utilize different algorithms. Those algorithms are mainly based on the principles of thermodynamics. Many of the candidate drugs, proposed by the computational methods, have so far been successfully brought to the market. This would indicate the importance of the computational methods. The methods of computational drug development have brought a new dimension to the solution of the problem.

Acknowledgment

The author would like to thank DST-FIST-II, UGC-SAP-DRSII, and University of Kalyani for support. DBT-Sponsored BIF Center (BT/PR40162/BTIS/137/48/2022 and SAN No. 102/IFD/SAN/653/2022-2023)

References

[1] J.G. Frey, C.L. Bird, Web-based services for drug design and discovery, Expert Opin. Drug Discovery 6 (9) (2011) 885–895, https://doi.org/10.1517/17460441.2011.598924.

[2] S. Morgan, P. Grootendorst, J. Lexchin, C. Cunningham, D. Greyson, The cost of drug development: a systematic review, Health Policy 100 (1) (2011) 4–17, https://doi.org/10.1016/j.healthpol.2010.12.002.

[3] L. Barnieh, F. Clement, A. Harris, M. Blom, C. Donaldson, S. Klarenbach, D. Husereau, D. Lorenzetti, B. Manns, A systematic review of cost-sharing strategies used within publicly-funded drug plans in member countries of the organization for economic co-operation and development, PLoS One 9 (3) (2014), e90434, https://doi.org/10.1371/journal.pone.0090434 (eCollection 2014).

[4] W.Z. Zhong, S.F. Zhou, Molecular science for drug development and biomedicine, Int. J. Mol. Sci. 15 (2014) 20072–20078, https://doi.org/10.3390/ijms151120072.

[5] X. Xiao, J.L. Min, W.Z. Lin, Z. Liu, iDrug-Target: predicting the interactions between drug compounds and target proteins in cellular networking via the benchmark dataset optimization approach, J. Biomol. Struct. Dyn. 33 (2015) 2221–2233, https://doi.org/10.1080/07391102.2014.998710.

[6] F. Mao, W. Ni, X. Xu, H. Wang, J. Wang, M. Ji, J. Li, Chemical structure-related drug-like criteria of global approved drugs, Molecules 21 (2016) 75, https://doi.org/10.3390/molecules21010075.

[7] G.P. Zhou, W.Z. Zhong, Perspective in medicinal chemistry, Curr. Top. Med. Chem. 16 (2016) 381–382, https://doi.org/10.2174/1568026616041510141140З0.

[8] S.F. Zhou, W.Z. Zhong, Drug design and discovery: principles and applications, Molecules 22 (2) (2017) 279, https://doi.org/10.3390/molecules22020279.

[9] A.A. Kaczor, D. Bartuzi, T.M. Stępniewski, D. Matosiuk, J. Selent, Protein-protein docking in drug design and discovery, Methods Mol. Biol. 1762 (2018) 285–305, https://doi.org/10.1007/978-1-4939-7756-7_15.

[10] D.A. Kessler, K.L. Feiden, Faster evaluation of vital drugs, Sci. Am. 272 (3) (1995) 48–54, https://doi.org/10.1038/scientificamerican0395-48.

[11] P. Agarwal, D.B. Searls, Literature mining in support of drug discovery, Brief. Bioinform. 9 (6) (2008) 479–492, https://doi.org/10.1093/bib/bbn035.

[12] M. Herschel, Portfolio decisions in early development: don't throw out the baby with the bathwater, Pharm. Med. 26 (2) (2012) 77–84, https://doi.org/10.1007/BF03256895.

[13] Y. Wang, Extracting knowledge from failed development programmes, Pharm. Med. 26 (2) (2012) 91–96, https://doi.org/10.1007/BF03256897.

[14] A.A. Ciociola, L.B. Cohen, P. Kulkarni, How drugs are developed and approved by the FDA: current process and future directions, Am. J. Gastroenterol. 109 (5) (2014) 620–623, https://doi.org/10.1038/ajg.2013.407.

[15] D. Taylor, The pharmaceutical industry and the future of drug development, in: Issues in Environmental Science and Technology, Royal Society of Chemistry, 2015, pp. 1–33, https://doi.org/10.1039/9781782622345-00001.

[16] A. Maxmen, Busting the billion-dollar myth: how to slash the cost of drug development, Nature 536 (7617) (2016) 388–390, https://doi.org/10.1038/536388a.

[17] J. Strovel, S. Sittampalam, N.P. Coussens, M. Hughes, J. Inglese, A. Kurtz, et al., Early drug discovery and development guidelines: for academic researchers, collaborators, and start-up companies, in: Assay Guidance Manual, Eli Lilly & Company and the National Center for Advancing Translational Sciences, 2016.

[18] A. Sertkaya, H.H. Wong, A. Jessup, T. Beleche, Key cost drivers of pharmaceutical clinical trials in the United States, Clin. Trials 13 (2) (2016) 117–126, https://doi.org/10.1177/1740774515625964.

[19] S. Marshall, R. Madabushi, E. Manolis, K. Krudys, A. Staab, K. Dykstra, S.A. Visser, Model-informed drug discovery and development: current industry good practice and regulatory expectations and future perspectives, CPT Pharmacometrics Syst. Pharmacol. 8 (2) (2019) 87–96, https://doi.org/10.1002/psp4.12372.

[20] A. Kabir, A. Muth, Polypharmacology: the science of multi-targeting molecules, Pharmacol. Res. 176 (2022) 106055, https://doi.org/10.1016/j.phrs.2021.106055.

[21] H.J. Böhm, The computer program LUDI: a new method for the de novo design of enzyme inhibitors, J. Comput. Aided Mol. Des. 6 (1992) 61–78.

[22] R. Abagyan, M. Totrov, D. Kuznetsov, ICM – a new method for protein modeling and design – applications to docking and structure prediction from the distorted native conformation, J. Comput. Chem. 15 (1994) 488–506.
[23] T.A. Ewing, S. Makino, A.G. Skillman, I. Kuntz, DOCK 4.0: search strategies for automated molecular docking of flexible molecule databases, J. Comput. Aided Mol. Des. 15 (2001) 411–428.
[24] R.D. Cramer, R.J. Jilek, K.M. Andrews, Dbtop: topomer similarity searching of conventional structure databases, J. Mol. Graph. Model. 20 (2002) 447–462.
[25] F. Ferrè, G. Ausiello, A. Zanzoni, M. Helmer-Citterich, SURFACE: a database of protein surface regions for functional annotation, Nucleic Acids Res. 32 (Database issue) (2004) D240–D244.
[26] J. Chen, S.J. Swamidass, Y. Dou, J. Bruand, P. Baldi, ChemDB: a public database of small molecules and related chemoinformatics resources, Bioinformatics 21 (2005) 4133–4139.
[27] G. Cruciani, E. Carosati, B. De Boeck, K. Ethirajulu, C. Mackie, T. Howe, R. Vianello, MetaSite: understanding metabolism in human cytochromes from the perspective of the chemist, J. Med. Chem. 48 (2005) 6970–6979.
[28] K. Arnold, L. Bordoli, J. Kopp, T. Schwede, The SWISS-MODEL workspace: a web-based environment for protein structure homology modelling, Bioinformatics 22 (2006) 195–201.
[29] J. Chen, L.H. Lai, Pocket v.2: further developments on receptor-based pharmacophore modeling, J. Chem. Inf. Model. 46 (2006) 2684–2691.
[30] S.L. Dixon, A.M. Smondyrev, E.H. Knoll, S.N. Rao, D.E. Shaw, R.A. Friesner, PHASE: a new engine for pharmacophore perception, 3D QSAR model development, and 3D database screening: 1. Methodology and preliminary results, J. Comput. Aided Mol. Des. 20 (2006) 647–671.
[31] J.H. Chen, E. Linstead, S.J. Swamidass, D. Wang, P. Baldi, ChemDB update—full-text search and virtual chemical space, Bioinformatics 23 (2007) 2348–2351.
[32] M. Brylinski, J. Skolnick, A threading-based method (FINDSITE) for ligand-binding site prediction and functional annotation, Proc. Natl. Acad. Sci. 105 (2008) 129–134.
[33] A. Durán, G.C. Martínez, M. Pastor, Development and validation of AMANDA, a new algorithm for selecting highly relevant regions in Molecular Interaction Fields, J. Chem. Inf. Model. 48 (2008) 1813–1823.
[34] S. Bar-Haim, A. Aharon, T. Ben-Moshe, Y. Marantz, H. Senderowitz, SeleX-CS: a new consensus scoring algorithm for hit discovery and lead optimization, J. Chem. Inf. Model. 49 (2009) 623–633.
[35] A. Grosdidier, V. Zoete, O. Michielin, SwissDock, a protein-small molecule docking web service based on EADock DSS, Nucleic Acids Res. 39 (2011) W270–W277.
[36] N.M. O'Boyle, et al., OpenBabel: an open chemical toolbox, J. Cheminform. 3 (2011) 33.
[37] V. Zoete, M.A. Cuendet, A. Grosdidier, O. Michielin, SwissParam: a fast force field generation tool for small organic molecules, J. Comput. Chem. 32 (2011) 2359–2368.
[38] F. Cheng, et al., admetSAR: a comprehensive source and free tool for assessment of chemical ADMET properties, J. Chem. Inf. Model. 52 (2012) 3099–3105.
[39] D. Gfeller, et al., Swiss Target Prediction: a web server for target prediction of bioactive small molecules, Nucleic Acids Res. 42 (2014) W32–W38.
[40] A. Singh, S. Shekhar, B. Jayaram, CADD: some success stories from Sanjeevini and the way forward, 2021, pp. 1–18, https://doi.org/10.1007/978-981-15-8936-2_1.
[41] R. Wang, S. Wang, How does consensus scoring work for virtual library screening? An idealized computer experiment, J. Chem. Inf. Comput. Sci. 41 (2001) 1422–1426.
[42] J. Bajorath, Integration of virtual and high-throughput screening, Nat. Rev. Drug Discov. 1 (2002) 882–894.
[43] J.A. Capra, R.A. Laskowski, J.M. Thornton, M. Singh, T.A. Funkhouser, Predicting protein ligand binding sites by combining evolutionary sequence conservation and 3D structure, PLoS Comput. Biol. 5 (2009), e1000585.
[44] A.C. Anderson, Structure-based functional design of drugs: from target to lead compound, Methods Mol. Biol. 823 (2012) 359–366.
[45] S. Zhong, A.D. MacKerell, Binding response: a descriptor for selecting ligand binding site on protein surfaces, J. Chem. Inf. Model. 47 (2007) 2303–2315.
[46] J. Wang, W. Wang, P.A. Kollman, D.A. Case, Automatic atom type and bond type perception in molecular mechanical calculations, J. Mol. Graph. Model. 25 (2006) 247–260.

[47] K. Vanommeslaeghe, A.D. MacKerell, Automation of the CHARMM General Force Field (CGenFF) I: bond perception and atom typing, J. Chem. Inf. Model. 52 (2012) 3144–3154.

[48] C.A. Lipinski, F. Lombardo, B.W. Dominy, P.J. Feeney, Experimental and computational approaches to estimate solubility and permeability in drug discovery and development settings, Adv. Drug Deliv. Rev. 46 (2001) 3–26.

[49] R. Todeschini, V. Consonni, H. Xiang, J. Holliday, M. Buscema, P. Willett, Similarity coefficients for binary chemoinformatics data: overview and extended comparison using simulated and real data sets, J. Chem. Inf. Model. 52 (2012) 2884–2901.

[50] D. Bernard, A. Coop, A.D. MacKerell, 2D conformationally sampled pharmacophore: a ligand-based pharmacophore to differentiate δ opioid agonists from antagonists, J. Am. Chem. Soc. 125 (2003) 3101–3107.

[51] Y.A. Cengel, M.A. Boles, Thermodynamics – An Engineering Approach, McGraw-Hill, 2005, ISBN: 978-0-07-310768-4.

[52] W. Gibbs, The Scientific Papers of J. Willard Gibbs, Volume One: Thermodynamics, 1993, ISBN: 978-0-918024-77-0.

[53] D.T. Haynie, Biological Thermodynamics, second ed., Cambridge University Press, 2008.

[54] I. Klotz, Chemical Thermodynamics: Basic Theory and Methods, John Wiley & Sons, Inc., Hoboken, New Jersey, 2008, p. 4, ISBN: 978-0-471-78015-1.

[55] M. Bailyn, A Survey of Thermodynamics, American Institute of Physics, AIP Press, Woodbury NY, 1994, p. 79, ISBN: 0883187973.

[56] J.S. Dugdale, Entropy and Its Physical Meaning, Taylor and Francis, 1998, ISBN: 978-0-7484-0569-5.

[57] H.C. Van Ness, Understanding Thermodynamics, Dover Publications, Inc., 1983, ISBN: 9780486632773.

[58] P. Perrot, A to Z of Thermodynamics, Oxford University Press, 1998, ISBN: 978-0-19-856552-9.

[59] R.A. Alberty, Biochemical thermodynamics: applications of mathematica, Methods Biochem. Anal. 48 (2006) 1–458. John Wiley & Sons, Inc. ISBN 978-0-471-75798-6 16878778.

[60] D.E. Barrick, Biomolecular Thermodynamics: From Theory to Applications, CRC Press, 2018, ISBN: 978-1-4398-0019-5.

[61] J. Mintseris, K. Wiehe, B. Pierce, R. Anderson, R. Chen, J. Janin, Z. Weng, Protein-Protein Docking Benchmark 2.0: an update, Proteins 60 (2) (2005) 214–216, https://doi.org/10.1002/prot.20560. 1598126.

[62] T. Vreven, I.H. Moal, A. Vangone, B.G. Pierce, P.L. Kastritis, M. Torchala, R. Chaleil, B. Jiménez-García, P.A. Bates, J. Fernandez-Recio, A.M. Bonvin, Z. Weng, Updates to the integrated protein-protein interaction benchmarks: docking benchmark version 5 and affinity benchmark version 2, J. Mol. Biol. 427 (19) (2015) 3031–3041, https://doi.org/10.1016/j.jmb.2015.07.016. PMC4677049.

[63] C. Nithin, P. Ghosh, J. Bujnicki, Bioinformatics tools and benchmarks for computational docking and 3D structure prediction of RNA-protein complexes, Genes 9 (9) (2018) 432, https://doi.org/10.3390/genes9090432. PMC6162694.

[64] R. Esmaielbeiki, J.C. Nebel, Scoring docking conformations using predicted protein interfaces, BMC Bioinformatics 15 (2014) 171, https://doi.org/10.1186/1471-2105-15-171. PMC4057934 24906633.

[65] C.J. Camacho, S. Vajda, Protein docking along smooth association pathways, Proc. Natl. Acad. Sci. 98 (19) (2008) 10636–10641, https://doi.org/10.1073/pnas.181147798. PMC58518 11517309.

[66] N.C. Strynadka, M. Eisenstein, E. Katchalski-Katzir, B.K. Shoichet, I.D. Kuntz, R. Abagyan, M. Totrov, J. Janin, J. Cherfils, F. Zimmerman, A. Olson, B. Duncan, M. Rao, R. Jackson, M. Sternberg, M.N. James, Molecular docking programs successfully predict the binding of a beta-lactamase inhibitory protein to TEM-1 beta-lactamase, Nat. Struct. Mol. Biol. 3 (3) (1996) 233–239, https://doi.org/10.1038/nsb0396-233. 8605624.

[67] H.A. Gabb, R.M. Jackson, M.J. Sternberg, Modelling protein docking using shape complementarity, electrostatics and biochemical information, J. Mol. Biol. 272 (1) (1997) 106–120, https://doi.org/10.1006/jmbi.1997.1203. 9299341.

[68] V.D. Badal, P.J. Kundrotas, I.A. Vakser, Natural language processing in text mining for structural modeling of protein complexes, BMC Bioinformatics 19 (1) (2018) 84, https://doi.org/10.1186/s12859-018-2079-4. PMC5838950.

[69] P.L. Kastritis, A.M. Bonvin, Are scoring functions in protein–protein docking ready to predict interactomes? Clues from a novel binding affinity benchmark, J. Proteome Res. 9 (5) (2010) 2216–2225, https://doi.org/10.1021/pr9009854.hdl:1874/202590. 20329755.

[70] J.J. Gray, S. Moughon, C. Wang, O. Schueler-Furman, B. Kuhlman, C.A. Rohl, D. Baker, Protein–protein docking with simultaneous optimization of rigid-body displacement and side-chain conformations, J. Mol. Biol. 331 (1) (2003) 281–299, https://doi.org/10.1016/S0022-2836(03)00670-3. 12875852.

[71] M. van Dijk, A.M. Bonvin, A protein-DNA docking benchmark, Nucleic Acids Res. 36 (14) (2008), e88, https://doi.org/10.1093/nar/gkn386. PMC2504314 18583363.

[72] A. Barik, C. Nithin, P. Manasa, R.P. Bahadur, A protein-RNA docking benchmark (I): nonredundant cases, Proteins 80 (7) (2012) 1866–1871, https://doi.org/10.1002/prot.24083. 22488669.

[73] L. Pérez-Cano, B. Jiménez-García, J. Fernández-Recio, A protein-RNA docking benchmark (II): extended set from experimental and homology modeling data, Proteins 80 (7) (2012) 1872–1882, https://doi.org/10.1002/prot.24075. 22488990.

[74] P.L. Kastritis, I.H. Moal, H. Hwang, Z. Weng, P.A. Bates, A.M. Bonvin, J. Janin, A structure-based benchmark for protein-protein binding affinity, Protein Sci. 20 (3) (2011) 482–491, https://doi.org/10.1002/pro.580. PMC3064828 21213247.

[75] F. Ballante, Protein-ligand docking in drug design: performance assessment and binding-pose selection, Methods Mol. Biol. 1824 (2018) 67–88, https://doi.org/10.1007/978-1-4939-8630-9_5. Rational Drug Design. ISBN 978-1-4939-8629-3. ISSN 1940-6029 30039402.

[76] J.J. Irwin, Community benchmarks for virtual screening, J. Comput. Aided Mol. Des. 22 (3–4) (2008) 193–199, https://doi.org/10.1007/s10822-008-9189-4. 18273555.

[77] M.J. Hartshorn, M.L. Verdonk, G. Chessari, S.C. Brewerton, W.T. Mooij, P.N. Mortenson, C.W. Murray, Diverse, high-quality test set for the validation of protein-ligand docking performance, J. Med. Chem. 50 (4) (2007) 726–741, https://doi.org/10.1021/jm061277y. 17300160.

[78] M. Ciemny, M. Kurcinski, K. Kamel, A. Kolinski, N. Alam, O. Schueler-Furman, S. Kmiecik, Protein-peptide docking: opportunities and challenges, Drug Discov. Today 23 (8) (2018) 1530–1537, https://doi.org/10.1016/j.drudis.2018.05.006. 29733895.

[79] Z. Zsoldos, D. Reid, A. Simon, S.B. Sadjad, A.P. Johnson, eHiTS: a new fast, exhaustive flexible ligand docking system, J. Mol. Graph. Model. 26 (1) (2007) 198–212, https://doi.org/10.1016/j.jmgm.2006.06.002. 16860582.

[80] A. Kahraman, R.J. Morris, R.A. Laskowski, J.M. Thornton, Shape variation in protein binding pockets and their ligands, J. Mol. Biol. 368 (1) (2007) 283–301, https://doi.org/10.1016/j.jmb.2007.01.086. 17337005.

[81] I. Schechter, Mapping of the active site of proteases in the 1960s and rational design of inhibitors/drugs in the 1990s, Curr. Protein Pept. Sci. 6 (6) (2005) 501–512, https://doi.org/10.2174/138920305774933286. 16381600.

[82] B.S. DeDecker, Allosteric drugs: thinking outside the active-site box, Chem. Biol. 7 (5) (2000) 103–107, https://doi.org/10.1016/S1074-5521(00)00115-0. 10801477.

[83] M. Zuercher, Structure-based drug design: exploring the proper filling of apolar pockets at enzyme active sites, J. Org. Chem. 73 (12) (2008) 4345–4361, https://doi.org/10.1021/jo800527n. 18510366.

[84] R. Powers, Comparison of protein active site structures for functional annotation of proteins and drug design, Proteins 65 (1) (2006) 124–135, https://doi.org/10.1002/prot.21092. 16862592.

[85] J. Yang, A. Roy, Y. Zhang, Protein-ligand binding site recognition using complementary binding-specific substructure comparison and sequence profile alignment, Bioinformatics 29 (2013) 2588–2595.

[86] U. Rester, From virtuality to reality – virtual screening in lead discovery and lead optimization: a medicinal chemistry perspective, Curr. Opin. Drug Discov. Devel. 11 (4) (2008) 559–568. 18600572.

[87] J.M. Rollinger, H. Stuppner, T. Langer, Virtual screening for the discovery of bioactive natural products, in: Natural Compounds as Drugs Volume I. Progress in Drug Research. Fortschritte der Arzneimittelforschung. Progrès des Recherches Pharmaceutiques, Progress in Drug Research, vol. 65, Springer, 2008, p. 211, https://doi.org/10.1007/978-3-7643-8117-2_6. 213–49, ISBN 978-3-7643-8098-4. PMC7124045. PMID 18084917.

[88] W.P. Walters, M.T. Stahl, M.A. Murcko, Virtual screening – an overview, Drug Discov. Today 3 (4) (1998) 160–178, https://doi.org/10.1016/S1359-6446(97)01163-X.

[89] C. McInnes, Virtual screening strategies in drug discovery, Curr. Opin. Chem. Biol. 11 (5) (2007) 494–502, https://doi.org/10.1016/j.cbpa.2007.08.033. 17936059.

[90] K. Santana, L.D. do Nascimento, A. Lima e Lima, V. Damasceno, C. Nahum, R.C. Braga, J. Lameira, Applications of virtual screening in bioprospecting: facts, shifts, and perspectives to explore the chemo-structural diversity of natural products, Front. Chem. 9 (2021), 662688, https://doi.org/10.3389/fchem.2021.662688 (ISSN 2296-2646. PMC8117418. PMID 33996755).

[91] H. Sun, Pharmacophore-based virtual screening, Curr. Med. Chem. 15 (10) (2008) 1018–1024, https://doi.org/10.2174/092986708784049630. 18393859.

[92] P. Willet, J.M. Barnard, G.M. Downs, Chemical similarity searching, J. Chem. Inf. Comput. Sci. 38 (6) (1998) 983–996, https://doi.org/10.1021/ci9800211.

[93] T.S. Rush, J.A. Grant, L. Mosyak, A. Nicholls, A shape-based 3-D scaffold hopping method and its application to a bacterial protein-protein interaction, J. Med. Chem. 48 (5) (2005) 1489–1495, https://doi.org/10.1021/jm040163o. 15743191.

[94] P.J. Ballester, I. Westwood, N. Laurieri, E. Sim, W.G. Richards, Prospective virtual screening with Ultrafast Shape Recognition: the identification of novel inhibitors of arylamine N-acetyltransferases, J. R. Soc. Interface 7 (43) (2010) 335–342, https://doi.org/10.1098/rsif.2009.0170. PMC2842611 19586957.

[95] A. Kumar, K.Y. Zhang, Advances in the development of shape similarity methods and their application in drug discovery, Front. Chem. 6 (2018) 315, https://doi.org/10.3389/fchem.2018.00315. PMC6068280 30090808.

[96] R.T. Kroemer, Structure-based drug design: docking and scoring, Curr. Protein Pept. Sci. 8 (4) (2007) 312–328, https://doi.org/10.2174/138920307781369382. 17696866.

[97] C.N. Cavasotto, A.J. Orry, Ligand docking and structure-based virtual screening in drug discovery, Curr. Top. Med. Chem. 7 (10) (2007) 1006–1014, https://doi.org/10.2174/156802607780906753. 1750893.

[98] A.J. Kooistra, H.F. Vischer, D. McNaught-Flores, R. Leurs, I.J. de Esch, C. de Graaf, Function-specific virtual screening for GPCR ligands using a combined scoring method, Sci. Rep. 6 (2016) 28288, https://doi.org/10.1038/srep28288. PMC4919634 27339552.

[99] J.J. Irwin, B.K. Shoichet, M.M. Mysinger, N. Huang, F. Colizzi, P. Wassam, Y. Cao, Automated docking screens: a feasibility study, J. Med. Chem. 52 (18) (2009) 5712–5720, https://doi.org/10.1021/jm9006966. PMC2745826 19719084.

[100] J.A. Grant, M.A. Gallard, B.T. Pickup, A fast method of molecular shape comparison: a simple application of a Gaussian description of molecular shape, J. Comput. Chem. 17 (1996) 1653–1666, https://doi.org/10.1002/(SICI)1096-987X(19961115)17:14<1653.

[101] A. Roy, J. Skolnick, LIGSIFT: an open-source tool for ligand structural alignment and virtual screening, Bioinformatics 31 (4) (2015) 539–544, https://doi.org/10.1093/bioinformatics/btu692. PMC4325547 25336501.

[102] H. Li, K.S. Leung, P.J. Ballester, M.H. Wong, istar: a web platform for large-scale protein-ligand docking, PLoS One 9 (1) (2014), e85678, https://doi.org/10.1371/journal.pone.0085678. PMC3901662 24475049.

[103] H. Zhou, J. Skolnick, FINDSITE(comb): a threading/structure-based, proteomic-scale virtual ligand screening approach, J. Chem. Inf. Model. 53 (1) (2013) 230–240, https://doi.org/10.1021/ci300510n. PMC3557555 23240691.

[104] A. Gaulton, L.J. Bellis, A.P. Bento, J. Chambers, M. Davies, A. Hersey, Y. Light, S. McGlinchey, D. Michalovich, B. Al-Lazikani, J.P. Overington, ChEMBL: a large-scale bioactivity database for drug discovery, Nucleic Acids Res. 40 (Database issue) (2012) D1100–D1107, https://doi.org/10.1093/nar/gkr777. PMC3245175 21948594.

[105] D.S. Wishart, C. Knox, A.C. Guo, S. Shrivastava, M. Hassanali, P. Stothard, Z. Chang, J. Woolsey, DrugBank: a comprehensive resource for in silico drug discovery and exploration, Nucleic Acids Res. 34 (Database issue) (2006) D668–D672, https://doi.org/10.1093/nar/gkj067. PMC1347430 16381955.

[106] M. Réau, F. Langenfeld, J.F. Zagury, N. Lagarde, M. Montes, Decoys selection in benchmarking datasets: overview and perspectives, Front. Pharmacol. 9 (2018) 11, https://doi.org/10.3389/fphar.2018.00011. PMC5787549 29416509.
[107] I. Wallach, A. Heifets, Most ligand-based classification benchmarks reward memorization rather than generalization, J. Chem. Inf. Model. 58 (5) (2018) 916–932, https://doi.org/10.1021/acs.jcim.7b00403. 29698607.
[108] F. Ballante, G.R. Marshall, An automated strategy for binding-pose selection and docking assessment in structure-based drug design, J. Chem. Inf. Model. 56 (1) (2016) 54–72, https://doi.org/10.1021/acs.jcim.5b00603. 26682916.
[109] F. Ballante, Protein-ligand docking in drug design: performance assessment and binding-pose selection. *Rational drug design*, Methods Mol. Biol. 1824 (2018) 67–88, https://doi.org/10.1007/978-1-4939-8630-9_5 (ISBN 978-1-4939-8629-3. ISSN 1940-6029. PMID 3003940).
[110] G. Klebe, T. Mietzner, A fast and efficient method to generate biologically relevant conformations, J. Comput. Aided Mol. Des. 8 (5) (1994) 583–606, https://doi.org/10.1007/BF00123667. 7876902.
[111] N.M. Cerqueira, N.F. Bras, P.A. Fernandes, M.J. Ramos, MADAMM: a multistaged docking with an automated molecular modeling protocol, Proteins 74 (1) (2009) 192–206, https://doi.org/10.1002/prot.22146. 18618708.
[112] M. Totrov, R. Abagyan, Flexible ligand docking to multiple receptor conformations: a practical alternative, Curr. Opin. Struct. Biol. 18 (2) (2008) 178–184, https://doi.org/10.1016/j.sbi.2008.01.004. PMC2396190 18302984.
[113] C. Hartmann, I. Antes, T. Lengauer, Docking and scoring with alternative side-chain conformations, Proteins 74 (3) (2009) 712–726, https://doi.org/10.1002/prot.22189. 18704939.
[114] R.D. Taylor, P.J. Jewsbury, J.W. Essex, FDS: flexible ligand and receptor docking with a continuum solvent model and soft-core energy function, J. Comput. Chem. 24 (13) (2003) 1637–1656, https://doi.org/10.1002/jcc.10295. 12926007.
[115] M.A. Murcko, Computational methods to predict binding free energy in ligand-receptor complexes, J. Med. Chem. 38 (26) (1995) 4953–4967, https://doi.org/10.1021/jm00026a001. 8544170.
[116] J.P. Arcon, A.G. Turjanski, M.A. Martí, S. Forli, Biased docking for protein–ligand pose prediction, in: F. Ballante (Ed.), Protein-Ligand Interactions and Drug Design, Methods in Molecular Biology, vol. 2266, Springer US, New York, NY, 2021, pp. 39–72, ISBN: 978-1-0716-1209-5, https://doi.org/10.1007/978-1-0716-1209-5_3.
[117] H. Gohlke, M. Hendlich, G. Klebe, Knowledge-based scoring function to predict protein-ligand interactions, J. Mol. Biol. 295 (2) (2000) 337–356, https://doi.org/10.1006/jmbi.1999.3371.
[118] B.D. Bursulaya, M. Totrov, R. Abagyan, C.L. Brooks, Comparative study of several algorithms for flexible ligand docking, J. Comput. Aided Mol. Des. 17 (11) (2003) 755–763, https://doi.org/10.1023/B:JCAM.0000017496.76572.6f. 15072435.
[119] B.K. Shoichet, I.D. Kuntz, D.L. Bodian, Molecular docking using shape descriptors, J. Comput. Chem. 13 (3) (2004) 380–397, https://doi.org/10.1002/jcc.540130311.
[120] W. Cai, X. Shao, B. Maigret, Protein-ligand recognition using spherical harmonic molecular surfaces: towards a fast and efficient filter for large virtual throughput screening, J. Mol. Graph. Model. 20 (4) (2002) 313–328, https://doi.org/10.1016/S1093-3263(01)00134-6. 11858640.
[121] R.J. Morris, R.J. Najmanovich, A. Kahraman, J.M. Thornton, Real spherical harmonic expansion coefficients as 3D shape descriptors for protein binding pocket and ligand comparisons, Bioinformatics 21 (10) (2005) 2347–2355, https://doi.org/10.1093/bioinformatics/bti337. 15728116.
[122] S.-Y. Huang, X. Zou, Advances and challenges in protein-ligand docking, Int. J. Mol. Sci. 2010 (11) (2010) 3016–3034.
[123] I.A. Guedes, C.S. Magalhães, L.E. Dardenne, Receptor-ligand molecular docking, Biophys. Rev. 6 (1) (2014) 75–87, https://doi.org/10.1007/s12551-013-0130-2.
[124] J. Schlosser, M. Rarey, Beyond the virtual screening paradigm: structure-based searching for new lead compounds, J. Chem. Inf. Model. 2009 (49) (2009) 800–809.
[125] A.R. Leach, Ligand docking to proteins with discrete side-chain flexibility, J. Mol. Biol. 1994 (235) (1994) 345–356.

[126] P.T. Lang, S.R. Brozell, S. Mukherjee, et al., DOCK 6: combining techniques to model RNA-small molecule complexes, RNA 2009 (15) (2009) 1219–1230.

[127] G. Wu, D.H. Robertson, C.L. Brooks, M. Vieth, Detailed analysis of grid-based molecular docking: a case study of CDOCKER?A CHARMm-based MD docking algorithm, J. Comput. Chem. 2003 (24) (2003) 1549–1562.

[128] J.-P. Changeux, S. Edelstein, Conformational selection or induced-fit? 50 years of debate resolved, Biol. Reprod. (2011), https://doi.org/10.3410/B3-19. F1000.

[129] C.J. Tsai, B. Ma, R. Nussinov, Folding and binding cascades: shifts in energy landscapes, Proc. Natl. Acad. Sci. U. S. A. 96 (1999) 9970–9972.

[130] G. Kar, O. Keskin, A. Gursoy, R. Nussinov, Allostery and population shift in drug discovery, Curr. Opin. Pharmacol. 10 (2010) 715–722, https://doi.org/10.1016/j.coph.2010.09.002.

[131] M. Petukh, S. Stefl, E. Alexov, The role of protonation states in ligand-receptor recognition and binding, Curr. Pharm. Des. 19 (2013) 4182–4190.

[132] M.Y. Mizutani, Y. Takamatsu, T. Ichinose, et al., Effective handling of induced-fit motion in flexible docking, Proteins 63 (2006) 878–891, https://doi.org/10.1002/prot.20931.

[133] S.B. Nabuurs, M. Wagener, J. de Vlieg, A flexible approach to induced fit docking, J. Med. Chem. 50 (2007) 6507–6518, https://doi.org/10.1021/jm070593p.

[134] J. Meiler, D. Baker, ROSETTALIGAND: protein-small molecule docking with full side-chain flexibility, Proteins 65 (2006) 538–548, https://doi.org/10.1002/prot.21086.

[135] V. Schnecke, L. Kuhn, Virtual screening with solvation and ligand induced complementarity, Perspect. Drug Discov. Des. 20 (2000) 171–190, https://doi.org/10.1023/A:1008737207775.

[136] J. Desmet, I.A. Wilson, M. De Joniau, et al., Computation of the binding of fully flexible peptides to proteins with flexible side chains, FASEB J. 11 (1997) 164–172.

[137] M. Nowosielski, M. Hoffmann, A. Kuron, et al., The MM2QM tool for combining docking, molecular dynamics, molecular mechanics, and quantum mechanics†, J. Comput. Chem. 34 (2013) 750–756, https://doi.org/10.1002/jcc.23192.

[138] A.H. Maghsoudi, F. Khodagholi, H. Hadi-Alijanvand, et al., Homology modeling, docking, molecular dynamics simulation, and structural analyses of coxsakievirus B3 2A protease: an enzyme involved in the pathogenesis of inflammatory myocarditis, Int. J. Biol. Macromol. 49 (2011) 487–492, https://doi.org/10.1016/j.ijbiomac.2011.05.023.

[139] P. Sokkar, V. Sathis, M. Ramachandran, Computational modeling on the recognition of the HRE motif by HIF-1: molecular docking and molecular dynamics studies, J. Mol. Model. 18 (2011) 1691–1700, https://doi.org/10.1007/s00894-011-1150-0.

[140] R.S. Armen, J. Chen, C.L. Brooks, An evaluation of explicit receptor flexibility in molecular docking using molecular dynamics and torsion angle molecular dynamics, J. Chem. Theory Comput. 5 (2009) 2909–2923, https://doi.org/10.1021/ct900262t.

[141] V. Venkatraman, D.W. Ritchie, Flexible protein docking refinement using pose-dependent normal mode analysis, Proteins 80 (2012) 2262–2274, https://doi.org/10.1002/prot.24115.

[142] M. Dietzen, E. Zotenko, A. Hildebrandt, T. Lengauer, On the applicability of elastic network normal modes in small-molecule docking, J. Chem. Inf. Model. 52 (2012) 844–856, https://doi.org/10.1021/ci2004847.

[143] C. Beier, M. Zacharias, Tackling the challenges posed by target flexibility in drug design, Expert Opin. Drug Discovery 5 (2010) 347–359, https://doi.org/10.1517/17460441003713462.

[144] M. Rueda, G. Bottegoni, R. Abagyan, Consistent improvement of cross-docking results using binding site ensembles generated with elastic network normal modes, J. Chem. Inf. Model. 49 (2009) 716–725, https://doi.org/10.1021/ci8003732.

[145] N. Brooijmans, I.D. Kuntz, Molecular recognition and docking algorithms, Annu. Rev. Biophys. Biomol. Struct. 32 (2003) 335–373, https://doi.org/10.1146/annurev.biophys.32.110601.142532.

[146] E.M. Novoa, L.R. de Pouplana, X. Barril, M. Orozco, Ensemble docking from homology models, J. Chem. Theory Comput. 6 (2010) 2547–2557, https://doi.org/10.1021/ct100246y.

[147] O. Sperandio, L. Mouawad, E. Pinto, et al., How to choose relevant multiple receptor conformations for virtual screening: a test case of Cdk2 and normal mode analysis, Eur. Biophys. J. 39 (2010) 1365–1372, https://doi.org/10.1007/s00249-010-0592-0.

[148] M.L. Teodoro, G.N. Phillips Jr., L.E. Kavraki, Understanding protein flexibility through dimensionality reduction, J. Comput. Biol. 10 (2003) 617–634, https://doi.org/10.1089/10665270360688228.
[149] M.L. Teodoro, L.E. Kavraki, Conformational flexibility models for the receptor in structure based drug design, Curr. Pharm. Des. 9 (2003) 1635–1648.
[150] G.M. Keserû, I. Kolossváry, Fully flexible low-mode docking: application to induced fit in HIV integrase, J. Am. Chem. Soc. 123 (2001) 12708–12709.
[151] R. Wang, Y. Lu, S. Wang, Comparative evaluation of 11 scoring functions for molecular docking, J. Med. Chem. 46 (2003) 2287–2303, https://doi.org/10.1021/jm0203783.
[152] E. Yuriev, P.A. Ramsland, Latest developments in molecular docking: 2010–2011 in review, J. Mol. Recognit. 26 (2013) 215–239, https://doi.org/10.1002/jmr.2266.
[153] K.L. Damm-Ganamet, R.D. Smith, J.B. Dunbar, et al., CSAR benchmark exercise 2011–2012: evaluation of results from docking and relative ranking of blinded congeneric series, J. Chem. Inf. Model. 53 (2013) 1853–1870.
[154] H.L.N. De Amorim, R.A. Caceres, P.A. Netz, Linear interaction energy (LIE) method in lead discovery and optimization, Curr. Drug Targets 9 (2008) 1100–1105.
[155] W.F. De Azevedo Jr., R. Dias, Computational methods for calculation of ligand-binding affinity, Curr. Drug Targets 9 (2008) 1031–1039.
[156] M.D. Eldridge, C.W. Murray, T.R. Auton, et al., Empirical scoring functions: I. The development of a fast empirical scoring function to estimate the binding affinity of ligands in receptor complexes, J. Comput. Aided Mol. Des. 11 (1997) 425–445.
[157] R.A. Friesner, J.L. Banks, R.B. Murphy, et al., Glide: a new approach for rapid, accurate docking and scoring. 1. Method and assessment of docking accuracy, J. Med. Chem. 47 (2004) 1739–1749, https://doi.org/10.1021/jm0306430.
[158] R. Vijayakrishnan, Structure-based drug design and modern medicine, J. Postgrad. Med. 55 (2009) 301–304.
[159] T.T. Talele, S.A. Khedkar, A.C. Rigby, Successful applications of computer aided drug discovery: moving drugs from concept to the clinic, Curr. Top. Med. Chem. 10 (2010) 127–141.
[160] J.H. Van Drie, Computer-aided drug design: the next 20 years, J. Comput. Aided Mol. Des. 21 (2007) 591–601.
[161] F. Bartoli, D. Cavaleri, B. Bachi, F. Moretti, I. Riboldi, C. Crocamo, G. Carrà, Repurposed drugs as adjunctive treatments for mania and bipolar depression: a meta-review and critical appraisal of meta-analyses of randomized placebo-controlled trials, J. Psychiatr. Res. 143 (2021) 230–238, https://doi.org/10.1016/j.jpsychires.2021.09.018. 34509090.
[162] S. Nabirotchkin, A.E. Peluffo, P. Rinaudo, J. Yu, R. Hajj, D. Cohen, Next-generation drug repurposing using human genetics and network biology, Curr. Opin. Pharmacol. 51 (2020) 78–92, https://doi.org/10.1016/j.coph.2019.12.004. 31982325.
[163] T.T. Ashburn, K.B. Thor, Drug repositioning: identifying and developing new uses for existing drugs, Nat. Rev. Drug Discov. 3 (8) (2004) 673–683, https://doi.org/10.1038/nrd1468. 15286734.
[164] G. Das, T. Das, N. Chowdhury, D. Chatterjee, A. Bagchi, Z. Ghosh, Repurposed drugs and nutraceuticals targeting envelope protein: a possible therapeutic strategy against COVID-19, Genomics 113 (1 Pt 2) (2021) 1129–1140, https://doi.org/10.1016/j.ygeno.2020.11.009. Epub 2020 Nov 13 33189776.
[165] S.H. Sleigh, C.L. Barton, Repurposing strategies for therapeutics, Pharm. Med. 24 (3) (2012) 151–159, https://doi.org/10.1007/BF03256811.
[166] V.P. Kale, H. Habib, R. Chitren, M. Patel, K.C. Pramanik, S.C. Jonnalagadda, et al., Old drugs, new uses: drug repurposing in hematological malignancies, Semin. Cancer Biol. 68 (2021) 242–248, https://doi.org/10.1016/j.semcancer.2020.03.005. PMID 32151704.
[167] R. Kumar, S. Harilal, S.V. Gupta, J. Jose, D.G. Thomas Parambi, M.S. Uddin, et al., Exploring the new horizons of drug repurposing: a vital tool for turning hard work into smart work, Eur. J. Med. Chem. 182 (2019), 111602, https://doi.org/10.1016/j.ejmech.2019.111602. PMC7127402 31421629.

CHAPTER 11

Drug discovery and repositioning for glioblastoma multiforme and low-grade astrocytic tumors

Asmita Dasgupta, Sanjukta Ghosh, Kastro Kalidass, and Shabnam Farisha
Department of Biochemistry and Molecular Biology, Pondicherry University, Pondicherry, India

Abstract

Among the tumors of the central nervous system (CNS), astrocytic tumors, including the high-grade, glioblastoma multiforme and low-grade astrocytomas, form a significant class that is often associated with poor prognosis and dismal patient outcome mostly due to the inherent molecular complexity of these tumors. With the recent World Health Organization 2021 classification for the tumors of the CNS adopting molecular diagnosis alongside the classical histopathological approach, the search for better therapy has taken a more definitive molecular approach. Hence, pharmacogenomic analysis, molecular network building, meta-analysis of the already available therapeutic responses, virtual screening, and drug repositioning are being significantly exploited as strategies for drug discovery for astrocytic tumors. Each of these approaches has been discussed with examples in the context of search for more effective therapies against astrocytic tumors. Among these approaches, the shortest route to a more effective drug is expected to come from drug repositioning. Drug repositioning for astrocytic tumors is more significantly aiming to use anticancer therapies originally approved or designed for cancers in organs other than the brain. Overall, there is still a lack of any significantly successful stride in identifying better therapies for astrocytic tumors, but the extensive number of ongoing studies remains a harbinger of hope for better therapeutics in the future.

Abbreviations

AA	anaplastic astrocytoma
ATRX	α thalassemia mental retardation X-linked
AUC-ROC	area under the receiver operating characteristics
BBB	blood-brain barrier
BED-ROC	Boltzmen-enhanced discrimination of ROC
BRAF	v-raf murine sarcoma viral oncogene homolog B
CADD	computer-aided drug design
CADM1	cell adhesion molecule1
CCNU	chloroethyl cyclohexyl nitrosourea
CDK4	cyclin-dependent kinase 4
CircNFIX	circular RNAs nuclear factor IX
CNS	central nervous system
CSCs	cancer stem cells
CTLA-4	T-lymphocyte-associated antigen4
D-2-HG	D-2-hydroxyglutarate

Computational Methods in Drug Discovery and Repurposing for Cancer Therapy
https://doi.org/10.1016/B978-0-443-15280-1.00013-3

EGCG epigallocatechin-3-gallate
EGFR epidermal growth factor receptor
ER endoplasmic reticulum
FDA Food and Drug Administration
FGF fibroblast growth factor
GBM glioblastoma multiforme
GC-GBM giant cell glioblastoma
GRP78 glucose-regulated protein 78
GSCs glioma stem cells
HGG high-grade glioma
HH/GLI hedgehog/glioma-associated oncogene homolog
HuR human antigen R
IC50 half-maximal inhibitory concentration
IDH isocitrate dehydrogenase
JAK Janus kinase
LGG low-grade glioma
METK met tyrosine protein kinase
mTOR mammalian target of rapamycin
O6GB O6-benzylguanine
OS overall survival
PCV procarbazine hydrochloride lomustine (CCNU) and vincristine sulfate
PDGFRα platelet-derived growth factor receptor alpha
PFS-6 6-month progression-free survival
PI3K phosphoinositide-3-kinase
QSAR quantitative structure-activity relationship
RB1 retinoblastoma susceptibility gene
RCT randomized clinical trial
RMSD root mean square deviation
RTKIs receptor tyrosine kinase inhibitors
SMO smoothened
SOC standard of care
TCGA the cancer genome atlas
TERT telomerase reverse transcriptase
TIICs tumor-infiltrating immune cells
TMZ temozolomide
TSC trans sodium crocetinate
VEGF vascular endothelial growth factor
VHL von Hippel-Lindau syndrome
WHO World Health Organization
WIP WASP-interacting protein

1. Introduction

Astrocytic tumors, though not one of the most common cancers, are definitely one of the leading causes of cancer-related deaths across the world. The dismal survival outcome observed in astrocytic tumor patients stems from the inherent complexity of the tumor phenotype. The heterogeneity within the astrocytic tumor classes with respect to their molecular phenotypes makes them difficult to diagnose correctly and treat with precision, making the prognostic outcome unfavorable for the patients. The most aggressive of these tumors with maximal dismal prognosis is glioblastoma multiforme (GBM) featuring tumor characterized by cellular and nuclear atypia, anaplasia, mitotic features, necrosis, and vascularization. The approved standard of care (SOC) is surgery, and thereafter radiation therapy many a times in combination with chemotherapy by means of an oral alkylating agent called temozolomide (TMZ). Classically, based on their clinical presentations, the high-grade gliomas (HGGs) as GBMs have been classified as primary or secondary with the secondary GBMs resulting from a preexisting lower-grade tumor after malignant progression while the primary GBMs are presented as advanced cancer at their first presentation from the outset [1]. Other than this, there are low-grade gliomas (LGGs), a group of diverse primary brain tumors, which include the World Health Organization (WHO)-classified grade I tumors that do not have any of the high-grade features, and grade II tumors that are characterized by just the presence of cytologic atypia. These LGGs include the WHO grade I tumors as subependymal giant cell astrocytoma and pilocytic astrocytoma and WHO grade II tumors as diffuse astrocytoma, pilomyxoid astrocytoma, and pleomorphic xanthoastrocytoma [2]. Treatment options for LGGs include surgery, radiation therapy, and chemotherapy or a combination of these based on the individual tumor presentation and patient characteristics. Risk factors include the age of the patient being above 40 years and the tumor size of 6 cm or more, especially when it crosses the midline and the patient shows neurological deficits [3].

Most of the malignant brain tumors affect mainly the adult population (between 20 and 60 years), especially the males older than 40 years, and the likelihood of the disease incidence in males is found to be 2.3 males to every 1 female [4–6]. The most aggressive of the astrocytic tumors is the WHO grade IV type of astrocytoma represented by 13.6% out of all malignant tumors of the brain, is common in adults with an incidence rate of 6.95 per 100,000, and has poor prognosis with a median overall survival (OS) of 12–14 months. Diffuse astrocytoma, WHO grade II type, is the second most prevalent brain tumor with a rate of 3.76 per 100,000 individuals, which is 7.9% of all brain tumors with an incidence rate of 0.57 per 100,000, and has slightly better prognosis with the rate of survival of the person diagnosed is at least 15 years [7]. Primary glioblastoma occurs most commonly in elderly patients with the median age of diagnosis ~65 years, and prognosis is poor with rapid progression and median OS of 16–18 months. Secondary GBM, which is only 5% of the total GBM incidence, has a lower median age of incidence ~45 years [1,6,8]. The incidence rate of malignant glioma with poor OS is approximately 4.7 per 100,000 individuals, with a significant male dominance determined by the male steroid hormones that lead to tumor progression [9,10], while the incidence of benign tumor is usually common in females [5]. However, recent studies have reported that a global trend in the incidence of pediatric

CNS tumors where the astrocytic type of tumors specifically called pilocytic astrocytoma is of greater severity followed by medulloblastoma, craniopharyngioma, and ependymoma, all of which can be seen particularly in the data from countries, such as Sweden, Germany, Brazil, Canada, Morocco, Korea, and India, but oligodendrogliomas and lymphomas were rare in children [5,11,12].

Most of the recent successes of cancer therapies have been achieved with the molecular approach to therapeutics. With the sequence of the human genome published at the turn of this millennium, precision therapy against tumors has become possible and drug discovery has taken a more resolute molecular approach. Human Protein Atlas, the Human HapMap Project, the Human Metabolome database, and other omics consortiums have contributed to the process [13–15]. Extensive tumor genomic data have accumulated since programs, such as The Cancer Genome Atlas (TCGA) by the National Cancer Institute, NIH, USA, and International Cancer Genomic Consortium (ICGC) led by Cancer Research, UK, have taken up the genomic analysis of tumors. TCGA has assessed 206 GBM cases. Based on this analysis, GBM subtypes have been classified as classical, mesenchymal, and pro-neural defined by the presence of epidermal growth factor receptor (EGFR), NF1, and PDGFRA/IDH1 mutations, respectively. More than 40% of GBM cases have mutations in chromatin-modifier regions with the frequently mutated genes, including TP53, PIK3R1, PIK3CA, IDH1, PTEN, RB1, and LZTR1 [1]. The lower-grade astrocytoma for which TCGA assessed some 293 cases is defined by three subtypes correlating with patient outcomes. These subtypes are all based on the status of IDH and 1p/19q loci and their combinations. Thus the subtypes are those with both IDH1 mutant and 1p/19q deletion, IDH mutant but without this 1p/19q deletion, and those with IDH wild type [16,17].

However, the integration of the genomic data to the tumor classification has happened only recently for the tumors of the central nervous system (CNS) with the updating of the WHO Classification of Tumors in 2021, which took into account the inherent genetic complexities in these tumors by the inclusion of molecular characteristics [18]. Aside from tumor classification, this opens up avenues for better understanding of the tumor mechanisms, identification of novel therapeutic targets, and thus more refined therapeutic strategies that can be expected to accelerate drug discovery against astrocytic tumors. This also enables the inclusion of the astrocytic tumor patients in clinical trials that approach therapy from the tumor's molecular perspective [8]. Concurrently, precision methods in protein structure determination have taken a long stride with improved resolution, enhanced scope of analysis and visualization through NMR, X-ray crystallography, and cryo-electron microscopy. In parallel, the evolution of algorithms in the tools for protein structure prediction by homology modeling and simulation also improved in accuracy, and overall, these have made the in silico approaches to drug discovery a very attractive option. Virtual screening followed by molecular dynamic simulations can easily screen large databases of either natural or synthetic molecules for appropriate candidate drugs which can shorten the bench-to-bedside journey for new molecules entering clinical trials for these almost fatal cancers. Another even quicker and more effective in silico approach is screening the drug molecule databases for candidate molecules to check their possibility of binding on novel therapeutic targets. Direct preclinical trials for off-label use can also be initiated based on the well-formed hypothesis on the possible efficacy of known drug molecules for the remission of fatal cancers such as astrocytic tumors. Either of the two ways would initiate a process of off-label use of known drug molecules that have already gone through clinical trials for some other therapeutic ends and open possibilities of drug repurposing toward astrocytic tumors.

In the following sections, we first discuss briefly the existing therapeutic options for astrocytic tumors. This is followed by an elaborate discussion on the progress made in recent times with drug discovery and drug repurposing for glioblastoma and the low-grade astrocytic tumors using pharmacogenomic analysis, network analysis, quantitative structure–activity relationships (QSARs), and meta-analysis, to identify candidate drug targets and their corresponding ligands. Virtual screening is an in silico strategy used to screen for candidate drugs from small-molecule databases to identify novel ligands to targets that are either new or already in use. Virtual screening of candidate drugs for astrocytic tumor therapeutics is discussed in detail in a subsequent section. Finally, we round up our perspective on in silico approaches to drug discovery against astrocytic tumors with a discussion of the clinical trials that have been completed with repurposed or repositioned drugs against astrocytic tumor therapy.

2. Approved therapeutics for astrocytic tumors

Currently there are a limited number of approved regimens for treating Astrocytic tumors as mentioned on the National Cancer Institute [19] webpage [20] (https://www.cancer.gov/about-cancer/treatment/drugs/brain). They include: (1) oral and injectable chemotherapeutics—everolimus, belzutifan, TMZ, lomustine, carmustine, carmustine implant, and PCV combination [procarbazine hydrochloride, lomustine [chloroethyl cyclohexyl nitrosourea (CCNU)] and vincristine sulfate]; (2) targeted therapies—bevacizumab, bevacizumab-AWWB, and bevacizumab-BVZR; and (3) tumor treatment fields [21]. In this section, the oral and injectable chemotherapeutics only would be discussed. Chemotherapy is a complementary therapy provided to patients with residual neoplasm after surgery or radiation. It can also be a concurrent therapy with radiation. It is provided in three forms: oral administration, intravenous injection, and implantation. Mostly, these drugs are either alkylating agents or specific mechanistic inhibitors and show a range of toxicities. Many times these drugs lead to tumor resistance necessitating better therapeutics for astrocytic tumors. The approved drugs and their toxicities are listed in Table 1 and briefly discussed in this section.

Table 1 List of approved drugs for astrocytic tumors and their common toxicities.

Treatment (initial year of approval)	Approved for (WHO grade 2016)	Route of administration	Mechanism of action	Common toxicities	Overall survival	References (randomized clinical trial)
Temozolomide (2005)	**Grade III and IV**	Oral	Methylation of DNA, mainly at O6 and N7 of guanine	Hematologic toxicity (16%): Thrombocytopenia (12%), leukopenia (7%), neutropenia (7%)	14.6–16.1 Months	[22]
Carmustine (BCNU) (1977)	Grade IV Recurrent GBM	Intra-venous	Nonspecific alkylation of nucleic acids	Pulmonary toxicity (<30%), ocular toxicity (>10%), bone marrow suppression (>10%)	11.75 Months	[23]
Carmustine wafer implant (1996, 2003)	**Grade IV** Recurrent GBM	Implant	Nonspecific alkylation of nucleic acids	Wound healing complications (12%), intracranial Infection (1%–10%), cerebral edema (1%–10%)	13.9 Months	[24]
Lomustine (1976)	**Grade III/ IV** Recurrent GBM	Oral	Nonspecific alkylation of nucleic acid.	Hematologic toxicity (49.7%)	11.5 Months	[25]
Everolimus (2009)	**Grade I**	Oral	mTOR inhibitor	mouth ulceration, stomatitis, convulsion, pyrexia	Not known	[26]
Belzutifan (2021)	Grade I	Oral	HIF-2α inhibitor	Anemia and fatigue	Not known	[27]

2.1 Alkylating agents

Alkylating agents that are more accepted in glioma therapy are TMZ, lomustine, and carmustine. Approved in the year 2005, TMZ is an oral drug that is cytotoxic due to nonspecific DNA methylation mostly at the O6 and N7 positions of guanine residues. TMZ is the current gold standard for the treatment of GBM. It is also effective for patients with refractory anaplastic astrocytoma. Resection of tumor, followed by concurrent TMZ and radiation therapy for 6 weeks and adjuvant therapy of TMZ for further 6 months, is the current SOC for GBM patients. It is also recommended for refractory anaplastic astrocytoma and newly diagnosed GBM [21,28]. 53.90% of patients show progression-free survival (PFS) at 6 months [22]. However, methylation by TMZ activates the methyl guanine methyl transferase (MGMT) DNA repair system; as a result, nearly 55% of GBM patients are TMZ resistant and also patients who show initial sensitivity and later acquire resistance to the drug. Other resistance mechanisms include the DNA repair system and autophagy [29]. This has led to the quest for newer or repurposed drugs/drug combination. For instance, TMZ can also be administered with O6-benzylguanine (O6GB) (NCT00613093), where O6GB is an O6-methylguanine-DNA methyltransferase inhibitor, and it increases the sensitivity of the drug-resistant cells to TMZ. However, according to a Phase II trial, it is not significantly effective in GBM patients with TMZ resistance. Nanoparticle-based drug delivery is also being tried to reduce TMZ resistance [30,31].

Another oral chemotherapeutic, lomustine or chloroethyl cyclohexyl nitrosourea (CCNU), is also a nonspecific alkylating agent, like TMZ, and thus crosslinks DNA and RNA to induce cytotoxicity in dividing cells leading to the death of tumor cells. Lomustine was approved by FDA in 1976 for HGG treatment [21,32]. In a randomized controlled trial (RCT) conducted in 1979, the median OS for this drug was reported to be 11.5 months [25]. Lomustine or carmustine (BCNU, *bis*-chloroethyl nitrosourea) alone or in combination with other chemotherapeutics, was the SOC following resection and/or radiation therapy till the early 21st century [21]. Lomustine currently is solely approved for recurrent HGGs [21,32]. CCNU is also a key component of PCV (P: procabazine, C: lomustine, and V: vincristine), a combination regimen approved by FDA for HGG treatment [33]. In an RCT that compared PCV treatment to TMZ treatment in patients with recurrent HGGs, there was no significant difference in PFS that was 3.6 months for PCV versus 4.7 months for TMZ, OS was recorded to be 6.7 for PCV versus 7.2 months for TMZ, and similarly, no significant difference in the quality of life and adverse events was observed. Hence, this regimen is less commonly prescribed compared to lomustine alone [34].

Carmustine or BCNU, an intravenous therapeutic, was approved in 1977 to treat HGGs [35]. In an RCT, the median OS of anaplastic glioma patients treated with carmustine was reported to be 11.75 months [23]. The mechanism of action of carmustine is similar to lomustine; it nonspecifically alkylates nucleic acid, leading to the crosslinking of

DNA and RNA. Pulmonary toxicity, ocular toxicity, and bone marrow suppression are the major toxicities reported due to this drug. Due to these reported toxicities and subsequent availability of alternate and more effective therapies, use of carmustine for the treatment of HGGs has decreased [21]. Carmustine wafer implants, a biodegradable polymer implanted in the cavities formed after the resection of tumors, were approved by FDA in 1996 for recurrent HGG treatment. It was also approved for new HGGs in 2003. This was intended to increase the efficacy and decrease the toxicity over intravenous carmustine [24,36]. However, it has not become the SOC, may due to its high expense, and reported high complications and challenges in handling the implant by operating room staffs [21].

2.2 Mechanistic inhibitors

Approved in 2009, everolimus is a mammalian target of rapamycin (mTOR) inhibitor used for the treatment of tuberous sclerosis complex, a genetic disease, that arises as a consequence of perpetual activation of mTOR leading to benign tumor growth in several organs, including brain. In a double-blind clinical trial, the group treated with everolimus showed 50% reduction of subependymal giant cell astrocytoma volume compared to the placebo leading to the approval of its use for grade I astrocytic tumors, tuberous sclerosis complex, and the benign subependymal giant cell astrocytoma [26]. Another mechanistic inhibitor that has been very newly approved is belzutifan, an inhibitor of HIF-2α developed by Peloton Therapeutics for treating von Hippel-Lindau syndrome (VHL) [37–39]. The VHL is an autosomal dominant disease, which is characterized by tumors, mostly benign in different parts of the body including the brain [40]. According to an ongoing (NCT03401788) clinical trial, 24 VHL patients with measurable CNS hemangioblastomas have been reported to have an overall response rate of 63% for these hemangioblastomas of CNS. Belzutifan shows side effects, such as anemia and fatigue [27].

3. Drug discovery approaches against astrocytic tumors

With the evolution of genomic and molecular profiling techniques, informed and guided therapeutics tailored against specific cancer genomic subtype have become possible. Several strategies have evolved toward the same and most start with a translational approach or patient-derived tumor cells/tissue. Workflows involve either performing the genomic, molecular, and pharmacological analyses directly from the patient-derived tissues followed by computational modeling to derive the genetic to pharmacological correlation based on the tumor cell's drug response profiles (Table 2) [41–43]. The workflow may also start with the secondary analysis of such primary genomic data already available with multiple repositories [44–47]. Other than these, a single predefined drug target or molecular pathway and their connectomes may be explored to derive novel

Table 2 Drug discovery against astrocytic tumors by *in silico* approaches.

Sl. No.	Methodology	Targets identified	Candidate drugs discovered	Experimentally validated candidates	Reference
1.	Molecular Network from Functional Genomics data	FoxM1, B-Myb, E2F2	Etoposide, Resveratrol, Monobenzone, Thioridazine, Methotrexate	TOP2A and PLK1 transcriptionally down-regulated in low-passage IDH1 mutant human tumor-derived TB98 cells after resveratrol exposure at nM concentrations.	[44]
2.	Meta-analysis of median overall survival and survival gain data of high-grade glioma patients	Topoisomerase II	Etoposide	None	[45]
3.	Computational model of brain endothelial cell signaling pathways	Therapeutic inhibition of AKT, Hif-1α, or cathepsin D	None	None	[46]
4.	Structure-activity relationship (SAR) and Molecular Docking	Human antigen R (HuR/ELAVL1)	SRI-42127	Inhibition of HuR dimerization	[48–50]
5.	QSAR, nanoscreen of 50,000 extracts for inhibition of HuR-induced anisotropy of TMR-labeled RNA followed by numerical simulations	Human antigen R (HuR/ELAVL1)	MS-444, dehydromutactin and okicenone	Inhibition of HuR dimerization	[51]

Continued

Table 2 Drug discovery against astrocytic tumors by *in silico* approaches—cont'd

Sl. No.	Methodology	Targets identified	Candidate drugs discovered	Experimentally validated candidates	Reference
6.	Construction of differentially expressed network, weighted gene correlation network (WGCNA), followed by identifying drug perturbations that reverse these dysregulations	Anaphase promoting complex, PDE9A, CAMK2G, MET kinase, CDK4/6, EGFR	Curcumin, proTAME, apcin, PDE9A inhibitor, W-13, V-4084, Kaempferol, PD-0332991, Dexamethasone, all-*trans*-retinoic acid, erlotinib	None	[47]
7.	Pharmacogenomic profiling using patient-derived glioma cultures	Pharmacological classes defined by p53 mutations and CDKN2A/B deletion	Proteasomal inhibitors	Bortezomib, and combinations	[41]
8.	Pharmacogenomic profiling using patient-derived short-term tumor-derived cultures including glioma	Pharmacological classes defined by EGFR/EGFRVIII amplifications compared to wild-type EGFR	EGFR inhibitors	Ibrutinib	[42]

therapeutic targets and/or drugs modulating the same [48–54]. All of these approaches require a subsequent preclinical validation of the candidate drug's remissive effects on the identified tumor subtype in either cultured cells or animal models with the xenograft of patient-derived tumor tissue before the proof of the principle is considered fulfilled and the drug can be proposed for clinical trials. Illustrative use of some of these strategies that have been recently applied to determine possible astrocytic tumor therapeutics is discussed.

3.1 Pharmacogenomic analysis

Pharmacogenomics is one of the finest evolving clinical tools in precision medicine that allows the clinician to understand how an individual patient's genetic background will affect the outcome of the treatment with an array of drugs either individually or in combinations and offer precise therapeutic guidelines according to the genetic variants [55]. Pharmacogenomic analysis thus increases the possibility of success of a trial drug by predefining the genetic backgrounds under which it would be most effective against a specific condition. This can help in the precise genomic definition of inclusion and exclusion criteria for a clinical trial increasing its chances of success [56]. In one of such global collaborative efforts to define the known and unknown pharmacological subclasses of GBM, genomic profiling was done for 100 patient-derived glioma cell cultures for mutations, copy number aberrations, DNA methylation, differential gene expression along with patient details, and tumor subtype. These cell cultures were next profiled for their pharmacological response with 1544 compounds with a range of doses and action for 72 h for 896 drug targets covering 116 mechanisms of action. The information was integrated into the genomic profile data followed by computational modeling to identify various active drug classes and their mechanism of action. The computational model thus built could inform about the key pathways associated with the drug response and possible combinatorial interventions based on the model-derived drug-pathway links. Mapping of the drug response of the glioma cell lines to the mechanism of action and molecular markers led to 51 distinct associations between drug classes and hallmark pathways. Of these, two mutually exclusive pharmacological classes could be defined from the differential sensitivity of glioma cell lines to the proteasomal inhibitors based on mutations in p53 and those with deletion of CDKN2A/B locus. These pharmacogenomic findings were subsequently validated in a smaller set of cell lines displaying a range of variability of mutations in these two loci, thus defining the distinct role of the p53 and cyclin-dependent kinase pathways in designing precision therapy against these tumors [41].

Proteasomal inhibitors induce apoptosis by accumulating ubiquitylated proteins leading to oxidative stress-induced mitochondrial dysfunction [57]. The pharmacogenomic analysis enabled the mechanistic classification of the proteasomal inhibitors as Bcl2 family inhibitors and p53 activators [41]. Based on the WHO 2021 classification of tumors that are associated with these molecular markers, it is speculated that these distinct classes of proteasomal inhibitors could be used in precision therapy for astrocytoma with IDH mutations that are associated with these molecular markers [18]. Combinatorial therapy using both classes of proteasomal inhibitors has been hypothesized to be effective for glioblastoma associated with germline mutations for both p53 and *CDKN2A/B* [41]. Bortezomib, an inhibitor of 26S proteasome, has both ongoing (Phase I/II, NCT03643549 for recurrent GBM with unmethylated MGMT promoter) and completed clinical trials (NCT00611325, NCT00998010). However, the results of the clinical trials completed so far are not very encouraging, which is possibly due to the poor permeability of bortezomib through the blood–brain barrier (BBB). An alternative is the irreversible pan proteasomal inhibitor, marizomib, a novel drug that displays strong inhibitory properties to all proteasomal subunits, has BBB permeability, and demonstrated significant anti-glioma activity in preclinical trials [58]. Marizomib has completed Phase I/II clinical trials evaluating the safety and preliminary efficacy for patients with recurrent glioblastoma where it was tried either as monotherapy or in combination with bevacizumab. The overall trial reported a 6-month PFS (PFS-6) rate of 29.8%, while the median OS was 9.1 months [59] A Phase III, randomized, controlled, open-label, superiority trial with marizomib is still underway for patients with histologically confirmed newly diagnosed glioblastoma ([60]; ClinicalTrials.gov Identifier: NCT03345095).

A similar strategy (Fig. 1) had been adopted to explore the pharmacogenomic landscape of 462 short-term patient-derived tumor cultures that included 14 cancer types including astrocytic tumors. Short-term cultures are expected to mimic the original tumor since they will be free from long-term culture-induced changes in genomic and expression profile. These cultures were scanned for somatic mutations, copy number aberrations, whole exome sequencing, as well as sequencing for full coding exons of 80 commonly mutated cancer genes toward their genomic profiling, and additionally, the glioma specimens were fully sequenced for glioma-associated genes.

The pharmacological landscape of these same cells was established by the screening of 60 compounds for 27,720 drug–tumor cell combinations to derive those drugs with median half-maximal inhibitory concentration (IC50) values ranging within 0.003–53.22 μM. Since IC50 of 1 μM is a common threshold for pharmacological relevance, molecules with low median IC50, such as AUY922 targeting HSP, BEZ235, PKI-587 targeting PI3K/mTOR, bortezomib, carfilzomib targeting proteasome, neratinib targeting EGFR, panobinostat targeting HDAC, and trametinib targeting MEK, were concluded to be more effective while those with median IC50 > 10 μM, such as dabrafenib targeting BRAF, olaparib targeting PARP, sotrastaurin targeting PKC, vismodegib targeting hedgehog, and XL147 targeting PI3K, were concluded to have low anti-tumor activities. Of the candidate drugs showing better pharmacological response, receptor tyrosine kinase blockers targeting EGFR, MET, FGFR, PDGFR, and PAM showed a broad range of drug sensitivities. Hence, tyrosine kinase genomic aberrations in these short-term

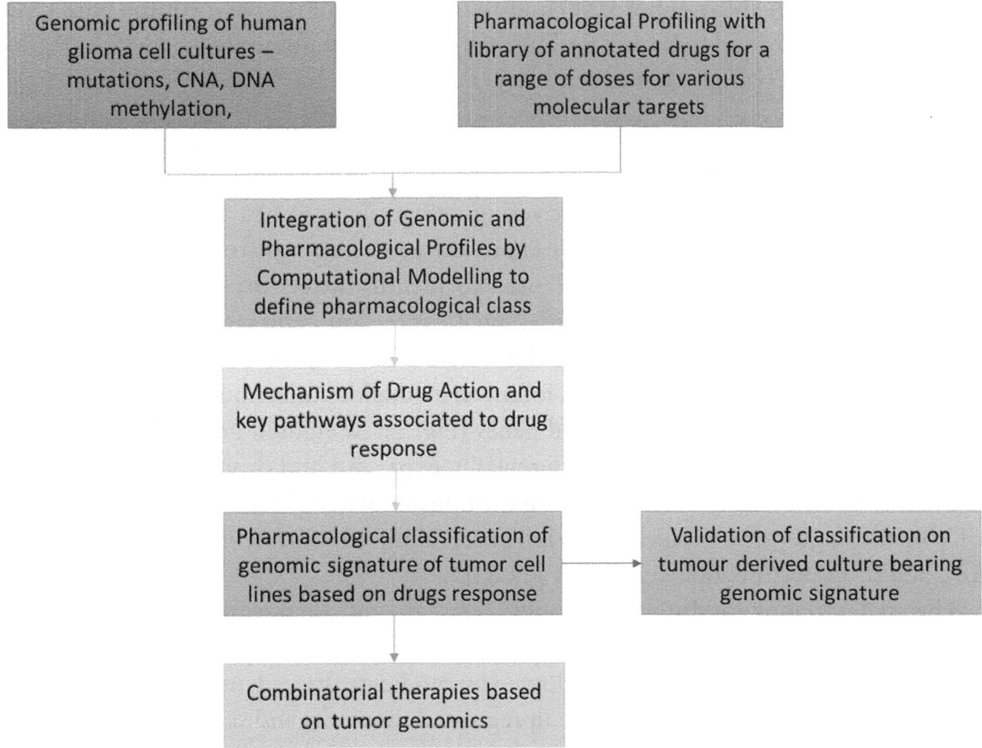

Fig. 1 Workflow of comprehensive integrated approach for pharmacogenomic analysis of astrocytic tumors.

primary tumor cell cultures were concluded to have a strong association with their pharmacological drug response. Computational modeling using topological data analysis from Mapper, by incorporating the most confident interactions of STRING human network (version 10.0) [61] and the gene-drug interactions from the Drug Gene Interactions Database [62], revealed tumor cell genotype-drug associations, such as erlotinib with PI3K, foretinib and BGJ398 with VEGFR, cediranib with FGFR, and ibrutinib with EGFR. Since ibrutinib was seen to significantly reduce the growth of *EGFR/EGFR VIII* amplification harboring cells from patient-derived GBM cell cultures compared to those with wild-type *EGFR*, the study supports repositioning ibrutinib for EGFR-specific glioma therapy and the same is also presently under clinical trials [42]. In an independent study, ibrutinib was shown to inactivate BMX-STAT3 in glioma stem cells without harming the neuronal stem cells in the process to specifically impair malignant growth and radio-resistance, thus increasing survival by ten times than the SOC drug in preclinical models [63]. Ongoing Phase I/II clinical trial NCT03535350 is looking into the feasibility of the use of ibrutinib following surgery alongside radiation therapy and with or without

TMZ. So far as of the November 2020 update of the trial, 420 mg of ibrutinib plus TMZ and radiation were found to be safe for both methylated and unmethylated MGMT glioblastoma (ClinicalTrials.gov Identifier: NCT03535350).

3.2 Network analysis

One of the rational approaches to discovering new drugs is to first find the drug targets using network analysis of differentially expressed genes derived from omics data. One such network-dependent strategy was used to identify novel drugs against astrocytic tumors through the construction of differential expression gene network derived from tumor transcriptome data. Identifying the differentially expressed genes, followed by Gene Ontology enrichment analysis, is followed by the identification of key driver genes for the upregulated and downregulated genes (Fig. 2). Weighted gene correlation networks are then constructed for the differentially expressed and driver genes. Candidate drug identification is thereafter done using existing annotated databases such as CREEDS that contain single-gene perturbation signatures, alongside disease versus normal signatures, and drug perturbation signatures [47,64].

The goal is to look for drugs that would reverse the disease signatures back to normal. When this workflow (Fig. 2) was used to first identify sets of upregulated and downregulated genes and their driver genes followed by candidate drug identification, four drugs could be identified that can reverse the upregulated networks and six molecules that can reverse the downregulated networks and thus prospectively stall tumor progression. Anti-tumor activity observed among the molecules reversing the upregulated genes are curcumin; anaphase promoting complexes (APC/C) inhibitors such as proTAME and apcin that target cell cycle proteins toward degradation through proteasomes;

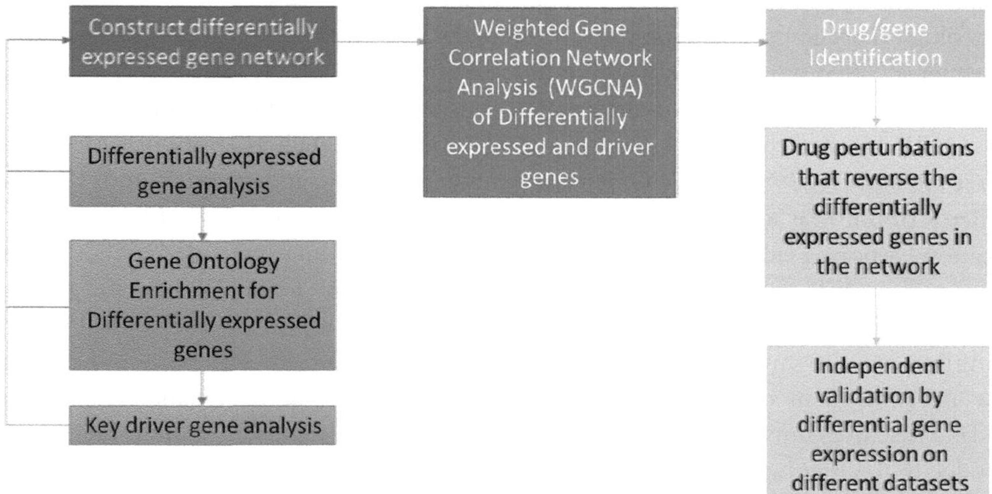

Fig. 2 Differential expression networks in the identification of drugs for astrocytic tumors.

PDE9A inhibitor; and a calmodulin antagonist, W-13, that can bind to CAMK2G protein. V-4084 selective inhibitor of MET kinase, Kaempferol, PD-0332991, selective CDK4/6 inhibitor, dexamethasone, all-*trans*-retinoic acid, and erlotinib are the small molecules that could reverse the downregulated networks [47]. Of these, erlotinib, the EGFR, had already completed multiple Phase I/II, I, and II clinical trials (NCT00672243, NCT00124657, NCT00445588, NCT00045110, NCT00112736, NCT00720356, NCT00671970, NCT00187486, NCT00301418) either singly or in combination. Erlotinib targets the tyrosine kinase domain of both the wild-type EGFR and its mutant constitutive form, the EGFR variant 3 (EGFRvIII) created by the erroneous deletion of exons 2–7. Thus erlotinib can downregulate EGFR/EGFR-vIII-mediated tumor growth and invasion. Overexpression of EGFR is observed in 40%–60% of GBM and is frequently associated with EGFRvIII. Hence, a number of these clinical trials were for GBM and some for recurrent GBM. In one such clinical trial, the single-agent activity of erlotinib was observed to be only slightly beneficial following radiation therapy for patients with nonprogressive GBM [65].

A similar approach to identifying the molecular target–drug correlation was applied to the functional genomics data of lower-grade astrocytoma and anaplastic astrocytoma toward target identification for these tumors for the determination of multitarget proliferation network. The differential co-expression between grade II and grade III, *IDH1*-mutated tumors, and 1p/19q co-deleted astrocytoma was first determined. This was followed by differential enrichment for genetic risk to cancer, and this information was combined with patient survival and the tumor genomic features to yield the molecular network of therapeutic targets primarily led by FoxM1, B-Myb, and E2F2. These targets could pull out candidate molecules, such as etoposide, resveratrol, monobenzone, thioridazine, and methotrexate. Of these, resveratrol was validated to transcriptionally downregulate topoisomerase 2A and polo kinase 1 at transcriptional level in IDH1-derived tumor cell lines in their early passages [44]. Previously, resveratrol has already been shown to enhance the therapeutic effect of TMZ by inhibiting its TMZ-induced autophagy that is mediated by the ROS/ERK pathway that otherwise protected the glioma cells from apoptosis. Co-administration of resveratrol with TMZ suppresses the ERK/ROS-mediated autophagy in the glioma cells and subsequently induces their apoptosis [66]. More recently, resveratrol has been shown to target AKT and p53 in GBM to suppress the tumor growth and infiltration of xenografts. Also, intracranial injection has been demonstrated to give desirable local drug concentrations without any toxicity, making it an attractive candidate to supplement the SOC treatment [67].

3.3 Quantitative structure-activity relationship

QSAR modeling is a drug discovery strategy that pertains to the construction of predictive models of biological activities based on the structural and molecular properties of libraries of structurally related forms or derivatives of the candidate drug molecule that helps to determine the structure that will give the desired drug-like activity. Inherent molecular properties of the candidate drugs like electronic properties, hydrophobicity, steric effects, and topology determined by either experimental or computational approach are correlated to the biological activity. A comparison of different derivatives gives an idea of the better candidate drug [68,69]. QSAR algorithms have been used to effectively pick specific ligands for the Human antigen R (HuR/ELAVL1), a second-level intermediary node in glioma network that works by stabilizing nascent mRNAs by binding through dimerization at their poly-U elements as well as AU-rich elements (AREs) in the 3′-UTR followed by cytoplasmic translocation of the RNA-protein complexes. By binding to transcripts of proteins significant for tumor growth, such as vascular endothelial growth factor (VEGF), hypoxia-inducible factor-1α (HIF-1α), matrix metalloproteinase 9 (MMP-9), urogenin plasminogen activator (uPA), B-cell lymphoma protein 2 (Bcl-2), cycloxygenase-2 (COX-2), and IL8 mRNA, and then moving them to the cytosol for translation, HuR enables these proteins to execute their role in key tumorigenic processes as angiogenesis, resistance to cell death, proliferation, metastasis, and immune evasion programs. Hence, targeting HuR can effectively target pathways in a combinatorial way, such as VEGFA, BDNF, NGF, and Wnt signaling, rendering the downstream targets unavailable for tumor establishment and maintenance [48]. MS-444 is a known blocker of HuR dimerization that was identified by a nanoscreen of 50,000 microbial, mycological, and plant extracts, of which 50 extracts showed >40% activity at 0.5% (v/v) concentration. Of these, 13 extracts from four different *Actinomyces* sp. had an IC50 below 0.5% (v/v) concentration. Reverse-phase HPLC of these revealed fractions bearing dehydromutactin, MS-444, okicenone, mutactin, and AUR367 as the main active inhibitors of HuR-ARE binding through inhibition of activity by a fluorescence anisotropy assay [51] by blocking HuR dimerization and prevention of the consequent downstream key tumor-associated pathological processes. Subsequently, a tanshinone group compound, 15,16-dihydrotanshinone-I, was also identified to inhibit the dimerization/multimerization of HuR [49,50]. In addition, dihydrotanshinone-I has been shown to induce ferroptosis in the U87 and U251 cells in vitro [70].

Computational modeling is another excellent tool for identifying new targets. The advantage of building such computational models is that they can be used to query for different combinatorial therapies by providing predictive power over how the nodes will be affected in such cases. HuR downstream targets, such as AKT, Hif-1α, or cathepsin D, were picked up as a target for glioma inhibition in a large-scale computational model integrating 63 nodes and 82 reactions picked targets, all of which are actually being addressed in various clinical trials [46]. Such models also allow the prediction of optimal combination therapies by testing multiple combinations of alterations in nodes and their overall effect on the network.

3.4 Meta-analysis

Meta-analysis has also been used as a tool to predict better drugs for these astrocytic tumors. In one such study to determine the more effective topoisomerase inhibitors to treat HGG (Fig. 3), meta-analysis of 624 HGG clinical trial studies that covered the median OS and survival gain data of 44,850 patients identified etoposide, a drug that works in G2 and S phases of the cell cycle, to significantly improve the median OS and survival gain in the HGG patients. Etoposide is a DNA synthesis inhibitor binding to topoisomerase II–DNA complexes and inhibiting the action of topoisomerase II, preventing the repair of double-stranded DNA breaks. Irinotecan, on the other hand, is a topoisomerase I inhibitor that prevents re-ligation of the DNA by binding to topoisomerase I–DNA complexes, prevents the movement of replication fork, and induces further double-stranded DNA breaks and replication arrest in dividing cells. In this metanalysis of the efficacy topoisomerase inhibitors to treat HGG, irinotecan correlated to worse overall median survival and gave a disadvantage in survival gain compared to patients treated without irinotecan [45]. The advantage of such studies is that they are comparing the patient's response to already completed clinical trials of these topoisomerase inhibitors in glioma patients. Hence, they enable informed advice for the future clinical trials.

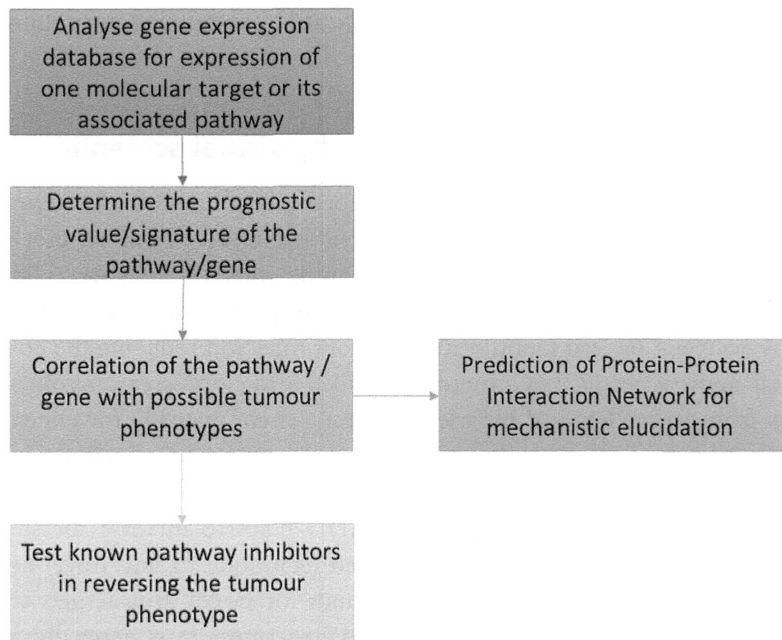

Fig. 3 Workflow of drug discovery by meta-analysis.

Inhibitors of the JAK/STAT pathway as AG490, a pharmacological inhibitor of Janus kinase (JAK) 2, the upstream activator of STAT3 has been shown to be inhibitory to the migratory and invasive potential of glioblastoma cell lines by preventing the phosphorylation of the tyrosine 705 of STAT3 by JAK2 [54]. When the expression profiles of JAK-STAT interactome were analyzed in selected glioblastoma GEO data sets, many dysregulations in the interactome were found to be significantly compared to the normal control, the key ones belonging to the STAT family of proteins. Some of these differential expressions could be validated in glioblastoma tissue [52]. More recently, the prognostic value of the STAT family of proteins, their expression, and role in tumor infiltration by immune cells for LGG and glioblastoma were investigated from publicly available databases using TIMER, a web server that has been developed for comprehensive analysis of tumor-infiltrating immune cells (TIICs) [71]. The expression of STAT members, particularly STAT1, STAT2, STAT3, STAT5A, and STAT6, was significantly higher and the same also positively correlated with IDH mutations. In contrast, the expression of STAT5B was lower in glioma and also negatively correlated with IDH mutations. Also, the group STAT1/2/3/5A/6 was upregulated in GBM with respect to the LGG tissues, while the expression of STAT5B was downregulated. These findings could be positively correlated to both TIICs and poorer OS in glioma in larger datasets from TCGA [53]. This entails the possibility of testing AG490 and other JAK2 inhibitors in improving PFS and OS in LGG. In these lines, STAT3 inhibitor WP1066 is already in clinical trials for patients with recurrent malignant glioma or progressive metastatic melanoma in the brain (ClinicalTrials.gov Identifier: NCT01904123).

4. Drug discovery for astrocytic tumors by virtual screening

Drug discovery and development are complex processes that include identifying and validating target molecules, identifying lead compounds, and optimizing preclinical and clinical trials, making novel drug development sufficiently challenging. The development of computer-aided drug design (CADD) technique has aided in the rational drug designing by accelerating lead identification and optimization reducing the cost faced by experimental approaches [72]. Computation-aided drug discovery involves deriving drug targets from large chemical libraries, screening them virtually for effective candidates, further optimizing compounds, and assessing the safety of the compounds in silico; the hit molecules are further evaluated by in vitro/in vivo experiments. Thus by removing the odd molecules from consideration, CADD helps to increase the success rate. Virtual screening is exhaustive knowledge-driven technique to find novel compounds with a required biological activity to act as ligands for novel drug targets with either known crystal structure or homology-modeled structures. It is generally affordable, decreasing the expenses of early-stage drug development. Virtual screening algorithms have resulted in an increased success rate in the identification of lead molecules [73]. Virtual screening workflows (Fig. 4) can involve two approaches: (1) structure-based virtual

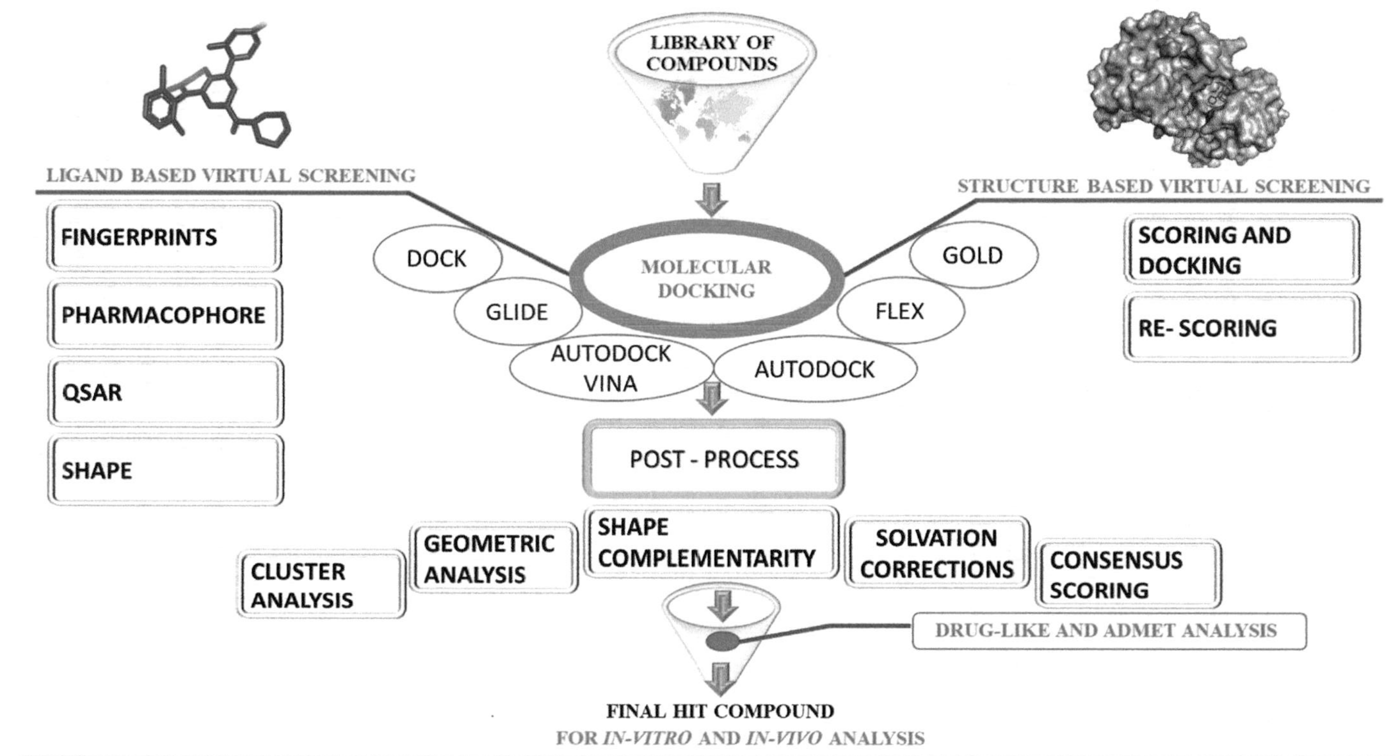

Fig. 4 Workflow for high-throughput virtual screening of ligand databases for drug discovery for known targets.

screening that focuses on to find the best binding site of compounds with the molecular target and (2) ligand-based virtual screening, which relies on the similarity of the candidate molecule of interest with the reference compound with known binding to the therapeutic target [74].

Virtual screening is a computational process that involves molecular docking of a batch of ligands in a random sequence by placing one ligand at a time in the three-dimensional space of the active site or the allosteric site target protein to find a configuration of the target and ligand with increased scoring function. The hit molecules are found based on their score and which are further processed for evaluating the possible noncovalent interactions at the binding site of the molecular target. The leads predicted through virtual screening need to be subsequently validated both in silico and experimentally to establish their actual efficacy [75]. Virtual screening always uses a reference molecule that has known activity on the target protein. Reference molecules are the reported molecules with high activity toward the target and are used to develop various thresholds for filters in the virtual screening procedure. The precise activity threshold at which a ligand is termed active is arbitrary; however, compounds are frequently considered active if their IC50, Ki, or EC50 activity levels are in the micromolar range. The higher the threshold determined by the reference molecule more is the restriction in virtual screening. Also, even if a lead molecule shows activity on the disease target, the action mechanism may differ from the action mechanism of the reference molecule used for virtual screening. This is especially true when the binding is sought at the allosteric sites. Since the binding modes are different, the virtual screening with a reference ligand for the orthosteric site would not be able to recognize molecules that could be active at the allosteric site and this in turn would reduce the performance of virtual screening. Thus using reference compounds with previously unknown protein-binding mechanism incorporates limitations during virtual screening and its subsequent validation steps. Inactive molecules are those that have been shown to have little action toward the target protein. Hit compounds similar to inactives have a higher likelihood of being inactive and should be avoided. In the same way, as actives have an arbitrary activity threshold below which compounds are inactive, an arbitrary activity threshold below which compounds are inactive may be established. The higher the threshold, the more difficult the virtual screening will be, because it is important to differentiate between active and inactive molecules with better precision due to the slighter dissimilarity in activity between the two groups. Another class of molecules that are relevant here is the decoy molecules. Decoy molecules are compounds that seem like active compounds but have not shown activity at the target of interest, and they are probably inert; it is also an inherent constraint for evaluating the efficiency of virtual screening [76]. Virtual screening effectively acts as a two-way classifier, labeling the output molecules as active or inactive based on the predefined active and inactive/decoy references [74]. Following the virtual screening, molecular dynamic simulation is performed to determine whether the protein-ligand complexes can reflect a complex that can be replicated in actual experiments. The molecular dynamic simulation is performed with the protein-ligand complexes in the presence of water and ions to determine whether the complexes produced by docking can be recreated in actual experiments to determine the root mean square deviation (RMSD), area under the receiver operating characteristics (AUC-ROC), and Boltzmen-enhanced discrimination of ROC (BED-ROC) in the presence of the enrichment factors. The RMSD plots against time are used to determine the stability of the protein–ligand complex in the presence of water and ions and the molecular interactions in that complex [77], The most difficult issue of virtual screening is distinguishing genuine positive hits from false positives. The area under the ROC curve is used for this purpose. The area under the ROC curve calculates the likelihood of a result being false. AUC-ROC shows the likelihood of recovering an active chemical over an inert compound. The range of AUC value can vary 0–1 with values close to 1 indicating excellent likelihood of an active compound and values <0.6 indicating a failure [78,79]. BED-ROC employs exponential weighting and gives early rankings of active compounds more weight than late rankings of such compounds. The enrichment factor is the amount of active compounds found in a proportion of 0–1 in comparison to the number of active compounds identified in a random search, with a maximum value of 1 and a minimum value of 0 [80]. There are multiple virtual screening software packages that employ various docking algorithms to make a virtual screening process easier by removing the requirement for sophisticated understanding of the algorithms and providing interfaces for researchers to conduct screening. Some of the algorithms used more often are AutoDock4, Autodock Vina, GOLD, Glide, etc. [81–83]. In this section, we discuss some of the novel compounds identified against targets for astrocytic tumors by virtual screening. The lead compounds against astrocytic tumors discovered by virtual screening are listed in Table 3. These listed molecules are next discussed in the context of the drug target protein or the molecular pathway against whom it was discovered.

4.1 IDH-mutant targeting therapies

Isocitrate dehydrogenases (IDH1/2) are enzymes that catalyze alpha-ketoglutarate formation step in Kreb's cycle. About 70%–80% of Grade II/III gliomas and secondary glioblastomas report associations with a mutant IDH1/2 [101]. These mutant enzymes produce oncometabolite D-2-hydroxyglutarate (D-2-HG) from α-KG due to mutation in Arg residues that are crucial for the cognate substrate recognition. R132 for IDH1 and R140 or R172 for IDH2 are the mutations associated with cancer. A high level of D2-HG is able to inhibit α-KG-dependent dioxygenases, viz. histone demethylases like lysine-specific demethylase (KDM) and DNA demethylation enzyme like the Ten-eleven translocation methyl cytosine dioxygenase [102]. This leads to the alteration in genome-wide histone and DNA methylation status [103]. Also, inhibition of histone

Table 3 Drugs against astrocytic tumors discovered by virtual screening.

Sl. No.	Molecule	Target protein	Mechanism	IC50	Drug discovery method(s)	Phase of development	Reference (s)
1.	**Isoliquiritigenin**	COX-2, mPGES-1 and CYP4A11	Inhibits lncRNA NEAT1/miR-194-5p/Akt mediated angiogenic pathway	8.1 μM, 17.4 μM and 10.3 μM	Structure-based virtual screening	In silico, Intracranial glioma model	[84]
2.	**CH625**	CYP4X1	Inhibits CYP4X, reduces 14,15-EET-EA production in tumor-associated macrophages via CB2 and EGFR-STAT3 signaling reduces VEGF and TGFβ expression	16.5 μM	Structure-based virtual screening	In silico, intracranial glioma model	[85]
3.	**AK-778/43420895**	ID2 (inhibitor of DNA binding 2)	Binds to and inhibits ID2	27.3 ± 3.7	Pharmacophore-based virtual screening followed by docking	In silico/ in vitro (U87)	[86]
4.	**VH1011 and VH1019 {((*E*)-N′-(2-hydroxy-5-methoxybenzylidene)-2-(p-tolylamino) acetohydrazide)}**	GRP78	Bind to GRP78 and show anti-proliferative activity in U87-MG	IC50 of 12.7 μM in MCF -7	Structure-based pharmacophore modeling and docking	In silico, in vitro (U87-MG)	[87]
5.	**Anthracyclines (10 + 10 small molecules)**	BRAF47-438del and PIK3R1-G376R proteins	Binds and inhibits mutated BRAF of the RAS-RAF-MAPK signaling pathway and mutated PI3KR1 of Akt/mTOR pathway	–	Structure-based virtual screening	In silico, in vitro	[88]

6.	**WM17 ($C_{24}H_{20}FN_3O_3$)**	Mutant IDH1 protein	WM17, binds to mutant IDH1, improving its thermostability and reverses genome-wide hypermethylation.	$IC_{50} = 8.86\,\mu M$ of mutant IDH1 activity	Structure-based virtual screening	In silico, in vitro {U87 (R132H/+)}	[89]
7.	**Gallic acid**	RAB13	Inhibits RAB13, a novel positive regulator of autophagy	–	Homology modeling followed by structure-based virtual screening	In silico, in vitro (SW1088)	[90]
8.	**L806-0255, V015-1671, and AQ-714/41674992**	Mutant IDH1 protein	Inhibits the mutant IDH1 enzyme at an allosteric site	28.3 ± 2.5, 23.8 ± 1.8, 20.8 ± 4.2 (Enzyme activity)	Comparative structure-based virtual screening, enzymatic activity	In silico, Enzyme assay	[91]
9.	**(7-((4-(diethylamino)phenyl)(pyridin-2-ylamino)methyl)-2-methylquinolin-8-ol), α-hydroxyquinoline**	GLI-1 (Glioma-associated oncogene 1)	Binds to GLI1–DNA complex and brings a conformational change, preventing GLI1 from functioning.	–	Structure-based virtual screening	In silico	[92]
10.	**SCHEMBL1250485 (PubChem CID: 66965667)**	VEGFR	Binds to the active site of VEGFR with high affinity and inhibits its functions.	–	Structure-based virtual training	In silico	[93]
11.	**ZX06**	mIDH1	Inhibits mIDH1 enzyme at its allosteric sites.	–	Cross docking-based virtual screening	In silico, in vitro (HEK-293 T IDH WT)	[94]

Continued

Table 3 Drugs against astrocytic tumors discovered by virtual screening—cont'd

Sl. No.	Molecule	Target protein	Mechanism	IC50	Drug discovery method(s)	Phase of development	Reference (s)
12.	**(*S*)-4-(Benz-hydryl-amino)-3-(2-(3-guanidinobenzamido)-acetamido)-4-oxobutanoic Acid**	MDM 2/4	It binds to MDM-2 and MDM-4 and inhibits their functions.	(MDM2 $IC_{50}=72.0\,nM$; MDM4 $IC_{50}=77.4\,nM$)	Structure-based virtual screening	In silico, in vitro	[95]
13.	**NSC232003**	UHRF1	It binds to the 5-mC pocket of UHRF1 and inhibits its function	15 μM	Structure-based virtual screening	In silico and in cellulo	[96]
14.	**SPB07479**	Chk1	It binds to the active site of Chk1 and inhibits it.	4.24 μM	Pharmacophore-based virtual screening	In silico, in vitro	[97]
15.	**ENMD-2076**	Aurora kinase A and VEGFR-2	It binds to Aurora kinase A and VEGFR-2	–	Structure-based virtual screening	Microarray, in silico, in vivo, in vitro	[98]
16.	**ZINC02145000 and ZINC32124203**	Oct4	They bind to POUHD and POUS domain of Oct4	–	High-throughput structure-based virtual screening	In silico	[99]
17.	**SRI-37683 and SRI-37684**	GLUT3	They bind to GLUT3 and inhibit glucose uptake	–	Structure-based virtual screening	In silico, In vitro, In vivo (xenograft)	[100]

demethylation by D2HG has been reported to impair cellular differentiation, which might implicate to IDH-mutated cancers [102]. WM17 is a novel inhibitor identified for this mutant enzyme, which on binding improves the thermostability of the protein. Through in vitro analysis, it has been found to reverse histone hypermethylation in IDH1-mutated cells caused by D2HG accumulation [89]. Novel inhibitors of IDH1 discovered by virtual screening for IDH1R132H protein are L806-0255, V015-1671, and AQ-714/41674992. The IC50 of enzyme activity of these compounds is less than 50 μM and possibly inhibits the protein via an allosteric pocket defined by hydrophobic residues VAL276, SER278, SER287, ILE128, and PRO118 [91]. ZX06, a lead compound screened from SPECS database through cross-docking-based virtual screening, inhibits IDH1 mutant via its allosteric site. In IDH WT cells, ZX06 shows low cytotoxicity but high BBB permeability [94].

4.2 Tumor vasculature normalization therapies

Angiogenic factors, such as VEGF and fibroblast growth factor (FGF), released by cancer cells serve to restructure the tumor vasculature that serves as a supply of oxygen and nutrients to the rapidly proliferating cells and also forms a route for metastasis [104]. Several angiogenic inhibitors have shown promising outcomes in the treatment of advanced cancers, since the approval of Avastin in 2004. However, recent studies have reported that antiangiogenic therapies are transient and lead to tumor recurrence after several months of treatment. This is because blockage of blood supply that results in hypoxic and acidic conditions makes the tumor cells more aggressive and metastatic [105]. Also, lack of hierarchial architecture of the vessels makes the tumor vasculature inherently defective as defined by their dilation, tortuosity, and leakiness, all of which contribute to tumor hypoxia and growth [106]. Hence, tumor vasculature normalization therapies have become the novel approach in anticancer research. Drugs that induce normalization of vasculature improve the anti-cancer drug delivery to the tumor microenvironment and the overall cancer treatment [107]. CH625, a flavonoid identified by structure-based virtual screening, inhibits CYP4X1 in M2-polarized macrophages and reduces 14,15-EET-EA synthesis, which in turn reduces tumor-associated macrophage (TAM)-derived VEGF and TGF-β via CB2 and EGFR-STAT3 signaling, which promotes vascular normalization in C6 and GL261 glioma, intracranial and subcutaneous models [85].

Similarly, isoliquiritigenin, a flavonoid identified by structure-based virtual screening, has been recently reported to have both antiangiogenic and vascular normalization effects in intracranial C6 model. Using in silico tools, it has been found to target COX-2, microsomal PGE synthase-1 (mPGES-1), and CYP4A and inhibit lncRNA NEAT1/miR-194-5p/Akt-FGF-2/TGF-β/VEGF pathway [84]. COX-2 and mPGES-1 are enzymes that convert arachidonic acid into prostaglandins that are mediators of tumor angiogenesis. Cytochrome P450 (CYP4A11), the third target enzyme for isoliquiritigenin, converts arachidonic acid to 20-hydroxyeicosatetraenoic acid that induces angiogenesis and downregulation of this protein has been reported to induce vascular normalization in glioma [84,108].

4.3 Unfolded protein response targeting therapies

Unfolded protein response (UPR) is an adaptive response of the endoplasmic reticulum (ER) during stress conditions to reduce the unfolded protein load and improve cellular viability and function [109]. Among the proteins involved in UPR, the glucose-regulated protein 78 (GRP78/BiP), a chaperone that is regulated by glucose, is an important protein involved in this adaptive response [110]. At basal condition, it binds and inactivates three UPR sensor proteins: PERK, IRE1, and ATF6. On increase in the defective protein load, these sensor proteins are released from GRP78/BiP, and the UPR cascade is initiated [111]. In cancer, the cellular conditions mimic ER stress, involving nutrient and oxygen deprivation, these are also conditions induced by anti-angiogenic drugs. However, due to the activation of GRP78-mediated UPR, the cells develop drug resistance. Thus GRP78 could be a better target for anticancer therapies [112]. Several agents have been proposed to target GRP78 to reduce cancer growth in the past two decades. These include natural compounds, such as AB5 subtilase cytotoxin [113], epigallocatechin-3-gallate (EGCG) [114], salicylic acid [115], and versipelostatin [116], and antibody regimens, such as C38, C107 [117], and anti-CTD [87,118]. Also, a series of adenosine derivatives have been presented that target the ATPase domain of GRP78 protein. They are the first inhibitors reported to target this domain [119]. By structure-based pharmacophore modeling followed by docking, VH1011 and VH1019 [((*E*)-*N*′-(2-hydroxy-5-methoxybenzylidene)-2-(*p*-tolylamino) acetohydrazide)] have been found to inhibit GRP78 and they also show concentration-dependent antiproliferative activity on U87-MG cancer cells over normal ones [87].

4.4 Hedgehog/glioma-associated oncogene homolog targeting therapeutics

Aberrant activation of Hedgehog/glioma (HH/GLI)-associated oncogene homolog targeting compounds pathway is implicated to various human cancers including brain [120]. This is an important signaling pathway that regulates the self-renewal of highly malignant and rare cancer stem cells (CSCs) that are responsible for tumor initiation, maintenance, metastatic spread, relapse, and drug resistance [121]. Therefore efficient regimes targeting CSC pathways, such as this pathway in combination with conventional therapies, are speculated to be more effective than the conventional therapies alone. There are some clinically approved drugs, viz. vismodegib, sonidegib, and glasdegib [122], that target the major effector, smoothened (SMO) of HH-pathway, and show high therapeutic efficacy in skin cancer patients. However, due to concomitant resistance to SMO inhibitors, such drugs limit the eradication of the CSCs [121]. Instead, GLI-1, the final effector of

HH pathway, might be a unique and potential anticancer target for various malignancies. (7-((4-(Diethylamino)-phenyl) (pyridin-2-ylamino) methyl)-2-methylquinolin-8-ol), a hydroxyquinoline, has been identified by virtual screening as a potential inhibitor of GLI-1, which binds to the protein-DNA complex and inhibits the transcription factor from functioning [92].

4.5 Octamer-binding transcription factor-4 targeting therapeutics

Octamer-binding transcription factor-4 (Oct4) is a core regulator of the stem-like properties of glioma stem cells (GSCs). It controls the stemness, self-renewal, and invasiveness of these cells and its overexpression inhibits the differentiation of glioma cells, thus promoting the tumor proliferation [123]. It has two sub-domains in the Pit-Oct-Unc (POU) domain, POU-specific domain (POUS) and POU-type homeodomain (POUHD) subdomains, that are essential for the Oct4 functioning for the generation of induced pluripotent stem cells from somatic cells leading to tumor initiation, invasion, relapse, and drug resistance [124,125]. Despite its pivotal role in GSC maintenance, there have been no drugs identified to target this protein, until recently. ZINC02145000 and ZINC32124203, two small molecules, have been identified by high-throughput structure-based virtual screening to interact with these two subdomains with high affinity and can be further analyzed for the development of potential drugs for GSC inhibition in glioma [99]. These compounds also show absorptive capacity at the BBB.

4.6 Apoptosis-inducing therapeutics

A significant proportion of research on anticancer therapeutics is dedicated to identifying the anti-cancer activity of compounds that directly or indirectly induce apoptosis. Some of the natural compounds that have been reported to do so are curcumin, EGCG, and genistein [126]. It has been found that $\alpha5\beta1$ integrin inhibitors are able to sensitize glioma cells to chemotherapeutics by favoring apoptotic death over premature senescence in cells that have a functional p53 pathway [127]. In one of the recent findings, MDM2/4 antagonists are shown to bind to $\alpha5\beta1/\alpha v\beta3$, by activating two convergent pathways in the regulation of glioma apoptosis, the MDM and the integrin pathways. Using the structure-based virtual screening, (*S*)-4-(benzhydrylamino)-3-(2-(3-guanidinobenzamido)-acetamido)-4-oxobutanoic acid has been identified as a novel compound that serves as antagonist both MDM and integrin and has been tested to arrest cell cycle, proliferation, and invasiveness of p53 wild-type glioma cells [95].

4.7 Autophagy targeting compounds

Self-eating or autophagy is a conserved intracellular catabolic process that prevents cellular damage and promotes survival primarily under conditions of energy or nutrient stress [128]. Though initially recognized as a protector process of cell death, it is now known to have both cytoprotective and cell death-inducing effects [129,130]. Signaling pathways, viz. ERK1/2, NF-κB, and PI3K/AKT/mTOR pathways, are autophagy-associated pathways and have been implicated to both tumor suppression and tumor protection against regimens that induce cytotoxicity in glioma cells [130]. A recent study analyzed LGG clinical data by multi-omics approaches and identified ZFP36L2 and RAB-13 as potential autophagic modulators in LGG. Out of the two RAB-13, a novel positive autophagy modulator was selected for in silico analysis. It was upregulated in LGG and was associated with the poor prognosis of the disease. Using the homology modeling followed by virtual screening of the Traditional Chinese Medicine database followed by in vitro analysis on the SW1088 cell line, gallic acid was identified as an inhibitor of RAB-13-mediated autophagy induction in LGG [90].

4.8 Glucose transporter targeting compounds

Cancer cells are highly dependent on glycolysis for the generation of ATP, even in the presence of adequate oxygen, which is called the Warburg effect. Glycolysis also generates additional metabolic intermediates that can be used by the tumor cells to grow in nutrient-deficient conditions [131]. To sustain increased glycolysis, these cells express high levels of glucose transporters (GLUTs), viz. GLUT1 and GLUT3 [132]. In addition, the knockdown of GLUT3 in brain tumor-initiating cells results in the inability of the cells to form tumors in vivo [133]. Pharmacological inhibition of GLUT1 has also been shown to decrease the tumor formation capacity of tumor-initiating cells [134]. Thus GLUTs can serve as unique targets of anti-cancer therapeutics. SRI-37683 and SRI-37684 are two potential small-molecule inhibitors of GLUT3 identified through a structure-based virtual screening. These compounds have also shown an inhibition of glucose uptake and a decrease in the growth of GBM patient-derived xenograft cells in-vitro [100].

5. Drug repositioning in astrocytic tumor therapy

Drug repositioning/repurposing is an approach for identifying alternative therapeutic applications for approved or investigational drugs for indications other than the purpose for which it has been initially approved by the regulatory authorities [135,136]. The key advantage of drug repositioning is that it saves the cost of drug development both in terms of time as well as money, cutting down the typical time of 12–16 years required from bringing a new molecule from its identification, to preclinical, clinical trials to market after regulatory clearances to just 6 years for a repositioned molecule and the financial cost for the same comes down from the typical \$1–2 billion to just \$300 million [137]. This clear advantage in drug repositioning in terms of time and financial cost has led to the clinical trials of a number of existing anticancer drugs toward astrocytic tumor therapy, and quite a few of these have completed the first few levels of trials. A recent review of drugs repositioned for GBM reported to include ALDH1 inhibitor disulfiram, the mTORC1 complex inhibitor rapamycin, and its derivatives, the biguanide anti-diabetic activator of AMPK and inhibitor for mTORC1 metformin, AF1980/lonidamine a reversible inhibitor of spermatogenesis, chloroquine and related antimalarial drugs, chloropromazine, and other dopamine receptor inhibitors of the class tricyclic anti-depressant [138], In this section, first, the anti-cancer drugs repurposed to astrocytic tumor therapy that have completed at least the Phase I clinical trials for astrocytic tumors are discussed. Following this, drugs approved for other conditions that have also entered the clinical trials for astrocytic tumor therapy are discussed. The repositioned drugs are discussed by their mechanism of action. The list of completed clinical trials of these repositioned drugs and their various combinations with conventional therapy is given in Table 4.

5.1 Repositioning anticancer drugs to astrocytic tumor therapy

A major proportion of anticancer drugs that are being repositioned for glioma therapy are receptor tyrosine kinase inhibitors (RTKIs). There are 58 proteins in this family of receptor that are identified to regulate the survival, growth, differentiation, and migration/motility in normal cells [139,140]. In cancer cells, aberrant activation of RTKs mostly leads to oncogenic trait by (1) overexpression of growth factors; (2) amplification and/or overproduction of the RTK itself, resulting in hypersensitivity to low level of ligand; (3) mutations in the ligand-binding site or kinase domains, and (4) fusion of kinase domains with unrelated proteins, or chromosomal translocation, forming chimeric kinase protein with enhanced activity [140]. Many of the RTKs such as EGFR and PDGFR are implicated to the pathophysiology of glioma [139,140]. EGFR is reported to be amplified in approximately 40–50% of GBM tumors and upregulated in more than 60% of patients [17,140,141]. The GBM dataset analysis by TCGA consortium revealed that about 55% of the patients have EGFR alterations. From the same dataset, PDGFRα was identified as the second most amplified receptor after EGFR in GBM [140]. Many anticancer drugs that target these RTKs have completed their early phase clinical trials for astrocytic tumors. These include erlotinib, sunitinib malate, tandutinib, sorafenib tosylate, dovitinib, tesevatinib, etc. ([142]; Table 4).

Erlotinib, an EGFR antagonist, originally a drug for small-cell lung cancer and advanced metastatic pancreatic cancer [143], has been tested on patients with glioblastoma, gliosarcoma, and giant cell glioblastoma in different Phase-I/II clinical trials. In a Phase II clinical trial (NCT00671970), patients with recurrent malignant glioma (GBM and anaplastic glioma) were given a combination therapy of bevacizumab and **erlotinib**. The PFS-6 and the median OS were 4% and 71 weeks for anaplastic glioma patients and 28% and 42 weeks for GBM patients, respectively. The PFS-6 and radiographic response rates were parallel or inferior to other combination therapies containing bevacizumab [144]. Another anticancer EGFR inhibitor like **afatinib** (NCT00977431) and **gefitinib** (NCT00085566, NCT00042991) has also gone through clinical trials for their efficacy in reducing brain tumors [142]. **Sunitinib**

Table 4 Repurposed drugs that completed clinical trials for astrocytic tumor therapy[a,b].

Sl. No.	Repurposed drug name	Current approved use	Mechanism of action	Conditions	NCT number	Phase completed I|II/II/III
Anti-cancer drugs						
1	**Irinotecan Hydrochloride**	Colorectal cancer	Inhibits topoisomerase I by binding to topoisomerase I-DNA complex and preventing re-ligation of DNA strand. This causes death by inducing ds DNA break.	Childhood Cerebral AA, Recurrent Childhood Brain Stem Glioma	NCT00381797	II
	Irinotecan			GBM	NCT00967330	II
	Irinotecan Hydrochloride			GBM, GS	NCT00979017	II
	Irinotecan Hydrochloride, Temozolomide			Adult—GB, GS; Recurrent Adult Brain Neoplasm	NCT00433381	II
	Irinotecan, Temozolomide			GB, GS, Brain Tumor	NCT00597402	II
2	**Zotiraciclib,** Temozolomide	**Novel drug** being tested on brain tumor	–	Brain Tumor, Astrocytoma, Astroglioma, GB, GS	NCT02942264	I|II
3	**Erlotinib,** sirolimus	Small cell lung cancers, advanced metastatic pancreatic cancers	Inhibits EGFR by reversibly binding to its ATP-binding site. Also, a potential inhibitor of JAK2V617F, a JAK2 (Tyrosine Kinase) mutant, which is reported in most patients with polycythemia vera, essential thrombocythemia and idiopathic myelofibrosis.	GB, GS	NCT00672243	II
	Erlotinib hydrochloride			Brain and Central Nervous System (CNS) Tumors	NCT00124657	I|II
	Erlotinib hydrochloride, Sorafenib tosylate			Adult—GC-GB, GB, GS; Recurrent Adult Brain Tumor	NCT00445588	II
	Erlotinib hydrochloride			Adult—AA, GC-GB, GB, GS; Recurrent Adult Brain Tumor	NCT00045110	I|II
	Erlotinib, Temsirolimus			Adult—AA, Diffuse Astrocytoma, GC-GB, GB, GSM, Mixed Glioma, Pilocytic	NCT00112736	I|II

				Astrocytoma, Astrocytoma, Subependymal GCA, Recurrent Adult Brain Tumor		
	Erlotinib hydrochloride			Brain and CNS Tumors	NCT00720356	II
	Erlotinib			GB, GS	NCT00671970	II
	Erlotinib, Temozolomide			GBM, GS	NCT00187486	II
	Erlotinib			GBM, AA	NCT00301418	I|II
4	**Sunitinib Malate**	Renal cell carcinoma, imatinib-resistant gastrointestinal stromal tumor	Inhibits various signaling pathways by binding to multiple RTKs including VEGFR and PDGFR.	Childhood—Cerebellar AA, Cerebral AA, Cerebral Astrocytoma, Mixed Glioma, Recurrent Childhood—Cerebellar Astrocytoma, Cerebral Astrocytoma, Subependymal GCA	NCT01462695	II
	Sunitinib Malate			Adult—AA, Diffuse Astrocytoma, GG-GB, GB, GS, Mixed Glioma, Pineal Gland Astrocytoma	NCT00499473	II
	Sunitinib Malate			AA, GB	NCT00606008	II
5	**Tandutinib**	Granted Fast-track status by FDA for AML patients, Phase I/II underway	Inhibits type III RTKs, including FLT3, PDGFR, and c-KIT.	Adult—Brain Tumor, GC-GB, GB, GS, Recurrent Adult Brain Tumor	NCT00379080	I|II
	Tandutinib			GB, GS, AA, Anaplastic Mixed Oligoastrocytoma (OA)	NCT00667394	II

Continued

Table 4 Repurposed drugs that completed clinical trials for astrocytic tumor therapy—cont'd

Sl. No.	Repurposed drug name	Current approved use	Mechanism of action	Conditions	NCT number	Phase completed I|II/II/III
6	**Sorafenib Tosylate**	For unresectable liver carcinoma and advanced renal carcinoma	An inhibitor of Raf kinase of Raf/Mek/Erk pathway, it also inhibits PDGFR, VEGFR-2 and 3, and c-Kit.	Adult—GB, GS, Recurrent Adult Brain Neoplasm	NCT00329719	I|II
	Sorafenib, Everolimus			Brain Tumor, GB, Anaplastic Glioma	NCT01434602	I|II
	Sorafenib, Temozolomide			Recurrent GBM	NCT00597493	II
	Sorafenib Tosylate, Erlotinib hydrochloride, Tipifarnib, Temisirolimus			Adult—GC-GB, GB, GS, Recurrent Adult Brain Tumor	NCT00335764	I|II
	Sorafenib, Temozolomide			GBM	NCT00544817	II
7	**Dovitinib**	Anticancer drug, not FDA approved yet	RTK inhibitor, inhibits PDGFR, VEGFR, FGFR.	Adult—GC-GB, GS, GB, Recurrent Adult Brain Tumor	NCT01753713	II
8	**Dasatinib**	Lymphoblastic or chronic myeloid leukemia with resistance/intolerance to prior therapy	TK inhibitor; inhibits BCR-ABL, c-KIT, EPHA2, PDGFRβ, Src- family (SRC, LCK, YES, FYN).	GBM	NCT00892177	II
	Dasatinib, Temozolomide			Brain and CNS Tumors	NCT00869401	I|II
	Dasatinib			Adult—GC-GB, GB, GS, Recurrent Adult Brain Neoplasm	NCT00423735	II
9	**Tesevatinib**	In trials for Stomach Cancer, Brain Metastases, Esophageal Cancer,	Inhibits multiple RTKs; EGRFR, HER2R, VEGFR, and EphB4, an RTK	GB, Recurrent GB, Brain Tumor	NCT02844439	II

		Leptomeningeal Metastasis	highly expressed in many tumors, promotes angiogenesis.			
10	**Tivozanib**	Renal cell carcinoma	Inhibits RTK-VEGFR	GB	NCT01846871	II
11	Pazopanib, **Topotecan**	Ovarian, cervical, small cell lung cancers	Inhibits Topoisomerase I, like Irinotecan.	GB, GBM, GS; Brain Neoplasms, CNS Neoplasms	NCT01931098	II
12	**Pazopanib,** Topotecan	Advanced renal cell cancer, advanced soft tissue sarcoma	2nd generation multitargeted tyrosine kinase inhibitor against VEGFR1/2/3, PDGFR, c-KIT.	GB, GBM, GS, Brain Neoplasms, CNS Neoplasms	NCT01931098	II
	Pazopanib hydrochloride			Adult—GC-GB, GB, GS; Recurrent Adult Brain Tumor	NCT00459381	II
13	**Imatinib mesylate,** Hydroxyurea	Leukemias; gastrointestinal stromal tumors	Inhibits BCR-ABL. Also inhibits PDGFR, c-KIT.	GB, GS GB, GS GBM, Astrocytoma	NCT00354913 NCT00615927 NCT00154375	II II III
14	Imatinib mesylate, **Hydroxyurea**	Antimetabolite for Sickle cell anemia	Induces cell death by DNA damage.	GB, GS	NCT00354913	II
15	**Afatinib (BIBW2992),** Temozolomide	Locally advanced or metastatic nonsmall-cell lung cancer	Irreversibly blocks ErbB family proteins.	GB	NCT00977431	I
16	**Ponatinib**	Various types of chronic myeloid leukemia)	Targets the chimeric Bcr-Abl tyrosine kinase.	GB	NCT02478164	II
17	**Lapatinib ditosylate**	HER-negative breast cancer	HER2/ERBB2 and EGFR tyrosine kinases inhibitor.	Recurrent Childhood—AA, Brain Stem Glioma, GC-GB, GB, GS	NCT00095940	I|II

Continued

Table 4 Repurposed drugs that completed clinical trials for astrocytic tumor therapy—cont'd

Sl. No.	Repurposed drug name	Current approved use	Mechanism of action	Conditions	NCT number	Phase completed I|II/II/III
18	**PF-299804 (Dacomitinib)**	Nonsmall-cell lung cancer with EGFR mutation	Irreversibly binds to EGFR family (EGFR/HER1, HER2, and HER4) tyrosine kinases and inhibits them.	GB, Brain Tumor	NCT01520870	II
19	**ZD6474 (Vandetanib),** Carboplatin	Medullary thyroid cancer	Selective inhibitor of VEGFR, EGFR, and RET tyrosine kinases.	GBM, GSM, AA, Anaplastic Mixed OA, GBM, GSM, AA	NCT00995007	II
20	**Carboplatin,** ZD6474 (Vandetanib)	Ovarian cancer	Alkylating agent, crosslinks in ds DNA prevents their separation during transcription.	Anaplastic Mixed OA	NCT00995007	II
21	**Gefitinib**	Nonsmall-cell lung carcinoma	Inhibits EGFR tyrosine kinase inhibitor.	Brain and CNS Tumors	NCT00085566	I|II
	Gefitinib			Untreated Childhood—AA, Brain Stem Glioma, GC-GB, GBM, Gliomatosis Cerebri, GSM	NCT00042991	I|II

22	**Bosutinib**	CML	Inhibitor of Src-family kinases. Its primary target is Bcr-Abl kinase.	GBM	NCT01331291	II
23	**Cediranib,** Lomustine	Liver cancer, nonsmall-cell lung cancer (NSCLC), colorectal cancer	Inhibits VEGFR.	Recurrent GBM	NCT00777153	III
24	**Cilengitide,** Temozolomide	Sarcoma, Gliomas, Lymphoma, Leukemia, and Lung Cancer	–	GBM	NCT00813943	II
	Cilengitide			GBM	NCT00093964	II
	Cilengitide, Temozolomide			Adult—GC-GBM, GBM, GSM	NCT00085254	I|II
	Cilengitide, Temozolomide			GBM	NCT00689221	III
	Cilengitide			Childhood high grade—Cerebellar Astrocytoma, Cerebral Astrocytoma, Recurrent Childhood—AA Brain Tumor, Cerebellar Astrocytoma, Cerebral Astrocytoma, GBM, Visual Pathway and Hypothalamic Glioma	NCT00679354	II

Continued

Table 4 Repurposed drugs that completed clinical trials for astrocytic tumor therapy—cont'd

Sl. No.	Repurposed drug name	Current approved use	Mechanism of action	Conditions	NCT number	Phase completed I|II/II/III
25	**Capecitabine**	Colon, colorectal and breast cancer	A prodrug, converted to a cytotoxic moiety by thymidine phosphorylase an enzyme that is overexpressed in many tumor cells. The final metabolites inhibit cell division and transcription.	Malignant Glioma	NCT00717197	II
26	**Tipifarnib (R115777),** Temozolomide	**Novel drug** being tested for AML	Inhibits farnesyltransferase transferase I which inhibits the proper functioning of Ras protein.	GBM	NCT00050986	I|II
27	**LDE225 (Sonidegib)**	Advanced recurrent basal cell carcinoma	Inhibits Smoothened and thus Hedge pathway.	Glioma, Astrocytoma	NCT01125800	I|II
28	**Thalidomide,** CPT-11 (Irinotecan)	Multiple myeloma and treats erythema nodosum leprosum	Inhibits VEGF secretion.	GB, GBM	NCT00412542	II

29	**6-Thioguanine,** Capecitabine**,** Celecoxib (Celebrex)**,** Temozolomide, Lomustine	Acute nonlymphocytic leukemias	Competes for the active site of HGPRTase and is converted into 6-thioguanilyic acid (TGMP), which prevents the synthesis of guanine nucleotides by inhibiting purine biosynthesis.	Anaplastic Glioma of Brain, Brain Cancer	NCT00504660	II
30	**Vorinostat**	Cutaneous T- cell lymphoma	Inhibits histone deacetylases leading to accumulation of acetylated histones that induces cell cycle arrest and/or apoptosis.	Adult GC-GB, GB, GS; Recurrent Adult Brain Tumor	NCT00238303	II
	Vorinostat			Malignant Glioma, Recurrent GB	NCT01266031	I|II
	Vorinostat, Bortezomib			Adult—GC-GB, GB, GS, Recurrent Adult Brain Tumor	NCT00641706	II
	Vorinostat, Temozolomide			Brain Tumor, Glioblastoma	NCT00939991	I|II
	Vorinostat			Recurrent GBM, Malignant Glioma, Adult Brain Tumor	NCT01738646	II
31	**Bortezomib**	Multiple myeloma	Inhibits 26S proteasome.	GB, GS	NCT00611325	II
	Bortezomib, Temozolomide			Brain and CNS Tumors	NCT00998010	II
32	**Bendamustine Hydrochloride**	Chronic lymphocytic leukemia and indolent B-cell non-Hodgkin lymphoma	Alkylating agent, crosslinks DNA and induces apoptosis.	Adult—AA, Adult GC-GB, GB, GS, Recurrent Adult Brain Neoplasm	NCT00823797	II
33	**Fotemustine**	Metastatic melanoma	Alkylating agent.	GBM	NCT01474239	II
34	**Etoposide**	Testicular and small cell lung tumors	Inhibits Topoisomerase II.	GB, GS	NCT00612430	II
	VP-16 (Etoposide), Temozolomide			GB, GS	NCT00613028	II

Continued

Table 4 Repurposed drugs that completed clinical trials for astrocytic tumor therapy—cont'd

<table>
<tr><th>Sl. No.</th><th>Repurposed drug name</th><th>Current approved use</th><th>Mechanism of action</th><th>Conditions</th><th>NCT number</th><th>Phase completed I|II/II/III</th></tr>
<tr><td>35</td><td>Vincristine sulfate, Carboplatin, Temozolomide,</td><td>Acute leukemia, malignant lymphoma, Hodgkin's disease, acute erythremia, acute panmyelosis</td><td>Interacts with tubulin and inhibits mitosis at metaphase.</td><td>Brain Tumor, CNS Tumor</td><td>NCT00077207</td><td>NA</td></tr>
<tr><td>36</td><td>ZD6474, temozolomide</td><td>Anticancer</td><td>Inhibits tyrosine kinases—VEGFR, EGFR, and RET.</td><td>GBM, GS</td><td>NCT00441142</td><td>I|II</td></tr>
<tr><td>37</td><td>Motexafin Gadolinium (Xcytrin), Temozolomide</td><td>Nonsmall-cell lung cancer (NSCLC) patients with brain metastases, rejected by FDA (Dec 2007)</td><td>Accumulates selectively in cancer cells and induces apoptosis by disrupting redox-dependent pathways through inhibition of Thioredoxin.</td><td>Adult—GC-GB, GB, GS</td><td>NCT00305864</td><td>I|II</td></tr>
<tr><td>38</td><td>Carboxyamidotriazole</td><td>Novel drug being used for the treatment of Lymphoma, Lung Cancer, Breast Cancer, Kidney Cancer, and Ovarian Cancer, in trials.</td><td>–</td><td>Adult—GC-GB, GB, GS</td><td>NCT00004146</td><td>II</td></tr>
</table>

Drugs not labeled for anti-cancer therapy						
39	**Disulfiram/Copper,** Temozolomide (TMZ)	Alcohol addiction	Inhibits alcohol oxidation at acetaldehyde stage of alcohol metabolism.	Recurrent GB	NCT03034135	II
40	**Donepezil**	Alzheimer's Disease and other types of dementia	Inhibits Acetylcholine esterase and downregulates NMDA receptors.	Brain and CNS Tumors	NCT00452868	Early Phase I
	Donepezil hydrochloride			Brain Tumors	NCT00369785	III
41	**Enzastaurin**	Novel drug being tried on brain cancer, Enzyme-inducing antiepileptic drugs (EIAED), Nonenzyme inducing antiepileptic drugs (NEIAED)	It is a Ser-Threonine kinase inhibitor and inhibits signaling through PKC-B and PI3K/AKT pathways.	GBM	NCT00509821	II
	Enzastaurin,			Recurrent GB	NCT00586508	II
	Enzastaurin, Temozolomide			GB, GBM, GS	NCT00402116	I|II
42	**poly ICLC**	–		Brain and CNS Tumors	NCT00058123	II
	poly ICLC, Temozolomide	–		GBM	NCT00262730	II
43	**Hydroxychloroquine,** Temozolomide	Antimalarial & Disease modifying anti-rheumatic drug	Inhibits Autophagy	Brain and CNS Tumors	NCT00486603	I|II
44	**Trans Sodium Crocetinate (TSC)**	Hemorrhagic stroke	Vitamin A analog increases O_2 diffusion in the plasma.	GB, GBM, Glioma	NCT01465347	I|II
45	**Valproic acid**	Anticonvulsant (Seizures)	Inhibits succinic semialdehyde dehydrogenase and indirectly promotes GABA-ergic neurotransmission.	Malignant Gliomas, GBM, AA, Gliomatosis Cerebri, GS, Brainstem Glioma, Diffuse Intrinsic Pontine Glioma	NCT00879437	II

Continued

Table 4 Repurposed drugs that completed clinical trials for astrocytic tumor therapy—cont'd

<table>
<tr><th>Sl. No.</th><th>Repurposed drug name</th><th>Current approved use</th><th>Mechanism of action</th><th>Conditions</th><th>NCT number</th><th>Phase completed I|II/II/III</th></tr>
<tr><td>46</td><td>Celecoxib, Isotretinoin, Temozolomide, Thalidomide</td><td>Used to treat severe recalcitrant acne</td><td>Interferes with the functioning of sebaceous gland cells.</td><td>Brain and CNS Tumors, GBM</td><td>NCT00112502</td><td>II</td></tr>
<tr><td>47</td><td>Plerixafor, Temozolomide</td><td>Hematopoietic stem cell mobilizer</td><td>Inhibits CXCR4 chemokine receptors on CD34+ cells, reversibly preventing binding of the cognate ligand, allowing the mobilization of progenitor cells.</td><td>Adult—GC-GB, GB, GS, Mixed Glioma</td><td>NCT01977677</td><td>I|II</td></tr>
<tr><td>48</td><td>Veliparib (ABT-888), Temozolomide</td><td>–</td><td></td><td>Brain and CNS Tumors</td><td>NCT01026493</td><td>I|II</td></tr>
<tr><td>49</td><td>Capecitabine, Celecoxib (Celebrex), Temozolomide, Lomustine, 6-Thioguanine</td><td>Nonsteroidal anti-inflammatory drug</td><td>Binds to the cadherin-11, protein involved in tumor progression and PDK-1 signaling mechanism. Also inhibits carbonic anhydrase-2 and 3, which enhances the anticancer effects.</td><td>Anaplastic Glioma of Brain, GBM, Brain Cancer</td><td>NCT00504660</td><td>II</td></tr>
</table>

50	**R-(−)-gossypol acetic acid**	**Novel drug** being tested on Recurrent Extensive-Stage Small Cell Lung Cancer and Brain tumor	–	Adult—GC-GB, GB, GS, Recurrent Adult Brain Tumor	NCT00540722	II
51	**Terameprocol**	**Novel drug** being tested on CNS tumor	–	Brain and CNS Tumors	NCT00404248	I|II

[a]Source: https://www.clinicaltrials.gov/ (Accessed 15 March 2022).

[b]Abbreviations: *AA*, anaplastic astrocytoma; *GB*, glioblastoma; *GBM*, glioblastoma multiforme; *GS*, gliosarcoma; *GC-GB*, giant cell glioblastoma; *CNS*, central nervous system; *GCA*, giant cell astrocytoma; *OA*, oligoastrocytoma.

malate is a multiple RTKI that is used for the treatment of renal cell carcinoma and imatinib-resistant gastrointestinal stromal tumor by binding to and inhibiting VEGFR and PDGFR [145]. This drug was used as a Phase-II (NCT01462695) regimen for the treatment of pediatric refractory or recurrent HGG or ependymoma. However, though well tolerated by pediatric patients, there was an insufficient activity of the drug as a monotherapy for refractory or recurrent HGG or ependymoma [146]. Other PDGFR antagonist anti-cancer drugs, such as **tandutinib, sorafenib tosylate, dovitinib** and **dasatinib**, have also been tested for their efficacy as a Glioblastoma therapy in monotherapy or combination with approved anti-glioma therapies [142]. Anti-angiogenic therapies targeting VEGFR have been studied either as a monotherapy or in combination therapies (Table 4). In these lines, **tivozanib**, an oral VEGFR antagonist used to treat renal cell cancer has been studied at Phase II level (NCT01846871) in patients with recurrent glioblastoma. However, it showed a limited anti-tumor effect; clear structural changes in vasculature were not observed and there was no significant change in the volume of the increasing tumor [147]. Similarly, pazopanib, a second-generation RTKI, used for the treatment of soft tissue sarcoma and renal cell cancer could not prolong PFS in patients suffering from recurrent glioblastoma in a Phase-II trial (NCT00459381) as a single agent [148].

Other than RTKIs there are several other anticancer drug classes that have been repurposed for glioma treatment. This includes the topoisomerase inhibitors (irinotecan and topotecan), Src and Src-family of protein kinase inhibitors (dasatinib and bosutinib), and alkylating agents (carboplatin) [142]. Src kinase is another important kinase that is upregulated in several solid tumors, including 61% of GBM tumor samples collected from patients after their first resection [149]. It is also upregulated after bevacizumab therapy. Upregulation of this kinase has been implicated in reduced cell adhesion and increased metastatic potential [150,151]. **Bosutinib** and **dasatinib** are two drugs that have been used in clinical trials for investigating the drugs' efficacy in treating recurrent glioblastoma patients as a monotherapy or as a combination therapy with bevacizumab, respectively. From the clinical trials, it can be concluded that bosutinib (NCT01331291) and dasatinib (NCT00892177) were not effective as a monotherapy or as a combination therapy, respectively, at ameliorating recurrent GBM [152,153]. **Irinotecan** is a topoisomerase I inhibitor and is originally prescribed for colorectal cancer. Irinotecan together with bevacizumab showed better PFS-6 rate and median PFS compared to single TMZ treatment in a clinical trial (NCT00967330). However, the OS of the patients did not improve comparatively [154].

5.2 Nonanticancer drug repurposing

Other than these antitumor drugs there are many nonanticancer drugs that have been researched on animal models for their potential anti-glioma activity and some of them are also being investigated at clinical levels [142]. **Disulfiram**, a drug that is widely used to treat alcohol abuse, has been found to suppress refractory GBM in preclinical studies. Being used for many decades, disulfiram has good safety profiles and is also absorbed in the BBB [155,156]. In a preclinical study, it inhibited the growth of TMZ-resistant glioma cells and did not affect the normal astrocytes. Downregulation of PLK1, a cell cycle kinase, by the drug has been implicated in its cytotoxicity [156]. In another independent study, disufiram/Cu combination has been found to target the glioma stem cell-like population [157]. Clinical trials are also underway to investigate the potential of disulfiram as a regimen for recurrent GBM. Treatment of GBM patients with **trans sodium crocetinate** (TSC) increases the efficacy of SOC for the disease. Originally this drug is used to increase the whole body oxygen supply and ameliorates symptoms of hemorrhagic stroke [158]. In a recent clinical trial; it has improved the efficacy of radiation therapy with 36% of full-dose TSC treated patients survived at 2 years compared to the historical SOC survival values of 27%–30% [158]. **Valproic acid**, a mood-stabilizer and an anticonvulsant, has been well studied for its anti-glioma activity. It inhibits glioma proliferation and also invasion. It downregulates Snail1 and Twist1 and relocalizes E-cadherin, thereby inhibiting the EMT process [159]. It also downregulates MMPs to inhibit invasion and induces cell-cycle arrest at G0/G1 phase and apoptosis by ERK/Akt pathway [160,161]. Valproic acid also inhibits angiogenesis by preventing endothelial proliferation and its tube formation and indirectly decreases the VEGF secretion by glioma cells [161,162]. Clinical trials are being conducted to study the effects of valproic acid on glioma patients.

6. Conclusion

Astrocytic tumors are one of the most difficult to treat solid tumors and both its poor prognosis and survival have initiated an enormous amount of research for therapy against these tumors. Of the various strategies used for drug discovery against astrocytic tumors, pharmacogenomic analysis, QSAR studies, molecular network-led hypothesis-driven strategies, virtual screening, and drug repositioning have been significant (Fig. 5). Among these drugs getting newly identified as a possible treatment against astrocytic tumors, the tyrosine kinase inhibitor ibrunitib is one drug that has been identified through multiple approaches as pharmacogenomic as well as independent hypothesis-driven strategies. Ibrunitib was demonstrated to be inhibitory to the glioblastoma stem cells that drive the malignant growth in GBM through the BMX-mediated activation of STAT3 while not affecting the neural stem cells that lack the BMX receptors. The drug is presently in the clinical trial for use in postsurgical adjuvant therapy either with or without TMZ against both methylated and unmethylated MGMT promoter-bearing GBM. Other than this there are quite a few drugs that have been identified by virtual screening and already in or past their preclinical trials and

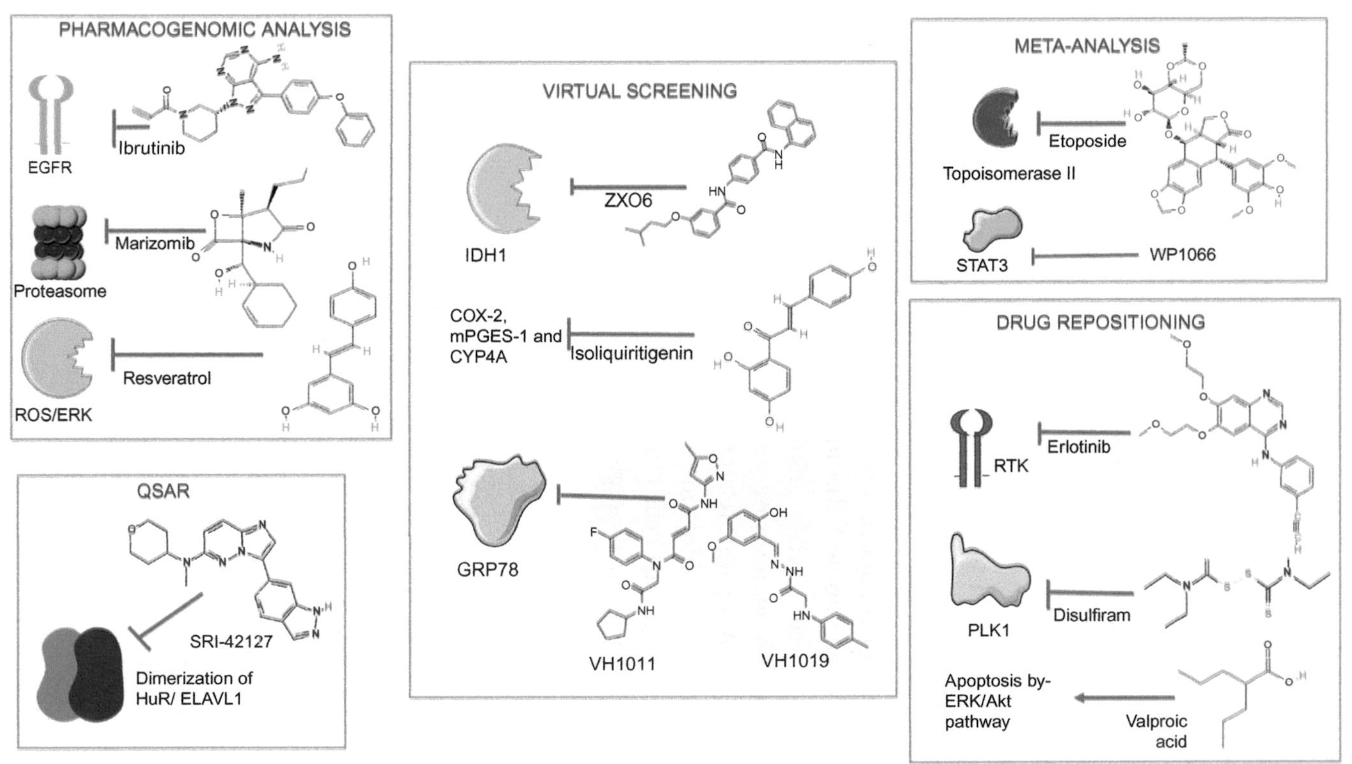

Fig. 5 Emerging drugs for astrocytic tumors identified by strategies involving in silico approaches.

presently on their way to the clinical studies. Anti-cancerous drugs not tried before for brain cancers, and other drugs presently approved for diverse diseases such as mood stabilizers, alcohol abuse, etc., are being repositioned to check their efficacy against astrocytic tumors. Considerable number of these repositioned drugs are presently in their Phase I/II clinical trials bringing us hope for better and more effective treatment against astrocytic tumors.

Acknowledgments

No funding was received specifically for writing this article.

Conflict of interest

None declared.

References

[1] D.W. Parsons, S. Jones, X. Zhang, J.C. Lin, R.J. Leary, P. Angenendt, P. Mankoo, H. Carter, I.M. Siu, G.L. Gallia, A. Olivi, R. McLendon, B.A. Rasheed, S. Keir, T. Nikolskaya, Y. Nikolsky, D.A. Busam, H. Tekleab, L.A. Diaz Jr., J. Hartigan, et al., An integrated genomic analysis of human glioblastoma multiforme, Science 321 (5897) (2008) 1807–1812, https://doi.org/10.1126/science.1164382.

[2] D.N. Louis, H. Ohgaki, O.D. Wiestler, eds., et al., WHO Classification of Tumours of the Central Nervous System, IARC Press, Lyon, France, 2007.

[3] D.A. Forst, B.V. Nahed, J.S. Loeffler, T.T. Batchelor, Low-grade gliomas, Oncologist 19 (4) (2014) 403–413, https://doi.org/10.1634/theoncologist.2013-0345.

[4] M. Krishnatreya, A.C. Kataki, J.D. Sharma, M. Bhattacharyya, P. Nandy, M. Hazarika, Brief descriptive epidemiology of primary malignant brain tumours from North-East India, Asian Pac. J. Cancer Prev. 15 (22) (2014) 9871–9873, https://doi.org/10.7314/apjcp.2014.15.22.9871.

[5] M. Kurdi, N.S. Butt, S. Baeesa, B. Alghamdi, Y. Maghrabi, A. Bardeesi, R. Saeedi, A.I. Lary, Epidemiological distribution of primary central nervous system tumours in the Western Province of Saudi Arabia: a local registry from neuroscience-affiliated centers, Epidemiol. Health 43 (2021), e2021037, https://doi.org/10.4178/epih.e2021037.

[6] K.D. Miller, Q.T. Ostrom, C. Kruchko, N. Patil, T. Tihan, G. Cioffi, H.E. Fuchs, K.A. Waite, A. Jemal, R.L. Siegel, J.S. Barnholtz-Sloan, Brain and other central nervous system tumour statistics, 2021, CA Cancer J. Clin. 71 (5) (2021) 381–406, https://doi.org/10.3322/caac.21693.

[7] A.S. Zhang, Q.T. Ostrom, C. Kruchko, L. Rogers, D.M. Peereboom, J.S. Barnholtz-Sloan, Complete prevalence of malignant primary brain tumours registry data in the United States compared with other common cancers, 2010, Neuro-Oncology 19 (5) (2017) 726–735, https://doi.org/10.1093/neuonc/now252.

[8] S. Gritsch, T.T. Batchelor, L.N. Gonzalez Castro, Diagnostic, therapeutic, and prognostic implications of the 2021 World Health Organization classification of tumors of the central nervous system, Cancer 128 (1) (2022) 47–58, https://doi.org/10.1002/cncr.33918.

[9] A. Hirtz, F. Rech, H. Dubois-Pot-Schneider, H. Dumond, Astrocytoma: a hormone-sensitive tumor? Int. J. Mol. Sci. 21 (23) (2020) 9114, https://doi.org/10.3390/ijms21239114.

[10] D.R. Johnson, P.D. Brown, E. Galanis, J.E. Hammack, Pilocytic astrocytoma survival in adults: analysis of the surveillance, epidemiology, and end results program of the National Cancer Institute, J. Neuro-Oncol. 108 (1) (2012) 187–193, https://doi.org/10.1007/s11060-012-0829-0.

[11] A. Jain, M.C. Sharma, V. Suri, S.S. Kale, A.K. Mahapatra, M. Tatke, G. Chacko, A. Pathak, V. Santosh, P. Nair, N. Husain, C. Sarkar, Spectrum of pediatric brain tumours in India: a multi-institutional study, Neurol. India 59 (2) (2011) 208–211, https://doi.org/10.4103/0028-3886.79142.
[12] M.K. Rana, T.S. Barwal, U. Sharma, R. Bansal, K. Singh, A. Rana, A. Jain, U. Khera, Current trends of carcinoma: experience of a tertiary care cancer center in North India, Cureus 13 (6) (2021), e15788, https://doi.org/10.7759/cureus.15788.
[13] The International Hap Map Consortium, The international hap map project, Nature 426 (2003) 789–796, https://doi.org/10.1038/nature02168.
[14] M. Uhlen, P. Oksvold, L. Fagerberg, E. Lundberg, K. Jonasson, M. Forsberg, M. Zwahlen, C. Kampf, K. Wester, S. Hober, H. Wernerus, L. Björling, F. Ponten, Towards a knowledge-based human protein atlas, Nat. Biotechnol. 28 (12) (2010) 1248–1250, https://doi.org/10.1038/nbt1210-1248.
[15] D.S. Wishart, D. Tzur, C. Knox, R. Eisner, A.C. Guo, N. Young, D. Cheng, K. Jewell, D. Arndt, S. Sawhney, C. Fung, L. Nikolai, M. Lewis, M.A. Coutouly, I. Forsythe, P. Tang, S. Shrivastava, K. Jeroncic, P. Stothard, G. Amegbey, D. Block, H.H. Hau, J. Wagner, J. Miniaci, M. Clements, M. Gebremedhin, N. Guo, Y. Zhang, G.E. Duggan, G.D. MacInnis, A.M. Weljie, R. Dowlatabadi, F. Bamforth, D. Clive, R. Greiner, L. Li, T. Marrie, B.D. Sykes, H.J. Vogel, L. Querengesser, HMDB: the human metabolome database, Nucleic Acids Res. 35 (Suppl 1) (2007) D521–D526, https://doi.org/10.1093/nar/gkl923.
[16] A. Blum, P. Wang, J.C. Zenklusen, SnapShot: TCGA-analyzed tumors, Cell 173 (2) (2018) 530, https://doi.org/10.1016/j.cell.2018.03.059.
[17] Cancer Genome Atlas Research Network, Comprehensive genomic characterization defines human glioblastoma genes and core pathways, Nature 455 (7216) (2008) 1061–1068, https://doi.org/10.1038/nature07385.
[18] D.N. Louis, A. Perry, P. Wesseling, D.J. Brat, I.A. Cree, D. Figarella-Branger, C. Hawkins, H.K. Ng, S.M. Pfister, G. Reifenberger, R. Soffietti, A. von Deimling, D.W. Ellison, The 2021 WHO classification of Tumors of the central nervous system: a summary, Neuro-Oncology 23 (8) (2021) 1231–1251, https://doi.org/10.1093/neuonc/noab106.
[19] National Cancer Institute, ClinicalTrials.gov Identifiers: …NCT00978458, 2022, Available from: http://www.cancer.gov/clinicaltrials. (Accessed 15 March 2022).
[20] Drugs Approved for Brain Tumors, National Cancer Institute, 2022, https://www.cancer.gov/about-cancer/treatment/drugs/brain. (Accessed 20 May 2022).
[21] J.P. Fisher, D.C. Adamson, Current FDA-approved therapies for high-grade malignant gliomas, Biomedicine 9 (3) (2021) 324, https://doi.org/10.3390/biomedicines9030324.
[22] R. Stupp, W.P. Mason, M.J. van den Bent, M. Weller, B. Fisher, M.J.B. Taphoorn, K. Belanger, A.A. Brandes, C. Marosi, U. Bogdahn, J. Curschmann, R.C. Janzer, S.K. Ludwin, T. Gorlia, A. Allgeier, D. Lacombe, J.G. Cairncross, E. Eisenhauer, R.O. Mirimanoff, et al., Radiotherapy plus concomitant and adjuvant temozolomide for glioblastoma, N. Engl. J. Med. 352 (10) (2005) 987–996, https://doi.org/10.1056/NEJMoa043330.
[23] M.D. Walker, E. Alexander, W.E. Hunt, C.S. MacCarty, M.S. Mahaley, J. Mealey, H.A. Norrell, G. Owens, J. Ransohoff, C.B. Wilson, E.A. Gehan, T.A. Strike, Evaluation of BCNU and/or radiotherapy in the treatment of anaplastic gliomas. A cooperative clinical trial, J. Neurosurg. 49 (3) (1978) 333–343, https://doi.org/10.3171/jns.1978.49.3.0333.
[24] M. Westphal, D.C. Hilt, E. Bortey, P. Delavault, R. Olivares, P.C. Warnke, I.R. Whittle, J. Jääskeläinen, Z. Ram, A phase 3 trial of local chemotherapy with biodegradable carmustine (BCNU) wafers (Gliadel wafers) in patients with primary malignant glioma, Neuro-Oncology 5 (2) (2003) 79–88, https://doi.org/10.1093/neuonc/5.2.79.
[25] F.H. Hochberg, R. Linggood, L. Wolfson, W.H. Baker, P. Kornblith, Quality and duration of survival in glioblastoma multiforme. Combined surgical, radiation, and lomustine therapy, JAMA 241 (10) (1979) 1016–1018.
[26] D.N. Franz, E. Belousova, S. Sparagana, E.M. Bebin, M. Frost, R. Kuperman, O. Witt, M.H. Kohrman, J.R. Flamini, J.Y. Wu, P. Curatolo, P.J. de Vries, V.H. Whittemore, E.A. Thiele, J.P. Ford, G. Shah, H. Cauwel, D. Lebwohl, T. Sahmoud, S. Jozwiak, Efficacy and safety of everolimus for subependymal giant cell astrocytomas associated with tuberous sclerosis complex (EXIST-1): a multicentre, randomised, placebo-controlled phase 3 trial, Lancet 381 (9861) (2013) 125–132, https://doi.org/10.1016/S0140-6736(12)61134-9.

[27] E. Jonasch, F. Donskov, O. Iliopoulos, W.K. Rathmell, V.K. Narayan, B.L. Maughan, S. Oudard, T. Else, J.K. Maranchie, S.J. Welsh, S. Thamake, E.K. Park, R.F. Perini, W.M. Linehan, R. Srinivasan, MK-6482-004 Investigators, Belzutifan for renal cell carcinoma in von Hippel-Lindau disease, N. Engl. J. Med. 385 (22) (2021) 2036–2046, https://doi.org/10.1056/NEJMoa2103425.
[28] C. Fernandes, A. Costa, L. Osório, R.C. Lago, P. Linhares, B. Carvalho, C. Caeiro, Current standards of care in glioblastoma therapy, in: S. De Vleeschouwer (Ed.), Glioblastoma, Codon Publications, 2017. http://www.ncbi.nlm.nih.gov/books/NBK469987/.
[29] S. Jiapaer, T. Furuta, S. Tanaka, T. Kitabayashi, M. Nakada, Potential strategies overcoming the temozolomide resistance for glioblastoma, Neurol. Med. Chir. 58 (10) (2018) 405–421, https://doi.org/10.2176/nmc.ra.2018-0141.
[30] J.N. Sarkaria, G.J. Kitange, C.D. James, R. Plummer, H. Calvert, M. Weller, W. Wick, Mechanisms of chemoresistance to alkylating agents in malignant glioma, Clin. Cancer Res. 14 (10) (2008) 2900–2908, https://doi.org/10.1158/1078-0432.CCR-07-1719.
[31] K. Wiwatchaitawee, J.C. Quarterman, S.M. Geary, A.K. Salem, Enhancement of therapies for glioblastoma (GBM) using nanoparticle-based delivery systems, AAPS PharmSciTech 22 (2) (2021) 71, https://doi.org/10.1208/s12249-021-01928-9.
[32] M. Weller, E. Le Rhun, How did lomustine become standard of care in recurrent glioblastoma? Cancer Treat. Rev. 87 (2020), 102029, https://doi.org/10.1016/j.ctrv.2020.102029.
[33] U. Lassen, M. Mau-Sørensen, H.S. Poulsen, Orphan drugs in glioblastoma multiforme: a review, Orphan Drugs Res. Rev. 4 (2014) 83–91, https://doi.org/10.2147/ODRR.S46018.
[34] M. Brada, S. Stenning, R. Gabe, L.C. Thompson, D. Levy, R. Rampling, S. Erridge, F. Saran, R. Gattamaneni, K. Hopkins, S. Beall, V.P. Collins, S.-M. Lee, Temozolomide versus procarbazine, Lomustine, and vincristine in recurrent high-grade glioma, J. Clin. Oncol. 28 (30) (2010) 4601–4608, https://doi.org/10.1200/JCO.2009.27.1932.
[35] C.G. Hadjipanayis, W. Stummer, 5-ALA and FDA approval for glioma surgery, J. Neuro-Oncol. 141 (3) (2019) 479–486, https://doi.org/10.1007/s11060-019-03098-y.
[36] D.A. Bota, A. Desjardins, J.A. Quinn, M.L. Affronti, H.S. Friedman, Interstitial chemotherapy with biodegradable BCNU (Gliadel) wafers in the treatment of malignant gliomas, Ther. Clin. Risk Manag. 3 (5) (2007) 707–715.
[37] E.D. Deeks, Belzutifan: first approval, Drugs 81 (16) (2021) 1921–1927, https://doi.org/10.1007/s40265-021-01606-x.
[38] No Authors, FDA OK's HIF2α inhibitor Belzutifan, Cancer Discov 11 (10) (2021) 2360–2361, https://doi.org/10.1158/2159-8290.CD-NB2021-0377.
[39] US Food and Drug Administration Center for Drug Evaluation and Research, 2022. https://www.fda.gov/drugs/resources-information-approved-drugs/fda-approves-belzutifan-cancers-associated-von-hippel-lindau-disease.
[40] S. Gläsker, E. Vergauwen, C.A. Koch, A. Kutikov, A.O. Vortmeyer, Von Hippel-Lindau disease: current challenges and future prospects, OncoTargets Ther. 13 (2020) 5669–5690, https://doi.org/10.2147/OTT.S190753.
[41] P. Johansson, C. Krona, S. Kundu, M. Doroszko, S. Baskaran, L. Schmidt, C. Vinel, E. Almstedt, R. Elgendy, L. Elfineh, C. Gallant, S. Lundsten, F.J. Ferrer Gago, A. Hakkarainen, P. Sipilä, M. Häggblad, U. Martens, B. Lundgren, M.M. Frigault, D.P. Lane, et al., A patient-derived cell atlas informs precision targeting of glioblastoma, Cell Rep. 32 (2) (2020), 107897, https://doi.org/10.1016/j.celrep.2020.107897.
[42] J.K. Lee, Z. Liu, J.K. Sa, S. Shin, J. Wang, M. Bordyuh, H.J. Cho, O. Elliott, T. Chu, S.W. Choi, D. Rosenbloom, I.H. Lee, Y.J. Shin, H.J. Kang, D. Kim, S.Y. Kim, M.H. Sim, J. Kim, T. Lee, Y.J. Seo, et al., Pharmacogenomic landscape of patient-derived tumor cells informs precision oncology therapy, Nat. Genet. 50 (10) (2018) 1399–1411, https://doi.org/10.1038/s41588-018-0209-6.
[43] M.J. Garnett, E.J. Edelman, S.J. Heidorn, C.D. Greenman, A. Dastur, K.W. Lau, P. Greninger, I.R. Thompson, X. Luo, J. Soares, Q. Liu, F. Iorio, D. Surdez, L. Chen, R.J. Milano, G.R. Bignell, A.T. Tam, H. Davies, J.A. Stevenson, S. Barthorpe, et al., Systematic identification of genomic markers of drug sensitivity in cancer cells, Nature 483 (7391) (2012) 570–575, https://doi.org/10.1038/nature11005.
[44] L. Laaniste, P.K. Srivastava, J. Stylianou, N. Syed, S. Cases-Cunillera, K. Shkura, et al., Integrated systems-genetic analyses reveal a network target for delaying glioma progression, Ann. Clin. Transl. Neurol. 6 (9) (2019) 1616–1638, https://doi.org/10.1002/acn3.50850.

[45] A. Leonard, J.E. Wolff, Etoposide improves survival in high-grade glioma: a meta-analysis, Anticancer Res. 33 (8) (2013) 3307–3315.
[46] C.M. Gorick, J.J. Saucerman, R.J. Price, Computational model of brain endothelial cell signaling pathways predicts therapeutic targets for cerebral pathologies, J. Mol. Cell. Cardiol. 164 (2022) 17–28, https://doi.org/10.1016/j.yjmcc.2021.11.005.
[47] B. Zhu, X. Mao, Y. Man, Potential drug prediction of glioblastoma based on drug perturbation-induced gene expression signatures, Biomed. Res. Int. 2021 (2021) 6659701, https://doi.org/10.1155/2021/6659701.
[48] A. Guha, S. Waris, L.B. Nabors, N. Filippova, M. Gorospe, T. Kwan, P.H. King, The versatile role of HuR in glioblastoma and its potential as a therapeutic target for a multi-pronged attack, Adv. Drug Deliv. Rev. 181 (2022), 114082, https://doi.org/10.1016/j.addr.2021.114082.
[49] N. Filippova, X. Yang, S. Ananthan, J. Calano, V. Pathak, L. Bratton, R.H. Vekariya, S. Zhang, E. Ofori, E.N. Hayward, D. Namkoong, D.K. Crossman, M.R. Crowley, P.H. King, J. Mobley, L.B. Nabors, Targeting the HuR oncogenic role with a new class of cytoplasmic dimerization inhibitors, Cancer Res. 81 (8) (2021) 2220–2233, https://doi.org/10.1158/0008-5472.CAN-20-2858.
[50] N. Filippova, X. Yang, S. Ananthan, A. Sorochinsky, J.R. Hackney, Z. Gentry, S. Bae, P. King, L.B. Nabors, Hu antigen R (HuR) multimerization contributes to glioma disease progression, J. Biol. Chem. 292 (41) (2017) 16999–17010, https://doi.org/10.1074/jbc.M117.797878.
[51] N.C. Meisner, M. Hintersteiner, K. Mueller, R. Bauer, J.M. Seifert, H.U. Naegeli, J. Ottl, L. Oberer, C. Guenat, S. Moss, N. Harrer, M. Woisetschlaeger, C. Buehler, V. Uhl, M. Auer, Identification and mechanistic characterization of low-molecular-weight inhibitors for HuR, Nat. Chem. Biol. 3 (8) (2007) 508–515, https://doi.org/10.1038/nchembio.2007.14.
[52] R. Jain, A. Dasgupta, A. Moiyadi, S. Srivastava, Transcriptional analysis of JAK/STAT signaling in glioblastoma multiforme, Curr. Pharmacogenomics Pers. Med. 10 (1) (2012) 54–69.
[53] W. Ji, Y. Liu, B. Xu, J. Mei, C. Cheng, Y. Xiao, K. Yang, W. Huang, J. Jiao, H. Liu, J. Shao, Bioinformatics analysis of expression profiles and prognostic values of the signal transducer and activator of transcription family genes in glioma, Front. Genet. 12 (2021), 625234, https://doi.org/10.3389/fgene.2021.625234.
[54] C. Senft, M. Priester, M. Polacin, K. Schröder, V. Seifert, D. Kögel, J. Weissenberger, Inhibition of the JAK-2/STAT3 signaling pathway impedes the migratory and invasive potential of human glioblastoma cells, J. Neuro-Oncol. 101 (3) (2011) 393–403, https://doi.org/10.1007/s11060-010-0273-y.
[55] J.K. Hockings, A.L. Pasternak, A.L. Erwin, N.T. Mason, C. Eng, J.K. Hicks, Pharmacogenomics: an evolving clinical tool for precision medicine, Cleve. Clin. J. Med. 87 (2) (2020) 91–99, https://doi.org/10.3949/ccjm.87a.19073.
[56] D.M. Roden, H.L. McLeod, M.V. Relling, M.S. Williams, G.A. Mensah, J.F. Peterson, S.L. Van Driest, Pharmacogenomics, Lancet 394 (10197) (2019) 521–532, https://doi.org/10.1016/S0140-6736(19)31276-0.
[57] Y.H. Ling, L. Liebes, Y. Zou, R. Perez-Soler, Reactive oxygen species generation and mitochondrial dysfunction in the apoptotic response to bortezomib, a novel proteasome inhibitor, in human H460 non-small cell lung cancer cells, J. Biol. Chem. 278 (36) (2003) 33714–33723, https://doi.org/10.1074/jbc.M302559200.
[58] P. Roth, W.P. Mason, P.G. Richardson, M. Weller, Proteasome inhibition for the treatment of glioblastoma, Expert Opin. Investig. Drugs 29 (10) (2020) 1133–1141, https://doi.org/10.1080/13543784.2020.1803827.
[59] D.A. Bota, W. Mason, S. Kesari, R. Magge, B. Winograd, I. Elias, S.D. Reich, N. Levin, M. Trikha, A. Desjardins, Marizomib alone or in combination with bevacizumab in patients with recurrent glioblastoma: phase I/II clinical trial data, Neuro-oncol. Adv. 3 (1) (2021), vdab142, https://doi.org/10.1093/noajnl/vdab142.
[60] P. Roth, J. Reijneveld, T. Gorlia, F. Dhermain, F. De Vos, M. Vanlancker, C. O'Callaghan, E. Le Rhun, M. van den Bent, W. Mason, M. Weller, P14.124 EORTC 1709/CCTG CE.8: a phase III trial of marizomib in combination with standard temozolomide-based radiochemotherapy versus standard temozolomide-based radiochemotherapy alone in patients with newly diagnosed glioblastoma, Neuro-Oncology 21 (Suppl 3) (2019) iii98, https://doi.org/10.1093/neuonc/noz126.359.
[61] A. Franceschini, D. Szklarczyk, S. Frankild, M. Kuhn, M. Simonovic, A. Roth, J. Lin, P. Minguez, P. Bork, C. von Mering, L.J. Jensen, STRING v9.1: protein-protein interaction networks, with

increased coverage and integration, Nucleic Acids Res. 41 (Database issue) (2013) D808–D815, https://doi.org/10.1093/nar/gks1094.

[62] M. Griffith, O.L. Griffith, A.C. Coffman, J.V. Weible, J.F. McMichael, N.C. Spies, J. Koval, I. Das, M.-B. Callaway, J.M. Eldred, C.A. Miller, J. Subramanian, R. Govindan, R.D. Kumar, R. Bose, L. Ding, J.R. Walker, D.E. Larson, D.J. Dooling, S.M. Smith, R.K. Wilson, DGIdb: mining the druggable genome, Nat. Methods 10 (12) (2013) 1209–1210, https://doi.org/10.1038/nmeth.2689.

[63] Y. Shi, O.A. Guryanova, W. Zhou, C. Liu, Z. Huang, X. Fang, X. Wang, C. Chen, Q. Wu, Z. He, W. Wang, W. Zhang, T. Jiang, Q. Liu, Y. Chen, W. Wang, J. Wu, L. Kim, R.C. Gimple, H. Feng, et al., Ibrutinib inactivates BMX-STAT3 in glioma stem cells to impair malignant growth and radioresistance, Sci. Transl. Med. 10 (443) (2018), eaah6816, https://doi.org/10.1126/scitranslmed.aah6816.

[64] Z. Wang, C.D. Monteiro, K.M. Jagodnik, N.F. Fernandez, G.W. Gundersen, A.D. Rouillard, S.L. Jenkins, A.S. Feldmann, K.S. Hu, M.G. McDermott, Q. Duan, N.R. Clark, M.R. Jones, Y. Kou, T. Goff, H. Woodland, F. Amaral, G.L. Szeto, O. Fuchs, S.M. Schüssler-Fiorenza Rose, et al., Extraction and analysis of signatures from the gene expression omnibus by the crowd, Nat. Commun. 7 (2016) 12846, https://doi.org/10.1038/ncomms12846.

[65] J.J. Raizer, L.E. Abrey, A.B. Lassman, S.M. Chang, K.R. Lamborn, J.G. Kuhn, W.K. Yung, M.R. Gilbert, K.A. Aldape, P.Y. Wen, H.A. Fine, M. Mehta, L.M. Deangelis, F. Lieberman, T.F. Cloughesy, H.I. Robins, J. Dancey, M.D. Prados, North American Brain Tumor Consortium, A phase II trial of erlotinib in patients with recurrent malignant gliomas and nonprogressive glioblastoma multiforme postradiation therapy, Neuro-Oncology 12 (1) (2010) 95–103, https://doi.org/10.1093/neuonc/nop015.

[66] C.J. Lin, C.C. Lee, Y.L. Shih, T.Y. Lin, S.H. Wang, Y.F. Lin, C.M. Shih, Resveratrol enhances the therapeutic effect of temozolomide against malignant glioma in vitro and in vivo by inhibiting autophagy, Free Radic. Biol. Med. 52 (2) (2012) 377–391, https://doi.org/10.1016/j.freeradbiomed.2011.10.487.

[67] P.A. Clark, S. Bhattacharya, A. Elmayan, S.R. Darjatmoko, B.A. Thuro, M.B. Yan, P.R. van Ginkel, A.S. Polans, J.S. Kuo, Resveratrol targeting of AKT and p53 in glioblastoma and glioblastoma stem-like cells to suppress growth and infiltration, J. Neurosurg. 126 (5) (2017) 1448–1460, https://doi.org/10.3171/2016.1.JNS152077.

[68] K. Funatsu, T. Miyao, M. Arakawa, Systematic generation of chemical structures for rational drug design based on QSAR models, Curr. Comput. Aided Drug Des. 7 (1) (2011) 1–9, https://doi.org/10.2174/157340911793743556.

[69] C. Nantasenamat, C. Isarankura-Na-Ayudhya, T. Naenna, V. Prachayasittikul, A practical overview of quantitative structure-activity relationship, EXCLI J. 8 (2009) 74–88.

[70] S. Tan, X. Hou, L. Mei, Dihydrotanshinone I inhibits human glioma cell proliferation via the activation of ferroptosis, Oncol. Lett. 20 (4) (2020) 122, https://doi.org/10.3892/ol.2020.11980.

[71] T. Li, J. Fan, B. Wang, N. Traugh, Q. Chen, J.S. Liu, B. Li, X.S. Liu, TIMER: a web server for comprehensive analysis of tumor-infiltrating immune cells, Cancer Res. 77 (21) (2017) e108–e110, https://doi.org/10.1158/0008-5472.CAN-17-0307.

[72] F.R. Makhouri, J.B. Ghasemi, In silico studies in drug research against neurodegenerative diseases, Curr. Neuropharmacol. 16 (6) (2017) 664–725, https://doi.org/10.2174/1570159x15666170823095628.

[73] A. Varela-Rial, M. Majewski, G. De Fabritiis, Structure based virtual screening: fast and slow, Wiley Interdiscip. Rev.: Comput. Mol. Sci. 12 (2) (2022) 1–17, https://doi.org/10.1002/wcms.1544.

[74] A. Gimeno, M.J. Ojeda-Montes, S. Tomás-Hernández, A. Cereto-Massagué, R. Beltrán-Debón, M. Mulero, G. Pujadas, S. Garcia-Vallvé, The light and dark sides of virtual screening: what is there to know? Int. J. Mol. Sci. 20 (6) (2019), https://doi.org/10.3390/ijms20061375.

[75] B. Suay-García, J.I. Bueso-Bordils, A. Falcó, G.M. Antón-Fos, P.A. Alemán-López, Virtual combinatorial chemistry and pharmacological screening: a short guide to drug design, Int. J. Mol. Sci. 23 (3) (2022) 1620, https://doi.org/10.3390/ijms23031620.

[76] T. Scior, A. Bender, G. Tresadern, J.L. Medina-franco, K. Mart, T. Langer, K. Cuanalo-contreras, D.K. Agrafiotis, 06_2012_JChemInfModel_52_867.pdf, 2012.

[77] K. Sargsyan, C. Grauffel, C. Lim, How molecular size impacts RMSD applications in molecular dynamics simulations, J. Chem. Theory Comput. 13 (4) (2017) 1518–1524, https://doi.org/10.1021/acs.jctc.7b00028.

[78] A. Hamza, N.N. Wei, C.G. Zhan, Ligand-based virtual screening approach using a new scoring function, J. Chem. Inf. Model. 52 (4) (2012) 963–974, https://doi.org/10.1021/ci200617d.

[79] S. Lätti, S. Niinivehmas, O.T. Pentikäinen, Rocker: open source, easy-to-use tool for AUC and enrichment calculations and ROC visualization, J. Cheminformatics 8 (1) (2016) 1–5, https://doi.org/10.1186/s13321-016-0158-y.

[80] J.F. Truchon, C.I. Bayly, Evaluating virtual screening methods: good and bad metrics for the "early recognition" problem, J. Chem. Inf. Model. 47 (2) (2007) 488–508, https://doi.org/10.1021/ci600426e.

[81] S. Cosconati, S. Forli, A.L. Perryman, R. Harris, D.S. Goodsell, A.J. Olson, Virtual screening with AutoDock: theory and practice, Expert Opin. Drug Discovery 5 (6) (2010) 597–607, https://doi.org/10.1517/17460441.2010.484460.

[82] S. Forli, R. Huey, M.E. Pique, M.F. Sanner, D.S. Goodsell, A.J. Olson, Computational protein-ligand docking and virtual drug screening with the AutoDock suite, Nat. Protoc. 11 (5) (2016) 905–919, https://doi.org/10.1038/nprot.2016.051.

[83] E.H.B. Maia, L.C. Assis, T.A. de Oliveira, A.M. da Silva, A.G. Taranto, Structure-based virtual screening: from classical to artificial intelligence, Front. Chem. 8 (April) (2020), https://doi.org/10.3389/fchem.2020.00343.

[84] C. Wang, Y. Chen, Y. Wang, X. Liu, Y. Liu, Y. Li, H. Chen, C. Fan, D. Wu, J. Yang, Inhibition of COX-2, mPGES-1 and CYP4A by isoliquiritigenin blocks the angiogenic Akt signaling in glioma through ceRNA effect of miR-194-5p and lncRNA NEAT1, J. Exp. Clin. Cancer Res. 38 (2019) 371, https://doi.org/10.1186/s13046-019-1361-2.

[85] C. Wang, Y. Li, H. Chen, K. Huang, X. Liu, M. Qiu, Y. Liu, Y. Yang, J. Yang, CYP4X1 inhibition by flavonoid CH625 normalizes glioma vasculature through reprogramming TAMs via CB2 and EGFR-STAT3 Axis, J. Pharmacol. Exp. Ther. 365 (1) (2018) 72–83, https://doi.org/10.1124/jpet.117.247130.

[86] G. Zhong, Y. Wang, Q. Wang, M. Wu, Y. Liu, S. Sun, Z. Li, J. Hao, P. Dou, B. Lin, Discovery of novel ID2 antagonists from pharmacophore-based virtual screening as potential therapeutics for glioma, Bioorg. Med. Chem. 49 (2021), 116427, https://doi.org/10.1016/j.bmc.2021.116427.

[87] A.N.I. Viswanath, J.W. Lim, S.H. Seo, J.Y. Lee, S.M. Lim, A.N. Pae, GRP78-targeted in-silico virtual screening of novel anticancer agents, Chem. Biol. Drug Des. 92 (2) (2018) 1555–1566, https://doi.org/10.1111/cbdd.13322.

[88] M.E.M. Saeed, O. Kadioglu, H.J. Greten, A. Yildirim, K. Mayr, F. Wenz, F.A. Giordano, T. Efferth, Drug repurposing using transcriptome sequencing and virtual drug screening in a patient with glioblastoma, Investig. New Drugs 39 (3) (2021) 670–685, https://doi.org/10.1007/s10637-020-01037-7.

[89] N. Zhang, B. Zheng, X. Yao, X. Huang, J. Du, Y. Shen, Z. Huang, J. Chen, Q. Lin, W. Lan, W. Lin, W. Ma, Identification and characterization of a novel mutant isocitrate dehydrogenase 1 inhibitor for glioma treatment, Biochem. Biophys. Res. Commun. 551 (2021) 38–45, https://doi.org/10.1016/j.bbrc.2021.02.112.

[90] S. Wei, M. Liao, H. Tan, Y. Chen, R. Zhao, W. Jin, S. Zhu, Y. Zhang, L. He, B. Liu, Identification of autophagic target RAB13 with small-molecule inhibitor in low-grade glioma via integrated multi-omics approaches coupled with virtual screening of traditional Chinese medicine databases, Cell Prolif. 54 (12) (2021), https://doi.org/10.1111/cpr.13135.

[91] Y. Wang, S. Tang, H. Lai, R. Jin, X. Long, N. Li, Y. Tang, H. Guo, X. Yao, E.L.-H. Leung, Discovery of novel IDH1 inhibitor through comparative structure-based virtual screening, Front. Pharmacol. 11 (2020), 579768, https://doi.org/10.3389/fphar.2020.579768.

[92] R.C. Dash, J. Wen, A.M. Zaino, S.R. Morel, L.Q. Chau, R.J. Wechsler-Reya, M.K. Hadden, Structure-based virtual screening identifies an 8-hydroxyquinoline as a small molecule GLI1 inhibitor, Mol. Ther. Oncolytics 20 (2021) 265–276, https://doi.org/10.1016/j.omto.2021.01.004.

[93] M. Yadav, R. Khandelwal, U. Mudgal, S. Srinitha, N. Khandekar, A. Nayarisseri, S. Vuree, S.K. Singh, Identification of potent VEGF inhibitors for the clinical treatment of glioblastoma, a virtual screening approach, Asian Pac. J. Cancer Prev. 20 (9) (2019) 2681–2692, https://doi.org/10.31557/APJCP.2019.20.9.2681.

[94] F. Zou, S. Pusch, J. Hua, T. Ma, L. Yang, Q. Zhu, Y. Xu, Y. Gu, A. von Deimling, X. Zha, Identification of novel allosteric inhibitors of mutant isocitrate dehydrogenase 1 by cross docking-based virtual screening, Bioorg. Med. Chem. Lett. 28 (3) (2018) 388–393, https://doi.org/10.1016/j.bmcl.2017.12.030.

[95] F. Merlino, S. Daniele, V. La Pietra, S. Di Maro, F.S. Di Leva, D. Brancaccio, S. Tomassi, S. Giuntini, L. Cerofolini, M. Fragai, C. Luchinat, F. Reichart, C. Cavallini, B. Costa, R. Piccarducci, S. Taliani, F. Da Settimo, C. Martini, H. Kessler, et al., Simultaneous targeting of RGD-integrins and dual murine double minute proteins in glioblastoma multiforme, J. Med. Chem. 61 (11) (2018) 4791–4809, https://doi.org/10.1021/acs.jmedchem.8b00004.

[96] V. Myrianthopoulos, P.F. Cartron, Z. Liutkevičiūtė, S. Klimašauskas, D. Matulis, C. Bronner, N. Martinet, E. Mikros, Tandem virtual screening targeting the SRA domain of UHRF1 identifies a novel chemical tool modulating DNA methylation, Eur. J. Med. Chem. 114 (2016) 390–396, https://doi.org/10.1016/j.ejmech.2016.02.043.

[97] V. Kumar, S. Khan, P. Gupta, N. Rastogi, D.P. Mishra, S. Ahmed, M.I. Siddiqi, Identification of novel inhibitors of human Chk1 using pharmacophore-based virtual screening and their evaluation as potential anti-cancer agents, J. Comput. Aided Mol. Des. 28 (12) (2014) 1247–1256, https://doi.org/10.1007/s10822-014-9800-9.

[98] S. Zhong, Y. Bai, B. Wu, J. Ge, S. Jiang, W. Li, X. Wang, J. Ren, H. Xu, Y. Chen, G. Zhao, Selected by gene co-expression network and molecular docking analyses, ENMD-2076 is highly effective in glioblastoma-bearing rats, Aging 11 (21) (2019) 9738–9766, https://doi.org/10.18632/aging.102422.

[99] C. Nayak, S.K. Singh, In silico identification of natural product inhibitors against octamer-binding transcription factor 4 (Oct4) to impede the mechanism of glioma stem cells, PLoS One 16 (10) (2021), e0255803, https://doi.org/10.1371/journal.pone.0255803.

[100] C.J. Libby, S. Zhang, G.A. Benavides, S.E. Scott, Y. Li, M. Redmann, A.N. Tran, A. Otamias, V. Darley-Usmar, M. Napierala, J. Zhang, C.E. Augelli-Szafran, W. Zhang, A.B. Hjelmeland, Identification of compounds that decrease glioblastoma growth and glucose uptake in vitro, ACS Chem. Biol. 13 (8) (2018) 2048–2057, https://doi.org/10.1021/acschembio.8b00251.

[101] X. Du, H. Hu, The roles of 2-hydroxyglutarate, Front. Cell Dev. Biol. 9 (2021), 651317, https://doi.org/10.3389/fcell.2021.651317.

[102] S. Han, Y. Liu, S.J. Cai, M. Qian, J. Ding, M. Larion, M.R. Gilbert, C. Yang, IDH mutation in glioma: molecular mechanisms and potential therapeutic targets, Br. J. Cancer 122 (11) (2020) 1580–1589, https://doi.org/10.1038/s41416-020-0814-x.

[103] W. Xu, H. Yang, Y. Liu, Y. Yang, P. Wang, S.-H. Kim, S. Ito, C. Yang, P. Wang, M.-T. Xiao, L. Liu, W. Jiang, J. Liu, J. Zhang, B. Wang, S. Frye, Y. Zhang, Y. Xu, Q. Lei, Y. Xiong, Oncometabolite 2-hydroxyglutarate is a competitive inhibitor of α-ketoglutarate-dependent dioxygenases, Cancer Cell 19 (1) (2011) 17–30, https://doi.org/10.1016/j.ccr.2010.12.014.

[104] N. Nishida, H. Yano, T. Nishida, T. Kamura, M. Kojiro, Angiogenesis in cancer, Vasc. Health Risk Manag. 2 (3) (2006) 213–219, https://doi.org/10.2147/vhrm.2006.2.3.213.

[105] B. Shang, Z. Cao, Q. Zhou, Progress in tumor vascular normalization for anticancer therapy: challenges and perspectives, Front. Med. 6 (1) (2012) 67–78, https://doi.org/10.1007/s11684-012-0176-8.

[106] D. Fukumura, J. Kloepper, Z. Amoozgar, D.G. Duda, R.K. Jain, Enhancing cancer immunotherapy using antiangiogenics: opportunities and challenges, Nat. Rev. Clin. Oncol. 15 (5) (2018) 325–340, https://doi.org/10.1038/nrclinonc.2018.29.

[107] P. Carmeliet, R.K. Jain, Principles and mechanisms of vessel normalization for cancer and other angiogenic diseases, Nat. Rev. Drug Discov. 10 (6) (2011) 417–427, https://doi.org/10.1038/nrd3455.

[108] C. Wang, Y. Li, H. Chen, J. Zhang, J. Zhang, T. Qin, C. Duan, X. Chen, Y. Liu, X. Zhou, J. Yang, Inhibition of CYP4A by a novel flavonoid FLA-16 prolongs survival and normalizes tumor vasculature in glioma, Cancer Lett. 402 (2017) 131–141, https://doi.org/10.1016/j.canlet.2017.05.030.

[109] C. Hetz, The unfolded protein response: controlling cell fate decisions under ER stress and beyond, Nat. Rev. Mol. Cell Biol. 13 (2) (2012) 89–102, https://doi.org/10.1038/nrm3270.

[110] R. Langer, M. Feith, J.R. Siewert, H.-J. Wester, H. Hoefler, Expression and clinical significance of glucose regulated proteins GRP78 (BiP) and GRP94 (GP96) in human adenocarcinomas of the esophagus, BMC Cancer 8 (1) (2008) 70, https://doi.org/10.1186/1471-2407-8-70.

[111] M. Schröder, R.J. Kaufman, The mammalian unfolded protein response, Annu. Rev. Biochem. 74 (2005) 739–789, https://doi.org/10.1146/annurev.biochem.73.011303.074134.

[112] M. Wang, S. Wey, Y. Zhang, R. Ye, A.S. Lee, Role of the unfolded protein response regulator GRP78/BiP in development, cancer, and neurological disorders, Antioxid. Redox Signal. 11 (9) (2009) 2307–2316, https://doi.org/10.1089/ars.2009.2485.

[113] A.W. Paton, T. Beddoe, C.M. Thorpe, J.C. Whisstock, M.C.J. Wilce, J. Rossjohn, U.M. Talbot, J.C. Paton, AB5 subtilase cytotoxin inactivates the endoplasmic reticulum chaperone BiP, Nature 443 (7111) (2006) 548–552, https://doi.org/10.1038/nature05124.

[114] S.P. Ermakova, B.S. Kang, B.Y. Choi, H.S. Choi, T.F. Schuster, W.-Y. Ma, A.M. Bode, Z. Dong, (−)-Epigallocatechin gallate overcomes resistance to etoposide-induced cell death by targeting the molecular chaperone glucose-regulated protein 78, Cancer Res. 66 (18) (2006) 9260–9269, https://doi.org/10.1158/0008-5472.CAN-06-1586.

[115] W.G. Deng, K.H. Ruan, M. Du, M.A. Saunders, K.K. Wu, Aspirin and salicylate bind to immunoglobulin heavy chain binding protein (BiP) and inhibit its ATPase activity in human fibroblasts, FASEB J. 15 (13) (2001) 2463–2470, https://doi.org/10.1096/fj.01-0259com.

[116] J. Matsuo, Y. Tsukumo, J. Sakurai, S. Tsukahara, H.-R. Park, K. Shin-ya, T. Watanabe, T. Tsuruo, A. Tomida, Preventing the unfolded protein response via aberrant activation of 4E-binding protein 1 by versipelostatin, Cancer Sci. 100 (2) (2009) 327–333, https://doi.org/10.1111/j.1349-7006.2008.01036.x.

[117] G.G. de Ridder, R. Ray, S.V. Pizzo, A murine monoclonal antibody directed against the carboxyl-terminal domain of GRP78 suppresses melanoma growth in mice, Melanoma Res. 22 (3) (2012) 225–235, https://doi.org/10.1097/CMR.0b013e32835312fd.

[118] U.K. Misra, S.V. Pizzo, Ligation of cell surface GRP78 with antibody directed against the COOH-terminal domain of GRP78 suppresses Ras/MAPK and PI 3-kinase/AKT signaling while promoting caspase activation in human prostate cancer cells, Cancer Biol. Ther. 9 (2) (2010) 142–152, https://doi.org/10.4161/cbt.9.2.10422.

[119] A.T. Macias, D.S. Williamson, N. Allen, J. Borgognoni, A. Clay, Z. Daniels, P. Dokurno, M.J. Drysdale, G.L. Francis, C.J. Graham, R. Howes, N. Matassova, J.B. Murray, R. Parsons, T. Shaw, A.E. Surgenor, L. Terry, Y. Wang, M. Wood, A.J. Massey, Adenosine-derived inhibitors of 78 kDa glucose regulated protein (Grp78) ATPase: insights into isoform selectivity, J. Med. Chem. 54 (12) (2011) 4034–4041, https://doi.org/10.1021/jm101625x.

[120] S. Teglund, R. Toftgård, Hedgehog beyond medulloblastoma and basal cell carcinoma, Biochim. Biophys. Acta 1805 (2) (2010) 181–208, https://doi.org/10.1016/j.bbcan.2010.01.003.

[121] E. Peer, S. Tesanovic, F. Aberger, Next-generation hedgehog/GLI pathway inhibitors for cancer therapy, Cancers 11 (4) (2019) 538, https://doi.org/10.3390/cancers11040538.

[122] H. Xie, B.D. Paradise, W.W. Ma, M.E. Fernandez-Zapico, Recent advances in the clinical targeting of hedgehog/GLI Signaling in cancer, Cell 8 (5) (2019) 394, https://doi.org/10.3390/cells8050394.

[123] J.K. Petersen, P. Jensen, M. Dahl Sørensen, B. Winther Kristensen, Expression and prognostic value of Oct-4 in astrocytic brain tumors, PLoS One 11 (12) (2016), e0169129, https://doi.org/10.1371/journal.pone.0169129.

[124] S. Jerabek, F. Merino, H.R. Schöler, V. Cojocaru, OCT4: dynamic DNA binding pioneers stem cell pluripotency, Biochim. Biophys. Acta 1839 (3) (2014) 138–154, https://doi.org/10.1016/j.bbagrm.2013.10.001.

[125] W. Jin, L. Wang, F. Zhu, W. Tan, W. Lin, D. Chen, Q. Sun, Z. Xia, Critical POU domain residues confer Oct4 uniqueness in somatic cell reprogramming, Sci. Rep. 6 (2016) 20818, https://doi.org/10.1038/srep20818.

[126] C.M. Pfeffer, A.T.K. Singh, Apoptosis: a target for anticancer therapy, Int. J. Mol. Sci. 19 (2) (2018) 448, https://doi.org/10.3390/ijms19020448.

[127] E. Martinkova, A. Maglott, D.Y. Leger, D. Bonnet, M. Stiborova, K. Takeda, S. Martin, M. Dontenwill, Alpha5beta1 integrin antagonists reduce chemotherapy-induced premature senescence and facilitate apoptosis in human glioblastoma cells, Int. J. Cancer 127 (5) (2010) 1240–1248, https://doi.org/10.1002/ijc.25187.

[128] I. Dikic, Z. Elazar, Mechanism and medical implications of mammalian autophagy, Nat. Rev. Mol. Cell Biol. 19 (6) (2018) 349–364, https://doi.org/10.1038/s41580-018-0003-4.

[129] D. Denton, S. Kumar, Autophagy-dependent cell death, Cell Death Differ. 26 (4) (2019) 605–616, https://doi.org/10.1038/s41418-018-0252-y.

[130] F. Feng, M. Zhang, C. Yang, X. Heng, X. Wu, The dual roles of autophagy in gliomagenesis and clinical therapy strategies based on autophagic regulation mechanisms, Biomed. Pharmacother. 120 (2019), 109441, https://doi.org/10.1016/j.biopha.2019.109441.

[131] S.Y. Lunt, M.G. Vander Heiden, Aerobic glycolysis: meeting the metabolic requirements of cell proliferation, Annu. Rev. Cell Dev. Biol. 27 (1) (2011) 441–464, https://doi.org/10.1146/annurev-cellbio-092910-154237.
[132] C.M. Labak, P.Y. Wang, R. Arora, M.R. Guda, S. Asuthkar, A.J. Tsung, K.K. Velpula, Glucose transport: meeting the metabolic demands of cancer, and applications in glioblastoma treatment, Am. J. Cancer Res. 6 (8) (2016) 1599–1608.
[133] W.A. Flavahan, Q. Wu, M. Hitomi, N. Rahim, Y. Kim, A.E. Sloan, R.J. Weil, I. Nakano, J.N. Sarkaria, B.W. Stringer, B.W. Day, M. Li, J.D. Lathia, J.N. Rich, A.B. Hjelmeland, Brain tumor initiating cells adapt to restricted nutrition through preferential glucose uptake, Nat. Neurosci. 16 (10) (2013) 1373–1382, https://doi.org/10.1038/nn.3510.
[134] K. Shibuya, M. Okada, S. Suzuki, M. Seino, S. Seino, H. Takeda, C. Kitanaka, Targeting the facilitative glucose transporter GLUT1 inhibits the self-renewal and tumor-initiating capacity of cancer stem cells, Oncotarget 6 (2) (2015) 651–661, https://doi.org/10.18632/oncotarget.2892.
[135] T.T. Ashburn, K.B. Thor, Drug repositioning: identifying and developing new uses for existing drugs, Nat. Rev. Drug Discov. 3 (8) (2004) 673–683, https://doi.org/10.1038/nrd1468.
[136] S. Pushpakom, F. Iorio, P.A. Eyers, K.J. Escott, S. Hopper, A. Wells, A. Doig, T. Guilliams, J. Latimer, C. McNamee, A. Norris, P. Sanseau, D. Cavalla, M. Pirmohamed, Drug repurposing: progress, challenges and recommendations. Nature reviews, Drug Discov. 18 (1) (2019) 41–58, https://doi.org/10.1038/nrd.2018.168.
[137] N. Nosengo, Can you teach old drugs new tricks? Nature 534 (7607) (2016) 314–316, https://doi.org/10.1038/534314a.
[138] C. Abbruzzese, S. Matteoni, M. Signore, L. Cardone, K. Nath, J.D. Glickson, M.G. Paggi, Drug repurposing for the treatment of glioblastoma multiforme, J. Exp. Clin. Cancer Res. 36 (1) (2017) 169, https://doi.org/10.1186/s13046-017-0642-x.
[139] M. Nakada, D. Kita, L. Teng, I.V. Pyko, T. Watanabe, Y. Hayashi, J.-I. Hamada, Receptor tyrosine kinases: principles and functions in glioma invasion, Adv. Exp. Med. Biol. 1202 (2020) 151–178, https://doi.org/10.1007/978-3-030-30651-9_8.
[140] M. Tilak, J. Holborn, L.A. New, J. Lalonde, N. Jones, Receptor tyrosine kinase Signaling and targeting in glioblastoma multiforme, Int. J. Mol. Sci. 22 (4) (2021) 1831, https://doi.org/10.3390/ijms22041831.
[141] K.J. Hatanpaa, S. Burma, D. Zhao, A.A. Habib, Epidermal growth factor receptor in glioma: signal transduction, neuropathology, imaging, and radioresistance, Neoplasia 12 (9) (2010) 675–684, https://doi.org/10.1593/neo.10688.
[142] ClinicalTrials.gov, 2022. March 15 https://www.clinicaltrials.gov/.
[143] C.M. Rocha-Lima, L.E. Raez, Erlotinib (tarceva) for the treatment of non-small-cell lung cancer and pancreatic cancer, P T 34 (10) (2009) 554–564.
[144] S. Sathornsumetee, A. Desjardins, J.J. Vredenburgh, R.E. McLendon, J. Marcello, J.E. Herndon, A. Mathe, M. Hamilton, J.N. Rich, J.A. Norfleet, S. Gururangan, H.S. Friedman, D.A. Reardon, Phase II trial of bevacizumab and erlotinib in patients with recurrent malignant glioma, Neuro-Oncology 12 (12) (2010) 1300–1310, https://doi.org/10.1093/neuonc/noq099.
[145] N. Mulet-Margalef, Sunitinib in the treatment of gastrointestinal stromal tumor: patient selection and perspectives, OncoTargets Ther. 9 (2016) 7573–7582, https://doi.org/10.2147/OTT.S101385.
[146] C. Wetmore, V.M. Daryani, C.A. Billups, J.M. Boyett, S. Leary, R. Tanos, K.C. Goldsmith, C.F. Stewart, S.M. Blaney, A. Gajjar, Phase II evaluation of sunitinib in the treatment of recurrent or refractory high-grade glioma or ependymoma in children: a children's oncology group study ACNS1021, Cancer Med. 5 (7) (2016) 1416–1424, https://doi.org/10.1002/cam4.713.
[147] J. Kalpathy-Cramer, V. Chandra, X. Da, Y. Ou, K.E. Emblem, A. Muzikansky, X. Cai, L. Douw, J.G. Evans, J. Dietrich, A.S. Chi, P.Y. Wen, S. Stufflebeam, B. Rosen, D.G. Duda, R.K. Jain, T.T. Batchelor, E.R. Gerstner, Phase II study of tivozanib, an oral VEGFR inhibitor, in patients with recurrent glioblastoma, J. Neuro-Oncol. 131 (3) (2017) 603–610, https://doi.org/10.1007/s11060-016-2332-5.
[148] F.M. Iwamoto, K.R. Lamborn, H.I. Robins, M.P. Mehta, S.M. Chang, N.A. Butowski, L.M. Deangelis, L.E. Abrey, W.-T. Zhang, M.D. Prados, H.A. Fine, Phase II trial of pazopanib (GW786034), an oral multi-targeted angiogenesis inhibitor, for adults with recurrent glioblastoma

(North American Brain Tumor Consortium Study 06-02), Neuro-Oncology 12 (8) (2010) 855–861, https://doi.org/10.1093/neuonc/noq025.

[149] J. Du, P. Bernasconi, K.R. Clauser, D.R. Mani, S.P. Finn, R. Beroukhim, M. Burns, B. Julian, X.P. Peng, H. Hieronymus, R.L. Maglathlin, T.A. Lewis, L.M. Liau, P. Nghiemphu, I.K. Mellinghoff, D.N. Louis, M. Loda, S.A. Carr, A.L. Kung, T.R. Golub, Bead-based profiling of tyrosine kinase phosphorylation identifies SRC as a potential target for glioblastoma therapy, Nat. Biotechnol. 27 (1) (2009) 77–83, https://doi.org/10.1038/nbt.1513.

[150] E. Avizienyte, A.W. Wyke, R.J. Jones, G.W. McLean, M.A. Westhoff, V.G. Brunton, M.C. Frame, Src-induced de-regulation of E-cadherin in colon cancer cells requires integrin signalling, Nat. Cell Biol. 4 (8) (2002) 632–638, https://doi.org/10.1038/ncb829.

[151] R.B. Irby, T.J. Yeatman, Increased Src activity disrupts cadherin/catenin-mediated homotypic adhesion in human colon cancer and transformed rodent cells, Cancer Res. 62 (9) (2002) 2669–2674.

[152] E. Galanis, S.K. Anderson, E.L. Twohy, X.W. Carrero, J.G. Dixon, D.D. Tran, S.A. Jeyapalan, D.M. Anderson, T.J. Kaufmann, R.W. Feathers, C. Giannini, J.C. Buckner, P.Z. Anastasiadis, D. Schiff, A phase 1 and randomized, placebo-controlled phase 2 trial of bevacizumab plus dasatinib in patients with recurrent glioblastoma: Alliance/North Central Cancer Treatment Group N0872, Cancer 125 (21) (2019) 3790–3800, https://doi.org/10.1002/cncr.32340.

[153] J.W. Taylor, J. Dietrich, E.R. Gerstner, A.D. Norden, M.L. Rinne, D.P. Cahill, A. Stemmer-Rachamimov, P.Y. Wen, R.A. Betensky, D.H. Giorgio, K. Snodgrass, A.E. Randall, T.T. Batchelor, A.S. Chi, Phase 2 study of bosutinib, a Src inhibitor, in adults with recurrent glioblastoma, J. Neuro-Oncol. 121 (3) (2015) 557–563, https://doi.org/10.1007/s11060-014-1667-z.

[154] U. Herrlinger, N. Schäfer, J.P. Steinbach, A. Weyerbrock, P. Hau, R. Goldbrunner, F. Friedrich, V. Rohde, F. Ringel, U. Schlegel, M. Sabel, M.W. Ronellenfitsch, M. Uhl, J. Maciaczyk, S. Grau, O. Schnell, M. Hänel, D. Krex, P. Vajkoczy, et al., Bevacizumab plus irinotecan versus temozolomide in newly diagnosed O6-methylguanine-DNA methyltransferase nonmethylated glioblastoma: the randomized GLARIUS trial, J. Clin. Oncol. 34 (14) (2016) 1611–1619, https://doi.org/10.1200/JCO.2015.63.4691.

[155] A. Paranjpe, R. Zhang, F. Ali-Osman, G.C. Bobustuc, K.S. Srivenugopal, Disulfiram is a direct and potent inhibitor of human O6-methylguanine-DNA methyltransferase (MGMT) in brain tumor cells and mouse brain and markedly increases the alkylating DNA damage, Carcinogenesis 35 (3) (2014) 692–702, https://doi.org/10.1093/carcin/bgt366.

[156] J. Triscott, C. Lee, K. Hu, A. Fotovati, R. Berns, M. Pambid, M. Luk, R.E. Kast, E. Kong, E. Toyota, S. Yip, B. Toyota, S.E. Dunn, Disulfiram, a drug widely used to control alcoholism, suppresses the self-renewal of glioblastoma and over-rides resistance to temozolomide, Oncotarget 3 (10) (2012) 1112–1123, https://doi.org/10.18632/oncotarget.604.

[157] P. Liu, S. Brown, T. Goktug, P. Channathodiyil, V. Kannappan, J.-P. Hugnot, P.-O. Guichet, X. Bian, A.L. Armesilla, J.L. Darling, W. Wang, Cytotoxic effect of disulfiram/copper on human glioblastoma cell lines and ALDH-positive cancer-stem-like cells, Br. J. Cancer 107 (9) (2012) 1488–1497, https://doi.org/10.1038/bjc.2012.442.

[158] J.L. Gainer, Trans-sodium crocetinate for treating hypoxia/ischemia, Expert Opin. Investig. Drugs 17 (6) (2008) 917–924, https://doi.org/10.1517/13543784.17.6.917.

[159] G. Riva, C. Cilibrasi, R. Bazzoni, M. Cadamuro, C. Negroni, V. Butta, M. Strazzabosco, L. Dalprà, M. Lavitrano, A. Bentivegna, Valproic acid inhibits proliferation and reduces invasiveness in glioma stem cells through Wnt/β catenin signalling activation, Genes 9 (11) (2018) E522, https://doi.org/10.3390/genes9110522.

[160] Y. Chen, Y.-H. Tsai, S.-H. Tseng, Valproic acid affected the survival and invasiveness of human glioma cells through diverse mechanisms, J. Neuro-Oncol. 109 (1) (2012) 23–33, https://doi.org/10.1007/s11060-012-0871-y.

[161] W. Han, Valproic acid: a promising therapeutic agent in glioma treatment, Front. Oncol. 11 (2021), 687362, https://doi.org/10.3389/fonc.2021.687362.

[162] S. Osuka, S. Takano, S. Watanabe, E. Ishikawa, T. Yamamoto, A. Matsumura, Valproic acid inhibits angiogenesis in vitro and glioma angiogenesis in vivo in the brain, Neurol. Med. Chir. 52 (4) (2012) 186–193, https://doi.org/10.2176/nmc.52.186.

CHAPTER 12

Repurposing of phytocompounds-derived novel bioactive compounds possessing promising anticancer and cancer therapeutic efficacy through molecular docking, MD simulation, and drug-likeness/ADMET studies

Rajalakshmi Manikkam[a,b,c], **Vijayalakshmi Periyasamy**[a,c], **and Indu Sabapathy**[a,c]
[a]DBT-BIF Centre, Holy Cross College (Autonomous), Tiruchirappalli, Tamil Nadu, India
[b]Department of Zoology, Holy Cross College (Autonomous), Tiruchirappalli, Tamil Nadu, India
[c]Department of Biotechnology, Holy Cross College (Autonomous), Tiruchirappalli, Tamil Nadu, India

Abstract

Though considerable success has been achieved in modern decades through chemotherapy, radiation, and surgery for efficient cancer therapy, cancers continue to be a significant burden on human health globally. Drug repurposing (or repositioning) is a relatively new concept that entails repurposing existing medications for new therapeutic applications. Phytochemicals isolated from medicinal plants have been generally ignored in this context, despite the fact that their pharmacological actions have been extensively studied in the past and they may hold significant repositioning potential. To find some potential novel ligands, molecular docking and virtual screening will be used. MD simulations will help to confirm the ligand-complex stability of the candidates discovered by molecular docking and screening. Exploiting the chemical variety of natural chemicals may help to expand the candidate pool of cancer chemotherapeutic and preventive agents.

Abbreviations

DeCoST	Drug Repurposing from Control System Theory
DGT	dihydroxy gymnemic triactate
DNN	deep neural networks
hTERT	human telomerase reverse transcriptase
HTS	high-throughput screening
NSAID	nonsteroidal antiinflammatory drugs
NSCLC	nonsmall-cell lung cancer
PAFR	platelet-activating factor receptor
PGE2	prostaglandin E2

Computational Methods in Drug Discovery and Repurposing for Cancer Therapy
https://doi.org/10.1016/B978-0-443-15280-1.00020-0

1. Drug repurposing

1.1 Introduction

Cancer is a disease that affects and kills millions of people throughout the world, and it has been the subject of intense research in both pathophysiology and therapy [1]. Several medications for the treatment of various cancers have been licensed by the US Food and Drug Administration. Chemotherapeutic drugs are well-known for their negative side effects, which dramatically lower quality of life. The most regularly used chemotherapeutics have serious side effects, such as low absorption, toxicity, nonspecificity, and the promotion of recurrence or metastasis, fatigue, headaches, musculoskeletal symptoms, blood clots, lymphedema, infertility, and memory loss [2,3]. For example, irinotecan, one of the most successful medications against a wide spectrum of tumors, can cause neutropenia, sensory neuropathy, and diarrhea, whereas doxorubicin causes cardiotoxicity in many people. Furthermore, alkylating drugs, such as oxaliplatin, melphalan, carboplatin, cisplatin, and cyclophosphamide, have been linked to nephrotoxicity, gastrointestinal toxicity, cardiovascular toxicity, pulmonary toxicity, and hematological toxicity. On a global scale, the cancer burden is gradually rising. Meanwhile, the number of cancer drugs approved by the FDA is decreasing [4]. As a result, drug repositioning may offer hope to cancer patients, as most noncancer drugs have little or manageable side effects. Simultaneously, the rising cost of newly licensed cancer medicines, such as immunotherapies or targeted drugs, is posing a significant financial challenge. In this situation, an alternate approach is needed to quickly increase the availability of innovative and effective anticancer therapies in a cost-efficient manner.

De novo identification and validation of new chemical entities is a time-consuming and expensive process in the traditional method to drug discovery. Only a few potential anticancer treatments is authorized by the FDA, and only 5% of oncology drugs that reach Phase I clinical trials are approved. Between Phase II and Phase III of clinical trials, the largest rate of failure is found, with 70% of projects failing. Poor pharmacokinetic qualities of the medicine under investigation is one of the reasons for phase II failures. This is owing to a lack of understanding about the interaction between dose, exposure, and the target of interest. By exploiting the understanding of interactions between the many system components, systems biology can be employed as an effective platform in drug discovery and development [5,6]. Rather than synthesis and design of new therapeutic modalities, numerous strategies for repurposing various existing licensed medications that may target this devastating disease should be considered [7]. In addition to drug design and production, in vitro and in vivo investigations are required to assess the drug's efficacy, toxicity, and pharmacokinetic and pharmacodynamic characteristics. Drug repositioning aims to create new medications from previously authorized drugs by uncovering novel effects or targets [8]. The demand for new cancer medicines continues to rise, and DR could provide a more efficient and cost-effective means to combat cancer [9]. The pharmacokinetic, pharmacodynamic, and toxicological characteristics of medications have previously been established in preclinical and Phase I research, which is a major advantage of this strategy. Drug candidates developed in animal studies can be safely administered to human participants to assess efficacy, allowing for full-fledged development of a new medicine if efficacy is established. FDA-approved repurposed pharmaceuticals, which will undergo shorter clinical trials due to their well-known safety and toxicological profile [10].

2. Strategies in drug repurposing

Drug repurposing has two methodologies in which already existing drugs could be repurposed, namely activity-based drug repositioning and in silico drug repositioning. Activity-based in vitro or in vivo assays are used to test genuine medications in drug repurposing [11]. In silico drug discovery uses public databases and bioinformatics technologies to systematically find drug-protein interaction networks [12]. Since the growth of bioinformatics and computational science, a vast amount of information on the structure of proteins and pharmacophores has been amassed over the past few decades. Computational approaches in drug development have been shown to be successful in terms of time and cost savings [13] and the availability of publicly available resources [14]. In silico drug repurposing has been extensively studied abroad in recent years [15–17].

3. Pros and cons of drug repurposing

Individual researchers and pharmaceutical companies have sought to systematically find drug-protein target interaction networks using artificial intelligence algorithms and other bioinformatics methods. In silico drug repositioning provides various advantages over activity-based medication repositioning, such as faster speed and lower cost. However, because it demands high-resolution structural knowledge of targets, it has several limitations. When a screen does not involve protein targets, it also requires disease/phenotype information or drug gene expression profiles. Repurposed medications are rarely successful as monotherapies, with anticancer activity being seen more frequently in combination with other repurposed pharmaceuticals or established cytotoxic agents. Furthermore, establishing sufficient performance with repositioned medications for novel uses may necessitate greater doses, a longer treatment term, or a different formulation than for traditional indications accompanied with side effects. In targeted therapy, only a few repurposed medications that directly target cancer cells have been identified. The majority of repurposed anticancer medications, on the other hand, target the tumor microenvironment [18]. Another disadvantage of repurposing medications is that they may have a variety of off-target and immunomodulatory effects. Because these medications target several targets, they are unlikely to be used as monotherapy for cancer treatment [19].

4. Computational advancements in oncology research

In cancer drug repurposing, exploratory research using in vitro and in silico approaches are used to find possible therapeutic candidates. The core principles of drug repurposing through the combination of system biology and bioinformatics are activity-based and in silico drug discovery. The experimental technique of activity-based drug repurposing is to examine the medication candidate for anticancer activity directly. Existing medications are assessed for cytotoxicity against cancer cells using this technology, allowing for high-throughput screening (HTS) of proven treatments for antineoplastic activity. A structurally comparable medicine is likely to have a similar target, biological action, and indications. When the same metabolic route or signaling is compromised in two diseases, medications that target that system can be utilized to treat both diseases, regardless of their structural differences. The off-target binding and effect of a drug that exhibits great efficacy in one disease can be studied further. Using algorithms from the data mining technology, existing medications are examined for their novel molecular targets in an in silico method. Recent breakthroughs in genomes, proteomics, transcriptomics, and metabolomics have revealed a wealth of information regarding the molecular and metabolic changes that occur in malignancies. For hit detection, this method employs virtual screening of molecular targets. Computational approaches are an indispensable aspect of the drug discovery producing fine structural details that can only be achieved by sophisticated experimental methods, such as HTS, X-ray crystallography, NMR, or electron microscopy; structure-based virtual screening, usually followed by molecular dynamics simulation, is one of the most common methods in predictive drug repurposing [20]. Computational drug-repurposing/repositioning system can easily predict the possibility of repurposing candidates based on a large amount of prior data, such as screening data, genomics, epigenomics, proteomics, phenomics, in vitro and in vivo results, pharmacokinetic data, and safety results [21].

Basic principles, such as activity-based and in silico drug discovery, underpin drug repurposing through the combination of system biology and bioinformatics. The pharmacodynamics, pharmacokinetics, dosage, adverse effects, metabolic profiles, and targeted molecular route of these medications are all well known [22]. Clinical development can now begin with a Phase II trial to test efficacy for a new indication or disease target. Sildenafil (Viagra) and Thalidomide are two examples of effective drug repositioning. Because of its antiangiogenic and antiinflammatory properties, the medication thalidomide, which was originally used to treat morning sickness but was shown to cause abnormalities in infants, was effectively repositioned for use in anticancer therapy. As a result, the FDA-approved thalidomide for use in combination with dexamethasone in patients with multiple myeloma [23] in the United States. In Japan, this medicine was re-approved in 2008 for treatment in patients with multiple myeloma and erythema nodosumleprosum. Pfizer first introduced Viagra as a treatment for hypertension and angina pectoris (1980). In a Phase I clinical trial, however, the patients got penile erections as a side effect. Later, the medication was created to treat erectile dysfunction.

5. Structure-based and target-based virtual screening

Structure-based virtual screening has recently become appealing because a computational docking system can virtually and easily predict free energy and binding conformations of small compounds or molecule ligands to macromolecular targets [24]. Traditional drug development is mostly based on the "one molecule, one target, one disease" paradigm, which ignores drug-protein interactions. However, it has been overlooked that many complex diseases are linked to a wide range of target proteins [25,26]. Furthermore, because of the "poly-pharmacological" features of certain medications, unexpected drug functionalities produced from off-targets are an unpredictable and unavoidable activity that may result in unwanted side effects. These are especially noticeable in the case of cancer medications. Pharmacological repositioning necessitates the identification of drug targets. As a result, data on pharmacological targets are required, which can be collected either from preclinical research or from enhanced computational in silico methods. Advanced molecular approaches have been employed in conjunction with machine learning and artificial intelligence (deep learning) technologies to elucidate multiple targets and pathways important for drug repurposing [27]. The development of computational in silico methodologies can increase biological important for medication repurposing for cancer. In silico screening has the potential to expand the arsenal of pharmaceuticals available for repurposing and thus overcome some limits of modern cancer therapies against both old and new therapeutic targets in oncology.

Docking can be used in a variety of ways in computational drug repositioning workflows. It is possible to discover new drug-target interactions by screening a single chemical against a library of protein structures [28]. Docking can be combined with other techniques and used at the end of the computational pipeline to evaluate candidates identified using other in silico methodologies. Molecular docking is a common structure-based methodology used in rational drug design that involves analyzing and predicting the binding patterns and interaction affinities between ligand and receptor proteins [29]. It can be divided into two types: hard docking and flexible docking according to the flexibility of the ligands involved in the computational process [30]. In a nutshell, the interactions between a medication and a target's binding sites are examined and quantified by determining the free energy of binding (G), with lower or more negative G values indicating more binding affinity. Docking programs use scoring functions, which are mathematical formulas that include physicochemical properties of the drug and protein, to determine the G. Another typical method is to compare protein binding sites. Several techniques for binding site prediction and comparison have been documented in recent years, including geometrical criteria as well as chemical descriptors, based on the notion that identical cavities might exhibit a similar pharmacological profile and hence accommodate the same ligands. Pharmacophore-based screening is a third structure-based technique. To repurpose a ligand to a new target, it is tested against a list of binding sites for matching protein-ligand 3D pharmacophoric characteristics [31], which were previously produced using a pharmacophore modeling technique. The binding affinity or binding energy is then calculated to determine the most suitable compounds and postures for the binding pocket, and possible compounds can then be picked after examining and inspecting [32,33]. After that, MD simulations for target-ligand complexes are frequently used, allowing researchers to explore their interactions in a more realistic environment including pressure, temperature, and solvent molecules [34,35].

6. Systems biology integrated approach in drug repositioning

Systems biology is the study of the entire biological system as it emerges through the interactions of individual biomolecules. As a result, rather than focusing on individual molecules, systems biology takes a holistic approach to analyzing interactions among multiple components. It combines wet-lab investigations that quantify cellular components with computational methodologies and models that allow for the analysis of various data sets or biological system recapitulation. It also uses a variety of computational methodologies to provide predictions that may be evaluated in the lab [36]. Furthermore, using systems biology to make drug development decisions for various diseases may be more efficient [37]. There are several examples of noncancer medications that have been repositioned using computational systems pharmacology to predict potential chemoadjuvants and their drug-target interactions in oncology. Although the anticancer properties of these medications were initially explained using numerous in silico approaches, they were repurposed based on clinical outcomes or in vitro screening of licensed drug collections. Systems biology techniques offer a lot of potential in medication repositioning for successful cancer treatment [17]. By systematically integrating and coordinating computation and bioinformatics, modeling (such as docking for structural modeling), experimentation, statistics, and machine learning, large data about drug-disease, gene expression (microarrays) or protein-protein interactions or gene-protein interactions or signaling pathway mapping, signature matching, and genome-wide association studies can be used for providing drug-disease gene association networking. Signature matching, structure and ligand-based virtual screening, genome association, pathway mapping, and other computational techniques have been employed in drug repurposing [38].

7. In silico databases and web-based tools for drug repurposing

Drug-based, disease-based, and profile-based repositioning techniques are now in use. To infer new disease-drug connections, drug-drug or disease-disease techniques use drug-drug or disease-disease similarities and current drug-treatment knowledge [39]. Pharmacological data, such as drug chemical structure and adverse effects, are frequently used to compare drugs. Disease phenotypic, disease genetic, and disease genomic data are frequently used to calculate disease similarities. Recently, profile-based repositioning techniques have been successful in identifying novel therapeutic candidates for inflammatory bowel disease and small cell lung cancer [40,41]. Existing profile-based medication repositioning approaches primarily use the gene expression profiles of pharmaceuticals and diseases. In addition, the recently published "Drug Repurposing from Control System Theory (DeCoST)" is a comprehensive platform for drug repurposing that addresses various limitations in previous databases, such as variation in the number of copies of the gene of interest, mutations, and a lack of reference for normal gene expression range in various diseases [42]. The most promising strategy for drug repositioning has been reported as a vigorously explored "network-based approach" by integrating the aforesaid resources for discovering possible target, route, and drug [43]. There are a variety of data resources that can be used for bioinformatics-based study and experimental validation of any drug repurposing potential in any disease. Similar gene expression profiles for medication phenotype in patients with various disorders, as mapped by connection map, Library Integrated Network-based Cellular Signatures, and expression signatures, could have similar therapeutic implications [44]. Gene set enrichment analysis for drug-drug similarity network [45]; DrugBank [46], online mendelian inheritance in men (OMIM) [47], and GEO [48] for predicting drug-disease network; KEGG, STRING, BioGrid [49], HAPPI [50], and Reactome [51] for pathway and/or protein-protein interactions; STITCH drug gene/protein database, TTD therapeutic target database [52], SFINX for drug-drug interactions [53]; and SIDER for drug side effects [54] are used.

Various cancer omics studies not only add to our understanding of tumor hallmarks at the molecular level but also provide large amounts of data that can be used to promote medication repurposing using advanced bioinformatics. A thorough framework built using computer processing can combine drug action mechanisms, phenotypes, and molecular biology properties of cancer to find novel drug-disease correlations and prospective drug repurposing opportunities. Overlapping cancer-associated genes and drug-targeted genes from DrugBank, a freely accessible database with over 13,000 medications and related pathways or targets (https://www.drugbank.ca/), are used to infer pharmaceuticals that target cancer. DrugBank and DGIdb are two repositories that collect not only drug information but also drug-target associations. Another freely available, computable Medication Indication Resource can be used to confirm the plausibility of inferred therapeutic indications with clinical promise. A computational profile-based drug-repurposing approach (DrugPredict) suggested that indomethacin could be utilized to treat epithelial ovarian cancer in another investigation [55]. Hurle et al. [56] developed a novel drug discovery strategy that combines a novel computational drug-repositioning system (DrugPredict) with experimental validation to rapidly identify repositioned drug candidates for the treatment of high-grade serious ovarian cancer [56].

Structure-based medication interaction prediction to novel targets is the most fundamental technique to computational drug repurposing. By using protein-ligand docking, Zhao et al. [57] discovered possible Ebola virus inhibitors that targeted viral protein 24 (VP24) and methyltransferase (MTase). Using AutoDock4 [58], AutoDockVina, PLANTS [59], and Surflex, FDA-approved 2005 pharmaceuticals from DrugBank were docked to the predicted binding sites of the proteins. Sinefungin and Indinavir were anticipated to be potential inhibitors of Ebola virus infection based on the consensus of docking data. Therapeutic-target interaction networks are a useful tool for analyzing patterns of interacting substances and targets, which can lead to the discovery of new drug targets. To capture properties of interacting compounds and targets, Nidhi et al. [60] employed extended-connectivity fingerprints to describe compounds and trained a multiple-category nave Bayesian model on the WOMBAT database [61] of compounds and their targets. When evaluated using a different database, MDDR (Elsevier MDL Home Page. http://www.mdli.com), the software correctly predicted a new histone deacetylase inhibitor, [*N*-(2-aminophenyl)-4-(3-hydroxypropanamido) benzamide], which is a close analog of a known histone deacetylase inhibitor. Cao et al. [62] trained random forest, a common machine learning technique, using the PDSP Ki database [63], which contains 514 target proteins and 3393 drug-like ligands. Deep-learning has recently been used to anticipate a novel drug-target interaction. Aliper et al. [64] used gene transcription data to train deep neural networks (DNN) to predict a drug's novel target disease. As a result, the DNN model could be used to reposition drugs. Zeng et al. [65] used a deep autoencoder, a recent deep learning-based technique, to integrate 10 networks, including drug-target, drug-disease, drug-side effect, and seven drug-drug networks, and discovered interaction patterns. A new target disease for a query target medicine can be predicted using the autoencoder. A few studies on mutation-specific inhibitors that were published in the literature were also important examples for NSCLC drug screening [66]. In recent years, for example, the structural and functional impact of a missense mutation in EGFR, a potential therapeutic target in cancer therapy, has been revealed [67]. Although there are still few medications that were designed primarily using computational methods and then approved and launched on the market, there is an increasing body of literature reporting potential pharmaceuticals and drug-target interactions discovered using computational methods. As a result, the influence of computational methodologies will only grow in the future.

8. Phytochemicals repurposed in cancer therapy

A few discoveries of phyto-drugs repurposed with anticancer activities are discussed below. Existing medications have a well-established dosing regimen, acceptable pharmacokinetics and pharmacodynamics features, and manageable side effects, making them useful sources for future anticancer drug discovery.

8.1 Metformin

The medication N',N'-dimethyl biguanide, a natural compound found in *Galega officinalis* is used to treat individuals with type 2 diabetes all around the world [68]. Metformin works mechanically by lowering insulin levels, which stimulates the phosphatidylinositol-4,5-bisphosphate 3-kinase (PI3K)-mTOR signaling pathway, preventing tumors with insulin receptor expression from proliferating [69]. According to statistical data, people treated with metformin for metabolic dysfunction, such as obesity or diabetes, had a lower risk of cancer [70]. Metformin absorption into the cell, which is mediated by OCT1 which shows anticancer action in breast cancer cells in vivo [71]. In order to reestablish equilibrium, metformin interacts directly with AMP-activated protein kinase (AMPK) after being taken up by OCT1 in breast cancer cells. Metformin also arrests the cell cycle, opens up apoptotic pathways, and inhibits PARP degradation in triple-negative breast cancer [72]. Metformin inhibits mTOR, mitogen-activated protein kinase (MAPK), and Akt, which result in apoptosis, antiangiogenic, and antiproliferative effects by blocking the STAT3 and TGF signaling pathways [73]. Metformin suppression of mTOR signaling is dependent on Ras-related GTPase but independent of AMPK [74]. Liu et al. [75] reported that metformin-mediated tumor cell-intrinsic mitochondrial metabolism in ovarian cancer. Because NF-kB plays a key role in chemoresistance, metformin may be the best solution for treating breast cancer by lowering its expression. Metformin also promotes SIRT1, a protein that has antiinflammatory properties and reduces inflammation [76]. Shi et al. [77] have shown that metformin can inhibit cycclooxygenase-2 (COX-2) expressions, suggesting that it may have the potential to be used in combination with other COX-2 inhibitors. Furthermore, patients with breast cancer who take metformin monotherapy or in combination with other drugs have reduced tumor growth and increases survival rate [78]. This combined investigation gave us the idea to employ metformin as an adjuvant medication for cancer treatment [79]. Metformin is a successful repurposing medicine that has progressed to Phase III and Phase IV for the treatment of prostate, oral, breast, pancreatic, and endometrial malignancies. Several mechanisms of action for the anticancer effect of metformin have been displayed and most of which involve the activation of AMPK: one being an indirect course with inhibition of insulin/IGF-1 pathway with resultant suppression of PI3K/AKT/mTOR and MAPK pathways, which slows the growth of precancerous and cancerous cells and induces cell cycle arrest and cell death [80], and another that targets the respiratory complex I of the electron transport chain in the mitochondria, thus hindering energy consumption in the cell [81].

8.2 Artemisinin

The active element in *Artemisia annua* L. is artemisinin, which is used to treat malaria is proposed to have anticancer potentials. According to recent findings, artemisinin and its derivatives have anticancer properties due to its ability to induce nonapoptotic programmed cell death [52]. Artemisinin when given orally to individuals with colorectal cancer had anticancer properties and was well tolerated [82].

8.3 Curcumin

Curcumin, an active element present in turmeric (*Curcuma longa*) is an antioxidant, anti-inflammatory, and even anticancer agent [83]. Curcumin's effect on telomerase has recently gained a lot of attention. It has been presented as a telomerase inhibitor with significant potential for drug repurposing in cancer therapy. Curcumin has been shown to inhibit human telomerase reverse transcriptase (hTERT) transcription and thereby mediate telomerase activity in breast cancer cells [84]. Curcumin's effects on the Wnt/β-catenin and Hippo/YAP signaling pathways have been verified in more research, with curcumin decreasing stemness or proliferation in a variety of malignancies [85,86]. Curcumin drug repurposing to target telomerase using highly bioavailable forms of curcumin could be advantageous for clinical translation.

8.4 Genistein

Genistein is an isoflavone found in beans (*Genista tinctoria* L.) that can be used to treat a variety of diseases, including menopause, osteoporosis, and obesity [87]. Genistein has been used to treat breast cancer as a phytoestrogen mimic of 17β-estradiol [88]. Following that, genistein was discovered to decrease telomerase activity and related on cosignaling pathways, suggesting that it could be used to treat a variety of malignancies [89]. In prostate cancer cells, it has been shown to decrease the transcriptional activation of hTERT by partially inhibiting c-Myc. As indicated by the downregulation of hTERT phosphorylation mediated by AKT in prostate cancer cells, genistein inhibits hTERT nuclear translocation posttranslationally [90]. Genistein has recently been shown to suppress Wnt/β-catenin signaling in several malignancies via regulating associated genes, microRNA, DNA methylation, and histone modification, resulting in the reduction of proliferation or apoptosis [91].

8.5 Berberine

Berberine is a plant-derived isoquinoline alkaloid found in *Coptis chinensis*, *Berberis vulgaris*, and *Hydrastis canadensis* first used to treat bacterial diarrhea [92]. Berberine, on the other hand, exhibits antioxidant [93], antiinflammatory [94], hypolipidemic [95], neuroprotective [96], anticancer [97], and antidiabetic [98] properties in vitro and in vivo. With a better understanding of berberine, it was discovered that its effect on lowering lipid levels is linked to the inhibition of HMG-CoA reductase, which has benefits for patients with nonalcoholic fatty liver disease [99]. Berberine has also been shown to lower the glycemic index via improving insulin action or restoring insulin sensitivity, as well as blocking AMPK activation or upregulating InsR expression [100]. Several recent investigations have found that berberine has anticancer properties, reducing invasion and metastasis in breast and colorectal cancers, as well as other cancers. Berberine, altered ephrin-B2 and inhibited MMP-2 and MMP-9 production via downregulating TGF-1, resulting in a reduction in breast cancer cell proliferation and metastasis. Berberine has been demonstrated to decrease migration, invasion, and metastasis in endometrial cancer via transcriptionally upregulating miR-101, which inhibits COX-2/prostaglandin E2 (PGE2) signaling pathways. Many publications on the anticancer impact of berberine have been published since Chang revealed antitumor effect of berberine via downregulation of Ki-ras2 in NT2/D1 teratoma cells. According to Ma et al. [101], berberine inhibited HIF-1 and P-gp, which had an anticancer effect on MCF-7 breast cancer cells. Berberine inhibited STAT3, nuclear factor-kappaB (NF-B), and ERK 1/2 in cholangiocarcinoma cells [102].

8.6 Levofloxacin

The antibiotic levofloxacin, derived from the *Lupinus luteus*, inhibits the mTOR and MAPK/ERK pathways, resulting in antiproliferative and apoptotic actions in breast cancer cells [103]. Song et al. [104] also found that increase in ROS, mitochondrial superoxide, hydrogen peroxide, and oxidative stress indicators (HEL and 4-HNE) causes levofloxacin to have antiproliferative and apoptotic effects in lung cancer cells.

8.7 Aspirin

Aspirin produced from *Spiraea ulmaria*. Aspirin, also known as acetylsalicylic acid, is a nonsteroidal antiinflammatory medicine that was licensed by the FDA in 1984 for modest pain relief and fever reduction and has been used as a COX-2 inhibitor for the prevention of colorectal cancer risk since FDA approval in 1992 [105]. It has antiplatelet [106], antiinflammatory [107], analgesic [108], and anticancer actions in breast [50], colon [109], prostate [110], lung [86], brain [111], and liver [112] malignancies. Aspirin inhibits COX-2 in cells, which has been thoroughly proven [113]. Aspirin inhibited LPS-induced PGE2 production and activation of COX-2, NFB, and PKC and IB degradation in alveolar macrophages, and aspirin inhibits angiogenesis in HCT-116, DLD-1, and HT-29 colon cancer cells via inhibition of COX-2 [114]. Aspirin reduces the growth of certain melanomas, according to Kumar et al. [115], via suppressing PGE2 and activating AMPK. Furthermore aspirin has been reported as a strong inhibitor of heparanase activity, which inhibits the proliferation of B16F10, MDA-MB-231, and MDA-MB-435 cancer cells. Aspirin has previously been utilized as an anticancer medicine repurposed for canner therapy, including colon cancer prevention as a COX-2 inhibitor.

8.8 Tanshinone

Tanshinone, is a major compound of Danshen (*Salvia miltiorrhiza*) [116]. Many anticancer mechanisms of tanshinones have been documented. Tanshinone I and IIA had a greater cytotoxic impact in P388 lymphocytic leukemia cells than dihydrotanshinone I and cryptotanshinone. Tanshinone I, for example, triggered apoptosis in monocyticleukemia cells (U937, THP-1, and SHI 1) by activating caspase-3, decreasing hTERT mRNA expression and telomerase activity, and downregulating survivin [117]. In addition, Won et al. [118] found that tanshinone IIA induces G1 arrest in LNCaP prostate cancer cells by activating p53 signaling and inhibiting AR, while Kim et al. [119] discovered that cryptotanshinone sensitizes TNF-induced apoptosis in human myeloid leukemia KBM-5 cells by activating caspase-8 and pp38 via ROS-dependent activation of caspase-8 and p38.

8.9 Digoxin

Digoxin, a cardiac glycoside produced from *Digitalis purpurea*, was recently licensed for the treatment of heart failure and atrial fibrillation. In Burkitt's lymphoma cells in an animal model, Digoxin had an anticancer impact by inhibiting TNF-stimulated NF-B activity and activation of caspases [68]. Digoxin also caused prostate cancer cells to undergo Cdk5/p25-related apoptosis [120], glioblastoma cells to undergo p38-related apoptosis [68], and breast cancer cells to undergo mitochondria-dependent apoptosis. Digoxin, a widely used cardiac glycoside for the treatment of various heart failure syndromes, has garnered attention for its anticancer properties, with encouraging results in prostate, breast, renal, and lung carcinomas, melanoma, and leukemia models. The suppression of the Na+/K+-ATPase pump and modification of downstream signaling cascades (i.e., MAPK, PLC, PI3K, and Src kinase) are thought to be the key mechanisms of digoxin's antiproliferative effects [121].

8.10 Ginkgolide

Ginkgolide B, a main active component of *Ginkgo biloba*, was found to trigger apoptosis in HepG2 cells via intracellular ROS production, activation of JNK and caspase-3, and DNA fragmentation. Ginkgolide B also decreased invasion by inhibiting miR-223-3p-mediated ZEB1 [122] and suppressed tumorigenesis and angiogenesis in colitis-associated cancer by targeting platelet-activating factor receptor (PAFR) [123]. In terms of anticancer drug combinations, ginkgolide B increased gemcitabine sensitivity in pancreatic cancer cell lines by inhibiting the PAFR/NF-κB pathway [124] and sensitized SKOV-3 ovarian cancer cells to cisplatin [125].

8.11 Hypericin

Hypericin, a key active ingredient in *Hypericum perforatum*, has been shown to have antidepressant, anticancer, and antiviral properties [126]. Hypericin-induced phototoxicity can inhibit tumor growth in EMT6 mouse mammary cancer cells. In colorectal cancer, esophageal cancer, glioma, hepatocellular carcinoma, urinary bladder cancer, pancreatic cancer, breast cancer, and thyroid cancer, hypericin exerts anticancer effects via photodynamic action [127,128]. According to Ferenc et al. [129], hypericin, in combination with genistein, inhibits BCL-2 and AKT in breast cancer cells.

8.12 Paclitaxel

In 1971, paclitaxel was isolated from pacific yew (*Taxus brevifolia*). It was a medication used to treat arterial restenosis. Paclitaxel promotes G2/M cell cycle arrest and is used to treat early, advanced, and metastatic breast cancer in pre- and postmenopausal women as neoadjuvant or adjuvant therapy, either alone or in combination with other chemotherapeutic drugs. Paclitaxel (175 mg/m^2 IV over 3 h 3 weeks four times with doxorubicin-containing regimen) was repositioned as chemotherapy adjuncts in breast cancer treatment regimens after that [130]. Clinicians all around the world utilize a variety of taxanes-containing combinatorial chemotherapy in the treatment of breast cancer [131].

8.13 Vinblastine

Vinblastine is a Vinca alkaloid that can be discovered in the white flowered periwinkle *Vinca rosea*. The researchers were more interested in determining the antidiabetic efficacy of *Vinca rosea* extract and revealed that rats given the extract had peripheral granulocytopenia and leukopenia. Finally, they discovered that *Vinca rosea* extract/vinblastine has carcinostatic action in rats with transplantable mammary adenocarcinoma and sarcoma. In 1965, vinblastine was licensed for the treatment of lymphoma. In addition, vinblastine (2–4 mg/mm^2 IV once weekly or every other week) in combination with mitomycin or MVP (mitomycin C, vinblastine, and cisplatin) has been used to treat advanced and metastatic breast cancer since the 1980s [132]. Vinblastine is mitotic inhibitor that works by altering microtubule dynamics to stop cell division or mitosis. This causes cell cycle arrest in the G2/M phase or inhibits spindle formation.

9. Antidiabetic phytocompounds repurposed for cancer therapy

A few phytocompounds derived from traditional medicinal plants reported in our research laboratory for antidiabetic activity have been repurposed for cancer with significant therapeutic evidences against prostate, colon, and breast cancers. Our studies explored the anticancer efficacies of phytocompounds from *Cassia fistula*, *Tinospora cordifoila*, *Gymnema sylvestre*, *Terminalia bellirica*, and *Costus speciosus*. The tetracyclic triterpenoids from *C. fistula* L. ethyl acetate extract having hypoglycemic potential were tested against a human colon cancer cell line (HT-29) showed depreciation in the rates of invasion and metastasis. Apoptotic was induced in cancer cells with chromatin condensation, DNA breakage, membrane leakage, and increased depolarization of the mitochondrial membrane, as well as cell cycle arrest at S phase and G2/M phase. The result of treated cell line was reported with the upregulation of p53 and downregulation of ERK2 expression. A novel polysaccharide isolated from the methanol extract of *T. cordifoila* has been previously reported for antidiabetic activity and also examined for its chemopreventive effects on breast cancer cell lines MCF-7 and MDA-MB-231 [133]. Dihydroxy gymnemic triacetate (DGT) is a new triterpinoidsaponin isolated from *G. sylvestre* that has been shown to have antidiabetic properties and repurposed for testing its anticancer potential in prostate cancer [134]. DGT inhibited PC-3 cell survival, prostate's PSA level is efficiently maintained and dramatically increased apoptosis by downregulating antiapoptotic proteins, Bcl-2 and Bcl-xL which was well substantiated by in silico studies. Costunolide, a bioactive secondary metabolite derived from *C. speciosus*, has been reported for antidiabetic, hepatoprotective, antimicrobial, and anticancer properties. Investigations of costunolide for breast cancer therapy revealed the anticancer efficacy of the compounds through regulation of intrinsic cancer signaling pathway. Costunolide treatment in the breast cancer cell lines showed decrease in the protein expressions of positive cell cycle regulators; furthermore, the compound has been reported with better antioxidant potential also. Another phytoconstituent eremanthin isolated from *C. speciosus* was reported for reducing the survival rate of cancer cell lines when tested in vitro. Octyl gallate and gallic acid were the two compounds isolated from the fruits of *T. bellirica* and both were reportedly proved to possess hypoglycemic and diabetes ameliorating effects [135]. These compounds when examined for anticancer activity against breast cancer reported a significant antiproliferative effect against breast cancer cell lines, also the assessment of tumor markers carcinoembryonic antigen and cancer antigen 15–3, hematology profile, antioxidant enzyme level and histology of breast tissue revealed the chemotherapeutic potential of eremanthin (Fig. 1).

10. Conclusion

The oncology community is interested in the clinical development of existing noncancer drugs that have shown anticancer activity rather than de novo medicines with the advancements in combinatorial chemistry, virtual screening, data mining, and molecular interaction and simulation studies.

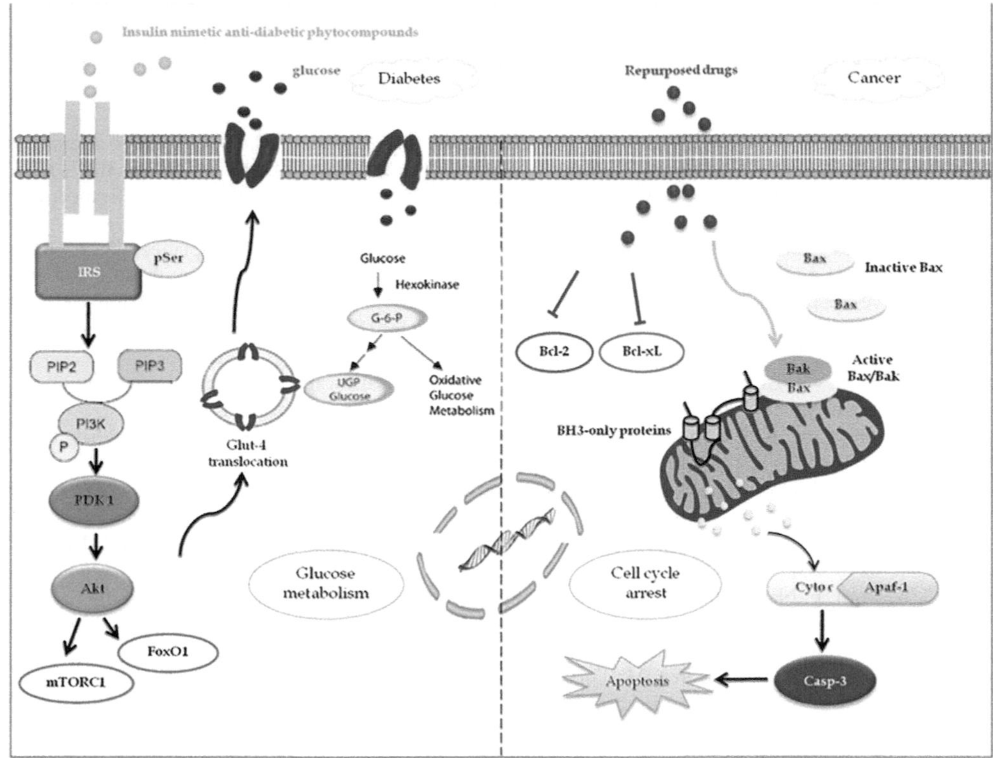

Fig. 1 The antidiabetic drugs reported in our laboratory have their mode of action via PI3K/IRS-1-mediated insulin signaling pathway promoting the effective Glut-4 translocation to the cell membrane, thereby reducing glucose load in the blood. These drugs also had chemopreventive efficacy when tested against breast cancer, they induced apoptosis through intrinsic pathway of apoptosis, which involved the process of mitochondrial outer membrane permeabilization. Once the apoptosis is triggered, the antiapoptotic proteins BcL-2 and BcL-xL are inhibited and BH3-only proteins activate Bax and Bak, which oligomerize and insert into the outer mitochondrial membrane and thus releasing cytochrome *c* into the cytosol. The cytochrome *c* forms a complex with Apaf-1 and assembled into an apoptosome with the subsequent activation of caspase-3 leading to apoptosis.

References

[1] J.A. Malik, S. Ahmed, B. Jan, O. Bender, T. Al Hagbani, A. Alqarni, S. Anwar, Drugs repurposed: an advanced step towards the treatment of breast cancer and associated challenges, Biomed. Pharmacother. 145 (2022), 112375, https://doi.org/10.1016/j.biopha.2021.112375.

[2] S.C. Gupta, B. Sung, S. Prasad, L.J. Webb, B.B. Aggarwal, Cancer drug discovery by repurposing: teaching new tricks to old dogs, Trends Pharmacol. Sci. 34 (9) (2013) 508–517, https://doi.org/10.1016/j.tips.2013.06.005.

[3] A.G. Waks, E.P. Winer, Breast cancer treatment, JAMA 321 (3) (2019) 288, https://doi.org/10.1001/jama.2018.19323.

[4] A. Mullard, 2020 FDA drug approvals, Nat. Rev. Drug Discov. 20 (2) (2021) 85–90, https://doi.org/10.1038/d41573-021-00002-0.

[5] E.C. Butcher, et al., Systems biology in drug discovery, Nat. Biotechnol. 22 (2004) 1253–1259.

[6] H. Kitano, Systems biology: a brief overview, Science 295 (2002) 1662–1664.

[7] E. Hernández-Lemus, M. Martínez-García, Pathway-based drug-repurposing schemes in cancer: the role of translational bioinformatics, Front. Oncol. 10 (2021), https://doi.org/10.3389/fonc.2020.605680.

[8] J. Langedijk, A.K. Mantel-Teeuwisse, D.S. Slijkerman, M.H.D.B. Schutjens, Drug repositioning and repurposing: terminology and definitions in literature, Drug Discov. Today 20 (2015) 1027–1034.

[9] J.S. Shim, J.O. Liu, Recent advances in drug repositioning for the discovery of new anticancer drugs, Int. J. Biol. Sci. 10 (2014) 654–663.

[10] M. Ávalos-Moreno, A. López-Tejada, J.L. Blaya-Cánovas, F.E. Cara-Lupiañez, A. González-González, J.A. Lorente, P. Sánchez-Rovira, S. Granados-Principal, Drug repurposing for triple-negative breast cancer, J. Personal. Med. 10 (4) (2020) 200, https://doi.org/10.3390/jpm10040200.

[11] B. Turanli, M. Grøtli, J. Boren, et al., Drug repositioning for effective prostate cancer treatment, Front. Physiol. 9 (2018) 500.

[12] V. Frattini, V. Trifonov, J.M. Chan, et al., The integrated landscape of driver genomic alterations in glioblastoma, Nat. Genet. 45 (2013) 1141–1149.

[13] Z. Liu, H. Fang, K. Reagan, et al., In silico drug repositioning: what we need to know, Drug Discov. Today 18 (2013) 110–115.

[14] L. Cardone, Biocomputing drug repurposing toward targeted therapies, Aging (Albany NY) 8 (2016) 2609–2610.

[15] F. Cheng, In silico oncology drug repositioning and polypharmacology, Methods Mol. Biol. 1878 (2019) 243–261.

[16] C. Mottini, F. Napolitano, Z. Li, X. Gao, L. Cardone, Computer-aided drug repurposing for cancer therapy: approaches and opportunities to challenge anticancer targets, Semin. Cancer Biol. (2019), https://doi.org/10.1016/j.semca ncer.2019.09.023.

[17] B. Turanli, O. Altay, J. Borén, H. Turkez, J. Nielsen, M. Uhlen, K.Y. Arga, A. Mardinoglu, Systems biology based drug repositioning for development of cancer therapy, Semin. Cancer Biol. 68 (2021) 47–58, https://doi.org/10.1016/j.semcancer.2019.09.020.

[18] P. Nowak-Sliwinska, L. Scapozza, A. Ruiz iAltaba, Drug repurposing in oncology: compounds, pathways, phenotypes and computational approaches for colorectal cancer, Biochim. Biophys. Acta Rev. Cancer 1871 (2) (2019) 434–454, https://doi.org/10.1016/j.bbcan.2019.04.005.

[19] M. Chartier, L. Morency, M.I. Zylber, R.J. Najmanovich, Large-scale detection of drug off-targets: hypotheses for drug repurposing and understanding side-effects, BMC Pharmacol. Toxicol. 18 (1) (2017), https://doi.org/10.1186/s40360-017-0128-7.

[20] X. Meng, H. Zhang, M. Mezei, M. Cui, Molecular docking: a powerful approach for structure-based drug discovery, Curr. Comput. Aided Drug Des. 7 (2) (2011) 146–157.

[21] A. Peyvandipour, N. Saberian, A. Shafi, M. Donato, S. Draghici, A novel computational approach for drug repurposing using systems biology, Bioinformatics 34 (16) (2018) 2817–2825.

[22] S. Pushpakom, F. Iorio, P.A. Eyers, K.J. Escott, S. Hopper, A. Wells, A. Doig, T. Guilliams, J. Latimer, C. McNamee, A. Norris, P. Sanseau, D. Cavalla, M. Pirmohamed, Drug repurposing: progress, challenges and recommendations, Nat. Rev. Drug Discov. 18 (1) (2019) 41–58.

[23] Y.M. Ning, J.L. Gulley, P.M. Arlen, S. Woo, S.M. Steinberg, J.J. Wright, H.L. Parnes, J.B. Trepel, M.J. Lee, Y.S. Kim, H. Sun, R.A. Madan, L. Latham, E. Jones, C.C. Chen, W.D. Figg, W.L. Dahut, Phase II trial of bevacizumab, thalidomide, docetaxel, and prednisone in patients with metastatic castration-resistant prostate cancer, J. Clin. Oncol. 28 (12) (2010) 2070–2076.

[24] S. Forli, R. Huey, M.E. Pique, M.F. Sanner, D.S. Goodsell, A.J. Olson, Computational protein-ligand docking and virtual drug screening with the AutoDock suite, Nat. Protoc. 11 (5) (2016) 905–919.

[25] A.L. Hopkins, Network pharmacology: the next paradigm in drug discovery, Nat. Chem. Biol. 4 (11) (2008) 682–690.

[26] Y. Yamanishi, M. Araki, A. Gutteridge, W. Honda, M. Kanehisa, Prediction of drug-target interaction networks from the integration of chemical and genomic spaces, Bioinformatics 24 (13) (2008) i232–i240.

[27] V. Palve, Y. Liao, L.L. RemsingRix, U. Rix, Turning liabilities into opportunities: off-target based drug repurposing in cancer, Semin. Cancer Biol. 68 (2021) 209–229, https://doi.org/10.1016/j.semcancer.2020.02.003.

[28] S. Ekins, J. Mestres, B. Testa, In silico pharmacology for drug discovery: methods for virtual ligand screening and profiling, Br. J. Pharmacol. 152 (1) (2007) 9–20, https://doi.org/10.1038/sj.bjp.0707305.

[29] L. Ferreira, R. Dos Santos, G. Oliva, A. Andricopulo, Molecular docking and structure-based drug design strategies, Molecules 20 (7) (2015) 13384–13421.

[30] I. Halperin, B. Ma, H. Wolfson, R. Nussinov, Principles of docking: an overview of search algorithms and a guide to scoring functions, Proteins Struct. Funct. Genet. 47 (4) (2002) 409–443.

[31] G. Wolber, T. Langer, LigandScout: 3-D pharmacophores derived from protein-bound ligands and their use as virtual screening filters, J. Chem. Inf. Model. 45 (1) (2004) 160–169, https://doi.org/10.1021/ci049885e.

[32] B.Q. Wei, W.A. Baase, L.H. Weaver, B.W. Matthews, B.K. Shoichet, A model binding site for testing scoring functions in molecular docking, J. Mol. Biol. 322 (2) (2002) 339–355.

[33] G.L. Warren, C.W. Andrews, A.-M. Capelli, B. Clarke, J. LaLonde, M.H. Lambert, M. Lindvall, N. Nevins, S.F. Semus, S. Senger, G. Tedesco, I.D. Wall, J.M. Woolven, C.E. Peishoff, M.S. Head, A critical assessment of docking programs and scoring functions, J. Med. Chem. 49 (20) (2006) 5912–5931.

[34] S.E. Nichols, R. Baron, A. Ivetac, J.A. McCammon, Predictive power of molecular dynamics receptor structures in virtual screening, J. Chem. Inf. Model. 51 (6) (2011) 1439–1446.

[35] T. Yang, J.C. Wu, C. Yan, Y. Wang, R. Luo, M.B. Gonzales, K.N. Dalby, P. Ren, Virtual screening using molecular simulations, Proteins Struct. Funct. Bioinform. 79 (6) (2011) 1940–1951.

[36] J. Zou, M.W. Zheng, G. Li, Z.G. Su, Advanced systems biology methods in drug discovery and translational biomedicine, Biomed. Res. Int. 2013 (2013), 742835.

[37] J. Bosley, C. Boren, S. Lee, M. Grøtli, J. Nielsen, M. Uhlen, J. Boren, A. Mardinoglu, Improving the economics of NASH/NAFLD treatment through the use of systems biology, Drug Discov. Today 22 (10) (2017) 1532–1538.

[38] R.A. Hodos, B.A. Kidd, K. Shameer, B.P. Readhead, J.T. Dudley, *In silico* methods for drug repurposing and pharmacology, WIREs Syst. Biol. Med. 8 (2016) 186–210.

[39] J. Li, S. Zheng, B. Chen, A.J. Butte, S.J. Swamidass, Z. Lu, A survey of current trends in computational drug repositioning, Brief. Bioinform. 17 (2016) 2–12.

[40] J.T. Dudley, M. Sirota, M. Shenoy, R.K. Pai, S. Roedder, A.P. Chiang, et al., Computational repositioning of the anticonvulsant topiramate for inflammatory bowel disease, Sci. Transl. Med. 3 (2011) 96ra76.

[41] M. Sirota, J.T. Dudley, J. Kim, A.P. Chiang, A.A. Morgan, A. Sweet-Cordero, et al., Discovery and preclinical validation of drug indications using compendia of public gene expression data, Sci. Transl. Med. 3 (2011) 96ra77.

[42] T.M. Nguyen, S.A. Muhammad, S. Ibrahim, L. Ma, J. Guo, B. Bai, B. Zeng, DeCoST: a new approach in drug repurposing from control system theory, Front. Pharmacol. 9 (2018) 583.

[43] A. Pujol, R. Mosca, J. Farres, P. Aloy, Unveiling the role of network and systems biology in drug discovery, Trends Pharmacol. Sci. 31 (3) (2010) 115–123.

[44] F. Iorio, R. Tagliaferri, D. di Bernardo, Identifying network of drug mode of action by gene expression profiling, J. Comput. Biol. 16 (2) (2009) 241–251.

[45] A. Subramanian, P. Tamayo, V.K. Mootha, S. Mukherjee, B.L. Ebert, M.A. Gillette, A. Paulovich, S.L. Pomeroy, T.R. Golub, E.S. Lander, J.P. Mesirov, Gene set enrichment analysis: a knowledge-based approach for interpreting genome-wide expression profiles, Proc. Natl. Acad. Sci. U. S. A. 102 (43) (2005) 15545–15550.

[46] V. Law, C. Knox, Y. Djoumbou, T. Jewison, A.C. Guo, Y. Liu, A. Maciejewski, D. Arndt, M. Wilson, V. Neveu, A. Tang, G. Gabriel, C. Ly, S. Adamjee, Z.T. Dame, B. Han, Y. Zhou, D.S. Wishart, DrugBank 4.0: shedding new light on drug metabolism, Nucleic Acids Res. 42 (Database issue) (2014) D1091–D1097.

[47] A. Hamosh, A.F. Scott, J.S. Amberger, C.A. Bocchini, V.A. McKusick, Online Mendelian Inheritance in Man (OMIM), a knowledgebase of human genes and genetic disorders, Nucleic Acids Res. 33 (Database issue) (2005) D514–D517.

[48] T. Barrett, S.E. Wilhite, P. Ledoux, C. Evangelista, I.F. Kim, M. Tomashevsky, K.A. Marshall, K.H. Phillippy, P.M. Sherman, M. Holko, A. Yefanov, H. Lee, N. Zhang, C.L. Robertson, N. Serova, S. Davis, A. Soboleva, NCBI GEO: archive for functional genomics data sets—update, Nucleic Acids Res. 41 (Database issue) (2013) D991–D995.

[49] A. Chatr-Aryamontri, B.J. Breitkreutz, S. Heinicke, L. Boucher, A. Winter, C. Stark, J. Nixon, L. Ramage, N. Kolas, L. O'Donnell, T. Reguly, A. Breitkreutz, A. Sellam, D. Chen, C. Chang, J. Rust, M. Livstone, R. Oughtred, K. Dolinski, M. Tyers, The BioGRID interaction database: 2013 update, Nucleic Acids Res. 41 (Database issue) (2013) D816–D823.

[50] J.Y. Chen, R. Pandey, T.M. Nguyen, HAPPI-2: a comprehensive and high-quality map of human annotated and predicted protein interactions, BMC Genomics 18 (1) (2017) 182.

[51] D. Croft, G. O'Kelly, G. Wu, R. Haw, M. Gillespie, L. Matthews, M. Caudy, P. Garapati, G. Gopinath, B. Jassal, S. Jupe, I. Kalatskaya, S. Mahajan, B. May, N. Ndegwa, E. Schmidt, V. Shamovsky, C. Yung, E. Birney, H. Hermjakob, P. D'Eustachio, L. Stein, Reactome: a database of reactions, pathways and biological processes, Nucleic Acids Res. 39 (Database issue) (2011) D691–D697.

[52] S. Zhu, et al., Ferroptosis: a novel mechanism of artemisinin and its derivatives in cancer therapy, Curr. Med. Chem. (2020), https://doi.org/10.2174/0929867327666200121124404.

[53] M.L. Andersson, Y. Bottiger, P. Bastholm-Rahmner, M.L. Ovesjo, A. Veg, B. Eiermann, Evaluation of usage patterns and user perception of the drug-drug interaction database SFINX, Int. J. Med. Inform. 84 (5) (2015) 327–333.

[54] M. Kuhn, I. Letunic, L.J. Jensen, P. Bork, The SIDER database of drugs and side effects, Nucleic Acids Res. 44 (D1) (2016) D1075–D1079.

[55] A.B. Nagaraj, Q.Q. Wang, P. Joseph, C. Zheng, Y. Chen, O. Kovalenko, S. Singh, A. Armstrong, K. Resnick, K. Zanotti, S. Waggoner, R. Xu, A. DiFeo, Using a novel computational drug-repositioning approach (DrugPredict) to rapidly identify potent drug candidates for cancer treatment, Oncogene 37 (3) (2017) 403–414, https://doi.org/10.1038/onc.2017.328.

[56] M.R. Hurle, L. Yang, Q. Xie, D.K. Rajpal, P. Sanseau, P. Agarwal, Computational drug repositioning: from data to therapeutics, Clin. Pharmacol. Ther. 93 (2013) 335–341.

[57] Z. Zhao, C. Martin, R. Fan, P.E. Bourne, L. Xie, Drug repurposing to target Ebola virus replication and virulence using structural systems pharmacology, BMC Bioinformatics 17 (2016) 90.

[58] G.M. Morris, R. Huey, W. Lindstrom, M.F. Sanner, R.K. Belew, D.S. Goodsell, A.J. Olson, AutoDock4 and AutoDockTools: automated docking with selective receptor flexibility, J. Comput. Chem. 30 (2009) 2785.

[59] O. Korb, T. Stuzle, T.E. Exner, Empirical scoring functions for advanced protein-ligand docking with PLANTS, J. Chem. Inf. Model. 49 (2009) 84.

[60] G.M. Nidhi, J.W. Davies, J.L. Jenkins, Prediction of biological targets for compounds using multiple-category Bayesian models trained on chemogeonics databases, J. Chem. Inf. Model. 46 (2006) 1124.

[61] M. Olah, M. Mracec, L. Ostopovici, R. Rad, A. Bora, N. Hadaruga, et al., WOMBAT: world of molecular bioactivity, in: T.I. Oprea (Ed.), Cheminformatics in Drug Discovery, Wiley-VCH, New York, 2004, pp. 223–239.

[62] D. Cao, Y. Liang, Z. Deng, Q. Hu, M. He, Q. Xu, G. Zhou, L. Zhang, Z. Deng, S. Liu, Genome-scale screening of drug-target associations relevant to Ki using a Chemogenomics approach, PLoS One 8 (4) (2013), e57680, https://doi.org/10.1371/journal.pone.0057680.

[63] T. Liu, Y. Lin, X. Wen, R.N. Jorissen, M.K. Gilson, BindingDB: a web-accesible database of experimentally determine protein-ligand binding affinities, Nucleic Acids Res. 35 (2007) D198–D201.

[64] A. Aliper, S. Plis, A. Artemov, A. Ulloa, P. Mamoshina, A. Zhavoronkov, Deep learning applications of drugs and drug repurposing using transcriptomic data, Mol. Pharm. 13 (2016) 2524.

[65] X. Zeng, S. Zhu, X. Liu, Y. Zhou, R. Nussinov, F. Cheng, DeepDR: a network-based deep learning approach to in silico drug repositioning, Bioinformatics 35 (24) (2019) 5191–5198.

[66] V. Kanakaveti, S. Rathinasamy, S.K. Rayala, M. Gromiha, Forging new scaffolds from old: combining scaffold hopping and hierarchical virtual screening for identifying novel Bcl-2 inhibitors, Curr. Top. Med. Chem. 19 (13) (2019) 1162–1172.

[67] P. Anoosha, R. Sakthivel, M.M. Gromiha, Investigating mutation-specific biological activities of small molecules using quantitative structure-activity relationship for epidermal growth factor receptor in cancer, Mutat. Res. 806 (2017) 19–26.

[68] T. Wang, P. Xu, F. Wang, D. Zhou, R. Wang, L. Meng, X. Wang, M. Zhou, B. Chen, J. Ouyang, Effects of digoxin on cell cycle, apoptosis and NF-kappaB pathway in Burkitt's lymphoma cells and animal model, Leuk. Lymphoma 58 (7) (2017) 1673–1685.

[69] H.K. Bronsveld, et al., The association of diabetes mellitus and insulin treatment with expression of insulin-related proteins in breast tumors, BMC Cancer 18 (2018) 224.

[70] S. Jiralerspong, P.J. Goodwin, Obesity and breast cancer prognosis: evidence, challenges, and opportunities, J. Clin. Oncol. 34 (2016) 4203–4216, https://doi.org/10.1200/JCO.2016.68.4480.

[71] Y. Shu, S.A. Sheardown, C. Brown, R.P. Owen, S. Zhang, R.A. Castro, A.G. Ianculescu, L. Yue, J.C. Lo, E.G. Burchard, C.M. Brett, K.M. Giacomini, Effect of genetic variation in the organic cation transporter 1 (OCT1) on metformin action, J. Clin. Investig. 117 (2007) 1422–1431, https://doi.org/10.1172/JCI30558.

[72] S.M. Hsieh Li, S.T. Liu, Y.L. Chang, C.L. Ho, S.M. Huang, Metformin causes cancer cell death through downregulation of p53-dependent differentiated embryo chondrocyte 1, J. Biomed. Sci. 25 (2018), https://doi.org/10.1186/S12929-018-0478-5.

[73] R.S. Wahdan-Alaswad, A.D. Thor, Metformin activity against breast cancer: mechanistic differences by molecular subtype and metabolic conditions, in: Metformin, IntechOpen, 2020, https://doi.org/10.5772/INTECHOPEN.91183 (Work. Title).

[74] A. Kalender, et al., Metformin, independent of AMPK, inhibits mTORC1 in a RAG GTPase-dependent manner, Cell Metab. 11 (2010) 390–401.

[75] X. Liu, et al., Metformin targets central carbon metabolism and reveals mitochondrial requirements in human cancers, Cell Metab. 24 (2016) 728–739.

[76] J. Faria, G. Negalha, A. Azevedo, F.F. Martel, Metformin and breast cancer: molecular targets, J. Mammary Gland Biol. Neoplasia 24 (2019) 111–123, https://doi.org/10.1007/S10911-019-09429-Z.

[77] B. Shi, X. Hu, H. He, W. Fang, Metformin suppresses breast cancer growth via inhibition of cyclooxygenase-2, Oncol. Lett. 22 (2021) 1–14, https://doi.org/10.3892/OL.2021.12876.

[78] M.H. Roshan, Y.K. Shing, N.P. Pace, Metformin as an adjuvant in breast cancer treatment, SAGE Open Med. 7 (2019), https://doi.org/10.1177/2050312119865114 (205031211986511).

[79] J. Lee, A.E. Yesilkanal, J.P. Wynne, C. Frankenberger, J. Liu, J. Yan, M. Elbaz, D.C. Rabe, F.D. Rustandy, P. Tiwari, E.A. Grossman, P.C. Hart, C. Kang, S.M. Sanderson, J. Andrade, D.K. Nomura, M.G. Bonini, J.W. Locasale, M.R. Rosner, Effective breast cancer combination therapy targeting BACH1 and mitochondrial metabolism, Nature 568 (5687751) (2019) 254–258, https://doi.org/10.1038/s41586-019-1005-x.

[80] G. Han, H. Gong, Y. Wang, S. Guo, K. Liu, AMPK/mtor-mediated inhibition of survivin partly contributes to metformin-induced apoptosis in human gastric cancer cell, Cancer Biol. Ther. 16 (1) (2014) 77–87, https://doi.org/10.4161/15384047.2014.987021.

[81] W.W. Wheaton, S.E. Weinberg, R.B. Hamanaka, S. Soberanes, L.B. Sullivan, E. Anso, A. Glasauer, E. Dufour, G.M. Mutlu, G.S. Budigner, N.S. Chandel, Author response: metformin inhibits mitochondrial complex I of cancer cells to reduce tumorigenesis, Elife (2014), https://doi.org/10.7554/elife.02242.019.

[82] S. Krishna, et al., A randomised, double blind, placebo-controlled pilot study of oral artesunate therapy for colorectal cancer, EBioMedicine 2 (2015) 82–90.

[83] S.S. Patel, et al., Cellular and molecular mechanisms of curcumin in prevention and treatment of disease, Crit. Rev. Food Sci. Nutr. 60 (2020) 887–939.

[84] M. Nasiri, et al., Curcumin and silibinin inhibit telomerase expression in T47D human breast cancer cells, Asian Pac. J. Cancer Prev. 14 (2013) 3449–3453.

[85] F.H. Sarkar, Y. Li, Z. Wang, D. Kong, The role of nutraceuticals in the regulation of Wnt and Hedgehog signaling in cancer, Cancer Metastasis Rev. 29 (2010) 383–394.

[86] S. Ye, M. Lee, D. Lee, E.H. Ha, E.M. Chun, Association of long-term use of low-dose aspirin as chemoprevention with risk of lung cancer, JAMA Netw. Open 2 (3) (2019), e190185.
[87] P. Thangavel, A. Puga-Olguin, J.F. Rodriguez-Landa, R.C. Zepeda, Genistein as potential therapeutic candidate for menopausal symptoms and other related diseases, Molecules 24 (2019) 3892.
[88] M. Verheus, et al., Plasma phytoestrogens and subsequent breast cancer risk, J. Clin. Oncol. 25 (2007) 648–655.
[89] C. Spagnuolo, et al., Genistein and cancer: current status, challenges, and future directions, Adv. Nutr. 6 (2015) 408–419.
[90] S. Jagadeesh, S. Kyo, P.P. Banerjee, Genistein represses telomerase activity via both transcriptional and posttranslational mechanisms in human prostate cancer cells, Cancer Res. 66 (2006) 2107–2115.
[91] Y. Zhang, Q. Li, H. Chen, DNA methylation and histone modifications of Wnt genes by genistein during colon cancer development, Carcinogenesis 34 (2013) 1756–1763.
[92] S. Bandyopadhyay, et al., Potential antibacterial activity of berberine against multi drug resistant enterovirulent Escherichia coli isolated from yaks (Poephagusgrunniens) with haemorrhagicdiarrhoea, Asian Pac. J. Trop. Med. 6 (2013) 315–319.
[93] P. Hasanein, M. Ghafari-Vahed, I. Khodadadi, Effects of isoquinoline alkaloid berberine on lipid peroxidation, antioxidant defense system, and liver damage induced by lead acetate in rats, Redox Rep. 22 (1) (2017) 42–50.
[94] K. Zou, Z. Li, Y. Zhang, H.Y. Zhang, B. Li, W.L. Zhu, J.Y. Shi, Q. Jia, Y.M. Li, Advances in the study of berberine and its derivatives: a focus on anti-inflammatory and anti-tumor effects in the digestive system, Acta Pharmacol. Sin. 38 (2) (2017) 157–167.
[95] L.M. Koppen, A. Whitaker, A. Rosene, R.D. Beckett, Efficacy of berberine alone and in combination for the treatment of hyperlipidemia: a systematic review, Evid. Based Complement. Alternat. Med. 22 (4) (2017) 956–968.
[96] H.M. Hussien, A. Abd-Elmegied, D.A. Ghareeb, H.S. Hafez, H.E.A. Ahmed, N.A. El-Moneam, Neuroprotective effect of berberine against environmental heavy metals-induced neurotoxicity and Alzheimer's-like disease in rats, Food Chem. Toxicol. 111 (2018) 432–444.
[97] D. Hou, G. Xu, C. Zhang, B. Li, J. Qin, X. Hao, Q. Liu, X. Zhang, J. Liu, J. Wei, Y. Gong, Z. Liu, C. Shao, Berberine induces oxidative DNA damage and impairs homologous recombination repair in ovarian cancer cells to confer increased sensitivity to PARP inhibition, Cell Death Dis. 8 (10) (2017), e3070.
[98] A. Pirillo, A.L. Catapano, Berberine, a plant alkaloid with lipid- and glucose-lowering properties: from in vitro evidence to clinical studies, Atherosclerosis 243 (2) (2015) 449–461.
[99] X. Chang, et al., Lipid profiling of the therapeutic effects of berberine in patients with nonalcoholic fatty liver disease, J. Transl. Med. 14 (2016) 266.
[100] G. Derosa, A. D'Angelo, A. Vanelli, P. Maffioli, An evaluation of a nutraceutical with berberine, curcumin, inositol, banaba and chromium picolinate in patients with fasting dysglycemia, Diabetes Metab. Syndr. Obes. 13 (2020) 653–661.
[101] W. Ma, et al., Berberine inhibits the proliferation and migration of breast cancer ZR-75-30 cells by targeting Ephrin-B2, Phytomedicine 25 (2017) 45–51.
[102] N. Puthdee, W. Seubwai, K. Vaeteewoottacharn, T. Boonmars, U. Cha'on, C. Phoomak, S. Wongkham, Berberine induces cell cycle arrest in cholangiocarcinoma cell lines via inhibition of NF-κB and STAT3 pathways, Biol. Pharm. Bull. 40 (6) (2017) 751–757.
[103] M. Yu, R. Li, J. Zhang, Repositioning of antibiotic levofloxacin as a mitochondrial biogenesis inhibitor to target breast cancer, Biochem. Biophys. Res. Commun. 471 (4) (2016) 639–645.
[104] M. Song, H. Wu, S. Wu, T. Ge, G. Wang, Y. Zhou, S. Sheng, J. Jiang, Antibiotic drug levofloxacin inhibits proliferation and induces apoptosis of lung cancer cells through inducing mitochondrial dysfunction and oxidative damage, Biomed. Pharmacother. 84 (2016) 1137–1143.
[105] F.D. Hart, E.C. Huskisson, Non-steroidal anti-inflammatory drugs. Current status and rational therapeutic use, Drugs 27 (3) (1984) 232–255.
[106] N. Agarwal, A.N. Mahmoud, N.K. Patel, A. Jain, J. Garg, M.K. Mojadidi, S. Agrawal, A. Qamar, H. Golwala, T. Gupta, N. Bhatia, R.D. Anderson, D.L. Bhatt, Meta-analysis of aspirin

versus dual antiplatelet therapy following coronary artery bypass grafting, Am. J. Cardiol. 121 (1) (2018) 32–40.

[107] S.M. Ratchford, K.M. Lavin, R.K. Perkins, B. Jemiolo, S.W. Trappe, T.A. Trappe, Aspirin as a COX inhibitor and anti-inflammatory drug in human skeletal muscle, J. Appl. Physiol. 123 (6) (2017) 1610–1616.

[108] M. Voelker, B.P. Schachtel, S.A. Cooper, S.C. Gatoulis, Efficacy of disintegrating aspirin in two different models for acute mild-to-moderate pain: sore throat pain and dental pain, Inflammopharmacology 24 (1) (2016) 43–51.

[109] S. Park, D.G. Lee, H. Shin, Network mirroring for drug repositioning, BMC Med. Inform. Decis. Mak. 17 (Suppl. 1) (2017) 55.

[110] C.J. Smith, T.H. Dorsey, W. Tang, S.V. Jordan, C.A. Loffredo, S. Ambs, Aspirin use reduces the risk of aggressive prostate cancer and disease recurrence in African–American men, Cancer Epidemiol. Biomark. Prev. 26 (6) (2017) 845–853.

[111] J. Ming, B. Sun, Z. Li, L. Lin, X. Meng, B. Han, R. Wang, P. Wu, J. Li, J. Cai, C. Jiang, Aspirin inhibits the SHH/GLI1 signaling pathway and sensitizes malignant glioma cells to temozolomide therapy, Aging 9 (4) (2017) 1233–1247.

[112] T. Wang, X. Fu, T. Jin, L. Zhang, B. Liu, Y. Wu, F. Xu, X. Wang, K. Ye, W. Zhang, L. Ye, Aspirin targets P4HA2 through inhibiting NF-kappaB and LMCD1-AS1/let-7g to inhibit tumour growth and collagen deposition in hepatocellular carcinoma, EBioMedicine 45 (2019) 168–180.

[113] M. Dovizio, A. Bruno, S. Tacconelli, P. Patrignani, Mode of action of aspirin as a chemopreventive agent, Recent Results Cancer Res. 191 (2013) 39–65.

[114] M.I. Shtivelband, H.S. Juneja, S. Lee, K.K. Wu, Aspirin and salicylate inhibit colon cancer medium- and VEGF-induced endothelial tube formation: correlation with suppression of cyclooxygenase-2 expression, J. Thromb. Haemost. 1 (10) (2003) 2225–2233.

[115] D. Kumar, H. Rahman, E. Tyagi, T. Liu, C. Li, R. Lu, D. Lum, S.L. Holmen, J.A. Maschek, J.E. Cox, M.W. VanBrocklin, D. Grossman, Aspirin suppresses PGE_2 and activates AMP kinase to inhibit melanoma cell motility, pigmentation, and selective tumor growth *in vivo*, Cancer Prev. Res. 11 (10) (2018) 629–642.

[116] J. Wang, X. Xiong, B. Feng, Cardiovascular effects of salvianolic acid B, Evid. Based Complement. Alternat. Med. 2013 (2013), 247948.

[117] X.D. Liu, R.F. Fan, Y. Zhang, H.Z. Yang, Z.G. Fang, W.B. Guan, D.J. Lin, R.Z. Xiao, R.W. Huang, H.Q. Huang, P.Q. Liu, J.J. Liu, Down-regulation of telomerase activity and activation of caspase-3 are responsible for Tanshinone I-induced apoptosis in monocyte leukemia cells in vitro, Int. J. Mol. Sci. 11 (6) (2010) 2267–2280.

[118] S.H. Won, H.J. Lee, S.J. Jeong, J. Lu, S.H. Kim, Activation of p53 signaling and inhibition of androgen receptor mediate tanshinone IIA induced G1 arrest in LNCaP prostate cancer cells, Phytother. Res. 26 (5) (2012) 669–674.

[119] J.H. Kim, S.J. Jeong, T.R. Kwon, S.M. Yun, J.H. Jung, M. Kim, H.J. Lee, M.H. Lee, S.G. Ko, C.Y. Chen, S.H. Kim, Cryptotanshinone enhances TNF-alpha-induced apoptosis in chronic myeloid leukemia KBM-5 cells, Apoptosis 16 (7) (2011) 696–707.

[120] H. Lin, J.L. Juang, P.S. Wang, Involvement of Cdk5/p25 in digoxin-triggered prostate cancer cell apoptosis, J. Biol. Chem. 279 (28) (2004) 29302–29307.

[121] J. Tian, T. Cai, Z. Yuan, H. Wang, L. Liu, M. Haas, E. Maksimova, X.Y. Huang, Z.J. Xie, Binding of Src to Na+/K+-ATPase forms a functional signaling complex, Mol. Biol. Cell 17 (1) (2006) 317–326.

[122] Y. Zhi, J. Pan, W. Shen, P. He, J. Zheng, X. Zhou, G. Lu, Z. Chen, Z. Zhou, Ginkgolide B inhibits human bladder cancer cell migration and invasion through MicroRNA-223-3p, Cell. Physiol. Biochem. 39 (5) (2016) 1787–1794.

[123] L. Sun, Z. He, J. Ke, S. Li, X. Wu, L. Lian, X. He, X. He, J. Hu, Y. Zou, X. Wu, P. Lan, PAF receptor antagonist Ginkgolide B inhibits tumourigenesis and angiogenesis in colitis-associated cancer, Int. J. Clin. Exp. Pathol. 8 (1) (2015) 432–440.

[124] C. Lou, H. Lu, Z. Ma, C. Liu, Y. Zhang, Ginkgolide B enhances gemcitabine sensitivity in pancreatic cancer cell lines via inhibiting PAFR/NF-small ka, CyrillicB pathway, Biomed. Pharmacother. 109 (2019) 563–572.

[125] W. Jiang, Q. Cong, Y. Wang, B. Ye, C. Xu, Ginkgo may sensitize ovarian cancer cells to cisplatin: antiproliferative and apoptosis-inducing effects of ginkgolide B on ovarian cancer cells, Integr. Cancer Ther. 13 (3) (2014) Np10–Np17.

[126] C.M. Shih, C.H. Wu, W.J. Wu, Y.M. Hsiao, J.L. Ko, Hypericin inhibits hepatitis C virus replication via deacetylation and down-regulation of heme oxygenase-1, Phytomedicine 46 (2018) 193–198.

[127] H. Kim, S.W. Kim, K.H. Seok, C.W. Hwang, J.C. Ahn, J.O. Jin, H.W. Kang, Hypericin-assisted photodynamic therapy against anaplastic thyroid cancer, Photodiagn. Photodyn. Ther. 24 (2018) 15–21.

[128] M. Majernik, R. Jendzelovsky, M. Babincak, J. Kosuth, J. Sevc, Z. TonelliGombalova, Z. Jendzelovska, M. Burikova, P. Fedorocko, Novel insights into the effect of Hyperforin and photodynamic therapy with hypericin on chosen angiogenic factors in colorectal micro-tumors created on chorioallantoic membrane, Int. J. Mol. Sci. 20 (12) (2019).

[129] P. Ferenc, P. Solar, J. Kleban, J. Mikes, P. Fedorocko, Down-regulation of Bcl-2 and Akt induced by combination of photoactivatedhypericin and genistein in human breast cancer cells, J. Photochem. Photobiol. B Biol. 98 (1) (2010) 25–34.

[130] J.M. Nabholtz, J. Gligorov, The role of taxanes in the treatment of breast cancer, Expert. Opin. Pharmacother. 6 (7) (2005) 1073–1094.

[131] J. Crown, M. O'Leary, W.S. Ooi, Docetaxel and paclitaxel in the treatment of breast cancer: a review of clinical experience, Oncologist 9 (Suppl. 2) (2004) 24–32.

[132] A. Urruticoechea, C.D. Archer, L.A. Assersohn, R.K. Gregory, M. Verrill, R. Mendes, G. Walsh, I.E. Smith, S.R. Johnston, Mitomycin C, vinblastine and cisplatin (MVP): an active and well-tolerated salvage regimen for advanced breast cancer, Br. J. Cancer 92 (3) (2005) 475–479.

[133] A. Ludas, A. Roy, R.M. Kumar, I. Sabapathy, R. Manikkam, A polysaccharide from Tinosporacordifolia stem induces cell cycle arrest in human breast cancer cell lines MCF-7 and MDA-MB-231, J. Endocrinol. Reprod. 21 (2017) 1–10.

[134] R. Pon Nivedha, J. Selvaraj, K. Govindaram Lalitha, M. Rajalakshmi, Effects of dihydroxygymnemic triacetate (DGT) on expression of apoptosis associated proteins in human prostate cancer cell lines (PC-3), J. Recept. Signal Transduct. Res. 35 (2015) 605–612.

[135] M.S. Sales, A. Roy, L. Antony, S.K. Banu, S. Jeyaraman, R. Manikkam, Octyl gallate and gallic acid isolated from Terminaliabellarica regulates normal cell cycle in human breast cancer cell lines, Biomed. Pharmacother. 103 (2018) 1577–1584.

CHAPTER 13

Old drugs and new opportunities—Drug repurposing in colon cancer prevention

Vemula Sarojamma[a], Manoj Kumar Gupta[b], Jeelan Basha Shaik[c], and Ramakrishna Vadde[b]

[a]Department of Microbiology, Government Medical College, Anantapur, India
[b]Department of Biotechnology and Bioinformatics, Yogi Vemana University, Kadapa, India
[c]Department of Chemistry, Yogi Vemana University, Kadapa, India

Abstract

Cancer is the major public health complication in increasing life expectancy and ranked second in the cause of deaths all over the world, and colorectal cancer is the most commonly diagnosed and the third leading cause of cancer deaths. Though new drugs are added every year to the anticancer arsenal, there are many impediments to reach the drugs into the markets and to patients, viz. long drug discovery progress, expensive (cost) of new drug, adverse side effects, and inefficiency of novel agents. These barriers can be overcome by the recent revolution in drug discovery, that is, drug repurposing. These repurposed drugs are already approved drugs but failed in efficacy in human clinical trials or drugs withdrawn from markets because of safety concerns. If these drugs are used in the drug discovery process for new uses, it can effectively reduce both cost and time. Currently, many of the companies are adopting this repurposing technology to redevelop some of their Food and Drug Administration (FDA)-approved and unsuccessful molecules as innovative therapies against various diseases, including cancers. Computer-aided drug repurposing is having high-impact patients through their novel personalized treatments. In this chapter, reviews on the drug repurposing, principles and tools used in drug repurposing, various classes of drugs used against human cancers and colorectal cancer, repurposed drugs used in colon cancer, and finally computational methods used in the development of drugs through drug repurposing are discussed. Integrating the computational approaches like artificial intelligence and machine learning with omics-study and other network-based tools will help in future repurposed drugs for colon cancer treatment. The computational approaches predicted that drug discoveries should be validated with preclinical and clinical trials and finally used as a novel drug in the treatment of colon cancer.

Abbreviations

ACE angiotensin-converting enzyme
CAPOX capecitabine and oxaliplatin
CMap connectivity map
COVID coronavirus disease
CPX ciclopirox
EGFR epidermal growth factor receptor

Computational Methods in Drug Discovery and Repurposing for Cancer Therapy
https://doi.org/10.1016/B978-0-443-15280-1.00010-8

FDA Food and Drug Administration
FOLFIRI FOLinic acid Fluorouracil IRInotecan regimen
FOLFOX folinic acid, fluorouracil, and oxaliplatin
FSC Financial Services Commission
GWAS genome-wide association studies
NSAID nonsteroidal antiinflammatory drugs
SIDER SIDe Effects Resource
TBZ thiabendazole
TFP trifluoperazine
VEGF vascular endothelial growth factor

1. Introduction

Globally, cancer is the major public health complication in the increasing life expectancy and ranked second in the cause of deaths in all countries. Prostate cancer in males and breast cancer in females are the leading cancerous deaths followed by lung and colorectal cancers. Colon cancer is the most frequently diagnosed cancer in humans and is the third leading cause of cancer deaths in the United States. According to cancer statistics 2022, the estimated new colorectal cancer cases by sex in the United States are 80,690 men and 70,340 women and estimated deaths are 28,400 men and 24,180 women [1]. Colorectal cancer occurs via stepwise mutational inactivation of tumor suppressor genes and oncogenes activation [2]. In recent years, a revolution was noticed in drug development, particularly for cancer treatment. Although new drugs are added every year to the anticancer arsenal, there are many impediments to reach the drugs into the markets, viz. long drug discovery progress, expensiveness (cost) of new drugs, adverse side effects, and inefficiency of novel agents. The average cost of a novel drug from its discovery to market comes around $2.0–3.0 billion and the complete process can take a long period of 10–15 years [3]. This long drug discovery process opens doors for alternative approaches to develop directly needed drugs.

One of the alternative approaches is drug repurposing. It is also referred to as drug reprofiling, drug repositioning, drug switching, or drug redirecting. It is a recently developed concept and provided definition by Ashburn and Thor as "drug repurposing is the process of finding new uses for the existing drugs" [4]. These repurposed drugs are already approved drugs but failed in efficacy in human clinical trials, or drugs withdrawn from markets because of safety concerns. If these drugs are used in the drug discovery process for new uses, it can effectively reduce both cost and time. Drug repurposing has several advantages over the new drug development process—low risk failure, less time consumption, and less investment in the process of drug development. Approval rate for a repurposed drug is 30% as compared to conventional drug development, which is 10%. Minimal risk, shortened developmental cycle, high approval rate, and reduced cost of repurposed drugs will help pharmaceutical companies to deliver drugs to cancer patients within a short period with an inexpensive price. Currently, many of the companies are adopting this repurposing technology to redevelop some of their Food and Drug Administration (FDA)-approved and unsuccessful molecules as innovative therapies for various diseases [5,6]. In this chapter, reviews on the principles and tools used in drug repurposing, various classes of drugs used against human cancers and colorectal cancer, repurposed drugs used in colon cancer, and finally computational methods used in the development of drugs through drug repurposing are discussed.

2. Principles and tools used in drug repurposing

New drug development needs a long, expensive, and complicated process and is associated with uncertainty. However, drug repurposing uses directly FDA-approved drugs to treat a variety of diseases on emergency times where no drug is available to treat the disease. Recently, in COVID-19 treatment, scientists are focused on drug repurposing to identify a curable drug. Drug repurposing strategy in the drug development pipeline involves three steps viz., right drug recognition (generation of hypothesis), evaluation of the effect of the drug systematically in clinical trials, and valuation of its efficacy in clinical Phase II phase [7,8]. These steps will be done skillfully by experimental and computational methods. Computational methods comprise databases and bioinformatics techniques to provide chemical structures of drug molecules, identify cancer-related gene expression, and finally select the candidate genes for drug development. The computational approaches include drug centric approaches, which replace the existing drug with side effects, target-based approach to study the drug effect on target protein for its response, knowledge-based screening consolidate the drug information and upgrade the prediction certainty, pathway- or network-based approach suggests unexpected and novel discoveries for drug development, and signature-based methods gives primary data analysis only (Fig. 1). One of the computational drug repurposing servers is DRUGSURV consisting of a large number of FDA-approved drugs [9]. In computational methods, in silico approaches are merged with molecular modeling tools in the novel drug-target discovery and later proceeded to validation steps through in vitro and in vivo systems. These methods identify many novel drug molecules for the treatment of diseases including cancer-related diseases. Broad Institute-established CMap (connectivity map) database comprises gene expression profiles produced by novel drugs in in vitro cell lines; this will make drug repositioning for cancer-related diseases. GWAS (genome-wide association studies) is used to study the genetic variations related to diseases and identified gene targets for novel drugs. Pathway-based methods using bioinformatics tools provide genetic information for particular genes which aid in drug repurposing [10,11]. Recently, Fiscon and Paci [12] developed a freely available tool SAveRUNNER (Searching off-lAble dRUg aNd NEtwoRk), a network-based technique/software for drug repurposing. It is promisingly detecting novel indications. It is an open-access software (available at https://github.com/giuliafisc on/SAveR UNNER. git with a user guide).

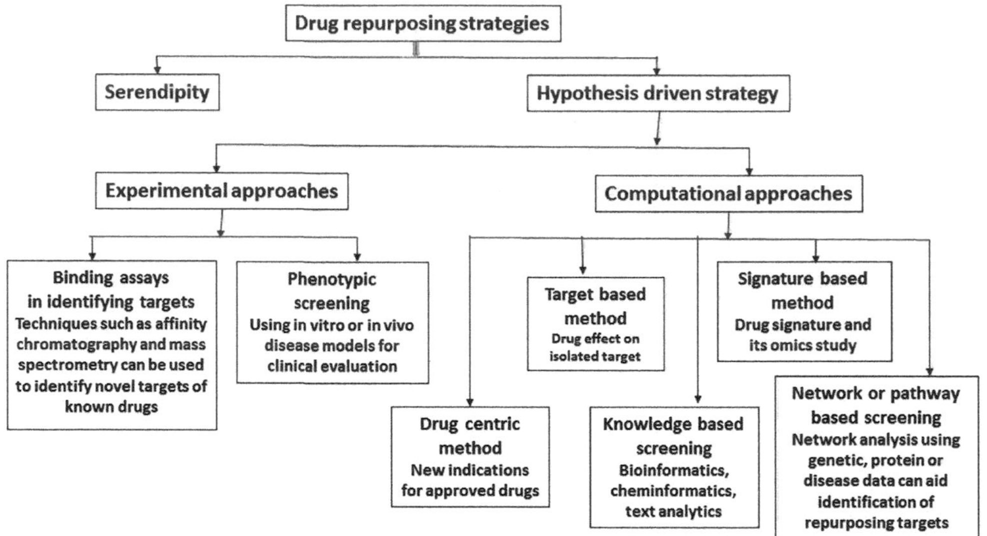

Fig. 1 Schematic representation of drug repurposing strategies.

Experimental methods used in drug repurposing for the identification of novel agents in the drug discovery process are DNA and RNA sequencing and generated data and proteomics generated data used in the discovery of novel binding partners for the already existing drugs and phenotypic approaches. Mapping of targets inside the cells using cellular thermos stability experiment. Still more variety of novel technologies needs to be explored for drug repositioning in the cancer treatment with clinical evidences.

Nowadays, drug repurposing is an appropriate and simple method for drug discovery as it reduces time and cost. Based on this, many scientists have identified novel methods of making databases or web resources for beneficial data content, and using in the finding of new application for existing drug [6,13,14]. Some of the important databases or web resources are used in drug repurposing are as follows:

- DrugBank (https://www.drugbank.ca/), SuperDRUG2 (http://cheminfo.charite.de/superdrug2/), DrugCentral (http://drugcentral.org/), Withdrawn (http://cheminfo.charite.de/withdrawn/index.html), Drug Repurposing Hub (https://clue.io/repurposing), BindingDB (https://www.bindingdb.org/bind/index.jsp), ChEMBL (https://www.ebi.ac.uk/chembl/), KEGG Drug (http://www.genome.jp/kegg/drug/), ZINC Database (http://zinc.docking.org/), Therapeutic TargetDB (http://bidd.nus.edu.sg/group/cjttd/), RepurposeDB (http://repurposedb.dudleylab.org/), Side Effect Resource (SIDER) (http://sideeffects.embl.de), Repurposing Drugs in Oncology (ReDO) (http://www.redo-project.org/db/), DSRV (http://www.bioprofiling.de/drugsurv), DrugComb+,* (https://drugcomb.fimm.fi/), Drug combination database (http://www.cls.zju.edu.cn/dcdb/), Medsafe

(https://medsafe.govt.nz/profs/class/classintro.asp), Cancer Therapeutics Response Portal (CTRP)+ (https://portals.broadinstitute.org/), and Profiling Relative Inhibition Simultaneously in Mixtures (PRISM)+,− (https://depmap.org/portal/prism/).
- BiGRID (https://thebiogrid.org/), STRING 9https://string-db.org/), HAPPI (http://discovery.informatics.uab.edu/HAPPI/), Cancer genome atlas (https://www.cancer.gov/about-nci/organization/ccg/research/structural-genomics/tcga), DeSigN (http://design-v2.cancerresearch.my/query), GenBank− (https://www.ncbi.nlm.nih.gov/genbank/), CMap (https://portals.broadinstitute.org/cmap/), OMIM (https://www.omim.org/), GEO (https://www.ncbi.nlm.nih.gov/geo/), Human Disease Network Database (DNetDB) (http://app.scbit.org/DNetDB/), STITCH (http://stitch.embl.de/), Ensembl (https://www.ensembl.org/index.html), DECIPHER (https://decipher.sanger.ac.uk), Molecular INTeraction database (MINT) (https://mint.bio.uniroma2.it), and PathwayCommon (http://www.pathwaycommons.org).

3. Categories of repurposed drugs against human cancers

Repurposed drugs used in the prevention of cancer are categorized based on the utilization of preexisting drugs against the disease, viz. antidiabetic drugs, antifungal drugs, antibiotic drugs, antipsychotic drugs, antiparasitic drugs, antiinflammatory drugs, and cardiovascular drugs. All these noncancerous drugs are used as an alternative in the treatment of human cancers and are developed as new agents for malignancies with less expensive prices around the globe [8]. Some of these are exhibiting anticancer capabilities in preclinical and clinical studies. All classes of repurposed drugs are discussed in Table 1.

4. Drugs used in the treatment of colon cancer

Globally, colorectal cancer is a frequently observed cancer, includes all the cancers of colon and rectum, and it is known as colon cancer. Colorectal cancer is the second leading cause of cancer deaths worldwide [1,15]. It has been proposed that colon cancer occurs via stepwise mutational inactivation of tumor suppressor genes and oncogenes activation [2]. The main factor for development of colon cancer is age and life style, and available treatment includes surgery, chemotherapy, radiation therapy, and immunotherapy [16–19]. Chemotherapy is the important strategy to control colon cancer where different drugs or drug combinations are used in reducing cell division. Chemotherapy has side effects viz. anemia, diarrhea, neutropenia, mucositis, fatigue, hand-foot syndrome, nausea, vomiting, gastrointestinal toxicity, and hematologic disorders. These chemotherapy treatments have not given satisfactory results; hence, surgery is the primary treatment to cure colon cancer. Despite using advanced therapies, still high mortality is observed due to the failure of current treatment regimen, and surgery at early stages to be

Table 1 Classes of repurposed drugs used in the treatment of human cancers.

S. no.	Class of drug	Drugs utilized in the prevention of disease
1.	Antidiabetic drugs	Metformin, troglitazone, pioglitazone, rosiglitazone, dapagliflozin, canagliflozin, empagliflozin, Vildagliptin, sitagliptin, saxagliptin
2.	Antibiotic drugs	Doxorubicin, doxycycline, nigericin, *N*-thiolated β-lactams, 4-alkylidene-β-lactams, and polyaromatic β-lactams, penicillin G, daunorubicin, duocarmycin, epirubicin, idarubicin, mitoxantrone, gemcitabine, landomycin, salinomycin, rapamycin
3.	Antifungal drugs	Itraconazole, thiabendazole (TBZ), triseofulvin, clotrimazole, ciclopirox (CPX), nannocystin A
4.	Antiinflammatory drugs	Asprin, ibuproten, diclofenac, indomethacin
5.	Antipsychotic drugs	Dopamine, lamotrigine, trifluoperazine (TFP), pimozide, penfluridol
6.	PDE inhibitors and ER antagonists	Sildenafil, celecoxib, tadalafil, sulindac sulfide, clomifene
7.	Antiparasitic drugs	Mebendazole, albendazole, ivermectin, suramin, nitazoxanide, clioquinol, atovaquone, potassium antimonyl tartrate chloroquine
8.	Cardiovascular agents	Digoxigenin, digoxin, digitalis, furosemide, bumetanide, propranolol, lovastatin, fluvastatin, simvastatin, nifedipine, amlodipine and nicardipine, nitroglycerin, isosorbide 5-mononitrate

done, but it is detected at advanced stages. Advanced-stage therapies include chemotherapy, immunotherapy, and radiotherapies used as adjuvant therapy for surgery and chemotherapy [15]. Tumor relapse and metastasis are also responsible for colon cancer as they are not effectively prevented. Finally, the current therapies are not effectively working against colorectal cancer and the response rates are also very less, that is, less than 20% [16,17]. As per NCCN guidelines, the first-line chemotherapy given to colon cancer is fluoropyrimidines (5-flurouracil) alone or in leucovorin combination or with other cytotoxic drugs—oxaliplatin or irinotecan. Second-line chemotherapy will be given to the patients who are having good organ function and resistance against first-line chemotherapy (irinotecan with FOLFOX or CAPOX) or FOLFIRI [15,20]. Colon cancer is treated even with the combination of chemotherapeutic drugs with proteins against VEGF and EGFR or monoclonal antibodies, for instance mAb bevacizumab [20]. These treatments have given new hope in the treatment of colon cancer even though they cannot stop relapse. For efficient treatment of colon cancer, we need to develop new drugs through novel approaches. One of the approaches is drug repurposing.

5. Drug repurposing in the prevention of colon cancer

The aim of new drug development is to find out a new molecule that is tumor specific and not causing normal cell damage. Also, the new drug should be cheaper and effective in treatment. Hence, it needs novel technologies to develop drug in an alternative approach by compromising all of the above qualities. Drug repurposing or drug switching is an effective alternative strategy to develop novel drugs from already available drugs, which are used in different diseases or failed drugs due to safety reasons. Scientific reasons for using drug repurposing in drug development is the sharing of same target and pleiotropic nature (shows action other than the specific disease for which it has been developed). Drug repurposing has a simple regulation process for approval because it is already approved and available in market and its pharmacokinetics, molecular target, mechanism of action, pharmacodynamics, and all properties have been described [21,22]. This will save a lot of time and money for companies and used as a best one in drug development. Monotherapy is the most common method for cancer treatment but it develops drug resistance. Hence, combination of drugs is the alternative one in the treatment in which synergetic effect will be seen and shows highest efficacy than monotherapy. However, in the treatment of colon cancer, the selected repurposed drugs are used alone or in combination [16], and these drugs are discussed in Table 2.

Table 2 Repurposed drugs used alone or in combination for the treatment of colon cancer [16].

Drug	Group	Originally used	Used in colon cancer prevention in combination
Acetylsalicylic acid	NSAID	Pain, fever	Yes
Amantadine	Antiviral drug	Viral infection and Parkinson's disease	Yes
Atorvastatin	Statins	High cholesterol levels	Yes
Captopril	ACE inhibitor	Hypertension	Yes
Celecoxib	NSAID	Pain and inflammation	Yes
Chloroquine	Antimalarial drug	Malaria	Yes
Clotam	NSAID	Pain	Yes
Diclofenac	NSAID	Pain	Yes
Hydroxychloroquine	Antimalarial drug	Malaria	Yes
Ivermectin	Anthelmintic drug	Parasitic infection	Yes

Continued

Table 2 Repurposed drugs used alone or in combination for the treatment of colon cancer—cont'd

Drug	Group	Originally used	Used in colon cancer prevention in combination
Metformin	Biguanide	Type 2 diabetes	Yes
Propranolol	Antianginal drug	Anginal	Yes
Sildenafil	PDE5 inhibitor	Anginal/erectile dysfunction	Yes
Sulindac	NSAID	Pain, fever, inflammation	Yes

6. Drug repurposing pitfalls

Drug repurposing saves time and money compared with classical drug development process. This cost-saving drug development approach is strongly welcomed by various pharma industries. Although repurposing drugs are approved quickly through safety, the overall success rate is only 6% as compared with 5% of de novo drug discovery. Lack of drug efficacy is higher and is the major problem observed in clinical trials. So, it needs more efforts to improve efficacy and also to determine the therapeutic route to ascertain the treatment strategy.

All the repositioned drugs used in colon cancer prevention are evaluated preclinical or clinical models. These drugs are used either alone or in combination in treatment at various stages of the disease. If combination is used, more studies are required as the off-patient drugs are increasing. With these basic points, it is essential to start "personalized medicine in repurposing." For this personalized medicine treatment, scientists are combining all genetic, biochemical, pharmacological, omics, clinic, and other data instigating the development of computational methods (bioinformatics tools) for the better understanding of biological systems complexity, drug development speed, and treatment of patient.

7. Computational approaches in drug repurposing for colorectal cancer

Cancers still have a high mortality rate because cancer targets do not have perfect drug or chemo-resistance. Along with these properties, the metastases, tumor heterogeneity and microenvironment, and other features aggravate the cancer. To overcome all these problems, the best option is to go for drug repurposing to control cancer. Drug repurposing results are serendipitous or sometimes time-consuming preclinical or clinical studies and to avoid in silico drug repurposing is developed by taking advantage of big data usage (e.g., key pathways identified through omics-study). Through computational tools, precise, efficient, and cost-effective drugs can be generated with improved version in the treatment of cancer along with the use of pharmacological studies [23,24]. In this review, we present all recently emerging computational approaches working under the principles of omics studies (genomics, transcriptomics, proteomics, and metabolomics) and network studies used in drug repurposing.

- Literature-based discovery or text-mining approaches

For existing drugs, new indications will be discovered through the text-mining approach by utilizing immense literature available in PubMed, MEDLINE, and other databases and generating novel hypothesis [23]. These text-mining tools give a solution to knowledge gap between structure and free text information and convert the text information to clinical information useful in the treatment of cancer [25]. CHAT (http://chat.lionproject.net), a supervised machine learning tool developed by Baker et al. [25], has the capability of retrieving or organizing cancer-related data from PUBMED into taxonomy. It has classified more than 150 million sentences and has 24 million abstracts and gives text-mining approach find connections and used in colon cancer prevention.

- Transcriptomics

The total RNA molecule content in a cell and their differential expression in diseased versus normal condition or drug-treated group versus control can be studied in this omics-study. These differentially expressed genes are used in the evaluation of dysregulated pathways. CMap is a platform of transcriptomic study to identify similarities or variation in genomic structures among complex disease [26].

- Genomics

GWAS has potential to allow to discover the new drug indication through drug repurposing. Colon cancer-related genes will be identified through genomics study. CMap is widely used in this genomics study [27].

- Phenotypes and side effects

Although genomics and transcriptomics are used in the identification of mutations concerned for colon cancer, it should support clinical response in patients. The doctor will examine and diagnose the patients based on phenotypic characteristics or symptoms of the patients, including physical properties, appearance, development, and behavior [28]. Even on treatment side effects are considering in this tool for identifying phenotypic biomarker in the prevention of cancer. SIDER database developed by Yang and Agarwal [29] has complete side effects of the repurposed drugs in disease. Side effects are contributed various factors including multiple factors, depend on patient and pharmacological data.

- Integrated approach

Different databases give different information and different results; when different databases are combined, we can get better results. Currently, all the methods are merging in a systematic way to predict the drug interaction and identification of novel drug indications in a cost-effective manner [30]. For instance, pharmacokinetic systematic analysis merged with computational and experimental approaches to develop an efficient drug in the prevention of colon cancer. Computational drug repurposing techniques designed for drug predictions helped in the process of drug discovery in drug repurposing. Drug-disease association networks can be used immediately for novel clinical applications after observing phenotypic and chemical structural similarities. These methods give insights into the mechanism of action of the existing drugs and finally unravel disease mechanism, which can be targeted by existing drug. A number of machine learning programs were developed recently for the studies of drug-target interactions and identification of cost-effective novel drug. These machine learning strategies are differential evolution (working based on phenotypic data), similarity between drug-drug and disease-disease (CMap and PREDICT used in measurement of similarities, gene-chemical structure target network, diseasome network, drug-target disease network, and Bayesian networks). All these strategies are used in the drug identification through drug repurposing. FSC platform is working on artificial intelligence. It has been applied successfully to investigate nine angiostatic drugs and ten anticancer drugs.

Various software toolboxes are available for drug repurposing drugs, which produced systematically for exciting assumptions in the development and identify many lead compounds through computational studies [31–33]. During this process, the repurposed drug clinical use and its combinations, doses, and route of administration are considered critically and systematically explored. In the realistic predictions, systems biology's omics-study with all its tools is used in the development of drug. Even the drug of repositioning has not alleviated the actions of small molecules, but it is a trend of shifting technology to future generated drugs [34]. The complex drug repurposing process involves so many factors viz. patents, commercial models, investment, development, and marketing and its demand. Government support is highly needed for speeding up this updated technology in the development of drugs. IPR is also playing a role in drug repurposing where IP protection is limited. Single-cell sequencing like new technologies are available for seeing new exciting directions in drug development with the help of bioinformatics tools along with pharmacology and systems biology. Databases available in medicine are extended to study the genetic variations between patients and computational tools that help in identifying suitable molecular target for specific populations of patients.

8. Conclusions and perspectives

New anticancer drug development is expensive and time consuming and has a less success rate. Improvement in the prognosis of cancer in patient is influenced by various factors like chemo-resistance, metastases, tumor heterogeneity, tumor microenvironment, and undruggable targets; these are the major barriers in the control of cancer in patients. Traditional methods of drug discovery have failed to provide efficient drugs to control these barriers, so the computational methods used for drug repurposing promise to control the cancer in patients and improve health by giving the data on molecular targets or phenotype identification for curing disease, and clinical data with biomarker for future drug discovery [35,36]. Computer-aided drug repurposing is having high impact in patients through their novel personalized treatments. In this drug repurposing, various innovative tools are using including omics studies, phenotypic studies, and machine learning approaches to discover new drugs quickly and benefit patients along with public and private organizations. Integrating the computational approaches with omics-study and other network-based tools will help in future repurposed drugs for cancer treatment. It is already demonstrated that repurposing drugs on combination with other agents is showing highest improvement in clinical outcome in patients suffering with cancer. Though drug repurposing is highly beneficial, but produced larger levels and having negative impact on environment and finally effects on ecosystem as it moves through food chain. So, scientists should give high priority to environmental friendly and ecosystem safety in the process of effective anticancer drug discovery to improve healthy and quality of life on the earth. Artificial intelligence and machine learning algorithms are used in predicting novel drug molecule against disease though integrated approaches. The computational approaches predicted drug discoveries should be validated preclinical and clinical trials and finally use as novel drugs in the treatment of colon cancer.

Conflicts of interest

None of the authors have any relevant conflicts of interests to declare.

References

[1] R.L. Siegel, K.D. Miller, H.E. Fuchs, A. Jemal, Cancer statistics, 2022, CA Cancer J. Clin. 72 (1) (2022) 7–33, https://doi.org/10.3322/caac.21708. Epub 2022 Jan 12 35020204.

[2] S.D. Markowitz, M.M. Bertagnolli, Molecular origins of cancer: molecular basis of colorectal cancer, N. Engl. J. Med. 361 (25) (2009) 2449–2460, https://doi.org/10.1056/NEJMra0804588. 20018966. PMC2843693.

[3] J.A. DiMasi, H.G. Grabowski, R.W. Hansen, Innovation in the pharmaceutical industry: new estimates of R&D costs, J. Health Econ. 47 (2016) 20–33, https://doi.org/10.1016/j.jhealeco.2016.01.012. Epub 2016 Feb 12 26928437.

[4] T.T. Ashburn, K.B. Thor, Drug repositioning: identifying and developing new uses for existing drugs, Nat. Rev. Drug Discov. 3 (8) (2004) 673–683, https://doi.org/10.1038/nrd1468. 15286734.

[5] V. Parvathaneni, N.S. Kulkarni, A. Muth, V. Gupta, Drug repurposing: a promising tool to accelerate the drug discovery process, Drug Discov. Today 24 (10) (2019) 2076–2085, https://doi.org/10.1016/j.drudis.2019.06.014. Epub 2019 Jun 22 31238113.

[6] V.P. Kale, H. Habib, R. Chitren, M. Patel, K.C. Pramanik, S.C. Jonnalagadda, K. Challagundla, M.K. Pandey, Old drugs, new uses: drug repurposing in hematological malignancies, Semin. Cancer Biol. 68 (2021) 242–248, https://doi.org/10.1016/j.semcancer.2020.03.005. Epub 2020 Mar 6 32151704.

[7] F.I. Pushpakom, P.A. Eyers, K.J. Escott, S. Hopper, et al., Drug repurposing: progress, challenges and recommendations, Nat. Rev. Drug Discov. 18 (1) (2019) 41–58.

[8] A. Kirtonia, K. Gala, S.G. Fernandes, G. Pandya, et al., Repurposing of drugs: an attractive pharmacological strategy for cancer therapeutics, Semin. Cancer Biol. (2021), https://doi.org/10.1016/j.semcancer.2020.04.006.

[9] I. Amelio, M. Gostev, R.A. Knight, A.E. Willis, G. Melino, A.V. Antonov, DRUGSURV: a resource for repositioning of approved and experimental drugs in oncology based on patient survival information, Cell Death Dis. 5 (2014), e1051.

[10] C.S. Greene, B.F. Voight, Pathway and network-based strategies to translate genetic discoveries into effective therapies, Hum. Mol. Genet. 25 (R2) (2016) R94–R98.

[11] A. Talevi, C.L. Bellera, Challenges and opportunities with drug repurposing: finding strategies to find alternative uses of therapeutics, Expert Opin. Drug Discovery 15 (4) (2020) 397–401, https://doi.org/10.1080/17460441.2020.1704729.

[12] G. Fiscon, P. Paci, SAveRUNNER: an R-based tool for drug repurposing, BMC Bioinformatics 22 (2021) 150, https://doi.org/10.1186/s12859-021-04076-w.

[13] Y. Masoudi-Sobhanzadeh, Y. Omidi, M. Amanlou, A. Masoudi-Nejad, Drug databases and their contributions to drug repurposing, Genomics 112 (2) (2020) 1087–1095, https://doi.org/10.1016/j.ygeno.2019.06.021. Epub 2019 Jun 18 31226485.

[14] Z. Tanoli, U. Seemab, A. Scherer, K. Wennerberg, J. Tang, M. Vähä-Koskela, Exploration of databases and methods supporting drug repurposing: a comprehensive survey, Brief. Bioinform. 22 (2) (2021) 1656–1678, https://doi.org/10.1093/bib/bbaa003. 32055842. PMC7986597.

[15] R. Vadde, G.P.C. Nagaraju, in: R. Vadde, G.P. Nagaraju (Eds.), Immunotherapy for Gastrointestinal Malignancies, Springer Nature, 2020, ISBN: 978-981-15-6486-4, https://doi.org/10.1007/978-981-15-6487-1.

[16] D. Duarte, N. Vale, Combining repurposed drugs to treat colorectal cancer, Drug Discov. Today 27 (1) (2022), https://doi.org/10.1016/j.drudis.2021.09.012.

[17] M.K. Gupta, R. Vadde, S. Vemula, Curcumin – a novel therapeutic agent in the prevention of colorectal cancer, Curr. Drug Metab. 20 (12) (2019) 977–987, https://doi.org/10.2174/1389200220666191007153238.

[18] M.K. Gupta, R. Vadde, Applications of computational biology in gastrointestinal malignancies, in: R. Vadde, G.P. Nagaraju (Eds.), Immunotherapy for Gastrointestinal Malignancies, Springer Nature, 2020, ISBN: 978-981-15-6486-4, https://doi.org/10.1007/978-981-15-6487-1.

[19] S. Bonala, M.K. Gupta, R. Vadde, Functional food in prevention of colorectal cancer, Crit. Rev. Oncog. 25 (2) (2020) 111–128, https://doi.org/10.1615/CritRevOncog.2020035112.

[20] E. Van Cutsem, A. Cervantes, B. Nordlinger, D. Arnold, The ESMO Guidelines Working Group, Metastatic colorectal cancer: ESMO clinical practice guidelines for diagnosis, treatment and follow-up, Ann. Oncol. 25 (2014) iii1–iii9.

[21] R.R. Shah, P.D. Stonier, Repurposing old drugs in oncology: opportunities with clinical and regulatory challenges ahead, J. Clin. Pharm. Ther. 44 (1) (2019) 6–22.

[22] J. Jourdan, R. Bureau, C. Rochais, P. Dallemagne, Drug repositing: a brief overview, J. Pharm. Pharmacol. 72 (9) (2020) 1145–1151.

[23] S. Zhao, R. Iyengar, Systems pharmacology: network analysis to identify multiscale mechanisms of drug action, Annu. Rev. Pharmacol. Toxicol. 52 (2012) 505–521.

[24] C. Mottini, F. Napolitano, Z. Li, X. Gao, Computer aided drug repusposing for cancer therapy: approaches and opportunities to challenge anticancer targets, Semin. Cancer Biol. 68 (2021) 59–74.

[25] S. Baker, I. Ali, I. Silins, S. Pyysalo, Y. Guo, J. Hogberg, U. Stenius, A. Korhonen, Cancer Hallmarks Analytics Tool (CHAT): a text mining approach to organize and evaluate scientific literature on cancer, Bioinformatics 33 (24) (2017) 3973–3981.

[26] J. Lamb, E.D. Crawford, D. Peck, J.W. Modell, I.C. Blat, M.J. Wrobel, et al., The Connectivity Map: using gene-expression signatures to connect small molecules, genes, and disease, Science 313 (5795) (2006) 1929–1935.

[27] X.A. Qu, D.K. Rajpal, Applications of connectivity map in drug discovery and development, Drug Discov. Today 17 (23–24) (2012) 1289–1298.

[28] Scitable, Nature Education, 2018. https://www.nature.com/scitable/definition/phenotype-phenotypes-35.

[29] L. Yang, Agarwal., Systematic drug repositioning based on clinical side-effects, PLoS One 6 (12) (2011), e28025.

[30] C. Mottini, F. Napolitano, Z. Li, X. Gao, L. Cardone, Computer-aided drug repurposing for cancer therapy: approaches and opportunities to challenge anticancer targets, Semin. Cancer Biol. 68 (2021) 59–74.

[31] B. Turanli, M. Grøtli, J. Boren, J. Nielsen, M. Uhlen, K.Y. Arga, A. Mardinoglu, Drug repositioning for effective prostate cancer treatment, Front. Physiol. 9 (500) (2018), https://doi.org/10.3389/fphys.2018.00500. eCollection 2018.

[32] A. Peyyandipour, N. Saberian, A. Shafi, M. Donato, S. Draghici, A novel computational approach for drug repurposing using systems biology, Bioinformatics 34 (16) (2018) 2817–2825, https://doi.org/10.1093/bioinformatics/bty133.

[33] B. Turanlia, O. Altaya, J.I. Borend, H. Turkeze, J. Nielsenf, M. Uhlena, K.Y. Argab, A. Mardinoglu, Systems biology based drug repositioning for development of cancer therapy, Semin. Cancer Biol. (2019), https://doi.org/10.1016/j.semcancer.2019.09.020.

[34] M. Duran-Frigola, L. Mateo, P. Aloy, Drug repositioning beyond the low-hanging fruits, Curr. Opin. Syst. Biol. (2019) 95–102, https://doi.org/10.1016/j.coisb.2017.04.010. Bioinformatics 2018;34 (16):2817–2825. doi: 10.1093/bioinformatics/bty133.

[35] M. Marusina, D.J. Welsch, L. Rose, D. Brock, N. Bahr, The CTSA Pharmaceutical Assets Portal – a public-private partnership model for drug repositioning, Drug Discov. Today Ther. Strateg. 8 (3–4) (2011) 77–83, https://doi.org/10.1016/j.ddstr.2011.06.006.

[36] M. Alison, NCATS launches drug repurposing program, Nat. Biotechnol. 30 (2012) 571–572.

CHAPTER 14

Repurposing cardiac glycosides as the hallmark of immunogenic modulators in cancer therapy

Honey Pavithran[a], **Angelina Job Kolady**[a], **and Ranjith Kumavath**[a,b]
[a]Department of Genomic Science, Central University of Kerala, Kasaragod, India
[b]Department of Biotechnology, School of Life Sciences, Pondicherry University, Puducherry, India

Abstract

Cancer endures a major threat to global disease burden and is prognosticated to rise its incidence in impending years, causing it to be an important barrier to increasing life expectancy worldwide. Cancer research consortium worldwide continues to learn different aspects to diagnose, treat, prevent, and survive cancer to ameliorate this circumstance. At the forefront of emerging research in cancer immunotherapy, it is providing remarkable advances in recent years. Targeted immunotherapy has improved several solid tumors, especially those with high mutational thrust. However, clinical trials to perceive novel therapeutics consume substantial time and resources. An alternative is to use drug repurposing (DR) that traces out the novel therapeutic concepts of the approved drugs. Cardiac glycosides (CGs), a class of FDA-approved drugs to increase rhythmic heart conditions, are now extensively studied to illustrate its anticancer activity. The compound is found to exert anticancer properties by inhibiting the sodium-potassium ion channel, thereby regulating the associated signaling cascade. Recent studies shed light on the immunomodulatory properties of the compounds causing immunogenic cell death in various cancer cells.

Moreover, CGs are known to render various immunomodulatory effects via regulating the transcription of immune response genes through STAT and NF-κB. Thus consequently recruiting immune cell ratios and levels of inflammatory signals in the tumor microenvironment. Due to its significance, immunotherapy from a clinically safe drug like CG is gaining forefront importance in cancer cure and therapy. Here, we illustrate our understanding and imprint the scope of DR CG as immunomodulatory in cancer.

Abbreviations

53BP1	p53-binding protein 1
Akt	Ak strain transforming
AMPK	AMP-activated protein kinase
ATF4	activating transcription factor 4
ATP	adenosine triphosphate
ATP1B3	ATPase Na+/K+-transporting subunit beta 3
Cal-12T	Center Antoine Lacassagne-12T
CD4	cluster of differentiation 4
CD8	cluster of differentiation 8
CDK 1	cyclin-dependent kinase 1
CG	cardiac glycosides

Computational Methods in Drug Discovery and Repurposing for Cancer Therapy
https://doi.org/10.1016/B978-0-443-15280-1.00018-2

CHOP	C/EBP homologous protein
CRT	calreticulin
DAMP	damage-associated molecular patterns
DR	drug repurposing
DR4	death receptor 4
H129	human nonsmall-cell lung carcinoma cell line
HBE	human bronchial epithelial cell lines
HIF 1 α	hypoxia-inducible factor alpha
HMGB1	high mobility group box 1 protein
HSP70	heat shock protein 70
HSP90	heat shock protein 90
ICD	immunogenic cell death
IDO1	indoleamine-2,3-dioxygenase 1
IFN	interferons
IKKβ	inhibitor of nuclear factor kappa b kinase
MAPK	mitogen-activated protein kinase
MCF 7	Michigan Cancer Foundation 7
NKA	Na+/K+-ATPase
NSCLC	nonsmall-cell lung cancer
NF kappa b	nuclear factor kappa b
PCa	prostate cancer
PERK	protein kinase R-like ER kinase
PI3K	phosphoinositide 3 kinase
PLC	phospholipase C
Src	sarcoma
STAT 1	signal transducers and activators of transcription 1
STAT 3	signal transducers and activators of transcription 3
SW1990	pancreatic adenocarcinoma
TMV	tumor micro environment
TRAIL	tumor necrosis factor-related apoptosis-inducing ligand
U-87	glioblastoma
Wnt/β catenin	wingless-related integration site beta catenin

1. Introduction

According to the World Health Organization, cancer ranks as the second leading cause of death globally. As reported by Global Cancer Observatory, it is estimated that in 2040, an increase of 28.9 million new cases will be observed, meaning a rise of ~49.7% in comparison to 2020, along with about 62.5% upsurge in death [1]. These statistics imply the importance of developing an anticancer drug. Still, the lengthy process of development [2] for the novel approach of drug repositioning mitigates the high cost, longer development time, and increased risk of failure. Drug repurposing (DR) identifies the pharmacological indications of an FDA-approved drug in the market. It examines its application in treating disease apart from its original therapeutic use [3].

Animal cells generally are present with an active transporter named Na^+/K^+-ATPase (NKA) pump on its plasma membrane. This transmembrane pump keeps the intracellular potassium high and sodium low to maintain the electrochemical gradient of the cell. This electrochemical gradient regulates various physiological processes. Pirahanchi and Aeddula [4] including calcium regulation, plays a crucial role in the contraction of cardiac muscles, thereby maintaining the cardiac output [5]. The intracellular sodium level regulates calcium entry in the sarcoplasmic reticulum [6]. An imbalance in calcium concentrations can affect myocardial function. Thus the NKA pump indirectly controls the function of the heart.

Cardiac glycosides (CGs) have ionotropic effects on the NKA pump. CG drugs inhibit the pump by binding on the α subunit of the NKA pump, which augments intracellular sodium. This causes an increment in intracellular calcium levels by sodium–calcium exchanger [7]. This enhances the rate of contractions in the myocardium and treats several heart disorders and heart failure. Colon cancer displays the high expression of NKA β2 subunits than the normal tissues [8]. Renal cell carcinoma exhibits a low expression of β subunit of NKA, which reduces the NKA activity in renal cell carcinoma membranes [9]. The binding of CGs to these pumps caused changes in the membrane potential and the transport activity of sodium and potassium ions and induced apoptosis of the cell. This proved the drugs' capacity to treat human tumor cells. CGs exploit the immune system, modulate the immune cells, and inhibit the growth of cancer cells. Reports prove the antiproliferative activity of CGs, such as gamabufotalin and arenobufagin, against U-87 and SW1990 cancer cell lines by decreasing the immunosuppressive regulatory T cells, thereby increasing the anticancerous immunity [10].

Scientific research reports have proved the importance of CG against cancer. Thus the DR of CG, which was used initially to treat heart failure and arrhythmias [11], was introduced. Drug repositioning of CG against cancer has a major advantage thin these drugs can be rapidly progressed into Phase II and Phase III clinical trials [12]. Thus they possess a promising anticancer activity and can act as a multipurpose drug for various diseases.

2. Repurposing cardiac glycosides in cancer treatment

CGs are organic compounds that can increase the rate of contractions by inhibiting the NKA pump and activating the calcium pump. These steroids are isolated from various sources of important drugs for treating various heart disorders. Digoxin manages and treats heart failure and arrhythmias. It is one of the most ancient drugs used for heart problems [13]. It inhibits the activity of the myocardial NKA pump, which causes an increase in the intracellular sodium ions, thereby resulting in the influx of calcium. This excess Ca is taken by the sarcoplasmic reticulum, leading to increased contractions.

2.1 Structural peculiarities of cardiac glycosides augmenting anticancer property

CGs are composed of two physical features: sugar (glycone) moiety and nonsugar (aglycone-steroid) moiety. The "aglycone" moiety is also known as "genin" moiety [14]. The general structure of a cardio glycoside includes a steroid ring attached to an unsaturated lactone ring in position 17, which is connected to a sugar moiety at the third position of the CGs structure. Lactone is cyclic esters [15] that get saturation on receptor binding. It is formed due to a condensation reaction between an alcohol group and a hydroxy carbonic acid molecule [16]. The steroid nucleus of a cardio glycoside is generally 5β,14β-androstenone-3β,14 diols [17]. It has 4 fused rings with 17 carbons attached to a lactone ring and different sugar residues. This structure is required to inhibit the NKA pumps as it causes conformational change at various stages of the transport activity [17]. The functional groups attached to the fused rings determine the molecule's biological activity. The sugar groups generally attached to the end of steroids are glucose, galactose, mannose, and rhamnose and digitalize. The potency of the cardio glycoside can be increased from 6 to 35 times when rhamnose is attached [18]. They help the glycoside be water soluble and bond to the heart muscle [14]. Detaching saccharide groups from the structure of a cardio glycoside makes the structure simpler. The glycosyl moiety attached to C_3 of the steroid is responsible for both pharmacological and pharmacokinetic activities [19].

Depending upon the R group attached to the 17th position of the lactone ring, CG can be classified into two groups as observed in nature. They are (1) cardenolides and (2) bufadienolides. The cardenolides are generally derived from plants and have an α,β-unsaturated five-membered butyrolactone ring attached to the 17-β positions [14]. It has a 5–6 membered lactone ring sugar moiety. A single, double bond is present at the end of the lactone. They are C_{23} steroids and have methyl groups at C_{10} and C_{13}. It contains a butanolide ring. The sugar molecule is bound with the β-OH group of the C_3 atom. Cardenolides target the α subunit of NKA present on the cellular membrane. An α subunit is the catalytic subunit of the enzyme and helps in binding Na+, K+, and ATP. This binding blocks the enzyme activity and affects the concentration of Na+ and K+ [20]. For example, cardenolide glycoside acovenoside (AcoA) isolated from pericarps of acokanthera oppositifolia induced cell death in nonsmall-cell lung cancer by generating reactive oxygen species (ROS) [21]. The cytotoxicity of digoxin, a cardenolide, is due to the interaction of hydroxyl groups at C_{12}, C_{14}, C_3, C_{17} lactone, and C_3 saccharide with NKA [22]. The steroidal moiety helps bind amino acids and recognizes the receptor. The sugar moiety is vital for the ATPase activity of the cardenolides. The P glycoprotein of cardenolides possesses inhibitory activity that makes them the target to treat cancer [23]. Other examples of cardenolides include acetyldigitoxins, digoxin, digitoxin, ouabain, medigoxin, strophanthidin, etc.

Bufadienolides are derived from the toad skin secretions [24]. It includes a polyhydroxy C_{24} steroid. It consists of a six-membered lactone (α-pyrone) ring at the C_{17} position. The pyrone ring is also called as Penta-2,4-dien-5-olide ring. It contains a δ-lactone ring. Here, the sugar molecule is bound with the β-OH group of the C_3 atom. It has higher member rings than cardenolides. Some major common CGs (Fig. 1) of bufadienolides include bufalin, convallamarin, and hellebrin. They include members of the genus *Kalanchoe* as well as the Crassulaceae subfamily. Accumulating evidence on the structural peculiarities of CG contributing to its anticancer activity suggests that the compound binds to the lactone cycle of the NKA signalosome, thereby inhibiting the NKA from triggering a signal cascade.

2.2 Anticancer effects of CGs in cancer cells

Inhibition of NKA [25] alterations in Ca^{2+} signaling [26] is some of the distinguished anticancer activities of CGs. It is also validated that CGs can repair double-stranded break and single-stranded break, which act as a novel anticancer mechanism. This feature has enhanced its effect on nontiny cell lungs [27]. It acts as a significant neuroblastoma growth inhibitor as it reduces the growth of human SH-SY5Y neuroblastoma cells in immunodeficient mice [28]. There is also evidence of this CG being useful to treat patients with overexpressing HIF-1 breast cancers [29]. Another CG, ouabain, used to treat congestive heart failure and supraventricular arrhythmias is repurposed against cancer for its tumor regression activity in immunodeficient mice injected with human Y79LUC retinoblastoma cells [30]. Effects of CGs on the immune system are also beneficial to cancer treatment. Ouabain has a significant impact on the immune system of leukemia mouse models. The ouabain-treated WEHI-3 generated leukemic mice increased CD19 cells, macrophage phagocytosis, and natural killer cell activities [31]. It is also proved that it contributes to the better survival of melanoma-injected mice and the preservation of B lymphocytes in the peripheral organs [32]. Bufalin is widely used in the treatment of heart failure by inhibiting the sodium pump. This drug is repurposed to target the PI3K-Akt (phosphoinositide 3 kinase-Ak strain transforming) pathway and treat cancers associated with sodium pump overexpression. Due to its high affinity toward the sodium pump in the E2P form, the cation exchange is blocked, inhibiting the sodium pump and inducing cell cycle arrest, apoptosis, and autophagy [33]. It can also inhibit the tumor necrosis factor (TNF) signaling, which in contrast would cause metastasis [34], bufotalin is a 24-carbon steroid derived from Chinese medicine *Venenum bufonis*. It acts as a chemotherapeutic agent on human malignant A375 cells by inhibiting the expression of CDK1 and thus arresting the cycle at the G2/M phase and inducing apoptosis [35]. It also exhibits inhibitory effects on human HepG2 hepatocarcinoma cells [36]. Arenobufagin is a natural bufadienolide compound derived from the venom of the toad. It has apoptotic activity on MCF-7 and MDA-MB-231 breast cancer cell lines [37].

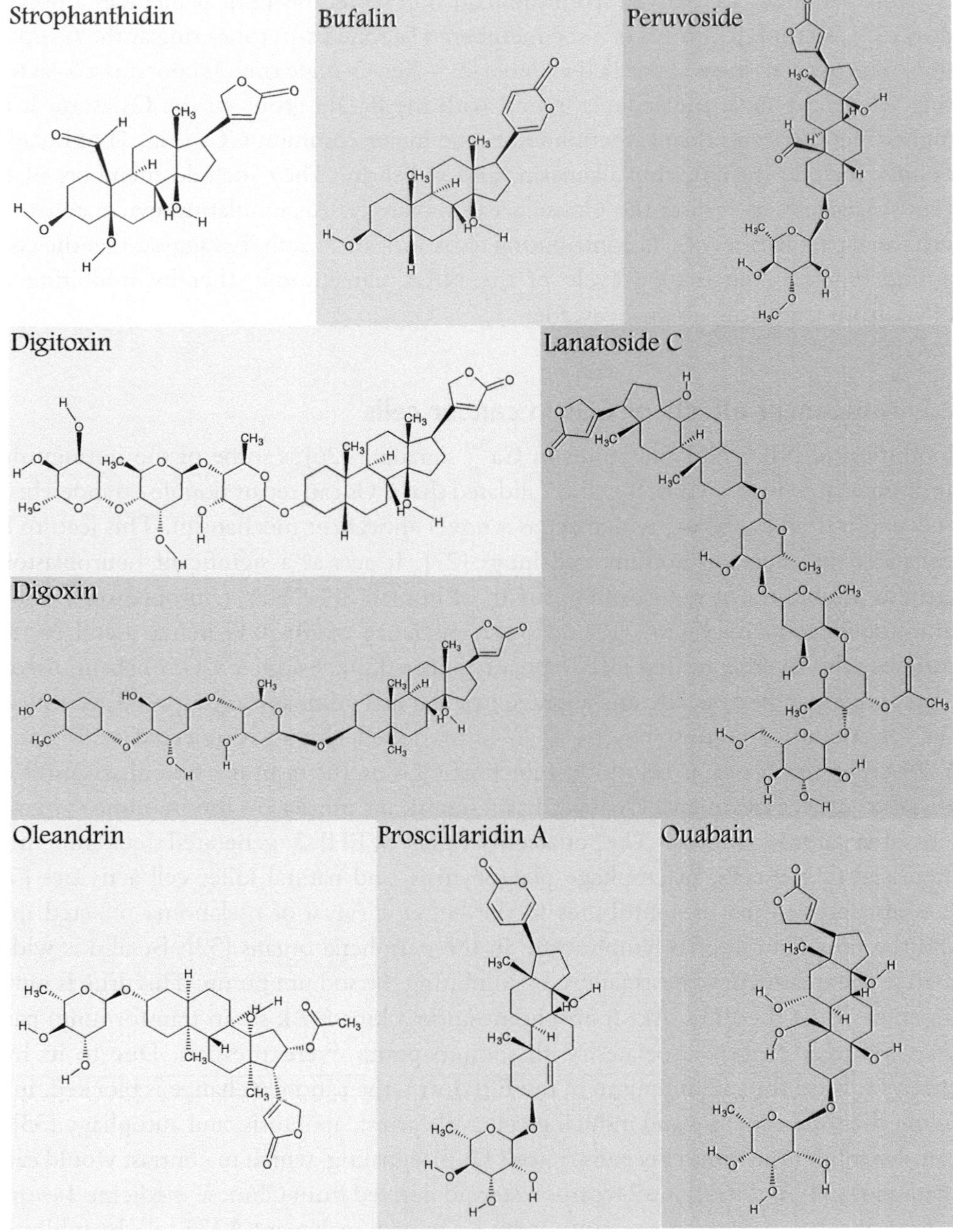

Fig. 1 Molecular structures of some common cardiac glycosides.

Arenobufagin inhibited the epithelial-mesenchymal transition of lung cancer cell line in vivo mouse models, and metastasis of lung cancer cell lines was reduced by downregulating the IKKβ/NF kappa β signal cascade [38]. It also displays anticancer activity against a wide range of cancers, such as hepatoma, breast, adenocarcinoma, cervix, lung, and colon [39]. Cancer growth is regulated by using transcription factors as targets. The digitoxin, which generally decreases heart rate, can inhibit the overexpressed HIF-1 α subunit, a transcription factor presents on cancer cells [18]. In addition, upon binding on the NKA pump, it activates various downstream signaling pathways, such as phospholipase C signaling, mitogen-activated protein kinase signaling, PI3K, and Src kinase signaling, that leads to the proapoptotic pathway and induces apoptosis [40]. Thus it has an enhanced activity on cancer cells. Strophanthidin inhibits the cell proliferation of A549, MCF-7, and HepG2 cancer cell lines. It inhibits the expression of cyclin-dependent kinase and causes a cascade of reactions, overexpressing caspases that result in the apoptosis of cancer cell lines [41]. However, peruvoside inhibits autophagy through the PI3K/AKT/mTOR signaling pathway and can also cause cell cycle arrest at G0/G1 phase for breast cancer cell lines [41].

DNA damage and inefficient DNA repair mechanism are the major reasons for tumorigenesis. Oleandrin is a C32 compound isolated from *Nerium oleander*. The oleandrin increases the concentration of RPA protein that contributes to DNA repair, recombination, replication, etc. It can, thus, cause apoptosis on A549 (adenocarcinoma), HBE (human bronchial epithelial cell lines), and H1299 (human nonsmall-cell lung carcinoma cell line) [42]. Proscillaridin A is involved in the antiproliferative activity and thus inhibits tumorigeneses [43]. It acts as a direct inhibitor of NKA pump, which activates the AMP-activated protein kinase pathway. It also enhanced the gene expression of the DR4 (death receptor 4) and suppressed tumor growth. Studies prove its anticancer effects on nonsmall-cell lung cancer [44]. It can alter the mitochondria membrane potential and generate ROS, inducing apoptosis. Janus kinase/STAT3 (signal transducer and activator of transcription) pathway helps tumor formation, inhibits proscillaridin A, and causes antiproliferative effects on prostate cancer (PCa) cells [45,46].

Combination drugs enhance the effectiveness of drugs on cancer cells. One of the examples includes lanatoside, in combination with TNF-related apoptosis-inducing ligand (TRAIL), which reduces tumor growth in mice [47]. Treatment of lanatoside C on MKN-45 cell line caused cell cycle arrest at G2/M phase, upregulation of caspase-9, and cleaved PARP that leads to the apoptotic pathway [48]. It downregulates c-Myc by inhibiting the Wnt/β catenin pathway that induces an antitumor effect [48]. The balance of the potassium ions is lost after the cancer cells are induced with lanatoside C, and this causes mitochondrial aggregation or degeneration, resulting in autophagy [49]. 53BP1 (p53 binding protein 1) was found in very low amounts in lanatoside C-treated HCT116 cancer cell lines [49], displaying antitherapeutic effects.

Cancers are gradually becoming resistant to chemotherapy, so recent studies show the importance of cardio glycosides against cancer [18]. The above examples prove that cardio glycosides can be repurposed as anticancer drugs for their various properties, such as antiproliferative activities, inducing apoptosis, inhibiting Na–K-ATPase pathway, and other immunomodulatory properties. It is also observed that the concentration required to treat cancers is less compared to the concentration required to treat cardiac disorders [39]. Various CGs are in their clinical trial phase for the treatment of tumors. Due to their specificity and efficacy, CGs could use as repurposed drugs to kill tumors and treat cancer (Table 1).

Table 1 The anticancerous activity of cardiac glycosides and their mechanism of action on various cancer cell lines.

Name of the cardiac glycoside	Anticancer activity mechanism of action			Reference
	Cell line	IC50 value		
Digoxin	MCF 7	24.1 ± 2.1 nM [50]	Inhibits NKA activity Treats HIF 1 in breast cancer, NSCLC Inhibits phosphorylation of Src and EGFR/STAT3 pathways in lung cancer cell lines	[25] [27] [28]
Ouabain	H460	10.44 nM [51]	Tumor regression Cause macrophage phagocytosis and high NK cell activity Treats melanoma Downregulates STAT3 and inhibits the signaling pathway	[31] [32]
Bufalin	HCT-116 SW620	12.823 ± 1.792 Nm [52]	Targets PI3K-Akt pathway Induce apoptosis and inhibits TNF Downregulates VEGF and deactivate tumor angiogenesis	[35] [33] [34]
Bufotalin	ESCC	0.8–3.6 μm [53]	Inhibits CDK1, arrests G2/M phase Treats HepG2 carcinoma	[35] [36]

Table 1 The anticancerous activity of cardiac glycosides and their mechanism of action on various cancer cell lines—cont'd

Name of the cardiac glycoside	Anticancer activity mechanism of action			Reference
	Cell line	IC50 value		
Arenobufagin	A549 NC1-H40 NC1H197	10 nM [51]	Treats MCF 7 and MDA-MB 231 Downregulates IKKβ/ NF kappa β signal Treats various cancers Inhibits metastasis of lung cancer cells	[37] [18] [38] [39]
Lanatoside C	MCF 7	1.2 μm [54]	Causes cell cycle arrest on MKN-45 upregulation of Caspase 9, inhibits Wnt/ β pathway. Treats HCT-116 Attenuates MAPK by inducing G2/M cell cycle arrest	[48] [49]
Digitoxin	MCF 7	10.2 ± 0.3 nM [55]	Inhibits HIF 1 α subunit overexpression Activates PLC, MAPK, PI3K, Src kinase pathway	[18]
Oleandrin	MDA - MB 231	24.62 nM [56]	Increases concentration of RPA protein Treats A549, HBE, and H1299	[34] [42]
Strophanthidin	A549	0.529 ± 0.05 μM [41]	Inhibits proliferation of cancer cells - A549, MCF 7 and HepG2 Inhibits expression of cyclin-dependent kinases in cancer cells Overexpresses initiator caspase-9 and further caspases, causing apoptosis.	[41]
Peruvoside	MCF 7	47.5 ± 13.1 nM [50]	Causes cell cycle arrest at G0/G1 phase. Inhibit autophagy by PI3K/AKT/mTOR signaling pathway	[41]
Proscillaridin A		70 nM [57]	Activates AMPK pathway Inhibit JAK/STAT3 pathway Treats NSCLC	[45] [44]

3. CGs hamper Na^+/K^+-ATPase signaling complex in cancer

The Na^+/K^+ pump is a transmembrane protein buried in the plasma membrane that perpetuates an ionic gradience across the membrane. The cell maintains an ionic imbalance with a higher concentration of K^+ intracellularly than outside and a higher concentration of Na + extracellularly than inside a cell through the pump. To maintain this ionic difference, the Na^+/K^+ pump needs to be provided with energy in the form of ATP, and hence, this pump is specifically referred to as NKA. Establishing this Na^+ and K^+ concentration gradient generates an action potential, maintains pH homeostasis, and regulates cell metabolism and growth [58]. Furthermore, to serve as an ion transporter, Na^+/K^+-pump also acts as receptors that interact with extracellular components and then mediate signals to the intracellular signaling cascade. The recent studies have recognized the Na^+/K^+ pump as an important integrator of various signals and a subunit of protein-protein interactions that form receptor complexes with important pharmacological implications [59].

The distinctive structural peculiarities of the NKA, comprising catalytic α subunit, β subunit, and an FXYD protein, make it a multi-facilitator as a transporter and a binding site [60]. In addition, the crucial importance of NKA for the metabolism of animal cells and numerous physiological functions mediated through the pump makes it a vital entity for targeted therapy. In 2014, Kubala et al. showed the NKA inhibition through the widely used chemotherapeutic agent cisplatin. They have provided essential evidence for cisplatin-NKA interactions, leading to the cisplatin nephrotoxicity [61]. Later Huličiak et al. showed that cisplatin binds to the cytoplasmic part of NKA through covalent bonding and impairs its normal functioning when cisplatin is administered in cancer therapy [62]. Other most scrutinized NKA inhibitors include natural derivatives of cardiotonic steroids.

A deeper look at the expressional studies revealed that the NKA activities are regulated at its transcriptional level through transcription factors, hormones, growth factors, and external agents. These factors modulate the transcription of NKA subunits and, in turn, alter its activity [63]. The catalytic α-subunit mainly imparts the transport activities, and the ß unit controls cell adhesion property. Studies showed that the NKA expression profile is often altered in various cancers, including lung, breast [64], colorectal, and liver. Based on a study conducted on nonsmall-cell lung cancer (NSCLC), Nilsson and his team have reported the elevated expression of the α-1 subunit of NKA in tissue samples from patients with NSCLC compared to standard control [65]. The same pattern was perceived from cancer cell line studies, including A549, Cal-12T, and NCI-H727. A similar study administered in colorectal and liver cancer cell lines showed that the α1, α2, and ß1 subunits of NKA were highly expressed in tumor cells at the metastatic stage [66]. It was also found that ß3 subunit of NKA was also found to be overexpressed in gastric cancer, which is the cause to promote cell progression influencing PI3K/AKT pathway. The study further revealed the elevated expression of the ATP1B3 gene encoding the ß3 subunit at the transcript and protein level in malignant gastric cells compared to the normal gastric epithelial cell lines. The study also provided the significance of ATP1B3 (ATPase Na+/K+ transporting subunit beta 3) gene knockout, consequently inhibiting cell proliferation, migration, colony-formation ability, and increased apoptosis through the PI3K/AKT signaling pathway. Hence, the subunits prove a potential therapeutic target for cancer [67]. Accordingly, the modulators of NKA are in the front line of cancer research as it is identified as an emerging cancer target.

There comes the importance of naturally derived cardiac steroidal compounds, such as CGs, which bind to NKA with high affinity and inhibit its membrane activity. As a result, the intracellular sodium concentration increases and consequently affects sodium–calcium exchanger (Na^{+}/Ca^{+}) by causing calcium ion (Ca^{2+}) accumulation in the cell [68]. Ca^{2+} homeostasis in the cell regulates various cellular processes, including gene transcription, cell proliferation, apoptosis, angiogenesis, etc. [69]. The intracellular calcium ions act as secondary messengers, thereby activating or inhibiting cellular signaling cascades and other Ca^{2+}-dependent processes. CGs including oleandrin, ouabain, and digoxin were studied and reported to induce apoptosis in PCa cell lines. The study further demonstrated that these CGs induce proapoptotic effects through intracellular Ca^{2+} fluxes [70]. The recent research aimed at delineating the anticancer activity of deslanoside in PCa further substantiated that the compound inhibited colony formation and tumor growth in multiple PCa cell lines through the induction of apoptosis (Fig. 2). Beyond being an intracellular messenger, Ca^{2+} controls diverse cellular functions, imparting cell death signals [71].

The intracellular Ca^{2+} concentration is maintained to an optimal range in normal cells. In contrast, its Ca^{2+} is present at high concentrations in cellular organelles such as sarcoplasmic and endoplasmic reticulum (SR/ER) [72]. They extend their review stating that the Ca^{2+} regulates the induction of apoptosis. Earlier reports confirm that the elevated cytosolic Ca^{2+} concentration results in the execution of apoptosis in cancer cell lines. An increased Ca^{2+} in the cytoplasm activates calpains, a cysteine protease. The activated enzyme further activates caspase-12, which induces cascade activation of caspase-9 and -3, initiating apoptosis. Apart from the induction of apoptosis, diverse molecular mechanisms exert the anticancer property of CGs. However, there is consistent evidence for cell cycle arrest and apoptosis induction through the involvement of NKA in cancer cells. The assumptions of CG derived anticancer activity through NKA signalosome are well illustrated in the reports of [73], where they tinted multiple structural proteins associated with NKA Src/EGFR/Ras/Raf/MEK/ERK and PI3K/Akt inhibition by means of CG related to its anticancer activity.

4. Role of the immune system in cancer

Interaction of the immune system and cancer had been the subject of epidemiological studies since William's nineteenth century. Busch and Fehleisen independently noticed regression of tumors in cancer patients infected by erysipelas. After two decades, William Cooley,

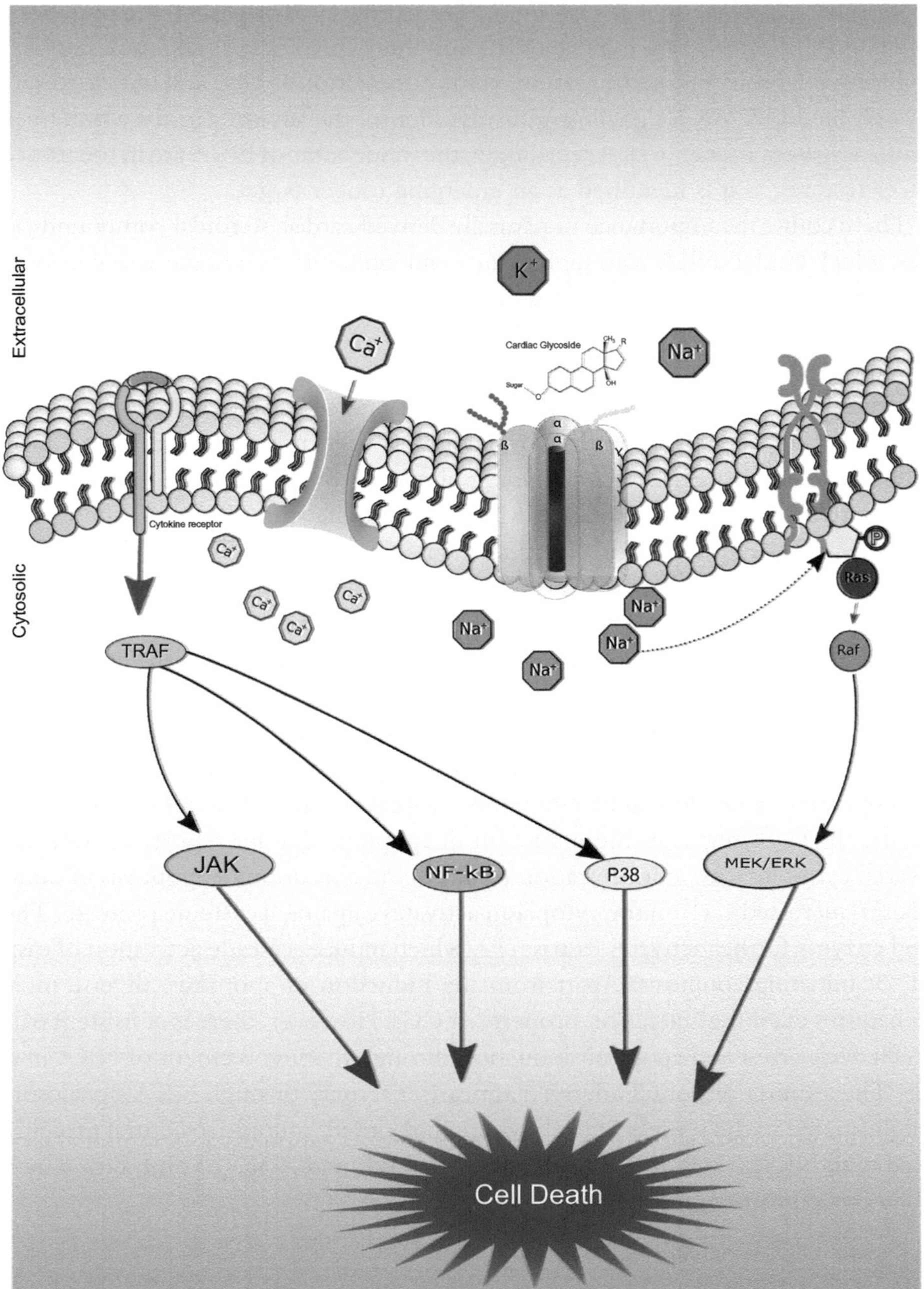

Fig. 2 Illustrating the Na^+/K^+-ATPase activity upon treatment with cardiac glycosides and its influence on calcium pump regulating Ca^{++} & Na+ in a cell obstructing cellular signaling and further leading to cell death.

often referred to as the "Father of Immunotherapy," took forward this research and reported significant regression and cure of sarcoma in patients through deliberately inducing erysipelas infection [74]. Immunotherapy is a gold standard in cancer therapeutics by drastically increasing life expectancy and quality in cancer patients. Esfahani elaborates in his recent review on cancer immunotherapy. He further extends the scope of tumor-specific vaccines by employing immune checkpoint inhibitors, targeting tumor immunogenicity, and attenuating antitumor immune responses released by cancer cells [75].

There is intimate crosstalk between the immune system and tumor cells and is recognized as an emerging hallmark in cancer [76]. According to the immune surveillance concept, formulated by Paul Ehrlich in 1909 stating that the "immune system of the host finds and prevents neoplastic cells from developing into tumors" [77]. Recent clinical and preclinical studies in human cancer prove that the particular immune cell type, effector molecules, and pathways can destroy nascent tumors. The advent of knockout mouse models experimentally demonstrates a link between immunodeficiency and cancer. An immune-deficient mouse that lacked both B and T cells developed intestinal and lung adenocarcinoma while STAT1 knockout increased the incidence of breast and colon adenocarcinomas or both in mice. In addition, mice lacking $CD8^+$ T cells and NK cells were found to develop lymphomas with age [78].

Cancer immune evasion is yet another major threat whereby the cancer cells evoke immune-suppressing responses to avoid the tumoricidal attack. This usually occurs by targeting the regulatory T-cell function or their secretions and producing immunosuppressive agents, thus modifying immune surveillance in the body. This generally occurs through altering the $CD8^+$ cytotoxic T cells and $CD4^+$ helper T cells, giving scopes to cancer development [79]. Cancer immunotherapy focuses on harnessing the antitumor activity of $CD8^+$ and $CD4^+$ cells by providing a sustained immune response against tumors [80]. The immunosuppressive circuitries established by suppressing the activity of T-helper cells further regulate transcription of the immune response genes through transcription factor units NF-κB.

Immunogenic cell death (ICD) is a type of regulated cell death induced through innate immune responses that recognize and destroys tumor cells and thereby is regarded as the regulatory mechanism in cellular metabolism and related diseases. The potent triggers of inflammation, released by dying tumor cells called damage-associated molecular patterns (DAMPs), bind and activate the dendritic cells (DCs), consequently promoting phagocytosis of the antigenic component by DC. DAMPs include nucleic acids like mtDNA, the cell surface ones such as calreticulin (CRT), secretions of adenosine triphosphate (ATP), type-1 interferons (IFNs), and heat shock proteins (HSP70 and HSP90) that assist cell uptake through antigen-presenting cells and mediate immunogenicity of cancer cells [81]. Following ICD, DAMPs further lead to the activation of T cells through macrophages, DCs, and NK cells, which progressively detect and eliminate other cancerous cells from the tumor microenvironment (TMV).

Induction of ICD in cancer cells through immunotherapy is the new therapeutic regimen equipping immune modulations and even proposing ICD-based cancer vaccine development [82]. Some of the widely studied classic ICD inducers include anthracyclines (doxorubicin, mitoxantrone), CG (lanatoside C, ouabain, digoxin, and digitoxin), shikonin, etc., which has reported to induce ICD and inhibition of tumor growth [83]. An authenticated ICD inducer should exhibit high therapeutic efficiency in in vivo studies (mice models). The preliminary studies should provide tumornaive, synergistic hosts immune-mediated prophylactic protection in the liver cancer cell system. Thus very few chemotherapeutic agents can cause cell demise by inducing ICD, including oxaliplatin, cyclophosphamide, idarubicin, epirubicin, etc. [84]. Hence, there is a tremendous demand for therapeutic drugs that are safe to use and exhibit potential immune response mechanisms that drove cell death in cancer treatment. Fucikova recently screened out a few characteristic features associated with ICD prompted by ICD inducers that triggered immunogenicity in malignant cells. These include a quantitative assessment of CALR, HSPs, IFNs' release, and ATP secretion following ICD in tumor cells.

Likewise, inhibition of RNA transcription and consequently ceasing protein translation are the salient features of ICD undergoing cells upon ICD inducers; details of assessment procedures are described elsewhere [85]. In this aspect of drug discovery, the employment of DR through clinically safe molecules is significant in targeting a particular disease. Such a family of compounds called CGs is gaining support against cancer by inducing ICD and immune-modulatory properties.

4.1 CGs as immunomodulators in cancer

Immunomodulators are a group of medications used to treat a disease by either activating or suppressing the patients' immune system [86]. In the case of tumor immunotherapy, comprising of immune checkpoint inhibitors, adoptive T-cell therapies have induced anticancer immune-response in eradicating cancer cells [87]. In general, immunomodulatory effects have been described from several molecular drugs used to treat diseases other than cancer. The CG is a class of drugs that has been widely studied and investigated for its anticancer activity [11,18,41]. Reports from several recent studies on CGs and cancer suggest a substantial immunomodulatory role of the compound and promote growth-suppressive agents for cancer [88]. Recent findings from the study of ouabain, a cardiotonic steroid, and specific NKA inhibitor, showed anticancer activity through downregulating STAT3 successively halting STAT3-mediated transcription and downstream target proteins [89]. A supporting study to the previous results was carried out using methotrexate-loaded poly nanocarrier drug-induced anticancer activity via immunomodulatory effects. The study mapped out the significance of STAT3 and NF-κB in regulating tumor-associated macrophage activity controlling crosstalk between immune and malignant cells [90]. A recent review report on CGs as immune system modulators [10] described the immunomodulatory effect of CGs through suppressing the activity of T-helper cells and further modulating transcription of immune response genes by dint of NF-κB. A recent study showed the mechanistic link between NKA inhibition through ouabain and digoxin, further downregulating immune checkpoint protein indole amine-pyrrole 2′,3′-deoxygenase 1 (IDO1) and STAT1 in lung and breast cancers, respectively. The study further demonstrated that ATP1A1 (α1 subunit of NKA) knockdown significantly affected STAT1 stabilization, decreasing IDO1 expression and affecting immune checkpoint proteins [91]. All this evidence suggests that CGs have far-reaching clinical implications as immunomodulators in cancer treatment and cure.

CGs are also distinguished inducers of ICD, thereby ensuing antitumor activity in various cancers. It is ascertained that CGs stimulate ICD due to tumor cell death, followed by the DAMP release of DAMPs, triggering an immune response [92]. Li et al. revealed that CG oleandrin, which inhibited NKA, further induced ICD in BC cells accompanying CRT, HMGB1, HSP70/90, and ATP (Fig. 3). Moreover, he demonstrated increased maturation and activation of DCs, which subsequently enhanced $CD8^+$ T-cell-driven cytotoxicity that indicated enhancement of tumor lymphocytes in oleandrin-treated cancer cells. The study also gathered in vivo mRNA-seq data, which

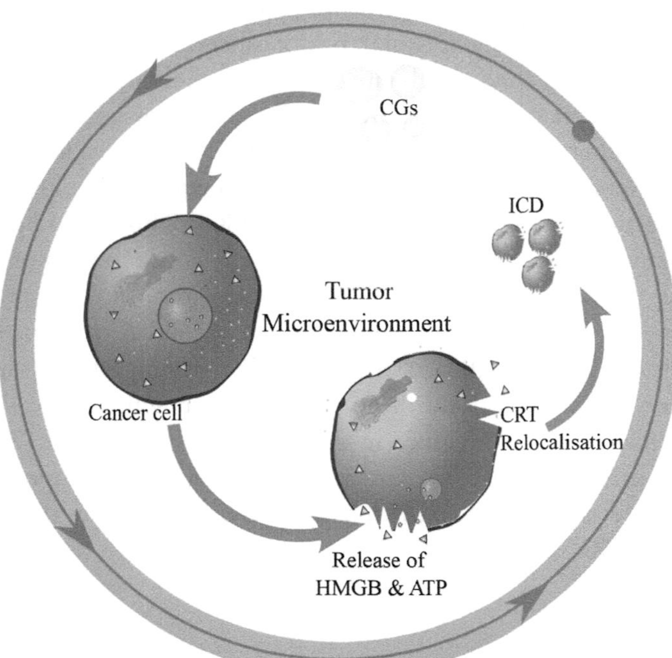

Fig. 3 A schematic representation of immunogenic cell death driven by cardiac glycosides in the tumor microenvironment. The release of DAMPS, including high mobility group box 1 protein and ATP.

further validated the results and confirmed ICD induction through the PERK/elF2α/ATF4/CHOP pathway [56]. The extensively studied CGs digoxin and digitoxin down-regulated TNF-α by inhibiting NF-κB-interfering NKA and increased intracellular Na^+ and inhibiting ATPase activity [13].

Hypoxia in the TMV is another crucial determinant driving tumor progression. A group of transcription factors called hypoxia-inducible factors (HIFs) regulates the expression of genes that assist tumor cells in adapting to hypoxic conditions. Among the HIFs, HIF-1α is associated with cancer progression, and it has been known to impart a crucial role in inflammatory responses by the immune system [93]. Myriads of data support that NF-κB and HIF-1α correspondingly contribute to inflammatory signals in hypoxia in tumor cells. Thus HIF-1α inhibition through CGs could be targeted to explore anticancer therapeutic properties [94]. Compiling all this information, we pinpoint the aforementioned molecular markers related to the immune system in regulating cancer growth through CGs.

5. Conclusions

Cancer, being one of the deadliest disorders in the world, persuades the discovery of drugs that inhibit the growth of cancer cells. Anticancer drugs have played a vital role in providing treatment and reducing high risk of cancer. DR can simplify the long-term drug development process and a high rate of success and requirement of low concentrations. Compounds obtained from natural sources and drugs for various disorders have been repositioned therapeutically. CGs are therapeutic agents used for multiple heart diseases but can be reprocessed against various cancers due to their antiproliferative activity and inhibiting action on several pathways, such as NKA. This impending action induces apoptosis and causes cell cycle arrest by increasing the concentration of Ca^+ and stimulating signaling pathways that make it an ionotropic agent. The exceptional activity of CG in inducing ICD also served to annihilate cancer cells. A combinatorial therapy of CG like lanatoside C and TRAIL can target multiple signaling pathways in tumor growth and thus enhance the efficacy of the drugs. Though the potential effects have been studied, the molecular pathways involved in the anticancer property of CGs are yet to be studied in the future. Ultimately, CGs represent many bioactive compounds with immunomodulatory effects in cancer and emphasize the potential clinical use of these compounds through DR.

Acknowledgments

The authors thank SERB-EMR/2016/003715 for partial financial assistance. HP and AJK thank the research facilities supported by the Central University of Kerala.

Consent for publication

Not applicable.

Ethics approval and consent to participate

Not applicable.

Conflict of interest

The authors have declared no competing interests.

References

[1] H. Sung, et al., Global cancer statistics 2020: GLOBOCAN estimates of incidence and mortality worldwide for 36 cancers in 185 countries, CA Cancer J. Clin. 71 (3) (2021) 209–249, https://doi.org/10.3322/caac.21660.

[2] I. Torjesen, Drug development: the journey of medicine from lab to shelf, Pharm. J. (2015), https://doi.org/10.1211/PJ.2015.20068196.

[3] M. Rudrapal, J.S. Khairnar, G.A. Jadhav, Drug repurposing (DR): an emerging approach in drug discovery, in: Drug Repurposing - Hypothesis, Molecular Aspects and Therapeutic Applications, 2020, https://doi.org/10.5772/intechopen.93193.

[4] Y. Pirahanchi, N.R. Aeddula, Physiology, Sodium-Potassium Pump (Na+ K+ Pump), StatPearls Publishing, Treasure Island, FL, 2019.

[5] H. Sutanto, J. Heijman, The role of calcium in the human heart: with great power comes great responsibility, Front. Young Minds 7 (65) (2019) 10–3389, https://doi.org/10.3389/frym.2019.00065.

[6] J. Tian, Z.J. Xie, The Na-K-ATPase and calcium-signaling microdomains, Physiology 23 (4) (2008) 205–211, https://doi.org/10.1152/physiol.00008.2008.

[7] A.R. Michell, The Clinical Biology of Sodium: The Physiology and Pathophysiology of Sodium in Mammals, Elsevier, 2014, https://doi.org/10.1016/b978-0-08-040842-2.50016-6.

[8] J. Avila, E. Lecuona, M. Morales, A. Soriano, T. Alonso, P.A.B.L.O. Martín-Vasallo, Opposite expression pattern of the human Na, K-ATPase β1 isoform in stomach and colon adenocarcinomas a, Ann. N. Y. Acad. Sci. 834 (1) (1997) 653–655, https://doi.org/10.1111/j.1749-6632.1997.tb52341.x.

[9] S.A. Rajasekaran, W.J. Ball, N.H. Bander, H. Liu, J.D. Pardee, A.K. Rajasekaran, Reduced expression of β-subunit of Na, K-ATPase in human clear-cell renal cell carcinoma, J. Urol. 162 (2) (1999) 574–580, https://doi.org/10.1091/mbc.e04-03-0222.

[10] J. Škubník, V. Pavlíčková, S. Rimpelová, Cardiac glycosides as immune system modulators, Biomol. Ther. 11 (5) (2021) 659, https://doi.org/10.3390/biom11050659.

[11] J. Škubník, J. Bejček, V.S. Pavlíčková, S. Rimpelová, Repurposing cardiac glycosides: drugs for heart failure surmounting viruses, Molecules 26 (18) (2021) 5627, https://doi.org/10.3390/molecules26185627.

[12] Z. Zhang, L. Zhou, N. Xie, E.C. Nice, T. Zhang, Y. Cui, C. Huang, Overcoming cancer therapeutic bottleneck by drug repurposing, Signal Transduct. Target. Ther. 5 (1) (2020) 1–25, https://doi.org/10.1038/s41392-020-00213-8.

[13] O. Kepp, L. Menger, E. Vacchelli, S. Adjemian, I. Martins, Y. Ma, A.Q. Sukkurwala, M. Michaud, L. Galluzzi, L. Zitvogel, G. Kroemer, Anticancer activity of cardiac glycosides, OncoImmunology 1 (9) (2012) 1640–1642, https://doi.org/10.4161/onci.21684.

[14] H.R. El-Seed, S.A. Khalifa, E.A. Taher, M.A. Farag, A. Saeed, M. Gamal, et al., Cardenolides: insights from chemical structure and pharmacological utility, Pharmacol. Res. 141 (2019) 123–175, https://doi.org/10.1016/j.phrs.2018.12.015.

[15] R. Tisserand, R. Young, Essential oil composition, in: Essential Oil Safety, Elsevier, Kanada, 2014, https://doi.org/10.1016/b978-0-443-06241-4.00002-3.
[16] I. Labuda, Flavor Compounds. Encyclopedia of Microbiology, Academic Press, 2009, https://doi.org/10.1016/B978-012373944-5.00148-6.
[17] W. Schönfeld, J. Weiland, C. Lindig, M. Masnyk, M.M. Kabat, A. Kurek, et al., The lead structure in CG is 5 β, 14 β-androstane-3 β, 14-diol, Naunyn Schmiedeberg's Arch. Pharmacol. 329 (4) (1985) 414–426, https://doi.org/10.1007/bf00496377.
[18] R. Kumavath, S. Paul, H. Pavithran, M.K. Paul, P. Ghosh, D. Barh, V. Azevedo, Emergence of cardiac glycosides as potential drugs: current and future scope for cancer therapeutics, Biomol. Ther. 11 (9) (2021) 1275, https://doi.org/10.3390/biom11091275.
[19] J.I. Ayogu, A.S. Odoh, Prospects and therapeutic applications of CG in cancer remediation, ACS Comb. Sci. 22 (11) (2020) 543–553, https://doi.org/10.1021/acscombsci.0c00082.
[20] W.J. Leu, H.S. Chang, S.H. Chan, J.L. Hsu, C.C. Yu, L.C. Hsu, et al., Reevesioside A, a cardenolide glycoside, induces anticancer activity against human hormone-refractory prostate cancers through suppression of c-myc expression and induction of G1 arrest of the cell cycle, PLoS One 9 (1) (2014), e87323, https://doi.org/10.1371/journal.pone.0087323.
[21] S. Hafner, M. Schmiech, S.J. Lang, The cardenolide glycoside acovenoside a interferes with epidermal growth factor receptor trafficking in non-small cell lung cancer cells, Front. Pharmacol. 12 (2021) 1067, https://doi.org/10.3389/fphar.2021.611657.
[22] Y. Ren, S. Wu, J.E. Burdette, X. Cheng, A.D. Kinghorn, Structural insights into the interactions of digoxin and Na+/K+-ATPase and other targets for the inhibition of cancer cell proliferation, Molecules 26 (12) (2021) 3672, https://doi.org/10.3390/molecules26123672.
[23] V.K. Sharma, Plant cardenolides in therapeutics, Int. J. Indig. Med. Plants (2015).
[24] C. Theurer, H.J. Treumann, T. Faust, U. May, W. Kreis, Glycosylation in cardenolide biosynthesis, in: Primary and Secondary Metabolism of Plants and Cell Cultures III, Springer, Dordrecht, 1994, pp. 327–335, https://doi.org/10.1007/978-94-011-0237-7_29.
[25] R.B. Zavareh, K.S. Lau, R. Hurren, A. Datti, D.J. Ashline, M. Gronda, et al., Inhibition of the sodium/potassium ATPase impairs N-glycan expression and function, Cancer Res. 68 (16) (2008) 6688–6697, https://doi.org/10.1158/0008-5472.CAN-07-6833.
[26] N.J.M. Raynal, J.T. Lee, Y. Wang, A. Beaudry, P. Madireddi, J. Garriga, et al., Targeting calcium signaling induces epigenetic reactivation of tumor suppressor genes in cancer, Cancer Res. 76 (6) (2016) 1494–1505, https://doi.org/10.1158/0008-5472.can-14-2391.
[27] Y. Wang, Q. Ma, S. Zhang, H. Liu, B. Zhao, B. Du, W. Wang, P. Lin, Z. Zhang, Y. Zhong, D. Kong, Digoxin enhances the anticancer effect on non-small cell lung Cancer while reducing the cardiotoxicity of Adriamycin, Front. Pharmacol. 11 (2020). https://www.frontiersin.org/article/10.3389/fphar.2020.00186.
[28] A. Svensson, F. Azarbayjani, U. Bäckman, T. Matsumoto, R. Christofferson, Digoxin inhibits neuroblastoma tumor growth in mice, Anticancer Res. 25 (1A) (2005) 207–212.
[29] C.C.L. Wong, H. Zhang, D.M. Gilkes, J. Chen, H. Wei, P. Chaturvedi, et al., Inhibitors of hypoxia-inducible factor 1 block breast cancer metastatic niche formation and lung metastasis, J. Mol. Med. 90 (7) (2012) 803–815, https://doi.org/10.1007/s00109-011-0855-y.
[30] C. Antczak, C. Kloepping, C. Radu, T. Genski, L. Müller-Kuhrt, K. Siems, et al., Revisiting old drugs as novel agents for retinoblastoma: in vitro and in vivo antitumor activity of cardenolides, Invest. Ophthalmol. Vis. Sci. 50 (7) (2009) 3065–3073, https://doi.org/10.1167/iovs.08-3158.
[31] Y.L. Shih, H.S. Shang, Y.L. Chen, S.C. Hsueh, H.M. Chou, H.F. Lu, et al., Ouabain promotes immune responses in WEHI-3 cells to generate leukemia mice through enhancing phagocytosis and natural killer cell activities in vivo, Environ. Toxicol. 34 (5) (2019) 659–665, https://doi.org/10.1002/tox.22732.
[32] J.M.C. da Silva, M.L.A. Campos, M.P. Teixeira, R. da Silva Faustino, R.C. Aleixo, F.J.P. Cavalcante, et al., Ouabain pre-treatment modulates B and T lymphocytes and improves survival of melanoma-bearing animals, Int. Immunopharmacol. 86 (2020) 106772, https://doi.org/10.1016/j.intimp.2020.106772.
[33] C.M. Xie, X.T. Lin, W. Di, Y. Tan, C.H. Cheng, J. Zhang, Cardiac glycoside bufalin blocks cancer cell growth by inhibition of Aurora A and Aurora B activation via PI3K-Akt pathway, Oncotarget 9 (17) (2018) 13783, https://doi.org/10.18632/oncotarget.24475.

[34] J. Ye, S. Chen, T. Maniatis, CG are potent inhibitors of interferon-β gene expression, Nat. Chem. Biol. 7 (1) (2011) 25–33, https://doi.org/10.1038/nchembio.476.
[35] Z. Pan, C. Qu, Y. Chen, X. Chen, X. Liu, W. Hao, W. Xu, L. Ye, P. Lu, D. Li, Q. Zheng, Bufotalin induces cell cycle arrest and cell apoptosis in human malignant melanoma A375 cells, Oncol. Rep. 41 (4) (2019) 2409–2417, https://doi.org/10.3892/or.2019.7032.
[36] D.-M. Zhang, J.-S. Liu, M.-K. Tang, A. Yiu, H. Cao, L. Jiang, J.Y.-W. Chan, H.-Y. Tian, K.-P. Fung, W.-C. Ye, Bufotalin from Venenum Bufonis inhibits growth of multidrug resistant HepG2 cells through G2/M cell cycle arrest and apoptosis, Eur. J. Pharmacol. 692 (1–3) (2012) 19–28, https://doi.org/10.1016/j.ejphar.2012.06.045.
[37] Y. Zhang, B. Yuan, B. Bian, H. Zhao, A. Kiyomi, H. Hayashi, Y. Iwatani, M. Sugiura, N. Takagi, Cytotoxic effects of hellebrigenin and arenobufagin against human breast cancer cells, Front. Oncol. 11 (2021) 711220, https://doi.org/10.3389/fonc.2021.711220.
[38] J. Zhao, Q. Zhang, G. Zou, G. Gao, Q. Yue, Arenobufagin, isolated from toad venom, inhibited epithelial-to-mesenchymal transition and suppressed migration and invasion of lung cancer cells via targeting IKKβ/NFκB signal cascade, J. Ethnopharmacol. 250 (2020) 112492, https://doi.org/10.1016/j.jep.2019.112492.
[39] D.M. Zhang, J.S. Liu, L.J. Deng, M.F. Chen, A. Yiu, H.H. Cao, et al., Arenobufagin, a natural bufadienolide from toad venom, induces apoptosis and autophagy in human hepatocellular carcinoma cells through inhibition of PI3K/Akt/mTOR pathway, Carcinogenesis 34 (6) (2013) 1331–1342, https://doi.org/10.1093/carcin/bgt060.
[40] H.A. Elbaz, T.A. Stueckle, W. Tse, Y. Rojanasakul, C.Z. Dinu, Digitoxin and its analogs as novel cancer therapeutics, Exp. Hematol. Oncol. 1 (1) (2012) 1–10, https://doi.org/10.1186/2162-3619-1-4.
[41] D. Reddy, R. Kumavath, D. Barh, V. Azevedo, P. Ghosh, Anticancer and antiviral properties of cardiac glycosides: a review to explore the mechanism of actions, Molecules (Basel, Switzerland) 25 (16) (2020) E3596, https://doi.org/10.3390/molecules25163596.
[42] Z. Bao, B. Tian, X. Wang, H. Feng, Y. Liang, Z. Chen, W. Li, H. Shen, S. Ying, Oleandrin induces DNA damage responses in cancer cells by suppressing the expression of Rad51, Oncotarget 7 (37) (2016) 59572–59579, https://doi.org/10.18632/oncotarget.10726.
[43] V. Pongrakhananon, Anticancer properties of CG, in: Cancer Treatment—Conventional and Innovative Approaches, Intech, 2013, pp. 65–83, https://doi.org/10.5772/55381.
[44] R.Z. Li, X.X. Fan, F.G. Duan, Z.B. Jiang, H.D. Pan, L.X. Luo, et al., Proscillaridin A induces apoptosis and suppresses non-small-cell lung cancer tumor growth via calcium-induced DR4 upregulation, Cell Death Dis. 9 (6) (2018) 1–14, https://doi.org/10.1038/s41419-018-0733-4.
[45] Y. He, M. Khan, J. Yang, M. Yao, S. Yu, H. Gao, Proscillaridin A induces apoptosis, inhibits STAT3 activation and augments doxorubicin toxicity in prostate cancer cells, Int. J. Med. Sci. 15 (8) (2018) 832, https://doi.org/10.7150/ijms.23270.
[46] M. Liu, Q. Huang, L. Li, X. Li, Z. Zhang, J. Dong, The cardiac glycoside deslanoside exerts anticancer activity in prostate cancer cells by modulating *multiple signaling pathways*, Cancers 13 (22) (2021) 5809.
[47] C.E. Badr, T. Wurdinger, J. Nilsson, J.M. Niers, M. Whalen, A. Degterev, B.A. Tannous, Lanatoside C sensitizes glioblastoma cells to tumor necrosis factor-related apoptosis-inducing ligand and induces an alternative cell death pathway, Neuro-Oncology 13 (11) (2011) 1213–1224, https://doi.org/10.1093/neuonc/nor067.
[48] Y. Hu, K. Yu, G. Wang, D. Zhang, C. Shi, Y. Ding, et al., Lanatoside C inhibits cell proliferation and induces apoptosis through attenuating Wnt/β-catenin/c-Myc signaling pathway in human gastric cancer cells, Biochem. Pharmacol. 150 (2018) 280–292, https://doi.org/10.1016/j.bcp.2018.02.023.
[49] M.A. Kang, M.S. Kim, W. Kim, J.H. Um, Y.J. Shin, J.Y. Song, J.H. Jeong, Lanatoside C suppressed colorectal cancer cell growth by inducing mitochondrial dysfunction and increased radiation sensitivity by impairing DNA damage repair, Oncotarget 7 (5) (2016) 6074, https://doi.org/10.18632/oncotarget.6832.
[50] V. Kaushik, N. Azad, J.S. Yakisich, A.K.V. Iyer, Antitumor effects of naturally occurring cardiac glycosides convallatoxin and peruvoside on human ER+ and triple-negative breast cancers, Cell Death Discov. 3 (2017) 17009, https://doi.org/10.1038/cddiscovery.2017.9.
[51] L. Ma, Y. Zhu, S. Fang, H. Long, X. Liu, Z. Liu, Arenobufagin induces apoptotic cell death in human non-small-cell lung cancer cells via the noxa-related pathway, Molecules 22 (9) (2017) 1525, https://doi.org/10.3390/molecules2209152.

[52] D. Wu, W.-Y. Zhou, X.-T. Lin, L. Fang, C.-M. Xie, Bufalin induces apoptosis via mitochondrial ROS-mediated caspase-3 activation in HCT-116 and SW620 human colon cancer cells, Drug Chem. Toxicol. 42 (4) (2019) 444–450, https://doi.org/10.1080/01480545.2018.1512611.
[53] S. Lin, J. Lv, P. Peng, C. Cai, J. Deng, H. Deng, X. Li, X. Tang, Bufadienolides induce p53-mediated apoptosis in esophageal squamous cell carcinoma cells in vitro and in vivo, Oncol. Lett. 15 (2) (2018) 1566–1572, https://doi.org/10.3892/ol.2017.7457.
[54] D. Reddy, R. Kumavath, P. Ghosh, D. Barh, Lanatoside C induces G2/M cell cycle arrest and suppresses cancer cell growth by attenuating MAPK, Wnt, JAK-STAT, and PI3K/AKT/mTOR signaling pathways, Biomol. Ther. 9 (12) (2019) 792, https://doi.org/10.3390/biom9120792.
[55] M. López-Lázaro, N. Pastor, S.S. Azrak, M.J. Ayuso, C.A. Austin, F. Cortés, Digitoxin inhibits the growth of cancer cell lines at concentrations commonly found in cardiac patients, J. Nat. Prod. 68 (11) (2005) 1642–1645, https://doi.org/10.1021/np050226l.
[56] X. Li, J. Zheng, S. Chen, F. Meng, J. Ning, S. Sun, Oleandrin, a cardiac glycoside, induces immunogenic cell death via the PERK/elF2α/ATF4/CHOP pathway in breast cancer, Cell Death Dis. 12 (4) (2021) 1–15, https://doi.org/10.1038/s41419-021-03605-y.
[57] E.M. Da Costa, G. Armaos, G. McInnes, A. Beaudry, G. Moquin-Beaudry, V. Bertrand-Lehouillier, M. Caron, C. Richer, P. St-Onge, J.R. Johnson, N. Krogan, Y. Sai, M. Downey, M. Rafei, M. Boileau, K. Eppert, E. Flores-Díaz, A. Haman, T. Hoang, et al., Heart failure drug proscillaridin A targets MYC overexpressing leukemia through global loss of lysine acetylation, J. Exp. Clin. Cancer Res. 38 (1) (2019) 251, https://doi.org/10.1186/s13046-019-1242-8.
[58] A.S. Pivovarov, F. Calahorro, R.J. Walker, Na+/K+-pump and neurotransmitter membrane receptors, Invertebr. Neurosci. 19 (1) (2018) 1, https://doi.org/10.1007/s10158-018-0221-7.
[59] K. Alevizopoulos, T. Calogeropoulou, F. Lang, C. Stournaras, Na+/K+ ATPase inhibitors in cancer, Curr. Drug Targets 15 (10) (2014) 988–1000.
[60] K. Geering, Functional roles of Na,K-ATPase subunits, Curr. Opin. Nephrol. Hypertens. 17 (5) (2008) 526–532, https://doi.org/10.1097/MNH.0b013e3283036cbf.
[61] M. Kubala, J. Geleticova, M. Huliciak, M. Zatloukalova, J. Vacek, M. Sebela, Na^+/K^+-ATPase inhibition by cisplatin and consequences for cisplatin nephrotoxicity, Biomed. Papers 158 (2) (2014) 194–200, https://doi.org/10.5507/bp.2014.018.
[62] M. Huličiak, J. Vacek, M. Šebela, E. Orolinová, J. Znaleziona, M. Havlíková, M. Kubala, Covalent binding of cisplatin impairs the function of Na+/K+-ATPase by binding to its cytoplasmic part, Biochem. Pharmacol. 83 (11) (2012) 1507–1513, https://doi.org/10.1016/j.bcp.2012.02.015.
[63] Z. Li, S.A. Langhans, Transcriptional regulators of Na,K-ATPase subunits, Front. Cell Dev. Biol. 3 (2015). https://www.frontiersin.org/article/10.3389/fcell.2015.00066.
[64] S.A. Perkov, A.K. Emelyanov, S.V. Shmakov, A.A. Bogdanov, Investigation of Na+/K+-ATPase role in cancer cells' functioning, J. Phys. Conf. Ser. 1124 (2018), 031023, https://doi.org/10.1088/1742-6596/1124/3/031023.
[65] B. Nilsson, T. Mijatovic, A. Mathieu, I. Roland, E. Van Quaquebeke, F. Van Vynckt, F. Darro, R. Kiss, Targeting Na+/K+-ATPase in non-small cell lung cancer (NSCLC), J. Clin. Oncol. 25 (18_suppl) (2007) 18144, https://doi.org/10.1200/jco.2007.25.18_suppl.18144.
[66] M. Baker Bechmann, D. Rotoli, M. Morales, M.D.C. Maeso, M.D.P. García, J. Ávila, A. Mobasheri, P. Martín-Vasallo, Na,K-ATPase isozymes in colorectal cancer and liver metastases, Front. Physiol. 7 (2016). https://www.frontiersin.org/article/10.3389/fphys.2016.00009.
[67] L. Li, R. Feng, Q. Xu, F. Zhang, T. Liu, J. Cao, S. Fei, Expression of the β3 subunit of Na+/K+-ATPase is increased in gastric cancer and regulates gastric cancer cell progression and prognosis via the PI3/AKT pathway, Oncotarget 8 (48) (2017) 84285–84299, https://doi.org/10.18632/oncotarget.20894.
[68] R.H.G. Schwinger, H. Bundgaard, J. Müller-Ehmsen, K. Kjeldsen, The Na, K-ATPase in the failing human heart, Cardiovasc. Res. 57 (4) (2003) 913–920, https://doi.org/10.1016/S0008-6363(02)00767-8.
[69] G.R. Monteith, D. McAndrew, H.M. Faddy, S.J. Roberts-Thomson, Calcium and cancer: targeting Ca2+ transport, Nat. Rev. Cancer 7 (7) (2007) 519–530, https://doi.org/10.1038/nrc2171.
[70] D.J. McConkey, Y. Lin, L.K. Nutt, H.Z. Ozel, R.A. Newman, Cardiac glycosides stimulate Ca2+ increases and apoptosis in androgen-independent, metastatic human prostate adenocarcinoma cells, Cancer Res. 60 (14) (2000) 3807–3812.

[71] R. Bagur, G. Hajnóczky, Intracellular Ca2+ sensing: role in calcium homeostasis and signaling, Mol. Cell 66 (6) (2017) 780–788, https://doi.org/10.1016/j.molcel.2017.05.028.
[72] A. Danese, S. Patergnani, M. Bonora, M.R. Wieckowski, M. Previati, C. Giorgi, P. Pinton, Calcium regulates cell death in cancer: roles of the mitochondria and mitochondria-associated membranes (MAMs), Biochim. Biophys. Acta Biomembr. – Bioenerg. 1858 (8) (2017) 615–627, https://doi.org/10.1016/j.bbabio.2017.01.003.
[73] J. Bejček, M. Jurášek, V. Spiwok, S. Rimpelová, Quo vadis cardiac glycoside research? Toxins 13 (5) (2021) 344, https://doi.org/10.3390/toxins13050344.
[74] S.J. Oiseth, M.S. Aziz, Cancer immunotherapy: a brief review of the history, possibilities, and challenges ahead, J. Cancer Metastatis Treat. 3 (2017) 250–261, https://doi.org/10.20517/2394-4722.2017.41.
[75] K. Esfahani, L. Roudaia, N. Buhlaiga, S.V. Del Rincon, N. Papneja, W.H. Miller, A review of cancer immunotherapy: from the past, to the present, to the future, Curr. Oncol. 27 (Suppl 2) (2020) S87–S97, https://doi.org/10.3747/co.27.5223.
[76] D. Hanahan, R.A. Weinberg, Hallmarks of cancer: the next generation, Cell 144 (5) (2011) 646–674, https://doi.org/10.1016/j.cell.2011.02.013.
[77] D. Ribatti, The concept of immune surveillance against tumors: the first theories, Oncotarget 8 (4) (2016) 7175–7180, https://doi.org/10.18632/oncotarget.12739.
[78] J.B. Swann, M.J. Smyth, Immune surveillance of tumors, J. Clin. Investig. 117 (5) (2007) 1137–1146, https://doi.org/10.1172/JCI31405.
[79] D.S. Vinay, E.P. Ryan, G. Pawelec, W.H. Talib, J. Stagg, E. Elkord, T. Lichtor, W.K. Decker, R.L. Whelan, H.M.C.S. KuArera, E. Signori, K. Honoki, A.G. Georgakilas, A. Amin, W.G. Helferich, C.S. Boosani, G. Guha, M.R. Ciriolo, S. Chen, et al., Immune evasion in cancer: mechanistic basis and therapeutic strategies, Semin. Cancer Biol. 35 (2015) S185–S198, https://doi.org/10.1016/j.semcancer.2015.03.004.
[80] R.E. Tay, E.K. Richardson, H.C. Toh, Revisiting the role of CD4+ T cells in cancer immunotherapy—new insights into old paradigms, Cancer Gene Ther. 28 (1) (2021) 5–17, https://doi.org/10.1038/s41417-020-0183-x.
[81] A. Ahmed, S.W.G. Tait, Targeting immunogenic cell death in cancer, Mol. Oncol. 14 (12) (2020) 2994–3006, https://doi.org/10.1002/1878-0261.12851.
[82] M.-Z. Jin, X.-P. Wang, Immunogenic cell death-based cancer vaccines, Front. Immunol. (2021) 12. https://www.frontiersin.org/article/10.3389/fimmu.2021.697964.
[83] K.P. Fabian, B. Wolfson, J.W. Hodge, From immunogenic cell death to immunogenic modulation: select chemotherapy regimens induce a Spectrum of immune-enhancing activities in the tumor micro-environment, Front. Oncol. 11 (2021). https://www.frontiersin.org/article/10.3389/fonc.2021.728018.
[84] I. Vanmeerbeek, J. Sprooten, D. De Ruysscher, S. Tejpar, P. Vandenberghe, J. Fucikova, R. Spisek, L. Zitvogel, G. Kroemer, L. Galluzzi, A.D. Garg, Trial watch: chemotherapy-induced immunogenic cell death in immuno-oncology, Oncoimmunology 9 (1) (2020) 1703449, https://doi.org/10.1080/2162402X.2019.1703449.
[85] J. Fucikova, O. Kepp, L. Kasikova, G. Petroni, T. Yamazaki, P. Liu, L. Zhao, R. Spisek, G. Kroemer, L. Galluzzi, Detection of immunogenic cell death and its relevance for cancer therapy, Cell Death Dis. 11 (11) (2020) 1–13, https://doi.org/10.1038/s41419-020-03221-2.
[86] X. Feng, W. Xu, Z. Li, W. Song, J. Ding, X. Chen, Immunomodulatory nanosystems, Adv. Sci. 6 (17) (2019) 1900101, https://doi.org/10.1002/advs.201900101.
[87] M. Matsushita, M. Kawaguchi, Immunomodulatory effects of drugs for effective cancer immunotherapy, J. Oncol. 2018 (2018) 8653489, https://doi.org/10.1155/2018/8653489.
[88] R. Dhanasekhar, G. Preetam, K. Ranjith, Strophanthidin attenuates MAPK, PI3K/AKT/mTOR, and Wnt/β-catenin signaling pathways in human cancers, Front. Oncol. 9 (2020) Retrieved from, https://www.frontiersin.org/articles/10.3389/fonc.2019.01469/full. (Accessed 17 March 2022).
[89] J. Du, L. Jiang, F. Chen, H. Hu, M. Zhou, Cardiac glycoside Ouabain exerts anticancer activity via downregulation of STAT3, Front. Oncol. 11 (2021). https://www.frontiersin.org/article/10.3389/fonc.2021.684316.
[90] R.S. Cavalcante, U. Ishikawa, E.S. Silva, A.A. Silva-Júnior, A.A. Araújo, L.J. Cruz, A.B. Chan, R.F. de Araújo Júnior, STAT3/NF-κB signalling disruption in M2 tumour-associated macrophages is a

major target of PLGA nanocarriers/PD-L1 antibody immunomodulatory therapy in breast cancer, Br. J. Pharmacol. 178 (11) (2021) 2284–2304, https://doi.org/10.1111/bph.15373.
[91] M.A. Shandell, A.L. Capatina, S.M. Lawrence, W.J. Brackenbury, D. Lagos, Inhibition of the Na+/K+-ATPase by cardiac glycosides suppresses expression of the IDO1 immune checkpoint in cancer cells by reducing STAT1 activation, J. Biol. Chem. 298 (3) (2022) 101707, https://doi.org/10.1016/j.jbc.2022.101707.
[92] C. Sansone, A. Bruno, C. Piscitelli, D. Baci, A. Fontana, C. Brunet, D.M. Noonan, A. Albini, Natural compounds of marine origin as inducers of immunogenic cell death (ICD): potential role for cancer interception and therapy, Cell 10 (2) (2021) 231, https://doi.org/10.3390/cells10020231.
[93] K. Balamurugan, HIF-1 at the crossroads of hypoxia, inflammation, and cancer, Int. J. Cancer 138 (5) (2016) 1058–1066, https://doi.org/10.1002/ijc.29519.
[94] J. Lin, M.A. Carducci, HIF-1α inhibition as a novel mechanism of cardiac glycosides in cancer therapeutics, Expert Opin. Investig. Drugs 18 (2) (2009) 241–243, https://doi.org/10.1517/13543780802683081.

CHAPTER 15

Systems biology tools for the identification of potential drug targets and biological markers effective for cancer therapeutics

Gayathri Ashok[a,c], P. Priyamvada[a,c], Sravan Kumar Miryala[a,c], Anand Anbarasu[a,b], and Sudha Ramaiah[a,c]

[a]Medical and Biological Computing Laboratory, School of Biosciences and Technology, Vellore Institute of Technology, Vellore, Tamil Nadu, India
[b]Department of Biotechnology, School of Biosciences and Technology, Vellore Institute of Technology, Vellore, Tamil Nadu, India
[c]Department of Bio-Sciences, School of Biosciences and Technology, Vellore Institute of Technology, Vellore, Tamil Nadu, India

Abstract

Oncogenesis involves complex network of genes and their expressed proteins that are linked to their cellular signaling changes. The cellular alterations cause selective pressure for the available drug treatments to encounter and cure cancers. There is an urgent need for new advanced approaches that should be implemented to inhibit the cancer progression by improving the methods of drug delivery and therapy. The systems biology approach using gene interaction networks is an emerging field that helps cancer biomarker discovery and novel drug target identification. When analyzed with gene ontology data, biological networks such as gene interactions and protein-protein interactions help us to understand the tumor proliferation mechanisms. Network analysis of the cancer genes plays an important role in identifying the essential regulatory genes in cancer prognosis. The regulatory genes being unique can be used for targeted therapy and precision medicine. In this chapter, we discuss about the databases and computational tools useful for interaction data curation, network construction, visualization, and analysis. Further, the chapter describes about different analyses that can be performed on the constructed gene networks, such as clustering, functional enrichment, and topological parameter analyses. Implementing a systems biology approach will assist in the identification of suitable therapeutic options for cancer treatment.

Abbreviations

BP biological processes
CA clustering analysis
CC cellular components
CNV copy number variation
CTD comparative toxicogenomic database
DDGI drug-drug-gene interactions
DGI drug-gene interactions
EPC edge percolated component

Computational Methods in Drug Discovery and Repurposing for Cancer Therapy
https://doi.org/10.1016/B978-0-443-15280-1.00015-7

FEA	functional enrichment analysis
GCN	gene co-expression network
GIN	gene interaction network
GO	gene ontology
GRN	gene regulatory networks
HCA	hierarchical clustering
MCC	maximal clique centrality
MCODE	molecular complex detection
MF	molecular functions
MNC	maximum neighborhood component
NCBI	national center for biotechnology information
PPI	protein-protein interactions
SNA	social network analysis
STN	signal transduction networks
TSG	tumor suppressor genes

1. Introduction

Cancer is a major public health condition where the cells proliferate abnormally, giving rise to an abnormal mass of tissue. Cancer can be differentiated into benign and malignant based on cell growth and the mode of transmission within the body. Benign tumors are the initial stage of cancer where cells grow slowly and do not spread whereas, in malignant tumors the cells grow rapidly, invade and destroy the nearby cells, and even spread to other parts of the body [1]. The transformation of normal cells to tumor cells might be because of different reasons such as oncogenic mutations, exposure to various kinds of carcinogens, and hereditary factors. Oncogenic mutations derange the cellular signaling systems responsible for influencing the fate of the cells [2]. Because tumor cells follow various kinds of hallmarks for their survival inside the body, it becomes necessary for researchers to focus on different aspects of cancer. For years, discoveries related to genetic alterations in cancer have been a major focus, leading to a significant degree of improvement in the detection of different cancer [3]. Various aspects of cancer are being investigated vigorously to improve the current treatment strategies to provide early detection. With advancements in medicine, specific strategies like hormonal therapy and targeted therapy have shown to be better treatment options when compared with chemo and radiation therapies, as the former offers lesser side effects.

Because the genetic alteration associated with cancer is not just limited to any one gene/protein, but rather to the signaling cascade of reactions, it is more appropriate to use the application of systems biology to study cancer. It is also important for the oncologist to focus on a gene or protein of interest rather than on the entire set of possible genes, as conventional knockout studies on cancer-responsible genes are time-consuming and not feasible. The amalgamation of biological networks with the incorporation of enriched gene ontology (GO) terms provides clinicians a clear idea on where to focus specifically whereas designing therapeutic strategies [4]. In this chapter, we will be discussing in detail the different tools available for the construction and analysis of gene interaction networks (GIN) to identify novel drug targets in cancer.

2. Current problems in cancer therapies

Designing any treatment option will depend on the different stages and the type of cancer. The treatment can be of primary type where the major goal is to kill all the cancer cells, whereas the adjuvant treatment kills those tumor cells that remain after the primary treatment. Traditional anticancer therapies include chemotherapy, radiotherapy, surgery, and bone marrow transplant, although immunotherapy, hormone therapy, cryotherapy, and targeted drug therapy are still emerging [5]. Surgery as a mode of treatment is effective against solid tumors but ineffective against conditions like leukemia, where the tumors are mass of white blood cells circulating in the blood. Chemotherapy involves the intravenous injection of chemotherapeutic drugs. Even though this treatment is most commonly used, the treatment options produce severe side effects such as hair loss, nausea, fatigue, constipation, as the drug is distributed through the blood and may result in the death of normal cells in addition to cancer cells. Another major disadvantage of chemotherapy is the chemo-resistance property developed by tumor cells leading to the reduction in the effectiveness of the treatment [6].

3. Need for alternative approaches in cancer

The need for alternative treatment options for cancer is important as the tumor cells easily adapt to the cellular environment making it difficult for early detection. The cells also alter and thus develop resistance, which hinders the efficiency of existing therapies. Therefore, researchers have designed targeted drug therapy where particular drug targets for a defined cancer are identified [7]. For the successful designing and execution of targeted drug therapy, it is essential to analyze the cancer types in detail. These analyses are needed to identify the differentially expressed genes and their enriched pathways responsible for the proliferation, invasion, and metastasis in cancer condition.

4. GIN: A systems biology approach

Systems biology is a computational approach aimed at modeling molecular systems and integrating huge metadata, reflecting a new aspect of cancer. The approach focuses on the biological interaction of biomolecules like genes or proteins at the systems level to decipher new insights [8]. Advancements in functional genomics have enabled easy characterization of molecular constituents of life as it fills the gap between the biological molecules and their physiology [9].

Systems biology can be categorized into two namely, data-driven and model-driven. The former deals with data mining to find patterns from large datasets, whereas the latter is based on models. The models include a network of biological entities like genes, proteins, small molecules, and the integration of already existing knowledge to understand cancer. The incorporation of pathway data and GO data will further help to understand the network models. Another aspect of systems biology is examining the level of proteins and nucleic acids (DNA/RNA), including the posttranslational modifications to understand the effect of these changes inside the biological system [10].

GINs are genetic interactions between two genes that are not physical, unlike the protein-protein interactions. The significant findings from GIN indicate a similar functional relationship between the interacting genes, which can be either biological processes or pathways. A set of genes involved in the network are represented as nodes, and the interaction between them are termed as edges. Because the genes code for proteins and the expressed protein interactions regulate the major biological processes required for cell proliferation, it is important to analyze the major processes using interactions of biological entities. Analyzing these protein interactions will help to understand the complex biological processes of the protein function and identify novel drug targets for different cancer [11–20].

Although analyzing networks, the use of functionally enriched GO terms aids in the identification of enriched processes, functions, and cellular components allowing researchers to concentrate on a specific biological function. The biological networks are used to identify drug targets by focusing on the topological parameters of the network. Different characteristics show the role of the nodes, indicating their biological importance in the network. A detailed schematic representation of GIN construction and analyses along with the tools and databases has been depicted in Fig. 1.

5. Types of biological networks

There are different types of biological networks constructed depending on the biological entity to be analyzed, such as GIN for genes, protein-protein interaction (PPI) for proteins, gene regulatory networks (GRN) for (miRNA-gene, TF-gene, miRNA-gene-TFs), and lncRNA interactions for long noncoding RNAs. Other kinds of the network include evolutionary networks, biochemical interaction networks, gene co-expression networks (GCNs), metabolic networks, drug-gene interaction (DGI) networks, and neural networks.

5.1 Protein-protein interaction (PPI) networks

PPI network provides a valuable structure for an easier and better understanding of the functional aspects of the proteome. The networks are essentially helpful for cancer research as identifying the hub proteins with their functional nature helps to understand the mechanism of tumor progression. The major takeaways from an interaction network

Fig. 1 Schematic representation depicting the identification of cancer drug targets and biomarker discovery using Gene Interaction Network (GIN).

are to figure out how the hub proteins are connected in a network, how strong their interactions are with other known cancer genes or proteins, and how the tumor progresses with the knockout of the particular hub protein. The approach also helps in saving time by focusing on a more significant cluster of nodes than those with no direct or indirect function in cancer progression [21,22].

5.2 GCN

GCNs are networks in which the nodes represent the genes and are connected only whether the genes involved are significantly co-expressed across tissues. The principle behind GCN is the network usage to describe the pairwise relationships between the nodes. It is also used to associate genes with unknown functions to the biological processes of known genes. The advances in GCN have allowed the identification of regulatory genes of respective phenotypes. GCN can be constructed using RNA-seq or microarray data for both signed and unsigned networks. Further clustering and functional enrichment analysis of the co-expressed clusters can be used to identify cancer biomarkers [23,24].

5.3 GRNs

GRN represent the developmental processes starting from cell differentiation to cell cycle and signal transduction. Regulatory elements like transcription factors (TFs) modulate the expression of genes in the system and thus holds the key role in designing cancer networks. Networks showing the interactions of the cancer hub genes with the TFs helps in evaluating the role of the hub genes, thereby determining their significance. GRN help in deciphering the mechanism of how the TFs modulate the expression of the target gene. The complexities are when the target gene is modulated by more than one TFs [25,26].

5.4 Metabolic networks

Cancer cells follow deregulated metabolism allowing them to survive inside the body. The deregulated metabolism leads to an increase in cancer metabolites. Metabolic networks are pathways consisting of biochemical reactions which lead to the synthesis of compounds required for cellular functioning. Metabolic networks are used in cancer to detect specific patterns that can better understand tumor proliferation. The ultimate aim of metabolic network analysis is to discover novel drug targets as well as to design new systems-based therapies [27,28].

5.5 Signal transduction networks (STNs)

STNs regulate the fundamental biological processes that help the cells to adjust the changing environmental cues by external and internal signals. These signaling is carried out by small sets of networks which are often affected in cancers because of genetic mutations. These mutations drastically lead to intrinsic epigenetic changes, which affect drug treatments. Computational modeling is a potent tool for analyzing STNs and their alterations to study the effects in cancer therapeutics [29].

5.6 Drug-gene interaction network (DGI)

DGI networks using the systems biology approach is a promising strategy that uses PPI networks to map and predict drug-drug interactions. The network consists of drugs, target genes, or side effects as nodes and the interactions representing the edges. DGI shows the association of a drug and a genetic variant and reflects the patient's response to the drug treatment. Drug-drug-gene interactions (DDGI) are constructed to identify the inhibitory, induction, and phenoconversion interactions. The inhibitory and induction interaction refers to the effect of drug pharmacokinetics to increase or decrease the drug concentrations respectively. DGI networks hold a key role in drug repurposing as they help prove the drug's effectiveness against the target gene, making it less complicated whereas designing cancer therapeutics [30–32].

6. Cancer databases

Biological databases are organized bodies for collecting specific genes and proteins related information. The data are easily accessible to the researchers and help to remove the redundancy of data. Various databases have been dedicated to different cancer types and can be categorized into comprehensive cancer databases, specific cancer databases, and microbial databases for host-pathogen interaction. Different databases categorized under these broad categories have been discussed below in detail.

6.1 Comprehensive tumor database

6.1.1 The Cancer genome atlas (TCGA)

TCGA is a publicly available database (http://tcga.github.io/Roadmap/) that generates and analyses many genomic sequences, expression, methylation, copy number variation (CNV) of over 33 different types of cancer. This has a high source of knowledge about cancer genetics, epigenetics profile, biomarkers, and drug targets. Also, the database has information for exome and genome sequencing analysis, providing genome number change, gene expression profiles, and miRNAs [33].

6.1.2 cBioPortal

cBioPortal (http://cbioportal.org/) is an open-access resource with multidimensional cancer genomics data. It collects nonsynonymous mutation, DNA copy number, methylation, mRNA, miRNA, protein-level, and phosphoprotein level data. Few germline mutations are also reported in cBioPortal. It is currently having more than 20 cancer studies and 5000 tumor samples. The query interface helps to explore the genetic alteration across genes and pathways. In addition, it provides graphical summaries of gene-level data, network visualization, and analyses. cBioPortal has an intuitive web interface that helps the researcher and the clinician facilitate the biological discoveries without any need for bioinformatics knowledge [34].

6.1.3 Catalog of somatic mutation in cancer (COSMIC)

The latest COSMIC v95 (https://cancer.sanger.ac.uk/cosmic) contains all the mechanisms promoting cancer through somatic mutations, noncoding mutations, CNVs, and drug resistance mutation. The information accommodated is based on base substitution, insertion, deletion, and translocation. Current version encompasses 15,984,979 genomic noncoding variants out of 23,393,188 total genomic variants. In addition, COSMIC-3D is a new tool that explores mutation in three-dimensional protein structure and their protein functional impacts (in-frame deletion and protein missense mutation), an implication for drugability [35].

6.1.4 International cancer genome consortium (ICGC)

ICGC (https://www.icgc.org/) integrates TCGA and Sanger cancer genome project data and characterizes the genomic abnormalities in more than 50 different types of cancer. This database uses a graphical user interface for quick and easy search and analysis of the available data. Data mainly includes single nucleotide mutation, somatic mutation, structural rearrangement, copy number alterations, gene expression, DNA methylation, miRNA, and exon junction [36].

6.1.5 Cancer genome project (CGP)

CGP helps to identify the somatic mutation and the genes involved in oncogenesis. CGP has data collected for both primary cancer and cancer cell lines. This database helps the researcher to discover therapeutic biomarkers using bioinformatic tools, helping in differentiating the drug-sensitive biomarkers from the inhibitor biomarkers. Accordingly, we can make personalized medicine for cancer patients. The database also has information on the epigenetic changes in the genome, where there is no specific gene mutation even whether there is a change in the gene function at the molecular level [37].

6.1.6 DriverDBv3

DriverDB database (http://ngs.ym.edu.tw/driverdb) incorporates somatic mutation, RNA expression, miRNA expression, methylation, and CNVs. It uses bioinformatics algorithms to identify the gene mutation drivers and incorporates computational tools to define the CNV and methylation drivers. The database also helps to explore the relationship between cancer and associated genes using survival analysis. It seeks to improve the study of integrative cancer omics datasets [38].

6.1.7 Human cancer proteome variation database (CanProVar 2.0)

CanProVar database (http://canprovar2.zhang-lab.org/) has entries for single amino acid change in human cancer. The query section can be protein IDs, cancer types, chromosome location, or pathway involved. CanProVar addresses the genomic alteration at the protein level. It also includes the functional data that potentially influence cancer-related variants on 3D protein interaction and the differential expression between cancer and the normal cells [39].

6.1.8 Network of cancer genes (NCG)

NCG (http://ncg.kcl.ac.uk/index.php) is a manually collected database for cancer genes and healthy drivers. This database has a collection of altered genes that drive cancer. Presently there are 591 canonical cancer drivers and 2756 candidate cancer drivers. This covers over 127 cancer types providing information like gene expression, protein expression, functional properties, orthology, drug target/biomarker, and evolutionally appearance [40].

6.2 Databases for specific cancer

6.2.1 HColonDB

HColonDB database has information related to drugs collected from Drug Bank and PubChem database for colorectal cancer. The relationship between genes and pathway networks are obtained from KEGG database. It has a collection of 81 genes, 112 pathways, 108 networks, and 15 drugs associated with colon cancer. There are 322 gene and pathway associations, 242 gene-network associations and 68 network-pathway associations [41].

6.2.2 Pancreatic cancer database (PCD)

PCD is a resource (http://www.pancreaticcancerdatabase.org) for manually curated molecular alteration in mRNA (8489), protein (2882), and miRNA (744). Individual entries are also linked to HPRD, OMIM, HGNC, and miRBase. It was developed using PHP (http://www.php.net/) as an application server, and for the storage it uses MySQL (http://www.mysql.com/). The query includes gene symbol, cancer/disease types, protein name, cell line, molecular alteration, and experimental methods. They address molecules based on their level of gene expression (upregulated or downregulated). The genes are reported to be differentially expressed, whether the gene expression represented using fold change is more than two in the pancreatic cell when compared with the normal cell. This helps in investigating biomarkers and prognostic factors specifically for pancreatic cancer [42].

6.2.3 Pancreatic expression database (PED)

PED (https://pancreasexpression.org/) is a resource for mining omics data (transcriptomics, proteomics, and genomics) for pancreatic cancer. It derives data from repositories like GEO, ArrayExpress, TCGA, CCLE, and GENIE. The database helps in the discovery of potent noninvasive biomarkers and the identification of the passenger deleted gene for the therapeutics. This gives additional benefits to the researcher to quickly search for the homozygous co-deleted genes present proximal to the tumor suppressor gene (TSG) and their paralogous isoforms. The analytical model of PED helps to point out the potential candidates for cancer therapeutics [43].

6.2.4 Cervical cancer database (CCDB)

CCDB (http://crdd.osdd.net/raghava/ccdb) has a collection of a manually curated genes, contributing to the etiology and pathogenesis at different stages of cervical cancer. It contains all the gene sequence and the protein sequence information, assigned with an accession number. Other information like-chromosomal position, size, architecture, GO, and homology with other eukaryotic genomes is also mentioned. A total of 537 genes has been recorded that are further classified based on GO—cellular component, molecular function, and biological process. In addition, the database also provides information for miRNA altered in cervical cancer. CCDB also facilitates the information about the TSGs found hypermethylated in cervical cancer. It also provides extensive cross-references to other websites such as Unigene, HPRD, HGNC, Ensemble, and OMIM that are supplementing the CCDB-specific data [44].

6.2.5 Gene-to-systems breast cancer database (G2SBC)

G2SBC (http://www.itb.cnr.it/breastcancer/) is a database that has more than 2000 human genes associated with breast cancer. It collects data about genes, proteins, transcripts, molecular networks, and cell populations that are being altered in breast cancer. This alteration may be because of mutation at the level of gene or expression variation of the protein or the transcripts. This has been coupled with some of the analysis tools concerning cellular, biochemical pathways, protein-protein physical interaction, and protein structure [45].

6.2.6 Human lung cancer database (HLungDB)

HLungDB (https://www.hsls.pitt.edu/) is a comprehensive resource of gene information and its relationships to lung cancer. This integrates lung cancer-related genes, gene promoters, TFs binding sites, proteins, SNPs, and miRNA. It has a collection of 2585 genes and 212 lung cancer-related miRNA. The database also incorporates the results from analyses of TFs-binding motifs, SNP sites, and each gene's promoter. Epigenetic changes have a role in lung cancer, so genes with epigenetic regulation have also been included [46].

6.2.7 Renal cancer gene database (RCDB)

RCDB (https://www.juit.ac.in/attachments/jsr/rcdb/homenew.html) is a repository for the coding and noncoding genes that contribute to the etiology and pathogenesis of renal cancer. This manually curated database has more than 240 protein-coding and 269 miRNA gene information contributing to renal cell carcinoma. It also collects miRNAs that are dysregulated in renal cell carcinoma. They have classified protein-coding genes into six categories—methylation silencing, overexpressed, downregulated, mutation, translocation, and unclassified that are responsible for renal cancer [47].

6.3 Microbial databases for host-pathogen interaction

In this postgenomic era, the systems biology approach helps to decipher the host-pathogen interaction network and predict the biomarkers [48]. Further study would help to identify the potent targets and to consider them for therapeutic approach to eliminate or reduce the severity of the disease. Various databases with host and pathogen-related data help to identify the gene-gene and protein-proteins interactions. Host-pathogen interactions are essential in cancer as various pathogens are associated with cancer that induce and proliferate the tumor cells. In terms of understanding infectious mechanisms, a systems biology approach of the entire PHI system is superior to looking at the pathogen or host separately [49]. The features of the host factors targeted by pathogens are especially important for the identification of host-oriented pharmacological targets for next-generation antiinfectious treatments. For easy access of the information, some of the host-pathogen interaction databases have been discussed below:

6.3.1 Host-pathogen interaction database (HPIDB 3.0)

The HPIDB 3.0 database (https://hpidb.igbb.msstate.edu/) helps to identify and analyze critical host-pathogen interactions for developing novel drug targets. Manually curated data from this database can be used for network analysis and improve the accuracy for predicting the targets by computational study. HPIDB's latest release contains 69,787 unique protein interactions reported in between 66 host and 668 pathogens. HPIDB is also a biocurator for host-host, pathogen-pathogen interaction from literature. It also collects GO functional information [50].

6.3.2 VirHostNet

VirHostNet is a database (https://virhostnet.prabi.fr/) for virus and host protein interaction based on a network formed. The interface is based on the Cytoscape web library to study the interaction networks between virus-virus, virus-host, and host-host PPI. It facilitates a systems biology approach to identify new molecular drug targets that help in drug designing. This integrates an extensive and original literature curated dataset of virus-virus and virus-host interactions. It has an interface that provides appropriate tools for allowing the query to search and visualize the cellular networks [51,52].

6.3.3 VirusMentha

VirusMentha (https://virusmentha.uniroma2.it/) is an archive for collecting all viral interactions in a comprehensive way. The data are manually curated from the PPI database and the database also provides various tools for analyzing selected proteins in the context of network interactions. An interactome study is important for antiviral drugs to understand the interaction between the viral host protein. The query for search has broad range from UniProt IDS, polypeptide names, gene names, keywords, to PMID. The interface of VirusMentha gives an option to restrict the search to a specific organism or viral families [53].

6.3.4 Hepatitis C virus protein interaction database (HCVpro)

HCVpro is a comprehensive database (https://www.cbrc.kaust.edu.sa/hcvpro/) for the HCV protein interactions. The data are manually curated from the literature and from databases and compiled in HCVpro comprising HCV and host human cellular proteins. Query section can be protein identifiers or chromosomal location. It provides information about the interactions and enriches the data on functional annotations, hepatocellular carcinoma-related gene expression, molecular data, drug development, GO, and biological pathways. The data information inferred can help in drug discovery, prediction of potent drug targets, and diagnostic biomarkers [54].

6.3.5 Pathogen-host interaction search tool (PHISTO)

PHISTO database (https://phisto.org/) has all data and relevant information for pathogen-host protein interaction. It enables a user-friendly interface to access the PHI protein data that is experimentally verified. This also has integrated tools for network visualization graph analysis. PHISTO facilitates studies that provide therapeutic drug targets for infectious disease. There are around 23,661 PHIs between humans and 300 strains of different pathogens. This database can help to study the various mechanisms behind the diseases caused by different pathogens [55].

7. Databases for interaction data curation

Interaction databases are comprehensive databases that store and manage the various interactions between biological entities. The interactions can range from direct physical interaction demonstrated by experimental methods to predicted interactions. Various interaction databases ranging from gene-gene, and gene-protein interactions are available. The PPIs have risen dramatically creating a variety of public database to disseminate the information. These database help in making use of genetic data to determine a structural or evolutionary link between protein pairs, or to anticipate novel interactions based on previously observed interactions [56,57].

7.1 Gene interaction databases

Databases for gene interaction provide access to unified sets of data for gene and protein interaction for the inquisitions of their function and analysis of network properties. These databases are freely available and provide physical and genetic interaction. The datasets are downloadable in text files and PSI-MI XML format. Different gene interaction databases include BioGRID and GeneMANIA that has been discussed in detail.

7.1.1 BioGRID

BioGRID is a repository database (https://thebiogrid.org/) for genetic, protein, chemical interactions, and posttranslational modification (PTM) data. Latest version 4.4 contains information for 2,306,028 protein and genetic interactions curated from 78,593 publications. There are 29,417 chemical interactions and 1,128,339 PTMs from most model organisms. The data are freely available and downloadable that can be incorporated into various applications available. An advantage is that it can annotate a genome-wide CRISPR/Cas9-based screen that reports the gene-phenotype and gene-gene relationships [58,59].

7.1.2 GeneMANIA

GeneMANIA (https://genemania.org/) generates hypotheses regarding gene function that prioritizes the gene for functional assays. It extends the query list with similar functional genes available via genomics or proteomics data. Datasets available in this are collected from the different databases such as GEO, BioGRID, IntAct, MINT, and Reactome. A genetic screen with phenotypic readout is performed using GeneMANIA. It helps in finding the genes related to a set of input genes. GeneMANIA represents a multiple association network integration algorithm with two parts—(i) linear regression algorithm—calculating the functional association between multiple data. (ii) propagation algorithm—predict the gene function from the functional association network. GeneMANIA currently has 2830 associated networks and 660,554,667 interactions mapped to 166,691 genes from nine model organisms. The prediction of gene function made by GeneMANIA is highly accurate as it removes the weak correlation between the interactions [60].

7.2 Protein-protein interaction databases

The databases collect data for PPIs, for multiple organisms. They collect datasets independently and provide nonredundant set of PPI data in standard file formats. These databases maintain interactions between multiple proteins and organisms that implement an internal data management system that have access to interaction datasets. Here, we discuss about STRING, MINT and IntAct.

7.2.1 Search tool for the retrieval of interacting genes (STRING)

STRING is a database (https://string-db.org/) for predicting the PPIs. The interactions can be direct interaction or indirect interaction, associated with physical and functional properties. Interaction is derived from different sources such as genomic context prediction, experimental lab data, co-expression, text mining, and previous knowledge in databases. It has currently 67,592,464 proteins from 14,094 organisms and 20,052,394,042 interactions. The interactions are scored and integrated into a final combined score scaled between zero and one, contributing to the evidence. It doesn't differentiate between splicing variant or posttranslationally modified proteins, isoforms, and represents a single canonical protein. STRING allows users to characterize their gene lists and functional genomics information in-depth to create and share highly personalized and augmented protein-protein connection networks [61].

7.2.2 Molecular interaction database (MINT)

MINT is a molecular interaction database (https://mint.bio.uniroma2.it/) that stores data based on the functional interaction between different proteins and enzymatic modification. Here, both direct and indirect interactions are considered, including information about the kinetic and binding constants and domains participating in the interaction. There are approximately more than 2,35,000 interactions collected from 5000 publications. It has interactions between proteins from more than 30 species such as *Homo sapiens*, *Mus musculus*, *Drosophila melanogaster*, and *Saccharomyces cerevisiae*. MINT also integrates the HomoMINT database of interactions between human proteins [62].

7.2.3 IntAct

IntAct (https://www.ebi.ac.uk/intact/home) is a free, open data source for molecular interaction. It has currently 1,155,201 interactions and 118,213 interactors. It is capable of curation at both IMEx and MIMIx-levels. The web interface allows the user to retrieve the interaction in XML format, providing both textual and graphical representation of protein interactions and exploring the networks based on GO of the interacting proteins. The binary view displays all the interacting partners and indicates the potential roles of the uncharacterized proteins [63].

8. Network construction and visualization

Once the interaction data are curated, there is a need to construct a network. For this purpose, various tools and software are developed to enable users to construct various networks. The visualization software helps in representing the constructed network in a specific manner, where the users can depict specifically the biological entity of interest and represent the network accordingly. The commonly used visualization software's are mentioned briefly and listed in Table 1.

Table 1 List of visualization tools with their features and references are provided below.

Sl. No.	Tools	Link/Reference
1.	Cytoscape	https://cytoscape.org/
2.	Gephi	https://gephi.org/
3.	Medusa	https://sites.google.com/site/medusa3visualization/
4.	BioLayout Express^{3D}	http://biolayout.org/
5.	GeNeCK	http://lce.biohpc.swmed.edu/geneck

8.1 Cytoscape

Cytoscape is a user-friendly and freely accessible software used as a standard tool for the integrated visualization and analysis of networks. It allows for the construction and visualization of biological entities such as genes, proteins, small metabolites represented as nodes, and the interaction between them represented using edges. Cytoscape has the provision of importing datasets such as gene expression or methylation, which can be incorporated to yield a better network and to show different aspects in addition to the existing network data. The software is a better candidate for a large input dataset as it provides a better layout option for the network. Another advantage of this software is the different plugins associated with it, which helps to incorporate other analyses such as functional enrichment analysis, pathway analysis, and GO analysis. The amalgamation of such a network gives a better outlook for further analysis. The software provides the option of downloading high-quality figure, which can be used for publishing as shown in Fig. 2 [64–66].

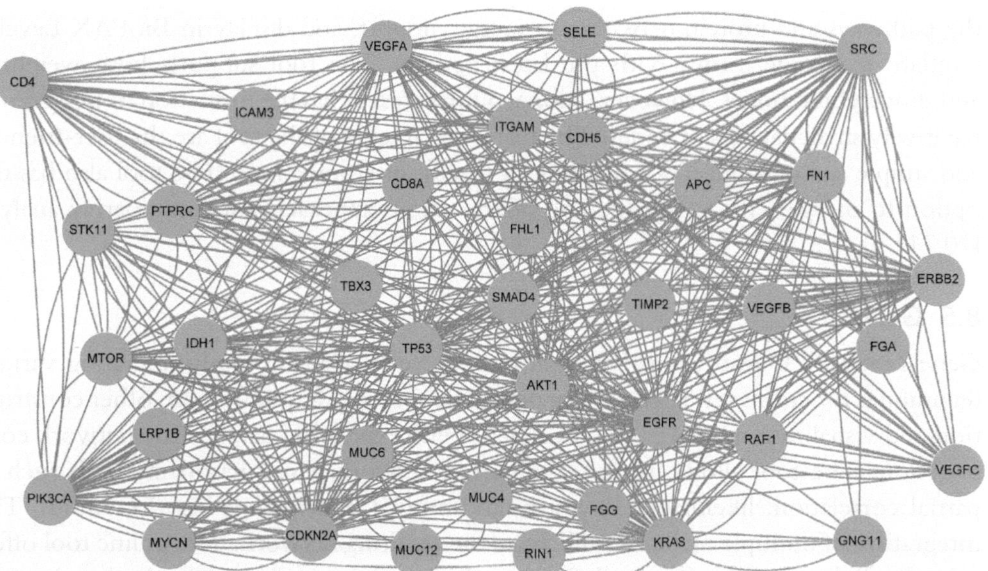

Fig. 2 Network construction and visualization using Cytoscape 3.8.2. The *green color* nodes are genes, and their interaction is represented using *gray edges*.

8.2 Gephi

Open graph visualization platform, Gephi is a freely available and easily accessible network analysis tool for all kinds of networks. Additional layouts plugins such as GeoLayout, NoverlapLayout, and Multimode Networks Transformation are incorporated in Gephi. The tool runs on Windows, Mac OS X, and Linux. The tool gives the advantage of handling large datasets with 100,000 nodes. Topological parameters such as degree and other centrality parameters are calculated, but the tool focuses more on visualization than analysis [67].

8.3 Medusa

Medusa is an open-source Java application based on the Fruchterman-Reingold algorithm, which provides a two-dimensional network representation of nodes. The tool is better suited for small datasets carrying medium-size nodes and edges. The open tool signifies the importance of the interaction by the varying thickness in the edges between the nodes and supports weighted graphs. It is best suited for multidimensional edge interactions with different edges reflecting different information. The tool is compatible with its text file format and is not compatible with other tool formats or data sources. The tool also supports expression-based studies, and the network can be saved to be reloaded anytime [68,69].

8.4 BioLayout Express^{3D}

The network analysis tool BioLayout^{3D} is designed to visualize and analyze biological data, especially those based on gene expression or pathway analysis. The tool allows the pathways and protein networks to merge, import, and display in BioPAX Level 3 standard exchange format with the latest updates. The tool supports both weighted and unweighted nodes. However, BioLayout Express^{3D} has the limitation of using comparatively small datasets of nodes. The major advantages of the tool are the user-friendly and simple use of input files consisting of the list of connections. The tool also has the option to merge with Cytoscape and offers various approaches for microarray analysis [70,71].

8.5 GeNeCK

Gene Network Construction Kit is an online, freely available tool integrating various techniques for constructing gene networks. The tool stands unique from other construction and visualization tools as GeNeCK uses gene expression data for the network construction. The tool allows using ten different network construction methods such as partial correlation, likelihood, Bayesian, and mutual information-based methods. The integration of multiple methods will create the resulting network. The online tool offers more flexibility for selecting the defined method, and the results will be displayed on the website once the job is done. The current version of the tool has the disadvantage of unable to download the network diagram whereas it allows the user to take screenshots of the result page. To further improve the biological network, the users are given the option of adding hub gene information [72].

9. Network analysis

Relationships between the biological nodes need to be analyzed accurately to yield meaningful biological insights. Network analysis is more powerful and provides an alternative to conventional enrichment analysis. The approach is less biased and gives greater coverage to known genes and proteins. The networks can be analyzed by clustering and topological analysis, where topological analysis constructs the graph depending on the different network parameters. In contrast, the clustering analysis constructs graphs depending on the nodes' similar functionality [73]. The commonly used tools (Table 2) for the analyses are given below:

9.1 Clustering analysis

Clustering analysis (CA) is a method to group a similar set of observations, in this scenario, a set of genes or proteins into a number of clusters. CA in biological networks provides valuable insights in understanding biological systems with complex nature. CA on the PPI network help in identifying stable complexes and is important because it provides functional annotations of subunit clusters that generally follow the same biological process.

A few popular kinds of CA are hierarchical clustering (HCA) and K Means clustering. HCA is a statistical method of identifying groups containing samples having more or less similar characteristics and using the similarity to quantify the structural characteristics of the samples. HCA structure the data using a dendrogram with the leaf corresponding to the clustered nodes and the branches conveying the clusters' relationship. K Means clustering is an iterative clustering that identifies the local maxima in each iteration. CA can produce a dendrogram with heatmap by incorporating expression levels, producing large molecular complexes, and identifying similar groups of proteins for classification [74]. Common tools used for CA are described below.

9.1.1 clusterMaker

clusterMaker is a freely available plugin in Cytoscape routinely used for CA, using nearly all clustering algorithms such as MCODE, community clustering, and hierarchical clustering. The algorithm is categorized into two namely, network clustering and attribute clustering. Network clustering is mainly used to identify protein-protein complexes from the network, whereas attribute clustering groups the nodes with similar node attributes [75].

Table 2 List of tools used for Clustering analysis, Functional enrichment analysis, Topological parameter analysis, and Hub gene identification are listed below with the features and reference.

Sl. No.	Tools	Link/Reference
Clustering Analysis Tools		
1.	clusterMaker	https://apps.cytoscape.org/apps/clustermaker2
2.	MCODE	https://apps.cytoscape.org/apps/mcode
3.	ClusterViz	https://apps.cytoscape.org/apps/clusterviz
Functional Enrichment Analysis Tools		
1.	DAVID	https://david.ncifcrf.gov/home.jsp
2.	FunRich	http://www.funrich.org
3.	BiNGO	https://www.psb.ugent.be/cbd/papers/BiNGO/Home.html
4.	GeneWeaver	https://www.geneweaver.org/
5.	GeneCodis3	https://genecodis.genyo.es/
Topological Parameter Analysis, and Hub Gene Identification Tools		
1.	Network Analysis Tool (NEAT)	http://rsat.sb-roscoff.fr/index_neat.html
2.	NetworkAnalyzer	http://med.bioinf.mpi-inf.mpg.de/networkanalyzer/
3.	CytoNCA	http://apps.cytoscape.org/apps/cytonca
4.	The Network Analysis Profiler (NAP)	http://bioinformatics.med.uoc.gr/NAP
5.	CentiScape	http://chianti.ucsd.edu/cyto_web/plugins/index.php
6.	cytoHubba	http://apps.cytoscape.org/apps/cytohubba
7.	Contextual Hub Analysis Tool (CHAT)	http://apps.cytoscape.org/apps/chat
8.	CyNetSVM	https://apps.cytoscape.org/apps/cynetsvm

9.1.2 MCODE

Molecular complex detection is a freely available plugin of Cytoscape used for CA using the molecular complex detection algorithm. The algorithm detects densely connected complexes from large PPI networks representing the molecular complexes. The algorithm focuses on vertex weighting using local neighborhood density and outward transversal. A major advantage of MCODE is it is not affected by false positives. It allows easy visualization of large networks and highlights the regions of importance as depicted in Fig. 3 [76].

9.1.3 ClusterViz

ClusterViz is another Cytoscape plugin for CA that works on three modules—the interface, algorithms, and visualization. The tool allows for the comparison of the obtained

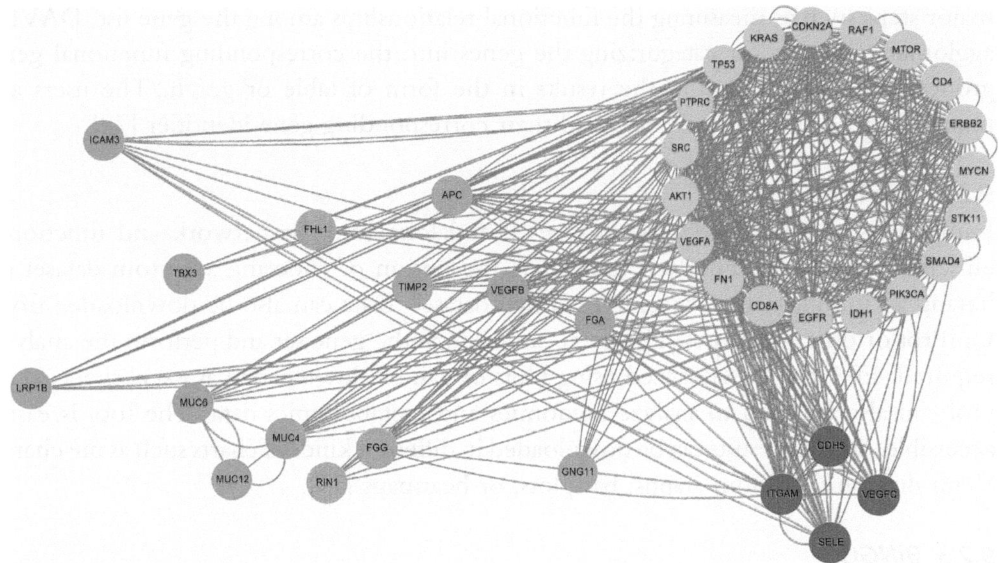

Fig. 3 Clustering analysis using MCODE. Network constructed using Cytoscape 3.8.2 was subjected to clustering analysis to yield clusters. Cluster 1 is represented in *green color*, and cluster 2 is represented in *violet color*.

results with other algorithms. The commonly included algorithms are MCODE, EAGLE, and FAG-EC. Because of the interface of ClusterViz, the plugin provides users with a easy and user-friendly approach for CA [77].

9.2 Functional enrichment analysis (FEA)

High-throughput data derive a huge amount of biological data that requires a proper pipeline to decode and obtain meaningful information. Huge efforts are required to functionally annotate every gene, associate the genes to their particular biological processes or the pathways they are involved in, to remove redundant data, and to view the interrelationships shared by the group of genes. For this purpose, a number of tools are developed that helps in facilitating the above-mentioned points. Functionally enriched terms can be classified into three GO terms, namely, biological process (BP), molecular functions (MF), and cellular components (CC). The analysis is critical in drug target and biomarker discovery as the hub genes identified using the network and clustering analyses can be ascertained for further validation using the GO terms. The commonly used tools for FEA are mentioned below:

9.2.1 The database for annotation, visualization, and integrated discovery (DAVID)

DAVID tool provides a module-centric FEA. The tool, in combination with DAVID functional annotation clustering tool, is developed using Java and functions in three major steps such as measuring the functional relationships among the gene list, DAVID agglomeration step for categorizing the genes into the corresponding functional gene groups, and visualization of the results in the form of table or graph. The users are required to paste the list of genes and their corresponding gene identifier [78].

9.2.2 FunRich

FunRich is a user-friendly, open-access standalone tool for network and functional enrichment analyses. FunRich tool offers the option of choosing a custom dataset or having an inbuilt human-specific FunRich dataset. Data can also be downloaded from UniProt or other databases. The users can provide the gene set and perform the analysis required. FEA can be visualized using plots or can be downloaded as excel sheets. The tool can also be used to analyze lipidomics and metabolomics data. The tool is easily accessible, and the results can be downloaded in different kinds of charts such as pie charts, Venn diagrams, column graphs, bar plots, or heatmaps [79].

9.2.3 BiNGO

The biological networks GO tool is a Cytoscape plugin that is freely downloadable from the app manager. The platform actively assesses the overrepresentation of GO terms in a biological network. A major advantage of BiNGO over other tools is the use of interactions integrated with the functionally enriched pathways. The tool offers flexibility in terms of annotations. The tool provides data for various organisms with default annotations available from NCBI and accepts various identifiers. The functional enrichment in the form of the network can later be saved in different ways. The result will be represented in colored gradient nodes, with the most intensely colored node being the more relevant one (Fig. 4) [80].

9.2.4 GeneWeaver

The freely available tool, GeneWeaver, is a web-based application presented by the ontological discovery environment. The tool is a curated repository for experimental genomic data, enabling users to identify the nature of the biological functions of a given gene. The tool contains data covering 80,000 genes from seven different species. Along with the gene's curated biological relationships and functional nature, the tool also integrates data from various databases such as comparative toxicogenomics databases, GeneNetwork, and other drug-related databases. GeneWeaver uses gene set similarity clustering for confining the large datasets into hierarchical clusters; this allows identifying the dissimilar group of genes/proteins from the input set [81].

9.2.5 GeneCodis3

GeneCodis3 is a valuable web-based tool that combines the data from different sources to identify the group of genes with similar biological function, process, or component. With

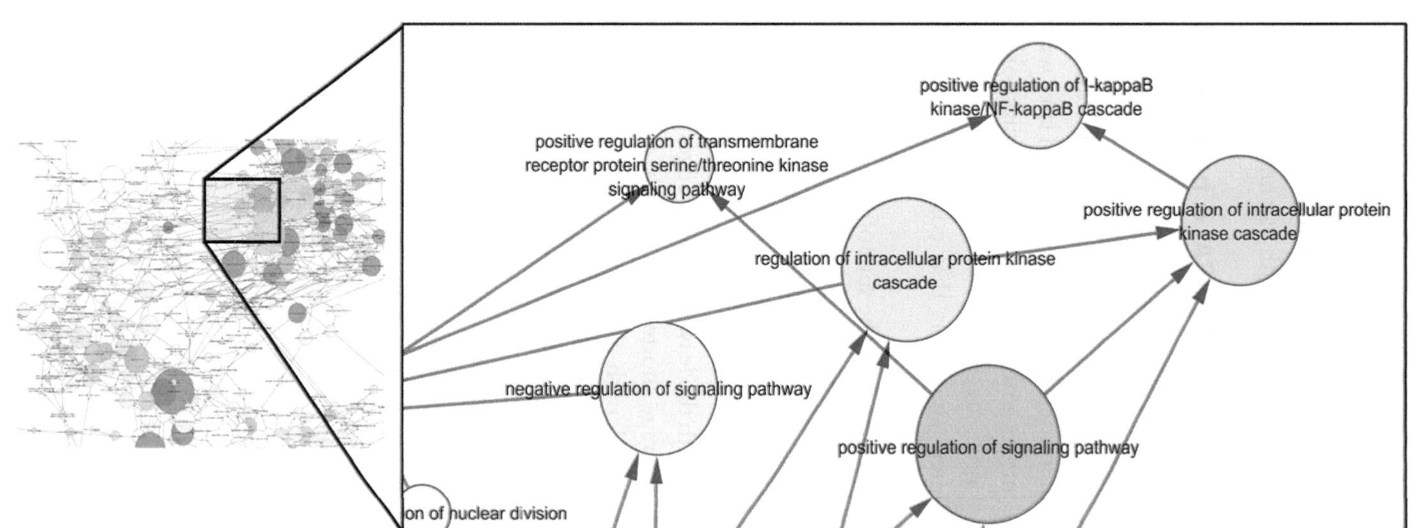

Fig. 4 Functional enrichment analysis using BiNGO. The Cytoscape plugin BiNGO was used to perform functional enrichment analysis. The *color gradient* represents the relevance, with *darker shade* depicting more relevance.

the latest update, the tool has made an effort to reduce the background noise and redundancy from the output results. The tool also has the feature to analyze exosomes by the inclusion of exosome IDs. In the latest update, the tool provides singular, nodal enrichment analyses, comparative analysis, functional annotations, pharmacological annotations, interactive visualization, and panther pathway annotations [82].

9.3 Topological parameter analysis (TPA) & hub gene identification

Network topology can be attained by calculating centrality parameters that help to configure the important nodes in a network. The centrality assigns rankings to the nodes, which determines the position of the nodes in terms of significance. The concept of centrality was first implemented in social network analysis and later was used to measure the significance of biological entities in the networks. The common centrality parameters used in GIN are node degree, average shortest path length, clustering coefficient, betweenness centrality. Other parameters that contribute to GIN includes radiality, closeness centrality, and stress.

The degree of a node corresponds to the sum of all the edges connected to that node. The degree is a simple and most commonly used parameter to determine the significance of a node in a network. In the case of directed networks, the degree can be defined as indegree and outdegree. The indegree is the number of edges directed to the node whereas the outdegree is the number of nodes that is directed to other nodes. The shortest path length refers to the path with the least number of edges between any two nodes in an unweighted network. The average shortest path length, also known as network diameter/distance, is the average path length of all node pairs in an entire network. The cohesive nature or aggregation property of the nodes in a network is determined using the clustering coefficient (CC). The nodes with greater tendency to gather other nodes will have a high clustering coefficient. CC in a network is calculated by the average ratio of the actual edge of a node in the network to all the edges. Betweenness centrality is a measure that quantifies the number of times a particular node acts as a bridge between the two other nodes with the shortest path length. Betweenness centrality is usually measured for nodes, whereas edge betweenness measured for edges. The parameter is applied to determine a biological entity's control on other genes in a biological network. The parameter is more preferred than degree centrality when the dataset contains expression together with interaction data [83]. TPA and hub gene identification can be performed using the following tools:

9.3.1 NEtwork analysis tools (NEAT)

NEAT provides an open and user-friendly web server for analyzing networks or clusters. The web-based server provides two sets of tools for analyzing. The first set supports basic operations on the graph, like comparing any two graphs, and path finding, and another set that helps to create links between the nodes in the clusters. The tool is flexible with its ability to analyze from various databases and can work on large datasets. The various tools can be performed separately for specific analysis by providing custom data [84].

9.3.2 NetworkAnalyzer

Cytoscape plugin NetworkAnalyzer provides an easy and simple execution of network analysis. The tool determines the type of edges it contains, such as directed or undirected. Further, it computes the topological parameters such as node degree distribution, average clustering coefficient distribution, topological coefficients, betweenness centralities, closeness centralities, stress centrality distribution, and shared neighbor distribution. Users can also analyze the local parameters of a subset of nodes. The statistics are available as downloadable graphs and saved using the save statistics option [85].

9.3.3 CytoNCA

CytoNCA is a Cytoscape plugin that supports calculating, evaluating, and visualization of eight different centrality measures. The plugin can be applied for both weighted and unweighted networks. The tool allows users to import supporting data of both nodes and edges so that the biological information can be integrated along with the topological data. The tool also allows multiple modes of visualization of the results in the form of graphs, charts, and tables [86].

9.3.4 The network analysis profiler (NAP)

The Network Analysis Profiler is a web tool designed to analyze complex biological conditions such as cancers using a systems biology approach. The tool performs network profiling and compares the intra and internetwork topologies. The tool fills the gap between graph theory, statistics, and network analysis. The tool is user-friendly and freely available that is being used by a broad range of sections—academics, researchers, and industrial sectors. NAP is constructed in R and shiny-based on the igraph library to analyze small to medium-sized networks with high-quality output plots [87].

9.3.5 CentiScaPe

For the enrichment of network data, a Cytoscape plugin called CentiScaPe was developed that helps in computing network centrality parameters, allowing the users to study the interacting nodes and their edges. The Boolean-based tool helps to characterize the nodes with significant centrality parameters and helps in proposing suitable drug targets for disease networks. Analyzing topological relevance based on several parameters is a significant benefit of this tool [88].

9.3.6 cytoHubba

cytoHubba is a commonly used Cytoscape plugin for identifying hub genes in a network. The plugin computes 11 topological parameters including degree, density of maximum

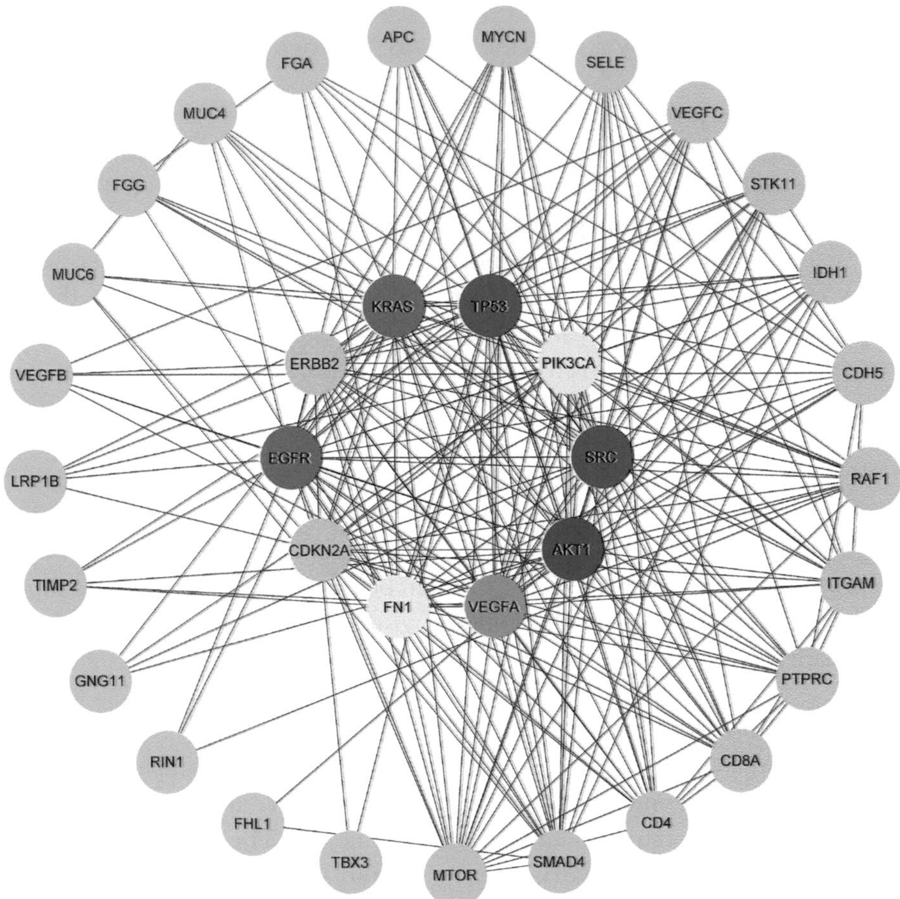

Fig. 5 Hub gene identification using cytoHubba. Network analysis tool cytoHubba was used to perform hub gene identification. The hub genes identified based on one of the 11 parameters are represented in a red to *yellow color gradient*, with *red* representing the top hub gene.

neighborhood component, edge percolated component, maximal clique centrality, and six other centralities. Once the tool computes the parameters, the graphical tool displays the hub genes according to the parameter chosen. The nodes are usually represented in a color gradient format, thus helping efficiently to visualize the computed hub genes. A major advantage of the tool is its compatibility with other plugins to yield novel analysis and provide new insights into the essential networks [89]. Fig. 5 depicts the various hub genes identified using cytoHubba.

9.3.7 CHAT contextual hub analysis tool

The contextual hub analysis tool is designed to analyze hub nodes that are significant in the network efficiently. A contextual node can be a differentially expressed gene/protein in a network and the identification of these nodes are unbiased for drug target identification. With the integration of contextual nodes, the analysis becomes more relevant for the particular condition under investigation. The tool is written in Java and is an open and freely available that prompts the users to provide a list of genes with various identifiers available depending on the database of choice. The tool has the advantage of comparing the contextual hub genes with those of degree-based hub genes [90].

9.3.8 CyNetSVM

CyNetSVM, a Cytoscape plugin incorporates the NetSVM method to identify the predictive biomarkers by combining expression and PPI data. CyNetSVM predicts patients' clinical outcomes and gives meaningful biological insights from the network. The tool is written in Java and can handle big datasets. The plugin provides the sensitivity and specificity of the prediction and graphically represents the network. The tool is particularly useful for cancer analysis where the proposed biomarker's clinical outcome can be predicted. The results can also be integrated with the functionally enriched signaling pathways [91].

10. How can the identified targets be used for cancer therapy?

The hub genes identified by GIN can be used in cancer therapeutics in two different ways, namely as cancer drug target or as cancer biomarkers. Drug targets are proteins or genes, which can be used to inhibit or hinder the proliferation of tumors. They may or may not be specific to any one type of cancer. Although a biomarker is a protein, which can be used as a measure to indicate the severity of the disease aiding in easy detection or diagnosis. Although drug targets aim to cover various cancers, biomarkers are cancer specific. Detection of biomarkers often helps in early diagnosis of cancer thereby impeding the tumor proliferation. Once the drug target and/or cancer biomarkers are identified various approaches, as depicted in Fig. 6, can be included to further validate the hub genes potentiality, making them more reliable for drug discovery and later for clinical translation.

Gene expression levels of the identified hub genes can be analyzed using various tools such as GEPIA [92], cBioPortal [93], BioXpress [94], and TNM plot [95]. The tools will help to compute the log2(Fold Change) value, which describes the increase in the fold change of protein or gene expression in tumor condition when compared with normal condition. The expression values reflect the level of deregulation of the genes, which can be further correlated using mutational signatures and epigenetic alterations. Mutational signatures can be identified using BioMuta [96] or OncoMX [97], mainly focusing on cancer gene mutations. MethHC [98], MethyCancer [99], and the SMART app [100] help in identifying methylation patterns in genes or proteins so that users can check for the epigenetic changes associated with the identified hub genes.

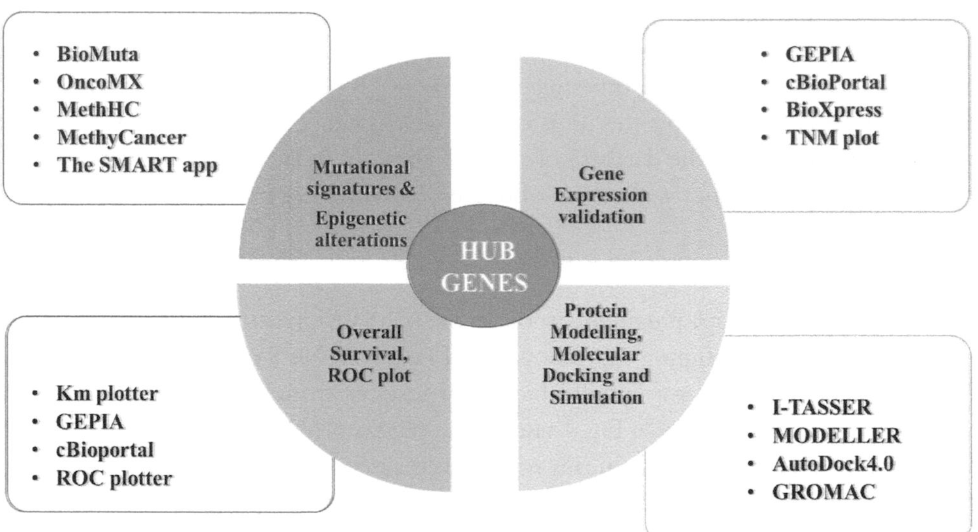

Fig. 6 Schematic representation depicting the future scope of the hub genes identified using gene interaction network for cancer therapy.

These mutational and epigenetic changes will help to identify the altered biological pathway responsible for tumor proliferation when incorporated with the pathway data. Overall survival and ROC plots can be constructed for the identified hub genes using GEPIA, km plotter [101], ROC plotter [102], that helps oncologists and clinicians to understand how the deregulated gene expression affect the patient's survival rate. More priority can be given to those targets that severely affect the patient's overall survival rate. Once the mutational signatures are identified in the active site of the drug target or cancer biomarker, they can be modeled using I-TASSER [103] and MODELER [104]. Virtual screening on the modeled protein will help to identify suitable ligands for a target, that helps in easy clinical translation of the drug. The stability of the modeled protein and docked complex consisting of target-drug can be analyzed after docking by molecular dynamic simulation using GROMAC. The stable complex can be further tested in vitro and in vivo, and positive results will promote the clinical translation of the drug for the pharmaceutical purposes. Advancements in systems biology approach will help us to opt for precision medicine against cancer.

11. Conclusion

In summary, cancer being a highly heterogeneous and complex disease imposes several hindrances to the existing treatment options. It becomes highly challenging to control the rate of mortality associated with cancer with the current therapeutic approaches. To create a breakthrough impact on cancer research and bring forth the next-generation treatment options of precision medicine into play, we highlight the significance of GIN in understanding the mechanism of cancer. GIN, an application of systems biology, involves the construction and analyses of the cancer gene networks. Analyses begin with the collection of a gene set associated with particular cancer and subsequent curation of interaction data among the genes. The interaction data curated is used to construct the network for further analysis. The different types of analyses starting from clustering, functional enrichment, and network analyses help in the identification of clusters, functionally enriched GO terms, and significant hub genes respectively that give an evident perception of the molecular mechanism of tumor proliferation. The hub genes identified when further validated can be used as a drug target and/or biomarker for the respective tumor. In this chapter, we highlighted the different steps involved in identifying the cancer drug targets and biomarkers using GIN and the different tools and databases that can be applied to perform each analysis.

Acknowledgments

AA, SR, MSK, PP, and GA would like to thank VIT management for providing the necessary facilities to perform this work. The authors gratefully acknowledge the Indian Council of Medical Research (ICMR), New Delhi, Government of India agency, for the research grant [IRIS ID: 2020-0690]. MSK thanks the ICMR for his senior research fellowship grant [IRIS ID: 2020-7788].

Conflict of interest

The authors declare that they have no known competing financial interests or personal relationships that could have appeared to influence the work reported in this paper.

Authors' contribution

Gayathri Ashok (GA): Data curation, Writing-Original Draft;

P. Priyamvada (PP): Data curation, Writing-Original Draft;

Sravan Kumar Miryala (MSK): Data curation, Writing-Original Draft;

Anand Anbarasu (AA): Funding Acquisition, Conceptualization, Project Administration;

Sudha Ramaiah (SR): Project Supervision, Conceptualization, Methodology, Draft Review.

References

[1] P.A. Jones, S.B. Baylin, The epigenomics of cancer, Cell 128 (2007) 683–692, https://doi.org/10.1016/J.CELL.2007.01.029.

[2] F.G. Giancotti, Deregulation of cell signaling in cancer, FEBS Lett. 588 (2014) 2558–2570, https://doi.org/10.1016/J.FEBSLET.2014.02.005.

[3] R.L. Siegel, K.D. Miller, H.E. Fuchs, A. Jemal, Cancer statistics, 2021, CA Cancer J. Clin. 71 (2021) 7–33, https://doi.org/10.3322/caac.21654.

[4] J.J. Hornberg, F.J. Bruggeman, H.V. Westerhoff, J. Lankelma, Cancer: a systems biology disease, Biosystems 83 (2006) 81–90, https://doi.org/10.1016/J.BIOSYSTEMS.2005.05.014.

[5] J. Han, L. Gao, J. Wang, J. Wang, Application and development of aptamer in cancer: from clinical diagnosis to cancer therapy, J. Cancer 11 (2020) 6902, https://doi.org/10.7150/JCA.49532.
[6] İ. Altun, A. Sonkaya, The most common side effects experienced by patients were receiving first cycle of chemotherapy, Iran. J. Public Health 47 (2018) 1218. PMCID PMC6123577: (accessed December 20, 2021).
[7] C. Pucci, C. Martinelli, G. Ciofani, Innovative approaches for cancer treatment: current perspectives and new challenges, Ecancermedicalscience 13 (2019), https://doi.org/10.3332/ECANCER.2019.961.
[8] S.K. Miryala, A. Anbarasu, S. Ramaiah, Discerning molecular interactions: a comprehensive review on biomolecular interaction databases and network analysis tools, Gene 642 (2018) 84–94, https://doi.org/10.1016/j.gene.2017.11.028.
[9] F.J. Bruggeman, H.V. Westerhoff, The nature of systems biology, Trends Microbiol. 15 (2007) 45–50, https://doi.org/10.1016/J.TIM.2006.11.003.
[10] M.W. Kirschner, The meaning of systems biology, Cell 121 (2005) 503–504, https://doi.org/10.1016/J.CELL.2005.05.005.
[11] S.K. Miryala, A. Anbarasu, S. Ramaiah, Systems biology studies in *Pseudomonas aeruginosa* PA01 to understand their role in biofilm formation and multidrug efflux pumps, Microb. Pathog. 136 (2019), 103668, https://doi.org/10.1016/j.micpath.2019.103668.
[12] S. Basu, A. Naha, B. Veeraraghavan, S. Ramaiah, A. Anbarasu, In silico structure evaluation of BAG3 and elucidating its association with bacterial infections through protein–protein and host-pathogen interaction analysis, J. Cell. Biochem. (2021) jcb.29953, https://doi.org/10.1002/jcb.29953.
[13] S.K. Miryala, A. Anbarasu, S. Ramaiah, Impact of bedaquiline and capreomycin on the gene expression patterns of multidrug-resistant *Mycobacterium tuberculosis* H37Rv strain and understanding the molecular mechanism of antibiotic resistance, J. Cell. Biochem. 120 (2019) 14499–14509, https://doi.org/10.1002/jcb.28711.
[14] S.K. Miryala, S. Ramaiah, Exploring the multi-drug resistance in *Escherichia coli* O157:H7 by gene interaction network: a systems biology approach, Genomics 111 (2019) 958–965, https://doi.org/10.1016/j.ygeno.2018.06.002.
[15] R. Debroy, S.K. Miryala, A. Naha, A. Anbarasu, S. Ramaiah, Gene interaction network studies to decipher the multi-drug resistance mechanism in *Salmonella enterica* serovar Typhi CT18 reveal potential drug targets, Microb. Pathog. 142 (2020), 104096, https://doi.org/10.1016/j.micpath.2020.104096.
[16] P.S. Shrivaishnavi, A. Naha, S. Ramaiah, A. Anbarasu, Deciphering the structural stability of bacterial exotoxins due to cation-π interactions using computational tools, in: 5th IITM-Tokyo Tech Symposium on "Current Trends in Bioinformatics: Big-Data Analysis, Machine Learning and Drug Design", 2020, pp. 2–3, https://doi.org/10.13140/RG.2.2.26833.68965.
[17] A. Naha, S. Kumar Miryala, R. Debroy, S. Ramaiah, A. Anbarasu, Elucidating the multi-drug resistance mechanism of *Enterococcus faecalis* V583: a gene interaction network analysis, Gene 748 (2020), 144704, https://doi.org/10.1016/J.GENE.2020.144704.
[18] C. Shankar, S. Basu, B. Lal, S. Shanmugam, K. Vasudevan, P. Mathur, S. Ramaiah, A. Anbarasu, B. Veeraraghavan, Aerobactin seems to be a promising marker compared with unstable RmpA2 for the identification of hypervirulent carbapenem-resistant *Klebsiella pneumoniae*: in silico and in vitro evidence, Front. Cell. Infect. Microbiol. 11 (2021) 1–18, https://doi.org/10.3389/fcimb.2021.709681.
[19] G. Ashok, S.K. Miryala, A. Anbarasu, S. Ramaiah, Integrated systems biology approach using gene network analysis to identify the important pathways and new potential drug targets for neuroblastoma, Gene Rep. 23 (2021), 101101, https://doi.org/10.1016/j.genrep.2021.101101.
[20] S.K. Miryala, S. Ramaiah, Cellular and molecular level host-pathogen interactions in *Francisella tularensis*: a microbial gene network study, Comput. Biol. Chem. 96 (2021), 107601, https://doi.org/10.1016/j.compbiolchem.2021.107601.
[21] J. Sun, Z. Zhao, A comparative study of cancer proteins in the human protein-protein interaction network, BMC Genomics 11 (2010) 1–10, https://doi.org/10.1186/1471-2164-11-S3-S5/TABLES/2.
[22] G. Kar, A. Gursoy, O. Keskin, Human cancer protein-protein interaction network: a structural perspective, PLoS Comput. Biol. 5 (2009), e1000601, https://doi.org/10.1371/JOURNAL.PCBI.1000601.
[23] S. van Dam, U. Võsa, A. van der Graaf, L. Franke, J.P. de Magalhães, Gene co-expression analysis for functional classification and gene–disease predictions, Brief. Bioinform. 19 (2018) 575–592, https://doi.org/10.1093/BIB/BBW139.

[24] B. Zhang, S. Horvath, A general framework for weighted gene co-expression network analysis, Stat. Appl. Genet. Mol. Biol. 4 (2005), https://doi.org/10.2202/1544-6115.1128/MACHINEREADABLECITATION/RIS.

[25] P. Khosravi, V.H. Gazestani, L. Pirhaji, B. Law, M. Sadeghi, B. Goliaei, G.D. Bader, Inferring interaction type in gene regulatory networks using co-expression data, Algorithms Mol. Biol. 10 (2015) 1–11, https://doi.org/10.1186/S13015-015-0054-4/FIGURES/11.

[26] E. Davidson, M. Levine, Gene regulatory networks, Proc. Natl. Acad. Sci. 102 (2005) 4935, https://doi.org/10.1073/PNAS.0502024102.

[27] A. Masoudi-Nejad, Y. Asgari, Metabolic cancer biology: structural-based analysis of cancer as a metabolic disease, new sights and opportunities for disease treatment, Semin. Cancer Biol. 30 (2015) 21–29, https://doi.org/10.1016/J.SEMCANCER.2014.01.007.

[28] A. Graudenzi, D. Maspero, M. Di Filippo, M. Gnugnoli, C. Isella, G. Mauri, E. Medico, M. Antoniotti, C. Damiani, Integration of transcriptomic data and metabolic networks in cancer samples reveals highly significant prognostic power, J. Biomed. Inform. 87 (2018) 37–49, https://doi.org/10.1016/J.JBI.2018.09.010.

[29] W. Kolch, M. Halasz, M. Granovskaya, B.N. Kholodenko, The dynamic control of signal transduction networks in cancer cells, Nat. Rev. Cancer 15 (2015) 515–527, https://doi.org/10.1038/nrc3983.

[30] Y. Zhou, V.M. Lauschke, Pharmacogenomic network analysis of the gene-drug interaction landscape underlying drug disposition, Comput. Struct. Biotechnol. J. 18 (2020) 52, https://doi.org/10.1016/J.CSBJ.2019.11.010.

[31] M.A. Malki, E.R. Pearson, Drug–drug–gene interactions and adverse drug reactions, Pharm. J. 20 (2019) 355–366, https://doi.org/10.1038/s41397-019-0122-0.

[32] V. Groza, M. Udrescu, A. Bozdog, L.L. Udrescu, Drug repurposing using modularity clustering in drug-drug similarity networks based on drug–gene interactions, Pharmaceutics 13 (2021) 2117, https://doi.org/10.3390/PHARMACEUTICS13122117.

[33] J.N. Weinstein, E.A. Collisson, G.B. Mills, K.R.M. Shaw, B.A. Ozenberger, K. Ellrott, C. Sander, J.M. Stuart, K. Chang, C.J. Creighton, C. Davis, L. Donehower, J. Drummond, D. Wheeler, A. Ally, M. Balasundaram, I. Birol, Y.S.N. Butterfield, A. Chu, E. Chuah, H.J.E. Chun, N. Dhalla, R. Guin, M. Hirst, C. Hirst, R.A. Holt, S.J.M. Jones, D. Lee, H.I. Li, M.A. Marra, M. Mayo, R.A. Moore, A.J. Mungall, A.G. Robertson, J.E. Schein, P. Sipahimalani, A. Tam, N. Thiessen, R.J. Varhol, R. Beroukhim, A.S. Bhatt, A.N. Brooks, A.D. Cherniack, S.S. Freeman, S.B. Gabriel, E. Helman, J. Jung, M. Meyerson, A.I. Ojesina, C.S. Pedamallu, G. Saksena, S.E. Schumacher, B. Tabak, T. Zack, E.S. Lander, C.A. Bristow, A. Hadjipanayis, P. Haseley, R. Kucherlapati, S. Lee, E. Lee, L.J. Luquette, H.S. Mahadeshwar, A. Pantazi, M. Parfenov, P.J. Park, A. Protopopov, X. Ren, N. Santoso, J. Seidman, S. Seth, X. Song, J. Tang, R. Xi, A.W. Xu, L. Yang, D. Zeng, J.T. Auman, S. Balu, E. Buda, C. Fan, K.A. Hoadley, C.D. Jones, S. Meng, P.A. Mieczkowski, J.S. Parker, C.M. Perou, J. Roach, Y. Shi, G.O. Silva, D. Tan, U. Veluvolu, S. Waring, M.D. Wilkerson, J. Wu, W. Zhao, T. Bodenheimer, D.N. Hayes, A.P. Hoyle, S.R. Jeffreys, L.E. Mose, J.V. Simons, M.G. Soloway, S.B. Baylin, B.P. Berman, M.S. Bootwalla, L. Danilova, J.G. Herman, T. Hinoue, P.W. Laird, S.K. Rhie, H. Shen, T. Triche, D.J. Weisenberger, S.L. Carter, K. Cibulskis, L. Chin, J. Zhang, C. Sougnez, M. Wang, G. Getz, H. Dinh, H.V. Doddapaneni, R. Gibbs, P. Gunaratne, Y. Han, D. Kalra, C. Kovar, L. Lewis, M. Morgan, D. Morton, D. Muzny, J. Reid, L. Xi, J. Cho, D. Dicara, S. Frazer, N. Gehlenborg, D.I. Heiman, J. Kim, M.S. Lawrence, P. Lin, Y. Liu, M.S. Noble, P. Stojanov, D. Voet, H. Zhang, L. Zou, C. Stewart, B. Bernard, R. Bressler, A. Eakin, L. Iype, T. Knijnenburg, R. Kramer, R. Kreisberg, K. Leinonen, J. Lin, Y. Liu, M. Miller, S.M. Reynolds, H. Rovira, I. Shmulevich, V. Thorsson, D. Yang, W. Zhang, S. Amin, C.J. Wu, C.C. Wu, R. Akbani, K. Aldape, K.A. Baggerly, B. Broom, T.D. Casasent, J. Cleland, D. Dodda, M. Edgerton, L. Han, S.M. Herbrich, Z. Ju, H. Kim, S. Lerner, J. Li, H. Liang, W. Liu, P.L. Lorenzi, Y. Lu, J. Melott, L. Nguyen, X. Su, R. Verhaak, W. Wang, A. Wong, Y. Yang, J. Yao, R. Yao, K. Yoshihara, Y. Yuan, A.K. Yung, N. Zhang, S. Zheng, M. Ryan, D.W. Kane, B.A. Aksoy, G. Ciriello, G. Dresdner, J. Gao, B. Gross, A. Jacobsen, A. Kahles, M. Ladanyi, W. Lee, K. Van Lehmann, M.L. Miller, R. Ramirez, G. Rätsch, B. Reva, N. Schultz, Y. Senbabaoglu, R. Shen, R. Sinha, S.O. Sumer, Y. Sun, B.S. Taylor, N. Weinhold, S. Fei, P. Spellman, C. Benz, D. Carlin, M. Cline, B. Craft, M.

Goldman, D. Haussler, S. Ma, S. Ng, E. Paull, A. Radenbaugh, S. Salama, A. Sokolov, T. Swatloski, V. Uzunangelov, P. Waltman, C. Yau, J. Zhu, S.R. Hamilton, S. Abbott, R. Abbott, N.D. Dees, K. Delehaunty, L. Ding, D.J. Dooling, J.M. Eldred, C.C. Fronick, R. Fulton, L.L. Fulton, J. Kalicki-Veizer, K.L. Kanchi, C. Kandoth, D.C. Koboldt, D.E. Larson, T.J. Ley, L. Lin, C. Lu, V.J. Magrini, E.-R. Mardis, M.D. McLellan, J.F. McMichael, C.A. Miller, M. O'Laughlin, C. Pohl, H. Schmidt, S.M. Smith, J. Walker, J.W. Wallis, M.C. Wendl, R.K. Wilson, T. Wylie, Q. Zhang, R. Burton, M.A. Jensen, A. Kahn, T. Pihl, D. Pot, Y. Wan, D.A. Levine, A.D. Black, J. Bowen, J. Frick, J.M. Gastier-Foster, H.A. Harper, C. Helsel, K.M. Leraas, T.M. Lichtenberg, C. McAllister, N.C. Ramirez, S. Sharpe, L. Wise, E. Zmuda, S.J. Chanock, T. Davidsen, J.A. Demchok, G. Eley, I. Felau, M. Sheth, H. Sofia, L. Staudt, R. Tarnuzzer, Z. Wang, L. Yang, J. Zhang, L. Omberg, A. Margolin, B.J. Raphael, F. Vandin, H.T. Wu, M.D.M. Leiserson, S.C. Benz, C.J. Vaske, H. Noushmehr, D. Wolf, L.V.T. Veer, D. Anastassiou, T.H.O. Yang, N. Lopez-Bigas, A. Gonzalez-Perez, D. Tamborero, Z. Xia, W. Li, D.Y. Cho, T. Przytycka, M. Hamilton, S. McGuire, S. Nelander, P. Johansson, R. Jörnsten, T. Kling, The cancer genome atlas pan-cancer analysis project, Nat. Genet. 45 (2013) 1113–1120, https://doi.org/10.1038/ng.2764.

[34] J. Gao, B.A. Aksoy, U. Dogrusoz, G. Dresdner, B. Gross, S.O. Sumer, Y. Sun, A. Jacobsen, R. Sinha, E. Larsson, E. Cerami, C. Sander, N. Schultz, Integrative analysis of complex cancer genomics and clinical profiles using the cBioPortal complementary data sources and analysis options, Sci. Signal. 6 (2014) 1–20, https://doi.org/10.1126/scisignal.2004088.Integrative.

[35] J.G. Tate, S. Bamford, H.C. Jubb, Z. Sondka, D.M. Beare, N. Bindal, H. Boutselakis, C.G. Cole, C. Creatore, E. Dawson, P. Fish, B. Harsha, C. Hathaway, S.C. Jupe, C.Y. Kok, K. Noble, L. Ponting, C.C. Ramshaw, C.E. Rye, H.E. Speedy, R. Stefancsik, S.L. Thompson, S. Wang, S. Ward, P.J. Campbell, S.A. Forbes, COSMIC: the catalogue of somatic mutations in cancer, Nucleic Acids Res. 47 (2019) D941–D947, https://doi.org/10.1093/nar/gky1015.

[36] J. Zhang, J. Baran, A. Cros, J.M. Guberman, S. Haider, J. Hsu, Y. Liang, E. Rivkin, J. Wang, B. Whitty, M. Wong-Erasmus, L. Yao, A. Kasprzyk, International cancer genome consortium data portal-a one-stop shop for cancer genomics data, Database 2011 (2011) 1–10, https://doi.org/10.1093/database/bar026.

[37] M.J. Garnett, E.J. Edelman, S.J. Heidorn, C.D. Greenman, A. Dastur, K.W. Lau, P. Greninger, I.R. Thompson, X. Luo, J. Soares, Q. Liu, F. Iorio, D. Surdez, L. Chen, R.J. Milano, G.R. Bignell, A.T. Tam, H. Davies, J.A. Stevenson, S. Barthorpe, S.R. Lutz, F. Kogera, K. Lawrence, A. McLaren-Douglas, X. Mitropoulos, T. Mironenko, H. Thi, L. Richardson, W. Zhou, F. Jewitt, T. Zhang, P. O'Brien, J.L. Boisvert, S. Price, W. Hur, W. Yang, X. Deng, A. Butler, H.G. Choi, J.W. Chang, J. Baselga, I. Stamenkovic, J.A. Engelman, S.V. Sharma, O. Delattre, J. Saez-Rodriguez, N.S. Gray, J. Settleman, P.A. Futreal, D.A. Haber, M.R. Stratton, S. Ramaswamy, U. McDermott, C.H. Benes, Systematic identification of genomic markers of drug sensitivity in cancer cells, Nature 483 (2012) 570–575, https://doi.org/10.1038/nature11005.

[38] S.H. Liu, P.C. Shen, C.Y. Chen, A.N. Hsu, Y.C. Cho, Y.L. Lai, F.H. Chen, C.Y. Li, S.C. Wang, M. Chen, I.F. Chung, W.C. Cheng, DriverDBv3: a multi-omics database for cancer driver gene research, Nucleic Acids Res. 48 (2020) D863–D870, https://doi.org/10.1093/nar/gkz964.

[39] M. Zhang, B. Wang, J. Xu, X. Wang, L. Xie, B. Zhang, Y. Li, J. Li, CanProVar 2.0: an updated database of human cancer proteome variation, J. Proteome Res. 16 (2017) 421–432, https://doi.org/10.1021/acs.jproteome.6b00505.

[40] D. Repana, J. Nulsen, J. Goldman, M. Pollit, Comparative assessment of genes driving cancer and somatic evolution in noncancer tissues: an update of the NCG resource, Genome Biol. 23 (2021) 1–46.

[41] X. Mao, Y. Xu, Z. Jiang, HColonDB: a database for human colon cancer research, J. Comput. Biol. 26 (2019) 218–224, https://doi.org/10.1089/cmb.2018.0193.

[42] J.K. Thomas, M.S. Kim, L. Balakrishnan, V. Nanjappa, R. Raju, A. Marimuthu, A. Radhakrishnan, B. Muthusamy, A.A. Khan, S. Sakamuri, S.G. Tankala, M. Singal, B. Nair, R. Sirdeshmukh, A. Chatterjee, T.S. Keshava Prasad, A. Maitra, H. Gowda, R.H. Hruban, A. Pandey, Pancreatic cancer database: an integrative resource for pancreatic cancer, Cancer Biol. Ther. 15 (2014) 963–967, https://doi.org/10.4161/cbt.29188.

[43] J. Marzec, A.Z. Dayem Ullah, S. Pirrò, E. Gadaleta, T. Crnogorac-Jurcevic, N.R. Lemoine, H.M. Kocher, C. Chelala, The pancreatic expression database: 2018 update, Nucleic Acids Res. 46 (2018) D1107–D1110, https://doi.org/10.1093/nar/gkx955.

[44] S.M. Agarwal, D. Raghav, H. Singh, G.P.S. Raghava, CCDB: a curated database of genes involved in cervix cancer, Nucleic Acids Res. 39 (2011) 975–979, https://doi.org/10.1093/nar/gkq1024.
[45] E. Mosca, R. Alfieri, I. Merelli, F. Viti, A. Calabria, L. Milanesi, A multilevel data integration resource for breast cancer study, BMC Syst. Biol. 4 (2010), https://doi.org/10.1186/1752-0509-4-76.
[46] L. Wang, Y. Xiong, Y. Sun, Z. Fang, L. Li, H. Ji, T. Shi, HlungDB: an integrated database of human lung cancer research, Nucleic Acids Res. 38 (2009) 665–669, https://doi.org/10.1093/nar/gkp945.
[47] J. Ramana, RCDB: renal cancer gene database, BMC Res. Notes 5 (2012) 2–5, https://doi.org/10.1186/1756-0500-5-246.
[48] D.G. Biron, D. Nedelkov, D.A. Missé, P. Holzmuller, Proteomics and host-pathogen interactions: a bright future? in: Genetics and Evolution of Infectious Disease, 2011, https://doi.org/10.1016/B978-0-12-384890-1.00011-X.
[49] M.F. Cesur, S. Durmuş, Systems biology modeling to study pathogen–host interactions, Methods Mol. Biol. 1734 (2018) 97–112, https://doi.org/10.1007/978-1-4939-7604-1_10.
[50] M.G. Ammari, C.R. Gresham, F.M. McCarthy, B. Nanduri, HPIDB 2.0: a curated database for host-pathogen interactions, Database (Oxford). 2016 (2016) 1–9, https://doi.org/10.1093/database/baw103.
[51] T. Guirimand, S. Delmotte, V. Navratil, VirHostNet 2.0: surfing on the web of virus/host molecular interactions data, Nucleic Acids Res. 43 (2015) D583–D587, https://doi.org/10.1093/nar/gku1121.
[52] V. Navratil, B. de Chassey, L. Meyniel, S. Delmotte, C. Gautier, P. André, V. Lotteau, C. Rabourdin-Combe, VirHostNet: a knowledge base for the management and the analysis of proteome-wide virus-host interaction networks, Nucleic Acids Res. 37 (2009) 661–668, https://doi.org/10.1093/nar/gkn794.
[53] A. Calderone, L. Licata, G. Cesareni, VirusMentha: a new resource for virus-host protein interactions, Nucleic Acids Res. 43 (2015) D588–D592, https://doi.org/10.1093/nar/gku830.
[54] S.K. Kwofie, U. Schaefer, V.S. Sundararajan, V.B. Bajic, A. Christoffels, HCVpro: hepatitis C virus protein interaction database, Infect. Genet. Evol. 11 (2011) 1971–1977, https://doi.org/10.1016/j.meegid.2011.09.001.
[55] S. Durmuş Tekir, T. Çakir, E. Ardiç, A.S. Sayilirbaş, G. Konuk, M. Konuk, H. Sariyer, A. Uğurlu, I. Karadeniz, A. Özgür, F.E. Sevilgen, K.Ö. Ülgen, PHISTO: pathogen-host interaction search tool, Bioinformatics 29 (2013) 1357–1358, https://doi.org/10.1093/bioinformatics/btt137.
[56] C.S. Goh, F.E. Cohen, Co-evolutionary analysis reveals insights into protein-protein interactions, J. Mol. Biol. 324 (2002) 177–192, https://doi.org/10.1016/S0022-2836(02)01038-0.
[57] S.K. Ng, Z. Zhang, S.H. Tan, Integrative approach for computationally inferring protein domain interactions, Bioinformatics 19 (2003) 923–929, https://doi.org/10.1093/bioinformatics/btg118.
[58] A. Chatr-Aryamontri, B.J. Breitkreutz, R. Oughtred, L. Boucher, S. Heinicke, D. Chen, C. Stark, A. Breitkreutz, N. Kolas, L. O'Donnell, T. Reguly, J. Nixon, L. Ramage, A. Winter, A. Sellam, C. Chang, J. Hirschman, C. Theesfeld, J. Rust, M.S. Livstone, K. Dolinski, M. Tyers, The BioGRID interaction database: 2015 update, Nucleic Acids Res. 43 (2015) D470–D478, https://doi.org/10.1093/nar/gku1204.
[59] R. Oughtred, C. Stark, B.J. Breitkreutz, J. Rust, L. Boucher, C. Chang, N. Kolas, L. O'Donnell, G. Leung, R. McAdam, F. Zhang, S. Dolma, A. Willems, J. Coulombe-Huntington, A. Chatr-Aryamontri, K. Dolinski, M. Tyers, The BioGRID interaction database: 2019 update, Nucleic Acids Res. 47 (2019) D529–D541, https://doi.org/10.1093/nar/gky1079.
[60] D. Warde-Farley, S.L. Donaldson, O. Comes, K. Zuberi, R. Badrawi, P. Chao, M. Franz, C. Grouios, F. Kazi, C.T. Lopes, A. Maitland, S. Mostafavi, J. Montojo, Q. Shao, G. Wright, G.D. Bader, Q. Morris, The GeneMANIA prediction server: biological network integration for gene prioritization and predicting gene function, Nucleic Acids Res. 38 (2010) W214–W220, https://doi.org/10.1093/NAR/GKQ537.
[61] D. Szklarczyk, A.L. Gable, K.C. Nastou, D. Lyon, R. Kirsch, S. Pyysalo, N.T. Doncheva, M. Legeay, T. Fang, L.J. Jensen, C. Von Mering, The STRING database in 2021: customizable protein-protein networks, and functional characterization of user-uploaded gene/measurement sets, Nucleic Acids Res. 49 (2021) 605–612, https://doi.org/10.1093/nar/gkaa1074.
[62] L. Licata, L. Briganti, D. Peluso, L. Perfetto, M. Iannuccelli, E. Galeota, F. Sacco, A. Palma, A.P. Nardozza, E. Santonico, L. Castagnoli, G. Cesareni, MINT, the molecular interaction database: 2012 update, Nucleic Acids Res. 40 (2012) 857–861, https://doi.org/10.1093/nar/gkr930.

[63] H. Hermjakob, L. Montecchi-Palazzi, C. Lewington, S. Mudali, S. Kerrien, S. Orchard, M. Vingron, B. Roechert, P. Roepstorff, A. Valencia, H. Margalit, J. Armstrong, A. Bairoch, G. Cesareni, D. Sherman, R. Apweiler, IntAct: an open source molecular interaction database, Nucleic Acids Res. 32 (2004) 452–455, https://doi.org/10.1093/nar/gkh052.
[64] C.T. Lopes, M. Franz, F. Kazi, S.L. Donaldson, Q. Morris, G.D. Bader, Cytoscape Web: an interactive web-based network browser, Bioinformatics 26 (2010) 2347–2348, https://doi.org/10.1093/bioinformatics/btq430.
[65] P. Shannon, A. Markiel, O. Ozier, N.S. Baliga, J.T. Wang, D. Ramage, N. Amin, B. Schwikowski, T. Ideker, Cytoscape: a software environment for integrated models of biomolecular interaction networks, Genome Res. (2003), https://doi.org/10.1101/gr.1239303.
[66] M.E. Smoot, K. Ono, J. Ruscheinski, P.L. Wang, T. Ideker, Cytoscape 2.8: new features for data integration and network visualization, Bioinformatics 27 (2011) 431–432, https://doi.org/10.1093/BIOINFORMATICS/BTQ675.
[67] G.A. Pavlopoulos, A.-L. Wegener, R. Schneider, A survey of visualization tools for biological network analysis, BioData Min. 1 (2008) 1–11, https://doi.org/10.1186/1756-0381-1-12.
[68] S.D. Hooper, P. Bork, Medusa: a simple tool for interaction graph analysis, Bioinformatics 21 (2005) 4432–4433, https://doi.org/10.1093/BIOINFORMATICS/BTI696.
[69] G.A. Pavlopoulos, S.D. Hooper, A. Sifrim, R. Schneider, J. Aerts, Medusa: a tool for exploring and clustering biological networks, BMC Res. Notes (2011), https://doi.org/10.1186/1756-0500-4-384.
[70] A. Theocharidis, S. van Dongen, A.J. Enright, T.C. Freeman, Network visualization and analysis of gene expression data using BioLayout Express3D, Nat. Protoc. 4 (2009) 1535–1550, https://doi.org/10.1038/nprot.2009.177.
[71] D.W. Wright, T. Angus, A.J. Enright, T.C. Freeman, Visualisation of BioPAX networks using BioLayoutExpress3D, F1000Research 3 (2014), https://doi.org/10.12688/F1000RESEARCH.5499.1.
[72] M. Zhang, Q. Li, D. Yu, B. Yao, W. Guo, Y. Xie, G. Xiao, GeNeCK: a web server for gene network construction and visualization, BMC Bioinf. 20 (2019) 1–7, https://doi.org/10.1186/S12859-018-2560-0/FIGURES/2.
[73] T. Charitou, K. Bryan, D.J. Lynn, Using biological networks to integrate, visualize and analyze genomics data, Genet. Sel. Evol. 48 (2016) 1–12, https://doi.org/10.1186/S12711-016-0205-1/FIGURES/4.
[74] J. Boccard, S. Rudaz, Mass spectrometry metabolomic data handling for biomarker discovery, in: Proteomic and Metabolomic Approaches to Biomarker Discovery, 2013, pp. 425–445, https://doi.org/10.1016/B978-0-12-394446-7.00027-3.
[75] J.H. Morris, L. Apeltsin, A.M. Newman, J. Baumbach, T. Wittkop, G. Su, G.D. Bader, T.E. Ferrin, ClusterMaker : a multi-algorithm clustering plugin for Cytoscape, 2011, pp. 1–14.
[76] G.D. Bader, C.W.V. Hogue, An automated method for finding molecular complexes in large protein interaction networks, BMC Bioinf. 4 (2003) 1–27, https://doi.org/10.1186/1471-2105-4-2/FIGURES/12.
[77] J. Wang, J. Zhong, G. Chen, M. Li, F.X. Wu, Y. Pan, ClusterViz: a cytoscape APP for cluster analysis of biological network, IEEE/ACM Trans. Comput. Biol. Bioinform. 12 (2015) 815–822, https://doi.org/10.1109/TCBB.2014.2361348.
[78] D.W. Huang, B.T. Sherman, Q. Tan, J.R. Collins, W.G. Alvord, J. Roayaei, R. Stephens, M.W. Baseler, H.C. Lane, R.A. Lempicki, The DAVID gene functional classification tool: a novel biological module-centric algorithm to functionally analyze large gene lists, Genome Biol. 8 (2007) 1–16, https://doi.org/10.1186/GB-2007-8-9-R183/TABLES/3.
[79] M. Pathan, S. Keerthikumar, C.S. Ang, L. Gangoda, C.Y.J. Quek, N.A. Williamson, D. Mouradov, O.M. Sieber, R.J. Simpson, A. Salim, A. Bacic, A.F. Hill, D.A. Stroud, M.T. Ryan, J.I. Agbinya, J.M. Mariadason, A.W. Burgess, S. Mathivanan, FunRich: an open access standalone functional enrichment and interaction network analysis tool, Proteomics 15 (2015) 2597–2601, https://doi.org/10.1002/pmic.201400515.
[80] S. Maere, K. Heymans, M. Kuiper, BiNGO: a cytoscape plugin to assess overrepresentation of gene ontology categories in biological networks, Bioinformatics 21 (2005) 3448–3449, https://doi.org/10.1093/BIOINFORMATICS/BTI551.

[81] E.J. Baker, J.J. Jay, J.A. Bubier, M.A. Langston, E.J. Chesler, GeneWeaver: a web-based system for integrative functional genomics, Nucleic Acids Res. 40 (2012) D1067–D1076, https://doi.org/10.1093/NAR/GKR968.

[82] D. Tabas-Madrid, R. Nogales-Cadenas, A. Pascual-Montano, GeneCodis3: a non-redundant and modular enrichment analysis tool for functional genomics, Nucleic Acids Res. 40 (2012) W478–W483, https://doi.org/10.1093/NAR/GKS402.

[83] X. Zhao, Z.P. Liu, Analysis of topological parameters of complex disease genes reveals the importance of location in a biomolecular network, Genes (Basel) 10 (2019), https://doi.org/10.3390/GENES10020143.

[84] S. Brohée, K. Faust, G. Lima-Mendez, O. Sand, R. Janky, G. Vanderstocken, Y. Deville, J. van Helden, NeAT: a toolbox for the analysis of biological networks, clusters, classes and pathways, Nucleic Acids Res. 36 (2008) W444–W451, https://doi.org/10.1093/NAR/GKN336.

[85] N.T. Doncheva, Y. Assenov, F.S. Domingues, M. Albrecht, Topological analysis and interactive visualization of biological networks and protein structures, Nat. Protoc. 7 (2012) 670–685, https://doi.org/10.1038/nprot.2012.004.

[86] Y. Tang, M. Li, J. Wang, Y. Pan, F.X. Wu, CytoNCA: a cytoscape plugin for centrality analysis and evaluation of protein interaction networks, Biosystems 127 (2015) 67–72, https://doi.org/10.1016/J.BIOSYSTEMS.2014.11.005.

[87] T. Theodosiou, G. Efstathiou, N. Papanikolaou, N.C. Kyrpides, P.G. Bagos, I. Iliopoulos, G.A. Pavlopoulos, NAP: the network analysis profiler, a web tool for easier topological analysis and comparison of medium-scale biological networks, BMC Res. Notes 10 (2017) 1–9, https://doi.org/10.1186/S13104-017-2607-8/FIGURES/5.

[88] G. Scardoni, M. Petterlini, C. Laudanna, Analyzing biological network parameters with CentiScaPe, Bioinformatics 25 (2009) 2857–2859, https://doi.org/10.1093/BIOINFORMATICS/BTP517.

[89] C.-H. Chin, S.-H. Chen, H.-H. Wu, C.-W. Ho, M.-T. Ko, C.-Y. Lin, cytoHubba: identifying hub objects and sub-networks from complex interactome, BMC Syst. Biol. 8 (2014) S11, https://doi.org/10.1186/1752-0509-8-S4-S11.

[90] T. Muetze, I.H. Goenawan, H.L. Wiencko, M. Bernal-Llinares, K. Bryan, D.J. Lynn, S. Orchard, E. Molecular, C.K. Tuggle, Contextual Hub Analysis Tool (CHAT): a cytoscape app for identifying contextually relevant hubs in biological networks [version 2; peer review: 2 approved] report, F1000Research (2016), https://doi.org/10.12688/f1000research.9118.1.

[91] X. Shi, S. Banerjee, L. Chen, L. Hilakivi-Clarke, R. Clarke, J. Xuan, CyNetSVM: a cytoscape app for cancer biomarker identification using network constrained support vector machines, PLoS One 12 (2017), e0170482, https://doi.org/10.1371/JOURNAL.PONE.0170482.

[92] C. Li, Z. Tang, W. Zhang, Z. Ye, F. Liu, GEPIA2021: integrating multiple deconvolution-based analysis into GEPIA, Nucleic Acids Res. 49 (2021) W242–W246, https://doi.org/10.1093/NAR/GKAB418.

[93] E. Cerami, J. Gao, U. Dogrusoz, B.E. Gross, S.O. Sumer, B.A. Aksoy, A. Jacobsen, C.J. Byrne, M.L. Heuer, E. Larsson, Y. Antipin, B. Reva, A.P. Goldberg, C. Sander, N. Schultz, The cBio cancer genomics portal: an open platform for exploring multidimensional cancer genomics data, Cancer Discov. 2 (2012) 401, https://doi.org/10.1158/2159-8290.CD-12-0095.

[94] Q. Wan, H. Dingerdissen, Y. Fan, N. Gulzar, Y. Pan, T.J. Wu, C. Yan, H. Zhang, R. Mazumder, BioXpress: an integrated RNA-seq-derived gene expression database for pan-cancer analysis, Database 2015 (2015) 19, https://doi.org/10.1093/DATABASE/BAV019.

[95] Á. Bartha, B. Győrffy, TNMplot.com: a web tool for the comparison of gene expression in normal, tumor and metastatic tissues, Int. J. Mol. Sci. 22 (2021) 2622, https://doi.org/10.3390/IJMS22052622.

[96] H.M. Dingerdissen, J. Torcivia-Rodriguez, Y. Hu, T.C. Chang, R. Mazumder, R. Kahsay, BioMuta and BioXpress: mutation and expression knowledgebases for cancer biomarker discovery, Nucleic Acids Res. 46 (2018) D1128–D1136, https://doi.org/10.1093/NAR/GKX907.

[97] H.M. Dingerdissen, F. Bastian, K. Vijay-Shanker, M. Robinson-Rechavi, A. Bell, N. Gogate, S. Gupta, E. Holmes, R. Kahsay, J. Keeney, H. Kincaid, C.H. King, D. Liu, D.J. Crichton, R. Mazumder, OncoMX: a knowledgebase for exploring cancer biomarkers in the context of related cancer and healthy data, JCO Clin. Cancer Inform. (2020) 210–220, https://doi.org/10.1200/cci.19.00117.

[98] W.Y. Huang, S. Da Hsu, H.Y. Huang, Y.M. Sun, C.H. Chou, S.L. Weng, H. Da Huang, MethHC: a database of DNA methylation and gene expression in human cancer, Nucleic Acids Res. 43 (2015) D856–D861, https://doi.org/10.1093/NAR/GKU1151.

[99] X. He, S. Chang, J. Zhang, Q. Zhao, H. Xiang, K. Kusonmano, L. Yang, Z.S. Sun, H. Yang, J. Wang, MethyCancer: the database of human DNA methylation and cancer, Nucleic Acids Res. 36 (2008) D836–D841, https://doi.org/10.1093/NAR/GKM730.

[100] Y. Li, D. Ge, C. Lu, The SMART app: an interactive web application for comprehensive DNA methylation analysis and visualization, Epigenetics Chromatin 12 (2019) 1–9, https://doi.org/10.1186/S13072-019-0316-3/TABLES/1.

[101] Z. Tang, C. Li, B. Kang, G. Gao, C. Li, Z. Zhang, GEPIA: a web server for cancer and normal gene expression profiling and interactive analyses, Nucleic Acids Res. 45 (2017), https://doi.org/10.1093/nar/gkx247.

[102] J.T. Fekete, B. Győrffy, ROCplot.org: validating predictive biomarkers of chemotherapy/hormonal therapy/anti-HER2 therapy using transcriptomic data of 3,104 breast cancer patients, Int. J. Cancer 145 (2019) 3140–3151, https://doi.org/10.1002/IJC.32369.

[103] A. Roy, A. Kucukural, Y. Zhang, I-TASSER: a unified platform for automated protein structure and function prediction, Nat. Protoc. 5 (2010) 725–738, https://doi.org/10.1038/nprot.2010.5.

[104] B. Webb, A. Sali, Comparative protein structure modeling using MODELLER, Curr. Protoc. Bioinformatics 54 (2016) 5.6.1–5.6.37, https://doi.org/10.1002/CPBI.3.

CHAPTER 16

Role of human body fluid biomarkers in liver cancer: A systematic review

Dahrii Paul, Vigneshwar Suriya Prakash Sinnarasan, Rajesh Das, Dinakara Rao Ampasala, and Amouda Venkatesan
Department of Bioinformatics, Pondicherry University, Puducherry, India

Abstract

Every year, thousands of liver cancer (LC) cases go undiagnosed. Despite the advances in LC diagnosis, treatment, and management, many patients continued to have rapid disease recurrence with poor outcomes. At present, physicians extensively rely on tissue tumor biopsy, which is invasive. Therefore, better noninvasive tools are urgently required to fight against such diseases. Human body fluids are a rich reservoir of potential biomarkers that are easily accessible and less invasive. But these body fluid proteins are complex and have a dynamic range of abundances, making it challenging to evaluate them efficiently. Thus, the study review and discuss a systematic analysis of LC human body fluid biomarkers and their clinical significance.

Abbreviations

A1AG1	alpha-1-acid glycoprotein 1
A1AT	alpha-1-antitrypsin
AACT	alpha-1-antichymotrypsin
AFP	alpha-fetoprotein
AFP-L3	*Lens culinaris* agglutinin-reactive alpha-fetoprotein
AGP	alpha-1 acid glycoprotein 1
AI	artificial intelligence
ANXA2	annexin II
AUC	area under the curve
B2M	beta-2-microglobulin
CA1	carbonic anhydrase I
CA19-9	carbohydrate antigen 19-9
CEA	carcinoembryonic antigen
CERU	ceruloplasmin
CP	calprotectin
DCP	des-gamma carboxyprothrombin
EGFR	epidermal growth factor receptor
ENO1	enolase-1
ERBB3	erb-b2 receptor tyrosine kinase 3
FDA	food and drug administration
FETUA	alpha-2-HS-glycoprotein
Gal-3BP	galectin 3 binding protein
HCC	hepatocellular carcinoma
HILIC	hydrophilic interaction liquid chromatography

Computational Methods in Drug Discovery and Repurposing for Cancer Therapy
https://doi.org/10.1016/B978-0-443-15280-1.00001-7

ICC	intrahepatic cholangiocarcinoma
IGF-I	insulin-like growth factors
LC	liver cancer
MC-LR	microcystin-LR
MDSCs	myeloid-derived suppressor cells
miRNA	microRNA
ML	machine learning
MVs	microvesicles
NASH	nonalcoholic steatohepatitis
PIVKA-II	prothrombin induced by vitamin K absence-II
PPP	pentose phosphate pathway
PRISMA	preferred reporting items for systematic reviews and meta-analyses
TALDO	transaldolase
WFA+-M2BP	WFA-positive Mac-2 binding protein
WFA	*Wisteria floribunda* agglutinin
WFA-sialylated MUC1	WFA-positive sialylated mucin 1

1. Introduction

Liver cancer (LC) is the 3rd deadliest cancer globally, with >905,000 new cases and >830,000 deaths annually [1]. By 2025, it is predicted that >1 million instances of LC will be impacted per year [2]. Hepatocellular carcinoma (HCC) and intrahepatic cholangiocarcinoma (ICC) is the most frequent types of LC, accounting for 75%–85% and 10%–15% of cases respectively [3]. Hepatoblastoma, angiosarcoma or haemangiosarcoma, and fibrolamellar carcinoma are other rare types of LC [4,5].The prognosis of LC depends on tumor stage and their survival rates drop from 34% for localized, 12% for regional, and 3% for distant metastases [6]. Hepatitis virus, aflatoxin B1, metabolic disorder, alcohol, tobacco, and nonalcoholic fatty liver disease are the major risk factor of LC [7]. Despite different guidelines and recommendations available, LC is often detected at a later stage when curative treatments are no longer effective. Thus, early diagnosis can drastically improve patient outcomes.

Currently, the diagnosis of LC is primarily based on histopathological or imaging [2]. Practice guidelines are increasingly advocating for molecularly characterized biopsies [8]. Computer imagining is highly sensitive and is being used extensively for LC diagnosis. Atiq et al. studies show that computer imagining methods may cause more bodily harm than molecular markers like alpha-fetoprotein (AFP) [9]. Thus, there has been an increasing interest in other noninvasive alternative techniques for screening LC. Because biological fluids are much more accessible, less invasive, do not require surgery, and can be performed repeatedly. Therefore, human body fluids may be safer and more valuable for LC diagnosis in a clinical setting. Approaches like liquid biopsy and omics-related methods have also made tremendous progress in identifying biomarkers [10]. Although wide usage of food and drug administration (FDA) approved molecular biomarkers like serum AFP, *L. culinaris* agglutinin-reactive alpha-fetoprotein (AFP-L3), and des-gamma carboxyprothrombin (DCP) they are found to be not a good diagnostic marker [11,12]. Several markers related to circulating nucleic acids, circulating tumor cells, and extracellular vesicles are also emerging as promising noninvasive biomarkers candidates [13]. Hence, the ability to identify new noninvasive biomarkers is the key to fighting against LC. Fig. 1 depicts the approaches used in the discovery of bodily fluid biomarkers. A systematic evaluation of LC human body fluid biomarkers and their clinical significance are discussed here.

2. Methods

A systematic literature search was performed using the PubMed database following the preferred reporting items for systematic reviews and meta-analyses (PRISMA) [14]. In April 2022, the literature search was performed using the MeSH term liver neoplasms, body fluids, and biomarkers tumor in the PubMed database. Along with the MeSH term, a free keyword term on body fluids, biological fluids, and biofluids search was also performed as shown in Table 1.

The criterion for the selection of papers in the article must be full-length human studies and published in English between 1st January 2000 and 30th April 2022. Publications such as editor comments, reader comments, book chapters, meta-analyses, and reviews were excluded. The final requirement is the articles based on LC bodily fluid biomarkers with the biomarkers being central to the research. The titles and abstracts were screened from the retrieved records. The articles were subjected to full-text evaluation based on the reported bodily fluids biomarkers. This systematic review discusses the type of biomarker, the samples collected, the number of patients studied, and the outcomes. Lack of data and variability in the studies, the statistical analyses were not performed.

3. Results

Collected 83 publications with full text by removing the redundant records out of 117 retrieved records. Based on the title and abstract, 19 articles were excluded and the remaining 64 full-texts were reviewed and rejected 38 articles, which does not fulfill the eligibility criteria. The current study considered 28 articles for the analysis. Fig. 2 summarizes the study selection procedure.

Samples reported were collected from serum, plasma, ascetic fluid, peripheral blood, and cyst fluid. Biomarkers measured were calprotectin (CP), *wisteria floribunda* agglutinin (WFA), microcystin-LR (MC-LR), DCP or prothrombin induced by vitamin K absence-II (PIVKA-II), glycoprotein, insulin-like growth factors (IGF-I), transaldolase (TALDO), microRNA (miRNA), carbonic anhydrase I (CA1), enolase-1 (ENO1), microvesicles (MVs), erb-b2 receptor tyrosine kinase 3 (ERBB3), annexin II (ANXA2), beta-2-microglobulin (B2M), metabolites, and myeloid-derived suppressor cells (MDSCs). Table 2 summarizes the details of the studies.

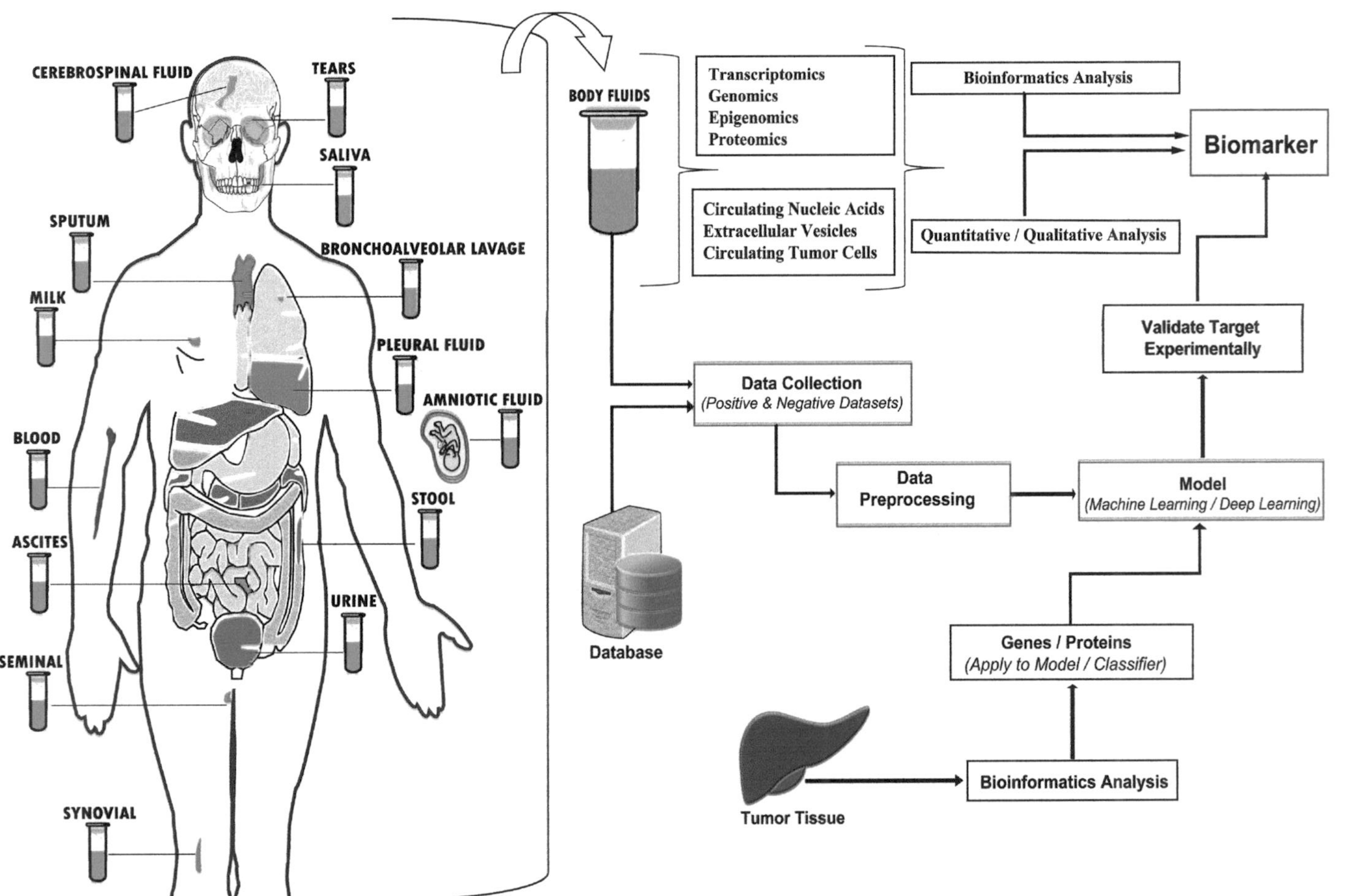

Fig. 1 Schematic representation of human body fluid biomarkers discovery strategy using an experimental and computational approach.

Table 1 Search strings.

S. No.	Search type	Key-string	Database	Date (dd-mm-yyyy)	Hits
1	MeSH term keywords search	(("Liver Neoplasms"[Mesh]) AND "Body Fluids"[Mesh]) AND "Biomarkers, Tumor"[Mesh]	PubMed	30-04-2022	34
2	MeSH term and free keywords search	((((body fluids) OR (bodily fluids)) OR (biological fluids)) OR (biofluids)) AND ("Liver Neoplasms"[Mesh]) AND ("Biomarkers, Tumor"[Mesh])	PubMed	30-04-2022	83

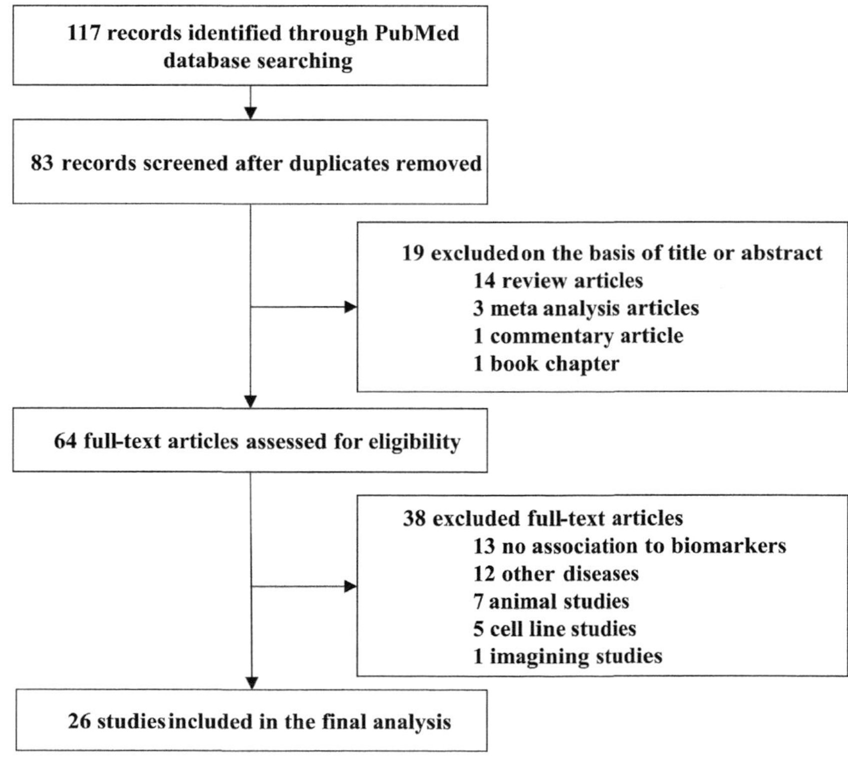

Fig. 2 Flow chart of the study selection procedure.

Table 2 A summary of the journals included in review.

Reference	Biomarkers	Total participants	Samples	AUC (area under curve)	LC types	Findings
[15]	CP	100	Ascetic fluid	0.95	HCC	Potential diagnostic marker
[16]	S100A9	94	Serum	0.83	HCC	Potential biomarker to distinguish HCC from liver cirrhosis
[17]	WFA-positive Mac-2 binding protein (WFA +-M2BP)	412	Serum	0.694	HCC	Potential prognostic marker
[18]	WFA-positive sialylated mucin 1 (WFA-sialylated MUC1)	144	Serum	–	HCC	WFA-sialylated MUC1 is a good prognostic marker complementing AFP & DCP
[19]	MC-LR	650	Serum	–	HCC	Worsen the prognosis
[20]	DCP	162	Serum	0.89	HCC	For the diagnosis of HCC, DCP beats AFP
[21]	PIVKA-II, AFP	81	Serum	–	HCC	PIVKA-II & AFP potential biomarkers for early detection of HCC
[22]	Galectin 3 binding protein (Gal-3BP)	220	Serum	0.898	HCC	Gal-3BP & AFP both boost diagnostic potential
[23]	Vitronectin, Alpha-1 acid glycoprotein 1 (AGP)	41	Plasma	0.955 (P04004), 0.880 (P04004), 0.907 (P02763)	HCC	Nonglycosylated peptides potential biomarkers HCC
[24]	Alpha-1-acid glycoprotein 1 (A1AG1), alpha-1-antitrypsin (A1AT), alpha-1-antichymotrypsin (AACT), CERU	(samples from 40 cases)	Serum	0.73–0.92	HCC	Glycoproteins are potent HCC biomarkers

[25]	A1AT, alpha-2-HS-glycoprotein (FETUA)	–	Plasma	–	HCC	Fucosylated glycoproteins, A1AT & FETUA were elevated in HCC
[26]	AFP	76,347	Serum	–	HCC	AFP elevations are closely linked to alanine transaminase (ALT) levels; adjusting the ALT values may improve prognostic and diagnostic results
[27]	AFP	655	Serum	–	HCC	AFP elevation was associated with HCC development
[28]	Fucosylated glycoproteins	29	Serum	–	HCC	Fucosylated glycoproteins a potential biomarkers
[29]	Carcinoembryonic antigen (CEA), Carbohydrate antigen 19–9 (CA19–9)	4	Serum & cyst fluid	–	Cystadenoma liver	Cyst fluid of CEA &CA19-9 levels were elevated
[30]	IGF-I	192	Serum	–	HCC	Low-baseline IGF-I levels correlate with poor prognosis
[31]	TALDO	(72 samples)	Serum	0.793	HCC	TALDO elevation in HCC patient's serum
[32]	miR-182, miR-301a, miR-373	52	Serum & ascitic fluid	–	HCC	Expression level were elevated in NASH-induced HCC
[33]	miR-26a-5p, miR-141-3p, miR-192-5p, miR-193b-5p, miR-199a-5p, miR-122-5p, miR-206, miR-486-5p	25	Serum	–	HCC	The differentially expressed miRNAs shown in cirrhosis progressed into hepatitis B virus-related HCC

Continued

Table 2 A summary of the journals included in review—cont'd

Reference	Biomarkers	Total participants	Samples	AUC (area under curve)	LC types	Findings
[34]	CA1, ENO1, fibrinogen	19	Ascetic fluid	–	HCC	CA1 predicts poor survival of HCC; ENO1and fibrinogen are potential biomarkers
[35]	MVs	116	Peripheral blood	0.83 (stage-I), 0.94 (stage-II)	HCC	MVs levels elevated in HCC
[36]	ERBB3	113	Serum	0.93 (chronic hepatitis), 0.70 (cirrhosis), 0.97 (ERBB3 & AFP-cirrhosis)	HCC	ERBB3 outperforms AFP & their combination increases the accuracy
[37]	ANXA2	382	Serum	0.734	HCC	ANXA2 was significantly elevated in HCC
[38]	B2M	37	Serum	–	HCC	B2M elevated in patients with HCV-related HCC
[39]	Lipids, *N*-acetyl glycoprotein, choline, glycerol, phosphatidylcholine/ glycerophosphocholine	120	Serum	0.87	HCC	Increase of lipids, *N*-acetyl glycoprotein, choline, glycerol, and decrease of phosphatidylcholine/ glycerophosphocholine in viral compared with nonviral HCC
[40]	MDSCs	60	Peripheral blood & ascitic fluid	–	HCC	Higher MDSCs were seen in HCC

4. Discussion

In the systematic review of 26 studies, 16 types of biomarkers were found to be independently associated with bodily fluids. Most of the studies cited in this review focus on HCC LC type and use AFP as the baseline biomarker to compare the new biomarkers. The area under the curve (AUC) of a biomarker is a good indicator of efficacy but not all research articles in this review address this issue. The AUC was reported in ~46% of the study. The majority of the biomarkers identified were serum based.

4.1 CP

CP is a heterodimeric complex comprised of S100A8 and S100A9 predominant in neutrophil cytosol [15]. They belong to the S100 protein family and bind to calcium and zinc proteins [41]. The application of CP was highlighted in Hanafy et al. and Sun et al. studies and was found to be elevated in HCC patients [15,16]. Both the studies suggest that CP levels are an indicator of HCC. CP is also used in diagnosing inflammatory bowel illness [42].

4.2 WFA

WFA is a purified extract from *W. floribunda* seeds, used as a disease probe, and known to bind to glycan moiety [43]. WFA+-M2BP has been used as a predictor of HCC. Lin et al. studies suggest that WFA+-M2BP is a good prognostic marker and a predictor of a survival rate [17]. Tamaki et al. reported that WFA-sialylated MUC1 can be a useful supplement to AFP and DCP as a prognostic marker [18]. It is also used as a probe in prostate cancer, ovarian cancer, and immunoglobulin A (IgA) nephropathy [43].

4.3 MC-LR

MC-LR is one of the most lethal types of MC variant produced by cyanobacteria, it can cause liver injury when it is exposed [44]. Humans are exposed to the toxin through ingestion, consumption of aquatic products, or direct contact. Lei et al. groups found that MC-LR worsens the prognosis by promoting oxidative stress in the body [19]. When MCs are absorbed into the blood circulation, they can be distributed to various organs such as the liver, brain, kidney, lung, heart, and reproductive system, amplifying cancer cell invasion and metastasis [45].

4.4 DCP

DCP or PIVKA-II is a blood-clotting protein that is generated abnormally in the liver. Hepatocytes may produce DCP/PIVKA-II as a result of a posttranslational flow in the vitamin K-dependent carboxylase [46]. Sultanik et al. and Kamel et al. reported that DCP/PIVKA-II serum level in HCC patients was higher and Sultanik et al. show that

DCP outperforms AFP [20,21]. The DCP/PIVKA-II threshold value for HCC diagnosis varies, and there are no well-established diagnostic cutoff values [20]. As a result, several metacentric studies are needed to evaluate the role of DCP/PIVKA-II.

4.5 Glycoprotein

Changes in glycoprotein distribution have been frequently linked to disease and are a common biomarker in inflammatory and cancer diseases [47]. Gal-3BP is a secreted glycoprotein predominantly expressed in epithelial cells. Serum Gal-3BP levels were elevated in HCC patients, and diagnostic accuracy was increased when paired with AFP [22]. Lee et al. targeted nonglycosylated peptides, revealing that vitronectin and AGP were promising biomarkers for HCC detection [23]. Proteomics analysis also showed that glycoproteins such as A1AG1, A1AT, AACT, CERU, and FETUA were able to discriminate between HCC from other groups [24,25]. An increase in AFP levels doesn't necessarily always correspond to the presence of HCC but also correlates to ALT. Therefore taking ALT into account could increase the AFP specificity in HCC [26]. Elevation AFP levels were associated with HCC development [27]. Fucosylated glycoproteins such as AACT, A1AT, CERU, FETUA, alpha-acid glycoprotein, alpha-2-macroglobulin, serotransferrin, complement factor B, IgG, IgA, and APO-D were elevated in the serum of HCC [28]. The fibrinogen level in HCC ascites was lower than in benign ascites, implying the potential to predict the prognosis in HCC patients [34]. The CEA and CA19-9 levels in cyst fluid were elevated in patients with liver cystadenomas. Thus, cyst fluid demonstrated a valuable indicator of the neoplastic character [29]. Human serum contains a large number of glycoproteins in varying amounts, but isolating and identifying low abundance glycoproteins is a difficult task [48]. Lectins, hydrazide chemistry, hydrophilic interaction liquid chromatography separation, and other techniques have been used to enrich the low abundance of glycoproteins but have reduced reproducibility [23]. However, advancements in various implementation methods are expected to improve the current assay options.

4.6 IGF-I

The liver produces a bulk of circulating IGF-I, reflecting the hepatic function. Patients with low IGF-I serum levels had a greater recurrence rate and a lower survival rate [30]. IGF-I levels are relatively stable and unaffected by food consumption. A drop in IGF-I levels has been linked to Laron syndrome, liver cirrhosis, and age-related cardiovascular and neurological disorders [49].

4.7 TALDO

TALDO expression decreased significantly during hepatocarcinogenesis but increased during tumor progression and metastasis. Serum levels of TALDO in HCC patients were also found to be elevated [31]. This TALDO enzyme participates in the pentose phosphate pathway and has also been linked to head, neck, breast, leukemia, colon, colorectal, esophageal, kidney, lung, and skin cancers [50].

4.8 miRNAs

The miRNA in cancer is well known that they can operate as tumor inducers or suppressor genes. The miR-182, miR-301a, and miR-373 were upregulated in both serum and ascetic fluid in nonalcoholic steatohepatitis and induces HCC [32]. MiRNAs such as miR-26a-5p, miR-141-3p, miR-192-5p, miR-193b-5p, miR-199a-5p, miR-122-5p, miR-206, and miR-486-5p were also differentially expressed hepatitis B virus-related HCC [33]. These miRNAs usually have multiple targets, and identifying the key targets is crucial for screening and treatment [51].

4.9 CA1

Carbonic anhydrases maintain acid-base balance in the blood and other tissues and transport carbon dioxide out of tissues. The CA1 is downregulated in HCC and could serve as an ascites-based biomarker for HCC [34]. CA1 is also a promising biomarker for schistosomiasis, breast, prostate, and nonsmall cell lung cancer [52].

4.10 ENO1

ENO1 in HCC is upregulated in the glycolysis/gluconeogenesis pathway and has been linked to tumor growth and therapeutic failure [34]. ENO1 levels are elevated in more than 70% of human cancer cases worldwide and are associated with poor prognosis [53].

4.11 MVs

MVs are plasma membrane-derived particles released into body fluids, consisting of proteins, lipids, nucleic acids, and other bioactive molecules. The MVs levels were elevated in patients with HCC and showed significantly higher MVs levels in the advanced stage compared with the early stage [35]. Tumor cells produce a considerable amount of MVs during treatment, which correlates with resistance to treatment [54].

4.12 ERBB3

ERBB3 is a member of the epidermal growth factor receptor/ERBB family that regulates cell proliferation, motility, and differentiation by transmitting extracellular signaling and relaying downstream intracellular signaling cascades. Serum ERBB3 isoforms outperform AFP in distinguishing between with and without HCC; combining with AFP significantly improves accuracy [36]. ErbB3 is also overexpressed in many other cancers and linked to a poor prognosis [55].

4.13 ANXA2

ANXA2 is a calcium-dependent phospholipid-binding protein involved in a wide range of biological activities, including antiinflammatory effects, Ca2+-dependent exocytosis, immune responses, Ca2+ transport, and phospholipase A2 regulation. Serum ANXA2 levels in HCC patients were significantly greater than in normal individuals, suggesting that it may play a vital role in LC progression [37]. ANXA2 is also overexpressed in various cancers and correlates positively with poor clinical outcomes [56].

4.14 B2M

Serum level of B2M has been reported to be elevated in chronic inflammatory disease, viral disease, and lymphomas. Ward et al. groups in proteomics studies found B2M to be elevated and most significantly associated with HCC [38]. B2M mutations occur in various malignant cells and affect MHC class I, which allows the immune system to escape tumor cells. This mutated B2M accumulates during cancer growth and treatment [57].

4.15 Metabolites

Metabolites have frequently been used as a prognostic or diagnostic marker and therapeutic screening for a disease. An increase of metabolites such as lipids, *N*-acetyl glycoprotein, choline, glycerol, and a decrease in phosphatidylcholine/glycerophosphocholine was observed by Goossens et al. group in viral compared with nonviral HCC [39]. Many serum metabolites markers have also been reported in other cancers [58].

4.16 MDSCs

MDSCs are a diverse group of cells, primarily of myeloid origin, suppressing various T-cell activities. An increasing number of MDSCs was reported in the blood of various cancer types [59]. A higher number of MDSCs in peripheral blood and ascitic fluid was also reported in HCC patients [40].

Although most of the papers cited in this review are in HCC, LC is a diverse malignancy that needs greater research on different LC forms. The majority of the article uses AFP as the baseline biomarker to compare the sensitivity and specificity of the new biomarkers. The sensitivity and specificity of biomarkers are useful indicators of their effectiveness, but not all studies included in this review discussed this. Despite the advances in technology and clinical practices, current bodily fluids biomarkers research for LC has provided limited success so far. The discovery of bodily fluids biomarkers has tough analytical challenges because of their low abundance, short half-life, tumor heterogeneity, reproducibility, masking by high abundance of nontumoral biomolecules, variability in test conditions, and lack of technology standardization [60–62]. Despite the technical difficulties in measuring body fluid biomarkers, they have significant advantages over traditional tissue biopsy. It is noninvasive with massive potential in clinical oncology and thus requires more research and attention. These findings revealed the changes in bodily fluids biomarker levels, which may be helpful in diagnosis and treatment strategy.

Leveraging available biological data and computer resources, artificial intelligence (AI) or machine learning (ML) could aid in the discovery of bodily fluid biomarkers and overcome the challenges faced in the analytical method. AI or ML have been used to predict urine excretory proteins, saliva-secretory proteins, and blood-secretory proteins, as well as to predict cancer biomarkers [63–72]. Thus integrating AI into liquid biopsy could improve the diagnosis and treatment in LC.

The limitation of this study is that the search was performed only against the PubMed database with restricted time and no statistical analysis was performed. The study only looks at English publications, it is not indicative of non-English journals. Many studies in this review have a small sample size, and sample selection was limited to one location. Therefore, extensive intervention trials research is required to improve biomarker reliability and reproducibility.

5. Conclusions

In conclusion, data in Table 2 indicates that there is clear evidence of how the levels of body fluid biomarkers alter depending on LC formation. In clinical practice, these markers can be used as an adjuvant to aid treatment and diagnosis. Bodily fluids, such as blood or urine, have long been used as a source of disease information for various noncancer illnesses; hence, the present progress of analytical detection technologies and integration of AI could improve their performance in clinical application.

References

[1] H. Sung, J. Ferlay, R.L. Siegel, M. Laversanne, I. Soerjomataram, A. Jemal, F. Bray, Global cancer statistics 2020: GLOBOCAN estimates of incidence and mortality worldwide for 36 cancers in 185 countries, CA Cancer J. Clin. 71 (2021) 209–249, https://doi.org/10.3322/caac.21660.

[2] J.M. Llovet, R.K. Kelley, A. Villanueva, A.G. Singal, E. Pikarsky, S. Roayaie, R. Lencioni, K. Koike, J. Zucman-Rossi, R.S. Finn, Hepatocellular carcinoma, Nat. Rev. Dis. Prim. 7 (2021), https://doi.org/10.1038/s41572-020-00240-3.

[3] Y. Murakami, S. Kubo, A. Tamori, S. Itami, E. Kawamura, K. Iwaisako, K. Ikeda, N. Kawada, T. Ochiya, Y.H. Taguchi, Comprehensive analysis of transcriptome and metabolome analysis in intrahepatic cholangiocarcinoma and hepatocellular carcinoma, Sci. Rep. 5 (2015) 1–4, https://doi.org/10.1038/srep16294.

[4] UK Cancer Research, Types of Liver Cancer. https://www.cancerresearchuk.org/about-cancer/liver-cancer/types. (Accessed 1 October 2021).

[5] Stanford Health Care, Liver Cancer Types. https://stanfordhealthcare.org/medical-conditions/cancer/liver-cancer/liver-cancer-types.html. (Accessed 1 October 2021).

[6] American Cancer Society, Liver Cancer Survival Rates. https://www.cancer.org/cancer/liver-cancer/detection-diagnosis-staging/survival-rates.html. (Accessed 2 October 2021).

[7] A. Forner, M. Reig, J. Bruix, Hepatocellular carcinoma, Lancet 391 (2018) 1301–1314, https://doi.org/10.1016/S0140-6736(18)30010-2.

[8] J.A. Marrero, L.M. Kulik, C.B. Sirlin, A.X. Zhu, R.S. Finn, M.M. Abecassis, L.R. Roberts, J.K. Heimbach, Diagnosis, staging, and management of hepatocellular carcinoma: 2018 practice guidance by the American Association for the Study of Liver Diseases, Hepatology 68 (2018) 723–750, https://doi.org/10.1002/hep.29913.
[9] O. Atiq, J. Tiro, A.C. Yopp, A. Muffler, J.A. Marrero, N.D. Parikh, C. Murphy, K. McCallister, A.G. Singal, An assessment of benefits and harms of hepatocellular carcinoma surveillance in patients with cirrhosis, Hepatology 65 (2017) 1196–1205, https://doi.org/10.1002/hep.28895.
[10] M. Chen, H. Zhao, Next-generation sequencing in liquid biopsy: cancer screening and early detection, Hum. Genomics 13 (2019) 34, https://doi.org/10.1186/s40246-019-0220-8.
[11] Y. Pan, H. Chen, J. Yu, Biomarkers in hepatocellular carcinoma: current status and future perspectives, Biomedicines 8 (2020), https://doi.org/10.3390/biomedicines8120576.
[12] M. Sherman, Serological Surveillance for hepatocellular carcinoma: time to quit, J. Hepatol. 52 (2010) 614–615, https://doi.org/10.1016/j.jhep.2009.11.026.
[13] F. Pelizzaro, R. Cardin, B. Penzo, E. Pinto, A. Vitale, U. Cillo, F.P. Russo, F. Farinati, Liquid biopsy in hepatocellular carcinoma: where are we now? Cancers (Basel). 13 (2021) 1–42, https://doi.org/10.3390/cancers13092274.
[14] A. Liberati, D.G. Altman, J. Tetzlaff, C. Mulrow, P.C. Gøtzsche, J.P.A. Ioannidis, M. Clarke, P.J. Devereaux, J. Kleijnen, D. Moher, The PRISMA statement for reporting systematic reviews and meta-analyses of studies that evaluate health care interventions: explanation and elaboration, PLoS Med. 6 (2009), https://doi.org/10.1371/journal.pmed.1000100.
[15] A.S. Hanafy, M.S. Mohamed, A.A. Alnagar, Ascitic calprotectin as an early predictor of hepatocellular carcinoma in patients with cirrhotic ascites, J. Cancer Res. Clin. Oncol. 146 (2020) 3207–3214, https://doi.org/10.1007/s00432-020-03363-y.
[16] W. Sun, B. Xing, L. Guo, Z. Liu, J. Mu, L. Sun, H. Wei, X. Zhao, X. Qian, Y. Jiang, F. He, Quantitative proteomics analysis of tissue interstitial fluid for identification of novel serum candidate diagnostic marker for hepatocellular carcinoma, Sci. Rep. 6 (2016) 1–8, https://doi.org/10.1038/srep26499.
[17] J. Lin, C.J. Ko, Y.J. Hung, P.Y. Lin, K.H. Lin, C.E. Hsieh, C. Te Chou, Y.L. Chen, Prognostic role of serum *Wisteria floribunda* agglutinin-positive mac-2 binding protein level in early stage hepatocellular carcinoma, Sci. Rep. 10 (2020) 1–9, https://doi.org/10.1038/s41598-020-62631-6.
[18] N. Tamaki, A. Kuno, A. Matsuda, H. Tsujikawa, K. Yamazaki, Y. Yasui, K. Tsuchiya, H. Nakanishi, J. Itakura, M. Korenaga, M. Mizokami, M. Kurosaki, M. Sakamoto, H. Narimatsu, N. Izumi, Serum *Wisteria floribunda* agglutinin-positive sialylated mucin 1 as a marker of progenitor/ biliary features in hepatocellular carcinoma, Sci. Rep. 7 (2017) 1–10, https://doi.org/10.1038/s41598-017-00357-8.
[19] F. Lei, X. Lei, R. Li, H. Tan, Microcystin-LR in peripheral circulation worsens the prognosis partly through oxidative stress in patients with hepatocellular carcinoma, Clin. Exp. Med. (2019) 235–243, https://doi.org/10.1007/s10238-019-00550-1.
[20] P. Sultanik, A. Ginguay, J. Vandame, T. Popovici, J.F. Meritet, L. Cynober, S. Pol, P.N. Bories, Diagnostic accuracy of des-gamma-carboxy prothrombin for hepatocellular carcinoma in a French cohort using the Lumipulse® G600 analyzer, J. Viral Hepat. 24 (2017) 80–85, https://doi.org/10.1111/jvh.12622.
[21] M.M. Kamel, M.F. Saad, A.A. Mahmoud, A.A. Edries, A.S. Abdel-Moneim, Evaluation of serum PIVKA-II and MIF as diagnostic markers for HCV/HBV induced hepatocellular carcinoma, Microb. Pathog. 77 (2014) 31–35, https://doi.org/10.1016/j.micpath.2014.10.009.
[22] T. Liu, D. Liu, R. Liu, H. Jiang, G. Yan, W. Li, L. Sun, S. Zhang, Y. Liu, K. Guo, Discovering potential serological biomarker for chronic hepatitis B virus-related hepatocellular carcinoma in Chinese population by MAL-associated serum glycoproteomics analysis, Sci. Rep. 7 (2017) 1–10, https://doi.org/10.1038/srep38918.
[23] J.Y. Lee, J.Y. Kim, M.H. Cheon, G.W. Park, Y.H. Ahn, M.H. Moon, J.S. Yoo, MRM validation of targeted nonglycosylated peptides from N-glycoprotein biomarkers using direct trypsin digestion of undepleted human plasma, J. Proteome 98 (2014) 206–217, https://doi.org/10.1016/j.jprot.2014.01.003.
[24] Y.H. Ahn, P.M. Shin, N.R. Oh, G.W. Park, H. Kim, J.S. Yoo, A lectin-coupled, targeted proteomic mass spectrometry (MRM MS) platform for identification of multiple liver cancer biomarkers in human plasma, J. Proteome 75 (2012) 5507–5515, https://doi.org/10.1016/j.jprot.2012.06.027.

[25] Y.H. Ahn, P.M. Shin, Y.S. Kim, N.R. Oh, E.S. Ji, K.H. Kim, Y.J. Lee, S.H. Kim, J.S. Yoo, Quantitative analysis of aberrant protein glycosylation in liver cancer plasma by AAL-enrichment and MRM mass spectrometry, Analyst 138 (2013) 6454–6462, https://doi.org/10.1039/c3an01126g.
[26] P. Richardson, Z. Duan, J. Kramer, J.A. Davila, G.L. Tyson, H.B. El-Serag, Determinants of serum alpha-fetoprotein levels in hepatitis C-infected patients, Clin. Gastroenterol. Hepatol. 10 (2012) 428–433, https://doi.org/10.1016/j.cgh.2011.11.025.
[27] M.G. Bruce, D. Bruden, B.J. McMahon, C. Christensen, C. Homan, D. Sullivan, H. Deubner, J. Williams, S.E. Livingston, D. Gretch, Clinical significance of elevated alpha-fetoprotein in Alaskan native patients with chronic hepatitis C, J. Viral Hepat. 15 (2008) 179–187, https://doi.org/10.1111/j.1365-2893.2007.00928.x.
[28] M.A. Comunale, M. Lowman, R.E. Long, J. Krakover, R. Philip, S. Seeholzer, A.A. Evans, H.W.L. Hann, T.M. Block, A.S. Mehta, Proteomic analysis of serum associated fucosylated glycoproteins in the development of primary hepatocellular carcinoma, J. Proteome Res. 5 (2006) 308–315, https://doi.org/10.1021/pr050328x.
[29] E. Dixon, F.R. Sutherland, P. Mitchell, G. McKinnon, V. Nayak, Cystadenomas of the liver: a spectrum of disease, Can. J. Surg. 44 (2001) 371–376.
[30] E.J. Cho, J.H. Lee, J.J. Yoo, W.M. Choi, M.J. Lee, Y. Cho, D.H. Lee, Y. Bin Lee, J.H. Kwon, S.J. Yu, J.M. Lee, K.S. Suh, K. Kim, Y.J. Kim, J.H. Yoon, C.Y. Kim, H.S. Lee, Serum insulin-like growth factor-i level is an independent predictor of recurrence and survival in early hepatocellular carcinoma: a prospective cohort study, Clin. Cancer Res. 19 (2013) 4218–4227, https://doi.org/10.1158/1078-0432.CCR-12-3443.
[31] C. Wang, K. Guo, D. Gao, X. Kang, K. Jiang, Y. Li, L. Sun, S. Zhang, C. Sun, X. Liu, W. Wu, P. Yang, Y. Liu, Identification of transaldolase as a novel serum biomarker for hepatocellular carcinoma metastasis using xenografted mouse model and clinic samples, Cancer Lett. 313 (2011) 154–166, https://doi.org/10.1016/j.canlet.2011.08.031.
[32] A.N. Muhammad Yusuf, R.A. Raja Ali, K.N. Muhammad Nawawi, N.M. Mokhtar, Potential biomarkers in Nash-induced liver cirrhosis with hepatocellular carcinoma: a preliminary work on roles of exosomal miR-182, miR-301a, and miR-373, Malays. J. Pathol. 42 (2020) 377–384.
[33] Y. Tan, B. Lin, Y. Ye, D. Wen, L. Chen, X. Zhou, Differential expression of serum microRNAs in cirrhosis that evolve into hepatocellular carcinoma related to hepatitis B virus, Oncol. Rep. 33 (2015) 2863–2870, https://doi.org/10.3892/or.2015.3924.
[34] J. Zhang, R. Liang, J. Wei, J. Ye, Q. He, J. Chunlingyuan, Y. Ye, Z. Li, Y.L. Liu, Identification of candidate biomarkers in malignant ascites from patients with hepatocellular carcinoma by iTRAQ-based quantitative proteomic analysis, Biomed Res. Int. 2018 (2018), https://doi.org/10.1155/2018/5484976.
[35] W. Wang, H. Li, Y. Zhou, S. Jie, Peripheral blood microvesicles are potential biomarkers for hepatocellular carcinoma, Cancer Biomarkers 13 (2013) 351–357, https://doi.org/10.3233/CBM-130370.
[36] S.Y. Hsieh, J.R. He, M.C. Yu, W.C. Lee, T.C. Chen, S.J. Lo, R. Bera, C.M. Sung, C.T. Chiu, Secreted ERBB3 isoforms are serum markers for early hepatoma in patients with chronic hepatitis and cirrhosis, J. Proteome Res. 10 (2011) 4715–4724, https://doi.org/10.1021/pr200519q.
[37] N.Y. Ji, M.-Y. Park, Y.H. Kang, C. Il Lee, D.G. Kim, Y. Il Yeom, Y.J. Jang, P.-K. Myung, J.W. Kim, H.G. Lee, J.W. Kim, K. Lee, E.Y. Song, Evaluation of annexin II as a potential serum marker for hepatocellular carcinoma using a developed sandwich ELISA method, Int. J. Mol. Med. 24 (2009) 765–771, https://doi.org/10.3892/ijmm_00000290.
[38] D.G. Ward, Y. Cheng, G. N'Kontchou, T.T. Thar, N. Barget, W. Wei, A. Martin, M. Beaugrand, P.J. Johnson, Preclinical and post-treatment changes in the HCC-associated serum proteome, Br. J. Cancer 95 (2006) 1379–1383, https://doi.org/10.1038/sj.bjc.6603429.
[39] C. Goossens, P. Nahon, L. Le Moyec, M.N. Triba, N. Bouchemal, R. Amathieu, N. Ganne-Carrié, M. Ziol, J.C. Trinchet, N. Sellier, A. Diallo, O. Seror, P. Savarin, Sequential serum metabolomic profiling after radiofrequency ablation of hepatocellular carcinoma reveals different response patterns according to etiology, J. Proteome Res. 15 (2016) 1446–1454, https://doi.org/10.1021/acs.jproteome.5b01032.
[40] N. Elwan, M.L. Salem, A. Kobtan, F. El-Kalla, L. Mansour, M. Yousef, A. Al-Sabbagh, A.A.A. Zidan, S. Abd-Elsalam, High numbers of myeloid derived suppressor cells in peripheral blood and

ascitic fluid of cirrhotic and HCC patients, Immunol. Investig. 47 (2018) 169–180, https://doi.org/10.1080/08820139.2017.1407787.

[41] Y. Nakatani, M. Yamazaki, W.J. Chazin, S. Yui, Regulation of S100A8/A9 (calprotectin) binding to tumor cells by zinc ion and its implication for apoptosis-inducing activity, Mediat. Inflamm. 2005 (2005) 280–292, https://doi.org/10.1155/MI.2005.280.

[42] A. Jukic, L. Bakiri, E.F. Wagner, H. Tilg, T.E. Adolph, Calprotectin: from biomarker to biological function, Gut (2021) 1978–1988, https://doi.org/10.1136/gutjnl-2021-324855.

[43] H. Narimatsu, T. Sato, *Wisteria floribunda* agglutinin positive glycobiomarkers: a unique lectin as a serum biomarker probe in various diseases, Expert Rev. Proteomics 15 (2018) 183–190, https://doi.org/10.1080/14789450.2018.1419066.

[44] R.D. Welten, J.P. Meneely, C.T. Elliott, A comparative review of the effect of microcystin-LR on the proteome, Expo. Heal. 12 (2020) 111–129, https://doi.org/10.1007/s12403-019-00303-1.

[45] I.Y. Massey, F. Yang, Z. Ding, S. Yang, J. Guo, C. Tezi, M. Al-Osman, R.B. Kamegni, W. Zeng, Exposure routes and health effects of microcystins on animals and humans: a mini-review, Toxicon 151 (2018) 156–162, https://doi.org/10.1016/j.toxicon.2018.07.010.

[46] M. Ono, H. Ohta, M. Ohhira, C. Sekiya, M. Namiki, Measurement of immunoreactive prothrombin precursor and vitamin-K-dependent gamma-carboxylation in human hepatocellular carcinoma tissues: decreased carboxylation of prothrombin precursor as a cause of des-gamma-carboxyprothrombin synthesis, Tumour Biol. J. Int. Soc. Oncodevelopmental Biol. Med. 11 (1990) 319–326, https://doi.org/10.1159/000217667.

[47] K. Chandler, R. Goldman, Glycoprotein disease markers and single protein-omics, Mol. Cell. Proteomics 12 (2013) 836–845, https://doi.org/10.1074/mcp.R112.026930.

[48] K. Sparbier, A. Asperger, A. Resemann, I. Kessler, S. Koch, T. Wenzel, G. Stein, L. Vorwerg, D. Suckau, M. Kostrzewa, Analysis of glycoproteins in human serum by means of glycospecific magnetic bead separation and LC-MALDI-TOF/TOF analysis with automated glycopeptide detection, J. Biomol. Tech. 18 (2007) 252–258.

[49] J.E. Puche, I. Castilla-Cortázar, Human conditions of insulin-like growth factor-I (IGF-I) deficiency, J. Transl. Med. 10 (2012) 1–29, https://doi.org/10.1186/1479-5876-10-224.

[50] A.K. Samland, G.A. Sprenger, Transaldolase: from biochemistry to human disease, Int. J. Biochem. Cell Biol. 41 (2009) 1482–1494, https://doi.org/10.1016/j.biocel.2009.02.001.

[51] Y. Peng, C.M. Croce, The role of microRNAs in human cancer, Signal Transduct. Target. Ther. 1 (2016), https://doi.org/10.1038/sigtrans.2015.4.

[52] S. Zamanova, A.M. Shabana, U.K. Mondal, M.A. Ilies, Carbonic anhydrases as disease markers, Expert Opin. Ther. Pat. 29 (2019) 509–533, https://doi.org/10.1080/13543776.2019.1629419.

[53] C.K. Huang, Y. Sun, L. Lv, Y. Ping, ENO1 and Cancer, Mol. Ther. Oncolytics 24 (2022) 288–298, https://doi.org/10.1016/j.omto.2021.12.026.

[54] K. Menck, S. Sivaloganathan, A. Bleckmann, C. Binder, Microvesicles in cancer: small size, large potential, Int. J. Mol. Sci. 21 (2020) 1–30, https://doi.org/10.3390/ijms21155373.

[55] U. Hafeez, A.C. Parslow, H.K. Gan, A.M. Scott, New insights into ErbB3 function and therapeutic targeting in cancer, Expert. Rev. Anticancer. Ther. 20 (2020) 1057–1074, https://doi.org/10.1080/14737140.2020.1829485.

[56] T. Wang, Z. Wang, R. Niu, L. Wang, Crucial role of Anxa2 in cancer progression: highlights on its novel regulatory mechanism, Cancer Biol. Med. 16 (2019) 671–687, https://doi.org/10.20892/j.issn.2095-3941.2019.0228.

[57] H. Wang, B. Liu, J. Wei, Beta2-microglobulin(B2M) in cancer immunotherapies: biological function, resistance and remedy, Cancer Lett. 517 (2021) 96–104, https://doi.org/10.1016/j.canlet.2021.06.008.

[58] M. Mamas, W.B. Dunn, L. Neyses, R. Goodacre, The role of metabolites and metabolomics in clinically applicable biomarkers of disease, Arch. Toxicol. 85 (2011) 5–17, https://doi.org/10.1007/s00204-010-0609-6.

[59] D.I. Gabrilovich, S. Nagaraj, Myeloid-derived suppressor cells as regulators of the immune system, Nat. Rev. Immunol. 9 (2009) 162–174, https://doi.org/10.1038/nri2506.

[60] P.H. Roos, N. Jakubowski, Methods for the discovery of low-abundance biomarkers for urinary bladder cancer in biological fluids, Bioanalysis 2 (2010) 295–309, https://doi.org/10.4155/bio.09.174.

[61] K. Page, J.A. Shaw, D.S. Guttery, The liquid biopsy: towards standardisation in preparation for prime time, Lancet Oncol. 20 (2019) 758–760, https://doi.org/10.1016/S1470-2045(19)30310-9.
[62] A. Di Meo, J. Bartlett, Y. Cheng, M.D. Pasic, G.M. Yousef, Liquid biopsy: a step forward towards precision medicine in urologic malignancies, Mol. Cancer 16 (2017) 1–14, https://doi.org/10.1186/s12943-017-0644-5.
[63] J. Wang, Y. Liang, Y. Wang, J. Cui, M. Liu, W. Du, Y. Xu, Computational prediction of human salivary proteins from blood circulation and application to diagnostic biomarker identification, PLoS One 8 (2013) 1–9, https://doi.org/10.1371/journal.pone.0080211.
[64] C.S. Hong, J. Cui, Z. Ni, Y. Su, D. Puett, F. Li, Y. Xu, A computational method for prediction of excretory proteins and application to identification of gastric cancer markers in urine, PLoS One 6 (2011) 2–9, https://doi.org/10.1371/journal.pone.0016875.
[65] J. Cui, Y. Chen, W.C. Chou, L. Sun, L. Chen, J. Suo, Z. Ni, M. Zhang, X. Kong, L.L. Hoffman, J. Kang, Y. Su, V. Olman, D. Johnson, D.W. Tench, I.J. Amster, R. Orlando, D. Puett, F. Li, Y. Xu, An integrated transcriptomic and computational analysis for biomarker identification in gastric cancer, Nucleic Acids Res. 39 (2011) 1197–1207, https://doi.org/10.1093/nar/gkq960.
[66] Y. Wang, W. Du, Y. Liang, X. Chen, C. Zhang, W. Pang, Y. Xu, PUEPro: a computational pipeline for prediction of urine excretory proteins, in: Lecture Notes in Computer Science (Including Subser. Lect. Notes Artif. Intell. Lect. Notes Bioinformatics), 10086, 2016, pp. 714–725, https://doi.org/10.1007/978-3-319-49586-6_51.
[67] D. Shao, L. Huang, Y. Wang, K. He, X. Cui, Y. Wang, Q. Ma, J. Cui, DeepSec: a deep learning framework for secreted protein discovery in human body fluids, Bioinformatics 38 (2021) 228–235, https://doi.org/10.1093/bioinformatics/btab545.
[68] L. Huang, D. Shao, Y. Wang, X. Cui, Y. Li, Q. Chen, J. Cui, Human body-fluid proteome: quantitative profiling and computational prediction, Brief. Bioinform. 22 (2021) 315–333, https://doi.org/10.1093/bib/bbz160.
[69] D. Shao, L. Huang, Y. Wang, X. Cui, K. He, Y. Wang, Computational prediction of human body-fluid protein, in: Proc. of 2019 IEEE Int. Conf. Bioinforma. Biomed. BIBM 2019, 2019, pp. 2735–2740, https://doi.org/10.1109/BIBM47256.2019.8982951.
[70] J. Cui, Q. Liu, D. Puett, Y. Xu, Computational prediction of human proteins that can be secreted into the bloodstream, Bioinformatics 24 (2008) 2370–2375, https://doi.org/10.1093/bioinformatics/btn418.
[71] W. Du, R. Pang, G. Li, H. Cao, Y. Li, Y. Liang, DeepUEP: prediction of urine excretory proteins using deep learning, IEEE Access 8 (2020) 100251–100261, https://doi.org/10.1109/ACCESS.2020.2997937.
[72] W. Du, Y. Sun, G. Li, H. Cao, R. Pang, Y. Li, CapsNet-SSP: multilane capsule network for predicting human saliva-secretory proteins, BMC Bioinform. 21 (2020) 1–17, https://doi.org/10.1186/s12859-020-03579-2.

CHAPTER 17

Study on biomarkers in endometrial cancer using transcriptome data: A machine learning approach

Vigneshwar Suriya Prakash Sinnarasan, Dahrii Paul, Rajesh Das, Dinakara Rao Ampasala, and Amouda Venkatesan
Department of Bioinformatics, Pondicherry University, Puducherry, India

Abstract

Endometrial cancer (EC) is women-related cancer and the most common malignancy worldwide. The prognosis of the EC remains poor because its diagnosis is only in an advanced stage. Potential diagnostic biomarkers are much needed to enhance EC diagnosis; however, machine learning (ML) derived remarkable results in biomarker discovery. The current study aimed to perform an integrated bioinformatics and ML analysis on publicly available data to explore the identification of novel biomarkers to diagnose EC. RNA-Seq data downloaded from the database, The Cancer Genome Atlas, and the aberrantly expressed significant genes extracted by data analysis. Subsequently, differentially expressed genes (DEGs) were identified and functionally annotated via gene ontology and also performed the pathway analysis. Through protein-protein interaction, the interaction between the proteins and hub genes is generated. The study resulted in 10 hub genes BUB1B, KIF20A, BIRC5, UBE2C, CDC20, CDCA8, DLGAP5, CCNB2, KIF2C, and TOP2A that involves in the progression of EC. In addition, the significant features of DEGs were selected using the recursive feature elimination method to predict the EC. Using ML models the diagnostic performance of the features is validated. The model identified ASF1B, SAPDC2, BIRC5, CDC25C, MAP3K20, TMEM196, IQGAP3, MK167, PRAME, GTSE1, GLRA4, and NEK2 as additional biomarkers. The overall results show that these diagnostic biomarkers achieved well-balanced accuracy in the prediction of EC.

Abbreviations

BIRC5	baculoviral IAP repeat containing 5
BUB1B	mitotic checkpoint serine/threonine kinase BUB1 beta
CCNB2	cyclin B2
CDCA8	cell division cycle associated 8
CDDC20	cell division cycle20
DEGs	differentially expressed genes
DLGAP2	DLG associated protein 5
DT	decision tree
EC	endometrial cancer
GO	gene ontologies

Computational Methods in Drug Discovery and Repurposing for Cancer Therapy
https://doi.org/10.1016/B978-0-443-15280-1.00019-4

KIF20A kinesin family member 20A
KIF2C kinesin family member 2C
MCODE molecular complex detection
MDA mean decrease accuracy
PPI protein-protein interaction
RF random forest
RFE recursive feature elimination
STRING search tool for the retrieval of interacting genes
SVM support vector machines
TCGA the cancer genome atlas
TOP2A topoisomerase II alpha
UBE2C ubiquitin-conjugating enzyme E2C

1. Introduction

Endometrial cancer (EC) is the neoplasm developed in the lining of the uterus (endometrium), the most frequent cancer of the female reproductive organs. EC is the sixth most often diagnosed cancer worldwide; in 2020, uterine corpus cancer with 417,000 newly diagnosed cases and 97,000 fatalities expected [1]. The incidence of EC is less in Asian countries when compared with western countries. The survival rates of EC patients have also increased because of the early detection, whereas the prognosis of EC patients varies according to the patient characteristics. A few factors like tobacco usage reduces EC patients' 5-years survival rate by 10% than the nonusers of tobacco [2]. The significant risk factors for EC are BMI, diabetes, late menopause, tamoxifen therapy, and endometrial hyperplasia (EH) [3–5]. Transvaginal ultrasonography (to measure endometrial thickness) and endometrial biopsy (from endometrial tissue sample) are used for the initial screening of EC [6]. Like other cancers, 5-year survival rate varies based on the stages of EC. The 5-year survival rate for initially diagnosed patients is 95%, but the survival rate 17% for the patients diagnosed in the later stage when the cancer spread to other parts of the body [7] (https://www.cancer.net/).The statistics reported that black women have a less risk of EC, however, this cohort has a poor survival rate because of the aggressiveness of the cancer [8]. Compared with the patients with bleeding postmenopausal, for the asymptomatic postmenopausal patients the survival rate is relatively low [9]. The prognosis of the EC is high when it is diagnosed in an early stage, but the screening in the early stage is a difficult task for physicians and researchers. Hence better screening procedures for early diagnosis of EC are required to increase the survival rate [10].

Nowadays, high-throughput sequencing (HTS) technologies make cancer research more comprehensive. The availability of public databases like The Cancer Genome Atlas (TCGA), and gene expression omnibus makes the researchers to access the different types of data (genome, transcriptome, epigenome, and clinical data) from numerous patients. Recent development in genome analysis let out several biomarkers responsible for the diagnosis and prognosis of several cancers [11–13]. A few studies have investigated the molecular markers involved in EC progression and prognosis [14–16]. HTS data are high in dimensions thus traditional statistical procedures may result in the loss of some essential information when large amounts of data are dealt with. Machine learning (ML) is used in biomarker discovery for the past two decades for any types of disease. It is a method of training a model to learn from data for a specific task using mathematical methodologies [17–19]. Recently, Chen et al., have applied ML algorithms to find the prognostic biomarkers in the tumor microenvironment of EC [7]. The more frequently used ML algorithms include random forest (RF), support vector machines (SVM), and decision tree (DT) [20–23]. The availability of HTS data in the TCGA database and ML algorithm together would result in more accurate prediction of diagnostic biomarkers.

Consider the significance of the early diagnosis of EC to increase the patient's prognosis. By data analysis, this study identified the differentially expressed genes (DEGs) using the data from the TCGA database considered for EC tissue and normal endometrial tissue. Further, using the integrated bioinformatics analysis found the hub genes responsible for the progression of EC. In addition, the potential diagnostic biomarkers are predicted using ML techniques. Further, the ML classification model is used to validate the diagnostic performance of the biomarkers. The goal of the study is to discover variables that influences the EC progression and makes the diagnosis easy.

2. Materials and methods

2.1 Dataset and preprocessing

Collected the transcriptome data of uterine corpus endometrial carcinoma (UCEC) by downloading from TCGA database (Fig. 1). The UCEC has 586 samples (551 cancer and

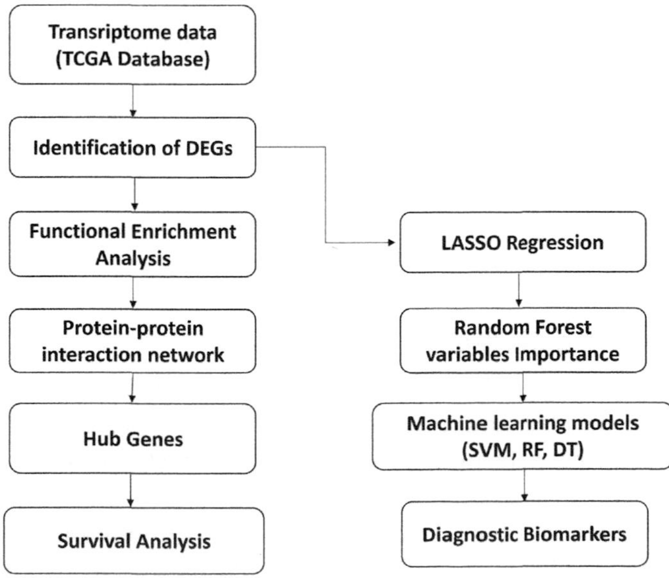

Fig. 1 Workflow of the study.

35 normal samples), the raw counts of the gene expression data, and their clinical information, were also downloaded from TCGA - GDC database using TCGAbiolinks [24].

2.2 Identification of DEGs

The TCGA - UCEC mRNA expression profile was analyzed using the DESeq2 package of R and Rstudio software [25]. Removal of the read counts with <10 and then the samples are mapped with clinical factors using clinical data to extract the DEGs. DEGs are selected using the criteria, log2FoldChange |(logFC)|<3 and false discovery rate *P*-value <.05. Using R package EnhancedVolcano [https://bioconductor.org/packages/EnhancedVolcano/], performed volcano plot analysis on DEGs to visualize the expression pattern.

2.3 Enrichment analysis

The identified DEGs were analyzed using the clusterProfiler (v4.0) package in R to show the gene ontology (GO) terms [26]. ClusterProfiler (v4.0) package is one of the most extensively used strategies for analyzing a set of genes from various HTS studies. GO annotate the biological processes (BP), molecular functions (MF), and cellular components (CC) by clustering the genes. Kyoto enrichment of genes and genomes (KEGG) pathway enrichment analysis was performed using clusterProfiler [27]. All enrichment analysis was performed in R and RStudio.

2.4 Protein-protein interaction network

Furthermore, using the identified DEGs built a protein-protein interaction (PPI) network, which showed the interaction between DEGs encoding proteins. By submitting the DEGs in the search tool for the retrieval of interacting genes (STRING), a publicly available database gives out the potential relationships among the encoding proteins [28]. The interaction between the DEGs with a combined score >0.9 (highest confidence score) was determined significant, and then the PPI was envisaged using Cytoscape software (3.9). The highly interacting genes obtained from the dense cluster of the constructed network checked using molecular complex detection (MCODE) [29]. The top 10 hub genes are selected based on the degrees using the cytoHubba module in the Cytoscape from highly interacted cluster [30].

2.5 Optimal diagnostic biomarkers

The study used statistical and ML methods to identify the optimal diagnostic biomarkers to predict EC. The most favorable features of DEGs were selected using feature selection techniques. To minimizes the prediction error of the model, calculated the variables and regression coefficients using least absolute shrinkage and selection operator (LASSO) [31]. The LASSO is a variable selection method for regression models and performed its analysis using the "glmnet" package in R (https://cran.r- 89project.org/web/

packages/glmnet/). Out of the lowest error rate result, the best parameters are chosen. The RF algorithm selected the potential features (which describe the complete set of data) from LASSO features [32]. The significance of each variable chosen randomly was prioritized from large to small depending on the mean decrease accuracy value. The maximum number of features selected was indicated by adding one DEG in the top-down method using an RF algorithm in 10-fold cross validation. The final step checked the diagnostic performance of the selected variables by implementing the classification models. The developed models using RF, SVM, and DT are evaluated for its accuracy and kappa score [33–35].

2.6 Survival analysis of hub genes

GEPIA is a tool used to investigate survival associations by contrasting clinical data with gene expression profiles of the TCGA - UCEC. It is used to check the prognostic impacts of the hub genes. Survival Analysis shows the association between hub genes and overall survival (OS) [36].

3. Results

3.1 Data processing and DEGs identification

The transcriptome expression count TCGA-UCEC data of 586 samples (551 EC tissue and 35 normal tissue) downloaded using TCGAbiolinks. *P*-value <.05 and log2FC >3 fixed as the cutoff criteria for selecting DEGs. From that total of 1386 DEGs (411 upregulated and 975 downregulated) were selected as significant DEGs by using DESeq2 analysis. The visualization of the DEG expressed pattern is demonstrated using the volcano plot in (Fig. 2).

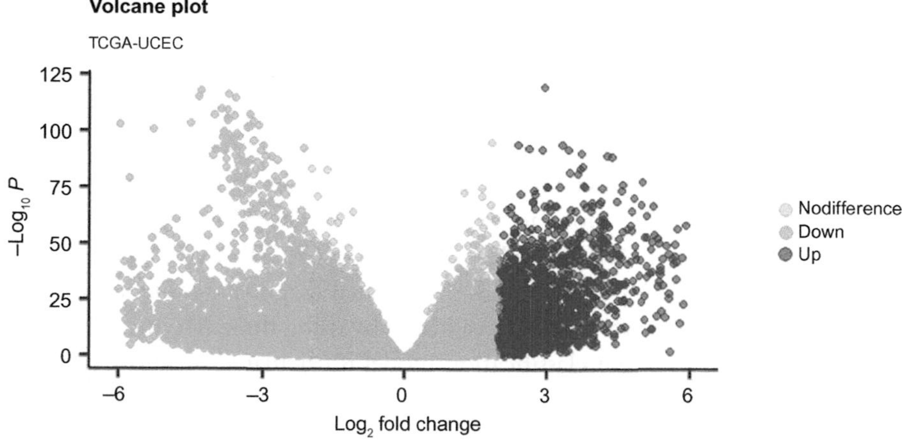

Fig. 2 Volcano plot for TCGA-UCEC.

3.2 Functional and pathway enrichment

The extracted DEGs were used to explore the biological functions by GO and KEGG pathway analysis. Mainly, the DEGs are enriched in BP associated with the cellular macromolecule metabolic process, developmental process, and anatomical structure development. Also, in MF and CC, the DEGs are enriched in nucleic acid binding, DNA binding, transcription regulator activity, intracellular membrane-bounded organelle, and nucleus (Fig. 3). The KEGG pathway analysis showed that the DEGs are mainly associated with calcium signaling pathway, alcoholism, and vascular smooth muscle contraction (Fig. 3).

3.3 Protein-protein interaction network

STRING database found the interaction between the DEGs coding proteins with the confidence >0.9 as scrutiny criteria to collect the more authenticated interactions. The network consists of 347 nodes and 2388 edges, among which, a highly connected protein cluster was found by performing MCODE analysis (Fig. 4). The MCODE analysis showed 34 nodes and 1008 edges as highly interacted clusters. Top 10 ten proteins identified from the clusters using cytoHubba with a cutoff degree >30. Finally, mitotic checkpoint serine/threonine kinase BUB1 beta (BUB1B), kinesin family member 20A (KIF20A), Baculoviral IAP repeat containing 5 (BIRC5), Ubiquitin-conjugating enzyme E2C (UBE2C), cell division cycle20 (CDC20), cell division cycle associated 8 (CDCA8), DLG associated protein 5 (DLGAP5), cyclin B2 (CCNB2), kinesin family member 2C (KIF2C), and topoisomerase II alpha (TOP2A) hub genes are found to be involved in the progression of the EC (Fig. 5). The expression values and *p*-values of the hub genes were given in Table 1.

3.4 Identification of optimal diagnostic biomarkers

Found the diagnostic molecular markers of EC using the expression values of DEGs between EC and normal tissue. Using *Z*-score normalization, the data of expression values are normalized, and the features were reduced to 300 variables by the LASSO regression analysis. Further analysis of the RFE-RF algorithm showed that randomly selected 12 variables have achieved the highest accuracy >95% (Fig. 6).The importance of the variables are found by mean decrease value to find the top 12 features, which contributes to prediction of EC more accurately (Fig. 7). The ASF1B, SAPDC2, BIRC5, CDC25C, MAP3K20, TMEM196, IQGAP3, MK167, PRAME, GTSE1, GLRA4, and NEK2 are top 12 features selected as the optimal diagnostic biomarkers. The diagnostic performance of the biomarkers is validated by using three ML models (SVM, DT, and RF). The accuracy of the classification model is calculated to know the predictive performance. It is found that the predictive performance of 12 biomarkers falls in the acceptable range. Although all three classifications models achieved well-balanced

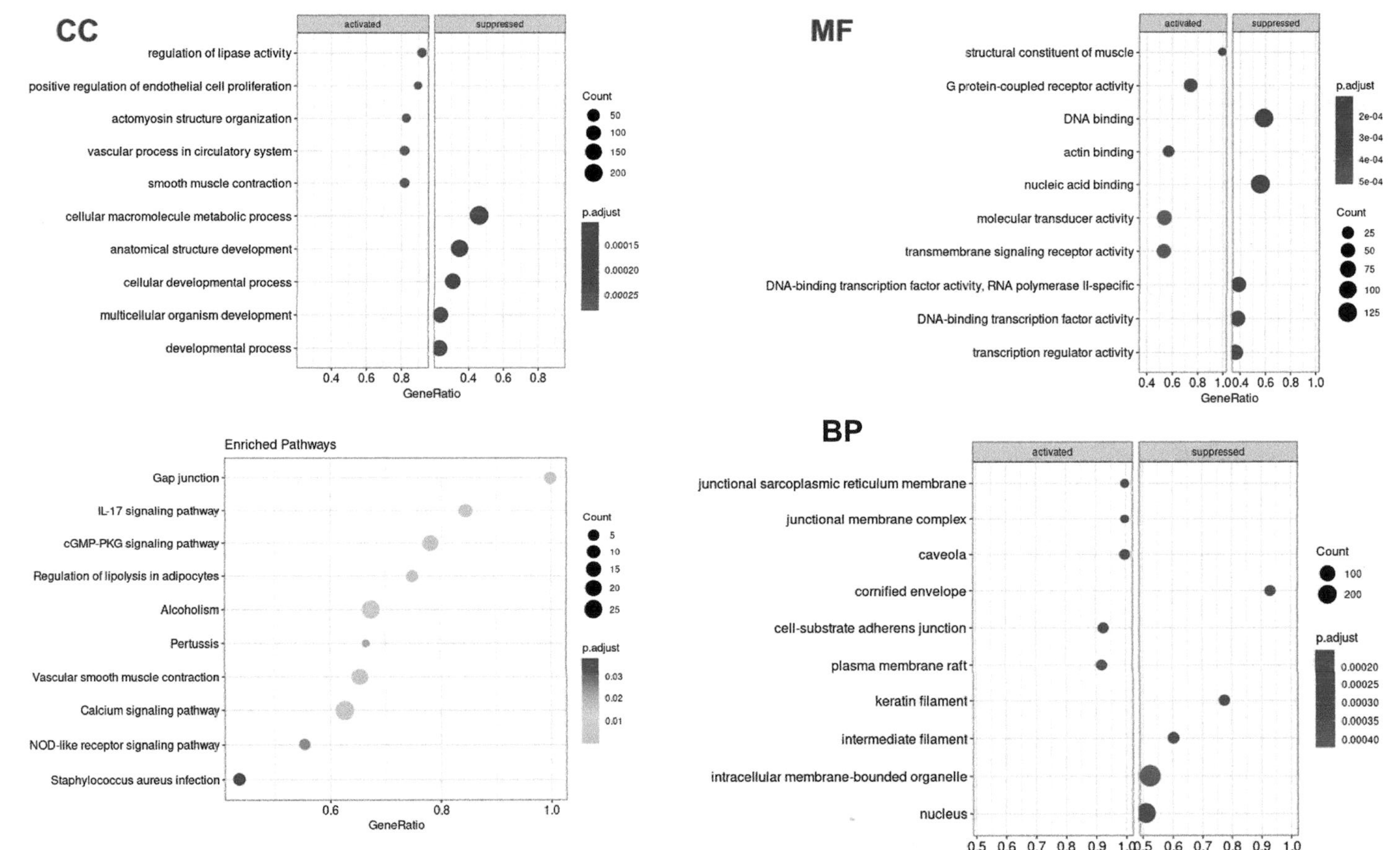

Fig. 3 GO enrichment analysis of significant DEGs. *CC*, cellular components; *MF*, molecular functions; *BP*, biological process; Enriched pathways.

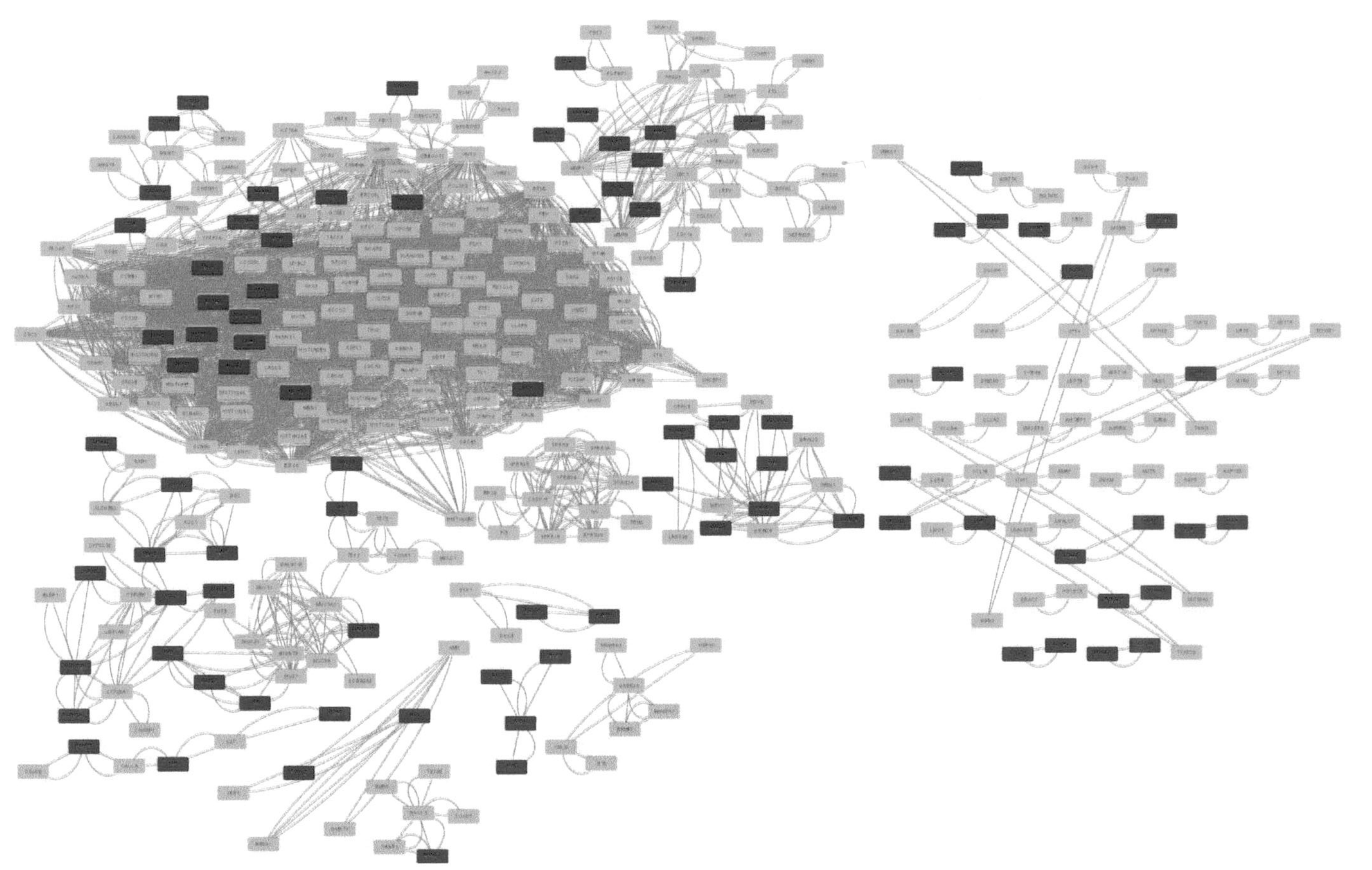

Fig. 4 Protein-protein interaction network for DEGs, the *red* nodes the up-regulated genes and *green* nodes denotes down-regulated genes.

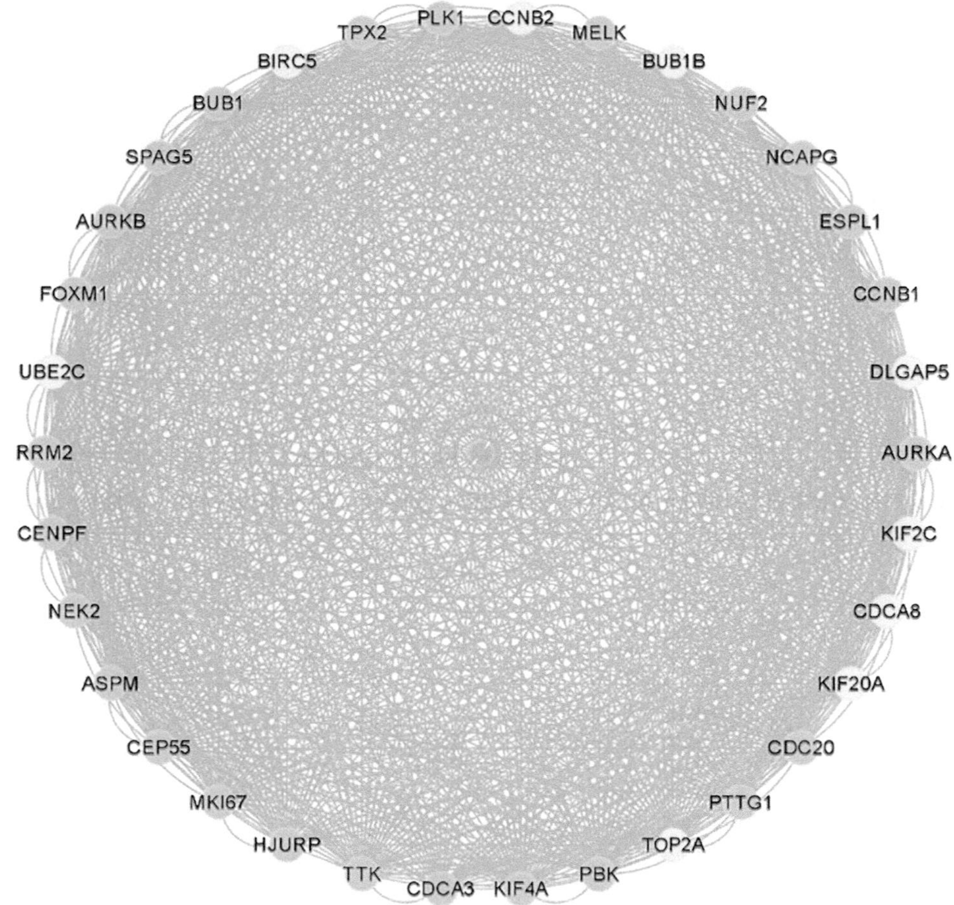

Fig. 5 Hub genes were denoted in *yellow color* node after MCODE and cytoHubba.

Table 1 Hub genes and the expression values.

Genes	log2FoldChange	*P*-value
BUB1B	−3.311792381	1.50E-81
KIF20A	−3.405754055	7.92E-88
BIRC5	−3.994493142	1.19E-92
UBE2C	−4.051654612	4.69E-90
CDC20	−4.277415626	5.55E-119
CDCA8	−3.583040861	8.67E-108
DLGAP5	−3.760374355	1.04E-88
CCNB2	−3.563403678	1.54E-115
KIF2C	−3.587811111	4.51E-94
TOP2A	−3.423944821	7.53E-81

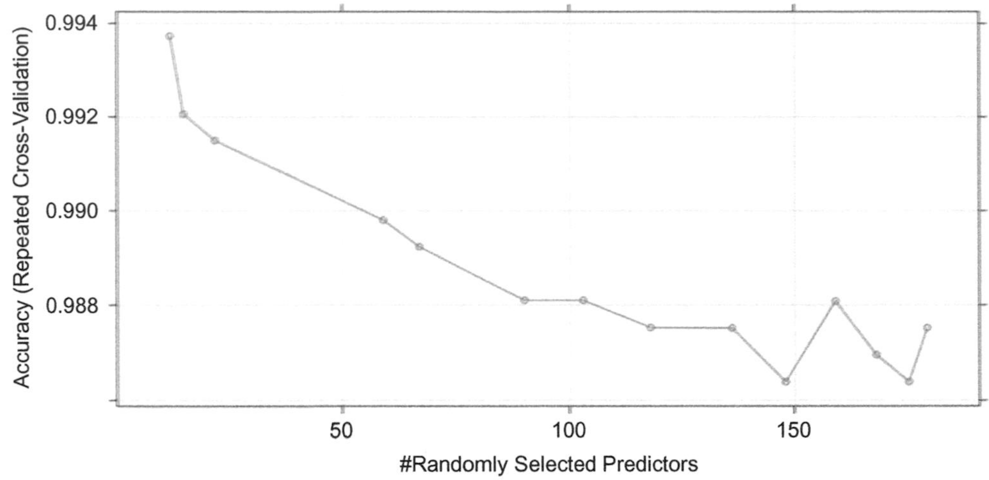

Fig. 6 Plot of RFE-RF algorithm to screen the feature genes under various cross-validation scores.

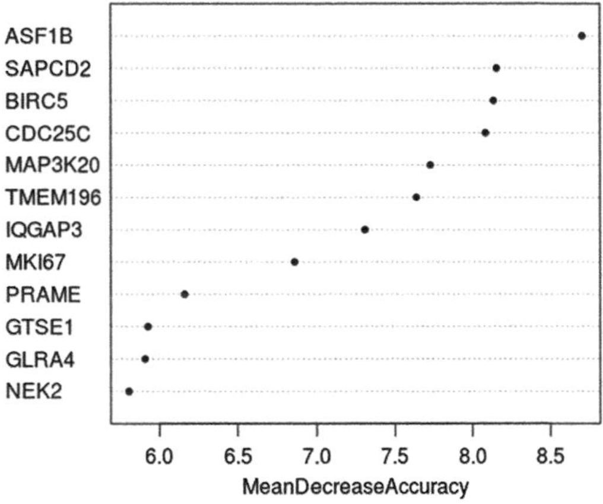

Fig. 7 Variables importance ranking based on mean decrease accuracy values.

accuracy (Fig. 8), SVM achieved a higher accuracy >95% compared with the other two models.

3.5 Survival analysis

GEPIA online web portal had used to analyze the prognostic value of the hub genes based on UCEC clinical data from the TCGA database. It showed that UBE2C had a significant difference in OS between high and low expression (*P*-value <.05). The outcome shows that the patients' survival with high expression of UBE2C is significantly lower than that of patients with low expression (Fig. 9).

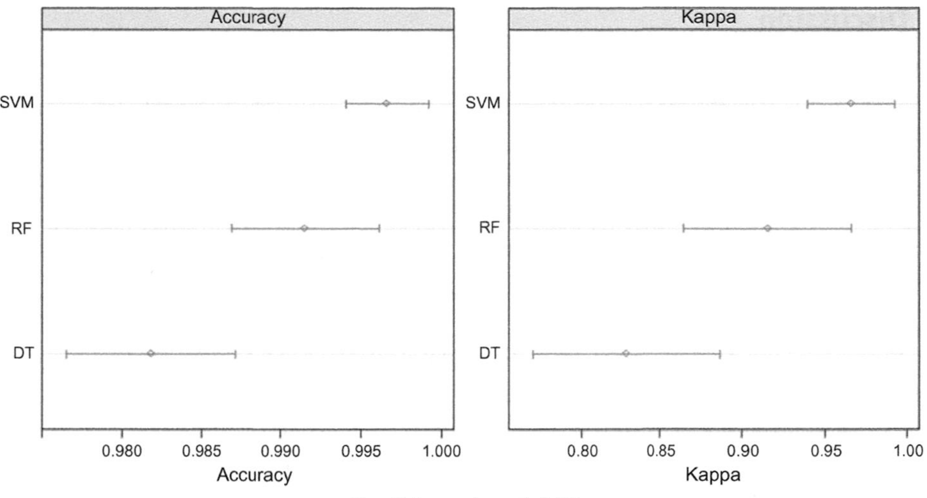

Fig. 8 Accuracy and kappa values of three models.

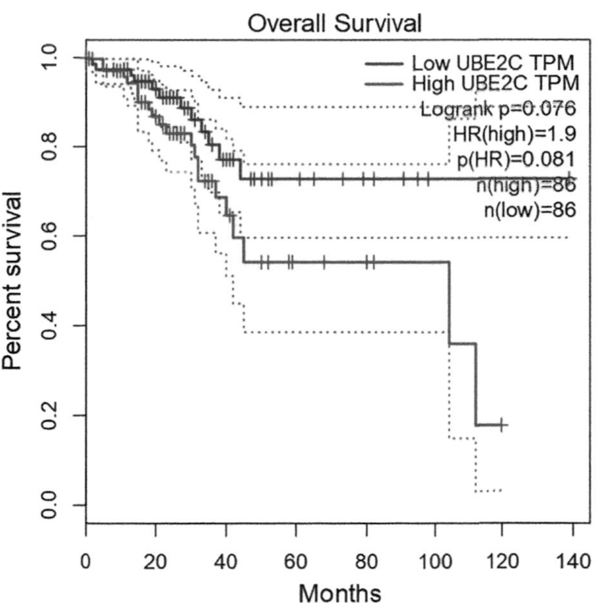

Fig. 9 KM plot for UBE2C.

4. Discussion

EC is female-related cancer, the most common malignant tumor worldwide. Recently, research in EC treatment has progressed but not well enough. Similarly, it is found that the diagnosing methods like transvaginal ultrasound, and cytology with less specificity [37]. The early diagnosis of EC can raise the chances of women living disease-free survival. In the recent two decades, the ML algorithms have made it easier to anticipate diagnostic biomarkers in the cancer research. As a result, publicly available HTS data are used to identify the DEGs for EC, which may aid in the early diagnosis in turn to develop effective therapeutics.

The study used transcriptome profile data containing 551 EC and 35 normal tissue samples and identified 1386 EC-related DEGs between the tumor and normal samples (411 upregulated and 975 downregulated DEGs). A total of 1386 DEGs were subject to GO analysis (BP, MF, and CC). As per GO analysis, the majority of DEGs are enriched in BP associated with the cellular macromolecule metabolic process, developmental process, and anatomical structure development. Also, in terms of MF and CC, the DEGs are mainly enriched in nucleic acid binding, DNA binding, transcription regulator activity, intracellular membrane-bounded organelle, and nucleus.

Further, KEGG pathway analysis shows that the DEGs are mainly associated with the calcium signaling pathway, alcoholism, and vascular smooth muscle contraction. Using the STRING database and Cytoscape software based on the DEGs built a PPI network. A network of 347 nodes and 2388 edges is generated as result of the input 1386 DEGs with a confidence score of 0.9. The clusters with highly interacting genes were scrutinized by MCODE analysis and the high-scored cluster with 34 nodes and 1008 edges is selected. The top 10 hub genes were selected with degrees >30 as selection criteria using the cytoHubba plugin. The selected hub genes BUB1B, KIF20A, BIRC5, UBE2C, CDC20, CDCA8, DLGAP5, CCNB2, KIF2C, and TOP2A are involved in the progression of EC. The Kaplan-Meier's analysis using GEPIA online portal showed that UBE2C had a significant difference in OS between high and low expression (P-value <.05). The outcome shows that patients' survival with a high expression of UBE2C is significantly lower than that of patients with low expression.

The overall aim of the study is to pick out the diagnostic biomarkers from the DEGs and start with LASSO regression analysis to filter uncorrelated genes. Out of 1386 DEGs, acquired farthest 300 variables. The RF algorithm predicted the variable importance, and the model with 12 variables has achieved the highest accuracy >95%. The 12 most significant variables: ASF1B, SAPDC2, BIRC5, CDC25C, MAP3K20, TMEM196, IQGAP3, MK167, PRAME, GTSE1, and GLRA4 are selected. The features may act as diagnostic biomarkers to predict the EC at an early stage. Three developed ML models (SVM, DT, and RF) predicted the diagnostic performance of the biomarkers, out of which SVM achieved the highest accuracy >95%. The overall results show that these diagnostic biomarkers achieved well-balanced accuracy in the prediction of EC.

The top 10 hub genes selected were compared with already reported or published results for confirmation. From the biological perspective, some related publications showed that the majority of discovered hub genes performed vital roles in EC progression. Similarly, Huang et al. found four-gene prognostic signatures inclusive of BUB1B, which act as independent prognostic predictions of EC, by using integrated bioinformatics and cox-regression analysis [38]. The BUB1B has been localized to the kinetochore and plays a role in the inhibition of the anaphase-promoting complex/cyclosome (APC/C), delaying the onset of anaphase and ensuring proper chromosome segregation. Several researchers have reported the association of BUB1B's overexpression with poor prognosis and its involvement in the progression of various cancers. The involved cancers such as prostate cancer, hepatocellular carcinoma, and ovarian cancer found using comprehensive bioinformatics approaches [39–42]. The KIF20A plays a significant role in mitosis such as microtubule assembly and spindle formation, and also it has several roles in meiosis. In the late stage of mitosis, Cdk1/cyclin B1 activity is decreased, and KIF20A is dephosphorylated and released. Fulfilled the activation and function of KIF20A by the reversal of Cdk1/cyclin B1-mediated inhibitory phosphorylation [43]. For ovarian cancer, the overexpression of KIF20A significantly reduces the fraction of apoptosis cells, whereas knockdown of KIF20A increased apoptosis cells compared with the normal cells [44]. KIF20A overexpression is associated with tumor progression and gives poor survival in various cancers [45–47]. However, the mechanisms and biological impact of KIF20A in EC are not yet studied.

UBE2C located in the nucleus and cytoplasm is essential for cell cycle progression. The previous studies stated that UBE2C has oncogenic characteristics, with high expression of mRNA [48]. High expression of UBE2C reduces the patients' survival in glioma, oral carcinoma, and prostate cancer [49–51]. Zhang et al. found that UBE2C is expressed significantly in EC samples and associated with poor survival [51]. The current study also found that the association of UBE2C with OS is analyzed, and the outcome shows that patients' survival with high expression of UBE2C is significantly lower than that of patients with low expression. It is understood from the findings that UBE2C will be an independent prognostic for the prediction of EC. The biological mechanism of UBE2C in EC needs to be analyzed in a precise manner. The CDC20 is involved in cell cycle progression, it activates the APC/C, thus modulating mitotic exit through the proteasomal degradation of proteins. CDC20 has oncogenic characteristics, and previous studies showed that it can be a potential therapeutic target for pan-cancer treatment [52,53]. An overexpression of CDC20 is associated with poor prognosis in other cancer types, gastric and colorectal cancer [54,55]. The CDCA8 is a regulatory gene in mitosis, and it plays a key role in promoting cell proliferation and invasion. The aberrant expression of CDCA8 is strongly associated with tumor pathogenesis. Shuai et al. showed that the CDCA8 act as an independent prognostic factor, and its overexpression is associated with poor survival in liver cancer patients [56]. BIRC5, CCNB2, KIF2C, and TOP2A genes were involved in the tumor progression and, the prognostic value and pathogenesis analyzed in several cancers [57–61]. These genes are strongly associated with the OS of the patients and found that an independent prognostic factor to predict the survival. Recently Zheng et al. found that DLGAP5 has oncogene characteristics, showing poor prognosis in EC when expressed abnormally [62]. However, the mechanism of action of DLGAP5 in EC progression requires an extensive research. The findings supported the theory that overexpression of ten hub genes leads to endometrial cell cycle instability that involves tumor progression, and they could be novel therapeutic targets for EC.

5. Conclusion

Integrated bioinformatics analysis identified ten hub genes (BUB1B, KIF20A, BIRC5, UBE2C, CDC20, CDCA8, DLGAP5, CCNB2, KIF2C, and TOP2A) involved in the progression of EC. The validation of the prognostic performance of the hub genes was performed through km-plot analysis and found UBE2C associated with the OS of the EC. The variable selection methods and ML models identified 12 diagnostic biomarkers: ASF1B, SAPDC2, BIRC5, CDC25C, MAP3K20, TMEM196, IQGAP3, MK167, PRAME, GTSE1, and GLRA4 for EC prediction.

References

[1] H. Sung, J. Ferlay, R.L. Siegel, M. Laversanne, I. Soerjomataram, A. Jemal, F. Bray, Global cancer statistics 2020: GLOBOCAN estimates of incidence and mortality worldwide for 36 cancers in 185 countries, CA Cancer J. Clin. 71 (2021) 209–249, https://doi.org/10.3322/caac.21660.

[2] G.A. Mishra, S.A. Pimple, S.S. Shastri, An overview of the tobacco problem in India, Indian J. Med. Paediatr. Oncol. 33 (2012) 139–145, https://doi.org/10.4103/0971-5851.103139.

[3] K. Lindemann, L.J. Vatten, M. Ellstrøm-Engh, A. Eskild, Body mass, diabetes and smoking, and endometrial cancer risk: a follow-up study, Br. J. Cancer 98 (2008) 1582–1585, https://doi.org/10.1038/sj.bjc.6604313.

[4] J. Zhao, Y. Hu, Y. Zhao, D. Chen, T. Fang, M. Ding, Risk factors of endometrial cancer in patients with endometrial hyperplasia: implication for clinical treatments, BMC Womens Health 21 (2021) 1–6, https://doi.org/10.1186/s12905-021-01452-9.

[5] Y. Gao, X. Dai, L. Chen, A.C. Lee, M. Tong, M. Wise, Q. Chen, Body mass index is positively associated with endometrial cancer in Chinese women, especially prior to menopause, J. Cancer 7 (2016) 1169–1173, https://doi.org/10.7150/jca.15037.

[6] M.M. Braun, E.A. Overbeek-Wager, R.J. Grumbo, Diagnosis and management of endometrial cancer, Am. Fam. Physician 93 (2016) 468–474.

[7] P. Chen, Y. Yang, Y. Zhang, S. Jiang, X. Li, J. Wan, Identification of prognostic immune-related genes in the tumor microenvironment of endometrial cancer, Aging (Albany NY) 12 (2020) 3371–3387.

[8] J.E. Allard, G.L. Maxwell, Race disparities between black and white women in the incidence, treatment, and prognosis of endometrial cancer, Cancer Control 16 (2009) 53–56, https://doi.org/10.1177/107327480901600108.
[9] O. Gemer, Y. Segev, L. Helpman, N. Hag-Yahia, R. Eitan, O. Raban, Z. Vaknin, S. Leytes, A. Ben Arie, A. Amit, T. Levy, A. Namazov, M. Volodarsky, I. Ben Shachar, I. Atlas, I. Bruchim, O. Lavie, Is there a survival advantage in diagnosing endometrial cancer in asymptomatic postmenopausal patients? An Israeli Gynecology Oncology Group study, Am. J. Obstet. Gynecol. 219 (181) (2018) e1–181.e6, https://doi.org/10.1016/j.ajog.2018.05.013.
[10] P. Vinklerová, P. Ovesná, M. Bednaříková, L. Minář, M. Felsinger, J. Hausnerová, V. Weinberger, Does an endometrial cancer diagnosis among asymptomatic patients improve prognosis? Cancers (Basel) 14 (2022) 1–11, https://doi.org/10.3390/cancers14010115.
[11] L. Liu, J. Lin, H. He, Identification of potential crucial genes associated with the pathogenesis and prognosis of endometrial cancer, Front. Genet. 10 (2019) 1–15, https://doi.org/10.3389/fgene.2019.00373.
[12] N. Gilani, R. Arabi Belaghi, Y. Aftabi, E. Faramarzi, T. Edgünlü, M.H. Somi, Identifying potential miRNA biomarkers for gastric cancer diagnosis using machine learning variable selection approach, Front. Genet. 12 (2022) 1–10, https://doi.org/10.3389/fgene.2021.779455.
[13] A. Hammad, M. Elshaer, X. Tang, Identification of potential biomarkers with colorectal cancer based on bioinformatics analysis and machine learning, Math. Biosci. Eng. 18 (2021) 8997–9015, https://doi.org/10.3934/mbe.2021443.
[14] S. Shi, Q. Tan, F. Feng, H. Huang, J. Liang, D. Cao, Z. Wang, Identification of core genes in the progression of endometrial cancer and cancer cell-derived exosomes by an integrative analysis, Sci. Rep. 10 (2020) 1–14, https://doi.org/10.1038/s41598-020-66872-3.
[15] J. Liu, M. Feng, S. Li, S. Nie, H. Wang, S. Wu, J. Qiu, J. Zhang, W. Cheng, Identification of molecular markers associated with the progression and prognosis of endometrial cancer: a bioinformatic study, Cancer Cell Int. 20 (2020) 1–18, https://doi.org/10.1186/s12935-020-1140-3.
[16] S. Hutt, A. Tailor, P. Ellis, A. Michael, S. Butler-Manuel, J. Chatterjee, The role of biomarkers in endometrial cancer and hyperplasia: a literature review, Acta Oncol. (Madr). 58 (2019) 342–352, https://doi.org/10.1080/0284186X.2018.1540886.
[17] Z. Jagga, D. Gupta, Machine learning for biomarker identification in cancer research developments toward its clinical application, Per. Med. 12 (2015) 371–387, https://doi.org/10.2217/PME.15.5.
[18] A.A. Tabl, A. Alkhateeb, W. ElMaraghy, L. Rueda, A. Ngom, A machine learning approach for identifying gene biomarkers guiding the treatment of breast cancer, Front. Genet. 10 (2019) 1–13, https://doi.org/10.3389/fgene.2019.00256.
[19] X. Mi, B. Zou, F. Zou, J. Hu, Permutation-based identification of important biomarkers for complex diseases via machine learning models, Nat. Commun. 12 (2021) 1–12, https://doi.org/10.1038/s41467-021-22756-2.
[20] A. Statnikov, L. Wang, C.F. Aliferis, A comprehensive comparison of random forests and support vector machines for microarray-based cancer classification, BMC Bioinform. 9 (2008) 1–10, https://doi.org/10.1186/1471-2105-9-319.
[21] K. Kourou, K.P. Exarchos, C. Papaloukas, P. Sakaloglou, T. Exarchos, D.I. Fotiadis, Applied machine learning in cancer research: a systematic review for patient diagnosis, classification and prognosis, Comput. Struct. Biotechnol. J. 19 (2021) 5546–5555, https://doi.org/10.1016/j.csbj.2021.10.006.
[22] T. Van den Bosch, A. Daemen, O. Gevaert, B. De Moor, D. Timmerman, Building decision trees for diagnosing intracavitary uterine pathology, Facts Views Vis. ObGyn. 1 (2009) 182–188. http://www.ncbi.nlm.nih.gov/pubmed/25489463%0Ahttp://www.pubmedcentral.nih.gov/articlerender.fcgi?artid=PMC4255509.
[23] K. Kourou, T.P. Exarchos, K.P. Exarchos, M.V. Karamouzis, D.I. Fotiadis, Machine learning applications in cancer prognosis and prediction, Comput. Struct. Biotechnol. J. 13 (2015) 8–17, https://doi.org/10.1016/j.csbj.2014.11.005.
[24] A. Colaprico, T.C. Silva, C. Olsen, L. Garofano, C. Cava, D. Garolini, T.S. Sabedot, T.M. Malta, S.M. Pagnotta, I. Castiglioni, M. Ceccarelli, G. Bontempi, H. Noushmehr, TCGAbiolinks: an R/Bioconductor package for integrative analysis of TCGA data, Nucleic Acids Res. 44 (2016), e71, https://doi.org/10.1093/nar/gkv1507.

[25] M.I. Love, W. Huber, S. Anders, Moderated estimation of fold change and dispersion for RNA-seq data with DESeq2, Genome Biol. 15 (2014) 1–21, https://doi.org/10.1186/s13059-014-0550-8.

[26] T. Wu, E. Hu, S. Xu, M. Chen, P. Guo, Z. Dai, T. Feng, L. Zhou, W. Tang, L. Zhan, X. Fu, S. Liu, X. Bo, G. Yu, clusterProfiler 4.0: a universal enrichment tool for interpreting omics data, Innov. 2 (2021), 100141, https://doi.org/10.1016/j.xinn.2021.100141.

[27] M. Kanehisa, M. Furumichi, M. Tanabe, Y. Sato, K. Morishima, KEGG: new perspectives on genomes, pathways, diseases and drugs, Nucleic Acids Res. 45 (2017) D353–D361, https://doi.org/10.1093/nar/gkw1092.

[28] D. Szklarczyk, A.L. Gable, K.C. Nastou, D. Lyon, R. Kirsch, S. Pyysalo, N.T. Doncheva, M. Legeay, T. Fang, P. Bork, L.J. Jensen, C. von Mering, The STRING database in 2021: customizable protein-protein networks, and functional characterization of user-uploaded gene/measurement sets, Nucleic Acids Res. 49 (2021) D605–D612, https://doi.org/10.1093/nar/gkaa1074.

[29] C.W. Hogue, M. Groll, An automated method for finding molecular complexes in large protein interaction networks, BMC Bioinform. 29 (2001) 137–140. https://academic.oup.com/nar/article-lookup/doi/10.1093/nar/29.1.137.

[30] C.H. Chin, S.H. Chen, H.H. Wu, C.W. Ho, M.T. Ko, C.Y. Lin, cytoHubba: identifying hub objects and sub-networks from complex interactome, BMC Syst. Biol. 8 (2014) S11, https://doi.org/10.1186/1752-0509-8-S4-S11.

[31] K.R. Lutchen, A.C. Jackson, Reliability of parameter estimates from models applied to respiratory impedance data, J. Appl. Physiol. 62 (1987) 403–413, https://doi.org/10.1152/jappl.1987.62.2.403.

[32] R. Díaz-Uriarte, S. Alvarez de Andrés, Gene selection and classification of microarray data using random forest, BMC Bioinform. 7 (2006) 1–13, https://doi.org/10.1186/1471-2105-7-3.

[33] F. Yin, X. Shao, L. Zhao, X. Li, J. Zhou, Y. Cheng, X. He, S. Lei, J. Li, J. Wang, Predicting prognosis of endometrioid endometrial adenocarcinoma on the basis of gene expression and clinical features using random forest, Oncol. Lett. 18 (2019) 1597–1606, https://doi.org/10.3892/ol.2019.10504.

[34] T.S. Furey, N. Cristianini, N. Duffy, D.W. Bednarski, M. Schummer, D. Haussler, Support vector machine classification and validation of cancer tissue samples using microarray expression data, Bioinformatics 16 (2000) 906–914, https://doi.org/10.1093/bioinformatics/16.10.906.

[35] R. López-Reig, A. Fernández-Serra, I. Romero, C. Zorrero, C. Illueca, Z. García-Casado, A. Poveda, J.A. López-Guerrero, Prognostic classification of endometrial cancer using a molecular approach based on a twelve-gene NGS panel, Sci. Rep. 9 (2019) 1–9, https://doi.org/10.1038/s41598-019-54624-x.

[36] Z. Tang, C. Li, B. Kang, G. Gao, C. Li, Z. Zhang, GEPIA: a web server for cancer and normal gene expression profiling and interactive analyses, Nucleic Acids Res. 45 (2017) W98–W102, https://doi.org/10.1093/nar/gkx247.

[37] M.E. Urick, D.W. Bell, Clinical actionability of molecular targets in endometrial cancer, Nat. Rev. Cancer 19 (2019) 510–521, https://doi.org/10.1038/s41568-019-0177-x.

[38] S. Huang, L. Pang, C. Wei, Identification of a four-gene signature with prognostic significance in endometrial cancer using weighted-gene correlation network analysis, Front. Genet. 12 (2021) 1–16, https://doi.org/10.3389/fgene.2021.678780.

[39] X. Fu, G. Chen, Z.D. Cai, C. Wang, Z.Z. Liu, Z.Y. Lin, Y.D. Wu, Y.X. Liang, Z.D. Han, J.C. Liu, W. De Zhong, Overexpression of BUBIB contributes to progression of prostate cancer and predicts poor outcome in patients with prostate cancer, Onco. Targets. Ther. 9 (2016) 2211–2220, https://doi.org/10.2147/OTT.S101994.

[40] Z. Long, T. Wu, Q. Tian, L.A. Carlson, W. Wang, G. Wu, Expression and prognosis analyses of BUB1, BUB1B and BUB3 in human sarcoma, Aging (Albany NY) 13 (2021) 12395–12408, https://doi.org/10.18632/aging.202944.

[41] J. Fu, X. Zhang, L. Yan, Y. Shao, X. Liu, Y. Chu, G. Xu, X. Xu, Identification of the hub gene BUB1B in hepatocellular carcinoma via bioinformatic analysis and in vitro experiments, PeerJ. 9 (2021) 1–22, https://doi.org/10.7717/peerj.10943.

[42] C. Dong, X. Tian, F. He, J. Zhang, X. Cui, Q. He, P. Si, Y. Shen, Integrative analysis of key candidate genes and signaling pathways in ovarian cancer by bioinformatics, J. Ovarian Res. 14 (2021) 1–12, https://doi.org/10.1186/s13048-021-00837-6.

[43] W. Da Wu, K.W. Yu, N. Zhong, Y. Xiao, Z.Y. She, Roles and mechanisms of Kinesin-6 KIF20A in spindle organization during cell division, Eur. J. Cell Biol. 98 (2019) 74–80, https://doi.org/10.1016/j.ejcb.2018.12.002.

[44] H. Li, W. Zhang, X. Sun, J. Chen, Y. Li, C. Niu, B. Xu, Y. Zhang, Overexpression of kinesin family member 20A is associated with unfavorable clinical outcome and tumor progression in epithelial ovarian cancer, Cancer Manag. Res. 10 (2018) 3433–3450, https://doi.org/10.2147/CMAR.S169214.
[45] Y. Kawai, K. Shibata, J. Sakata, S. Suzuki, F. Utsumi, K. Niimi, R. Sekiya, T. Senga, F. Kikkawa, H. Kajiyama, KIF20A expression as a prognostic indicator and its possible involvement in the proliferation of ovarian clear-cell carcinoma cells, Oncol. Rep. 40 (2018) 195–205, https://doi.org/10.3892/or.2018.6401.
[46] X. Cui, Comprehensive analysis of immune correlation of KIF20A in Pan-cancer, Res. Square (2020) 1–20.
[47] W. Zhang, W. He, Y. Shi, H. Gu, M. Li, Z. Liu, Y. Feng, N. Zheng, C. Xie, Y. Zhang, High expression of KIF20A is associated with poor overall survival and tumor progression in early-stage cervical squamous cell carcinoma, PLoS One 11 (2016) 1–21, https://doi.org/10.1371/journal.pone.0167449.
[48] C. Xiang, H. Yan, Ubiquitin conjugating enzyme E2 C (UBE2C) may play a dual role involved in the progression of thyroid carcinoma, Cell Death Discov. 8 (2022), https://doi.org/10.1038/s41420-022-00935-4.
[49] W. Alafate, J. Zuo, Z. Deng, X. Guo, W. Wu, W. Zhang, W. Xie, M. Wang, J. Wang, Combined elevation of AURKB and UBE2C predicts severe outcomes and therapy resistance in glioma, Pathol. Res. Pract. 215 (2019), 152557, https://doi.org/10.1016/j.prp.2019.152557.
[50] Y. Wang, J. Wang, Q. Tang, G. Ren, Identification of UBE2C as hub gene in driving prostate cancer by integrated bioinformatics analysis, PLoS One 16 (2021) 1–18, https://doi.org/10.1371/journal.pone.0247827.
[51] P.F. Liu, C.F. Chen, C.W. Shu, H.M. Chang, C.H. Lee, H.H. Liou, L.P. Ger, C.L. Chen, B.H. Kang, UBE2C is a potential biomarker for tumorigenesis and prognosis in tongue squamous cell carcinoma, Diagnostics 10 (2020) 1–17, https://doi.org/10.3390/diagnostics10090674.
[52] S. Cheng, V. Castillo, D. Sliva, CDC20 associated with cancer metastasis and novel mushroom-derived CDC20 inhibitors with antimetastatic activity, Int. J. Oncol. 54 (2019) 2250–2256, https://doi.org/10.3892/ijo.2019.4791.
[53] Z. Wang, L. Wan, J. Zhong, H. Inuzuka, P. Liu, F.H. Sarkar, W. Wei, Cdc20: a potential novel therapeutic target for cancer treatment, Curr. Pharm. Des. 19 (2013) 3210–3214, https://doi.org/10.2174/1381612811319180005.
[54] Z.Y. Ding, H.R. Wu, J.M. Zhang, G.R. Huang, D.D. Ji, Expression characteristics of CDC20 in gastric cancer and its correlation with poor prognosis, Int. J. Clin. Exp. Pathol. 7 (2014) 722–727.
[55] W.J. Wu, K.S. Hu, D.S. Wang, Z.L. Zeng, D.S. Zhang, D.L. Chen, L. Bai, R.H. Xu, CDC20 overexpression predicts a poor prognosis for patients with colorectal cancer, J. Transl. Med. 11 (2013) 1–8, https://doi.org/10.1186/1479-5876-11-142.
[56] Y. Shuai, E. Fan, Q. Zhong, Q. Chen, G. Feng, X. Gou, G. Zhang, CDCA8 as an independent predictor for a poor prognosis in liver cancer, Cancer Cell Int. 21 (2021) 1–10, https://doi.org/10.1186/s12935-021-01850-x.
[57] L. Xu, W. Yu, H. Xiao, K. Lin, BIRC5 is a prognostic biomarker associated with tumor immune cell infiltration, Sci. Rep. 11 (2021) 1–13, https://doi.org/10.1038/s41598-020-79736-7.
[58] S. Wu, R. Su, H. Jia, Cyclin B2 (CCNB2) stimulates the proliferation of triple-negative breast cancer (TNBC) cells in vitro and in vivo, Dis. Markers 2021 (2021), https://doi.org/10.1155/2021/5511041.
[59] Z. Gao, H. Jia, F. Yu, H. Guo, B. Li, KIF2C promotes the proliferation of hepatocellular carcinoma cells in vitro and in vivo, Exp. Ther. Med. 22 (2021) 1–9, https://doi.org/10.3892/etm.2021.10528.
[60] J.M. Ye, Z. He, W.D. Li, Z. Chen, I. Liu, A TOP2A-derived cancer panel drives cancer progression in papillary renal cell carcinoma, Oncol. Lett. 16 (2018) 4169–4178.
[61] Y.F. Pei, X.M. Yin, X.Q. Liu, TOP2A induces malignant character of pancreatic cancer through activating β-catenin signaling pathway, Biochim. Biophys. Acta Mol. Basis Dis. 1864 (2018) 197–207, https://doi.org/10.1016/j.bbadis.2017.10.019.
[62] R. Zheng, Z. Shi, W. Li, J. Yu, Y. Wang, Q. Zhou, Identification and prognostic value of DLGAP5 in endometrial cancer, PeerJ. 8 (2020) 1–17, https://doi.org/10.7717/peerj.10433.

CHAPTER 18

Drug targeting PIWI like protein-piRNA complex, a novel paradigm in the therapeutic framework of retinoblastoma

Rupa Roy[a,*], Muthuramalingam Karpagavalli[a,*], Athira Ramesh[a,*], Jayamuruga Pandian Arunachalam[b], Sudha Rani Sadras[a], and Subbulakshmi Chidambaram[a]

[a]Department of Biochemistry and Molecular Biology, Pondicherry University, Puducherry, India
[b]Central Inter-Disciplinary Research Facility, Sri Balaji Vidyapeeth (Deemed to be University), Pondicherry, India

Abstract

Cancer is a disease with a prodigious effect on global health. Metastatic progression of cancer and resistance to many therapeutic treatments make it further detrimental and fatal as well. Retinoblastoma (RB) is one of the common primary intraocular cancers where mutation takes place in both *RB1* alleles in a susceptible developing retinal cell. Many advancements and new therapeutic approaches have been made, but the underlying mechanism behind the onset and progression of RB and other cancers is still obscure. Recently, a small noncoding RNA, P-element-induced wimpy testis (PIWI)-interacting RNA (piRNA), along with its protein partner PIWI is emerging as a strong candidate in the progression of cancer. PIWI/piRNAs may act as oncogenes or tumor suppressors and may involve in the initiation of invasion, metastasis, apoptosis, or providing resistance to cell death and sustaining proliferative signaling, etc. An increasing number of studies have further shown the aberrant expression of PIWI/ piRNA in numerous cancers, which may act as potential biomarkers and therapeutic targets for diagnosis, treatment, or monitoring of the prognosis of cancer. Targeting PIWI/piRNA in combination with other existing therapeutic approaches could be an innovative treatment against cancer. This chapter encompasses the involvement of PIWI/piRNA in different cancers, with an insight on its therapeutic use for RB.

Abbreviations

5HT	5-hydroxytryptamine/serotonin
AFAP1-AS1	actin filament-associated protein 1-antisense RNA-1
Ago	argonaute
AKT	Ak strain transforming
Aub	Aubergine
BCL-2	B-cell lymphoma 2
BCL-XL	B-cell lymphoma-extra large
BDNF-AS	brain-derived neurotrophic factor antisense
BMP-4	bone morphogenetic protein 4
CAF1	chromatin assembly factor 1

* Authors have contributed equally.

Computational Methods in Drug Discovery and Repurposing for Cancer Therapy
https://doi.org/10.1016/B978-0-443-15280-1.00006-6

CCR4-NOT	carbon catabolite repression-negative on TATA-less
CDCs	cardiosphere-derived cells
CDK4	cyclin-dependent kinase 4
CDKI	cyclin-dependent kinase inhibitor
CF	cardiofibroblasts
CREB	cAMP resposnse element-binding protein
CSR-1	chromosome segregation and RNAi deficient
CYCS	cytochrome C, somatic
DNMT	DNA-methyl transferase
FGF8	fibroblast growth factor 8
HDACs	histone deacetylases
HMTs	histone methyltransferases
HoP	HSP90 organizing protein
HP1A	histone-protein-1A
HSP90	heat shock protein 90
IAP	intracisternal A-particle
KPNA6	karyopherin subunit alpha 6
LINE1	long interspersed nuclear elements
lncRNA	long noncoding RNA
miRNA	microRNA
ncRNA	noncoding RNA
NFκβ	nuclear factor kappa B
OTX2	orthodenticle homeobox2
PEV	position effect variegation
PI3K	phosphoinositide 3-kinase
piRISC	piRNA-induced silencing complex
piRNA	PIWI-interacting RNA
PIWI	P-element-induced wimpy testis
pRB	retinoblastoma protein
PRG-1	piwi (fruit fly)-related gene-1 (piwi-like protein of *C. elegans*)
Rab-11A	Ras-related protein
RB	retinoblastoma
RCC	renal cell carcinoma
RNAi	RNA interference
RPCs	retinal progenitor cells
RPE	retinal pigment epithelium
SMEDWI-2	*S. mediterranea* PIWI-2
STAT	signal transducer and activator of transcription
TEs	transposable elements
TGF-β1	transforming growth factor-β1
WAGO	Worm AGO

1. Introduction

Globally, cancer is one of the lethal and alarming diseases affecting thousands of human lives [1,2]. According to WHO, cancer has accounted for nearly 10 million deaths in 2020, or nearly one in six deaths. Cancer is the inclusion of many complex or heterogeneous diseases. It implies that not only the variances exist in cancer cells of different samples, but also the heterogenicity is observed between cancer cells within a single sample. This disease is persistently modifying its characteristics to invade the defense system of the cell, making new interventions difficult to be effective [3]. To treat cancer, the present conventional approach encompassed chemotherapeutic agents, radiation, surgical removal, etc. However, these treatments have serious side effects and toxicity, further leading to compromised lives for patients. In addition to this, cancer cells have been shown to induce resistance to current therapeutic approaches, further making the situation worst [4,5]. Therefore, new approaches are needed to understand the associated mechanisms of gene regulation in cancer and to identify new molecular targets to improve targeted therapy and the prognosis of cancer patients.

One of the commonest intraocular malignancies in childhood is retinoblastoma (RB) [6,7]. Initially, mutation of both RB1 alleles in the developing retinal cell occurs, later on, a limited proliferation of an RB1−/− retinal cells causes a nonmalignant retinal tumor. Through genetic or epigenetic alterations, finally, it experiences unrestrained proliferation and malignant transformation [8]. With high birth rates and a large population, Asia and Africa experience an escalating number of RB cases [9]. Despite improved techniques in diagnosis and treatment, working against RB is still difficult, especially in the developing world. It has been reported that 50% or more patients die due to this disease, and those who need therapeutic interventions have already been found to be in a progressive stage [10,11]. Nonetheless, new approaches and techniques in ophthalmic diagnostics and the use of ultrasonography, magnetic resonance imaging, and computed tomography have enhanced the diagnostic accuracy and detection of extraocular RB. However, much more progress is needed for easy and quick treatment against RB.

Noncoding RNAs (ncRNAs) are a group of RNAs transcribed from DNA but are not translated into proteins and are involved significantly in the development and homeostasis [12,13]. ncRNAs include small interfering RNAs (siRNAs), microRNAs (miRNAs), and P-element induced wimpy testis (PIWI)-interacting RNAs (piRNAs) [14–17]. piRNAs were discovered recently and they are 25–32 nucleotides long [18–21]. piRNA along with its cognate partner, PIWI protein, are involved in many pivotal roles, like transposon silencing, stem cell maintenance, transcription and posttranscription regulation, etc. [22–28].

Reports have suggested that a plethora of regulatory molecules including small regulatory RNAs control the expression of genes in cancer cells and tissues. In cancer, miRNA has been studied more profoundly than the other two ncRNAs [29,30]. PIWI/piRNAs are comparatively new players in cancer research. Changes in PIWI/piRNA pathway may contribute to epigenetic changes or may alter gene regulation, which can associate with diverse diseases such as cancers [31–33]. Studies have shown the altered expression of PIWI/piRNA in many cancer types predicting their vital indulgence in the development of human cancers [32,34–36]. Our lab has also delineated the aberrant expression of PIWI-like protein, PIWIL4 (HIWI2) in RB cells and further suggested that it might alter the cell cycle through orthodenticle homeobox2 (OTX2) [37]. Existing shreds of evidence and new findings revealed many unprecedented mechanisms of PIWI/piRNA including regulation of gene expression in cancer; thus, making them a promising tool against cancer. In this chapter, we provide a brief functional review of PIWI/piRNA in normal physiology followed by their indulgence in various cancers including RB. Finally, their potential use as biomarkers in the near future is discussed.

2. Biological functions of PIWI/piRNA in physiological conditions

PIWI/piRNA is essentially found in the germline and cancer cells. Recent studies have shown their less investigated functional significance in the somatic cells. The implications of PIWI/piRNA in the germline cells were well established, such as transposon silencing, maintenance of stem cell integrity, and regulations through posttranscriptional modification. PIWI protein family is conserved in a broad range of organisms. In human, four PIWI-like protein isoforms are present, namely: PIWIL1/HIWI, PIWIL2/HILI, PIWIL3, and PIWIL4/HIWI2 [38]. Similarly, three in mice: MIWI, MILI, and MIWI2 [27,39,40]; three in *Drosophila*: PIWI, Aubergine (Aub), and AGO3 (Argonate3); two in *C. elegans* PRG-1 (piwi-related gene-1) and PRG-2 [24,41–44]; Ziwi (zebrafish PIWI) and Zili (zebrafish PIWI like) in Zebrafish [45,46]; SMEDWI-2 (*S. mediterranea* PIWI-2) and SMEDWI-3 in Planaria [47]. However, the role of PIWI in the somatic cells has not been explored explicitly. In this segment, we discuss various functions of PIWI/piRNA at cellular and physiological levels both in the germline and somatic cells.

The PIWI family proteins were first identified in the *Drosophila* salivary gland [48], ovary [49], and testis [50] and are involved in various functions, both in the somatic and germline cells [51,52]. Among these, Aub and Ago3 are significant in the germline cells of *Drosophila* for the functional maintenance by transposon silencing and posttranscriptional modifications of the transcripts [53,54]. Either sense or antisense strands of piRNAs are bound to Aub and Ago3 for the transposon silencing mechanism. It has been shown that Aub-associated piRNAs bind to the antisense strand, whereas Ago3-complexed piRNAs bind to the sense strand of the transposon transcript, thus leading to the reciprocal cleavage of the transposons [41,55]. Transcripts are cleaved by slicer endonuclease activity exhibited by Aub/Ago3 through which the translation silencing is established [56]. The fragments of cleaved transcripts are reported to be taken up for piRNA biogenesis that later becomes mature piRNAs. This function implies that the transposon silencing in the germline cells is coupled with piRNA biogenesis [24,42]. Recently, it is observed that piRNA and related proteins are present both in the somatic and germline cells of the *Drosophila* ovary, where they are involved in the transcriptional silencing of transposons for which the PIWI protein must be present inside the nucleus [57]. Studies have shown that transposon silencing was carried out by the PIWI-piRNA-induced silencing complex (piRISC) complex [58]. If PIWI protein is attached to piRNA, the N-terminal domain promotes its nuclear entry. However, it was observed that PIWI can also enter the nucleus independently under specific conditions. Nuclear machinery for PIWI nuclear transport and nuclear localization signal in the binding of piRNA is still obscure.

Research has shown that PIWI protein works as a functional regulator of transcription. It was first observed in *Drosophila* salivary gland polytene chromosome [48,59]. They hypothesized that the binding of PIWI with histone-protein-1A (HP1A) makes it stable for the posttranscriptional silencing of heterochromatin in the somatic cells. The binding of HP1A to all genomic sites is not ubiquitous; thus, this epigenetic modification program carried out by PIWI combined with HP1A would not be universal [48]. However, similar mechanisms can be functional in the germline cells by which the PIWI might play a key role in the epigenetic modification [60,61]. Later, studies have revealed the presence and significance of PIWI proteins in the somatic cells as well. It has been demonstrated that in *Aplysia*, the PIWI-piRNA pathway is crucial for memory formation and synaptic plasticity, which in turn proves the existence of PIWI protein in neurons [62]. Interestingly, PIWI is also functionally visualized in the somatic follicle cells in *Drosophila* [63].

In this section, we will be discussing the somatic and germline functions of PIWI/piRNA uncovered to date. This mainly includes different modes of gene silencing and regulatory mechanisms (Table 1) such as transposon silencing, transcriptional and posttranscriptional gene silencing, repression, epigenetic regulations, DNA repair, and chromatinmaintenance.

2.1 Transposon silencing and gene repressions

Since the discovery, multiple functions of PIWI/piRNA have been identified in the germline and stem cells, especially in the maintenance of cell integrity during the cell division process. The insertion of transposons drives instability to mRNAs, affecting their integral function. Transposons in the genome act as a major *Cis* regulatory activity source. There are two types of transposable elements (TEs), one which requires RNA intermediate and the other one is a DNA transposon [64,65]. TEs and their role in evolution are significant because of their ultimate potential in transitioning and also the presence of various promoter sites, transcriptional factor binding sites, etc. One of the most popular ways to regulate the expression and function of certain genes is through transposon silencing where transcriptional level modification occurs through DNA and histone (H3k9Me3) methylation [66]. piRNAs that are derived from transposons exhibit striking periodicity in their functions. Similar to transposon-derived piRNAs, transposon-derived mRNAs are observed which have transposon sequences in their 5′UTR. For the regulation of these mRNAs, piRNAs with the complementary transposon sequence in 3′UTR are supposed to be involved

Table 1 Functional relevance of PIWI/piRNA in various organisms.

Sl. no.	Organism	Functions	References
1	Zebrafish	Transposon silencing	[46,120]
2	Drosophila	Mitotic chromosome condensation and segregation	[48,101,102]
		Transposon silencing	[53,54]
		mRNA degradation	[79,80]
		Epigenetic silencing	[84]
		Epigenetic activation	[59]
		Genome maintenance and telomere protection	[104]
3	Silkworm	Transcriptional regulation	[61]
		Sex determination	[81]
4	Mouse	Transposon repression	[39,76]
5	*C. elegans*	Transgenerational regulation	[94,97,124]
		Epigenetic memory	[96]
		Promoting and preventing gene silencing	[89,143]
		Genome-wide surveillance	[88]
		Maternal mRNA degradation	[98]
6	*Aplasia*	Memory-related synaptic plasticity	[62]
7	Human	Stem cell maintenance	[31]
		DNA repair	[114]
		Neuronal polarization and migration	[129]
		Cardiac differentiation	[135]

directly. These regulations are prominent in the zebrafish germline cells [67]. In *Drosophila*, repression of transposons is carried out by cytoplasmic Aub and Ago3 in the presence of piRNAs [68,69]. During this process, posttranscriptional cleavage of transcripts happens that produces antisense piRNA. These piRNAs further take part in transcriptional silencing. In mice, methylation initiated by Mili and Miwi2 is necessary to preserve the stability of transposon repressions and silencing [39,70,71]. Moreover, in higher mammals, the importance of piRNAs for stem cell reprogramming and epigenetic silencing of TEs such as long interspersed nuclear elements (LINE1) (L1) and intracisternal A-particle (IAP) is unavoidable. A specific piRNA knockdown effectively reversed the silencing of LINE1, suggesting that decreased expression of piRNA increases the TE activity in the system [22,72]. Additionally, PIWI protein is also involved in a phenomenon called canalization by which it suppresses transposons by interacting with HSP90 and HSP90-organizing protein (HoP). HSP90 has a role in piRNA biogenesis as well [73].

Posttranscriptional regulations overseen by piRNAs are extremely essential during spermatogenesis, where the meiotic and spermatoid genome maintenance is done by PIWI/piRNA duos. The piRNAs involved in this regulation are commonly called pachytene piRNAs, which are generated by primary biogenesis and bound to Miwi protein in the pachytene stage of spermatocyte formation. In mice, it has been suggested that the knockdown of Miwi did not affect the initiation of spermatogenesis but was arrested at the early-round spermatoid stage. Further, the L1 transposons that got escaped from getting silenced during spermatogenesis were "taken care of" by Miwi posttranscriptionally. This states the significance of Miwi in the germline maintenance and L1 transposon silencing [74,75]. Furthermore, Miwi and pachytene piRNAs have a role during later stages of spermatogenesis, where they are involved in the elimination of mRNAs. In the elongated spermatid stage, deadenylation and removal of unwanted mRNAs are done by Miwi in association with chromatin assembly factor 1 (CAF1) deadenylase protein. The mechanism behind the refined association of Miwi with CAF1 is still unknown. Also, the genes involved in the postmeiotic stage of spermatogenesis are stabilized by the association of Miwi [76,77]. Similarly, PRG-1 mutants of *C. elegans* turn out to have reduced expression of mRNAs required for spermatogenesis [78]. In addition, the replacement of maternal mRNA is another fascinating function performed by PIWI/piRNA during the developmental stage in *Drosophila*, where maternal mRNAs are replaced by zygotic mRNAs. The transition and decay of maternal mRNAs are done by the piRNA-Aub complex in association with the carbon catabolite repression-negative on TATA-less (CCR4-NOT) deadenylase complex. Nanos mRNA degradation is an example of deadenylation by the piRNA-Aub complex resulting in Aub mutant embryos lacking this degradation [79,80].

Besides the germline, developmental, and embryonic involvement, PIWI/piRNA also plays a key role in the sex determination in certain species. In silkworms with ZW sex (ZZ-male and ZW-female) determination system, a piRNA precursor for *fem* piRNA is present and specifically expressed in the W chromosome. The *fem* piRNA is the master regulator of feminization in silkworms, and the silencing of *fem* piRNA with antisense RNAs leads to a process called sex reversal where the females are changed into male worms. Interestingly, multiple copies of this single piRNA are only needed for the efficient sex reversal process [81–83]. This implies the significance of PIWI/piRNA in the maintenance of the sexual integrity of the organism.

2.2 Epigenetic regulations

The mammalian PIWI/piRNA system is conserved and dynamic which effectively plays a pivotal role in gene regulation at transcriptional and posttranscriptional levels. PIWI, Ago3, and Aub proteins, which belong to the argonaute family, were first identified in the germline cells of flies performing transposon silencing [60]. Later, the epigenetic regulations executed by them were revealed in flies, especially by Aub and PIWI which are the position effect variegation (PEV) regulators in flies. During this regulation, the piRNA pathway silences euchromatic gene expression and promotes heterochromatin assembly. PIWI in the nucleus tends to physically interact with heterochromatin and colocalize with HP1 in many sites of chromosomes [84]. This interaction of PIWI with HP1 determines heterochromatin formation and PEV. It has been found that the flies lacking PIWI-HP1 interaction exhibit ineffective PEV. HP1a and histone methyltransferase (HMT) Su(var)3–9 are recruited by piRNAs to their complementary sites in the genome guided by PIWI protein [85–87]. However, in some cases, the PIWI/piRNA duo also acts as an epigenetic activator for euchromatic genes in the subtelomeric region. The recruitment of RNA polymerase II in the genome is also overseen by PIWI as suggested by the varied level of euchromatin RNA polymerase II in PIWI mutants [59,60]. As discussed earlier, PIWI/piRNA also plays a gene inhibitory role. It is quite astonishing that the same protein is able to carry out both gene activation and repression at the genomic level depending upon the functional requirement.

2.3 Transgenerational memory and silencing

PIWI/piRNA is the conserved class of small ncRNAs that recognizes and silences the complimentary transcripts in the system. Target selection exhibited by PIWI/piRNAs seems to be very mysterious, because they usually target transposons and repetitive elements with high sequence diversity. Both in flies and mammals, genomic integrity is promoted by canonical piRNA pathways, where the mobile elements are entrapped in the genomic piRNA clusters which also induce biogenesis of piRNA and further silence the replicas positioned elsewhere in the genome. In progenies, maternally inherited PIWI/piRNAs are involved in genomic surveillance [88]. In *C. elegans*, piRNAs act through siRNAs where piRNA initiates heritable transcriptional and posttranscriptional silencing [89]. In this phenomenon, chromosome segregation and RNA interference (RNAi) deficient (CSR-1) 22G, an endogenous siRNA plays a key role which is vital for chromatin segregation during embryonic mitotic division. Self-genes or the endogenous protein-coding genes in *C. elegans* are protected by the CSR-1-dependent "licensing" process, from PRG-1 (PIWI ortholog in worms)-dependent WAGO 22G RNA silencing effect. These "licensed" genes were later on inherited without getting further silenced by piRNAs [78,90,91]. piRNAs have the ability to initiate inheritable transcriptional and posttranscriptional silencing which is triggered by foreign RNAi and PRG-1-dependent silencing, called RNA-induced epigenetic silencing or transgenerational silencing. Here, within a lengthy foreign sequence, transgene copy gets inserted leading to permanent PRG-1-dependent silencing. Still, after several generations, self-genes targeted by exogenous RNAi could reverse the silencing effect and may show resistance in permanent silencing due to the reduction in transgene copies. Normally, in the PIWI knock-out condition, the organism was found to have defects in spermatogenesis, germline proliferation, etc., but in *C. elegans*, PRG-1 mutants have not shown any effect on fertility and germline cell integrity. Studies stated that the worms have some special feature called "transgenerational memory" of WAGO class RNA production. When the silencing process occurs in the presence of PRG-1, that "memory" had been taken forward to the next-generation even in the absence of PRG-1. Mounting evidence has shown that PRG-1 is necessary only for the initiation of transgenerational silencing but not for the maintenance [92–97].

Another interesting fact in worms is that the maternal piRNAs have an eminent role in fertility. WAGO class 22G RNA which is transferred from the mother in addition to the complement RNAi factor is adequate to improve fertility in *C. elegans*. Resetting of RNAi in the absence of piRNA and the apoptosis of germline cells before entering the pachytene stage causes recognizable defect in meiosis progression and germline proliferation [23,98–100]. These facts determine the impeccable role of PRG-1 in worms in genomic surveillance and maintenance.

2.4 PIWI in DNA repair, chromosome dynamics, cell cycle progression, and apoptosis

The surveillance of genome integrity is one of the crucial roles played by PIWI which has an influence on chromosome dynamics and DNA repair. Various research groups have identified the involvement of PIWI in DNA repair and in chromosome architecture and dynamics [101,102]. Histone acetylation converts heterochromatin to euchromatin during the initiation of DNA repair, but in Mili mutants, the acetylase activity was found to be reduced. Furthermore, Alu retrotransposon-derived piRNAs are associated with DNA repair and chromatin reorganization proteins. During the double-strand breaks, small RNA which may also include piRNAs that were recruited near the break employs histone modifiers and DNA repairing molecules at the site of the break. Khurana et al. put forward the possible involvement of piRNA pathways in chromosome end protection via telomere capping [103–106].

In various cancer conditions such as lung carcinoma, piRNAs functions as a cell cycle promoter by regulating cyclin D1 and cyclin-dependent kinase 4 (CDK4) expression [107,108]. Additionally, it also navigates the cell's entry to the S phase in the leukemia cell line. In *Drosophila*, DEAD-box RNA helicase Vasa (Vas) that interacts with piRNA in PIWI/piRNA-mediated transposon silencing acts as a positive regulator of mitotic chromosome condensation. In flies, during mitosis, Aub and Spn-E are reported to function together with Vas. Aub-Spn-E mutants tend to show defects in chromosome segregation, entry to prometaphase, and Barr chromosomal localization. Thus, the interaction of PIWI family proteins with Vas regulates chromosomal condensation, segregation, and cell division [101,102,109–112]. Besides, piRNA-guided protein recruitment in the pericentric region during mitosis has been reported in the germline cells. It has been demonstrated that PIWI protein in these cases might be acting as a mitotic promoter since the downregulation of PIWI leads to decreased cell division in the germline cells while overexpression provides an increased division. The role of specific piRNAs has been established in cell proliferation through various pathways [113,114]. A few of them are piRNA-54,265 which binds to PIWIL2 and initiates STAT3 signaling. An increased piR-Hep1 promotes Ak strain transforming (AKT) phosphorylation and increased hepatic cell proliferation during hepatic carcinoma. The decreased level of piRNA-DQ722010 activated phosphoinositide 3-kinase (PI3K)/AKT pathway during prostate hyperplasia. Also, in normal conditions, piR-823 acts as a positive regulator for cell proliferation [115,116].

The piRNAs involved in the cell cycle are of two categories: the proproliferative or antiapoptotic piRNAs and the other one is antiproliferative or proapoptotic piRNAs. The role of PIWI/piRNA has been studied in apoptosis with a limitation in the germline and cancer cells. PIWI/piRNAs are significant for germline survival, so possibly the apoptosis can be considered as an indirect consequence of the absence of the protein-RNA pair. In mice, PIWI/piRNA is essential for germline cell survival. Miwi mutants have shown a reduced survival rate in later stages of spermatogenesis, but in the case of Mili and Miwi2, sudden cell cycle arrest was observed in the prophase of meiosis-I itself. In zebrafish, Ziwi and Zili mutation have shown diverse effects, a narrow loss of Ziwi diminished cell survival and further increased the rate of apoptosis during the growth period of the cell. However, Zili mutants have not shown any potential apoptosis [45,46,117–120]. Furthermore, the interaction of PIWI/piRNA with antiapoptotic, proapoptotic, and prosurvival molecules through various signaling pathways, especially the STAT3 pathway, signifies their indulgence in apoptosis. The prosurvival molecules such as nuclear factor kappa B (NFκβ) and B-cell lymphoma 2 (BCL-2) are activated by the PIWI/piRNA complex to maintain the survival of germ cells. PIWIL2 which is proposed to be an upstream molecule for the STAT3 signaling pathway regulates the antiapoptotic gene B-cell lymphoma-extra large (BCL-XL), and in the HeLa cell line, it inhibits p53 promoter by histone modification by forming a complex with STAT3 and SRC and acts as an antiapoptotic factor by itself. The same property is exhibited by PIWIL1 but with a different antiapoptotic molecule, fibroblast growth factor 8 (FGF8), which accelerates cellular viability and reduces the number of proapoptotic factors such as Bax and p21 [31,114,121,122].

Thus, the overexpression of PIWI/piRNA in various cancers demonstrated a role in cell proliferation by the initiation of various signaling pathways apart from DNA repair activities and maintaining the chromosome dynamics.

2.5 PIWI in neurons and other somatic tissues

The first somatic expression of PIWI/piRNA was reported in ovarian somatic cells of *Drosophila* [63,123]. Later on, the expression has been identified in several other cell types in different organisms. Interaction of PIWI/piRNA with various transcription factors such as NFκβ, cAMP resposnse element-binding (CREB) protein, and signal transducer and activator of transcription (STAT) protein further suggests their importance in the regulation of diverse mechanisms [124,125]. One significant role was identified in Aplysia neurons, where PIWI/piRNA has been identified in the neuronal nucleus which effectively denotes its transcriptional regulatory role. Furthermore, neuromodulators which are important for learning and memory formation have been shown to be regulated by PIWI/piRNAs. In Aplysia, the transcription factor CREB2 is methylated by PIWI/piRNA complex which later on involves long-term memory storage. PIWI also has a role in 5-hydroxytryptamine (5HT)-dependent long-term facilitation through the regulation of various genes, where CREB2 acts as a transcriptional repressor and CREB1 as a transcriptional activator [62,126].

piRNAs have been spotted in several mouse tissues like the brain, heart, liver, lung, spleen, kidney, and testis. Studies established the probability for Miwi to be a vital member of the PIWI clade in the mouse nervous system rather than Mili and Miwi2. It has been identified in mice that, in dendritic spine development and neuronal morphogenesis also piRNA has an eminent role [126]. Mounting evidence has revealed the involvement of PIWIL1 in the regulation of cortical neurons which are associated to fear memory and PIWIL2 and PIWIL4 in autism [127–129]. Aub and Ago3 were observed in drosophila neurons and fat bodies which were supposed to be associated with memory formation [130,131]. The expression of PIWI/piRNA has been recognized in the retina, the retinal pigment epithelium (RPE) and vitreous humor [132,133], cardiac progenitor cells such as cardiofibroblasts (CFs), cardiosphere-derived cells (CDCs), and cardiospheres. The possible role for piRNAs here could be for mRNA and transposon regulation. During myocardial infarction, one specific piRNA (piR-2106027) was increased and many were reduced in patients with cardiac failure which could act as biomarkers for the same [134–136]. Dysregulation of piRNAs is observed in Alzheimer's disease [137,138], Parkinson's disease (PD) [139,140], diabetic nephropathy [141], and rheumatoid arthritis [142] conditions as well. Reports have shown the involvement of piRNAs in trafficking and homeostasis maintenance of neurons. For example, piR38240, piR34393, and piR40666 were found to interact with *cycs, kpna6,* and *rab11a* genes in neurons. In PD, the upregulation of these piRNAs has been reported to initiate apoptosis and degeneration of the cells [33]. The presence and functions of PIWI/piRNA in the somatic cells are not well explored. Further studies on its presence and functional roles in various cell types would benefit the pharmacological and therapeutic fields. PIWI/piRNAs are executing significant functions (Fig. 1) in various organisms, especially in gene silencing both in the somatic and germline cells. But still, many of its functional possibilities are yet to be discovered (Table 1).

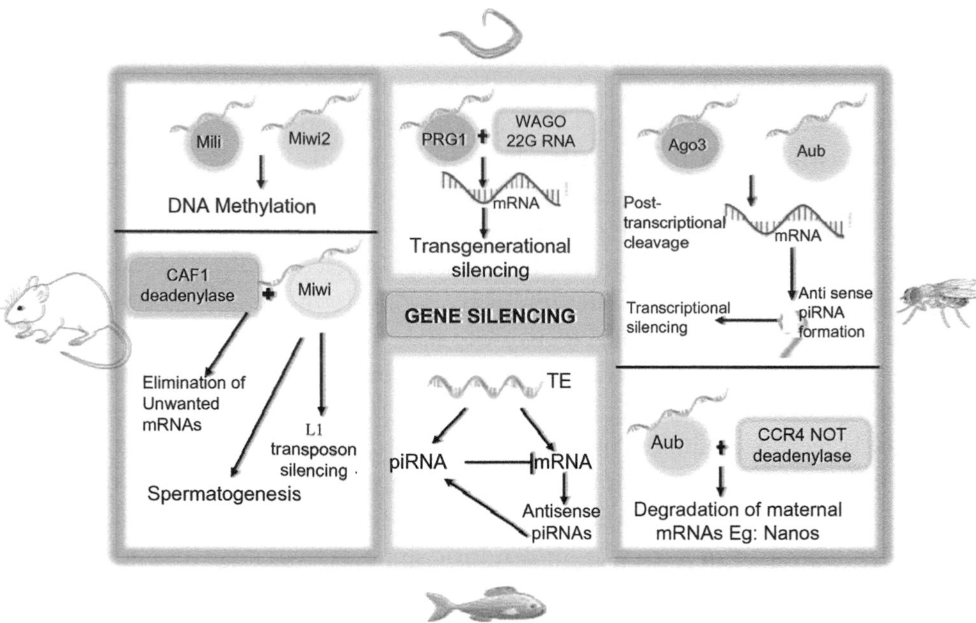

Fig. 1 Gene silencing exhibited by PIWI orthologs with piRNA in Mouse, *C. elegans*, *Drosophila*, and zebrafish. In mouse, Miwi2- and Mili-mediated gene regulation is done by DNA methylation, while Miwi employs deadenylation; *C. elegans* PRG-1 acts through transgenerational silencing. In zebrafish, piRNA functions via transposon silencing, and in *Drosophila*, Ago3 and Aub execute transcriptional and posttranscriptional mRNA cleavage, in addition, Aub uses deadenylation to maintain the gene regulation.

3. Emerging significance of PIWI/piRNA in various cancers

Germ cells, stem cells, and cancer cells are shown to have many similar characteristics such as infinite self-renewal, rapid proliferation, and growth. It will be worth saying that germline factors might have underlying involvement in oncogenesis too. This opens a new area of research namely germline-specific factors in cancer research [144–147]. These findings bring focus on PIWI/piRNA and their involvement in cancer as they are also reported to present in all the above-mentioned cells. In this section, we highlight the role of PIWI/piRNA in various cancers, focus on their potential participation in different pathways or their interaction with different proteins in tumorigenesis.

3.1 An insight of piRNAs in different cancers

Accumulating reports have shown the presence of both oncogenic piRNAs and tumor-suppressive piRNAs in numerous cancers [148]. It has been found that intensified proliferation of the cell, increased growth, enhanced migration and intrusion of cells, and impediment of apoptosis are the few processes contributed by oncogenic piRNAs [32,149,150].

On the other hand, the expression of some piRNAs has been reported to be diminished during tumorigenesis; thus, these piRNAs are known to be tumor-suppressor genes. To restrict the development of tumors, tumor-suppressor piRNAs enhanced the expression of tumor-suppressor genes and decreased the oncogenes. Interestingly, studies have proved that piRNA expression profiles can vary between tumor cells and noncancer cells, indicating their significance as cancer biomarkers in the near future [151].

3.1.1 piRNA in breast cancer

One of the most common cancers in the world is breast cancer (WHO), and it is the leading cause of cancer-related death in women. Reports have shown an enormous number of altered expressions of piRNAs in breast cancer, like piR-016975, piR-823, piR-932, piR-021285, piR-016658, piR-36712, and piR-4987. Recently, Qian [152] and his team have shown the expression of 415 piRNAs in human breast cancer cell line MCF-7; however, out of this, 27 have been shown to get dysregulated by pro-oncogene cyclin D1 [108]. Similarly, Hashim et al. have reported 100 piRNAs in tumor biopsies and breast cancer cell lines through RNA-Seq analysis [153].

Estrogen and its receptors-induced breast cancer has been well documented in recent years. It has been demonstrated that estrogen receptor alpha (Era), along with ncRNAs, has an interaction with piRNAs [154]. However, in the case of estrogen receptor beta (ERb), the underlying mechanism between ERb and ncRNAs in breast cancer is still elusive. Although many studies have shown the presence of piRNAs in human breast cancer, only a very few studies showed the molecular mechanisms and regulatory functions [152]. For instance, the first piRNA shown to have a regulatory effect on breast cancer cells was piR-021285 which exerts its effect via an epigenetic mechanism, DNA methylation. In this case, by comparing genome-wide methylation profiles in MCF7 cells transfected either with wild-type or variant piR-021285, differences in methylation have been observed in several cancer-related genes [155]. Further, the expression of piR-36712 was found to be low in breast cancer tumors and functions as a tumor suppressor in the presence of Selenoprotein W1 (SEPW1) and p53 protein. Reports have suggested that the downregulation of piR-36712 leads to higher expression of SEPW1 which in turn suppresses the expression levels of p53, p21, and E-cadherin [156]. Similar to the piR-021285, piR-823 has also shown regulatory function through an epigenetic mechanism. It has been delineated that the presence or absence of estrogen receptors helps piR-823 to impart carcinogenicity in breast cancer. Administration of estrogen externally has been found to escalate the expression of piR-823 in estrogen receptor-negative MDA-MB-231 cells, while reduced piR-823 levels were found in estrogen receptor-positive MCF-7 cells [157]. Increased cases of breast cancer have made the scientific world think of new strategies. Easy and early diagnostic approaches can make a difference against this disease. In future therapeutics, monitoring the expression of piRNAs can be one of the advantageous arts of war to counteract breast cancer.

3.1.2 piRNA in lung cancer

In lung cancer, reports have suggested that piRNAs affect the expression of cancer-related genes, a similar mechanism as shown by miRNAs, thus involved in the regulation of cancerous cells. piR-55490 was found to be associated with 3′UTR of mTOR mRNA and encourage its degradation in lung cancer cells [158]. Similar to the "seed sequence" of miRNAs, the 5′ end of piRNA-55490 can be complementary to the 3′UTR of mTOR mRNA. Moreover, the expression of piR-55490 was found to be diminished in lung carcinoma specimens and cell lines. Interestingly, the restoration of piR-55490-repressed cell proliferation by downregulating Akt/mTOR pathway in lung cancer [158].

In a different study, piRNAs have been shown to regulate human cancer cells by transcriptional factors. It has been elucidated that upregulation of piR-34871 and piR-52200 and downregulation of piR-35127 and piR-46545 were done by the Ras Association Domain Family Member 1C (RASSF1C) in lung cancer cell line H1299 and tumor tissues of lungs. The overexpression of piR-35127 and piR-46545 and the suppression of piR-34871 and piR-52200 significantly reduced cell proliferation in both lung cancer cell lines (A549 and H1299) and breast cancer cell lines (Hs578T and MDA-MB-231) [159]. From the above findings, it has been suggested that the altered expression of piRNA is potentially associated with the invasion, metastasis, and tumorigenesis of lung cancer, which possibly can be used as novel biomarkers and new targets for precision medicine [33].

3.1.3 piRNA in colorectal cancer

In the year 2020, colorectal cancer has the third position after breast and lung cancer, respectively. However, in terms of the most common deaths due to cancer, colorectal cancer has jumped to the second position (916,000 deaths) (WHO), indicating its alarming increase in incidence and fatality [160]. It has been proposed that several piRNAs can work as oncogenes in colorectal cancer. Increased expression of piR-1245 has been reported to enhance colorectal cancer cell growth, encourage invasion and migration, and inhibit apoptosis. piR-1245 binds to the intronic regions of its targeted mRNAs like, activating transcription factor 3 (ATF3), BTGantiproliferation factor 1 (BTG), dual specificity phosphatase 1 (DUSP1), Fas cell surface death receptor (FAS), NFκB inhibitor alpha (NFκBIA), uridine phosphorylase 1 (UPP1), sestrin 2 (SESN2), tumor protein P53 inducible nuclear protein 1 (TP53INP1) via sequence complementarity. These targeted mRNAs are involved in vital tumor-suppressive pathways and degrade mRNA through nuclear exosomes. Increased expression of piR-1245 has been observed in poorly differentiated colorectal tissues, distant metastasis, lymph node metastasis, and overall poor survival [161].

Interestingly, one study has reported that piRNA induces colorectal cancer by forming a complex with its cognate PIWI partner and other proteins. For example, PIWIL2/phosphorylated-SRC/piR-54265 stimulates the phosphorylation of STAT3. Once phosphorylated, STAT3 enters the nucleus and induces the expression of a plethora of different genes, like antiapoptotic and invasion-related genes such as matrix metallopeptidases. This in turn promotes tumor proliferation, invasion, and metastasis [35]. These studies have given a new dimension to the existing information on the involvement of PIWI-piRNA in the development of colorectal cancer by forming ribonucleoprotein complex and by phosphorylation of proteins [35]. Another study has revealed that in colorectal cancer, piR-823 inhibits the expression of heat shock protein (HSP), binds to HSF1, a general transcription factor of HSPs, and accelerates phosphorylation at Ser326, thus, promoting cancer [116]. Also, piRNA-823 has been found to suppress the ubiquitination of hypoxia-inducible factor (HIF-1a), this leads to increased cell proliferation, invasion, and resistance to apoptosis thereby accelerating the glucose consumption of cancer cells and inhibiting intracellular reactive oxygen species [162]. In a study, the downregulation of piR-1245 has been demonstrated to be crucial for the activation of the p53 pathway and thus in the promotion of colorectal cancer [161]. In addition to this, piR-1245, piR-18849, and piR-19521 have shown novel and independent prognostic characteristics in colorectal cancer [161,163]. Elevated cases of colon cancer have suggested that existing therapeutics are not enough and new dimensions are needed to reduce its severity and fatalities. A better understanding of the pathophysiological functions of piRNAs in the colon can deliver vital insight into the microenvironment of this cancer and thus can be used as a diagnostic strategy.

3.1.4 piRNA in liver cancer

Liver cancer is the sixth most commonly diagnosed cancer and in the year 2020, it was the third leading cause of cancer death [164,165]. In the last 8 years (from 2013 to 2021), the prevalence of liver cancer has escalated in both men and women [166]. Liver cancer can be categorized into several stages, cirrhotic nodules, low-grade dysplastic nodules, high-grade dysplastic nodules, primary hepatocellular carcinoma, and progressing hepatocellular carcinoma. piRNAs were found to be present in each stage. Studies on liver cancer have shown the expression of piR-LLi-24894 in cirrhotic nodules; piR-LLi-30552 and hsa-piR-020498 were chiefly found in high-grade dysplastic nodules, primary hepatocellular carcinoma, and progressed hepatocellular carcinoma [167]. Law et al. have shown the upregulated piR-Hep1 in 46.6% of liver carcinoma tissues compared with adjacent normal liver tissues [168]. The downregulation of piR-Hep1 repressed proliferation, migration, and invasion capability of hepatocellular carcinoma cells. In addition to this, silencing of piR-Hep1 also reduced the phosphorylation level of AKT, thus repressing other pathways associated with AKT in cancer [168–170].

In a compelling study in hepatic stellate cells, the expression of piR-823 was found to be remarkably upregulated. The overexpression of piR-823 was found to encourage the proliferation of hepatic stellate cells and the production of alpha-smooth-muscle actin and collagen-type 1 alpha 1 chain, including components of extracellular matrix, which finally resulted in cirrhosis. Interestingly, inhibition of piR-823 can inhibit the activity of hepatic stellate cells. This study has also demonstrated that a combination of piR-823 along with eukaryotic initiation factor 3B (EIF3B) activates hepatic stellate cells in liver fibrogenesis via upregulating transforming growth factor-β1 (TGF-β1) [171]. piRNA in liver cancer and their underlying specific regulatory mechanism are still obscure and in-depth studies are needed to understand its mechanism.

3.1.5 piRNA in gastric cancer

Among the top five most frequently occurring malignant tumors worldwide, gastric cancer is the third most deadly cancer [164,172]. When comparing men and women, the prevalence of gastric cancer is higher in men than in women, but the number varies between countries [173].

piRNA profiles have shown the copious presence of piRNAs in the human stomach [174]. Transcript analysis of normal gastric tissues and gastric cancer cells revealed that almost half of the piRNAs were upregulated in cancer samples [175]. This indicates that piRNAs might have a vital role in the progression of gastric cancer. Studies have shown significant suppression of piR-823 in gastric cancer tissues. Further, reports have suggested that mimicking piR-823 can halt cell proliferation. A study has proved that piR-823 inhibits tumor growth in a xenograft nude mouse model [176]. Additionally, the expression of piR-651 and piR-823 was found to be low in the peripheral blood of gastric cancer patients. In contrary, high expression of piR-32105, piR-58099, and piR-9056 was reported in gastric cancer tissues [177]. In human, piR-651 was highly expressed in gastric, breast, lung, and hepatic carcinoma cell lines, indicating its crucial role as an oncogene in tumorigenesis. piR-651 accelerates cell proliferation by promoting gastric cancer cells to enter the G2/M phase. Elevated levels of piR651 have been related to tumor-node-metastasis stages and also in less differentiated cancers. Studies revealed that the dose-dependent use of piR-651 inhibitors in gastric cancer cells reduced cell growth, implying piR-651 can act as a potential target for cancer therapy [178].

It is widely known that surgery or endoscopic treatment can cure the preliminary stage of gastric cancer, but the prognosis of later stages in gastric cancer is not satisfactory; thus, new approaches are needed for better prognosis and diagnosis.

3.1.6 piRNA in ovarian cancer

Globally, ovarian cancer is one of the primary causes of death in women. Ovarian cancer is responsible for the second highest death among all gynecological cancers [164,179]. Out of different ovarian cancer types and subtypes, endometrioid ovarian cancer (ENOCa) and serous ovarian cancer (SOCa) (subtype of EOCa) are recurrently observed and found to be extremely lethal [180]. In ENOCa cells, upregulation of piR-52207 has been demonstrated to repress four critical genes responsible for proliferation, migration, and tumorigenesis [181]. The four vital genes were nucleoside diphosphate-linked moiety X-type motif 4 (NUDT4), methionine synthetase (MTR), eukaryotic translation initiation factor 2 subunit 3 (EIF2S3), and M-phase phosphoprotein 8 (MPHOSPH8).

These are associated with different pathways, namely, 3-phosphoinositide biosynthesis, D-myo-inositol-5-phosphate biosynthesis, folate transformation, vascular endothelial growth factor (VEGF), and EIF2 signaling pathways. In SOCa, piR-33733 interacts with lipoic acid synthase at 3′UTRs, whereas piR-52207 interacts with actin-related protein 10 (ACTR10) and pleckstrin homology domain-containing family A member 5 (PLEKHA5) at 3′UTRs and 5′UTRs. The result of this interaction was found to enhance antiapoptotic and decrease proapoptotic proteins [181].

Mutations of breast cancer susceptibility genes (BRCA1 and BRCA2) have been found to contribute to almost 40% of ovarian cancer cases in women with a family history of the disease [182]. It will be interesting to understand whether piRNAs are interrelated to BRCA mutation or not, if it is so, they can be used as factors for genomic evaluation and indicators for anti-BRCA and antiovarian drug resistance.

3.1.7 piRNA in kidney/renal cell cancer

Renal cell carcinoma (RCC) is one of the most frequently occurring malignant tumors of the urinary system, and it contributes to approximately 2%–3% of all adult malignancies [183,184]. There are different types of renal cancers, out of them, clear cell renal cell carcinoma (ccRCC) is the most prominent type of RCC, which accounts for 60%–85% of all RCC cases [164,185]. Treatment and diagnosis of kidney cancer are difficult, and its underlying molecular mechanism is poorly understood [186].

The overexpression of piR-43607, piR 32051, and piR-39894 has been critically associated with advanced tumor stage, metastasis, and cancer-specific survival in RCC [187]. piR-57125 expression was found to be less in metastatic than in nonmetastatic malignancies. In contrast, piR-38756 and piR30924 are related to cancer metastasis, with higher expression in metastatic and lower expression in nonmetastatic tumors [188]. Du and his team explored the expression of piRNAs in six pairs of ccRCC tissues and revealed that piR-31115 was upregulated which accelerates cell proliferation and invasion through epithelial-mesenchymal transition and PI3K/AKT signaling pathway in ccRCC [189]. Studies of piRNA in kidney cancer are still in infancy and further investigations are needed to understand the complete mechanism.

3.1.8 piRNA in glioblastoma cancer

Glioblastoma is an extremely malignant and invasive intracranial tumor with the worst prognosis and it is derived from neuroepithelium [190]. Studies have reported decreased expression of piR-30188 and PIWIL3 in glioblastoma and they are further negatively correlated with pathological grade glioma. piR-30188 was found to inhibit tumor cell proliferation, invasion, and migration and encourage apoptosis [191]. Bartos et al. have shown that few piRNAs were significantly suppressed in glioblastoma. Out of them, piR-9491 and piR-12488 diminish the ability to form tumor cell colonies in vitro. It will be exciting to reveal further functions of these two piRNAs as therapeutic targets in glioblastoma. piR-23231 expression was connected with the overall survival of patients, suggesting that some piRNAs could also be used as prognostic biomarkers in glioblastoma [192]. In glioma-conditioned endometrium cancers, piR-DQ590027 was found to be expressed very less. However, it has been observed that the overexpression of piR-DQ590027 could reduce ZO-1, occludin, and claudin-5, this, in turn, increases the permeability of glioma-conditioned blood-brain barrier by piR-DQ590027/MIR17HG/miR-153(miR-377)/FOXR2 pathway.

Similar to piR-DQ590027, other piRNAs might also have distinct partners and pathways via which they could execute specific functions under pathological conditions. It will be interesting to decode different molecular functions of piRNAs to use them against glioblastoma as a new therapeutic strategy [193].

3.1.9 piRNA multiple myeloma

Multiple myeloma (MM) is generally diagnosed as hematological neoplasm. This disease is highly progressive in nature and mostly not curable [194]. Increased expression of piR-823 represses the caspase-3/Bax signaling pathway and induces endothelial cell proliferation. It was also found to increase angiogenesis by inducing VEGF and interleukin (IL)-6 secretion. Moreover, piR-823 increases the invasion of endothelial cells by inducing intercellular adhesion molecule 1 (ICAM-1) and C-X-C motif chemokine receptor 4 (CXCR4) [195]. One more study has reported that piRNA-823 instigated DNA methylation through DNA-methyl transferase (DNMTs), DNMT3A, and DNMT3B, and it repressed a methylation-silenced tumor suppressor protein, p16INK4A [196]. Myeloid myeloma cells have also shown higher expression of piRNA-4987 and piRNA-Hep1 [197]. Although many studies have predicted the importance of piRNA in multiple myeloma, in-depth studies are needed to uncover the mechanism behind the aberrant expression and thus, their use in precision medicine.

So far, the cancers which have a high prevalence of extensive mortality rate have been discussed. However, altered expression of piRNAs has been found in many other cancers, like bladder cancer, osteosarcoma, head, and neck squamous cell carcinoma, fibro-blastoma, etc. [34,198,199]. Existing techniques need further assistance to tackle cancer. PIWI/piRNA is one of the emerging fields that can be used in cancer diagnosis and treatment. Although piRNA field is in its infancy, the potential of piRNAs cannot be overlooked and in the future, they can be used as diagnostic or prognostic markers or as a therapeutic target.

3.2 PIWI-like proteins in cancer

In this segment, we have highlighted and discussed the involvement of PIWI in various cancers, explaining their expression-related outcomes, and epigenetic modifications in malignant cells.

3.2.1 PIWIL1 (HIWI)

Out of all the PIWI proteins, PIWIL1 has been studied extensively and has been found to control gene expression, cell cycle, cell proliferation, and apoptosis [200,201]. Janic et al. have reported that in *Drosophila*, two PIWI proteins, PIWI and AUB, were associated with the progression of tumors [202]. The expression of PIWI in cancer was first reported in seminomas, a cancer of male germ cells [203]. Although the expression of PIWIL1 (HIWI) was present in seminomas, it was not detected in spermatocytic seminomas or testicular tumors, nonseminomas derived from somatic cells such as Sertoli cells and Leydig cells [203]. Studies have suggested that the overexpression of PIWIL1 in lung cancer might promote cancer cell proliferation, invasion, and migration and finally affect the overall survival rate in patients with lung adenocarcinoma or malignant lung cancer phenotypes [204]. In the pathogenesis of retinal cell carcinoma, PIWIL1 along with piR-823 play a significant role. Lower expression of the PIWIL1 gene has been associated with aggressive tumor phenotype and poor survival rate, suggesting that PIWIL1 might serve as a prognostic biomarker in patients with retinal cell carcinoma [205,206].

In a knockout study, the CRISPR-Cas9 system has been used to suppress the PIWIL1 gene in the AGP01 gastric carcinoma cell line. This report revealed that the knockout of the PIWIL1 gene has diminished the cell migration and invasiveness of AGP01 gastric cancer cells. Furthermore, this study has also explored the altered expression of many crucial genes such as dedicator of cytokinesis 2 (DOCK2), zinc finger protein 503 (ZNF503), phosphodiesterase 4D (PDE4D), tyrosine-protein kinase ABL1, and ABL2. Interestingly, proteins encoded by these genes are involved in cellular invasion and migration [207]. In gastric cancer, a correlation between the expression of a proliferation marker Ki67 and HIWI has been observed [208]. The study has demonstrated that suppressing HIWI leads to cell cycle arrest in the G2/M phase and diminishes the progression of gastric cancer cells [208].

HIWI expression was high in cervical cancer as well, however, their functional aspect in these cells is elusive [209]. In an interesting finding in colon cancers without lymph-node metastasis, Kaplan-Meier analysis has been done. It was observed that patients with HIWI-positive tumors had a significantly lower life expectancy than those with HIWI-negative tumors [210]. In gliomas, patients with high HIWI expression had shown adverse clinical outcomes, this showed that the expression level of HIWI can be correlated positively with the grade of the tumor [211]. Pancreatic cancer patients with an altered level of HIWI mRNA had shown a high risk of cancer-related deaths [212]. In endometrial cancer, PIWIL1 has been shown to initiate epithelial-to-mesenchymal transition and bestow cells with stem-like properties, such as migration of malignant cells, invasion, sphere-forming activity, and viability. In addition, increased accumulation of common endometrial cancer stem cell markers, CD44, and aldehyde dehydrogenase (ALDH) were found in PIWIL1 overexpressed endometrium cancer cells [213,214]. PTEN protein (phosphatase and tensin homologs deleted on chromosome ten) work as a tumor suppressor through DNMT1-

mediated PTEN hypermethylation. Reports have shown loss of PTEN in upregulated PIWIL1 endometrium cancer cells, suggesting a potential functional relationship between these two proteins [213,214]. It will be interesting to reveal the possibility of using PIWIL1 as an innovative treatment strategy against endometrium cancer. Increased expression of PIWIL1 and PIWIL2 has also been reported in invasive ductal carcinoma, which facilitates cancer progression by anomalous methylation of DNA resulting in silencing of genes and promoting stemness property of cancer cells [215].

3.2.2 PIWIL2 (HILI)

In each stage of breast cancer, PIWIL2 has been reported to show a distinctive pattern of expression. PIWIL2 can be well detected in invasive and metastatic breast cancers, particularly both in the nucleus and cytoplasm of cancer cells. On the contrary, in breast precancers, because of the distinctive expression of PIWIL2, it is expressed only in the nucleus, indicating PIWIL2 might work as a novel biomarker [216]. c-Myc facilitates NME/NM23 nucleoside diphosphate kinase 2 (NME2) to bind to the G4-motif region within the c-Myc promoter, this, in turn, regulates proliferation, invasion, and metastasis in many human tumors. Interestingly, Yao et al. [217] have found that PIWIL2 can upregulate c-Myc, indicating the involvement of PIWIL2 in breast cancer although the underlying mechanism is yet to be deciphered. Zeng et al. reported that in liver cancer, the nuclear co-expression of PIWIL2/PIWI4 had a worse prognostic phenotype [218]. Moreover, HILI was also found to be expressed in seminomas, and overexpression of HILI in a mouse cell line, NIH3T3, further revealed its contribution to cell adhesion, growth, and apoptosis [121].

It is important to know that PIWIL2 (HILI) has numerous variants. PIWIL2-like (PL2L) proteins have been reported in a broad spectrum of cancers [219]. One study has shown that PL2L60 (one variant of PIWIL2) was present in all tested human cancer cell lines, and its level was correlated with that of NFκB in the nucleus. Further, aberrant regulation of NFκB has been associated with oncogenesis [220]. In glioma, relatively high expression of PIWIL2 is associated with poor patient prognosis. In vivo studies in glioma cells have shown that knockdown of PIWIL2 arrests the cell cycle, accelerates apoptosis, and diminishes migration of glioma cells [221]. PIWIL2 via epigenetic regulation was found to contribute to the transformation of cervical epithelial cells to tumor-initiating cells. In cervical cancer tumorigenesis, oncoproteins E6 and E7 of the human papillomavirus (HPV) were found to reactivate PIWIL2. This leads to H3K9 acetylation, but the reduction in H3K9 trimethylation, in short, contributes to epigenetic reprogramming and maintenance of embryonic stem cells [222].

Till now many factors have been found and many are yet to be deciphered that are essential in the biogenesis of piRNA. However, it might be possible that PIWI protein works independently via different pathways. Vourekas et al. have found that MIWI independently interacts and stabilizes mRNAs without any guidance from piRNAs [223]. Further studies are required to investigate the role of PIWI in cancer biology and whether the choice of activation of signaling pathways differs during physiological and cancerous conditions. Moreover, along with piRNAs, whether other RNAs can also accompany PIWI proteins in cancer cells or not are a few questions that need to be addressed.

3.2.3 PIWIL3

In glioma cells, the expression of PIWIL3 is low and its expression is negatively correlated with the pathological grade of glioma. One study has shown the association between PIWIL3, piR-30188, OIP5-AS1, and miR-367-3p in regulating the migration and invasion of glioma cells. Further, their target gene CEBPA is involved in the regulation of PIWIL3 and TNF receptor associated, thus orchestrating a feedback loop to regulate the cellular growth [191]. Also, the expression level of PIWIL3 has been associated with glioma cell proliferation, migration, and invasion. Moreover, reports have suggested their downregulation reduces the development of glioma cells through JAK2/STAT3 signaling pathway [224]. It has been found that increased PIWIL3 is present in more destructive primary malignant melanoma and metastatic disease [225].

Reports of PIWIL3 are fewer but recent advancements in ncRNAs have suggested that in the future they can also be considered as a therapeutic marker. Their limitation in the cancer study is probably due to their expression being restricted to some species [226]. This in turn can be beneficial in framing different but specific prognostic or diagnostic approaches.

3.2.4 PIWIL4 (HIWI2)

In breast cancer tissues, extensive expression of PIWIL4 has been reported, in addition, they are also elevated in triple-negative breast cancer-derived cell lines. Moreover, they were found to encourage cell survival, division, and migration of cancer by activating TGF-β, MAPK/ERK, and FGF signaling pathways, which are significant players in cancer. Zhang et al. have demonstrated that in prostate cancer, PIWIL4 along with piR-31470 control the methylation of glutathione *S*-transferase P by recruiting multiple DNA methylation enzymes, thus contributing to the development of prostate cancer [227]. Reports have suggested that PIWIL4 suppresses the expression of MHC class II molecules, this, in turn, assists cancer cells to avoid immune recognition and response [228].

In hepatocellular carcinoma, localization and co-expression of PIWIL2/PIWIL4 were suggested to be a useful prognostic indicator for tumors. This is because PIWIL2/PIWIL4 reflects that tumors are in the primary stage of tumorigenesis. On contrary, the presence of PIWIL2/PIWIL4 in the nucleus but not in the cytoplasm

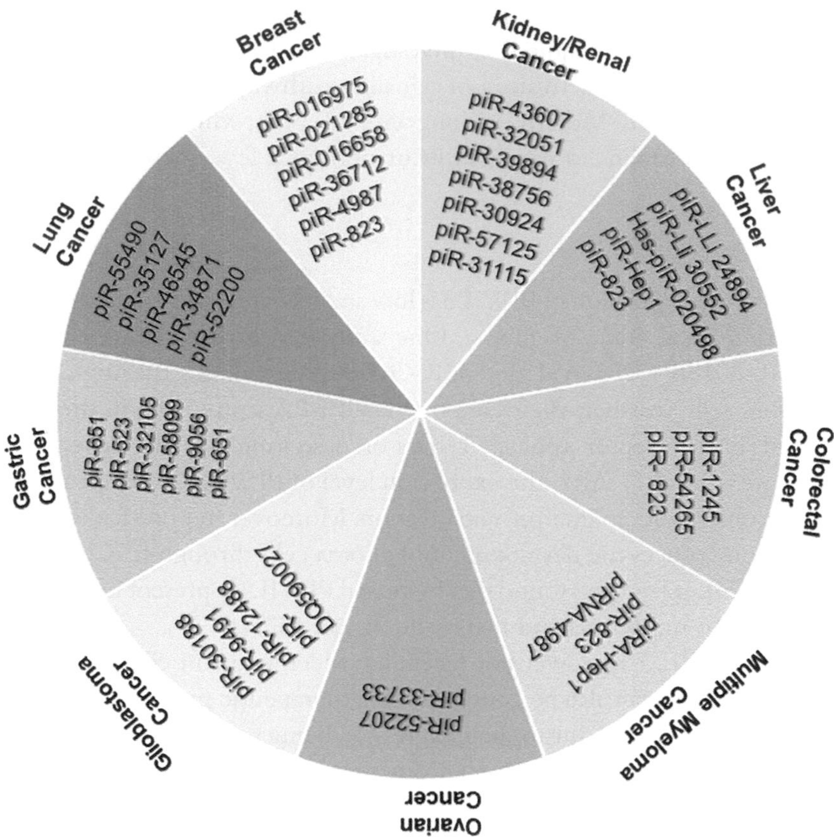

Fig. 2 Schematic illustration of the altered expression of piRNAs in different cancers. The diagram depicts significantly altered piRNAs in breast, kidney, lung, liver, and gastric cancers followed by glioblastoma, ovarian, and multiple myeloma cancers.

was correlated with more severe malignancy and poor hepatocellular carcinoma prognosis [218]. In diverse cancer cells, the ectopic expression of PIWI/piRNA has been reported. Studies on PIWI/piRNA are mostly at a correlative stage and their function in cancer is still not clear. Further studies are needed to locate their functional and regulatory targets and the molecular understanding of PIWI/piRNA-mediated mechanisms in cancer. A schematic representation of the expression of piRNAs is given in Fig. 2.

Before describing the potential role of PIWI/piRNA in RB, we have given an outline of the retina and its structure, heterogeneous environment, the functions of RB protein, and the involvement of different molecules in the formation of RB.

4. Retina and its structure

Diseases associated with the retina, including RB, have affected children's health and are being posed to cause a financial and economic burden across the world. RB has been a suitable model for studying human cancer genetics and biology due to their less molecular and cellular heterogeneity across patients [229–231]. In addition, this particular cancer is easy to detect and monitor; thus, making it easy to track the progression of the disease in patients [232]. Surprisingly, environmental factors and their association with RB are not much evident, making it less difficult to identify its molecular and cellular origin [233].

The retina is a multilayered structure of diverse cellular subtypes of retinal cells formed by retinogenesis. This process involves the proliferation of retinal progenitor cells (RPCs), whose tight regulation is necessary for the timed generation of cells for proper morphogenesis, histogenesis, and functionality [234–240]. During retinogenesis, retinal ganglion cells (RGCs) are formed in the initial stage of differentiation in the mammalian retina, followed by cones, horizontal interneurons, amacrine cells, rods, bipolar, and muller glial cells in evolutionarily conserved birth order [241,242].

Each retinal cell type exhibits distinct behavior during phototransduction, starting from the conversion of light energy to a change in membrane potential in the photoreceptors, which augments the release of neurotransmitters. Photoreceptors can be broadly classified into rods and cones. Rods have greater sensitivity to light and are thus responsible for dim-light vision [243,244]. Cones have lesser sensitivity, $\sim$100 times lesser than rods; therefore, compensated by faster response kinetics in cones during phototransduction. Cones are of different types depending on the wavelength of the light absorbed. For example, there are three types of cones in humans, with each responding to a specific wavelength of light, that is, short (S, blue), middle (M, green), and long (L, red). Thus, cones are involved in bright light and high sensitivity color vision. Further, in response to a light signal, photoreceptors release glutamate and transmit the membrane potential via synaptic connections with bipolar cells in the outer plexiform layer (OPL) to ganglion cells (outer layer of the retina). In addition, horizontal cells modulate the synaptic transmission between photoreceptors and bipolar cells. Similarly, amacrine cells regulate the excitation of the RGCs at the inner plexiform layer (IPL). Significantly, muller glial cells play a crucial role in the maintenance of the retinal homeostasis as well as in providing metabolic support to all the retinal cells [245]. This interconnected network of different cells in the retina is involved in the propagation and modulation of the signal through the entire complex to the visual centers for processing the information as schematically represented in Fig. 3 [246]. Importantly, any imbalance in the pattern of proliferation and differentiation of the retinal neurons leads to the formation of compromised retinal structure which can undergo degeneration or malignant transformation depending upon the intrinsic and extrinsic factors as in the case of RB [233]. A detailed view of RB, its cell of origin and pathophysiological functions, etc. are discussed in the next segment.

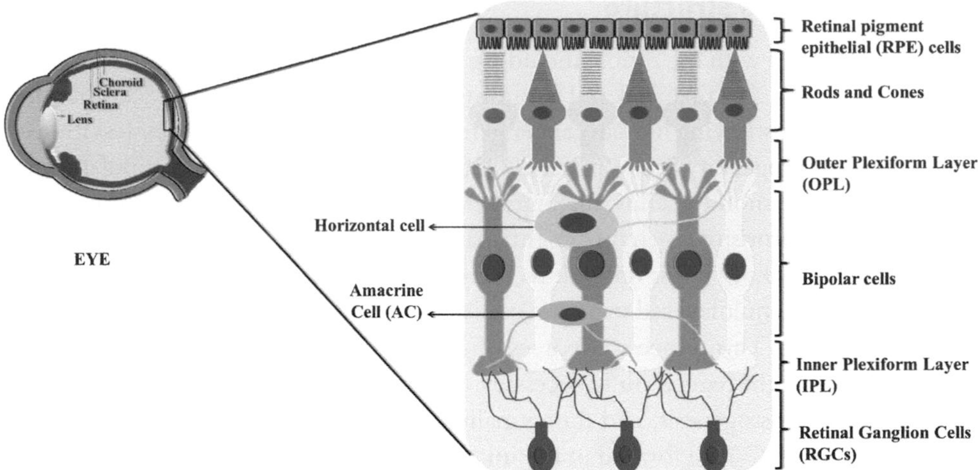

Fig. 3 Structure of retina. The outermost layer of the retina consists of photoreceptor cells (rods and cones) that are innervated into the cilia of RPE cells and form synapses with the bipolar and horizontal cells. The nerve plexus formed by photoreceptor, horizontal, and bipolar cells is called the outer plexiform layer (OPL). Bipolar cells form a synapse with retinal ganglion cells (RGCs) and amacrine cells (ACs). The nerve plexus formed by RGCs, bipolar cells, and ACs is called the inner plexiform layer.

4.1 Retinoblastoma

4.1.1 Pathologies of retinoblastoma

RB can be unilateral (tumor affecting one eye) and bilateral (tumor affecting both the eyes). Particularly, a bilateral form of RB is found to be multifocal (more than one focal tumors) and heritable due to the presence of mutations in the germline cells. RB in the retina is a form of sporadic cancer due to mutations in the somatic tissue [247] and can be categorized as intraocular RB and extraocular RB. There are different classification systems for RB to predict the treatment results and enable proper prognosis to be given to the patients. Among them, International Intraocular Retinoblastoma Classification Scheme (IIRC) and International Classification of Retinoblastoma (ICRB) have been used as the main classification system for intraocular RB [248]. As it is classified internationally, Stage-I starts with the formation of nonmalignant tumor in the retina; Stage-II tumor is extended by cuff of subretinal fluid from the base of the benign tumor; Stage-III progresses to form vitreous or subretinal seeds along with discrete retinal tumors of different sizes; Stage-IV is an advanced form with extensive vitreous or subretinal seeding; and in Stage-V, diffusion of tumor occurs to lens in conjunction with irreversible neovascular glaucoma, intraocular hemorrhage, and aseptic orbital cellulitis as shown in Fig. 4. However, extraocular RB is the malignant one that has penetrance to the eye globe wall and to the central nervous system. It can even diffuse via the blood stream to different parts of the body exhibiting metastasis [249].

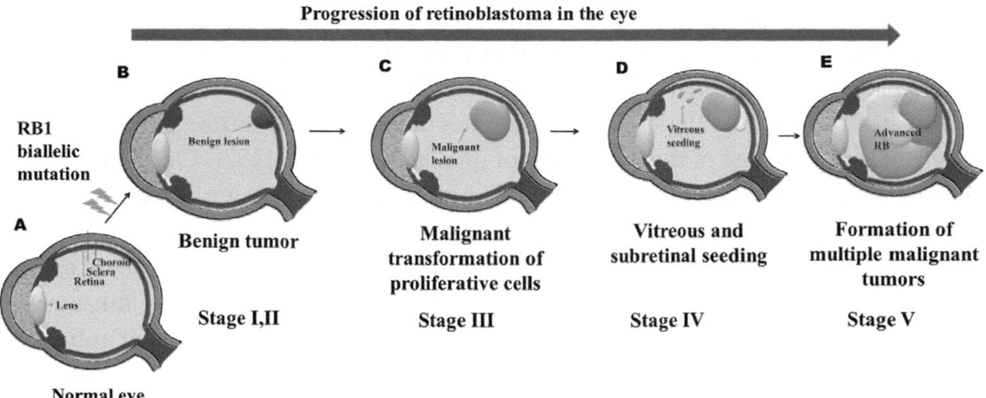

Fig. 4 Progression of retinoblastoma. (A) Normal eye; (B) biallelic mutation of RB1 gene transforms retinal cell into the nonmalignant tumor extended by cuff of subretinal fluid from the base of the tumor, RB Stage-I, II; (C) malignant transformation of proliferative cell, RB Stage-III; (D) progression of the tumor via vitreous and subretinal seeding, RB Stage-IV; and (E) formation of multiple malignant tumors, RB Stage-V.

Mouse models of RB have revealed mechanistic insight into the RB pathogenesis. The development of RB in the retina of mice requires inactivation of p107 or p130 genes in addition to the mutation of retinoblastoma protein (pRB) gene [250–254]. On the contrary, a biallclic mutation in RB1 gene in humans is sufficient to induce ectopic cell division in the retina to form a tumor [255]. It is believed that the suppression of pocket protein family (p107, p130, and RB1) is the defining event for the formation of nonmalignant retinoma in humans and mice. Furthermore, mutation in other genes, such as cancer-related genes, may transform the proliferative cell into a malignant cell. For instance, mutated MYCN (a cancer-related gene) undergoes amplification (MYCNA) to promote tumorigenesis in RB mutated or no RB mutated cells [230,256]. The $RB^{++}/MYCN^{A}$ tumors were found to have a unilateral pattern with distinct histology, earlier onset, and highly aggressive behavior compared with $RB^{-/-}$ tumors [256]. Therefore, species-specific genetic lesions contribute differently to disease progression which further depends upon the cell of origin. As RB is a developmental disease that originates from the diverse cell of origin, studying the biology of the different cell types would increase the understanding of RB tumor biology.

4.1.2 Cell of origin

RB in the retina may derive from RPCs (cells that can differentiate into any cell type) [253,254] or retinal transition cells (postmitotic cells that are biased to a particular fate). Both retinal progenitor and retinal transition cells exhibit distinct epigenetic features. This epigenetic heterogeneity could promote differential responses of various cell types to RB1 disruption. Here, epigenetic differences are related to the developmental potential of different progenitors or transition cells [255]. RB derived from retinal progenitors might exhibit variations in marker expression (both progenitor and differentiation markers) within individual tumors [253,254]. Since RPCs are multipotent, RB inactivated cells tend to undergo different states of competence during development that may result in a change in the expression of markers over time [257]. On the other hand, transition cell-derived RB may divide indefinitely after migrating to their final destination and could display markers specific to a postmitotic neuron as described in Fig. 5. For instance, the basal region of RB/p107-null retina consisted of ectopic S-phase cells that expressed BRN3B [250], a ganglion cell marker [258], or PAX6, a ganglion/amacrine marker [259,260]. Other than the expressed markers, the localization of tumor cells within the retina can also be used to differentiate the cell of origin of the tumor. For instance, tumor derived from the neuroblastic layer (proliferative zone of the inner optic cup) of the retina consists of RPCs. Whereas, tumor in the innermost layer of the retina contains mitotic transition cells and differentiated cells, such as amacrine and ganglion cells followed by the outer retina, which is the layer of photoreceptor-differentiation [250,251]. Accordingly, the malignant lesion may consist of multiple tumors with each

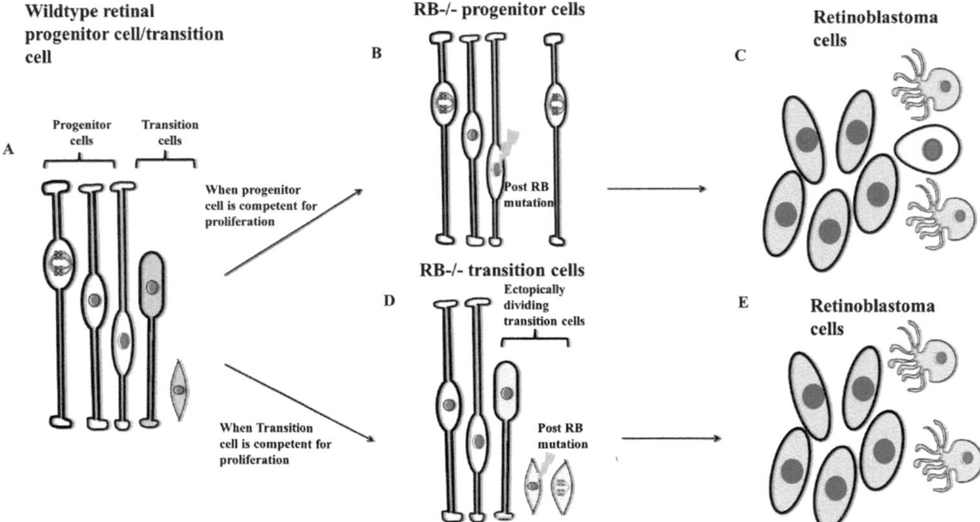

Fig. 5 Development of retinoblastoma from retinal progenitor and transition cells. (A) Retinal progenitor (RPC) and transition cells are present in the retina, (B) RPC is competent for proliferation under RB−/− mutation, (C) RB−/− mutated RPC along with post-RB mutation (shown by a lightning bolt) give rise to different retinoblastoma cell types, viz.; terminally differentiated cells with aberrant morphology (*blue* cytoplasm), ectopically dividing transition cells (*yellow* cytoplasm) and cells with self-renewal ability and indefinite dividing capacity (*white* cytoplasm). (D) RB−/− mutated transition cells undergo ectopic division and upon post-RB mutation, it produces (E) transition cells with self-renewal ability and indefinite division capacity (*yellow* cytoplasm) and terminally differentiated cells with aberrant morphology (*blue* cytoplasm). *RPC*, retinal progenitor cells; *RB*, retinoblastoma.

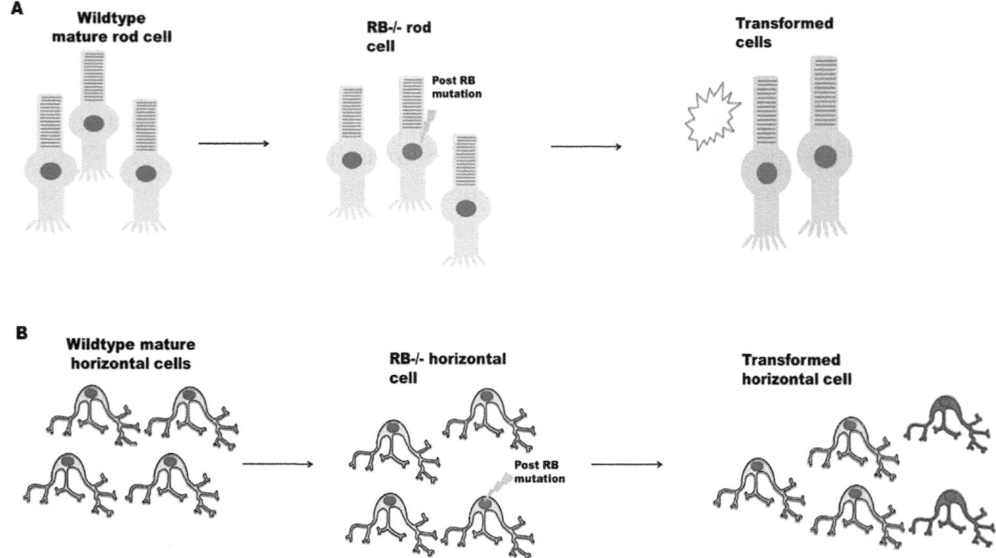

Fig. 6 Cellular pliancy model. (A) RB−/− mutated mature rod cells do not undergo cell cycle entry after post-RB mutations but rather degenerate (cell with *white* cytoplasm) or can have aberrant morphology (cell with *orange* cytoplasm). (B) RB−/− mutated mature horizontal cells undergo cell cycle entry after post-RB mutation. Cell with *orange* nucleus exhibit self-renewal ability and indefinite division capacity and cell with *blue* cytoplasm has aberrant morphology.

tumor having distinct morphology and cell types which depends upon the cell of origin. Moreover, the tumor can also be derived from differentiated cells of the retina.

The retina in RB can acquire malignant nature or undergo degeneration depending upon the cellular pliancy, which contributes to the progression of the corresponding disease. Cellular pliancy is defined as the property of cells with a propensity toward either death or cell cycle reentry after sustaining a specific oncogenic insult in pediatric cancers. In this context, rods are more prone to undergo degeneration as they are less able to respond to stress related to extrinsic or intrinsic perturbations such as oxidative stress. By contrast, horizontal cells have high pliancy, making them more adaptable to such changes and rendering them resistance to programmed cell death or necrosis [261] as explained in Fig. 6. In addition, cell-cycle reentry of horizontal neurons may predispose them to oncogenic lesions since they can survive long enough to acquire all the hallmarks of cancer [262]. This differential susceptibility of rods and horizontal cells to death and cell cycle reentry, respectively, can be explained due to the distinct organization of the epigenome [263,264]. Hence, epigenetic lesions are specific to individual cell types undergoing proliferation to malignant transformation in response to RB mutation.

4.1.3 The physiological role of retinoblastoma protein

RB1 is the first human tumor suppressor gene (TSG) that was identified in children with inherited RB [265,266], and this data supported Knudson's two hit-hypothesis for the initiation of cancer via inactivation of tumor suppressors [267]. The RB1 gene has 27 exons scattered over a 180-kb region at chromosome 13q14 [268]. It encodes pRB (928 amino acid long) [269–272], a pocket protein that along with the other similar proteins, p107 and p130, constitute the pocket protein family of "cell cycle regulators" [273–275]. These proteins bind with E2F family of transcription factors (E2F1–7) to regulate the transcription of cell cycle-related genes [276–284]. pRB binds with E2F under hypophosphorylated state in resting or G0 cells to facilitate the regulation over G1 to S phase transition. Hyperphosphorylation of pRB reduces its own binding affinity with E2F to allow the expression of genes that mediate S phase entry [285,286]. Dephosphorylation and phosphorylation of pRB are mediated by protein phosphatase 1 [287] and cyclin/Cdk proteins (protein kinases essential for cell cycle regulations), respectively [288,289]. pRB interacts with E2F(1–3) [274,290–292] proteins, whereas p107 and p130 form complex with E2F4 and E2F5 to exert their growth-suppressive effect on the cells in G0 and early G1 phases. In contrast, E2F3b, E2F6, and E2F7 exhibit repressive functions independent of pRB, p107, and p130 through other means [293]. In many cases, they recruit chromatin modifiers, type 1 histone deacetylases (HDACs) for the removal of an acetyl group from histones H3 and H4 [294–297] or HMTs for the deposition of H3K9me3 mark to repress E2F-regulated genes [298]. Other than the transcriptional regulation, pRB modulates its own phosphorylation status in response to environmental signals or interacts with discrete repressors and co-repressors to mediate specific and selective regulation of certain E2F responsive genes [299]. Thus, the interplay of pRB and its related proteins, p107 and p130 with E2Fs, that is, pocket protein-E2F network can induce different states of E2F-responsive promoters during different cell cycle phases which depends upon the binding factors recruited to the promoter sites [293].

Pocket proteins (p107 and p130) independent of E2Fs also regulate cell cycle transitions via regulating Cdk proteins [300–302]. Importantly, pRB may play an important role in suppressing RB, as evident in several "low-penetrance" RB mutants. These mutants retain the partial activity of pRB protein which is sufficient enough to suppress RB despite that they are defective in binding E2F [303,304]. This is achieved via inducing p27 (cyclin-dependent kinase inhibitor, CDKI) [305], and PML nuclear bodies [306], promoting differentiation-associated gene expression, suppressing Ras signaling [307], and cooperating with hLin-9 in differentiation [308]. However, several cellular aberrations lead to tumor formation such as mutational loss of pRB and binding of pRB with oncoproteins of HPV disrupt pRB-E2F interactions which in turn promotes the cell division [309,310]. In another instance, inhibition of $p16^{INK4A}$ protein (inhibitor of cdk4/cdk6) or overexpression of D-cyclins causes an increase in the phosphorylation of pRB and the resulting unmasked E2Fs regulate genes related to the contextual cues [289,311,312]. ncRNAs and their interaction with different proteins act as a regulating platform for many disease etiologies including RB as discussed below.

4.1.4 Novel regulators of RB

Altered regulation of cell cycle regulators has been profoundly implicated in the progression of RB. Aberrant ncRNAs (miRNAs, long noncoding RNAs (lncRNAs), circRNAs, and piRNAs) can act upstream of these regulators to mediate their silencing or activation effect during RB pathogenesis. For instance, miR-186 [313] has a potential tumor-suppressive effect that regulated the disheveled-axin domain containing 1 (DIXDC1) to inhibit the Wnt/β-catenin signaling pathway, which is mainly responsible for RB cell proliferation, migration, and invasion. In a study, Zhao and Cui found that miR-361-3p was downregulated in RB tissues and serum, and in human RB cell lines as well. miR-361-3p has been found to regulate sonic hedgehog signaling by targeting GLI zinc fingers 1 and 3 [314]. Another miRNA, miR-140-5p, regulates the proliferation of RB tumor cells by blocking c-met/Akt/mTOR regulatory axis. Similarly, miR-494 affects RB tumor progression by targeting PTEN, this in turn regulates PI3K/Akt pathway [315]. Alternatively, miR-29a modulates signal transducer and an activator of transcription 3 (STAT3) to affect the downstream genes cyclinD1 and MMP-2, common factors behind RB progression [316]. Overexpression of miR-204 in RB cell line was reported to reduce the level of cyclin D2 and MMP-9, thereby being found to control the RB cell proliferation and invasion [317]. Zhang et al. showed that downregulated miR-125a-5p in RB cell line and tissue led to upregulation of transcriptional co-activator with PDZ-binding motif (TAZ) which in turn activated EGFR pathway to induce RB cell proliferation [318]. In another instance, the binding of miR-106b with Runx3 target mRNA reduced the development of the malignant phenotype of RB [319]. Similarly, miR-504 [320] and miR-492 [321] controlled the aggressiveness of RB by regulating the astrocyte elevated gene 1 (AEG-1) and large tumor-suppressor kinase 2 (LATS 2), a serine/threonine kinase, respectively. Moreover, targeting the miRNA cluster is another method to control the proliferation of RB cells. Here, pri-miRNA-17–92 aptamer can directly target the primary miRNA precursor from mir17–92 cluster (oncomir-1 cluster having cancerous potential) in order to reduce the proliferative capacity of RB cell lines [322]. Compelling studies have revealed that downregulation of miR-125a-5p and upregulation of miR-125b at the same time in RB tissues and cells have targeted DNA damage regulated autophagy modulator 2 to suppress apoptosis and promoted cell proliferation [318].

In some studies, negative regulation of TSGs such as TP-53 and PDCD4 enhances cancer cell proliferation. TP-53 is regulated by nuclear-localized E3 ubiquitin ligase (MDM2) which is responsible for its proteasomal degradation. MDM2 is inhibited by cyclin-dependent kinase inhibitor 2A (p14ARF) to stimulate the expression of TP-53 target gene [323]. In the case of RB, the expression of miR-24 was elevated as demonstrated in a study by To et al. This specific miRNA inhibits p14ARF and further increases MDM2 level to destabilize the expression of TP-53 to cause tumor progression [324]. Another TSG, programmed cell death 4 (PDCD4) has been negatively regulated by miR-21 to promote RB cell proliferation and migration [325]. Apart from the above-mentioned miRNAs, many differentially expressed miRNAs have been reported in tissues and serum of children with RB, few of them are upregulated (miR-103, miR-513, miR-106b, miR-143, miR-148b, miR-17, miR-16, miR-183, miR-182, miR-19a, miR18a, miR-29a, miR-29b, miR-29c, miR-20a, miR-30b, miR-30d, miR-34a, miR-494, miR-378, miR-142-5b, miR-513-1, miR-513-2, miR-518c, miR-96) and some are downregulated miRNAs (miR216a, miR-217, let-7a, let-7i, let-7f, miR-9, miR-92a, miR-99b) [326]. These miRNAs can be used as biomarkers in the diagnosis of RB disease.

Aberrant regulation of lncRNAs has been found to have a disease implication during RB progression. Upregulation of HOTAIR lncRNA is a common characteristic of different cancer cell types including RB. HOTAIR has been reported to mediate pathogenesis by regulating the Notch signaling pathway [327]. Additionally, lncRNA shows miRNA sponging effect to suppress the effect of miRNAs over the corresponding targets. HOTAIR lncRNA sponged miR-613 to increase the expression of tyrosine protein kinase met (c-met) to affect the RB development [328]. Similarly, Zhang et al. showed that the upregulation of lncRNA CCAT1 negatively regulated miR-218-5p in RB cells to promote proliferation and migration [329]. Furthermore, a lncRNA named, differentiation antagonizing nonprotein coding RNA (DANCR) diminished the effect of tumor suppressor miRNAs, miR-613 and miR-34c via sponging mechanism to facilitate the RB cell proliferation by inducing MMP-9 expression [330]. Actin filament-associated protein 1-antisense RNA-1 (AFAP1-AS1) is another lncRNA whose level was increased in RB cells and promotes cell proliferation, invasion, and migration [331]. Another lncRNA, brain-derived neurotrophic factor antisense (BDNF-AS) associated with BDNF has shown reverse effects by suppressing the growth of neurons and their survival. Consistent with this, their forced expression in RB cells leads to cell cycle arrest due to the downregulation of proteins such as cyclin E and CDC42 [332]. Additionally, H19 lncRNA significantly suppressed the miR-17-92 cluster whose target is p21, a cell cycle regulator. Downregulation of p21 by the miR-17-92 cluster causes STAT3 activation and consequently results in cancer cell proliferation [333]. LncRNA-UCA1 promoted cell proliferation and invasion via activating PI3K/Akt pathway in RB tissues and cell lines [334].

CircRNAs are also dysregulated in RB tumors; for example, hsa_circ_0001649 has been demonstrated to affect the Akt/mTOR signaling pathway, but the exact mechanism remains elusive. In RB, the level of hsa_circ_0001649 has been reported to be reduced. Transfection of hsa_circ_0001649 to xenografts leads to decreased phosphorylation of Akt and mTOR and thus, negatively regulates the proliferation of RB tumor cells [335]. Similarly, circRNA TET1-hsa_circ_0093996 predicted to sponge miR-183 to regulate the TSG target PDCD4 in modulating the RB cell proliferation [336]. After learning about the different roles of miRNAs, lncRNAs, and circRNAs in RB pathogenesis, it is clear that ncRNAs are significantly involved in the RB progression, which can be used as therapeutics in the future. Besides the ncRNAs mentioned above, PIWI and piRNAs have significant importance in the RB pathogenesis.

5. Potential role of PIWI and piRNA in RB

We have shown that the piRNA-binding protein PIWIL4 (HIWI2) is aberrantly expressed in Y79 cells (RB cells). Silencing of HIWI2 leads to downregulation of OTX2 [37]. OTX2 is a transcription factor that plays important role in embryo patterning, brain regionalization, and lineage specification [337]. In addition, OTX2 can also act as an intrinsic determinant of embryonic stem cells differentiation into epiblast stem cells. OTX2 along with bone morphogenetic protein 4 (BMP4) and fgf2 promotes telencephalic and mesencephalic differentiation from embryonic stem cells-derived neural progenitor [338]. Some studies have shown that through an epigenetic mechanism, OTX2 may augment the suppression of differentiation markers by inducing stem-cell like properties in a cell. In accordance with the above, upregulation of OTX2 in group 3 medulloblastoma has been linked to a more aggressive tumor phenotype and adverse clinical outcome [339–341]. Briefly, OTX2 bound promoters exhibited a bivalent-like state, that is, promoters with both activation (H3K4me3 and H3K9ac) and repression marks (H3K27me3). Upon silencing of OTX2, there has been a drop in the level of H3K27me3 mark which affects the proliferation of cancer cells. Here, OTX2 maintains the bivalent state of promoters by regulating histone methylases and demethylases to sustain the H3K27me3 mark, an important function of OTX2 in medulloblastoma [342]. Similarly, OTX2 also plays a very critical role in cell fate determination of the photoreceptors by stimulating the expression of genes responsible for the differentiation of RPCs to photoreceptors [343]. Consistent with the above finding, alteration in the level of OTX2 has been found to increase cell proliferation via hyperphosphorylation of pRb [344].

PIWIL4 and its role in epigenetic regulation of transposons have been widely recognized in the germline [73] and cancer cells [345]. They are predominantly involved in depositing heterochromatin marks, H3K9me3 repressive marks at the transposon [70], and the genic loci to regulate their expressions. In some cases, they are also involved in the histone demethylation process to activate the expression of target genes, depending on the cellular context [346]. Interestingly, PIWIL proteins have an established role in the germline stem cell maintenance and embryo patterning in diverse organisms (*Drosophila* and zebrafish) [26,46], similar to OTX2. Moreover, RB1 mutation in a cell leads to rapid gene expression changes as epigenetics is the primary mechanism behind RB progression. The other tumor types rely on sequential deposition of genetic lesions that alter cancer gene expression [231]. Thus, HIWI2 and OTX2 can regulate cancer cell proliferation through epigenetic mechanisms via depositing repressive histone marks to maintain the stem cell properties under specific conditions.

PIWI/piRNA regulates different biological processes during physiological and pathological conditions. Studies have revealed that in many cancers, piRNA can function independently of PIWI. For instance, piR-823 has been upregulated in MM patients and found to modulate cell cycle protein such as cyclin D1 and CDK4 expression including the level of phosphorylated-Rb [197]. In addition, piR-823 has stimulated the proliferation of colorectal cancer cells via regulating the expression of cyclin D1 and CDK4 [116]. Wu et al. have shown that piR-011186 promoted the entry of cells into the S-phase of the cell cycle in leukemia [317]. In another case, piR-651 assisted the cell cycle entry via regulating cyclin D1 and CDK4 expression in nonsmall cell lung carcinoma [107]. Moreover, piRNAs can also block the cell cycle entry under different disease conditions. piR-8041 induced cell cycle arrest at the G1/S transition in glioma cells [347]. In mouse testis, the overexpression of mmu_piR_003399 was reported to arrest the cell cycle at the G1-phase via inhibiting the expression of CDK6 [178]. Thus, previous data and recent paramount research on PIWI/piRNAs signify their diverse role in many cancers and their potential use against different malignancies.

6. PIWI/piRNA as future biomarkers in cancer

In the last few years, several approaches of noninvasive biomarkers are encouraging researchers to investigate and bring more compelling techniques to study cancer. One of the constraints in this field is that cancer-related symptoms will arise only after they will spread maximally, and this brings hurdles to the therapeutic approaches and makes interventions less effective. It is important to find out novel biomarkers that can be used effectively at the primary stage of cancer for screening purposes. This will help to decrease the fatalities and will enhance the survival chances. A lot more remains to be understood including their complete molecular mechanism for clinical application, but paramounting studies have shown the possible use of circulating ncRNAs such as miRNAs as positive and noninvasive biomarkers for early screening of cancer [348–352]. On the other hand, complex functions and epigenetic regulation of piRNAs in the somatic cells indicate their contribution to human diseases including cancer [73,353–355]. Owing to the rise of next-generation sequencing technologies, it is suggested that, piRNAs might involve in vital functions in the progression of cancer and possibly serve as diagnostic and prognostic biomarkers in the future [356–359].

6.1 piRNAs as biomarkers

Similar to miRNAs, piRNAs have been reported to be stable in biofluids such as plasma [360]. Further, they can remain stable for a longer time in human plasma and serum even after frequent cycles of freeze-thaw or in an extended incubation time at room temperature [46,360]. Above mentioned advantages of piRNA (or ncRNAs) can be used in categorizing novel piRNA biomarkers for early-stage detection of cancer.

Earlier findings and recent studies have shown that altered expression of piRNAs is allied with different characteristics of cancer patients. In many regulatory and signaling pathways, piRNAs were found to be present as early products. This gives an idea that they might be a crucial component in the early detection and treatment of cancers [33,150,361]. One more benefit of these small ncRNAs is that they can pass through the cell membrane, without being degraded in the circulation, this, in turn, makes them a strong contender in the field of cancer treatment [362].

In lung cancer, the level of piRNAs was corelated with the progression of cancer cells [33]. In breast cancer, reports have shown that eight piRNAs, namely, piR-34736, piR-31106, piR-36249, piR-36026, piR-36318, piR-34377, piR-35407, and piR-36743, were highly elevated, giving a possibility that these piRNAs can be used as an independent prognostic biomarker [150]. piRNAs isolated from pancreatic cancer, colorectal cancer, and prostate cancer were found to be dysregulated [363]. In gastric cancer, overexpressed piR-823 was found to suppress the tumor development, signifying its potential as a promising therapeutic agent [176]. Also, lower expression of piR-823 and piR-651 in serum of the gastric cancer patients demonstrated its usefulness as a diagnostic biomarker [364]. Following serum and plasma, piRNAs were also found to be present in exosomes or as free-circulating RNA in saliva and stool, this, in turn, can make them potential noninvasive biomarkers [177,205,206,365–369]. However, studies on the prognostic role of circulating piRNAs are still in the preliminary stage and it needs an in-depth study.

The tissue-specific expression profile of piRNAs further indicated that, in the coming years, they might be utilized as tissue-based diagnostic and prognostic biomarkers for cancer [148]. As no enzymes are needed for the processing of piRNAs, it is an advantage to utilize synthetic piRNAs with specific targets [361]. It should be noted that further validation of these piRNAs should be done in independent studies with higher sample sizes and long-term clinical trials. It will be interesting to find out how the combination of circulating miRNAs and piRNAs can be used to enhance the specificity and sensitivity toward early prognosis and diagnosis of cancer [148]. In DNA methylation, piRNA silences the genes at the level of transcription, this suggested that piRNAs are capable of inhibiting the expression of certain oncogenes or their functions by degrading RNA posttranscriptionally stating their advantage as therapeutics against cancer. Moreover, RNAi is used to silence the genes of cancerous cells, this technique can also be utilized for selective silencing of oncogenic piRNAs [362]. Effective in vivo delivery strategies and enhanced studies will be of prime importance before using piRNAs as biomarkers against cancer [370]. There will be a lot of challenges that need to be addressed before using piRNA-related therapies from bench to bedside. Further research and multicentric medical testings might be useful in the future to understand the elusive molecular mechanisms and basic biological functions of piRNAs in normal and diseased conditions. Table 2 depicts the potential use of piRNAs in the therapeutic arena.

Table 2 Expression of piRNAs in different cancers and their possible therapeutic applications.

Type of cancer	piRNAs	Expression (high/low)	Therapeutic/ physiological relevance	References
Breast cancer	piR-34736	High	All as a prognostic marker	[371]
	piR-31106	High		
	piR-36249	High		
	piR-36026	High		
	piR-36318	High		
	piR-34377	High		
	piR-35407	High		
	piR-36743	High		
	piR-932	High		
Lung cancer	piR-55490	Low	Therapeutic target	[158]
	piR-651	High	Therapeutic target	[107]
	piR-L-163	Low	Diagnostic marker	[357]
Colorectal cancer	piR-1245	High	Prognostic marker	[372]
	piR-015551	Low	Critical/risk valuation	[161]
Liver cancer	piR-Hep1	High	Prognostic marker	[168]
Gastric cancer	piR-651	Low in peripheral blood High expression during tumor-node-metasis stage Low	Therapeutic target	[177]
	piR-823		Therapeutic/ diagnostic	[177]
Multiple-myeloma cancer	piR-823	High	Therapeutic target	[197]

Breast, lung, liver, and colon cancers depict explicit altered expression of piRNAs.

6.2 PIWI as biomarkers for various cancers

PIWI subfamily proteins were also found to be crucial players in the progression and biogenesis of tumors [373] (Table 3). A study has demonstrated the oncogenic association of PIWIL1 (HIWI) protein in breast cancer [380]. Later on, in an interesting finding, Krishnan et al. suggested that for breast cancer prognosis, PIWI proteins can act as novel markers. They found that PIWIL1 and PIWIL3 were upregulated but were not statistically meaningful, but PIWIL2 and PIWIL4 genes were downregulated and were statistically significant ($P < .05$) [379]. Earlier findings have explained the correlation between

Table 3 PIWI as potential biomarkers in different cancers.

Potential PIWI as a biomarker	Type of cancer	Expression	Significance in therapeutic approach/physiological relevance	References
PIWIL1	Breast cancer	High	Prognosis	[374]
	Colorectal cancer	High	Proliferation	[375]
	Hepatocellular cancer	High	Proliferation and migration	[376]
	Gastric cancer	High	Prognosis and diagnosis	[208]
	Renal cancer	High	Prognosis	[205,206]
	Ovarian cancer	High	Diagnosis	[377]
	Chronic myeloid leukemia	High	Growth and migration	[373]
	Glioma	High	Prognosis and diagnosis	[211]
PIWIL2	Colorectal cancer	High	Prognosis and diagnosis	[378]
	Ovarian cancer	High	Diagnosis	[377]
	Glioma	High	Prognosis	[221]
	Renal cell carcinoma	High	Prognosis	[205,206]
PIWIL3	Breast cancer	High	Prognosis	[379]
	Colorectal cancer	High	Prognosis	[382]
	Gastric cancer	High	Proliferation, migration, and invasion	[224]
PIWIL4	Breast cancer	High	Prognosis	[379]
	Colorectal cancer	High	Prognosis	[382]
	Renal cell carcinoma	High	Prognosis	[205,206]
	Ovarian cancer	High	Diagnosis	[377]
	Cervical cancer	High	Diagnosis and prognosis	[359]

PIWI protein and colorectal cancer. For instance, PIWIL2 positive cells are positively correlated to the advancement of colorectal cancer [381]. One more work on colorectal cancer emphasized that the expression of PIWIL1 (HIWI) (mRNA level) is associated with the expression of OCT4, and its expression was highly elevated in colorectal cancer tissues. This, in turn, indicates that PIWIL1 (HIWI) might be involved in the pathogenesis of colorectal cancer [378]. In colon cancer, PIWIL2 was found to regulate the transcriptional activity of matrix metallopeptidase 9. This study has further suggested that assessing the level of PIWIL1 (HIWI) can be used to predict the invasiveness of tumors [210].

An in vivo study in glioma cells stated that suppressing PIWIL1 (HIWI) decreases the progression of the tumor, and PIWIL1 (HIWI) is involved as an oncogene in the development of glioma [383]. Further studies have suggested that PIWIL1 (HIWI) can be used as a significant molecular marker for malignant gliomas; both in diagnosis and in prognosis of cancer [211]. Downregulation of PIWIL1 (HIWI) by shRNA decreased the proliferation and migration of hepatocarcinoma cells. This indicated that PIWIL1 (HIWI) may have underlying functions in the advancement of hepatocarcinoma and can possibly be used as a target for anticancer therapy [376]. In addition, PIWIL2 and PIWIL4 were found to be associated with the progression and metastasis of hepatocellular carcinoma cells. In the future, they can act as possible prognostic factors, especially in well-differentiated cells [218,384]. Interestingly, PIWI was found to be quite evident in the germline cells. A report has suggested that in cervical cancer, PIWIL4 might play a carcinogenic role through p14ARF (ARF tumor suppressor)/p53 pathway and can be a novel therapeutic target in near future [385]. Moreover, altered PIWI proteins also contribute to aberrant expression of piRNAs in a cell [131,386]. At this point, it is worthy to understand how the altered expression of PIWI could potentially modulate piRNAs expression in a cancer cell and thus can help restore the homeostasis of the cell.

7. Conclusion

Accumulating reports have indicated the novel and potential functions of PIWI/piRNAs in various diseases including cancer. PIWI/piRNA has been shown to affect the growth of cancer cells, their proliferation, invasiveness, motility, inhibition of apoptosis, etc. Recent studies have established them as active participants in converting a normal cell into a malignant one. However, there are still many questions remain to be answered, such as, whether the aberrant expression of piRNA has any impact on genes that reflect into phenotypes. It will be interesting to understand the functional implication of PIWI/piRNAs in different subtypes of cancers along with histological classification. Another significant question will be to study the response of PIWI/piRNAs in various therapeutic approaches against different kinds of cancers.

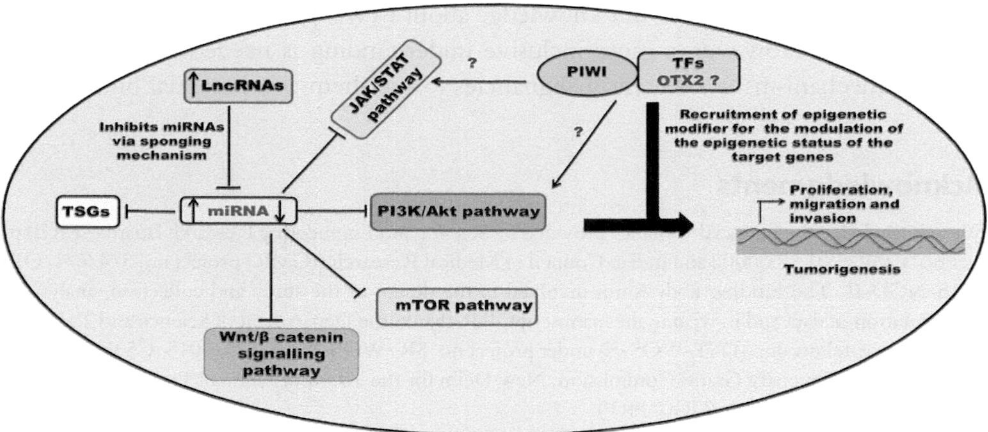

Fig. 7 Overall schematic view of regulation in RB cell by ncRNAs. In RB pathogenesis, downregulation of certain miRNAs diminishes their suppressive effect on tumor-promoting signaling pathways (JAK-STAT, PI3K/Akt, mTOR, and Wnt/β catenin signaling pathways), and upregulation of miRNAs suppresses the TSGs. An increase in the level of lncRNAs also has an inhibiting effect on miRNAs via a sponging mechanism to regulate the tumor-promoting signaling pathways. To promote tumorigenesis, PIWI possibly forms a complex with OTX2 or activates the PI3K/Akt and JAK/STAT pathways via recruiting epigenetic modifiers to alter the epigenetic status of target genes. *TSG*, tumor suppressor gene.

RB is a pediatric tumor, and its related studies have led to fundamental discoveries in cancer biology. It has provided impetus for many studies to look at pediatric cancers as aberrant epigenetic diseases that may promote tumor progression under additional genetic lesions. Interestingly, upregulation of HIWI2 and OTX2 in RB cells could be explained in the epigenetic context to the disease pathogenesis. PIWIL proteins have an established role in the germline stem cell maintenance and embryo patterning similar to OTX2. In this line, HIWI2 and OTX2 may work in partnership to sustain the stem-cell-like properties, a precursor for tumor formation. Since RB could be derived from progenitor cells or transition cells, those tumors could exhibit variation in the expression of ncRNAs and their corresponding RNA-binding proteins during the development of the retina. Hence, stage-specific ncRNAs and their complementary protein partner would affect tumor biology, which needs to be studied to employ them as therapeutics as represented in Fig. 7. The appropriate strategies to characterize the expression of piRNAs in different stages of RB will be a challenging task. As each cell type has a distinct epigenetic organization, correlating the expression of ncRNAs with the cellular epigenetic status might give comprehensive knowledge and better insight of the molecular interactions in the pathogenesis of RB.

Understanding the complexity of the molecular road-maps used by PIWI/piRNA in physiological conditions and cancer will be crucial in the diagnostic field. Nevertheless, recent studies have increased our knowledge about PIWI/piRNA as a promising area in tumorigenesis. However, a more inclusive understanding is needed to decipher their obscure mechanisms in different malignancies to use them as a potential biomarker.

Acknowledgments

We acknowledge the financial assistance provided by Science and Engineering Research Board (SERB) project no. EMR/2017/000002 and Indian Council of Medical Research (ICMR) project no. 5/4/6/1/OPH/2015-NCD-II. The funding body is not involved in the design of the study and collection, analysis, and interpretation of data and in writing the manuscript. RR thanks the Department of Science and Technology (DST) for the fellowship (DST-WOS-A) under project no. SR/WOS-A/LS-388/2018. CS thanks the support from the University Grants Commission, New Delhi for the award of Assistant Professorship under its Faculty Recharge Program (UGC-FRP).

Declaration of competing interest

The authors have declared no conflict of interest.

References

[1] S. Hema, S. Thambiraj, D.R. Shankaran, Nano formulations for targeted drug delivery to prostate cancer: an overview, J. Nanosci. Nanotechnol. 18 (8) (2018) 5171–5191, https://doi.org/10.1166/jnn.2018.15420.

[2] X. Xu, E. Kharazmi, Y. Tian, et al., Risk of prostate cancer in relatives of prostate cancer patients in Sweden: a nationwide cohort study, PLoS Med. 18 (6) (2021) 1–17, https://doi.org/10.1371/journal.pmed.1003616.

[3] A.M. Bode, Z. Dong, Precision oncology—the future of personalized cancer medicine? NPJ Precis Oncol. 1 (1) (2017) 1–2, https://doi.org/10.1038/s41698-017-0010-5.

[4] F. Raza, H. Zafar, M.W. Khan, et al., Recent advances in the targeted delivery of paclitaxel nanomedicine for cancer therapy, Mater. Adv. 3 (5) (2022) 2268–2290, https://doi.org/10.1039/D1MA00961C.

[5] M.M. Yallapu, P.K. Nagesh, M. Jaggi, S.C. Chauhan, Therapeutic applications of curcumin nano formulations, AAPS J. 17 (6) (2015) 1341–1356, https://doi.org/10.1208/s12248-015-9811-z.

[6] J.O. Bishop, E.C. Madsen, Retinoblastoma: review of current status, Surv. Ophthalmol. 19 (6) (1975) 342–366. https://pubmed.ncbi.nlm.nih.gov/1145423/.

[7] A.N. Pandey, Retinoblastoma: an overview, Saudi J. Opthalmol. 28 (4) (2014) 310–315, https://doi.org/10.1016/j.sjopt.2013.11.001.

[8] H. Dimaras, K. Kimani, E.A. Dimba, et al., Retinoblastoma, Lancet 379 (984) (2012) 1436–1446, https://doi.org/10.1016/S0140-6736(11)61137-9.

[9] M. Jain, D. Rojanaporn, B. Chawla, et al., Retinoblastoma in Asia, Eye (London) 33 (1) (2019) 87–96, https://doi.org/10.1038/s41433-018-0244-7.

[10] C.L. Shields, J.A. Shields, Diagnosis and management of retinoblastoma, Cancer Control 11 (5) (2004) 317–327, https://doi.org/10.1177/107327480401100506.

[11] U. Singh, D. Katoch, S. Kaur, et al., Retinoblastoma: a sixteen-year review of the presentation, treatment, and outcome from a tertiary care institute in Northern India, Ocul. Oncol. Pathol. 4 (1) (2017) 23–32, https://doi.org/10.1159/000477408.

[12] S.R. Eddy, Non-coding RNA genes and the modern RNA world, Nat. Rev. Genet. 2 (12) (2001) 919–929, https://doi.org/10.1038/35103511.

[13] X. Zhu, S. Jiang, Z. Wu, et al., Long non-coding RNA TTN antisense RNA 1 facilitates hepatocellular carcinoma progression via regulating miR-139-5p/SPOCK1 axis, Bioengineered 12 (1) (2021) 578–588, https://doi.org/10.1080/21655979.2021.1882133.

[14] H. Dana, G.M. Chalbatani, H. Mahmoodzadeh, et al., Molecular mechanisms and biological functions of siRNA, Int. J. Biomed. Sci. 13 (2) (2017) 48–57. https://pubmed.ncbi.nlm.nih.gov/28824341/.

[15] O.V. Klimenko, Small non-coding RNAs as regulators of structural evolution and carcinogenesis, Non-coding RNA Res. 2 (2) (2017) 88–92, https://doi.org/10.1016/j.ncrna.2017.06.002.

[16] G. Mahmoodi Chalbatani, H. Mahmoodzadeh, H. Gharagozlou, et al., Micro-RNA a new gate in cancer and human disease, J. Biol. Sci. 17 (6) (2017) 247–254, https://doi.org/10.3923/jbs.2017.247.254.

[17] J.C. Van Wolfswinkel, R.F. Ketting, The role of small non-coding RNAs in genome stability and chromatin organization, J. Cell Sci. 123 (pt11) (2010) 1825–1839, https://doi.org/10.1242/jcs.061713.

[18] A. Aravin, D. Gaidatzis, S. Pfeffer, et al., A novel class of small RNAs bind to MILI protein in mouse testes, Nature 442 (7099) (2006) 203–207, https://doi.org/10.1038/nature04916.

[19] A. Girard, R. Sachidanandam, G.J. Hannon, M.A. Carmell, A germline-specific class of small RNAs binds mammalian piwi proteins, Nature 442 (7099) (2006) 199–202, https://doi.org/10.1038/nature04916.

[20] S.T. Grivna, E. Beyret, Z. Wang, H. Lin, A novel class of small RNAs in mouse spermatogenic cells, Genes Dev. 20 (13) (2006) 1709–1714, https://doi.org/10.1101/gad.1434406.

[21] T. Watanabe, A. Takeda, T. Tsukiyama, et al., Identification and characterization of two novel classes of small RNAs in the mouse germline: retrotransposon-derived siRNAs in oocytes and germline small RNAs in testes, Genes Dev. 20 (13) (2006) 1732–1743, https://doi.org/10.1101/gad.1425706.

[22] A.A. Aravin, R. Sachidanandam, A. Girard, et al., Developmentally regulated piRNA clusters implicate MILI in transposon control, Science 316 (5825) (2007) 744–747, https://doi.org/10.1126/science.1142612.

[23] P.J. Batista, J.G. Ruby, J.M. Claycomb, et al., PRG-1 and 21U-RNAs interact to form the piRNA complex required for fertility in C. elegans, Mol. Cell 31 (1) (2008) 67–78, https://doi.org/10.1016/j.molcel.2008.06.002.

[24] J. Brennecke, A.A. Aravin, A. Stark, et al., Discrete small RNA-generating loci as master regulators of transposon activity in Drosophila, Cell 128 (6) (2007) 1089–1103, https://doi.org/10.1016/j.cell.2007.01.043.

[25] Y. Cheng, Q. Wang, W. Jiang, et al., Emerging roles of piRNAs in cancer: challenges and prospects, Aging (Albany NY) 11 (21) (2019) 9932–9946, https://doi.org/10.18632/aging.102417.

[26] D.N. Cox, A. Chao, H. Lin, Piwi encodes a nucleoplasmic factor whose activity modulates the number and division rate of germline stem cells, Development 127 (3) (2000) 503–514, https://doi.org/10.1242/dev.127.3.503.

[27] W. Deng, H. Lin, Miwi, a murine homolog of piwi, encodes a cytoplasmic protein essential for spermatogenesis, Dev. Cell 2 (6) (2002) 819–830, https://doi.org/10.1016/s1534-5807(02)00165-x.

[28] S. Zhao, L.T. Gou, M. Zhang, et al., piRNA-triggered MIWI ubiquitination and removal by APC/C in late spermatogenesis, Dev. Cell 24 (1) (2013) 13–25, https://doi.org/10.1016/j.devcel.2012.12.006.

[29] F. Corra, C. Agnoletto, L. Minotti, et al., The network of noncoding RNAs in cancer drug resistance, Front. Oncol. 8 (2018) 1–25, https://doi.org/10.3389/fonc.2018.00327.

[30] T.A. Farazi, J.I. Spitzer, P. Morozov, T. Tuschl, miRNAs in human cancer, J. Pathol. 223 (2011) 102–115, https://doi.org/10.1002/path.2806.

[31] H. Huang, X. Yu, X. Han, et al., Piwil1 regulates glioma stem cell maintenance and glioblastoma progression, Cell Rep. 34 (1) (2021) 1–28, https://doi.org/10.1016/j.celrep.2020.108522.

[32] Y. Liu, M. Dou, X. Song, et al., The emerging role of the piRNA/piwi complex in cancer, Mol. Cancer 18 (1) (2019) 1–15, https://doi.org/10.1186/s12943-019-1052-9.

[33] X. Wu, Y. Pan, Y. Fang, et al., The biogenesis and functions of piRNAs in human diseases, Mol. Ther. Nucleic Acids 21 (2020) 108–120, https://doi.org/10.1016/j.omtn.2020.05.023.

[34] H. Chu, G. Hui, L. Yuan, et al., Identification of novel piRNAs in bladder cancer, Cancer Lett. 356 (2 Pt B) (2015) 561–567, https://doi.org/10.1016/j.canlet.2014.10.004.

[35] D. Mai, P. Ding, L. Tan, et al., PIWI-interacting RNA-54265 is oncogenic and a potential therapeutic target in colorectal adenocarcinoma, Theranostics 8 (19) (2018) 5213–5230, https://doi.org/10.7150/thno.28001.
[36] S. Muller, S. Raulefs, P. Bruns, et al., Next-generation sequencing reveals novel differentially regulated mRNAs, lncRNAs, miRNAs, sdRNAs and a piRNA in pancreatic cancer, Mol. Cancer 14 (94) (2015) 1–18, https://doi.org/10.1186/s12943-015-0358-5.
[37] S. Sivagurunathan, J.P. Arunachalam, S. Chidambaram, PIWI-like protein, HIWI2 is aberrantly expressed in retinoblastoma cells and affects cell-cycle potentially through OTX2, Cell Mol. Biol. Lett. 22 (2017) 1–8, https://doi.org/10.1186/s11658-017-0048-y.
[38] T. Sasaki, A. Shiohama, S. Minoshima, N. Shimizu, Identification of eight members of the Argonaute family in the human genome small star, filled, Genomics 82 (3) (2003) 323–330, https://doi.org/10.1016/s0888-7543(03)00129-0.
[39] M.A. Carmell, A. Girard, H.J. van de Kant, et al., MIWI2 is essential for spermatogenesis and repression of transposons in the mouse male germline, Dev. Cell 12 (4) (2007) 503–514, https://doi.org/10.1016/j.devcel.2007.03.001.
[40] S. Kuramochi-Miyagawa, T. Kimura, K. Yomogida, et al., Two mouse piwi-related genes: miwi and mili, Mech. Dev. 108 (1–2) (2001) 121–133, https://doi.org/10.1016/s0925-4773(01)00499-3.
[41] D.N. Cox, A. Chao, J. Baker, et al., A novel class of evolutionarily conserved genes defined by piwi are essential for stem cell self-renewal, Genes Dev. 12 (23) (1998) 3715–3727, https://doi.org/10.1101/gad.12.23.3715.
[42] L.S. Gunawardane, K. Saito, K.M. Nishida, et al., A slicer-mediated mechanism for repeatassociated siRNA 5′ end formation in Drosophila, Science 315 (5818) (2007) 1587–1590, https://doi.org/10.1126/science.1140494.
[43] A.N. Harris, P.M. MacDonald, Aubergine encodes a Drosophila polar granule component required for pole cell formation and related to eIF2C, Development 128 (14) (2001) 2823–2832, https://doi.org/10.1242/dev.128.14.2823.
[44] H. Lin, A.C. Spradling, A novel group of pumilio mutations affects the asymmetric division of germline stem cells in the Drosophila ovary, Development 124 (12) (1997) 2463–2476, https://doi.org/10.1242/dev.124.12.2463.
[45] S. Houwing, E. Berezikov, R.F. Ketting, Zili is required for germ cell differentiation and meiosis in zebrafish, EMBO J. 27 (20) (2008) 2702–2711, https://doi.org/10.1038/emboj.2008.204.
[46] S. Houwing, L.M. Kamminga, E. Berezikov, et al., A role for Piwi and piRNAs in germ cell maintenance and transposon silencing in Zebrafish, Cell 129 (1) (2007) 69–82, https://doi.org/10.1016/j.cell.2007.03.026.
[47] P.W. Reddien, N.J. Oviedo, J.R. Jennings, et al., SMEDWI-2 is a PIWI-like protein that regulates planarian stem cells, Science 310 (5752) (2005) 1327–1330, https://doi.org/10.1126/science.1116110.
[48] B. Brower-Toland, S.D. Findley, L. Jiang, et al., Drosophila PIWI associates with chromatin and interacts directly with HP1a, Genes Dev. 21 (18) (2007) 2300–2311, https://doi.org/10.1101/gad.1564307.
[49] F.J. King, A. Szakmary, D.N. Cox, H. Lin, Yb modulates the divisions of both germline and somatic stem cells through piwi- and hh-mediated mechanisms in the Drosophila ovary, Mol. Cell 7 (3) (2001) 497–508, https://doi.org/10.1016/s1097-2765(01)00197-6.
[50] A.I. Kalmykova, M.S. Klenov, V.A. Gvozdev, Argonaute protein PIWI controls mobilization of ret rotransposons in the Drosophila male germline, Nucleic Acids Res. 33 (6) (2005) 2052–2059, https://doi.org/10.1093/nar/gki323.
[51] Z. Jin, A.S. Flynt, E.C. Lai, Drosophila piwi mutants exhibit germline stem cell tumors that are sustained by elevated Dpp signaling, Curr. Biol. 23 (15) (2013) 1442–1448, https://doi.org/10.1016/j.cub.2013.06.021.
[52] H.B. Megosh, D.N. Cox, C. Campbell, H. Lin, The role of PIWI and the miRNA machinery in Drosophila germline determination, Curr. Biol. 16 (19) (2006) 1884–1894, https://doi.org/10.1016/j.cub.2006.08.051.
[53] F. Jankovics, M. Bence, R. Sinka, et al., Drosophila small ovary gene is required for transposon silencing and heterochromatin organization, and ensures germline stem cell maintenance and differentiation, Development 145 (23) (2018) 1–13, https://doi.org/10.1242/dev.170639.

[54] S.H. Wang, S.C. Elgin, Drosophila Piwi functions downstream of piRNA production mediating a chromatin-based transposon silencing mechanism in female germ line, Proc. Natl. Acad. Sci. U. S. A. 108 (52) (2011) 21164–21169, https://doi.org/10.1073/pnas.1107892109.
[55] Han B.W., Wang W., Li C., et al., Noncoding RNA. piRNA-guided transposon cleavage initiates Zucchini-dependent, phased piRNA production, Science 348 (2015) 817–821, doi:10.1126/science.aaa1264 25977554.
[56] H. Huang, Y. Li, K.E. Szulwach, G. Zhang, P. Jin, D. Chen, AGO3 Slicer activity regulates mitochondria-nuage localization of Armitage and piRNA amplification, J. Cell Biol. 206 (2) (2014) 217–230, https://doi.org/10.1083/jcb.201401002.
[57] H. Ohtani, Y.W. Iwasaki, A. Shibuya, H. Siomi, M.C. Siomi, K. Saito, DmGTSF1 is necessary for Piwi-piRISC-mediated transcriptional transposon silencing in the Drosophila ovary, Genes Dev. 27 (15) (2013) 1656–1661, https://doi.org/10.1101/gad.221515.113.
[58] H. Ishizu, A. Nagao, H. Siomi, Gatekeepers for Piwi-piRNA complexes to enter the nucleus, Curr. Opin. Genet. Dev. 21 (4) (2011) 484–490, https://doi.org/10.1016/j.gde.2011.05.001.
[59] H. Yin, H. Lin, An epigenetic activation role of Piwi and a Piwi-associated piRNA in Drosophila melanogaster, Nature 450 (7167) (2007) 304–308, https://doi.org/10.1038/nature06263.
[60] X.A. Huang, H. Yin, S. Sweeney, et al., A major epigenetic programming mechanism guided by piRNAs, Dev. Cell 24 (5) (2013) 502–516, https://doi.org/10.1016/j.devcel.2013.01.023.
[61] T. Tatsuke, L. Zhu, Z. Li, et al., Roles of Piwi proteins in transcriptional regulation mediated by HP1s in cultured silkworm cells, PLoS One 9 (3) (2014) 1–9, https://doi.org/10.1371/journal.pone.0092313.
[62] P. Rajasethupathy, I. Antonov, R. Sheridan, et al., A role for neuronal piRNAs in the epigenetic control of memory-related synaptic plasticity, Cell 149 (3) (2012) 693–707, https://doi.org/10.1016/j.cell.2012.02.057.
[63] C.D. Malone, J. Brennecke, M. Dus, et al., Specialized piRNA pathways act in germline and somatic tissues of the drosophila ovary, Cell 137 (3) (2009) 522–535, https://doi.org/10.1016/j.cell.2009.03.040.
[64] Z. Durdevic, R.S. Pillai, A. Ephrussi, Transposon silencing in the Drosophila female germline is essential for genome stability in progeny embryos, Life Sci. Alliance 1 (5) (2018) 1–9, https://doi.org/10.26508/lsa.201800179.
[65] M.R. Branco, E.B. Chuong, Crossroads between transposons and gene regulation, Philos. Trans. R. Soc. Lond. Ser. B Biol. Sci. 375 (1795) (2020) 1–4, https://doi.org/10.1098/rstb.2019.0330.
[66] J.L. Miller, P.A. Grant, The role of DNA methylation and histone modifications in transcriptional regulation in humans, Subcell. Biochem. 61 (2013) 289–317, https://doi.org/10.1007/978-94-007-4525-4_13.
[67] H. Knaut, H. Steinbeisser, H. Schwarz, C. Nusslein-Volhard, An evolutionary conserved region in the vasa 3′UTR targets RNA translation to the germ cells in the zebrafish, Curr. Biol. 12 (6) (2002) 454–466, https://doi.org/10.1016/s0960-9822(02)00723-6.
[68] N.V. Rozhkov, M. Hammell, G.J. Hannon, Multiple roles for Piwi in silencing Drosophila transposons, Genes Dev. 27 (4) (2013) 400–412, https://doi.org/10.1101/gad.209767.112.
[69] V.V. Vagin, A. Sigova, C. Li, H. Seitz, V. Gvozdev, P.D. Zamore, A distinct small RNA pathway silences selfish genetic elements in the germline, Science 313 (5785) (2006) 320–324, https://doi.org/10.1126/science.1129333.
[70] A. Le Thomas, A.K. Rogers, A. Webster, et al., Piwi induces piRNA-guided transcriptional silencing and establishment of a repressive chromatin state, Genes Dev. 27 (4) (2013) 390–399, https://doi.org/10.1101/gad.209841.112.
[71] S.A. Manakov, D. Pezic, G.K. Marinov, et al., MIWI2 and MILI have differential effects on piRNA biogenesis and DNA methylation, Cell Rep. 12 (8) (2015) 1234–1243, https://doi.org/10.1016/j.celrep.2015.07.036.
[72] D. Pezic, S.A. Manakov, R. Sachidanandam, A.A. Aravin, piRNA pathway targets active LINE1 elements to establish the repressive H3K9me3 mark in germ cells, Genes Dev. 28 (13) (2014) 1410–1428, https://doi.org/10.1101/gad.240895.114.
[73] J.C. Peng, H. Lin, Beyond transposons: the epigenetic and somatic functions of the Piwi-piRNA mechanism, Curr. Opin. Cell Biol. 25 (2) (2013) 190–194, https://doi.org/10.1016/j.ceb.2013.01.010.

[74] M. Reuter, P. Berninger, S. Chuma, et al., Miwi catalysis is required for piRNA amplification-independent LINE1 transposon silencing, Nature 480 (7376) (2011) 264–267, https://doi.org/10.1038/nature10672.
[75] K. Zheng, P.J. Wang, Blockade of pachytene piRNA biogenesis reveals a novel requirement for maintaining post-meiotic germline genome integrity, PLoS Genet. 8 (11) (2012) 1–12, https://doi.org/10.1371/journal.pgen.1003038.
[76] D. Ding, J. Liu, K. Dong, et al., PNLDC1 is essential for piRNA 3′ end trimming and transposon silencing during spermatogenesis in mice, Nat. Commun. 8 (1) (2017) 1–10, https://doi.org/10.1038/s41467-017-00854-4.
[77] L.T. Gou, P. Dai, J.H. Yang, et al., Pachytene piRNAs instruct massive mRNA elimination during late spermiogenesis, Cell Res. 24 (6) (2014) 680–700, https://doi.org/10.1038/cr.2014.41.
[78] G. Wang, V.A. Reinke, C. elegans Piwi, PRG-1, regulates 21U-RNAs during spermatogenesis, Curr. Biol. 18 (12) (2008) 861–867, https://doi.org/10.1016/j.cub.2008.05.009.
[79] C. Rouget, C. Papin, A. Boureux, et al., Maternal mRNA deadenylation and decay by the piRNA pathway in the early Drosophila embryo, Nature 467 (7319) (2010) 1128–1132, https://doi.org/10.1038/nature09465.
[80] C. Temme, M. Simonelig, E. Wahle, Deadenylation of mRNA by the CCR4-NOT complex in Drosophila: molecular and developmental aspects, Front. Genet. 5 (2014) 1–11, https://doi.org/10.3389/fgene.2014.00143.
[81] T. Kiuchi, H. Koga, M. Kawamoto, et al., A single female-specific piRNA is the primary determiner of sex in the silkworm, Nature 509 (7502) (2014) 633–636, https://doi.org/10.1038/nature13315.
[82] Z. Li, L. You, D. Yan, et al., Bombyx mori histone methyltransferase BmAsh2 is essential for silkworm piRNA-mediated sex determination, PLoS Genet. 14 (2) (2018) 1–19, https://doi.org/10.1371/journal.pgen.1007245.
[83] X. Yang, K. Chen, Y. Wang, et al., The sex determination cascade in the silkworm, Genes (Basel) 12 (2) (2021) 1–11, https://doi.org/10.3390/genes12020315.
[84] Y.C. Lee, The role of piRNA-mediated epigenetic silencing in the population dynamics of transposable elements in Drosophila melanogaster, PLoS Genet. 11 (6) (2015) 1–24, https://doi.org/10.1371/journal.pgen.1005269.
[85] T. Gu, S.C. Elgin, Maternal depletion of Piwi, a component of the RNAi system, impacts heterochromatin formation in Drosophila, PLoS Genet. 9 (9) (2013) 1–14, https://doi.org/10.1371/journal.pgen.1003780.
[86] N. Moshkovich, E.P. Lei, HP1 recruitment in the absence of argonaute proteins in Drosophila, PLoS Genet. 6 (3) (2010) 1–15, https://doi.org/10.1371/journal.pgen.1000880.
[87] A.L. Todeschini, L. Teysset, V. Delmarre, S. Ronsseray, The epigenetic trans-silencing effect in Drosophila involves maternally-transmitted small RNAs whose production depends on the piRNA pathway and HP1, PloS One 5 (6) (2010) 1–7. el https://doi.org/10.1371/journal.pone.0011032.
[88] H.C. Lee, W. Gu, M. Shirayama, E. Youngman, D. Conte Jr., C.C. Mello, C. elegans piRNAs mediate the genome-wide surveillance of germline transcripts, Cell 150 (1) (2012) 78–87, https://doi.org/10.1016/j.cell.2012.06.016.
[89] M.J. Luteijn, P. van Bergeijk, L.J. Kaaij, et al., Extremely stable Piwi-induced gene silencing in Caenorhabditis elegans, EMBO J. 31 (16) (2012) 3422–3430, https://doi.org/10.1038/emboj.2012.213.
[90] J.M. Claycomb, P.J. Batista, K.M. Pang, et al., The Argonaute CSR-1 and its 22G-RNA cofactors are required for holocentric chromosome segregation, Cell 139 (1) (2009) 123–134, https://doi.org/10.1016/j.cell.2009.09.014.
[91] M. Seth, M. Shirayama, W. Gu, et al., The C. elegans CSR-1 argonaute pathway counteracts epigenetic silencing to promote germline gene expression, Dev. Cell 27 (6) (2013) 656–663, https://doi.org/10.1016/j.devcel.2013.11.014.
[92] A. Ashe, A. Sapetschnig, E.M. Weick, et al., piRNAs can trigger a multigenerational epigenetic memory in the germline of C. elegans, Cell 150 (1) (2012) 88–99, https://doi.org/10.1016/j.cell.2012.06.018.
[93] M.P. Bagijn, L.D. Goldstein, A. Sapetschnig, et al., Function, targets, and evolution of Caenorhabditis elegans piRNAs, Science 337 (6094) (2012) 574–578, https://doi.org/10.1126/science.1220952.

[94] T.M. Guerin, F. Palladino, V.J. Robert, Transgenerational functions of small RNA pathways in controlling gene expression in C. elegans, Epigenetics 9 (1) (2014) 37–44, https://doi.org/10.4161/epi.26795.
[95] K.J. Reed, J.M. Svendsen, K.C. Brown, et al., Widespread roles for piRNAs and WAGO-class siRNAs in shaping the germline transcriptome of Caenorhabditis elegans, Nucleic Acids Res. 48 (4) (2020) 1811–1827, https://doi.org/10.1093/nar/gkz1178.
[96] M. Shirayama, M. Seth, H.C. Lee, et al., piRNAs initiate an epigenetic memory of nonself RNA in the C. elegans germline, Cell 150 (1) (2012) 65–77, https://doi.org/10.1016/j.cell.2012.06.015.
[97] S. Dai, X. Tang, L. Li, et al., A family of C. elegans VASA homologs control Argonaute pathway specificity and promote transgenerational silencing, bioRxiv (2022), https://doi.org/10.1101/2022.01.18.476504. 2022.01.18.476504.
[98] P. Quarato, M. Singh, E. Cornes, et al., Germline inherited small RNAs facilitate the clearance of untranslated maternal mRNAs in C. elegans embryos, Nat. Commun. 12 (1) (2021) 1–14. Published 2021 Mar 4 https://doi.org/10.1038/s41467-021-21691-6.
[99] B. Heestand, M. Simon, S. Frenk, et al., Transgenerational sterility of Piwi mutants represents a dynamic form of adult reproductive diapause, Cell Rep. 23 (1) (2018) 156–171, https://doi.org/10.1016/j.celrep.2018.03.015.
[100] J.J. Wang, D.Y. Cui, T. Xiao, et al., The influences of PRG-1 on the expression of small RNAs and mRNAs, BMC Genom. 15 (1) (2014) 1–11, https://doi.org/10.1186/1471-2164-15-321.
[101] J.W. Pek, T. Kai, A role for vasa in regulating mitotic chromosome condensation in Drosophila, Curr. Biol. 21 (1) (2011) 39–44, https://doi.org/10.1016/j.cub.2010.11.051.
[102] J.W. Pek, T. Kai, DEAD-box RNA helicase Belle/DDX3 and the RNA interference pathway promote mitotic chromosome segregation, Proc. Natl. Acad. Sci. U. S. A. 108 (29) (2011) 12007–12012, https://doi.org/10.1073/pnas.1106245108.
[103] W. Fang, X. Wang, J.R. Bracht, et al., Piwi-interacting RNAs protect DNA against loss during Oxytricha genome rearrangement, Cell 151 (6) (2012) 1243–1255, https://doi.org/10.1016/j.cell.2012.10.045.
[104] J.S. Khurana, J. Xu, Z. Weng, W.E. Theurkauf, Distinct functions for the Drosophila piRNA pathway in genome maintenance and telomere protection, PLoS Genet. 6 (12) (2010) 1–8, https://doi.org/10.1371/journal.pgen.1001246.
[105] H.M. Kurth, K. Mochizuki, 2′-O-methylation stabilizes Piwi-associated small RNAs and ensures DNA elimination in Tetrahymena, RNA 15 (4) (2009) 675–685, https://doi.org/10.1261/rna.1455509.
[106] M. Nowacki, V. Vijayan, Y. Zhou, et al., RNA-mediated epigenetic programming of a genome-rearrangement pathway, Nature 451 (7175) (2008) 153–158, https://doi.org/10.1038/nature06452.
[107] D. Li, Y. Luo, Y. Gao, et al., piR-651 promotes tumor formation in non-small cell lung carcinoma through the upregulation of cyclin D1 and CDK4, Int. J. Mol. Med. 38 (3) (2016) 927–936, https://doi.org/10.3892/ijmm.2016.2671.
[108] J. Lu, Q. Zhao, X. Ding, et al., Cyclin D1 promotes secretion of pro-oncogenic immuno-miRNAs and piRNAs, Clin. Sci. (Lond.) 134 (7) (2020) 791–805, https://doi.org/10.1042/CS20191318.
[109] M. Dehghani, P. Lasko, C-terminal residues specific to Vasa among DEAD-box helicases are required for its functions in piRNA biogenesis and embryonic patterning, Dev. Genes Evol. 226 (6) (2016) 401–412, https://doi.org/10.1007/s00427-016-0560-5.
[110] M. Dehghani, P. Lasko, In vivo mapping of the functional regions of the DEAD-box helicase Vasa, Biol. Open 4 (4) (2015) 450–462, https://doi.org/10.1242/bio.201410579.
[111] S. Shpiz, I. Olovnikov, A. Sergeeva, et al., Mechanism of the piRNA-mediated silencing of Drosophila telomeric retrotransposons, Nucleic Acids Res. 39 (20) (2011) 8703–8711, https://doi.org/10.1093/nar/gkr552.
[112] J. Xiol, P. Spinelli, M.A. Laussmann, et al., RNA clamping by Vasa assembles a piRNA amplifier complex on transposon transcripts, Cell 157 (7) (2014) 1698–1711, https://doi.org/10.1016/j.cell.2014.05.018.
[113] M. Spichal, B. Heestand, K.K. Billmyre, et al., Germ granule dysfunction is a hallmark and mirror of Piwi mutant sterility, Nat. Commun. 12 (1) (2021) 1–15, https://doi.org/10.1038/s41467-021-21635-0.

[114] D.T. Yin, Q. Wang, L. Chen, et al., Germline stem cell gene PIWIL2 mediates DNA repair through relaxation of chromatin, PLoS One 6 (11) (2011) 1–12, https://doi.org/10.1371/journal.pone.0027154.

[115] R. Han, L. Zhang, W. Gan, et al., piRNA-DQ722010 contributes to prostate hyperplasia of the male offspring mice after the maternal exposed to microcystin-leucine arginine, Prostate 79 (7) (2019) 798–812, https://doi.org/10.1002/pros.23786.

[116] J. Yin, X.Y. Jiang, W. Qi, et al., piR-823 contributes to colorectal tumorigenesis by enhancing the transcriptional activity of HSF1, Cancer Sci. 108 (9) (2017) 1746–1756, https://doi.org/10.1111/cas.13300.

[117] J. Bao, Y. Zhang, A.S. Schuster, et al., Conditional inactivation of Miwi2 reveals that MIWI2 is only essential for prospermatogonial development in mice, Cell Death Differ. 21 (5) (2014) 783–796, https://doi.org/10.1038/cdd.2014.5.

[118] M.C. Siomi, S. Kuramochi-Miyagawa, RNA silencing in germlines—exquisite collaboration of Argonaute proteins with small RNAs for germline survival, Curr. Opin. Cell Biol. 21 (3) (2009) 426–434, https://doi.org/10.1016/j.ceb.2009.02.003.

[119] T. Watanabe, X. Cui, Z. Yuan, et al., MIWI2 targets RNAs transcribed from piRNA-dependent regions to drive DNA methylation in mouse prospermatogonia, EMBO J. 37 (18) (2018) 1–15, https://doi.org/10.15252/embj.201695329.

[120] N. Zamudio, J. Barau, A. Teissandier, et al., DNA methylation restrains transposons from adopting a chromatin signature permissive for meiotic recombination, Genes Dev. 29 (12) (2015) 1256–1270, https://doi.org/10.1101/gad.257840.114.

[121] J.H. Lee, D. Schutte, G. Wulf, et al., Stem-cell protein Piwil2 is widely expressed in tumors and inhibits apoptosis through activation of Stat3/Bcl-XL pathway, Hum. Mol. Genet. 15 (2) (2006) 201–211, https://doi.org/10.1093/hmg/ddi430.

[122] W. Zhu, G.M. Pao, A. Satoh, et al., Activation of germline-specific genes is required for limb regeneration in the Mexican axolotl, Dev. Biol. 370 (1) (2012) 42–51, https://doi.org/10.1016/j.ydbio.2012.07.021.

[123] R. Yashiro, Y. Murota, K.M. Nishida, et al., Piwi nuclear localization and its regulatory mechanism in drosophila ovarian somatic cells, Cell Rep. 23 (12) (2018) 3647–3657, https://doi.org/10.1016/j.celrep.2018.05.051.

[124] R.S. Moore, R. Kaletsky, C.T. Murphy, Piwi/PRG-1 Argonaute and TGF-β mediate transgenerational learned pathogenic avoidance, Cell 177 (7) (2019) 1827–1841, https://doi.org/10.1016/j.cell.2019.05.024.

[125] P. Sousa-Victor, A. Ayyaz, R. Hayashi, et al., Piwi is required to limit exhaustion of aging somatic stem cells, Cell Rep. 20 (11) (2017) 2527–2537, https://doi.org/10.1016/j.celrep.2017.08.059.

[126] E.J. Lee, S. Banerjee, H. Zhou, et al., Identification of piRNAs in the central nervous system, RNA 17 (6) (2011) 1090–1099, https://doi.org/10.1261/rna.2565011.

[127] I. Iossifov, B.J. O'Roak, S.J. Sanders, et al., The contribution of de novo coding mutations to autism spectrum disorder, Nature 515 (7526) (2014) 216–221, https://doi.org/10.1038/nature13908.

[128] L.J. Leighton, W. Wei, P.R. Marshall, et al., Disrupting the hippocampal Piwi pathway enhances contextual fear memory in mice, Neurobiol. Learn. Mem. 161 (2019) 202–209, https://doi.org/10.1016/j.nlm.2019.04.002.

[129] P.P. Zhao, M.J. Yao, S.Y. Chang, et al., Novel function of PIWIL1 in neuronal polarization and migration via regulation of microtubule-associated proteins [published correction appears in Mol Brain. 2016;9:21], Mol. Brain. 8 (2015) 1–12, https://doi.org/10.1186/s13041-015-0131-0.

[130] B.C. Jones, J.G. Wood, C. Chang, et al., A somatic piRNA pathway in the Drosophila fat body ensures metabolic homeostasis and normal lifespan, Nat. Commun. 7 (2016) 1–9, https://doi.org/10.1038/ncomms13856.

[131] P.N. Perrat, S. DasGupta, J. Wang, et al., Transposition-driven genomic heterogeneity in the Drosophila brain, Science 340 (6128) (2013) 91–95, https://doi.org/10.1126/science.1231965.

[132] S. Sivagurunathan, K. Palanisamy, J.P. Arunachalam, S. Chidambaram, Possible role of HIWI2 in modulating tight junction proteins in retinal pigment epithelial cells through Akt signaling pathway, Mol. Cell. Biochem. 27 (1–2) (2017) 145–156, https://doi.org/10.1007/s11010-016-2906-8.

[133] S. Sivagurunathan, R. Raman, S. Chidambaram, PIWI-like protein, HIWI2: a novel player in proliferative diabetic retinopathy, Exp. Eye Res. 177 (2018) 191–196, https://doi.org/10.1016/j.exer.2018.08.018.

[134] X.Q. Gao, Y.H. Zhang, F. Liu, et al., The piRNA CHAPIR regulates cardiac hypertrophy by controlling METTL3-dependent N^6-methyladenosine methylation of Parp10 mRNA, Nat. Cell Biol. 22 (2020) 1319–1331, https://doi.org/10.1038/s41556-020-0576-y.

[135] A. La Greca, M.A. Scarafía, M.C. Hernandez Canas, et al., PIWI-interacting RNAs are differentially expressed during cardiac differentiation of human pluripotent stem cells, PLoS One 15 (5) (2020) 1–22, https://doi.org/10.1371/journal.pone.0232715.

[136] K.S. Rajan, G. Velmurugan, P. Gopal, et al., Abundant and altered expression of PIWI-interacting RNAs during cardiac hypertrophy, Heart Lung Circ. 25 (10) (2016) 1013–1020, https://doi.org/10.1016/j.hlc.2016.02.015.

[137] G. Jain, A. Stuendl, P. Rao, et al., A combined miRNA-piRNA signature to detect Alzheimer's disease, Transl. Psychiatry 9 (1) (2019) 1–12, https://doi.org/10.1038/s41398-019-0579-2.

[138] W. Qiu, X. Guo, X. Lin, et al., Transcriptome-wide piRNA profiling in human brains of Alzheimer's disease, Neurobiol. Aging 57 (2017) 170–177, https://doi.org/10.1016/j.neurobiolaging.2017.05.020.

[139] M. Schulze, A. Sommer, S. Plotz, et al., Sporadic Parkinson's disease derived neuronal cells show disease-specific mRNA and small RNA signatures with abundant deregulation of piRNAs, Acta Neuropathol. Commun. 6 (1) (2018) 1–18, https://doi.org/10.1186/s40478-018-0561-x.

[140] T. Zhang, G. Wong, Dysregulation of human somatic piRNA expression in Parkinson's disease subtypes and stages, Int. J. Mol. Sci. 23 (5) (2022) 1–23, https://doi.org/10.3390/ijms23052469.

[141] X. He, G. Kuang, Y. Zuo, et al., The role of non-coding RNAs in diabetic nephropathy-related oxidative stress, Front. Med. (Lausanne) 8 (2021) 1–13, https://doi.org/10.3389/fmed.2021.626423.

[142] L. Plestilova, M. Neidhart, G. Russo, et al., Expression and regulation of PIWIL-proteins and PIWI-interacting RNAs in rheumatoid arthritis, PLoS One 11 (11) (2016) 1–14, https://doi.org/10.1371/journal.pone.0166920.

[143] B.E. Montgomery, T. Vijayasarathy, T.N. Marks, et al., Dual roles for piRNAs in promoting and preventing gene silencing in C. elegans, Cell Rep. 37 (10) (2021) 1–28, https://doi.org/10.1016/j.celrep.2021.110101.

[144] O.L. Caballero, Y.T. Chen, Cancer/testis (CT) antigens: potential targets for immunotherapy, Cancer Sci. 100 (11) (2009) 2014–2221, https://doi.org/10.1111/j.1349-7006.2009.01303.x.

[145] Y.H. Cheng, E.W. Wong, C.Y. Cheng, Cancer/testis (CT) antigens, carcinogenesis and spermatogenesis, Spermatogenesis 1 (3) (2011) 209–220, https://doi.org/10.4161/spmg.1.3.17990.

[146] F.F. Costa, K. Le Blanc, B. Brodin, Concise review: cancer/testis antigens, stem cells, and cancer, Stem Cells 25 (3) (2007) 707–711, https://doi.org/10.1634/stemcells.2006-0469.

[147] A.J. Simpson, O.L. Caballero, A. Jungbluth, et al., Cancer/testis antigens, gametogenesis and cancer, Nat. Rev. Cancer 5 (8) (2005) 615–625, https://doi.org/10.1038/nrc1669.

[148] H. Jeong, K.H. Park, Y. Lee, et al., The regulation and role of piRNAs and PIWI proteins in cancer, Processes 9 (7) (2021) 1–14, https://doi.org/10.3390/pr9071208.

[149] B. Guo, D. Li, L. Du, X. Zhu, piRNAs: biogenesis and their potential roles in cancer, Cancer Metastasis Rev. 39 (2) (2020) 567–575, https://doi.org/10.1007/s10555-020-09863-0.

[150] W. Weng, H. Li, A. Goel, Piwi-interacting RNAs (piRNAs) and cancer: emerging biological concepts and potential clinical implications, Biochim. Biophys. Acta Rev. Cancer 1871 (1) (2019) 160–169, https://doi.org/10.1016/j.bbcan.2018.12.005.

[151] G. Fonseca Cabral, A. Dos Santos, J. Pinheiro, A.F. Vidal, et al., piRNAs in gastric cancer: a new approach towards translational research, Int. J. Mol. Sci. 21 (6) (2020) 1–17, https://doi.org/10.3390/ijms21062126.

[152] L. Qian, H. Xie, L. Zhang, et al., Piwi-interacting RNAs: a new class of regulator in human breast cancer, Front. Oncol. 11 (695077) (2021) 1–7, https://doi.org/10.3389/fonc.2021.695077.

[153] A. Hashim, F. Rizzo, G. Marchese, et al., RNA sequencing identifies specific PIWI-interacting small non-coding RNA expression patterns in breast cancer, Oncotarget 5 (20) (2014) 9901–9910, https://doi.org/10.18632/oncotarget.2476.

[154] C.M. Klinge, Non-coding RNAs in breast cancer: intracellular and intercellular communication, Noncoding RNA 4 (4) (2018) 1–34, https://doi.org/10.3390/ncrna4040040.
[155] A. Fu, D.I. Jacobs, A.E. Hoffman, et al., PIWI-interacting RNA 021285 is involved in breast tumorigenesis possibly by remodeling the cancer epigenome, Carcinogenesis 36 (10) (2015) 1094–1102, https://doi.org/10.1093/carcin/bgv105.
[156] L. Tan, D. Mai, B. Zhang, et al., PIWI-interacting RNA36712 restrains breast cancer progression and chemoresistance by interaction with SEPW1 pseudogene SEPW1P RNA, Mol. Cancer 18 (1) (2019) 1–15, https://doi.org/10.1186/s12943-019-0940-3.
[157] C. Oner, D. Turgut Coşan, E. Çolak, Estrogen and androgen hormone levels modulate the expression of PIWI interacting RNA in prostate and breast cancer, PLoS One 11 (7) (2016) 1–15, https://doi.org/10.1371/journal.pone.0159044.
[158] L. Peng, L. Song, C. Liu, et al., piR-55490 inhibits the growth of lung carcinoma by suppressing mTOR signaling, Tumour Biol. 37 (2) (2016) 2749–2756, https://doi.org/10.1007/s13277-015-4056-0.
[159] M.E. Reeves, M. Firek, A. Jliedi, Y.G. Amaar, Identification and characterization of RASSF1C piRNA target genes in lung cancer cells, Oncotarget 8 (21) (2017) 34268–34282, https://doi.org/10.18632/oncotarget.15965.
[160] W. Chen, R. Zheng, P.D. Baade, et al., Cancer statistics in China, 2015, CA Cancer J. Clin. 66 (2) (2016) 115–132, https://doi.org/10.3322/caac.21338.
[161] W. Weng, N. Liu, Y. Toiyama, et al., Novel evidence for a PIWI-interacting RNA (piRNA) as an oncogenic mediator of disease progression, and a potential prognostic biomarker in colorectal cancer, Mol. Cancer 17 (1) (2018) 1–12, https://doi.org/10.1186/s12943-018-0767-3.
[162] J. Feng, M. Yang, Q. Wei, et al., Novel evidence for oncogenic piRNA-823 as a promising prognostic biomarker and a potential therapeutic target in colorectal cancer, J. Cell. Mol. Med. 24 (16) (2020) 9028–9040, https://doi.org/10.1111/jcmm.15537.
[163] J. Yin, W. Qi, C.G. Ji, et al., Small RNA sequencing revealed aberrant piRNA expression profiles in colorectal cancer, Oncol. Rep. 42 (1) (2019) 263–272, https://doi.org/10.3892/or.2019.7158.
[164] F. Bray, J. Ferlay, I. Soerjomataram, et al., Global cancer statistics 2018: GLOBOCAN estimates of incidence and mortality worldwide for 36 cancers in 185 countries, CA Cancer J. Clin. 68 (6) (2018) 394–424, https://doi.org/10.3322/caac.21492.
[165] WHO. https://www.who.int/news-room/fact-sheets/detail/cancer.
[166] A.B. Ryerson, C.R. Eheman, S.F. Altekruse, et al., Annual report to the Nation on the status of cancer, 1975–2012, Featuring the increasing incidence of liver cancer, Cancer 122 (9) (2016) 1312–1337, https://doi.org/10.1002/cncr.29936.
[167] F. Rizzo, A. Rinaldi, G. Marchese, et al., Specific patterns of PIWI-interacting small noncoding RNA expression in dysplastic liver nodules and hepatocellular carcinoma, Oncotarget 7 (34) (2016) 54650–55466, https://doi.org/10.18632/oncotarget.10567.
[168] P.T. Law, H. Qin, A.K. Ching, et al., Deep sequencing of small RNA transcriptome reveals novel non-coding RNAs in hepatocellular carcinoma, J. Hepatol. 58 (6) (2013) 1165–1173, https://doi.org/10.1016/j.jhep.2013.01.032.
[169] K. Nakanishi, M. Sakamoto, S. Yamasaki, et al., Akt phosphorylation is a risk factor for early disease recurrence and poor prognosis in hepatocellular carcinoma, Cancer 103 (2) (2005) 307–312, https://doi.org/10.1002/cncr.20774.
[170] S. Whittaker, R. Marais, A.X. Zhu, The role of signaling pathways in the development and treatment of hepatocellular carcinoma, Oncogene 29 (36) (2010) 4989–5005, https://doi.org/10.1038/onc.2010.236.
[171] X. Tang, X. Xie, X. Wang, et al., The combination of piR-823 and eukaryotic initiation factor 3 B (EIF3B) activates hepatic stellate cells via upregulating TGF-β1 in liver fibrogenesis, Med. Sci. Monit. 24 (2018) 9151–9165, https://doi.org/10.12659/MSM.914222.
[172] P. Rawla, A. Barsouk, Epidemiology of gastric cancer: global trends, risk factors and prevention, Prz. Gastroenterol. 14 (1) (2019) 26–38, https://doi.org/10.5114/pg.2018.80001.
[173] L.A. Torre, F. Bray, R.L. Siegel, et al., Global cancer statistics, 2012, CA Cancer J. Clin. 65 (2) (2015) 87–108, https://doi.org/10.3322/caac.21262.

[174] X. Lin, Y. Xia, D. Hu, et al., Transcriptome wide piRNA profiling in human gastric cancer, Oncol. Rep. 41 (5) (2019) 3089–3099, https://doi.org/10.3892/or.2019.7073.
[175] V.D. Martinez, K.S.S. Enfield, D.A. Rowbotham, W.L. Lam, An Atlas of gastric PIWI-interacting RNA transcriptomes and their utility for identifying signatures of gastric cancer recurrence, Gastric Cancer 19 (2) (2016) 660–665, https://doi.org/10.1007/s10120-015-0487-y.
[176] J. Cheng, H. Deng, B. Xiao, et al., piR823, a novel non-coding small RNA, demonstrates in vitro and in vivo tumor-suppressive activity in human gastric cancer cells, Cancer Lett. 315 (1) (2012) 12–17, https://doi.org/10.1016/j.canlet.2011.10.004.
[177] L. Cui, Y. Lou, X. Zhang, et al., Detection of circulating tumor cells in peripheral blood from patients with gastric cancer using piRNAs as markers, Clin. Biochem. 44 (13) (2011) 1050–1057, https://doi.org/10.1016/j.clinbiochem.2011.06.004.
[178] J. Cheng, J.M. Guo, B.X. Xiao, et al., piRNA, the new non-coding RNA, is aberrantly expressed in human cancer cells, Clin. Chim. Acta 412 (17–18) (2011) 1621–1625, https://doi.org/10.1016/j.cca.2011.05.015.
[179] E. Lee, N.A. Lokman, M.K. Oehler, et al., A comprehensive molecular and clinical analysis of the piRNA pathway genes in ovarian cancer, Cancers 13 (1) (2021) 1–23, https://doi.org/10.3390/cancers13010004.
[180] M. Devouassoux-Shisheboran, C. Genestie, Pathobiology of ovarian carcinomas, Chin. J. Cancer 34 (1) (2015) 50–55, https://doi.org/10.5732/cjc.014.10273.
[181] G. Singh, J. Roy, P. Rout, B. Mallick, Genome-wide profiling of the PIWI-interacting RNA-mRNA regulatory networks in epithelial ovarian cancers, PLoS One 13 (1) (2018) 1–24, https://doi.org/10.1371/journal.pone.0190485.
[182] K. Alsop, S. Fereday, C. Meldrum, et al., BRCA mutation frequency and patterns of treatment response in BRCA mutation-positive women with ovarian cancer: a report from the Australian ovarian cancer study group, J. Clin. Oncol. 30 (21) (2012) 2654–2663, https://doi.org/10.1200/JCO.2011.39.8545.
[183] H.T. Cohen, F.J. McGovern, Renal-cell carcinoma, N. Engl. J. Med. 353 (23) (2005) 2477–2490, https://doi.org/10.1056/NEJMra043172.
[184] H.M. Li, B. Heng, P. Ouyang, et al., Comprehensive profiling of circRNAs and the tumor suppressor function of circHIPK3 in clear cell renal carcinoma, J. Mol. Histol. 51 (3) (2020) 317–327, https://doi.org/10.1007/s10735-020-09882-9.
[185] E.M. Wallen, R.S. Pruthi, G.F. Joyce, M. Wise, Urologic diseases in America project kidney cancer, J. Urol. 177 (6) (2007) 2006–2018. discussion 2018–2019 https://doi.org/10.1016/j.juro.2007.01.126.
[186] B. Owens, Kidney cancer, Nature 537 (7620) (2016) S97, doi:10.1038/537S97a.
[187] Y. Li, X. Wu, H. Gao, et al., Piwi-interacting RNAs (piRNAs) are dysregulated in renal cell carcinoma and associated with tumor metastasis and cancer-specific survival, Mol. Med. 21 (1) (2015) 381–388, https://doi.org/10.2119/molmed.2014.00203.
[188] J. Busch, B. Ralla, M. Jung, et al., Piwi-interacting RNAs as novel prognostic markers in clear cell renal cell carcinomas, J. Exp. Clin. Cancer Res. 34 (1) (2015) 1–11, https://doi.org/10.1186/s13046-015-0180-3.
[189] X. Du, H. Li, X. Xie, et al., piRNA-31115 promotes cell proliferation and invasion via PI3K/AKT pathway in Clear Cell Renal Carcinoma, Dis. Markers 2021 (2021) 1–8, https://doi.org/10.1155/2021/6915329.
[190] Q.T. Ostrom, H. Gittleman, P. Farah, et al., CBTRUS statistical report: primary brain and central nervous system tumors diagnosed in the United States in 2006–2010, Neuro-Oncology 15 (Suppl. 2) (2013) ii1–56, https://doi.org/10.1093/neuonc/not151.
[191] X. Liu, J. Zheng, Y. Xue, et al., PIWIL3/OIP5-AS1/ miR-367-3p/CEBPA feedback loop regulates the biological behavior of glioma cells, Theranostics 8 (4) (2018) 1084–1105, https://doi.org/10.7150/thno.21740. eCollection 2018.
[192] M. Bartos, F. Siegl, A. Kopkova, et al., Small RNA sequencing identifies PIWI-interacting RNAs deregulated in glioblastoma—piR-9491 and piR-12488 reduce tumor cell colonies in vitro, Front. Oncol. 11 (2021) 1–11, https://doi.org/10.3389/fonc.2021.707017.

[193] X. Leng, J. Ma, Y. Liu, et al., Mechanism of piRDQ590027/MIR17HG regulating the permeability of glioma conditioned normal BBB, J. Exp. Clin. Cancer Res. 37 (1) (2018) 1–17, https://doi.org/10.1186/s13046-018-0886-0.

[194] R.L. Siegel, K.D. Miller, A. Jemal, CA Cancer J. Clin. 66 (1) (2016) 7–30, https://doi.org/10.3322/caac.21332.

[195] B. Li, J. Hong, M. Hong, et al., piRNA-823 delivered by multiple myeloma-derived extracellular vesicles promoted tumorigenesis through re-educating endothelial cells in the tumor environment, Oncogene 38 (26) (2019) 5227–5238, https://doi.org/10.1038/s41388-019-0788-4.

[196] L. Ai, S. Mu, C. Sun, et al., Myeloid-derived suppressor cells endow stem-like qualities to multiple myeloma cells by inducing piRNA-823 expression and DNMT3B activation, Mol. Cancer 18 (1) (2019) 1–12, https://doi.org/10.1186/s12943-019-1011-5.

[197] H. Yan, Q.L. Wu, C.Y. Sun, et al., piRNA-823 contributes to tumorigenesis by regulating de novo DNA methylation and angiogenesis in multiple myeloma, Leukemia 29 (1) (2015) 196–206, https://doi.org/10.1038/leu.2014.135.

[198] A.R. Krishnan, A. Korrapati, A.E. Zou, et al., Smoking status regulates a novel panel of PIWI-interacting RNAs in head and neck squamous cell carcinoma, Oral Oncol. 65 (2017) 68–75, https://doi.org/10.1016/j.oraloncology.2016.12.022.

[199] B. Das, J. Roy, N. Jain, B. Mallick, Tumor suppressive activity of PIWI interacting RNA in human fibrosarcoma mediated through repression of RRM2, Mol. Carcinog. 58 (3) (2019) 344–357, https://doi.org/10.1002/mc.22932.

[200] A. Ritter, M. Hirschfeld, K. Berner, et al., Circulating non-coding RNA-biomarker potential in neoadjuvant chemotherapy of triple negative breast cancer? Int. J. Oncol. 56 (1) (2020) 47–68, https://doi.org/10.3892/ijo.2019.4920.

[201] Q.E. Wang, C. Han, K. Milum, A.A. Wani, Stem cell protein Piwil2 modulates chromatin modifications upon cisplatin treatment, Mutat. Res. 708 (1–2) (2011) 59–68, https://doi.org/10.1016/j.mrfmmm.2011.02.001.

[202] A. Janic, L. Mendizabal, S. Llamazares, et al., Ectopic expression of germline genes drives malignant brain tumor growth in Drosophila, Science 330 (6012) (2010) 1824–1827, https://doi.org/10.1126/science.1195481.

[203] D. Qiao, A.M. Zeeman, W. Deng, et al., Molecular characterization of hiwi, a human member of the piwi gene family whose overexpression is correlated to seminomas, Oncogene 21 (25) (2002) 3988–3999, https://doi.org/10.1038/sj.onc.1205505.

[204] K. Xie, K. Zhang, J. Kong, et al., Cancer-testis gene PIWIL1 promotes cell proliferation, migration, and invasion in lung adenocarcinoma, Cancer Med. 7 (1) (2018) 157–166, https://doi.org/10.1002/cam4.1248.

[205] R. Iliev, M. Fedorko, T. Machackova, et al., Expression levels of PIWI-interacting RNA, piR-823, are deregulated in tumor tissue, blood serum and urine of patients with renal cell carcinoma, Anticancer Res. 36 (12) (2016) 6419–6423, https://doi.org/10.21873/anticanres.11239.

[206] R. Iliev, M. Stanik, M. Fedorko, et al., Decreased expression levels of PIWIL1, PIWIL2, and PIWIL4 are associated with worse survival in renal cell carcinoma patients, OncoTargets Ther. 9 (2016) 217–222, https://doi.org/10.2147/OTT.S91295.

[207] T. Araujo, A. Khayat, L. Quintana, et al., Piwi like RNA-mediated gene silencing 1 gene as a possible major player in gastric cancer, World J. Gastroenterol. 24 (47) (2018) 5338–5350, https://doi.org/10.3748/wjg.v24.i47.5338.

[208] X. Liu, Y. Sun, J. Guo, et al., Expression of hiwi gene in human gastric cancer was associated with proliferation of cancer cells, Int. J. Cancer 118 (8) (2006) 1922–1929, https://doi.org/10.1002/ijc.21575.

[209] W.K. Liu, X.Y. Jiang, Z.X. Zhang, Expression of PSCA, PIWIL1 and TBX2 and its correlation with HPV16 infection in formalin-fixed, paraffin-embedded cervical squamous cell carcinoma specimens, Arch. Virol. 155 (5) (2010) 657–663, https://doi.org/10.1007/s00705-010-0635-y.

[210] C. Liu, L. Qu, B. Dong, et al., Combined phenotype of 4 markers improves prognostic value of patients with colon cancer, Am. J. Med. Sci. 343 (4) (2012) 295–302, https://doi.org/10.1097/MAJ.0b013e31822cb4cd.

[211] G. Sun, Y. Wang, L. Sun, et al., Clinical significance of Hiwi gene expression in gliomas, Brain Res. 1373 (2011) 183–188, https://doi.org/10.1016/j.brainres.2010.11.097.

[212] L.F. Grochola, T. Greither, H. Taubert, et al., The stem cell-associated Hiwi gene in human adenocarcinoma of the pancreas: expression and risk of tumour-related death, Br. J. Cancer 99 (7) (2008) 1083–1088, https://doi.org/10.1038/sj.bjc.6604653.

[213] Z. Chen, Q. Che, X. He, et al., Stem cell protein Piwil1 endowed endometrial cancer cells with stem-like properties via inducing epithelial-mesenchymal transition, BMC Cancer 15 (2015) 1–13, https://doi.org/10.1186/s12885-015-1794-8.

[214] Z. Chen, Q. Che, F.Z. Jiang, et al., Piwil1 causes epigenetic alteration of PTEN gene via upregulation of DNA methyltransferase in type I endometrial cancer, Biochem. Biophys. Res. Commun. 463 (4) (2015) 876–880, https://doi.org/10.1186/s12885-015-1794-8.

[215] M. Litwin, A. Szczepanska-Buda, D. Michalowska, et al., Aberrant expression of PIWIL1 and PIWIL2 and their clinical significance in ductal breast carcinoma, Anticancer Res. 38 (4) (2018) 2021–2030, https://doi.org/10.21873/anticanres.12441.

[216] J.J. Liu, R. Shen, L. Chen, et al., Piwil2 is expressed in various stages of breast cancers and has the potential to be used as a novel biomarker, Int. J. Clin. Exp. Pathol. 3 (2010) 328–337. https://pubmed.ncbi.nlm.nih.gov/20490325/.

[217] Y. Yao, C. Li, X. Zhou, et al., PIWIL2 induces c-Myc expression by interacting with NME2 and regulates c-Myc-mediated tumor cell proliferation, Oncotarget 5 (18) (2014) 8466–8477, https://doi.org/10.18632/oncotarget.2327.

[218] G. Zeng, D. Zhang, X. Liu, et al., Co-expression of Piwil2/Piwil4 in nucleus indicates poor prognosis of hepatocellular carcinoma, Oncotarget 8 (3) (2017) 4607–4617, https://doi.org/10.18632/oncotarget.13491.

[219] Y. Ye, D.T. Yin, L. Chen, et al., Identification of Piwil2-like (PL2L) proteins that promote tumorigenesis, PLoS One 5 (10) (2010) 1–15, https://doi.org/10.1371/journal.pone.0013406.

[220] N. Perkins, The diverse and complex roles of NF-κB subunits in cancer, Nat. Rev. Cancer 12 (2) (2012) 121–132, https://doi.org/10.1038/nrc3204.

[221] J. Li, L. Xu, Z. Bao, et al., High expression of PIWIL2 promotes tumor cell proliferation, migration and predicts a poor prognosis in glioma, Oncol. Rep. 38 (1) (2017) 183–192, https://doi.org/10.3892/or.2017.5647.

[222] K.Y. Dingqing Feng, Y. Zhou, H. Liang, et al., Piwil2 is reactivated by HPV oncoproteins and initiates cell reprogramming via epigenetic regulation during cervical cancer tumorigenesis, Oncotarget 7 (40) (2016) 64575–64588, https://doi.org/10.18632/oncotarget.11810.

[223] A. Vourekas, Q. Zheng, P. Alexiou, et al., Mili and Miwi target RNA repertoire reveals piRNA biogenesis and function of Miwi in spermiogenesis, Nat. Struct. Mol. Biol. 19 (8) (2012) 773–781, https://doi.org/10.1038/nsmb.2347.

[224] L. Jiang, W.J. Wang, Z.W. Li, X.Z. Wang, Downregulation of Piwil3 suppresses cell proliferation, migration and invasion in gastric cancer, Cancer Biomark. 20 (4) (2017) 499–509, https://doi.org/10.3233/CBM-170324.

[225] T. Gambichler, C. Kohsik, A.K. Hoh, et al., Expression of PIWIL3 in primary and metastatic melanoma, J. Cancer Res. Clin. Oncol. 143 (3) (2017) 433–437, https://doi.org/10.1007/s00432-016-2305-2.

[226] J. Gutierrez, R. Platt, J.C. Opazo, et al., Evolutionary history of the vertebrate Piwi gene family, PeerJ 9 (2021) 1–22, https://doi.org/10.7717/peerj.12451.

[227] L. Zhang, X. Meng, C. Pan, et al., piR-31470 epigenetically suppresses the expression of glutathione S-transferase pi 1 in prostate cancer via DNA methylation, Cell. Signal. 67 (2020) 1–12, https://doi.org/10.1016/j.cellsig.2019.109501.

[228] Z. Wang, N. Liu, S. Shi, et al., The role of PIWIL4, an Argonaute family protein, in breast cancer, J. Biol. Chem. 291 (20) (2016) 10646–10658, https://doi.org/10.1074/jbc.M116.723239.

[229] C.A. Benavente, J.D. McEvoy, D. Finkelstein, et al., Cross-species genomic and epigenomic landscape of retinoblastoma, Oncotarget 4 (6) (2013) 844–859, https://doi.org/10.18632/oncotarget.1051.

[230] J. McEvoy, P. Nagahawatte, D. Finkelstein, et al., RB1 gene inactivation by chromothripsis in human retinoblastoma, Oncotarget 5 (2) (2014) 438–450, https://doi.org/10.18632/oncotarget.1686.

[231] J. Zhang, C.A. Benavente, J. McEvoy, et al., A novel retinoblastoma therapy from genomic and epigenetic analyses, Nature 481 (7381) (2012) 329–334, https://doi.org/10.1038/nature10733.

[232] C. Rodriguez-Galindo, M. Wilson, M. Dyer, Retinoblastoma. Hematology and Oncology of Infancy and Childhood, Retinoblastoma | SpringerLink, 2015, pp. 1747–1778.

[233] M.A. Dyer, Lessons from retinoblastoma: implications for cancer, development, evolution, and regenerative medicine, Trends Mol. Med. 22 (10) (2016) 863–876, https://doi.org/10.1016/j.molmed.2016.07.010.

[234] F. Cremisi, A. Philpott, S. Ohnuma, Cell cycle and cell fate interactions in neural development, Curr. Opin. Neurobiol. 13 (1) (2003) 26–33, https://doi.org/10.1016/s0959-4388(03)00005-9.

[235] S.L. Donovan, M.A. Dyer, Regulation of proliferation during central nervous system development, Semin. Cell Dev. Biol. 16 (3) (2005) 407–421, https://doi.org/10.1016/j.semcdb.2005.02.012.

[236] M.A. Dyer, C.L. Cepko, Regulating proliferation during retinal development, Nat. Rev. Neurosci. 2 (5) (2001) 333–342, https://doi.org/10.1038/35072555.

[237] L.M. Farkas, W.B. Huttner, The cell biology of neural stem and progenitor cells and its significance for their proliferation versus differentiation during mammalian brain development, Curr. Opin. Cell Biol. 20 (6) (2008) 707–715, https://doi.org/10.1016/j.ceb.2008.09.008.

[238] J. Malicki, Cell fate decisions and patterning in the vertebrate retina: the importance of timing, asymmetry, polarity and waves, Curr. Opin. Neurobiol. 14 (1) (2004) 15–21, https://doi.org/10.1016/j.conb.2004.01.015.

[239] S. Ohnuma, W.A. Harris, Neurogenesis and the cell cycle, Neuron 40 (2) (2003) 199–208, https://doi.org/10.1016/s0896-6273(03)00632-9.

[240] W. Zhong, W. Chia, Neurogenesis and asymmetric cell division, Curr. Opin. Neurobiol. 18 (1) (2008) 4–11, https://doi.org/10.1016/j.conb.2008.05.002.

[241] R.W. Young, Cell proliferation during postnatal development of the retina in the mouse, Brain Res. 353 (2) (1985) 229–239, https://doi.org/10.1016/0165-3806(85)90211-1.

[242] R.W. Young, Cell differentiation in the retina of the mouse, Anat. Rec. 212 (2) (1985) 199–205, https://doi.org/10.1002/ar.1092120215.

[243] F. Rieke, Mechanisms of single-photon detection in rod photoreceptors, Methods Enzymol. 316 (2000) 186–202, https://doi.org/10.1016/s0076-6879(00)16724-2.

[244] A.P. Sampath, F. Rieke, Selective transmission of single photon responses by saturation at the rod-to-rod bipolar synapse, Neuron 41 (3) (2004) 431–443, https://doi.org/10.1016/s0896-6273(04)00005-4.

[245] A. Bringmann, T. Pannicke, J. Grosche, et al., Muller cells in the healthy and diseased retina, Prog. Retin. Eye Res. 25 (4) (2006) 397–424, https://doi.org/10.1016/j.preteyeres.2006.05.003.

[246] M. Hoon, H. Okawa, L. Della Santina, R.O. Wong, Functional architecture of the retina: development and disease, Prog. Retin. Eye Res. 42 (2014) 44–84, https://doi.org/10.1016/j.preteyeres.2014.06.003.

[247] P.R. Mendoza, H.E. Grossniklaus, The biology of retinoblastoma, Prog. Mol. Biol. Transl. Sci. 134 (2015) 503–516, https://doi.org/10.1016/bs.pmbts.2015.06.012.

[248] C. Scelfo, J.H. Francis, V. Khetan, et al., An international survey of classification and treatment choices for group D retinoblastoma, Int. J. Ophthalmol. 10 (6) (2017) 961–967, https://doi.org/10.18240/ijo.2017.06.20.

[249] I.D. Fabian, A. Reddy, M.S. Sagoo, Classification and staging of retinoblastoma, Community Eye Health 31 (101) (2018) 11–13. https://pubmed.ncbi.nlm.nih.gov/29915461/.

[250] D. Chen, I. Livne-bar, J.L. Vanderluit, et al., Cell-specific effects of RB or RB/p107 loss on retinal development implicate an intrinsically death-resistant cell-of-origin in retinoblastoma, Cancer Cell 5 (6) (2004) 539–551, https://doi.org/10.1016/j.ccr.2004.05.025.

[251] D. MacPherson, J. Sage, T. Kim, et al., Cell type-specific effects of Rb deletion in the murine retina, Genes Dev. 18 (14) (2004) 1681–1694, https://doi.org/10.1101/gad.1203304.

[252] E. Robanus-Maandag, M. Dekker, M. van der Valk, et al., p107 is a suppressor of retinoblastoma development in pRb-deficient mice, Genes Dev. 12 (11) (1998) 1599–1609, https://doi.org/10.1101/gad.12.11.1599.

[253] J. Zhang, J. Gray, L. Wu, et al., Rb regulates proliferation and rod photoreceptor development in the mouse retina, Nat. Genet. 36 (4) (2004) 351–360, https://doi.org/10.1038/ng1318.
[254] J. Zhang, B. Schweers, M.A. Dyer, The first knockout mouse model of retinoblastoma, Cell Cycle 3 (7) (2004) 952–959. https://pubmed.ncbi.nlm.nih.gov/15190215/.
[255] M.A. Dyer, R. Bremner, The search for the retinoblastoma cell of origin, Nat. Rev. Cancer 5 (2) (2005) 91–101, https://doi.org/10.1038/nrc1545.
[256] D.E. Rushlow, B.M. Mol, J.Y. Kennett, et al., Characterization of retinoblastomas without RB1 mutations: genomic, gene expression, and clinical studies, Lancet Oncol. 14 (4) (2013) 327–334, https://doi.org/10.1016/S1470-2045(13)70045-7.
[257] C.L. Cepko, C.P. Austin, X. Yang, et al., Cell fate determination in the vertebrate retina, Proc. Natl. Acad. Sci. U. S. A. 93 (2) (1996) 589–595, https://doi.org/10.1073/pnas.93.2.589.
[258] W. Liu, S.L. Khare, X. Liang, et al., All Brn3 genes can promote retinal ganglion cell differentiation in the chick, Development 127 (15) (2000) 3237–3247, https://doi.org/10.1242/dev.127.15.3237.
[259] T. Marquardt, R. Ashery-Padan, N. Andrejewski, et al., Pax6 is required for the multipotent state of retinal progenitor cells, Cell 105 (1) (2001) 43–55, https://doi.org/10.1016/s0092-8674(01)00295-1.
[260] P.X. Xu, X. Zhang, S. Heaney, A. Yoon, A.M. Michelson, R.L. Maas, Regulation of Pax6 expression is conserved between mice and flies, Development 126 (2) (1999) 383–395, https://doi.org/10.1242/dev.126.2.383.
[261] X. Chen, A. Pappo, M.A. Dyer, Pediatric solid tumor genomics and developmental pliancy, Oncogene 34 (41) (2015) 5207–5215, https://doi.org/10.1038/onc.2014.474.
[262] D. Hanahan, R.A. Weinberg, Hallmarks of cancer: the next generation, Cell 144 (5) (2011) 646–674, https://doi.org/10.1016/j.cell.2011.02.013.
[263] A. Mo, C. Luo, F.P. Davis, et al., Epigenomic landscapes of retinal rods and cones, Elife 5 (2016) 1–29 (Published 2016 Mar 7) https://doi.org/10.7554/eLife.11613.
[264] I. Solovei, M. Kreysing, C. Lanctot, et al., Nuclear architecture of rod photoreceptor cells adapts to vision in mammalian evolution, Cell 137 (2) (2009) 356–368, https://doi.org/10.1016/j.cell.2009.01.052.
[265] T.P. Dryja, S. Friend, R.A. Weinberg, Genetic sequences that predispose to retinoblastoma and osteosarcoma, Symp. Fundam. Cancer Res. 39 (1986) 115–119. https://pubmed.ncbi.nlm.nih.gov/3480547/.
[266] S.H. Friend, R. Bernards, S. Rogelj, et al., A human DNA segment with properties of the gene that predisposes to retinoblastoma and osteosarcoma, Nature 323 (6089) (1986) 643–646, https://doi.org/10.1038/323643a0.
[267] A.G. Knudson Jr., Mutation and cancer: statistical study of retinoblastoma, Proc. Natl. Acad. Sci. U. S. A. 68 (4) (1971) 820–823, https://doi.org/10.1073/pnas.68.4.820.
[268] J. Toguchida, T.L. McGee, J.C. Paterson, et al., Complete genomic sequence of the human retinoblastoma susceptibility gene, Genomics 17 (3) (1993) 535–543, https://doi.org/10.1006/geno.1993.1368.
[269] K. Buchkovich, L.A. Duffy, E. Harlow, The retinoblastoma protein is phosphorylated during specific phases of the cell cycle, Cell 58 (6) (1989) 1097–1105, https://doi.org/10.1016/0092-8674(89)90508-4.
[270] D. Cobrinik, S.F. Dowdy, P.W. Hinds, et al., The retinoblastoma protein and the regulation of cell cycling, Trends Biochem. Sci. 17 (8) (1992) 312–315, https://doi.org/10.1016/0968-0004(92)90443-d.
[271] J.A. DeCaprio, J.W. Ludlow, D. Lynch, et al., The product of the retinoblastoma susceptibility gene has properties of a cell cycle regulatory element, Cell 58 (6) (1989) 1085–1095, https://doi.org/10.1016/0092-8674(89)90507-2.
[272] W.H. Lee, J.Y. Shew, F.D. Hong, et al., The retinoblastoma susceptibility gene encodes a nuclear phosphoprotein associated with DNA binding activity, Nature 329 (6140) (1987) 642–645, https://doi.org/10.1038/329642a0.
[273] D. Cobrinik, Regulatory interactions among E2Fs and cell cycle control proteins, Curr. Top. Microbiol. Immunol. 208 (1996) 31–61, https://doi.org/10.1007/978-3-642-79910-5_2.

[274] N. Dyson, The regulation of E2F by pRB-family proteins, Genes Dev. 12 (15) (1998) 2245–2262, https://doi.org/10.1101/gad.12.15.2245.

[275] J.R. Nevins, Toward an understanding of the functional complexity of the E2F and retinoblastoma families, Cell Growth Differ. 9 (8) (1998) 585–593.

[276] S. Bagchi, R. Weinmann, P. Raychaudhuri, The retinoblastoma protein copurifies with E2F-I, an E1A-regulated inhibitor of the transcription factor E2F, Cell 65 (6) (1991) 1063–1072, https://doi.org/10.1016/0092-8674(91)90558-g.

[277] L.R. Bandara, N.B. La Thangue, Adenovirus E1a prevents the retinoblastoma gene product from complexing with a cellular transcription factor, Nature 351 (6326) (1991) 494–497, https://doi.org/10.1038/351494a0.

[278] L. Cao, B. Faha, M. Dembski, et al., Independent binding of the retinoblastoma protein and p107 to the transcription factor E2F, Nature 355 (6356) (1992) 176–179, https://doi.org/10.1038/355176a0.

[279] S.P. Chellappan, S. Hiebert, M. Mudryj, et al., The E2F transcription factor is a cellular target for the RB protein, Cell 65 (6) (1991) 1053–1061, https://doi.org/10.1016/0092-8674(91)90557-f.

[280] T. Chittenden, D.M. Livingston, W.G. Kaelin Jr., The T/E1A-binding domain of the retinoblastoma product can interact selectively with a sequence-specific DNA-binding protein, Cell 65 (6) (1991) 1073–1082, https://doi.org/10.1016/0092-8674(91)90559-h.

[281] D. Cobrinik, P. Whyte, D.S. Peeper, et al., Cell cycle-specific association of E2F with the p130 E1A-binding protein, Genes Dev. 7 (12A) (1993) 2392–2404, https://doi.org/10.1101/gad.7.12a.2392.

[282] S.H. Devoto, M. Mudryj, J. Pines, et al., A cyclin A-protein kinase complex possesses sequence-specific DNA binding activity: p33cdk2 is a component of the E2F-cyclin A complex, Cell 68 (1) (1992) 167–176, https://doi.org/10.1016/0092-8674(92)90215-x.

[283] S.W. Hiebert, S.P. Chellappan, J.M. Horowitz, J.R. Nevins, The interaction of RB with E2F coincides with an inhibition of the transcriptional activity of E2F, Genes Dev. 6 (2) (1992) 177–185, https://doi.org/10.1101/gad.6.2.177.

[284] S. Shirodkar, M. Ewen, J.A. DeCaprio, et al., The transcription factor E2F interacts with the retinoblastoma product and a p107-cyclin A complex in a cell cycle-regulated manner, Cell 68 (1) (1992) 157–166, https://doi.org/10.1016/0092-8674(92)90214-w.

[285] E.K. Flemington, S.H. Speck, W.G. Kaelin Jr., E2F-1-mediated transactivation is inhibited by complex formation with the retinoblastoma susceptibility gene product, Proc. Natl. Acad. Sci. U. S. A. 90 (15) (1993) 6914–6918, https://doi.org/10.1073/pnas.90.15.6914.

[286] K. Helin, E. Harlow, A. Fattaey, Inhibition of E2F-1 transactivation by direct binding of the retinoblastoma protein, Mol. Cell. Biol. 13 (10) (1993) 6501–6508, https://doi.org/10.1128/mcb.13.10.6501-6508.1993.

[287] J.W. Ludlow, C.L. Glendening, D.M. Livingston, J.A. DeCarprio, Specific enzymatic dephosphorylation of the retinoblastoma protein, Mol. Cell. Biol. 13 (1) (1993) 367–372, https://doi.org/10.1128/mcb.13.1.367-372.1993.

[288] S. Mittnacht, Control of pRB phosphorylation, Curr. Opin. Genet. Dev. 8 (1) (1998) 21–27, https://doi.org/10.1016/s0959-437x(98)80057-9.

[289] R.A. Weinberg, The retinoblastoma protein and cell cycle control, Cell 81 (3) (1995) 323–330, https://doi.org/10.1016/0092-8674(95)90385-2.

[290] A. Aslanian, P.J. Iaquinta, R. Verona, J.A. Lees, Repression of the Arf tumor suppressor by E2F3 is required for normal cell cycle kinetics, Genes Dev. 18 (12) (2004) 1413–1422, https://doi.org/10.1101/gad.1196704.

[291] D. Ginsberg, E2F3-a novel repressor of the ARF/p53 pathway, Dev. Cell 6 (6) (2004) 742–743, https://doi.org/10.1016/j.devcel.2004.05.012.

[292] G. Leone, F. Nuckolls, S. Ishida, et al., Identification of a novel E2F3 product suggests a mechanism for determining specificity of repression by Rb proteins, Mol. Cell. Biol. 20 (10) (2000) 3626–3632, https://doi.org/10.1128/MCB.20.10.3626-3632.2000.

[293] D.K. Dimova, N.J. Dyson, The E2F transcriptional network: old acquaintances with new faces, Oncogene 24 (17) (2005) 2810–2826, https://doi.org/10.1038/sj.onc.1208612.

[294] R. Ferreira, I. Naguibneva, M. Mathieu, et al., Cell cycle-dependent recruitment of HDAC-1 correlates with deacetylation of histone H4 on an Rb-E2F target promoter, EMBO Rep. 2 (9) (2001) 794–799, https://doi.org/10.1093/embo-reports/kve173.

[295] A.J. Morrison, C. Sardet, R.E. Herrera, Retinoblastoma protein transcriptional repression through histone deacetylation of a single nucleosome, Mol. Cell. Biol. 22 (3) (2002) 856–865, https://doi.org/10.1128/MCB.22.3.856-865.2002.
[296] J.B. Rayman, Y. Takahashi, V.B. Indjeian, et al., E2F mediates cell cycle-dependent transcriptional repression in vivo by recruitment of an HDAC1/mSin3B corepressor complex, Genes Dev. 16 (8) (2002) 933–947, https://doi.org/10.1101/gad.969202.
[297] Y. Takahashi, J.B. Rayman, B.D. Dynlacht, Analysis of promoter binding by the E2F and pRB families in vivo: distinct E2F proteins mediate activation and repression, Genes Dev. 14 (7) (2000) 804–816. https://pubmed.ncbi.nlm.nih.gov/10766737/.
[298] M. Narita, S. Nunez, E. Heard, et al., Rb-mediated heterochromatin formation and silencing of E2F target genes during cellular senescence, Cell 113 (6) (2003) 703–716, https://doi.org/10.1016/s0092-8674(03)00401-x.
[299] M.V. Frolov, N.J. Dyson, Molecular mechanisms of E2F-dependent activation and pRB-mediated repression, J. Cell Sci. 117 (Pt 11) (2004) 2173–2181, https://doi.org/10.1242/jcs.01227.
[300] T. Chibazakura, S.G. McGrew, J.A. Cooper, et al., Regulation of cyclin-dependent kinase activity during mitotic exit and maintenance of genome stability by p21, p27, and p107, Proc. Natl. Acad. Sci. U. S. A. 101 (13) (2004) 4465–4470, https://doi.org/10.1073/pnas.0400655101.
[301] S. Coats, P. Whyte, M.L. Fero, et al., A new pathway for mitogen-dependent cdk2 regulation uncovered in p27(Kip1)-deficient cells, Curr. Biol. 9 (4) (1999) 163–173, https://doi.org/10.1016/s0960-9822(99)80086-4.
[302] L. Zhu, E. Harlow, B.D. Dynlacht, p107 uses a p21CIP1-related domain to bind cyclin/cdk2 and regulate interactions with E2F, Genes Dev. 9 (14) (1995) 1740–1752, https://doi.org/10.1101/gad.9.14.1740.
[303] J.W. Harbour, Molecular basis of low-penetrance retinoblastoma, Arch. Ophthalmol. 119 (11) (2001) 1699–1704, https://doi.org/10.1001/archopht.119.11.1699.
[304] G.A. Otterson, W. Chen, A.B. Coxon, et al., Incomplete penetrance of familial retinoblastoma linked to germ-line mutations that result in partial loss of RB function, Proc. Natl. Acad. Sci. U. S. A. 94 (22) (1997) 12036–12040, https://doi.org/10.1073/pnas.94.22.12036.
[305] P. Ji, H. Jiang, K. Rekhtman, et al., An Rb-Skp2-p27 pathway mediates acute cell cycle inhibition by Rb and is retained in a partial-penetrance Rb mutant, Mol. Cell 16 (1) (2004) 47–58, https://doi.org/10.1016/j.molcel.2004.09.029.
[306] W. Fang, T. Mori, D. Cobrinik, Regulation of PML-dependent transcriptional repression by pRB and low penetrance pRB mutants, Oncogene 21 (36) (2002) 5557–5565, https://doi.org/10.1038/sj.onc.1205666.
[307] K.Y. Lee, M.H. Ladha, C. McMahon, M.E. Ewen, The retinoblastoma protein is linked to the activation of Ras, Mol. Cell. Biol. 19 (11) (1999) 7724–7732, https://doi.org/10.1128/MCB.19.11.7724.
[308] S. Gagrica, S. Hauser, I. Kolfschoten, et al., Inhibition of oncogenic transformation by mammalian Lin-9, a pRB-associated protein, EMBO J. 23 (23) (2004) 4627–4638, https://doi.org/10.1038/sj.emboj.7600470.
[309] N. Dyson, P.M. Howley, K. Munger, E. Harlow, The human papilloma virus-16 E7 oncoprotein is able to bind to the retinoblastoma gene product, Science 243 (4893) (1989) 934–937, https://doi.org/10.1126/science.2537532.
[310] H.H. Zur, Viruses in human cancers, Science 254 (5035) (1991) 1167–1173, https://doi.org/10.1126/science.1659743.
[311] M. Serrano, G.J. Hannon, D. Beach, A new regulatory motif in cell-cycle control causing specific inhibition of cyclin D/CDK4, Nature 366 (6456) (1993) 704–707, https://doi.org/10.1038/366704a0.
[312] C.J. Sherr, Cancer cell cycles, Science 274 (5293) (1996) 1672–1677, https://doi.org/10.1126/science.274.5293.1672.
[313] X. Che, Y. Qian, D. Li, Suppression of disheveled-Axin domain containing 1 (DIXDC1) by microRNA-186 inhibits the proliferation and invasion of retinoblastoma cells, J. Mol. Neurosci. 64 (2) (2018) 252–261, https://doi.org/10.1007/s12031-017-1017-7.

[314] D. Zhao, Z. Cui, MicroRNA-361-3p regulates retinoblastoma cell proliferation and stemness by targeting hedgehog signaling, Exp. Ther. Med. 17 (2) (2019) 1154–1162, https://doi.org/10.3892/etm.2018.7062.

[315] F. Xu, G. Liu, L. Wang, et al., miR-494 promotes progression of retinoblastoma via PTEN through PI3K/AKT signaling pathway, Oncol. Lett. 20 (2) (2020) 1952–1960, https://doi.org/10.3892/ol.2020.11749.

[316] S. Liu, X. Zhang, C. Hu, et al., miR-29a inhibits human retinoblastoma progression by targeting STAT3 [published correction appears in Oncol Rep. 2021;46(2)], Oncol. Rep. 39 (2) (2018) 739–746, https://doi.org/10.3892/or.2017.6144.

[317] D. Wu, H. Fu, H. Zhou, et al., Effects of novel ncRNA molecules, p15-piRNAs, on the methylation of DNA and histone H3 of the CDKN2B promoter region in U937 cells, J. Cell. Biochem. 116 (12) (2015) 2744–2754, https://doi.org/10.1002/jcb.25199.

[318] Y. Zhang, C. Xue, X. Zhu, et al., Suppression of microRNA-125a-5p upregulates the TAZ-EGFR signaling pathway and promotes retinoblastoma proliferation, Cell. Signal. 28 (8) (2016) 850–860, https://doi.org/10.1016/j.cellsig.2016.04.002.

[319] G. Yang, Y. Fu, L. Zhang, et al., miR106b regulates retinoblastoma Y79 cells through Runx3, Oncol. Rep. 38 (5) (2017) 3039–3043, https://doi.org/10.3892/or.2017.5931.

[320] L. Wang, X. Lyu, Y. Ma, et al., MicroRNA-504 targets AEG-1 and inhibits cell proliferation and invasion in retinoblastoma, Mol. Med. Rep. 19 (4) (2019) 2935–2942, https://doi.org/10.3892/mmr.2019.9923.

[321] Z. Sun, A. Zhang, L. Zhang, Inhibition of microRNA-492 attenuates cell proliferation and invasion in retinoblastoma via directly targeting LATS2, Mol. Med. Rep. 19 (3) (2019) 1965–1971, https://doi.org/10.3892/mmr.2018.9784.

[322] N. Subramanian, J.R. Kanwar, R.K. Kanwar, S. Krishnakumar, Blocking the maturation of Onco-miRNAs using pri-miRNA-17∼92 aptamer in retinoblastoma, Nucleic Acid Ther. 25 (1) (2015) 47–52, https://doi.org/10.1089/nat.2014.0507.

[323] C.J. Sherr, Divorcing ARF and p53: an unsettled case, Nat. Rev. Cancer 6 (9) (2006) 663–673, https://doi.org/10.1038/nrc1954v.

[324] K.H. To, S. Pajovic, B.L. Gallie, B.L. Theriault, Regulation of p14ARF expression by miR-24: a potential mechanism compromising the p53 response during retinoblastoma development, BMC Cancer 12 (2012) 69, https://doi.org/10.1186/1471-2407-12-69.

[325] F. Shen, M.H. Mo, L. Chen, et al., MicroRNA-21 down-regulates Rb1 expression by targeting PDCD4 in retinoblastoma, J. Cancer 5 (9) (2014) 804–812, https://doi.org/10.7150/jca.10456.

[326] M. Beta, N. Venkatesan, M. Vasudevan, et al., Identification and insilico analysis of retinoblastoma serum microRNA profile and gene targets towards prediction of novel serum biomarkers, Bioinform. Biol. Insights 7 (2013) 21–34, https://doi.org/10.4137/BBI.S10501.

[327] C. Dong, S. Liu, Y. Lv, et al., Long non-coding RNA HOTAIR regulates proliferation and invasion via activating Notch signalling pathway in retinoblastoma, J. Biosci. 41 (4) (2016) 677–687, https://doi.org/10.1007/s12038-016-9636-7.

[328] G. Yang, Y. Fu, X. Lu, et al., LncRNA HOTAIR/miR-613/c-met axis modulated epithelial-mesenchymal transition of retinoblastoma cells, J. Cell. Mol. Med. 22 (10) (2018) 5083–5096, https://doi.org/10.1111/jcmm.13796.

[329] H. Zhang, J. Zhong, Z. Bian, et al., Long non-coding RNA CCAT1 promotes human retinoblastoma SO-RB50 and Y79 cells through negative regulation of miR-218-5p, Biomed. Pharmacother. 87 (2017) 683–691, https://doi.org/10.1016/j.biopha.2017.01.004.

[330] J.X. Wang, Y. Yang, K. Li, Long noncoding RNA DANCR aggravates retinoblastoma through miR-34c and miR-613 by targeting MMP-9, J. Cell. Physiol. 233 (10) (2018) 6986–6995, https://doi.org/10.1002/jcp.26621.

[331] F. Hao, Y. Mou, L. Zhang, et al., LncRNA AFAP1-AS1 is a prognostic biomarker and serves as oncogenic role in retinoblastoma, Biosci. Rep. 38 (3) (2018) 1–8, https://doi.org/10.1042/BSR20180384.

[332] W. Shang, Y. Yang, J. Zhang, Q. Wu, Long noncoding RNA BDNF-AS is a potential biomarker and regulates cancer development in human retinoblastoma, Biochem. Biophys. Res. Commun. 497 (4) (2018) 1142–1148, https://doi.org/10.1016/j.bbrc.2017.01.134.

[333] A. Zhang, W. Shang, Q. Nie, et al., Long non-coding RNA H19 suppresses retinoblastoma progression via counteracting miR-17-92 cluster, J. Cell. Biochem. 119 (4) (2018) 3497–3509, https://doi.org/10.1002/jcb.26521.

[334] Z. Yuan, Z. Li, Long noncoding RNA UCA1 facilitates cell proliferation and inhibits apoptosis in retinoblastoma by activating the PI3K/Akt pathway, Transl. Cancer Res. 9 (2) (2020) 1012–1022, https://doi.org/10.21037/tcr.2019.12.47.

[335] L. Xing, L. Zhang, Y. Feng, Z. Cui, L. Ding, Downregulation of circular RNA hsa_circ_0001649 indicates poor prognosis for retinoblastoma and regulates cell proliferation and apoptosis via AKT/mTOR signaling pathway, Biomed. Pharmacother. 105 (2018) 326–333, https://doi.org/10.1016/j.biopha.2018.05.141.

[336] J. Lyu, Y. Wang, Q. Zheng, et al., Reduction of circular RNA expression associated with human retinoblastoma, Exp. Eye Res. 184 (2019) 278–285, https://doi.org/10.1016/j.exer.2019.03.017.

[337] A. Simeone, E. Puelles, D. Acampora, The Otx family, Curr. Opin. Genet. Dev. 12 (4) (2002) 409–415, https://doi.org/10.1016/s0959-437x(02)00318-0.

[338] D. Acampora, L.G. Di Giovannantonio, A. Simeone, Otx2 is an intrinsic determinant of the embryonic stem cell state and is required for transition to a stable epiblast stem cell condition, Development 140 (1) (2013) 43–55, https://doi.org/10.1242/dev.085290.

[339] D.C. Adamson, Q. Shi, M. Wortham, et al., OTX2 is critical for the maintenance and progression of Shh-independent medulloblastomas, Cancer Res. 70 (1) (2010) 181–191, https://doi.org/10.1158/0008-5472.CAN-09-2331.

[340] R.Y. Bai, V. Staedtke, H.G. Lidov, et al., OTX2 represses myogenic and neuronal differentiation in medulloblastoma cells, Cancer Res. 72 (22) (2012) 5988–6001, https://doi.org/10.1158/0008-5472.CAN-12-0614.

[341] R. Kaur, C. Aiken, L.C. Morrison, et al., OTX2 exhibits cell-context-dependent effects on cellular and molecular properties of human embryonic neural precursors and medulloblastoma cells, Dis. Model. Mech. 8 (10) (2015) 1295–1309, https://doi.org/10.1242/dmm.020594.

[342] J. Bunt, N.A. Hasselt, D.A. Zwijnenburg, et al., OTX2 sustains a bivalent-like state of OTX2-bound promoters in medulloblastoma by maintaining their H3K27me3 levels, Acta Neuropathol. 125 (3) (2013) 385–394, https://doi.org/10.1007/s00401-012-1069.

[343] A. Nishida, A. Furukawa, C. Koike, et al., Otx2 homeobox gene controls retinal photoreceptor cell fate and pineal gland development, Nat. Neurosci. 6 (12) (2003) 1255–1263, https://doi.org/10.1038/nn1155.

[344] J. Li, C. Di, J. Jing, et al., OTX2 is a therapeutic target for retinoblastoma and may function as a common factor between C-MYC, CRX, and phosphorylated RB pathways, Int. J. Oncol. 47 (5) (2015) 1703–1710, https://doi.org/10.3892/ijo.2015.3179.

[345] J. Liu, S. Zhang, B. Cheng, Epigenetic roles of PIWI-interacting RNAs (piRNAs) in cancer metastasis, Oncol. Rep. 40 (5) (2018) 2423–2434, https://doi.org/10.3892/or.2018.6684.

[346] I. Nagamori, H. Kobayashi, T. Nishimura, et al., Relationship between PIWIL4-mediated H3K4me2 demethylation and piRNA-dependent DNA methylation, Cell Rep. 25 (2) (2018) 350–356, https://doi.org/10.1016/j.celrep.2018.09.017.

[347] D.I. Jacobs, Q. Qin, A. Fu, et al., piRNA-8041 is downregulated in human glioblastoma and suppresses tumor growth invitro and invivo, Oncotarget 9 (102) (2018) 37616–37626, https://doi.org/10.18632/oncotarget.26331.

[348] G.A. Calin, C.M. Croce, MicroRNA signatures in human cancers, Nat. Rev. Cancer 6 (11) (2006) 857–866, https://doi.org/10.1038/nrc1997.

[349] X. Chen, Y. Ba, L. Ma, et al., Characterization of microRNAs in serum: a novel class of biomarkers for diagnosis of cancer and other diseases, Cell Res. 18 (10) (2008) 997–1006, https://doi.org/10.1038/cr.2008.282.

[350] K. Hur, Y. Toiyama, Y. Okugawa, et al., Circulating microRNA-203 predicts prognosis and metastasis in human colorectal cancer, Gut 66 (4) (2017) 654–665, https://doi.org/10.1136/gutjnl-2014-308737.

[351] B. Mayr, E.E. Mueller, C. Schafer, et al., Pitfalls of analysis of circulating miRNA: role of hematocrit, Clin. Chem. Lab. Med. 55 (5) (2017) 622–625, https://doi.org/10.1515/cclm-2016-0323.

[352] C.C. Pritchard, E. Kroh, B. Wood, et al., Blood cell origin of circulating microRNAs: a cautionary note for cancer biomarker studies, Cancer Prev. Res. 5 (3) (2012) 492–497, https://doi.org/10.1158/1940-6207.CAPR-11-0370.
[353] Y.W. Iwasaki, M.C. Siomi, H. Siomi, PIWI-interacting RNA: its biogenesis and functions, Annu. Rev. Biochem. 84 (2015) 405–433, https://doi.org/10.1146/annurev-biochem-060614-034258.
[354] R.J. Ross, M.M. Weiner, H. Lin, PIWI proteins and PIWI-interacting RNAs in the soma, Nature 505 (7483) (2014) 353–359, https://doi.org/10.1038/nature12987.
[355] S. Siddiqi, I. Matushansky, Piwis and piwi-interacting RNAs in the epigenetics of cancer, J. Cell. Biochem. 113 (2) (2012) 373–380, https://doi.org/10.1002/jcb.23363.
[356] C.B. Assumpcao, D.Q. Calcagno, T.M. Araujo, et al., The role of piRNA and its potential clinical implications in cancer, Epigenomics 7 (6) (2015) 975–984, https://doi.org/10.2217/epi.15.37.
[357] Y. Mei, Y. Wang, P. Kumari, et al., A piRNA-like small RNA interacts with and modulates p-ERM proteins in human somatic cells, Nat. Commun. 6 (2015) 1–12, https://doi.org/10.1038/ncomms8316.
[358] K.W. Ng, C. Anderson, E.A. Marshall, et al., Piwi-interacting RNAs in cancer: emerging functions and clinical utility, Mol. Cancer 15 (5) (2016) 1–13, https://doi.org/10.1186/s12943-016-0491-9.
[359] F. Zhong, N. Zhou, K. Wu, et al., A SnoRNA-derived piRNA interacts with human interleukin-4 pre-mRNA and induces its decay in nuclear exosomes, Nucleic Acids Res. 43 (21) (2015) 10474–10491, https://doi.org/10.1093/nar/gkv954.
[360] X. Yang, Y. Cheng, Q. Lu, et al., Detection of stably expressed piRNAs in human blood, Int. J. Clin. Exp. Med. 8 (8) (2015) 13353–13358. https://pubmed.ncbi.nlm.nih.gov/26550265/.
[361] D. Meseure, K.D. Alsibai, Part 2: Deregulated expressions of PIWI proteins and piRNAs as new candidate biomarkers and potential therapeutic tools in cancer, in: C. Logie, T.A. Knoch (Eds.), Chromatin and Epigenetics, IntechOpen, London, United Kingdom, 2020, pp. 263–274, https://doi.org/10.5772/intechopen.81738.
[362] Y. Mei, D. Clark, L. Mao, Novel dimensions of piRNAs in cancer, Cancer Lett. 336 (1) (2013) 46–52, https://doi.org/10.1016/j.canlet.2013.04.008.
[363] T. Yuan, X. Huang, M. Woodcock, et al., Plasma extracellular RNA profiles in healthy and cancer patients, Sci. Rep. 6 (1) (2016) 1–11, https://doi.org/10.1038/srep19413.
[364] H. Zhou, J.M. Guo, Y.R. Lou, et al., Detection of circulating tumor cells in peripheral blood from patients with gastric cancer using microRNA as a marker, J. Mol. Med. 88 (7) (2010) 709–717, https://doi.org/10.1007/s00109-010-0617-2.
[365] X. Gu, C. Wang, H. Deng, et al., Exosomal piRNA profiling revealed unique circulating piRNA signatures of cholangiocarcinoma and gallbladder carcinoma, Acta Biochim. Biophys. Sin. Shanghai 52 (5) (2020) 475–484, https://doi.org/10.1093/abbs/gmaa028.
[366] Y. Ogawa, Y. Taketomi, M. Murakami, et al., Small RNA transcriptomes of two types of exosomes in human whole saliva determined by next generation sequencing, Biol. Pharm. Bull. 36 (1) (2013) 66–75, https://doi.org/10.1248/bpb.b12-00607.
[367] P. Vychytilova-Faltejskova, K. Stitkovcova, L. Radova, et al., Circulating PIWI-interacting RNAs piR-5937 and piR-28876 are promising diagnostic biomarkers of colon cancer, Cancer Epidemiol. Biomark. Prev. 27 (9) (2018) 1019–1028, https://doi.org/10.1158/1055-9965.EPI-18-0318.
[368] Z. Wang, H. Yang, D. Ma, et al., Serum PIWI-interacting RNAs piR-020619 and piR-020450 are promising novel biomarkers for early detection of colorectal cancer, Cancer Epidemiol. Prev. Biomarkers 29 (5) (2020) 990–998, https://doi.org/10.1158/1055-9965.EPI-19-1148.
[369] X. Zhou, J. Liu, A. Meng, et al., Gastric juice piR-1245: a promising prognostic biomarker for gastric cancer, J. Clin. Lab. Anal. 34 (4) (2020) 1–7, https://doi.org/10.1002/jcla.23131.
[370] A. Sarkar, Z. Ghosh, Rejuvenation of piRNAs in Emergence of Cancer and Other Diseases, Bibekan and Mallick AGO-Driven Non-Coding RNAs, Elsevier, USA, 2019, pp. 319–333. https://www.elsevier.com/books/ago-driven-non-coding-rnas/mallick/978-0-12-815669-8.
[371] H. Zhang, Y. Ren, H. Xu, et al., The expression of stem cell protein Piwil2 and piR-932 in breast cancer, Surg. Oncol. 22 (4) (2013) 217–223, https://doi.org/10.1016/j.suronc.2013.07.001.
[372] H. Chu, L. Xia, X. Qiu, et al., Genetic variants in noncoding PIWI-interacting RNA and colorectal cancer risk, Cancer 121 (12) (2015) 2044–2052, https://doi.org/10.1002/cncr.29314.

[373] Y. Wang, Y. Jiang, N. Ma, et al., Overexpression of Hiwi inhibits the growth and migration of chronic myeloid leukemia cells, Cell Biochem. Biophys. 73 (1) (2015) 117–124, https://doi.org/10.1007/s12013-015-0651-3.

[374] J. Cao, G. Xu, J. Lan, et al., High expression of piwi-like RNA-mediated gene silencing 1 is associated with poor prognosis via regulating transforming growth factor-beta receptors and cyclin-dependent kinases in breast cancer, Mol. Med. Rep. 13 (3) (2016) 2829–2835, https://doi.org/10.3892/mmr.2016.4842.

[375] L. Yang, L. Bi, Q. Liu, et al., Hiwi promotes the proliferation of colorectal cancer cells via upregulating global DNA methylation, Dis. Markers 2015 (2015) 1–10, https://doi.org/10.1155/2015/383056.

[376] Y. Xie, Y. Yang, D. Ji, et al., Hiwi downregulation, mediated by shRNA, reduces the proliferation and migration of human hepatocellular carcinoma cells, Mol. Med. Rep. 11 (12) (2015) 1455–1461, https://doi.org/10.3892/mmr.2014.2847.

[377] C. Chen, J. Liu, G. Xu, Overexpression of PIWI proteins in human stage III epithelial ovarian cancer with lymph node metastasis, Cancer Biomark. 13 (5) (2013) 315–321, https://doi.org/10.3233/CBM-130360.

[378] M. Litwin, J. Dubis, K. Arczyńska, et al., Correlation of HIWI and HILI expression with cancer stem cell markers in colorectal cancer, Anticancer Res. 35 (6) (2015) 3317–3324. https://pubmed.ncbi.nlm.nih.gov/26026091/.

[379] P. Krishnan, S. Ghosh, K. Graham, et al., Piwi-interacting RNAs and PIWI genes as novel prognostic markers for breast cancer, Oncotarget 7 (25) (2016) 37944–37956, https://doi.org/10.18632/oncotarget.9272.

[380] D.W. Wang, Z.H. Wang, L.L. Wang, et al., Overexpression of hiwi promotes growth of human breast cancer cells, Asian Pac. J. Cancer Prev. 15 (18) (2014) 7553–7558, https://doi.org/10.7314/APJCP.2014.15.18.7553.

[381] S.J. Oh, S.M. Kim, Y.O. Kim, H.K. Chang, Clinicopathologic implications of PIWIL2 expression in colorectal cancer, Korean J. Pathol. 46 (4) (2012) 318–323, https://doi.org/10.4132/KoreanJPathol.2012.46.4.318.

[382] G.R. Thomas, Y. Shnayder, Chapter 40—Genomic evaluation of head and neck cancer A2—Ginsburg, Geoffrey S, in: H.F. Willard (Ed.), Essentials of Genomic and Personalized Medicine, Academic Press, 2010, pp. 511–521.

[383] X. Wang, X. Tong, H. Gao, et al., Silencing HIWI suppresses the growth, invasion and migration of glioma cells, Int. J. Oncol. 45 (6) (2014) 2385–2392, https://doi.org/10.3892/ijo.2014.2673.

[384] Y.M. Zhao, J.M. Zhou, L.R. Wang, et al., HIWI is associated with prognosis in patients with hepatocellular carcinoma after curative resection, Cancer 118 (10) (2012) 2708–2717, https://doi.org/10.1002/cncr.26524. PMID:21989785.

[385] C. Su, Z.J. Ren, F. Wang, et al., PIWIL4 regulates cervical cancer cell line growth and is involved in down-regulating the expression of p14ARF and p53, FEBS Lett. 586 (9) (2012) 1356–1362, https://doi.org/10.1016/j.febslet.2012.03.053.

[386] J.A. Erwin, M.C. Marchetto, F.H. Gage, Mobile DNA elements in the generation of diversity and complexity in the brain, Nat. Rev. Neurosci. 15 (8) (2014) 497–506, https://doi.org/10.1038/nrn3730. Epub 2014 Jul 9.

Further reading

A. Dharap, V.P. Nakka, R. Vemuganti, Altered expression of PIWI RNA in the rat brain after transient focal ischemia, Stroke 42 (4) (2011) 1105–1109, https://doi.org/10.1161/STROKEAHA.110.598391.

J.E. Freedman, M. Gerstein, E. Mick, et al., Diverse human extracellular RNAs are widely detected in human plasma, Nat. Commun. 7 (2016) 1–14, https://doi.org/10.1038/ncomms11106.

D. Gebert, R.F. Ketting, H. Zischler, D. Rosenkranz, piRNAs from Pig testis provide evidence for a conserved role of the Piwi pathway in post-transcriptional gene regulation in mammals, PLoS One 10 (5) (2015) 1–22, https://doi.org/10.1371/journal.pone.0124860.

S. Huang, Y. Ichikawa, K. Yoshitake, S. Kinoshita, et al., Conserved and widespread expression of piRNA-like molecules and PIWI-like genes reveal dual functions of transposon silencing and gene regulation in Pinctada fucata (Mollusca), Front. Mar. Sci. 8 (2019) 1–15, https://doi.org/10.3389/fmars.2021.730556.

X. Huang, G. Wong, An old weapon with a new function: PIWI-interacting RNAs in neurodegenerative diseases, Transl. Neurodegener. 10 (1) (2021) 1–21, https://doi.org/10.1186/s40035-021-00233-6.

C.E. Juliano, A. Reich, N. Liu, et al., PIWI proteins and PIWI-interacting RNAs function in Hydra somatic stem cells, Proc. Natl. Acad. Sci. U. S. A. 111 (1) (2014) 337–342, https://doi.org/10.1073/pnas.1320965111.

C. Kim, C.M. Rubin, C.W. Schmid, Genome-wide chromatin remodeling modulates the Alu heat shock response, Gene 276 (1–2) (2001) 127–133, https://doi.org/10.1016/s0378-1119(01)00639-4.

M.A. Li, J.D. Alls, R.M. Avancini, K. Koo, D. Godt, The large Maf factor Traffic Jam controls gonad morphogenesis in Drosophila, Nat. Cell Biol. 5 (11) (2003) 994–1000, https://doi.org/10.1038/ncb1058.

F.J. Livesey, C.L. Cepko, Vertebrate neural cell-fate determination: lessons from the retina, Nat. Rev. Neurosci. 2 (2) (2001) 109–118, https://doi.org/10.1038/35053522.

S.R. Mani, H. Megosh, H. Lin, PIWI proteins are essential for early Drosophila embryogenesis, Dev. Biol. 385 (2) (2014) 340–349, https://doi.org/10.1016/j.ydbio.2013.10.017.

A. Qu, W. Wang, Y. Yang, et al., A serum piRNA signature as promising non-invasive diagnostic and prognostic biomarkers for colorectal cancer, Cancer Manag. Res. 11 (2019) 3703–3720, https://doi.org/10.2147/CMAR.S193266.

Z.G. Venkei, C.P. Choi, S. Feng, et al., A kinesin Klp10A mediates cell cycle-dependent shuttling of Piwi between nucleus and nuage [published correction appears in PLoS Genet. 2020;16(10):e1009147], PLoS Genet. 16 (3) (2020) 1–26, https://doi.org/10.1371/journal.pgen.1008648.

Y. Wang, Y. Liu, X. Shen, et al., The PIWI protein acts as a predictive marker for human gastric cancer, Int. J. Clin. Exp. Pathol. 5 (4) (2012) 315–325. https://pubmed.ncbi.nlm.nih.gov/22670175/.

Z. Williams, P. Morozov, A. Mihailovic, S. Juranek, et al., Discovery and characterization of piRNAs in the human fetal ovary, Cell Rep. 13 (2015) 854–863, https://doi.org/10.1016/j.celrep.2015.09.030.

CHAPTER 19

Emerging role of biosimilars: Focus on Bevacizumab and hepatocellular carcinoma

Anum Jalil[a], James Wert[b], Akriti Gupta Jain[c], and Sarfraz Ahmad[d]
[a]Department of Hospital Medicine, PeaceHealth Southwest Medical Center, Vancouver, WA, United States
[b]Department of Hematology-Oncology, University of Mississippi Medical Center, Jackson, MS, United States
[c]Department of Hematology-Oncology, H. Lee Moffitt Cancer Center and Research Institute, Tampa, FL, United States
[d]AdventHealth Cancer Institute, FSU and UCF Colleges of Medicine, Orlando, FL, United States

Abstract

Biosimilar is an emerging class of medications, that is, similar in safety and efficacy to the original reference product but is a better cost alternative to biologics. In this chapter, we explore the role of biosimilars with special focus on antineoplastic agent Bevacizumab (Avastin) and hepatocellular carcinoma (HCC), which is among the leading causes of cancer-related mortality in the world. Mvasi was the first ever approved biosimilar to Bevacizumab as well as the first biosimilar approved in the United States for the treatment of certain cancers, including colorectal, lung, brain, kidney, and cervical cancers. Increasing attention is being directed toward the development of biosimilars given the economic strain on healthcare systems caused by cancer management and it is imperative that clinicians familiarize themselves with the role of biosimilars. A critical appraisal of the Food and Drug Administration-approved biosimilars, their mechanism(s) of action, indications, usage, and clinical trials with special focus on Bevacizumab and HCC are succinctly covered in this chapter.

Abbreviations

BPCIA	biologics price competition and innovation act
CD	cluster differentiation
CKD	chronic kidney disease
EMA	European Medicines Agency
ERK	extracellular signal-regulated kinase
EU	European Union
FDA	Food and Drug Administration
GCSF	granulocyte colony stimulating factor
GSF	granulocyte stimulating factor
HCC	hepatocellular carcinoma
HER2	human epidermal growth factor receptor 2
IQVIA	I (IMS health), Q (quintiles), and VIA (by way of)
LGF	leukocyte growth factor
MAPK	mitogen-activated protein kinase
NHL	non-Hodgkin's lymphoma
Non-sq-NSCLC	non-squamous non-small-cell lung cancer

Computational Methods in Drug Discovery and Repurposing for Cancer Therapy
https://doi.org/10.1016/B978-0-443-15280-1.00003-0

NSCLC	non-small-cell lung cancer
OS	overall survival
PD1	programmed cell death protein 1
PD-L1	programmed death-ligand 1
PFS	progression-free survival
RAF	rapidly accelerated fibrosarcoma
TNF	tumor necrosis factor
UC	ulcerative colitis
VEGF	vascular endothelial growth factor
VEGFR	vascular endothelial growth factor receptor

1. Introduction

Cancer care and treatment put a significant burden on the US healthcare system. According to a report published in May 2020 by IQVIA Institute, the US expenditure on cancer is expected to increase by 11%–14% over the coming 5 years [1]. Biosimilars can play a substantial role in somewhat combating this immense financial and economic burden, especially considering the fact that drug patents for many biologics will expire in the upcoming years. The availability and use of biosimilars are growing day-by-day and can reduce the costs of drugs by US $100 billion over the next 5 years according to a new report from the IQVIA Institute for Human Data Science [2]. The biosimilar development is expanding at a rapid pace over the past few years, and it is of paramount importance that clinicians (especially oncologists and related healthcare professionals) make themselves familiar with these drugs to decrease the myths, negative concepts, and general doubts associated with them [1,2]. Cook et al. [3] reported that 74% of oncology clinicians including physicians, pharmacists, and advance practice providers could not tell the basic definition of biosimilars, which is an alarming fact. This further emphasizes the growing need for physicians to familiarize themselves with this emerging class of medications [3].

2. Biologics and biosimilars

Biologics have become the corner stone of cancer management. Significant financial issues are arising due to their high cost and healthcare systems are bearing the brunt of it. One of the aims behind the development of biosimilars is to aid the healthcare system with respect to cost savings (as noted above) [4]. Biosimilars are very similar to biologics; but not the same as generic, originating, or reference drug [5]. Strict regulations are required for the approval of biosimilars. The regulatory infrastructure for biosimilar approval was established in Europe in 2003, and several years later, in March 2010, the US Congress passed the Biologics Price Competition and Innovation Act of 2009 (BPCIA), which was the first authorization in the United States of an approval pathway for biosimilars [6]. The definition criteria of biosimilar mentioned in the

BPCIA must be satisfied before an approval can be granted by the Food and Drug Administration (FDA). As mentioned in the statue: "a biosimilar is highly similar to the reference product (notwithstanding minor differences in clinically inactive components) and has no clinically meaningful differences in safety, purity, and potency from the reference product" [6,7].

Although biosimilar has structural and complexity differences with the reference biologic drug, it should not have clinically significant difference in the safety and efficacy outcomes. Thus, in any patient a biosimilar is expected to have the same clinical outcomes as the generic biologic product [8]. The European Medicines Agency definition provides further insights and states: "a biosimilar demonstrates similarity to the [originator] in terms of quality characteristics, biological activity, safety, and efficacy based on a comprehensive comparability exercise" [9].

3. FDA approved biosimilars to date

The first biosimilar drug was approved in 2015 by the name of Zarxiom (filgrastim-sndz), a biosimilar to the granulocyte stimulating factor, filgrastim [10]. After that, more than 30 biosimilars have been approved by the FDA, including biosimilars to important oncology drugs like Bevacizumab, transtuzumab, and rituximab, etc. (Table 1). The first ever approved biosimilar to Bevacizumab (Avastin) was Mvasi (Bevacizumab-awwb). Mvasi was the first biosimilar approved in the United States for the treatment of certain cancers, including colorectal, lung, brain, kidney, and cervical cancers [12,13].

4. Role of Bevacizumab and its biosimilar in hepatocellular carcinoma

Bevacizumab is a monoclonal antibody that works by targeting vascular endothelial growth factor (VEGF), thus inhibiting angiogenesis. Angiogenesis is a crucial step in tumorigenesis and plays central roles in the survival of many kinds of tumor cells. Similar case is seen in hepatocellular carcinoma (HCC). Hypoxia inside tumor environment stimulates new vessel formation, to sustain and propagate the tumor. It acts via upregulation of hypoxia-inducible factor proteins that leads to overexpression of VEGF, ultimately leading to angiogenesis in HCC tumor cells [14,15]. In addition to Bevacizumab, many of the other approved treatments for liver cancer also act through the angiogenesis pathways, including the first-line drug Sorafenib and Lenvainib (as shown in Fig. 1). With the approval of Alymsys in April 2022, a total of three biosimilars to Bevacizumab have been approved by the FDA to date (as also mentioned in Table 1; the other two being bevacizumab-bvzr [Zirabev, Pfizer] approved in 2019 and bevacizumab-awwb [Mvasi, Amgen] approved in 2017). It is imperative that more

Table 1 A summary list of the FDA-approved biosimilars in the United States to date with their mechanism(s) of action, indications, and usage [11].

Biosimilar	Reference drug	Mechanism(s) of action	Indications and usage	Date of FDA approval
Pegfilgrastim-pbbk (Fylnetra)	Pegfilgrastim (Neulasta)	Leukocyte growth factor (LGF)	To decrease infection, as manifested by febrile neutropenia, in patients with nonmyeloid malignancies receiving myelosuppressive anticancer drugs	May 2022
Bevacizumab-maly (Alymsys)	Bevacizumab (Avastin)	Vascular endothelial growth factor (VEGF) inhibitor	Metastatic colorectal cancer, in combination with ifluorouracil-based chemotherapy or with fluoropyrimidineirinotecan- or fluoropyrimidine-oxaliplatin-based chemotherapy	April 2022
Filgrastim-ayow (Releuko)	Filgrastim (Neupogen)	LGF	To decrease infection, as manifested by febrile neutropenia, in patients with nonmyeloid malignancies receiving myelosuppressive anticancer drugs	February 2022
Adalimumab-aqvh (Yusimry)	Adalimumab (Humira)	Tumor necrosis factor (TNF) blocker	Rheumatoid Arthritis, Juvenile Idiopathic Arthritis, Psoriatic Arthritis, Ankylosing Spondylitis, Crohn's disease, Ulcerative colitis (UC)	December 2021
Insulin glargine-aglr (Rezvoglar)	Lantus (Insulin glargine)	Long-acting human insulin analog	Type 1 and Type 2 Diabetes Mellitus	December 2021
Ranibizumab-nuna (Byooviz)	Ranibizumab (Lucentis)	VEGF inhibitor	Age-related Macular Degeneration, Macular Edema Following Retinal Vein Occlusion, Myopic Choroidal Neovascularization	September 2021
Insulin glargine-yfgn (Semglee)	Lantus (Insulin glargine)	Long-acting human insulin analog	Type 1 and Type 2 Diabetes Mellitus	July 2021

Rituximab-arrx (Riabni)	Rituximab (Rituxan)	CD20-directed cytolytic antibody	Non-Hodgkin's Lymphoma, Chronic Lymphocytic Leukemia, Granulomatosis with Polyangiitis and Microscopic Polyangiitis	December 2020
Adalimumab-fkjp (Hulio)	Adalimumab (Humira)	TNF blocker	Rheumatoid Arthritis, Juvenile Idiopathic Arthritis, Psoriatic Arthritis, Ankylosing Spondylitis	July 2020
Pegfilgrastim-apgf (Nyvepria)	Pegfilgrastim (Neulasta)	LGF	To decrease infection, as manifested by febrile neutropenia, in patients with nonmyeloid malignancies receiving myelosuppressive anticancer drugs	June 2020
Infliximab-axxq (Avsola)	Infliximab (Remicade)	TNF blocker	Crohn's Disease, Ulcerative Colitis, Rheumatoid Arthritis in combination with methotrexate	December 2019
Adalimumab-afzb (Abrilada)	Adalimumab (Humira)	TNF blocker	Rheumatoid Arthritis, Juvenile Idiopathic Arthritis, Psoriatic Arthritis, Ankylosing Spondylitis	November 2019
Pegfilgrastim-bmez (Ziextenzo)	Pegfilgrastim (Neulasta)	LGF	To decrease infection, as manifested by febrile neutropenia, in patients with nonmyeloid malignancies receiving myelosuppressive anticancer drugs	November 2019
Adalimumab-bwwd (Hadlima)	Adalimumab (Hamira)	TNF blocker	Rheumatoid Arthritis, Juvenile Idiopathic Arthritis, Psoriatic Arthritis, Ankylosing Spondylitis	July 2019
Rituximab-pvvr (Ruxience)	Rituximab (Rituxan)	Cluster differentiation (CD) 20-directed cytolytic antibody	Non-Hodgkin's Lymphoma, Chronic Lymphocytic Leukemia, Granulomatosis with Polyangiitis and Microscopic Polyangiitis	July 2019
Bevacizumab-bvzr (Zirabev)	Bevacizumab (Avastin)	VEGF inhibitor	Metastatic colorectal cancer, in combination with ifluorouracil-based chemotherapy or with fluoropyrimidineirinotecan- or fluoropyrimidine-oxaliplatin-based chemotherapy	June 2019

Continued

Table 1 A summary list of the FDA-approved biosimilars in the United States to date with their mechanism(s) of action, indications, and usage —cont'd

Biosimilar	Reference drug	Mechanism(s) of action	Indications and usage	Date of FDA approval
Trastuzumab-anns (Kanjinti)	Trastuzumab (Herceptin)	Human epidermal growth factor receptor 2 (HER2)/ neu receptor antagonist	HER2 overexpressing breast cancer, HER2 overexpressing metastatic gastric or gastroesophageal junction adenocarcinoma	June 2019
Etanercept-ykro (Eticovo)	Etanercept (Enbrel)	TNF blocker	Rheumatoid Arthritis, Polyarticular Juvenile Idiopathic Arthritis, Psoriatic Arthritis, Ankylosing Spondylitis, Plaque Psoriasis	April 2019
Trastuzumab-qyyp (Trazimera)	Trastuzumab (Herceptin)	HER2/neu receptor antagonist	HER2 overexpressing breast cancer, HER2 overexpressing metastatic gastric or gastroesophageal junction adenocarcinoma.	March 2019
Trastuzumab-dttb (Ontruzant)	Trastuzumab (Herceptin)	HER2/neu receptor antagonist	HER2 overexpressing breast cancer, HER2 overexpressing metastatic gastric or gastroesophageal junction adenocarcinoma	January 2019
Trastuzumab-pkrb (Herzuma)	Trastuzumab (Herceptin)	HER2/neu receptor antagonist	HER2 overexpressing breast cancer, HER2 overexpressing metastatic gastric or gastroesophageal junction adenocarcinoma.	December 2018
Rituximab-abbs (Truxima)	Rituximab (Rituxan)	CD20-directed cytolytic antibody	Adult patients with CD20-positive, B-cell non-Hodgkin's lymphoma (NHL)	November 2018
Pegfilgrastim-cbqv (Udenyca)	Pegfilgrastim (Neulasta)	LGF	To decrease infection, as manifested by febrile neutropenia, in patients with nonmyeloid malignancies receiving myelosuppressive anticancer drugs	November 2018
Adalimumab-adaz (Hyrimoz)	Adalimumab (Humira)	TNF blocker	Rheumatoid Arthritis, Juvenile Idiopathic Arthritis, Psoriatic Arthritis, Ankylosing Spondylitis	October 2018
Filgrastin-aafi (Nivestym)	Filgrastin (Neupogen)	LGF	To decrease infection, as manifested by febrile neutropenia, in patients with nonmyeloid malignancies receiving myelosuppressive anticancer drugs	July 2018
Pegfilgrastim-jmdb (Fulphilia)	Pegfilgrastim (Neulasta)	LGF	To decrease infection, as manifested by febrile neutropenia, in patients with nonmyeloid malignancies receiving myelosuppressive anticancer drugs	June 2018

Epoetin Alfa-epbx (Retacrit)	Epoetin Alfa (Epogen/ Procrit)	Erythropoietin	Anemia, Chronic Kidney Disease (CKD)	May 2018
Infliximab-qbtx Ixifi	Infliximab (Remicade)	TNF blocker	Crohn's Disease, UC, Rheumatoid Arthritis in combination with methotrexate	December 2017
Transtuzumab-dkst (Ogivri)	Transtuzumab (Herceptin)	HER2/neu receptor antagonist	HER2 overexpressing breast cancer, HER2 overexpressing metastatic gastric or gastroesophageal junction adenocarcinoma	December 2017
Bevacizumab-awwb (Mvasi)	Bevacizumab (Avastin)	VEGF inhibitor	Metastatic colorectal cancer, in combination with ifluorouracil-based chemotherapy or with fluoropyrimidineirinotecan- or fluoropyrimidine-oxaliplatin-based chemotherapy	September 2017
Adalimumab-adbm (Cyltezo)	Adalimumab (Humira)	TNF blocker	Rheumatoid Arthritis, Juvenile Idiopathic Arthritis, Psoriatic Arthritis, Ankylosing Spondylitis	August 2017
Infliximab-abda (Renflexis)	Infliximab (Remicade)	TNF blocker	Crohn's Disease, UC, Rheumatoid Arthritis in combination with methotrexate	May 2017
Adalimumab-atto (Amjevita)	Adalimumab (Humira)	TNF-α inhibitor	Rheumatoid Arthritis, Juvenile Idiopathic Arthritis, Psoriatic Arthritis, Ankylosing Spondylitis	September 2016
Etanercept-szzs (Erelzi)	Etanercept (Enbrel)	TNF-α inhibitor	Rheumatoid Arthritis, Polyarticular Juvenile Idiopathic Arthritis, Psoriatic Arthritis, Ankylosing Spondylitis, Plaque Psoriasis	August 2016
Infliximab-dyyb (Inflectra)	Infliximab (Remicade)	TNF-α inhibitor	Crohn's Disease, UC, Rheumatoid Arthritis in combination with methotrexate	April 2016
Filgrastim-sndz1 (Zarxio)	Filgrastim (Neupogen/ Amgen)	Granulocyte colony stimulating Factor	To decrease infection, as manifested by febrile neutropenia, in patients with nonmyeloid malignancies receiving myelosuppressive anticancer drugs	March 2015

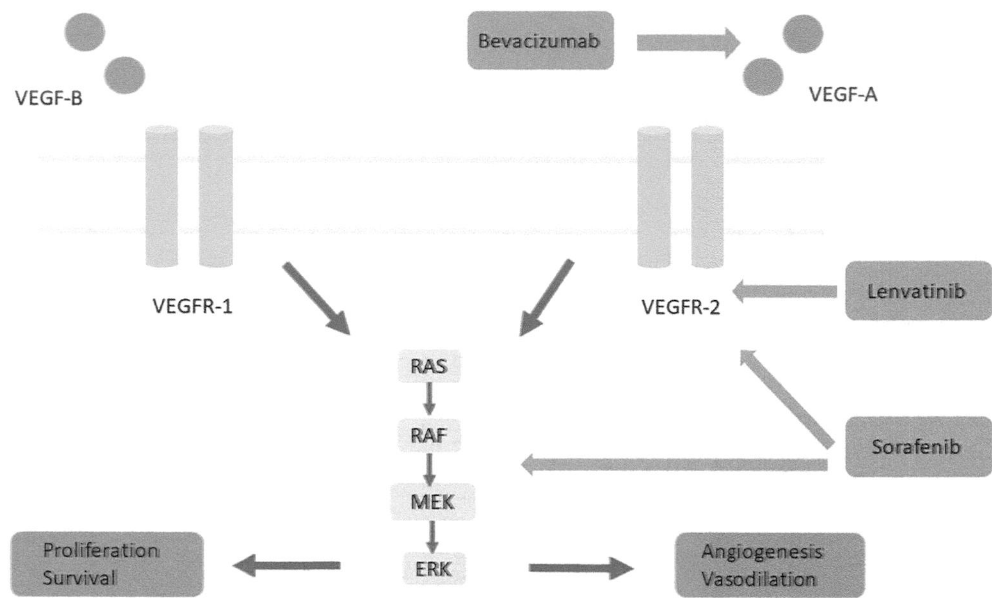

Fig. 1 Schematic representation of the angiogenesis pathways of Bevacizumab and its biologicals in HCC. Bevacizumab inhibits VEGF binding to VEGFR, ultimately leads to inhibition of the MAPK/ERK pathway (also known as the Ras-Raf-MEK-ERK pathway), thus inhibiting angiogenesis in tumor cells. Sorafenob and Lenvatinib inhibit VEGFR and downstream signaling pathways to inhibit tumor angiogenesis. Abbreviations: *VEGF*, vascular endothelial growth factor; *VEGFR*, vascular endothelial growth factor receptor; *MAPK*, mitogen-activated protein kinase; *ERK*, extracellular signal-regulated kinase; *RAF*, rapidly accelerated fibrosarcoma; *MEK*, mitogen-activated protein kinase.

biosimilar options are developed to provide better cost alternative options for Bevacizumab given the importance of combination therapy with Bevacizumab in advanced HCC as mentioned in Fig. 1.

5. Clinical trials with Bevacizumab and its biosimilar in HCC

In Table 2, we summarize some of the key and most recent clinical trials on Bevacizumab biosimilars for HCC. As examples, a few clinical trials are described with more specifics below.

5.1 Atezolizumab plus Bevacizumab in unresectable HCC

Clinical trial IMBrave 150 (NCT03434379) compared combination therapy with Bevacizumab and Atezolizumab (anti-PD-L1 monoclonal antibody) to Sorafenib monotherapy for patients with unresectable HCC, and results demonstrated better overall survival (S) as well as progression-free survival (PFS) with combination therapy [43]. On May 29,

Table 2 A summary of key recent clinical trials with various biosimilars for Bevacizumab [2016–present].

Biosimilar	Clinical trial/study	Description, results, outcomes	Reference
FKB238	Randomized, double-blind, parallel-group study	Study showed pharmacokinetic similarity of FKB238 to both US-sourced and EU-sourced Bevacizumab	Boyce et al. [16]
BCD-021	International multicenter phase III clinical trial	Results showed therapeutic equivalence of BCD-021 with original Bevacizumab	Stroyakovskiy et al. [17]
MIL60	Phase III randomized, double-blind study	Similar efficacy, safety, and immunogenicity for advanced or recurrent non-squamous non-small-cell lung cancer (NSCLC)	Wan et al. [18]
MYL-1402O	Phase III double-blind study	Found to be therapeutically equivalent for patients with stage IV NSCLC	Socinski et al. [19]
BI 695502	Phase III, multicenter, randomized, double-blind trial	Equivalent overall response rate and similar efficacy, safety, pharmacokinetics after 18 weeks treatment with either BI 695502 or Bevacizumab in patients of advanced non-squamous NSCLC	Kim et al. [20]
HD204	Randomized phase I study to evaluate pharmacokinetic equivalence	Results showed pharmacokinetic equivalence compared with both US-sourced and EU-sourced Bevacizumab	Demarchi et al. [21]
MB02	Phase I, randomized, double-blind, single-dose, parallel-group study	Study showed pharmacokinetic similarity to both US-sourced and EU-sourced Bevacizumab	Sinn et al. [22]

Continued

Table 2 A summary of key recent clinical trials with various biosimilars for Bevacizumab [2016–present]—cont'd

Biosimilar	Clinical trial/study	Description, results, outcomes	Reference
GB222	Randomized, double-blind, single-dose, parallel-group clinical trial	Comparable results to Bevacizumab in terms of pharmacokinetics, safety, and immunogenicity for healthy Chinese males	Dong et al. [23]
FKB238	Multicenter, double-blind, parallel, randomized, comparative clinical trial	Results showed no meaningful differences in efficacy and safety between FKB238 or bevacizumab in patients of non-squamous-NSCLC	Syrigos et al. [24]
LY01008	Multicenter, randomized, double-blinded, phase III trial	Similarity in efficacy and safety in Chinese patients with advanced or recurrent non-squamous NSCLC	Shi et al. [25]
SB8	Randomized phase III, double-blind study	Results largely showed equivalence, trial done on patients with metastatic or recurrent non-squamous-NSCLC	Reck et al. [26]
BVZ-BC (bevacizumab-biosimilar candidate)	Analytical comparison	Proposed biosimilar to Bevacizumab, similar biochemical characteristics, biological activity, etc.	Yu et al. [27]
QL1101	Randomized, double-blind, single-dose study in healthy male subjects	Demonstrated pharmacokinetic equivalence to Avastin	Liu et al. [28]
PF-06439535	Multinational, double-blind, randomized, parallel-group phase III clinical trial	For advanced non-squamous-NSCLC, similar efficacy, comparable safety profile of PF-06439535 and bevacizumab-EU, both combined with paclitaxel and carboplatin	Reinmuth et al. [29]
IBI305	Randomized, double-blind, multicenter, phase III clinical trial	Similar efficacy and safety of IBI305 vs. Bevacizumab plus paclitaxel/carboplatin for the treatment of locally advanced, metastatic or recurrent non-squamous-NSCLC	Yang et al. [30]

Table 2 A summary of key recent clinical trials with various biosimilars for Bevacizumab [2016–present]—cont'd

Biosimilar	Clinical trial/study	Description, results, outcomes	Reference
TAB008	Phase I, randomized, double-blind, parallel controlled study in 100 healthy Chinese male subjects	Pharmacokinetic similarity to Bevacizumab, safe, well tolerated	Wang et al. [31]
ABP 215	Randomized, double-blind, phase III study	Similar clinical efficacy and safety in advanced non-squamous-NSCLC	Thatcher et al. [32]
BAT1706	Randomized, double-blinded, phase I clinical trial in 128 healthy adult male subjects	Comparable pharmacokinetics and safety, immunogenicity	Wu et al. [33]
CT-P16	Randomized, double-blind, parallel-group phase I trial in 144 healthy adult males were randomized	Comparable pharmacokinetics and safety, immunogenicity	Cho et al. [34]
BEVZ92	Multicenter, open-label, randomized controlled trial	Pharmacokinetically bioequivalent, no appreciable differences in efficacy, immunogenicity, and safety profiles as first-line treatment in combination with FOLFOX or FOLFIRI in patients with metastatic colorectal cancer	Romera et al. [35]
PF-06439535	Non-clinical assessment, structural/functional assays, peptide mapping, cell growth assay, in vivo studies for monkey/rat toxicity, etc.	Proposed biosimilar to Bevacizumab. Nonclinical assessment. Similar structure, function but limited in vivo value in studies on rats/ monkeys	Peraza et al. [36]
Hetero-Bevacizumab	Prospective, randomized, multiple-dose, multicenter, comparative clinical study	Along with chemotherapy (XELOX or FOLFOX-4) regimen, comparable efficacy to reference Bevacizumab in Indian patients with metastatic colorectal cancer	Advani et al. [37]

Continued

Table 2 A summary of key recent clinical trials with various biosimilars for Bevacizumab [2016–present]—cont'd

Biosimilar	Clinical trial/study	Description, results, outcomes	Reference
DRL_BZ	Randomized, double-blind, parallel-group, phase I trial in 149 healthy adult male subjects	Comparable pharmacokinetics and safety, immunogenicity	Wynne et al. [38]
CT-P16	Double-blind, randomized, active-controlled, parallel-group, phase III clinical trial by Celltrion	To compare efficacy and safety of CT-P16 and EU-approved Avastin as first-line treatment for metastatic or recurrent non-squamous NSCLC (ongoing)	NCT03676192 [39]
BI 695502	Randomized, single-blind, phase I trial (INVICTAN-1) in healthy male subjects	Bioequivalence, similar safety profile.	Hettema et al. [40]
	Multicenter, multinational, safety and efficacy phase IIIb trial (INVICTAN-3)	Trial of BI 695502 plus mFOLFOX6 in patients with previously untreated metastatic colorectal cancer to assess safety and efficacy (ongoing)	NCT02776683 [41]
PF-06439535	Phase I, double-blind, randomized, parallel-group, single-dose, three-arm study was conducted in one center in the United States	Similar pharmacokinetics and safety profile compared to Bevacizumab sourced from the European Union (bevacizumab-EU) and USA (bevacizumab-US)	Knight et al. [42]

2020, the combination of Bevacizumab and Atezolizumab was approved by the FDA for the treatment of patients with advanced HCC.

5.2 Sintilimab plus Bevacizumab biosimilar for advanced HCC

According to a phase III, randomized, open label study (ORIENT-32) by Ren et al. [44] conducted in China between February 11, 2019 and January 15, 2020, Sintilimab (a PD-1 inhibitor) in combination with Bevacizumab biosimilar (IBI305) showed significantly improved OS as well as PFS in patients with advanced HBV-associated HCC, when compared with Sorafenib [44].

6. Conclusions and future perspectives

Biosimilars provide a more cost-effective alternative to the biologics which are widely utilized for cancer care all over the world. Before approval is granted by the FDA (or related global agencies), the proposed biosimilar drug is tested rigorously and must meet standard safety and efficacy criteria. Efforts should be made to increase awareness and education among clinicians and other healthcare professionals regarding the appropriate use of biosimilars. Combination of Bevacizumab and Atezolizumab has now become the standard first-line therapy for patients with advanced hepatocellular cancer. To date, three biosimilars for Bevacizumab have been approved by the FDA. Given the vital importance of Bevacizumb in HCC as well as in the treatment of numerous other cancers, it is imperative that further clinical trials should be done to explore additional biosimilar options.

Funding

This research article did not receive any specific grant from funding agencies in the public, commercial, or not-for-profit sectors.

Authors' contribution

All authors made a significant contribution to the work reported, whether that is in the conception, study design, execution, acquisition of data, analysis and interpretation, or in all these areas; took part in drafting, revising, or critically reviewing the article; gave final approval of the version to be published; have agreed on the publisher to which the article has been submitted; and agree to be accountable for all aspects of the work.

References

[1] IQVIA, Biosimilars Reach Inflection Point - on Track to Reduce Drug Costs by $100 Bn over Next Five Years, 2020, October https://www.iqvia.com/newsroom/2020/10/iqvia-institute-for-human-data-science-study-biosimilars-reach-inflection-point- -on-track-to-reduce. (Accessed 4 September 2022).

[2] IQVIA, Oncology Landscape: More Demand, Demands More, 2020, May https://www.iqvia.com/locations/united-states/library/white-papers/oncology-landscape-more-demands. (Accessed 4 September 2022).

[3] J.W. Cook, M.K. McGrath, M.D. Dixon, J.M. Switchenko, R.D. Harvey, R.D. Pentz, Academic oncology clinicians' understanding of biosimilars, and information needed before prescribing, Ther. Adv. Med. Oncol. 11 (2019), 1758835918818335, https://doi.org/10.1177/1758835918818335.

[4] P. Cornes, The economic pressures for biosimilar drug use in cancer medicine, Target. Oncol. 7 (Suppl. 1) (2012) S57–S67, https://doi.org/10.1007/s11523-011-0196-3.

[5] S. Konstantinidou, A. Papaspiliou, E. Kokkotou, Current and future roles of biosimilars in oncology practice, Oncol. Lett. 19 (2020) 45–51.

[6] H. Koyfman, Biosimilarity and interchangeability in the biologics price competition and innovation act of 2009 and FDA's 2012 draft guidance for industry, Biotechnol. Law Rep. 32 (2013) 238–251, https://doi.org/10.1089/blr.2013.9884.

[7] P. Declerck, R. Danesi, D. Petersel, I. Jacobs, The language of biosimilars: clarification, definitions, and regulatory aspects, Drugs 77 (2017) 671–677, https://doi.org/10.1007/s40265-017-0717-1.

[8] A.D. Zelenetz, P.S. Becker, The role of biosimilars, J. Natl. Compr. Cancer Netw. 14 (5 Suppl) (2016) 626–629, https://doi.org/10.6004/jnccn.2016.0178.

[9] European Medicines Agency, Guidelines on Similar Biological Medicinal Products (CHMP/437/04 Rev 1), European Medicines Agency, London, 2014.

[10] The State of Cancer Care in America, 2016: a report by the American Society of Clinical Oncology, JCO Oncol. Pract. 12 (2016) 339–383.

[11] FDA, Research C for DE and Biosimilar Product Information, 2020. https://www.fda.gov/drugs/biosimilars/biosimilar-product-information. (Accessed 4 September 2022).

[12] M. Thomas, N. Thatcher, J. Goldschmidt, Y. Ohe, H.J. McBride, V. Hanes, Totality of evidence in the development of ABP 215, an approved bevacizumab biosimilar, Immunotherapy 11 (2019) 1337–1351, https://doi.org/10.2217/imt-2019-0125.

[13] FDA, Commissioner O of the FDA Approves First Biosimilar for the Treatment of Cancer, 2019. http://www.fda.gov/news-events/press-announcements/fda-approves-first-biosimilar-treatment-cancer. (Accessed 4 September 2022).

[14] S.R. McKeown, Defining normoxia, physoxia and hypoxia in tumors-implications for treatment response, Br. J. Radiol. 87 (2014) 20130676.

[15] M.A. Morse, W. Sun, R. Kim, et al., The role of angiogenesis in hepatocellular carcinoma, Clin. Cancer Res. 25 (2019) 912–920.

[16] M. Boyce, D. Wilkes, H. Kaito, M. Takanuma, Y. Arai, Pharmacokinetics, safety, tolerability, and immunogenicity of FKB238, a new biosimilar of bevacizumab, in healthy participants, Int. J. Clin. Pharmacol. Ther. 60 (2022) 280–290, https://doi.org/10.5414/CP204211.

[17] D.L. Stroyakovskiy, N.V. Fadeeva, M.P. Matrosova, et al., Randomized double-blind clinical trial comparing safety and efficacy of the biosimilar BCD-021 with reference bevacizumab, BMC Cancer 22 (2022) 129, https://doi.org/10.1186/s12885-022-09243-7.

[18] R. Wan, X. Dong, Q. Chen, et al., Efficacy and safety of MIL60 compared with bevacizumab in advanced or recurrent non-squamous non-small cell lung cancer: a phase 3 randomized, double-blind study, EClinicalMedicine 42 (2021), 101187, https://doi.org/10.1016/j.eclinm.2021.101187.

[19] M.A. Socinski, C.F. Waller, T. Idris, et al., Phase III double-blind study comparing the efficacy and safety of proposed biosimilar MYL-1402O and reference bevacizumab in stage IV non-small-cell lung cancer, Ther. Adv. Med. Oncol. 13 (2021), 17588359211045845, https://doi.org/10.1177/17588359211045845.

[20] E.S. Kim, S. Balser, K.B. Rohr, R. Lohmann, B. Liedert, D. Schliephake, Phase 3 trial of BI 695502 plus chemotherapy versus bevacizumab reference product plus chemotherapy in patients with advanced non-squamous NSCLC, JTO Clin. Res. Rep. 3 (2021), 100248, https://doi.org/10.1016/j.jtocrr.2021.100248.

[21] M. Demarchi, P. Coliat, P. Barthelemy, et al., A randomized phase I study comparing the pharmacokinetics of a bevacizumab (HD204) biosimilar to European Union- and United States of America-sourced bevacizumab, PLoS One 16 (2021), e0248222, https://doi.org/10.1371/journal.pone.0248222.

[22] A. Sinn, F. García-Alvarado, V. Gonzalez, C. Huerga, F. Bullo, A randomized, double-blind, single-dose, comparative study of the pharmacokinetics, safety and immunogenicity of MB02 (bevacizumab biosimilar) and reference bevacizumab in healthy male volunteers, Br. J. Clin. Pharmacol. 88 (2022) 1063–1073, https://doi.org/10.1111/bcp.15032.

[23] W. Dong, M. Chen, S. Niu, et al., Pharmacokinetic bioequivalence, safety, and immunogenicity of GB222, a bevacizumab biosimilar candidate, and bevacizumab in Chinese healthy males: a randomized clinical trial, Expert. Opin. Biol. Ther. 22 (2022) 253–262, https://doi.org/10.1080/14712598.2021.1954157.

[24] K. Syrigos, I. Abert, Z. Andric, AVANA Investigators, et al., Efficacy and safety of bevacizumab biosimilar FKB238 versus originator bevacizumab: results from AVANA, a phase III trial in patients with non-squamous non-small-cell lung cancer (non-sq-NSCLC), BioDrugs 35 (2021) 417–428, https://doi.org/10.1007/s40259-021-00489-4.

[25] Y. Shi, K. Lei, Y. Jia, et al., Bevacizumab biosimilar LY01008 compared with bevacizumab (Avastin) as first-line treatment for Chinese patients with unresectable, metastatic, or recurrent non-squamous non-small-cell lung cancer: a multicenter, randomized, double-blinded, phase III trial, Cancer Commun. (Lond.). 41 (2021) 889–903, https://doi.org/10.1002/cac2.12179.

[26] M. Reck, A. Luft, I. Bondarenko, et al., A phase III, randomized, double-blind, multicenter study to compare the efficacy, safety, pharmacokinetics, and immunogenicity between SB8 (proposed bevacizumab biosimilar) and reference bevacizumab in patients with metastatic or recurrent non-squamous non-small cell lung cancer, Lung Cancer 146 (2020) 12–18, https://doi.org/10.1016/j.lungcan.2020.05.027.

[27] C. Yu, F. Zhang, G. Xu, et al., Analytical similarity of a proposed biosimilar BVZ-BC to bevacizumab, Anal. Chem. 92 (2020) 3161–3170, https://doi.org/10.1021/acs.analchem.9b04871.

[28] Y.-N. Liu, J. Huang, C. Guo, et al., A randomized, double-blind, single-dose study to evaluate the biosimilarity of QL1101 with bevacizumab in healthy male subjects, Cancer Chemother. Pharmacol. 85 (2020) 555–562, https://doi.org/10.1007/s00280-019-04014-x.

[29] N. Reinmuth, M. Bryl, I. Bondarenko, et al., PF-06439535 (a bevacizumab biosimilar) compared with reference bevacizumab (Avastin®), both plus paclitaxel and carboplatin, as first-line treatment for advanced non-squamous non-small-cell lung cancer: a randomized, double-blind study, BioDrugs Clin. Immunother. Biopharm. Gene Ther. 33 (2019) 555–570, https://doi.org/10.1007/s40259-019-00363-4.

[30] Y. Yang, B. Wu, L. Huang, et al., Biosimilar candidate IBI305 plus paclitaxel/carboplatin for the treatment of non-squamous non-small cell lung cancer, Transl. Lung Cancer Res. 8 (2019) 989–999, https://doi.org/10.21037/tlcr.2019.12.23.

[31] J. Wang, L. Qi, L. Liu, et al., A phase I, randomized, single-dose study evaluating the biosimilarity of TAB008 to bevacizumab in healthy volunteers, Front. Pharmacol. 10 (2019) 905, https://doi.org/10.3389/fphar.2019.00905.

[32] N. Thatcher, J.H. Goldschmidt, M. Thomas, et al., Efficacy and safety of the biosimilar ABP 215 compared with bevacizumab in patients with advanced non-squamous non-small cell lung cancer (MAPLE): a randomized, double-blind, phase III study, Clin. Cancer Res. 25 (2019) 2088–2095, https://doi.org/10.1158/1078-0432.CCR-18-2702 (Erratum in: Clin. Cancer Res. 2019; 25: 3193. PMID: 30617139).

[33] X. Wu, C. Wynne, C. Xu, et al., A global phase I clinical study comparing the safety and pharmacokinetics of proposed biosimilar BAT1706 and bevacizumab (Avastin®) in healthy male subjects, BioDrugs Clin. Immunother. Biopharm. Gene Ther. 33 (2019) 335–342, https://doi.org/10.1007/s40259-019-00352-7.

[34] S.-H. Cho, S. Han, J.-L. Ghim, et al., A randomized, double-blind trial comparing the pharmacokinetics of CT-P16, a candidate bevacizumab biosimilar, with its reference product in healthy adult males, BioDrugs 33 (2019) 173–181, https://doi.org/10.1007/s40259-019-00340-x.

[35] A. Romera, S. Peredpaya, Y. Shparyk, et al., Bevacizumab biosimilar BEVZ92 versus reference bevacizumab in combination with FOLFOX or FOLFIRI as first-line treatment for metastatic colorectal cancer: a multi-center, open-label, randomized controlled trial, Lancet Gastroenterol. Hepatol. 3 (2018) 845–855, https://doi.org/10.1016/S2468-1253(18)30269-3.

[36] M.A. Peraza, K.E. Rule, M.H.I. Shiue, et al., Nonclinical assessments of the potential biosimilar PF-06439535 and bevacizumab, Regul. Toxicol. Pharmacol. 95 (2018) 236–243, https://doi.org/10.1016/j.yrtph.2018.03.020.

[37] S. Advani, G. Biswas, S. Sinha, et al., A prospective, randomized, multiple-dose, multi-center, comparative clinical study to evaluate the efficacy, safety, immunogenicity of a biosimilar bevacizumab (test product, hetero) and reference medicinal product (bevacizumab, Roche) in patients of metastatic colorectal cancer, J. Assoc. Physicians India 66 (2018) 55–59.

[38] C. Wynne, C. Schwabe, S.S. Batra, L. Lopez-Lazaro, S. Kankanwadi, A comparative pharmacokinetic study of DRL_BZ, a candidate biosimilar of bevacizumab, with Avastin® (EU and US) in healthy male subjects, Br. J. Clin. Pharmacol. 84 (2018) 2352–2364, https://doi.org/10.1111/bcp.13691.

[39] ClinicalTrials.gov, To compare efficacy and safety of CT-P16 and EU-approved Avastin as first-line treatment for metastatic or recurrent non-squamous non-small cell lung cancer. https://clinicaltrials.gov/ct2/show/NCT03676192. (Accessed 4 September 2022).
[40] W. Hettema, C. Wynne, B. Lang, et al., A randomized, single-blind, phase I trial (INVICTAN-1) assessing the bioequivalence and safety of BI 695502, a bevacizumab biosimilar candidate, in healthy subjects, Expert Opin. Investig. Drugs 26 (2017) 889–896, https://doi.org/10.1080/13543784.2017.1347635.
[41] ClinicalTrials.gov, Open-label, single arm trial of BI 695502 in patients with previously untreated metastatic colorectal cancer. https://clinicaltrials.gov/ct2/show/NCT02776683. (Accessed 4 September 2022).
[42] B. Knight, D. Rassam, S. Liao, R. Ewesuedo, A phase I pharmacokinetics study comparing PF-06439535 (a potential biosimilar) with bevacizumab in healthy male volunteers, Cancer Chemother. Pharmacol. 77 (2016) 839–846, https://doi.org/10.1007/s00280-016-3001-2.
[43] R.S. Finn, S. Qin, M. Ikeda, et al., Atezolizumab plus bevacizumab in unresectable hepatocellular carcinoma, N. Engl. J. Med. 382 (2020) 1894–1905, https://doi.org/10.1056/NEJMoa1915745.
[44] Z. Ren, J. Fan, J. Xu, et al., Sintilimab plus bevacizumab biosimilar vs sorafenib as first-line treatment for advanced hepatocellular carcinoma (ORIENT-32)2, Ann. Oncol. 31 (Suppl_6) (2020) S1287–S1318, https://doi.org/10.1016/annonc/annonc356.

CHAPTER 20

Integrated computational approaches to aid precision medicine for cancer therapy: Present scenario and future prospects

Hithesh Kumar[a,b], Sravan Kumar Miryala[a,b], Anand Anbarasu[a,c], and Sudha Ramaiah[a,b]
[a]Medical and Biological Computing Laboratory, School of Biosciences and Technology, Vellore Institute of Technology, Vellore, Tamil Nadu, India
[b]Department of Bio-Sciences, School of Biosciences and Technology, Vellore Institute of Technology, Vellore, Tamil Nadu, India
[c]Department of Biotechnology, School of Biosciences and Technology, Vellore Institute of Technology, Vellore, Tamil Nadu, India

Abstract

Cancer is a heterogeneous disease that involves uncontrolled growth of cells leading to the formation of tumor. It is the second most predominant disease causing highest number of deaths globally. Majority of cancer cases are due to the changes in environmental factors such as dietary, exposure to chemicals and pollution, while the remaining cases are due to the alterations in the genetic makeup. The current treatment strategies available against cancer include surgery, chemotherapy, and radiation therapy. The major drawback of these approaches is the severe side effects resulting from its nonspecific nature. In addition, the cells also acquire resistance against chemotherapy and radiotherapy, making it necessary to improve the existing cancer therapies. A major breakthrough in cancer treatment is the application of targeted therapy (precision therapy/personalized therapy), which deals with small molecules that can directly act on specific drug targets based on the genomic and metabolic profile of individuals. Despite the advantages of targeted therapy, there are constraints in terms of time, economy and accuracy. The huge pool of genomic, transcriptomic, and expression data along with the relevant clinical profiles requires ardent modes for efficient consolidation. Integrated computational pipelines and bioinformatics approaches can address these aspects to escalate clinical translation of precision medicine. This chapter summarizes the current scenario and future perspectives of precision medicine under the lens of computational biology thereby addressing the drawbacks and solutions.

Abbreviations

BCR-ABL	breakpoint cluster region protein—tyrosine-protein kinase ABL
BRCA	BReast CAncer gene
CHIP	chromatin immunoprecipitation
CpG	5′—C—phosphate—G—3′
CTLA4	cytotoxic T-lymphocyte associated protein 4
DNA	deoxyribonucleic acid

Computational Methods in Drug Discovery and Repurposing for Cancer Therapy
https://doi.org/10.1016/B978-0-443-15280-1.00008-X

EGFR	epidermal growth factor receptor
ENCODE	Encyclopedia of DNA Elements
HER2/EBBR2	human epidermal growth factor receptor 2/Erb-B2 receptor tyrosine kinase 2
HGP	Human Genome Project
INDELS	insertions or deletions
INSDC	International Nucleotide Sequence Database Collaboration
NGS	next generation sequencing
NIH	National Institute of Health
PCM	precision cancer medicine
PD-1/PD-L1	programmed death-1/programmed cell death ligand 1
PM	personalized medicine
SNPs	single nucleotide polymorphism
SRSF2	serine and arginine rich splicing factor 2
SVs	structural variations

1. Introduction

World Health Organization reported cancer to be the second leading cause of deaths worldwide, with an estimated 19.3 million new cases and ~10 million deaths in 2020. Among the cancer cases registered, breast cancer is the most reported cancer while lung cancer causes the highest global mortality. The Asian continent has been reporting around half of the global cancer cases [1].

Cancer is a very complex and heterogeneous disease which follows a set of hallmarks for their proliferation inside the body. Generally, there are more than 200 different types and subtypes of cancer present based on the site of tumor occurrence such as carcinoma for epithelial cells, sarcoma for connective tissue, leukemia for blood cancer, lymphoma for lymphocytes, and melanoma for skin cancer [2]. The most common cancers found in men are lung, prostate, colorectal, stomach, and liver cancers, while breast, colorectal, lung, cervical, and thyroid cancers are commonly found in women [3].

The major two classes of genes in cancer are oncogenes and tumor-suppressor genes which on activation and inhibition, respectively, will lead to the uncontrolled proliferation of cells. These specific genes are responsible for cell division, apoptosis, and cell death which upon alteration due to any kind of mutation such as deletion, insertion, or translocation may result in deregulated genetic makeup [4]. Tumor cells follow certain adaptive measures which help them in surviving as well as proliferating in the body. The hallmarks include resisting cell death, replicative immortality, invasion and metastasis, evading growth suppressors, sustaining proliferative signaling, inducing angiogenesis, metabolic reprogramming, and evading immune cell destruction [5,6]. It should also be noted that these hallmarks vary and not all tumor cells follow the same patterns for tumor growth. This heterogenous nature leads to the failure of nonspecific therapeutics which causes cancer to relapse. Nonspecific treatment for most cancer types also results in deterioration of the patient's overall health. Furthermore, the mutations in regulatory genes leading to cancer evoke cancer cells to continuously proliferate even in the presence of antitumor agents. These secondary mutations apart from oncogenic mutations make it impossible for an effective medicine to work, leading to increased drug resistance in cancer [7,8]. In such circumstances, the only effective way of increasing the efficiency of cancer treatment is by focusing on targeted therapy.

Understanding the biological drivers of cancer has led to effective treatments against tyrosine kinases, nuclear receptors, and other molecular targets. The initial success of estrogen receptor and androgen receptor antagonists and *BCR-ABL*, *HER2*, and EGFR inhibitors prompted a significant effort to develop medicines that target oncogenes [9]. Oncological therapy has advanced notably in recent years due to the arrival of numerous immunological techniques to detect cancer. Anti-CTLA4 12 and anti-PD-1/PD-L1 13 monoclonal antibodies that block the adaptive immune system's negative regulators or checkpoints have shown promising antitumor activity [10].

The advent of Human Genome Project (HGP) and INSDC consortium validated 22,000 genes in the human genome catalogue that played an instrumental role in the genomic surveillance against cancer [11,12]. Furthermore, the Encyclopedia of DNA Elements' (ENCODE) investigations have produced an annotated road map of significantly modified DNA and deciphered the functioning of genomes switches in complicated illness like cancer [13]. Extensive analyses of genomic profiles pertaining to specific cancer cases and genomic mapping-based targeted therapies can lead to a new era of cancer medicine.

Therapies available for cancer include surgery, radiation therapy, stem cell therapy, immunotherapy, hormone therapy, and chemotherapy [14]. In radiation therapy, high-energy radiation like X-rays and gamma rays damages the DNA of the cancerous cells resulting in their death. It also produces the free radicals inside the cells, thereby killing the normal cells in addition to cancerous cells [15,16]. The immunotherapy deals with the use of immune markers to identify the tumor cells and subsequent lysis [17,18]. Stem cell therapy is used as an adjuvant therapy after chemo and radiotherapy, as the latter results in the destruction of stem cells. This therapy helps in restoring the stem cells and stimulate bone marrow growth [19,20]. Hormone therapy, commonly used to treat breast cancer or prostate cancer, involves the inhibition of hormones, which are utilized by cancerous cells [21]. Polychemotherapy or the combined administration of agents with nonoverlapping modes of action was adapted from the antimicrobial therapy concept as the first response to the problem of single-agent chemotherapy resistance. Chemotherapy is also paired with radiation for surgical resection in patients with locally advanced illness and these combination treatment modalities enhance clinical results [22–24]. However, chemotherapeutic drugs are deleterious to the other healthy cells as well. Hence, more sustainable, less harmful, and efficient approaches are being explored [25].

The existing treatment options helped in treating patients but with significant side effects [26]. Another major concern prevailing in current treatment methods is the ability of the tumor cells to acquire resistance to the anticancerous agents [27]. Moreover, the present diagnostic and therapeutic procedures are time consuming. Fast, accurate, and economical theranostic methods need to be designed taking into account the diverse hallmarks of cancer by amalgamating computational tools besides molecular techniques. A more targeted approach should be devised which can yield better results.

2. Precision cancer medicine: Prospects and hurdles

Precision cancer medicine (PCM) refers to the treatments and medicines best suited for an individual while taking both genetic and environmental variables that influence response to therapy into account for better patient care and more personal attention [28,29]. It has been demonstrated that there is a significant amount of variability in drug response due to change in genetic composition, age, nutrition, health status, environmental exposure, epigenetic variables, and concurrent therapy [30]. To achieve such a pharmacological treatment with a reasonably predictable outcome, variable drug response patterns among geographically and ethnically heterogeneous groups must also be considered. This newer discipline aims to understand all of the genetic underpinnings of medication response. In addition to genomic and proteomic technologies, metabolomics plays an important role in designing tailored personalized medicine (PM) [31].

PCM confers with right diagnostics and prognostics information, by using the genomic complexity of the oncogenic drivers. This is achieved by using sequencing technologies (whole-genome studies, transcriptomics, epigenetics and chromatin immunoprecipitation (CHIP) seq) and genome profiling [32,33]. A set of protocols are made by this treatment regime as one decision point, mapping of patient data for recommended action. This therapy is more effective and precise with least toxicity for the patient's care. The therapy has been gaining momentum for the treatment of rare cancer diseases [34]. The HGP initiated as new era of genomic medicine, which enabled the individual patient's genome sequences to identify the disorder or disease and to prescribe the proper treatment. Treatment is based on molecular phenotypes to group the patients with standard underlying biology and a step forward in customizing medicine. Stratified medicine is recognized as a critical strategic approach for disease diagnosis and treatment that is heavily reliant on the integration of existing data sets to form a comprehensive personal healthcare record and the generation of new data describing patient characteristics genotype and phenotype to enable stratification [11,35].

Various international consortia were associated with launching trials using the application of genomics and transcriptomics biomarker platforms to boost precision oncology across the world [36]. However, despite the extensive international network and participation of candidates, the cases with PMs mostly suggested had a progression-free survival ratio way below the expected percentage. Some of the important examples of precision therapeutic consortia are mentioned in Table 1. Rodon et al. suggested that genomic and transcriptome profiling can help improve therapy recommendations, patient outcomes and increase individualized cancer treatment options [49].

Table 1 PM consortiums around the globe adapted from Gomez-Lopez et al. [37] can provide information for computational genomics studies.

Name of consortium	Descriptions	Designated capacity	Weblink
PMI Cohort Program [38]	• Program initiated by National Institute of Health (NIH) • This program collects information of genetic data	>1 million subjects from multiple centers	https://allofus.nih.gov/
MyCode community a Health Initiative [39]	• Geisinger's started this program • It is a DNA sequencing program	~275,000 participations	https://www.geisinger.org/precision-health/mycode
ICGCmed	• International Cancer Genome Consortium for Medicine started in 2007	25,000 individual types cancer genomes; 50 tumor types	http://www.icgcmed.org/
Genome-Asia100k [40]	• Sequencing mission • Designed for Asian individuals	~100 thousand genomes (projected)	https://genomeasia100k.org/
Project GENIE [41]	• Devised by American association for cancer research (AACR) • International pan-cancer genomics consortium	19 international cancer centers collaborated to generate >40,000 tumor genomics information	https://www.aacr.org/professionals/research/aacr-project-genie/
Worldwide Innovative Networking (WIN) Consortium in personalized cancer medicine [42]	• WIN consortium has leading cancer centers worldwide for precision medicine clinical trials and research projects	26 premiere academic centers across 18 countries and 4 continents	http://www.winconsortium.org/
100,000 Genomes Project [43]	• This project initiated by Genomics England	~85,000 patients affected by rare disease or cancer	https://www.genomicsengland.co.uk/about-genomics-england/the-100000-genomes-project/
The ICPerMed [44]	• ICPerMed is a public accessible international consortia for personalized medicine information and guidance	Collaboration of 30 funding bodies from EU state members	https://www.icpermed.eu/

Continued

Table 1 PM consortiums around the globe adapted from Gomez-Lopez et al. can provide information for computational genomics studies—cont'd

Name of consortium	Descriptions	Designated capacity	Weblink
France Médicine Génomique 2025 [45]	• The objective of this project is to sequence patients and their families	~10,000 WGS corresponding to 20,000 patients with rare diseases ~50,000 patients with metastatic and refractory cancer	https://pfmg2025.aviesan.fr/en/
Scottish Genomes Partnership (SGP)	• SGP was a major Scotland-research program • Genome sequencing project	~2588 genomes with 12 collaborators and 4 Scottish centers	https://www.scottishgenomespartnership.org/
Danish Strategy for Personalized Medicine 2021–2022	• Devised by Danish National Genome Center • Genome sequencing project	~60,000 whole genomes in healthcare (projected till 2024)	https://eng.ngc.dk/
Qatar Genome Programme (QGP) [46]	• A large-scale population-based genome project to implement precision medicine in Qatar	Not mentioned	https://www.qatargenome.org.qa/
Genome of the Netherlands Consortium (GoNL) [47]	• Devised to sequence genetic variations of Dutch population	~769 whole genomes among Dutch population	https://www.nlgenome.nl/
Australian National Genomic Healthcare Initiative [48]	• Australian genomics is a government national collaboration of supporting the translation genomic research into clinical practice	Not mentioned	https://www.australiangenomics.org.au/

3. Next generation sequencing and computational genomics in PCM

Advancements in novel technologies like next generation sequencing (NGS) have amplified the growth of precision medicine in cancer research and over the decades, the cost of sequencing has been declining with the refinement in technologies [50]. In the last two decades, the development of genomic data analysis was made easier through high-throughput technologies like NGS, microarray and single cell sequencing techniques, which strengthened the development of PM in oncology. This advancement in technologies made cancer research apply the extensive use data application as a part of research globally. Several cancer-specific data repositories work with research institutes and government entities to manage and store high-throughput data [51]. Due to this expansion, most of the data available through these biomedical data repositories is too vast or complicated to be processed, analyzed, or displayed using standard methods. This type of data, often known as big data, provides a variety of benefits as well as difficulties in the pharmaceutical business [52,53]. Big data is often described by a collection of qualities, including abnormally high volume, velocity, and diversity. To put it another way, big data is too vast, too quick, or too difficult to process with conventional technologies [54]. The big data, hence, demand the use of computational models and algorithms rather than typical direct analysis.

The cost of the sequencing is reducing considerably due to high demand and availability of dedicated low-cost computational tools, which are leading to proportional increase in generated datasets. The efficient bioinformatics systems are reliable on the data being generated and assist in the translation of knowledge from the biological data toward molecular targeting and diagnosis. Many steps in the clinical trials are being dilated using the PM with the help of computational genomics data to cut down the time and accuracy in finding the targeted drug molecule [55].

Some of the application of the bioinformatics approaches like biomarkers identification, genome-wide characterization of molecular profiles, the gene-expression microarrays have been a part of signature pipelines for diagnostic and prognostic purposes (Fig. 1). These gene signatures are being used as clinical tools for many types of cancer. Majority of the bioinformatics approach in PM are integrating the biomarkers identification in individual patients. These markers may be the single nucleotide polymorphism (SNPs), structural variation, circulating DNAs [56,57]. The availability of human genome enabled the individual patient's genomic determinants to identify the disorder or disease and prescribe the PMs [11,35].

Genetic alterations in tumor cells have led to the increase in resistance to chemotherapy and radiotherapy in cancer. Sequencing technologies and computational genomics have increased the specificity of identifying the markers by substituting the single-gene testing and targeted conventional testing [58]. Cancer genomic analysis can be performed to analyze the SNPs, copy number variations, structural variations, INDELS, and

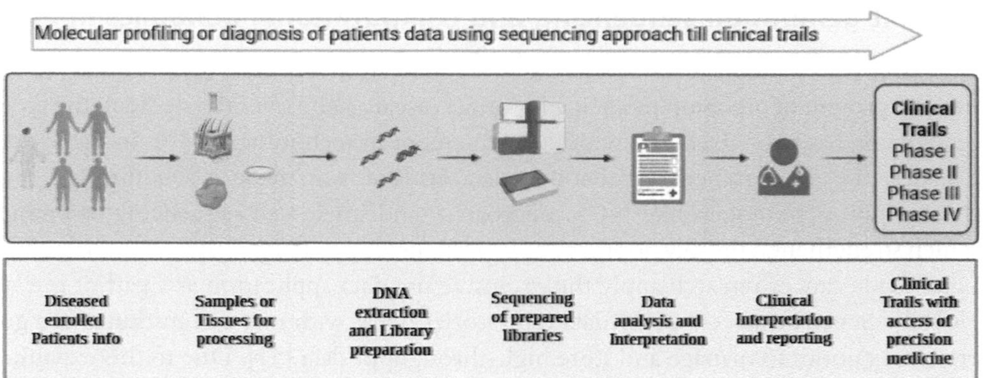

Fig. 1 Schematic representation of designing precision medicine using molecular diagnostic profiling.

chromosomal translocations. Genomic technologies can be used in the detection of gene fusion and gene deletions [32,59,60].

Microarray helps to gain an insight about the changes in gene expression that could be correlated to the cancer treatment. Microarray analyses aim at finding the significant biomarker which help in classifying the cancer on the basis of diagnostic biomarkers [61]. It is a group of microscopic DNA spots attached to the biochip; it has become the most eminent tool for the researcher's community. DNA microarrays on the basis of mode of preparation are categorized into two types, namely, in situ synthesized and spotted microarrays [62]. In situ synthesized are microarrays consisting of an oligonucleotide of 20–60 nucleotide in length on a solid base [63]. Spotted arrays are made by robotic micro spotting of DNA fragments or longer oligonucleotides onto the solid support like glass. Gene expression profiling of multiple genes is monitored to study the effects of cancer treatments and disorders. Breast cancer research has progressed immensely using transcriptomics, microarray, CHIP Seq, single-cell sequencing. Hereditary breast and ovarian cancers are caused by mutations in the *BRCA* genes, which account for up to 60% of all cases [64]. However, there is no single mutation responsible for all of these occurrences. Researchers have already detected over 800 distinct mutations in *BRCA1*. The DNA microarray is a technique for determining whether a person's DNA contains mutations in genes like *BRCA1* and *BRCA2*. Standardizing array manufacturing procedures, assay protocols, and analytical methodologies utilized to interpret the data are still needed before microarrays that may be used routinely in clinical practice. Furthermore, integrating microarray data with clinical and epidemiological factors is one of the major challenges in the advancement of this approach. The research studies on the microarray in cancer research summarize the key contributions and highlight several significant challenges that must be addressed to improve the efficacy of this potentially transformative technology in clinical oncology [65]. The vast expression data requires ardent

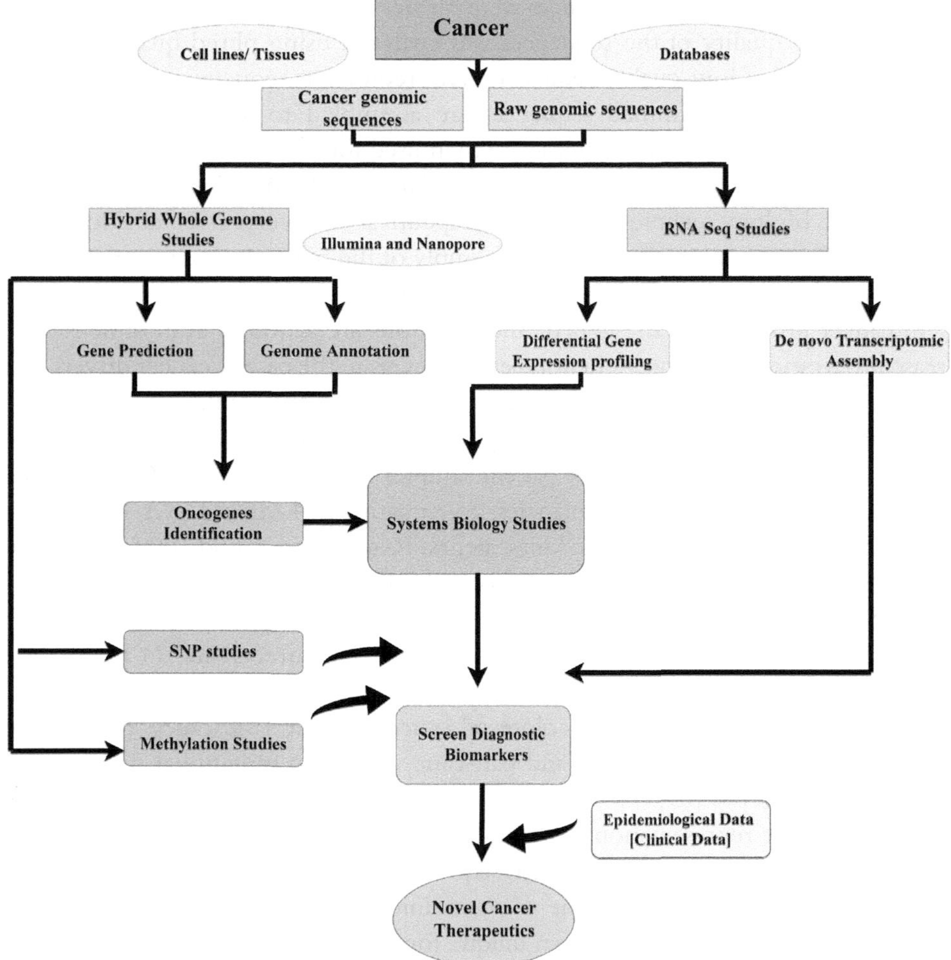

Fig. 2 Schematic representation of integrated computational approaches for therapeutic discovery using PCM.

computational programming for conclusive evidence based on the expression patterns thereby helping in PCM designing [66].

The cancer genomic pipeline for novel cancer therapeutics discovery has been described in Fig. 2. The tumor biopsy sample or tissues are initially extracted from the cancer patients. Further isolation of DNA from the tissue and quality and quantity of DNA are analyzed. NGS library is being prepared for the generation of raw sequences; either using high-throughput data from Illumina (NGS), Oxford Nanopore Technologies (Third generation sequencing technologies) or the raw data sequences are retrieved from the databases. The raw sequences were further processed for quality check and data trimming. The quality of the sequences was analyzed using phred quality scores (Q). Sequence adapters, low-quality sequences, and redundant sequences were trimmed in data trimming step. Trimmed sequences are assembled to attain the hybrid whole genome assembly. Assembled genome are then used for genome annotation and ontology analysis. The secondary analyses can be used to identify the oncogene biomarkers by using systems biology techniques for the therapeutical discovery. In parallel to the whole genome studies, de novo transcriptome assembly of the transcripts of tumor samples can be performed alongside gene expression profiling.

In cancer progression, the genetic modifications are acquired as in dimension with disease progression and cancer phenotype. However, in the case of cancer drivers, a small set of genes are responsible for the critical alterations and sustainability of the disease. Initially, big data and high-throughput sequencing technologies were used to find the mutant driver genes in a group of patient samples [67]. The Cancer Genome Project studied 210 different human malignancies, investigating 274 Mb of DNA, corresponding to the coding exons of 518 protein kinase genes. Researchers found 1000 somatic mutations and used a statistical technique to rank each of the kinases investigated based on the likelihood of a driver mutation [68]. Vogelstein and colleagues looked at exons from 18,191 genes that represented 20,857 transcripts in 11 colorectal and 11 breast cancers. The frequency of gene mutation was more than predicted as likely to be drivers. They also described the first breast and colorectal cancer genetic landscapes. Researches are mainly focusing on disease-based and pan-cancer somatic mutational data to identify mutation driver genes [69].

The schematic representation workflow shown in Fig. 3 represents the hybrid whole genome data analysis using two different sequencing platforms like Illumina and Oxford nanopore technologies (ONT). The raw genomic sequences from Illumina sequencers and ONT are generated in their own unique format (e.g., bcl and fast5) and are binary encoded file. The nucleotide bases are called using base-callers and are demultiplexed using bcl2fastq and Guppy base-caller in case of Illumina and ONT, respectively. Quality of the raw sequences are identified using FastQC and PoreQC [70]. The adapter sequences, low-quality reads, and redundant sequences were trimmed using trimmomatic and Porechop [71]. The filtered Illumina and Nanopore reads were used to construct the hybrid whole genome assembly using MaSuRCA genome assembler [72]. The scaffolding of the genome was processed for reducing the number of contigs, this process was performed using pyScaf or npScaf. The N50 value of genome can be analyzed and genome QC can be performed using BUSCO or QUAST [73,74]. The assembled genome can be further used for secondary analysis like genome visualization (BRIG or Circos tool), gene prediction (Prokka for prokaryote or Augustus for eukaryote), genome annotation, and genome comparative studies (Mauve or OrthoVenn), respectively [75–80].

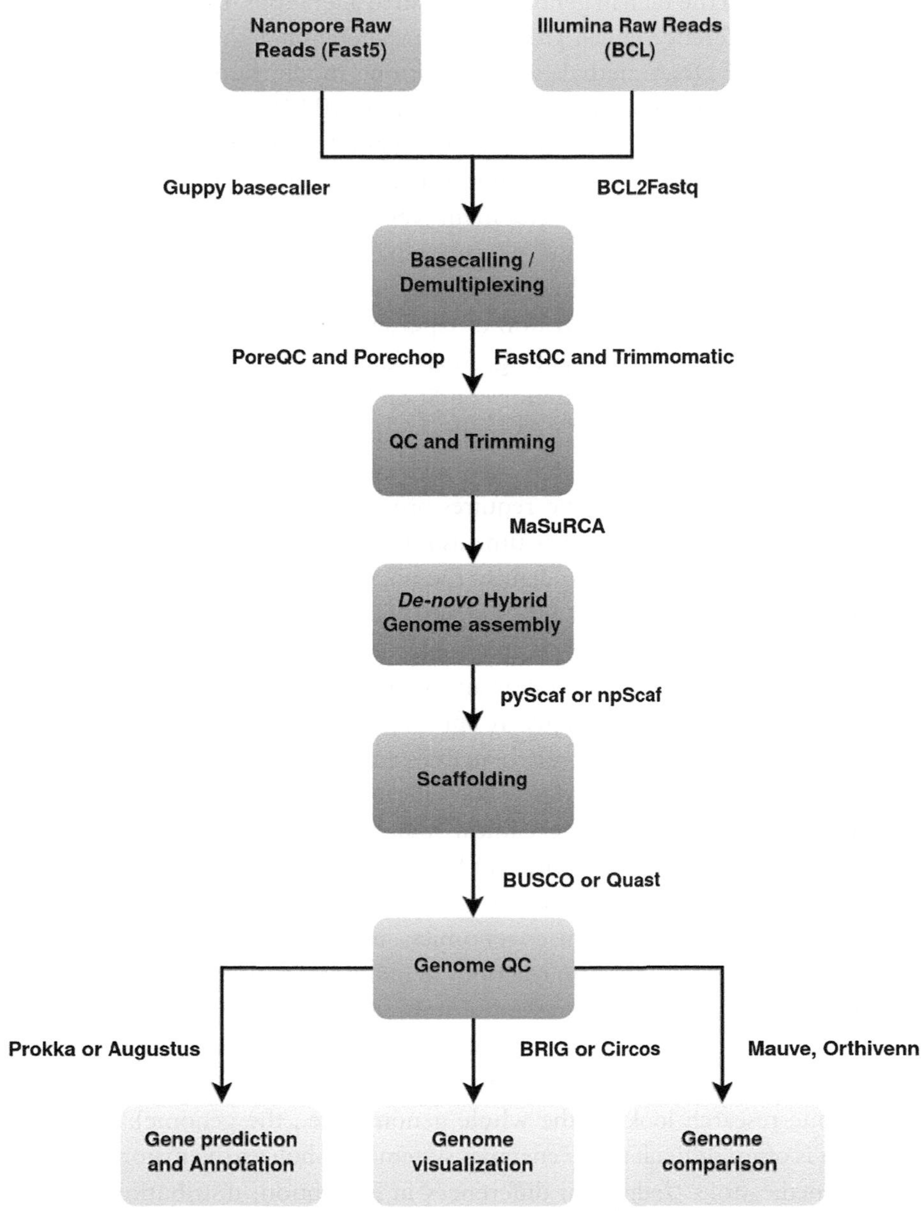

Fig. 3 Workflow representing the NGS-Hybrid whole genome data analysis using Illumina and Oxford Nanopore sequencing technologies.

Modifications in the human genome will lead to alterations in transcriptional activity, resulting in the difference in cell growth and proliferation architecture. Genome-wide epigenetic maps of DNA methylation and histone modifications are being produced by International Human Epigenetic Consortium or NIH Roadmap Epigenomics Mapping Consortium [81]. Epigenetic mapping is intended to understand tumor biology and potential therapeutic biomarkers for clinical use. The function of epigenetic modifications in oncogenesis and cancer development is becoming more evident, paving the path for early therapeutic intervention or pharmacological targeting [82]. Differential DNA methylation patterns observed while comparing tumor with normal samples can predict the prognosis and survival. Methylation of CpG sites, a kind of epigenetic regulation of gene expression, results in gene silencing. Analyzing these patterns helps in predicting the expression of associated genes in tumor condition like in lung cancer, colorectal cancer and breast cancer. Genome-scale DNA methylation mapping reveals temporal and spatial heterogeneity in different tumors [83]. Although epigenetic targeting as a precision medicine technique is complicated and requires prospective clinical assessment, the field's therapeutic potential will grow over time as more understanding is gained [84].

Global research investigations identify the novel biomarkers with clinical relevance that may subsequently be used as a new standard of care clinical diagnostic test to optimize patient benefit [85]. Many tumor-specific molecular changes including protein overexpression, driver gene mutations, or rearrangements are well-established biomarkers for response to selective targeted therapy, are appearing all the time. The continuous prediction of biomarkers requires a thorough analysis and validation using high-performance computer algorithms which can detect the efficacy of the biomarkers when translated for clinical study. As a result, the clinical molecular pathology analysis followed by detailed validation has become an efficient laboratory tool for characterizing tumor biology and guiding therapy decisions [86,87].

Pharmacogenetics and pharmacogenomics, in general, are concerned with the genetic basis of varying medication reactions in individual patients and is an essential part of PM. In traditional pharmacogenetic research, sequence variations in candidate genes that are thought to affect medicine response are examined. The study of how genetic variations affect medication development is known as pharmacogenomics, whereas pharmacogenomic research looks at the whole genome (i.e., the genome). The candidate gene search is often difficult as the enzymes system metabolizes the majority of currently accessible medications. Individual differences in absorption, distribution, metabolism, and excretion are caused by these enzymes and their variants [88]. As a result, even tiny differences such as a single nucleotide base misspelling might have clinically significant repercussions that can be extensively studied under PM. New genomic technologies like NGS-enable broader identification over the entire genome due to their incredible speed and specificity [89].

4. Drug repositioning using translational bioinformatics

Many bioinformatics methods are available for drug designing and development. However, in the case of acquired antibiotic resistance, the available drugs in the market require drug repositioning. The existing ligand-binding positions are replaced with the novel treatment target of binding affinity. Designing a new drug is a lengthy process and high price validation followed by target identification [90]. Additional targets are not determined for a drug molecule and clinical applications are not yet discovered [91]. The repositioning of drug molecules will be a novel strategy for current treatments, as some of the most commercially successful drugs are used for reasons other than those originally intended when they were developed. The drugs such as Sildenafil, Minoxidil, and Thalidomide are just a few of the many instances. Different approaches are available in drug repositioning, from blind screening of libraries to data-driven computational methods integrating the linkage between the drugs and diseases with multiple forms of biocompounds [92].

There are different types of drug-based approaches in drug repositioning. The drug similarity approach in drug repositioning shows the property of each compound and classifies them based on the chemical constituents of the molecule. This approach has QSAR models and Pharmacophore studies, which allow to share the properties of similarity between the drugs and identify the important therapeutic applications [93]. Other approaches available are metabotropic glutamate (mGlu) conceptual approach, similarity ensemble approach, molecular activity similarity, molecular docking [94]. There is another major type of approach called disease-based approaches for drug repositioning. The association between the drugs and diseases is being used, specificity of the generic disease is termed in the way to treat with proper drug molecules [95]. Our research group has explored the prognostic biomarkers and potential therapeutic targets to counteract neuroblastoma through extensive gene-interaction network approach [96]. Genome-based network analyses, in-silico structural biology approaches, and therapeutic predictions can sustainably address complex human diseases through biomarker and therapeutic predictions [97–100]. Some of the tools and databases for integrated bioinformatics analysis were mentioned in Table 2.

5. Future perspectives

> *... What if matching a cancer cure to our genetic code was just as easy, just as standard? What if figuring out the right dose of medicine was as simple as taking our temperature?*
>
> ***Barack Obama (2015)***

Former US President and Nobel laureate Barack Obama launched the "Precision Medicine Initiative" (PMI) in January 2015 to accelerate "biomedical discoveries and provide

Table 2 Tools and programs for integrated bioinformatics approach to address PCM development.

Application	Software	Link
Assembly	SPAdes UniCycler MaSuRCA	https://github.com/ablab/spades https://github.com/rrwick/Unicycler https://github.com/alekseyzimin/masurca
Annotation	RAST NCBI	https://rast.nmpdr.org/ https://blast.ncbi.nlm.nih.gov/Blast.cgi
Alignment	Mauve	http://darlinglab.org/mauve/mauve.html
GWAS and Pangenome analysis	Roary Panseq gwas-clustering	https://sanger-pathogens.github.io/Roary/ https://github.com/chadlaing/Panseq https://github.com/johhorn/gwas-clustering
Visualization and comparative genomics	MEGA EasyFig ACT	http://wishart.biology.ualberta.ca/cgview/ https://mjsull.github.io/Easyfig/ http://sanger-pathogens.github.io/Artemis/ACT/
Interaction network construction and visualization	STRING PHIDIAS CYTOSCAPE	https://string-db.org/ http://www.phidias.us/ https://cytoscape.org/
Molecular docking	Autodock4.2 AutodockVina Sybyl 2.0	http://autodock.scripps.edu/news/autodock4-2.6 http://vina.scripps.edu/ ***Paid and licensed product***
Pharmaco-kinetics and toxicity of drug candidates	Molinspiration SwissADME pkCSM	https://www.molinspiration.com/ http://www.swissadme.ch/ http://biosig.unimelb.edu.au/pkcsm/
Virtual screening	DockBlaster MTIOpenScreen	https://blaster.docking.org/ https://bioserv.rpbs.univ-paris-diderot.fr/services/MTiOpenScreen/
Mutation screening	I-Mutant SIFT	https://folding.biofold.org/i-mutant/i-mutant2.0.html https://sift.bii.a-star.edu.sg/
Epitope prediction	BepiPred CTLPred NetMHCIIpan	https://services.healthtech.dtu.dk/service.php?BepiPred-2.0 http://crdd.osdd.net/raghava/ctlpred/ https://services.healthtech.dtu.dk/service.php?NetMHCIIpan-4.0
Molecular dynamics simulation	GROMACS AMBER Schrodinger	http://www.gromacs.org/ https://ambermd.org/ https://www.schrodinger.com/pipeline

clinicians with new tools, knowledge, and therapies to select which treatments will work best for which patients." It was motivated by a futuristic vision that precision medicine will enable health-care providers to design treatment and prevention strategies based on people's unique characteristics. Extensive computational studies from genomics to metabolomics besides clinical data integration can serve the purpose of active/real-time monitoring. A successful implementation will make health data portable, which can easily be shared between providers, researchers, and most importantly, patients and research participants [101].

The sequencing of the human genome has brought the most significant advancement in technologies concerning precision medicine. Sequencing has become cheaper recently to look for rare genetic variations in the genome and many common variants play significant roles in causing diseases. Multiple sites on the genome, most of which are relevant genes, have been linked to common diseases. Even though many more remain to be discovered, work can be carried out to develop diagnostics and investigate therapeutic possibilities for certain diseases. The only way to discover rare genetic variations is to sequence an individual's entire genome. That approach is now becoming feasible as the cost of sequencing falls below $1000 per genome. HGP has provided common sequencing scaffolds, where every gene and control element can now be mapped to its correct site on the genome allowing all of the system's working parts to be related to one another. Genome-wide association studies, despite their detractors has provided new biological insights into some prevalent diseases or polygenic features, making it easier to design new and improved treatments and preventive measures based on these findings. The significant progress being made through meta-analyses predicts that many more common variations conferring risk of disease will be found in the coming years, resulting in increased stability of individual risk estimates. Once risk estimations are more consistent, the value of genetic screening for each illness must be considered and suggestions for potential interventions for people whose anticipated risk exceeds a certain threshold must be made. Appropriate recommendations are urgently needed in advising patients on how to interpret the results as they become more stable and when to act on them.

6. Conclusion

Cancer heterogeny has been a persistent complication that needs rapid attention. One approach to tackle the difficulty is to customize the therapeutic strategies depending on the type of tumor. Advancements in genomic technologies have highlighted the use of PCM in the detection as well as in designing cancer therapeutics. The time, cost, and accuracy of existing cancer therapies can be addressed by designing integrated translational bioinformatics protocols to escalate the development of PCM candidates. An effective amalgamation of NGS, big data analysis, computational genotype-correlations and structure-based drug repurposing can create new paradigm in PCM development.

Acknowledgment

The authors would like to thank Mr. Soumya Basu (ICMR-RA) and Ms. Gayathri Ashok (TRA), Ms. Priyamvada (TRA), Mr. Aniket Naha (ICMR-RA), Ms. Reetika Debroy (TRA) VIT-Vellore for their expert contributions in the manuscript. The authors also thank VIT management for providing the necessary facilities to carry out this work. The authors gratefully acknowledge the Indian Council of Medical Research (ICMR), New Delhi, Government of India agency, for the research grant [IRIS ID: 2020-0690].

Author contributions

Hithesh Kumar (HK): Data curation, Writing-Original Draft;

Miryala Sravan Kumar (MSK): Data curation, Writing-Original Draft;

Anand Anbarasu (AA): Funding Acquisition, Conceptualization, Project Administration;

Sudha Ramaiah (SR): Project Supervision, Conceptualization, Methodology, Draft Review.

Declaration of interests

The authors declare that they have no known competing financial interests or personal relationships that could have appeared to influence the work reported in this paper.

References

[1] H. Sung, J. Ferlay, R.L. Siegel, M. Laversanne, I. Soerjomataram, A. Jemal, F. Bray, Global cancer statistics 2020: GLOBOCAN estimates of incidence and mortality worldwide for 36 cancers in 185 countries, CA Cancer J. Clin. 71 (2021) 209–249, https://doi.org/10.3322/caac.21660.

[2] G. Benstead-Hume, S.K. Wooller, F.M.G. Pearl, 'Big data' approaches for novel anti-cancer drug discovery, Expert Opin. Drug Discov. 12 (2017) 599–609, https://doi.org/10.1080/17460441.2017.1319356.

[3] K. Cooper, H. Squires, C. Carroll, D. Papaioannou, A. Booth, R. Logan, C. Maguire, D. Hind, P. Tappenden, Chemoprevention of colorectal cancer: systematic review and economic evaluation, Health Technol. Assess. (Rockv) 14 (2010) 1–205, https://doi.org/10.3310/hta14320.

[4] S.E. Yost, Accurate Identification of Somatic Mutations in Clinical Tumor Specimens, San Diego ProQuest Dissertations Publishing, 2013, 3588307.

[5] K. Pietras, A. Östman, Hallmarks of cancer: interactions with the tumor stroma, Exp. Cell Res. 316 (2010) 1324–1331, https://doi.org/10.1016/j.yexcr.2010.02.045.

[6] N.N. Pavlova, C.B. Thompson, The emerging hallmarks of cancer metabolism, Cell Metab. 23 (2016) 27–47, https://doi.org/10.1016/j.cmet.2015.12.006.

[7] D.G. Nathan, The cancer treatment revolution, Trans. Am. Clin. Climatol. Assoc. 118 (2007) 317–323, https://doi.org/10.1001/jama.299.7.836.

[8] P.L. Germain, Cancer cells and adaptive explanations, Biol. Philos. 27 (2012) 785–810, https://doi.org/10.1007/s10539-012-9334-2.

[9] B.N. Rexer, J.A. Engelman, C.L. Arteaga, Overcoming resistance to tyrosine kinase inhibitors: lessons learned from cancer cells treated with EGFR antagonists, Cell Cycle 8 (2009) 18–22, https://doi.org/10.4161/cc.8.1.7324.

[10] M. Abramovitz, C. Williams, P.K. De, N. Dey, S. Willis, B. Young, E. Andreopoulou, W.F. Symmans, J.K. Sicklick, R.L. Schilsky, V. Lazar, C. Bresson, J. Mendelsohn, R. Kurzrock, B. Leyland-Jones, in: S. Badve, G.L. Kumar (Eds.), Precision Medicine Clinical Trials: Successes and Disappointments, Challenges and Opportunities – Lessons Learnt BT – Predictive Biomarkers in

Oncology: Applications in Precision Medicine, Springer International Publishing, Cham, 2019, pp. 593–603, https://doi.org/10.1007/978-3-319-95228-4_53.

[11] K.K. Jain, Textbook of personalized medicine, Expert Opin. Pharmacother. (2009), https://doi.org/10.1517/14656566.6.9.1463.

[12] H. Chial, DNA Sequencing Technologies Key to the Human Genome Project Thanks to the Human Genome Project, researchers have sequenced all 3.2 billion base pairs in the human genome. How did researchers complete this chromosome map years ahead of schedule? Initi, Nat. Educ. 1 (1) (2008) 219.

[13] D.J. Thomas, K.R. Rosenbloom, H. Clawson, A.S. Hinrichs, H. Trumbower, B.J. Raney, D. Karolchik, G.P. Barber, R.A. Harte, J. Hillman-Jackson, R.M. Kuhn, B.L. Rhead, K.E. Smith, A. Thakkapallayil, A.S. Zweig, D. Haussler, W.J. Kent, The ENCODE project at UC Santa Cruz, Nucleic Acids Res. 35 (2007) 4, https://doi.org/10.1093/nar/gkl1017.

[14] A. Sudhakar, J. Cancer Sci. Ther. 1 (2009) 1–4, https://doi.org/10.4172/1948-5956.100000e2.History.

[15] M.B. Goldman, F. Maloof, R.R. Monson, A. Aschengrau, D.S. Cooper, E.C. Ridgway, Radioactive iodine therapy and breast cancer: a follow-up study of hyperthyroid women, Am. J. Epidemiol. 127 (1988) 969–980, https://doi.org/10.1093/oxfordjournals.aje.a114900.

[16] N.N.Y. Janssen, J. Nijkamp, T. Alderliesten, C.E. Loo, E.J.T. Rutgers, J.J. Sonke, M.T.F.D. Vrancken Peeters, Radioactive seed localization in breast cancer treatment, Br. J. Surg. 103 (2016) 70–80, https://doi.org/10.1002/bjs.9962.

[17] T.A. Waldmann, Immunotherapy: past, present and future, Nat. Med. 9 (2003) 269–277, https://doi.org/10.1038/nm0303-269.

[18] J. Couzin-Frankel, Cancer immunotherapy, Science (80-.) 342 (2013) 1432–1433, https://doi.org/10.1126/science.342.6165.1432.

[19] S.U. Kim, J. de Vellis, Stem cell-based cell therapy in neurological diseases: a review, J. Neurosci. Res. 87 (2009) 2183–2200, https://doi.org/10.1002/jnr.22054.

[20] B.E. Strauer, R. Kornowski, Stem cell therapy in perspective, Circulation 107 (2003) 929–934, https://doi.org/10.1161/01.CIR.0000057525.13182.24.

[21] M. Arruebo, N. Vilaboa, B. Sáez-Gutierrez, J. Lambea, A. Tres, M. Valladares, Á. González-Fernández, Assessment of the evolution of cancer treatment therapies, Cancers (Basel) 3 (2011) 3279–3330, https://doi.org/10.3390/cancers3033279.

[22] P. Srinivasan, T. Shanmugam, Understanding cancer therapies, Choice Rev. Online (2007), https://doi.org/10.5860/CHOICE.45-0308.

[23] J. Zugazagoitia, C. Guedes, S. Ponce, I. Ferrer, S. Molina-Pinelo, L. Paz-Ares, Current challenges in cancer treatment, Clin. Ther. 38 (2016) 1551–1566, https://doi.org/10.1016/j.clinthera.2016.03.026.

[24] A. Wigfield, J. Eccles, D. Rodriguez, Cancer Chemotherapy, Immunotherapy and Biotherapy, Lippincott Williams & Wilkins (LWW), 2013.

[25] C.Y. Huang, D.T. Ju, C.F. Chang, P. Muralidhar Reddy, B.K. Velmurugan, A review on the effects of current chemotherapy drugs and natural agents in treating non-small cell lung cancer, Biomedicine 7 (2017) 12–23, https://doi.org/10.1051/bmdcn/2017070423.

[26] D.A. Gewirtz, M.L. Bristol, J.C. Yalowich, Toxicity issues in cancer drug development, Curr. Opin. Investig. Drugs 11 (2010) 612–614.

[27] E.R. Lepper, K. Nooter, J. Verweij, M.R. Acharya, W.D. Figg, A. Sparreboom, Mechanisms of resistance to anticancer drugs: the role of the polymorphic ABC transporters ABCB1 and ABCG2, 6 (2005) 115–138, https://doi.org/10.1517/14622416.6.2.115.

[28] C. Le Tourneau, E. Borcoman, M. Kamal, Molecular profiling in precision medicine oncology, Nat. Med. 25 (2019) 711–712, https://doi.org/10.1038/s41591-019-0442-2.

[29] R. Srivas, J.P. Shen, C.C. Yang, S.M. Sun, J. Li, A.M. Gross, J. Jensen, K. Licon, A. Bojorquez-Gomez, K. Klepper, J. Huang, D. Pekin, J.L. Xu, H. Yeerna, V. Sivaganesh, L. Kollenstart, H. van Attikum, P. Aza-Blanc, R.W. Sobol, T. Ideker, A network of conserved synthetic lethal interactions for exploration of precision cancer therapy, Mol. Cell 63 (2016) 514–525, https://doi.org/10.1016/j.molcel.2016.06.022.

[30] N. Crawley, M. Thompson, A. Romaschin, Theranostics in the growing field of personalized medicine: an analytical chemistry perspective, Anal. Chem. 86 (2014) 130–160, https://doi.org/10.1021/ac4038812.

[31] F.R. Vogenberg, C.I. Barash, M. Pursel, Personalized medicine – Part 1: evolution and development into theranostics, P T 35 (2010) 560–576.

[32] E.R. Malone, M. Oliva, P.J.B. Sabatini, T.L. Stockley, L.L. Siu, Molecular profiling for precision cancer therapies, Genome Med. 12 (2020) 1–19, https://doi.org/10.1186/s13073-019-0703-1.

[33] A.V. Uzilov, W. Ding, M.Y. Fink, Y. Antipin, A.S. Brohl, C. Davis, C.Y. Lau, C. Pandya, H. Shah, Y. Kasai, J. Powell, M. Micchelli, R. Castellanos, Z. Zhang, M. Linderman, Y. Kinoshita, M. Zweig, K. Raustad, K. Cheung, D. Castillo, M. Wooten, I. Bourzgui, L.C. Newman, G. Deikus, B. Mathew, J. Zhu, B.S. Glicksberg, A.S. Moe, J. Liao, L. Edelmann, J.T. Dudley, R.G. Maki, A. Kasarskis, R.F. Holcombe, M. Mahajan, K. Hao, B. Reva, J. Longtine, D. Starcevic, R. Sebra, M.J. Donovan, S. Li, E.E. Schadt, R. Chen, Development and clinical application of an integrative genomic approach to personalized cancer therapy, Genome Med. 8 (2016) 1–20, https://doi.org/10.1186/s13073-016-0313-0.

[34] M.R. Kosorok, E.B. Laber, Precision medicine, Annu. Rev. Stat. Appl. 6 (2019) 263–286, https://doi.org/10.1146/annurev-statistics-030718-105251.

[35] S.H. Shin, A.M. Bode, Z. Dong, Precision medicine: the foundation of future cancer therapeutics, NPJ Precis. Oncol. 1 (2017) 1–2, https://doi.org/10.1038/s41698-017-0016-z.

[36] J. Rodon, J.-C. Soria, R. Berger, W.H. Miller, V. Lazar, E. Rubin, A.M. Tsimberidou, P. Saintigny, A. Ackerstein, I. Brana, Y. Loriot, M. Afshar, V.A. Miller, F. Wunder, C. Bresson, J.-F. Martini, J. Mendelsohn, R.L. Schilsky, J.J. Lee, R. Kurzrock, WINTHER: an international WIN Consortium precision medicine trial using genomic and transcriptomic analysis in patients with advanced malignancies, J. Clin. Oncol. 36 (2018) 12011, https://doi.org/10.1200/JCO.2018.36.15_suppl.12011.

[37] G. Gomez-Lopez, J. Dopazo, J.C. Cigudosa, A. Valencia, F. Al-Shahrour, Precision medicine needs pioneering clinical bioinformaticians, Brief. Bioinform. 20 (2017) 752–766, https://doi.org/10.1093/bib/bbx144.

[38] P.L. Sankar, L.S. Parker, The Precision Medicine Initiative's All of Us Research Program: an agenda for research on its ethical, legal, and social issues, Genet. Med. 19 (2017) 743–750, https://doi.org/10.1038/gim.2016.183.

[39] M. [professor Murtuza Rampurwala, MD, MPH [clinical instructor], Kari B. Wisinski, MD [associate professor], and Ruth O'Regan, 心提取 HHS Public Access, Physiol. Behav. 176 (2017) 139–148. https://doi.org/10.1038/gim.2015.187.

[40] J.D. Wall, E.W. Stawiski, A. Ratan, H.L. Kim, C. Kim, R. Gupta, K. Suryamohan, E.S. Gusareva, R.-W. Purbojati, T. Bhangale, V. Stepanov, V. Kharkov, M.S. Schröder, V. Ramprasad, J. Tom, S. Durinck, Q. Bei, J. Li, J. Guillory, S. Phalke, A. Basu, J. Stinson, S. Nair, S. Malaichamy, N.K. Biswas, J.C. Chambers, K.C. Cheng, J.T. George, S.S. Khor, J.I. Kim, B. Cho, R. Menon, T. Sattibabu, A. Bassi, M. Deshmukh, A. Verma, V. Gopalan, J.Y. Shin, M. Pratapneni, S. Santhosh, K. Tokunaga, B.M. Md-Zain, K.G. Chan, M. Parani, P. Natarajan, M. Hauser, R.R. Allingham, C. Santiago-Turla, A. Ghosh, S.G.K. Gadde, C. Fuchsberger, L. Forer, S. Schoenherr, H. Sudoyo, J.S. Lansing, J. Friedlaender, G. Koki, M.P. Cox, M. Hammer, T. Karafet, K.C. Ang, S.Q. Mehdi, V. Radha, V. Mohan, P.P. Majumder, S. Seshagiri, J.S. Seo, S.C. Schuster, A.S. Peterson, The GenomeAsia 100K Project enables genetic discoveries across Asia, Nature 576 (2019) 106–111, https://doi.org/10.1038/s41586-019-1793-z.

[41] W. Dakkak, AACR Project GENIE: Powering Precision M, Physiol. Behav. 176 (2017) 139–148, https://doi.org/10.1158/2159-8290.CD-17-0151.AACR.

[42] J. Rodon, J.C. Soria, R. Berger, G. Batist, A. Tsimberidou, C. Bresson, J.J. Lee, E. Rubin, A. Onn, R.L. Schilsky, W.H. Miller, A.M. Eggermont, J. Mendelsohn, V. Lazar, R. Kurzrock, Challenges in initiating and conducting personalized cancer therapy trials: perspectives from WINTHER, a Worldwide Innovative Network (WIN) Consortium trial, Ann. Oncol. 26 (2015) 1791–1798, https://doi.org/10.1093/annonc/mdv191.

[43] D. Smedley, K.R. Smith, A. Martin, E.A. Thomas, E.M. McDonagh, V. Cipriani, J.M. Ellingford, G. Arno, A. Tucci, J. Vandrovcova, G. Chan, H.J. Williams, T. Ratnaike, W. Wei, K. Stirrups, K. Ibanez, L. Moutsianas, M. Wielscher, A. Need, M.R. Barnes, L. Vestito, J. Buchanan, S. Wordsworth, S. Ashford, K. Rehmström, E. Li, G. Fuller, P. Twiss, O. Spasic-Boskovic, S. Halsall, R.A. Floto,

K. Poole, A. Wagner, S.G. Mehta, M. Gurnell, N. Burrows, R. James, C. Penkett, E. Dewhurst, S. Gräf, R. Mapeta, M. Kasanicki, A. Haworth, H. Savage, M. Babcock, M.G. Reese, M. Bale, E. Baple, C. Boustred, H. Brittain, A. de Burca, M. Bleda, A. Devereau, D. Halai, E. Haraldsdottir, Z. Hyder, D. Kasperaviciute, C. Patch, D. Polychronopoulos, A. Matchan, R. Sultana, M. Ryten, A.L.T. Tavares, C. Tregidgo, C. Turnbull, M. Welland, S. Wood, C. Snow, E. Williams, S. Leigh, R.E. Foulger, L.C. Daugherty, O. Niblock, I.U.S. Leong, C.F. Wright, J. Davies, C. Crichton, J. Welch, K. Woods, L. Abulhoul, P. Aurora, D. Bockenhauer, A. Broomfield, M.A. Cleary, T. Lam, M. Dattani, E. Footitt, V. Ganesan, S. Grunewald, S. Compeyrot-Lacassagne, F. Muntoni, C. Pilkington, R. Quinlivan, N. Thapar, C. Wallis, L.R. Wedderburn, A. Worth, T. Bueser, C. Compton, C. Deshpande, H. Fassihi, E. Haque, L. Izatt, D. Josifova, S. Mohammed, L. Robert, S. Rose, D. Ruddy, R. Sarkany, G. Say, A.C. Shaw, A. Wolejko, B. Habib, G. Burns, S. Hunter, R.J. Grocock, S.J. Humphray, P.N. Robinson, M. Haendel, M.A. Simpson, S. Banka, J. Clayton-Smith, S. Douzgou, G. Hall, H.B. Thomas, R.T. O'Keefe, M. Michaelides, A.T. Moore, S. Malka, N. Pontikos, A.C. Browning, V. Straub, G.S. Gorman, R. Horvath, R. Quinton, A.M. Schaefer, P. Yu-Wai-Man, D.M. Turnbull, R. McFarland, R.W. Taylor, E. O'Connor, J. Yip, K. Newland, H.R. Morris, J. Polke, N.W. Wood, C. Campbell, C. Camps, K. Gibson, N. Koelling, T. Lester, A.H. Németh, C. Palles, S. Patel, N.B.A. Roy, A. Sen, J. Taylor, P. Cacheiro, J.O. Jacobsen, E.G. Seaby, V. Davison, L. Chitty, A. Douglas, K. Naresh, D. McMullan, S. Ellard, I.K. Temple, A.D. Mumford, G. Wilson, P. Beales, M. Bitner-Glindzicz, G. Black, J.R. Bradley, P. Brennan, J. Burn, P.F. Chinnery, P. Elliott, F. Flinter, H. Houlden, M. Irving, W. Newman, S. Rahman, J.A. Sayer, J.C. Taylor, A.R. Webster, A.O.M. Wilkie, W.H. Ouwehand, F.L. Raymond, J. Chisholm, S. Hill, D. Bentley, R.H. Scott, T. Fowler, A. Rendon, M. Caulfield, 100,000 Genomes Pilot on rare-disease diagnosis in health care—Preliminary Report, N. Engl. J. Med. 385 (2021) 1868–1880, https://doi.org/10.1056/nejmoa2035790.

[44] A.M. Vicente, W. Ballensiefen, J.I. Jönsson, How personalised medicine will transform healthcare by 2030: the ICPerMed vision, J. Transl. Med. 18 (2020) 1–4, https://doi.org/10.1186/s12967-020-02316-w.

[45] F. Lethimonnier, Y. Levy, Genomic medicine France 2025, Ann. Oncol. 29 (2018) 783–784, https://doi.org/10.1093/annonc/mdy027.

[46] G. Thareja, Y. Al-Sarraj, A. Belkadi, M. Almotawa, S. Ismail, W. Al-Muftah, R. Badji, H. Mbarek, D. Darwish, T. Fadl, H. Yasin, M. Ennaifar, R. Abdellatif, F. Alkuwari, M. Alvi, Y. Al-Sarraj, C. Saad, A. Althani, E. Fethnou, F. Qafoud, E. Alkhayat, N. Afifi, S. Tomei, W. Liu, S. Lorenz, N. Syed, H. Almabrazi, F.R. Vempalli, R. Temanni, T.A. Saqri, M. Khatib, M. Hamza, T.A. Zaid, A. El Khouly, T. Pathare, S. Poolat, R. Al-Ali, O. Albagha, S. Al-Khodor, M. Alshafai, R. Badii, L. Chouchane, X. Estivill, K. Fakhro, Y. Mokrab, J. Puthen, Z. Tatari, K. Suhre, O.M.E. Albagha, Whole genome sequencing in the Middle Eastern Qatari population identifies genetic associations with 45 clinically relevant traits, Nat. Commun. 12 (2021), https://doi.org/10.1038/s41467-021-21381-3.

[47] D.I. Boomsma, C. Wijmenga, E.P. Slagboom, M.A. Swertz, L.C. Karssen, A. Abdellaoui, K. Ye, V. Guryev, M. Vermaat, F. Van Dijk, L.C. Francioli, J.J. Hottenga, J.F.J. Laros, Q. Li, Y. Li, H. Cao, R. Chen, Y. Du, N. Li, S. Cao, J. Van Setten, A. Menelaou, S.L. Pulit, J.Y. Hehir-Kwa, M. Beekman, C.C. Elbers, H. Byelas, A.J.M. De Craen, P. Deelen, M. Dijkstra, J.T. Den Dunnen, P. De Knijff, J. Houwing-Duistermaat, V. Koval, K. Estrada, A. Hofman, A. Kanterakis, D. Van Enckevort, H. Mai, M. Kattenberg, E.M. Van Leeuwen, P.B.T. Neerincx, B. Oostra, F. Rivadeneira, E.H.D. Suchiman, A.G. Uitterlinden, G. Willemsen, B.H. Wolffenbuttel, J. Wang, P.I.W. De Bakker, G.J. Van Ommen, C.M. Van Duijn, The Genome of the Netherlands: design, and project goals, Eur. J. Hum. Genet. 22 (2014) 221–227, https://doi.org/10.1038/ejhg.2013.118.

[48] Z. Stark, T. Boughtwood, P. Phillips, J. Christodoulou, D.P. Hansen, J. Braithwaite, A.J. Newson, C.L. Gaff, A.H. Sinclair, K.N. North, Australian genomics: a federated model for integrating genomics into healthcare, Am. J. Hum. Genet. 105 (2019) 7–14, https://doi.org/10.1016/j.ajhg.2019.06.003.

[49] J. Rodon, J.C. Soria, R. Berger, W.H. Miller, E. Rubin, A. Kugel, A. Tsimberidou, P. Saintigny, A. Ackerstein, I. Braña, Y. Loriot, M. Afshar, V. Miller, F. Wunder, C. Bresson, J.F. Martini, J. Raynaud, J. Mendelsohn, G. Batist, A. Onn, J. Tabernero, R.L. Schilsky, V. Lazar, J.J. Lee, R.

Kurzrock, Genomic and transcriptomic profiling expands precision cancer medicine: the WINTHER trial, Nat. Med. 25 (2019) 751–758, https://doi.org/10.1038/s41591-019-0424-4.
[50] I. Regel, J. Mayerle, M. Ujjwal Mukund, Current strategies and future perspectives for precision medicine in pancreatic cancer, Cancers 12 (2020), https://doi.org/10.3390/cancers12041024.
[51] A.H.H. Wong, C.X. Deng, Precision medicine for personalized cancer therapy, Int. J. Biol. Sci. 11 (2015) 1410–1412, https://doi.org/10.7150/ijbs.14154.
[52] E.A. Ashley, Towards precision medicine, Nat. Rev. Genet. 17 (2016) 507–522, https://doi.org/10.1038/nrg.2016.86.
[53] A.A. Friedman, A. Letai, D.E. Fisher, K.T. Flaherty, Precision medicine for cancer with next-generation functional diagnostics, Nat. Rev. Cancer 15 (2015) 747–756, https://doi.org/10.1038/nrc4015.
[54] A.M. Tsimberidou, A.M.M. Eggermont, R.L. Schilsky, Precision cancer medicine: the future is now, only better, Am. Soc. Clin. Oncol. Educ. Book (2014) 61–69, https://doi.org/10.14694/edbook_am.2014.34.61.
[55] N. Servant, J. Roméjon, P. Gestraud, P. La Rosa, G. Lucotte, S. Lair, V. Bernard, B. Zeitouni, F. Coffin, G. Jules-Clément, F. Yvon, A. Lermine, P. Poullet, S. Liva, S. Pook, T. Popova, C. Barette, F. Prud'homme, J.G. Dick, M. Kamal, C. Le Tourneau, E. Barillot, P. Hupé, Bioinformatics for precision medicine in oncology: principles and application to the SHIVA clinical trial, Front. Genet. 5 (2014) 152, https://doi.org/10.3389/FGENE.2014.00152/BIBTEX.
[56] H. Li, J. Guo, G. Cheng, Y. Wei, S. Liu, Y. Qi, G. Wang, R. Xiao, W. Qi, W. Qiu, Identification and validation of SNP-containing genes with prognostic value in gastric cancer via integrated bioinformatics analysis, Front. Oncol. 11 (2021) 1434, https://doi.org/10.3389/FONC.2021.564296/BIBTEX.
[57] P. Anker, H. Mulcahy, X.Q. Chen, M. Stroun, Detection of circulating tumour DNA in the blood (plasma/serum) of cancer patients, Cancer Metastasis Rev. 18 (1) (1999) 65–73, https://doi.org/10.1023/A:1006260319913.
[58] Z. Gamie, D. Karthikappallil, E. Gamie, S. Stamiris, E. Kenanidis, E. Tsiridis, Molecular sequencing technologies in the diagnosis and management of prosthetic joint infections, Expert. Rev. Mol. Diagn. (2021) 1–21, https://doi.org/10.1080/14737159.2021.1894929.
[59] L. Hartwell, D. Mankoff, A. Paulovich, S. Ramsey, E. Swisher, Cancer biomarkers: a systems approach, Nat. Biotechnol. 24 (2006) 905–908, https://doi.org/10.1038/nbt0806-905.
[60] A.N. Bhatt, R. Mathur, A. Farooque, A. Verma, B.S. Dwarakanath, Cancer biomarkers – current perspectives, Indian J. Med. Res. 132 (2010) 129–149.
[61] I.-J. Kim, H.C. Kang, J.-G. Park, Microarray applications in cancer research, Cancer Res. Treat. 36 (2004) 207, https://doi.org/10.4143/crt.2004.36.4.207.
[62] S. Katsuma, G. Tsujimoto, Genome medicine promised by microarray technology, Expert. Rev. Mol. Diagn. 1 (2001) 377–382, https://doi.org/10.1586/14737159.1.4.377.
[63] R. Govindarajan, J. Duraiyan, K. Kaliyappan, M. Palanisamy, Microarray and its applications, J. Pharm. Bioallied Sci. 4 (2012) S310–S312, https://doi.org/10.4103/0975-7406.100283.
[64] M.F. Templin, D. Stoll, M. Schrenk, P.C. Traub, C.F. Vöhringer, T.O. Joos, Protein microarray technology, Drug Discov. Today 7 (2002) 815–822, https://doi.org/10.1016/S1359-6446(00)01910-2.
[65] L. Gabriele, F. Moretti, M.A. Pierotti, F.M. Marincola, R. Foà, F.M. Belardelli, The use of microarray technologies in clinical oncology, J. Transl. Med. 4 (2006) 1–5, https://doi.org/10.1186/1479-5876-4-8.
[66] X. Yu, N. Schneiderhan-Marra, T.O. Joos, Protein microarrays for personalized medicine, Clin. Chem. 56 (2010) 376–387, https://doi.org/10.1373/clinchem.2009.137158.
[67] U.D. Akavia, O. Litvin, J. Kim, F. Sanchez-Garcia, D. Kotliar, H.C. Causton, P. Pochanard, E. Mozes, L.A. Garraway, D. Pe'Er, An integrated approach to uncover drivers of cancer, Cell 143 (2010) 1005–1017, https://doi.org/10.1016/j.cell.2010.11.013.
[68] A. Gonzalez-Perez, N. Lopez-Bigas, Functional impact bias reveals cancer drivers, Nucleic Acids Res. 40 (2012) 1–10, https://doi.org/10.1093/nar/gks743.
[69] A. Butera, G. Melino, I. Amelio, Epigenetic "Drivers" of cancer, J. Mol. Biol. 433 (2021), https://doi.org/10.1016/j.jmb.2021.167094.

[70] S. Andrews, FastQC: A Quality Control Tool for High Throughput Sequence Data, 2010. http://www.bioinformatics.babraham.ac.uk/projects/fastqc/.
[71] A.M. Bolger, M. Lohse, B. Usadel, Trimmomatic: a flexible trimmer for Illumina sequence data, Bioinformatics 30 (2014) 2114–2120.
[72] A.V. Zimin, G. Marçais, D. Puiu, M. Roberts, S.L. Salzberg, J.A. Yorke, The MaSuRCA genome assembler, Bioinformatics 29 (2013) 2669–2677.
[73] F.A. Simão, R.M. Waterhouse, P. Ioannidis, E.V. Kriventseva, E.M. Zdobnov, BUSCO: assessing genome assembly and annotation completeness with single-copy orthologs, Bioinformatics 31 (2015) 3210–3212, https://doi.org/10.1093/bioinformatics/btv351.
[74] A. Gurevich, V. Saveliev, N. Vyahhi, G. Tesler, QUAST: quality assessment tool for genome assemblies, Bioinformatics 29 (2013) 1072–1075.
[75] A.C.E. Darling, B. Mau, F.R. Blattner, N.T. Perna, Mauve: multiple alignment of conserved genomic sequence with rearrangements, Genome Res. 14 (2004) 1394–1403, https://doi.org/10.1101/gr.2289704.
[76] L. Xu, Z. Dong, L. Fang, Y. Luo, Z. Wei, H. Guo, G. Zhang, Y.Q. Gu, D. Coleman-Derr, Q. Xia, OrthoVenn2: a web server for whole-genome comparison and annotation of orthologous clusters across multiple species, Nucleic Acids Res. 47 (2019) W52–W58.
[77] M. Stanke, O. Keller, I. Gunduz, A. Hayes, S. Waack, B. Morgenstern, AUGUSTUS: ab initio prediction of alternative transcripts, Nucleic Acids Res. 34 (2006) W435–W439.
[78] T. Seemann, Prokka: rapid prokaryotic genome annotation, Bioinformatics 30 (2014) 2068–2069, https://doi.org/10.1093/bioinformatics/btu153.
[79] N.F. Alikhan, N.K. Petty, N.L. Ben Zakour, S.A. Beatson, BLAST Ring Image Generator (BRIG): simple prokaryote genome comparisons, BMC Genomics 12 (2011), https://doi.org/10.1186/1471-2164-12-402.
[80] M. Krzywinski, J. Schein, I. Birol, J. Connors, R. Gascoyne, D. Horsman, S.J. Jones, M.A. Marra, Circos: an information aesthetic for comparative genomics, Genome Res. 19 (2009) 1639–1645.
[81] Pevzner, 心 提 取 HHS Public Access, Physiol. Behav. 176 (2017) 139–148, https://doi.org/10.1097/PPO.0000000000000281.Epigenetics.
[82] A.M. Tsimberidou, E. Fountzilas, L. Bleris, R. Kurzrock, Transcriptomics and solid tumors: the next frontier in precision cancer medicine, Semin. Cancer Biol. (2020), https://doi.org/10.1016/j.semcancer.2020.09.007.
[83] J.E. Dancey, P.L. Bedard, N. Onetto, T.J. Hudson, The genetic basis for cancer treatment decisions, Cell 148 (2012) 409–420, https://doi.org/10.1016/j.cell.2012.01.014.
[84] A.P. Feinberg, Epigenetics at the epicenter of modern medicine, JAMA – J. Am. Med. Assoc. 299 (2008) 1345–1350, https://doi.org/10.1001/jama.299.11.1345.
[85] B. Heidecker, J.M. Hare, The use of transcriptomic biomarkers for personalized medicine, Heart Fail. Rev. 12 (2007) 1–11, https://doi.org/10.1007/s10741-007-9004-7.
[86] W.B. McKean, J.C. Moser, D. Rimm, S. Hu-Lieskovan, Biomarkers in precision cancer immunotherapy: promise and challenges, Am. Soc. Clin. Oncol. Educ. Book (2020) e275–e291, https://doi.org/10.1200/edbk_280571.
[87] F. Andre, E. Mardis, M. Salm, J.C. Soria, L.L. Siu, C. Swanton, Prioritizing targets for precision cancer medicine, Ann. Oncol. 25 (2014) 2295–2303, https://doi.org/10.1093/annonc/mdu478.
[88] M.C.E. McFadyen, W.T. Melvin, G.I. Murray, Cytochrome P450 enzymes: novel options for cancer therapeutics, Mol. Cancer Ther. 3 (2004) 363–371.
[89] U.M. Zanger, K. Klein, Pharmacogenetics of cytochrome P450 2B6 (CYP2B6): advances on polymorphisms, mechanisms, and clinical relevance, Front. Genet. 4 (2013) 1–12, https://doi.org/10.3389/fgene.2013.00024.
[90] J.T. Dudley, T. Deshpande, A.J. Butte, Exploiting drug–disease relationships for computational drug repositioning, Brief. Bioinform. 12 (2011) 303–311.
[91] C.R. Chong, D.J. Sullivan, New uses for old drugs, Nature 448 (2007) 645–646.
[92] M.J. Keiser, B.L. Roth, B.N. Armbruster, P. Ernsberger, J.J. Irwin, B.K. Shoichet, Relating protein pharmacology by ligand chemistry, Nat. Biotechnol. 25 (2007) 197–206.
[93] M.A. Lill, Multi-dimensional QSAR in drug discovery, Drug Discov. Today 12 (2007) 1013–1017.

[94] T. Noeske, B.C. Sasse, H. Stark, C.G. Parsons, T. Weil, G. Schneider, Predicting compound selectivity by self-organizing maps: cross-activities of metabotropic glutamate receptor antagonists, ChemMedChem 1 (2006) 1066.
[95] A.P. Chiang, A.J. Butte, Systematic evaluation of drug–disease relationships to identify leads for novel drug uses, Clin. Pharmacol. Ther. 86 (2009) 507–510.
[96] G. Ashok, S.K. Miryala, A. Anbarasu, S. Ramaiah, Integrated systems biology approach using gene network analysis to identify the important pathways and new potential drug targets for neuroblastoma, Gene Rep. 23 (2021) 101101, https://doi.org/10.1016/j.genrep.2021.101101.
[97] R. Debroy, S.K. Miryala, A. Naha, A. Anbarasu, S. Ramaiah, Gene interaction network studies to decipher the multi-drug resistance mechanism in Salmonella enterica serovar Typhi CT18 reveal potential drug targets, Microb. Pathog. 142 (2020) 104096, https://doi.org/10.1016/j.micpath.2020.104096.
[98] S. Basu, A. Naha, B. Veeraraghavan, S. Ramaiah, A. Anbarasu, In silico structure evaluation of BAG3 and elucidating its association with bacterial infections through protein-protein and host-pathogen interaction analysis, J. Cell. Biochem. (2021), https://doi.org/10.1002/jcb.29953.
[99] A. Naha, S. Vijayakumar, B. Lal, B.A. Shankar, Genome sequencing and molecular characterisation of XDR Acinetobacter baumannii reveal complexities in resistance: novel combination of sulbactam-durlobactam holds promise for therapeutic intervention, 122, J. Cell. Biochem., 2021, pp. 1946–1957. 30156.
[100] C. Shankar, S. Basu, B. Lal, S. Shanmugam, K. Vasudevan, P. Mathur, S. Ramaiah, A. Anbarasu, B. Veeraraghavan, Aerobactin, seems to be a promising marker compared to unstable RmpA2 for the identification of hypervirulent carbapenem-resistant Klebsiella pneumoniae: in-silico and in-vitro evidence, Front. Cell. Infect. Microbiol. 776 (2021), https://doi.org/10.3389/fcimb.2021.709681.
[101] The White House, Precision Medicine Initiative: Privacy and Trust Principles, 2015, pp. 1–4.

Index

Note: Page numbers followed by *f* indicate figures and *t* indicate tables.

D

E

F

G

H

I

N

O

P

Q

R

S

9780443152801